THE I TATTI
RENAISSANCE LIBRARY

James Hankins, General Editor

BOCCACCIO

GENEALOGY OF THE PAGAN GODS

VOLUME I

ITRL 46

GIOVANNI BOCCACCIO

✦ ✦ ✦

GENEALOGY OF THE PAGAN GODS

VOLUME I ✦ BOOKS I–V

EDITED AND TRANSLATED BY

JON SOLOMON

THE I TATTI RENAISSANCE LIBRARY

HARVARD UNIVERSITY PRESS

CAMBRIDGE, MASSACHUSETTS

LONDON, ENGLAND

2011

Series design by Dean Bornstein

Library of Congress Cataloging-in-Publication Data

Boccaccio, Giovanni, 1313–1375.
[Genealogia deorum. English & Latin]
Genealogy of the pagan gods / Giovanni Boccaccio ; edited and
translated by Jon Solomon.
p. cm. — (The I Tatti Renaissance library ; v. 46)
Includes bibliographical references and index.
ISBN 978-0-674-05710-4 (v. 1 : alk. paper)   1. Mythology, Classical.
2. Geography, Medieval.   3. Boccaccio, Giovanni, 1313–1375. Genealogia
deorum.   I. Solomon, Jon, 1950–   II. Title.   III. Series.
PQ4274.G6E5 2011
292.2′11 — dc22   2010042690

Contents

ॐ।।ॐ

Introduction

※※※

Giovanni Boccaccio's *Genealogy of the Pagan Gods* (*Genealogia deorum gentilium*) is an ambitious synthesis of ancient mythological information, Greek and Latin poetry, medieval and humanistic scholarly research, and poetic manifesto. Boccaccio divided this large work into fifteen books. The first thirteen contain a mythological genealogy meticulously organized within a single, all-encompassing genealogical matrix. The scope is enormous: 723 chapters include well over 1000 citations from over 200 different Greek, Roman, medieval, and Trecento authors and scholars to identify and describe approximately 950 Greco-Roman mythological individuals and groups and account for dozens of additional names of spouses, mothers, and unnamed siblings as well as mythological beasts and even quasi-personified geophysical phenomena. Boccaccio incorporates into most of these entries an array of allegorical, historical, and scientific analyses of the fabulous and iconographic elements embedded in the ancient tales, and he expands many of these passages by comparing and evaluating previous interpretations selected from his medieval predecessors. In Books 14 and 15 Boccaccio writes a compelling defense of poetry in general and a more specific defense of his *Genealogy*. In doing so he offers a brief history of the origins of poetry as well as a dexterous and unabashed justification for the study of pagan literature within a Christian context.

Much more than a prose collection of pagan myths, the *Genealogy* incorporates hundreds of relevant poetic excerpts, applies scholarly analyses that represent the new scientific spirit of Italian humanism, and argues that this method of studying ancient mythological poetry ultimately affirms God's truths. As one of the first works of classical scholarship in the Renaissance, as a comprehen-

sive treatment of classical mythology, and as a historical, theoretical, and practical endorsement of the value of poetry, the *Genealogy* would remain a treatise of enduring influence for several centuries.

History of the Work

We do not know exactly when Boccaccio began writing the *Genealogy*, although we can identify numerous stages of development and production that spanned four decades.

- Near the conclusion of the *Genealogy*, Boccaccio informs us that he had become interested in pagan mythology "while still a youth" (15.6: *Ego iuvenculus adhuc*). This would have been during the 1330s, when as a teenager Boccaccio studied with Paul of Perugia, head librarian at King Robert's Angevin court at Naples, from whom he collected material which would eventually be cited in or incorporated into his *Genealogy*.
- In the *Preface* of the *Genealogy* Boccaccio explains to his patron, King Hugo IV of Cyprus, why he was reluctant to accept the enormous undertaking when first petitioned by the king's minister Donnino di Parma. It has been suggested that the meeting took place between 1347 and 1349, when Boccaccio was residing primarily in Ravenna and Forlì while working on the *Decameron* and, as it would turn out, escaping the initial impact of the plague in Florence in 1348.
- Near the end of the *Genealogy* (15.13) Boccaccio apologizes to the king for not seriously engaging in the project prior to further urging from Becchino Bellincioni, who after traveling from Cyprus met with Boccaccio in Ravenna, and Paul the Geometer, who showed him signed and sealed orders from the king. This Ravenna sojourn is thought to

have taken place in 1350, the year before the Senate of
Florence sent Boccaccio to Padua to offer Petrarch a chair
at the Florentine Studium.[1] Indeed, it was in 1350 and 1351
that two inspiring personal encounters with Petrarch in
Florence and Padua were dramatically transforming
Boccaccio's literary focus from vernacular Italian romance
and poetry to scholarly Latin prose treatises.[2]

+ One would like to think that the abdication of Hugo in
November 1358 and his subsequent death in October 1359
provide obvious *termini ante quem* for the initial completion
of the project: Boccaccio addresses the king throughout the
work as if he were alive. But Boccaccio also frequently cites
Leontius Pilatus, whom he employed as his Greek tutor
during Leontius' tenure at the Florentine Studium from
1360 to 1362, so the Greek passages in the *Genealogy* prove
that work continued during these years.[3]

+ A decade later, in a letter written to fellow humanist Pietro
Piccolo da Monteforte on April 5, 1372, Boccaccio describes
his manuscript as "incomplete" (*non perfectum*).[4] Giuseppe
Billanovich, Vittorio Zaccaria, and others have identified
the corrections Piccolo made in the margins of this extant
autograph copy of the *Genealogy*, and these and subsequent
corrections and additions made by Boccaccio were
incorporated into a subsequent redaction.[5]

The text of Boccaccio's autograph reveals the status of the *Genealogy* as a work undergoing periodic revision that would continue
in later copies, now lost. In its margins we find references to sources
Boccaccio had previously neglected, e.g., Tacitus (3.23),[6] Pliny
(3.19, 25), Martial (3.20), and Columella (11.1).[7] His neat, semi-
Gothic script is altered on many leaves with erasures, corrections,
and additions which often continue into the margins. The discussion of Atlas (4.31) alone contains two corrected genealogies and a

parenthetical addition as well as an appended citation from the elder Pliny. Nearing the end of the project, Boccaccio compiled a lengthy table of rubrics listing in order all 723 entries in the *Genealogy*, subsequently adjusting it to include final additions, e.g., 2.76, on Scythes. A leaf representing Scythes was added as well to the colorful and naturalistic genealogical trees Boccaccio had painted earlier to introduce each of the first thirteen books.[8] Even so, the lack of rubrication throughout the autograph reveals the autograph's incomplete state.[9]

As the fifteenth century approached and commenced, interest in the *Genealogy* expanded, and several humanists made the work even more valuable as a veritable encyclopedia of mythological information. Coluccio Salutati, who was serving as Chancellor of Florence when Boccaccio died, commissioned Domenico Bandini,[10] the Aretine teacher of rhetoric and grammar working in Florence, to compile an alphabetic glossary for the *Genealogy*. The result, containing 1966 entries—keyed to book and chapter numbers, and alphabetized to the second letter—was one of the most comprehensive indices applied to a work of European scholarly literature at that time and one of the first to be committed to print.[11] Two additional indices were compiled in the final decades of the fourteenth century, one by Matteo d'Orgiano and the other anonymous, but it was Bandini's that would continue to appear in most of the subsequent printed editions. Domenico Silvestri, who like Boccaccio had studied Greek with Leontius and specialized in the writing of Latin verse epigrams, composed eighteen Latin hexameters featuring seriatim the name of the progenitor of each of the thirteen books of the *Genealogy*. Like Bandini's index, Silvestri's versified table of contents became attached to the subsequent tradition of the *Genealogy*.

Although less than a century separated Boccaccio's death and the first printed edition of the work, forty-seven extant codi-

ces contain the first thirteen books or complete versions of both strands of the manuscript tradition, and another forty-two contain several books, single books, extracts, or paraphrases; we know of over three dozen additional early fifteenth-century manuscripts which included all or portions of the *Genealogy* but are no longer extant.[12] As just one marker of its influence, in the early fifteenth century Boccaccio's *Genealogy* was already providing source material for John Lydgate's *Siege of Thebes* (e.g., 3.3537–42).[13]

In 1472 Wendelin of Speyer issued the *editio princeps* of the *Genealogy* in gilt vellum; the text of this version was corrected by the Istrian humanist Raffaele Zovenzoni. Although he chose not to print the illustrated trees, Wendelin did print a passage (3.22) with Greek type nearly two decades before Aldus Manutius began printing his influential Greek texts in Venice. In the next year Johann Veldener, the first printer in Louvain, issued an anonymously paraphrased Latin compendium of the first thirteen books.[14] Thereafter, printed Latin editions of the *Genealogy* proliferated. Editions appeared in Reggio in 1481, Vicenza in 1487, and Venice in 1494 and 1497, followed by Parisian and Venetian editions in 1511 and Jacob Mycillus' 1532 Basel edition with annotations and a new, even larger index. None included any Greek text, but most included Boccaccio's table of contents, Bandini's index, and Silvestri's epigram followed by a printed version of Boccaccio's *On Mountains*. Some, beginning with the 1494 Venetian edition, include woodcut renditions of the genealogical trees.

Vernacular translations made the treatise accessible to a wider audience. In 1498 a French translation of the first thirteen books (*De la génénealogie des dieux*) was published by Antoine Vérard in Paris in a large-format, gilt-edged volume accompanied by a generous number of unattributed woodcut images; this was reset in 1531 in a smaller format with fewer of the woodcuts. The French translation has been attributed to the humanist Laurent de Premierfait,

who is known to have translated Boccaccio's Latin works on illustrious men and women (*De casibus virorum illustrium*, 1400; *De mulieribus claris*, 1409) as well as the *Decameron* (1414–18).[15]

The earliest Italian translation was rendered by an equally prominent man of letters, Giuseppe Betussi. A member of Padua's Accademia degli Infiammati and sponsored by Sperone Speroni, Betussi was at the avant-garde of those promoting the substitution of Italian for Latin as the language of scholarly literature.[16] From 1544 to 1547 he was in the service of Count Collaltino di Collalto, to whom his version of Boccaccio's *Genealogy* is dedicated, as are his translations of two other major Latin scholarly works by Boccaccio. Betussi's *La genealogia de gli dei de' gentili* was published first in Venice by Comino da Trino di Monferrato in 1547, and this was followed by nearly a dozen subsequent editions into the seventeenth century. Most of these include Betussi's ten-page biography of Boccaccio, and their alphabetical indices are keyed to page numbers, not book and chapter. Indicative of the continuing interest specifically in the mythological content of Boccaccio's *Genealogy*, many of the Betussi editions were published along with contemporary publications of Lilio Gregorio Giraldi's *De deis gentium* (1548), Vincenzo Cartari's *Imagini de i dei de gli antichi* (1556), and Natale Conti's *Mythologiae* (1567).[17]

Although the works by Giraldi, Cartari, and Conti put an end to the dominance of Boccaccio's *Genealogy* as a mythological reference, near the end of the sixteenth century it still served as an important source for Edmund Spenser's Christianized paganism.[18] Thereafter the visibility of Boccaccio's *Genealogy* was mostly limited to lexica of the seventeenth to nineteenth centuries, but as a monumental artistic and intellectual model, it would continue to influence the Greco-Roman mythological tradition. Perhaps most noteworthy is Boccaccio's identification of Demogorgon as the ultimate progenitor of the entire race of pagan divinities. In the seventeenth century John Milton included Demogorgon among

Satan's netherworld conspirators in *Paradise Lost* (2.965), and in the nineteenth century Acts II and III of Percy Bysshe Shelley's *Prometheus Unbound* featured Demogorgon as the sole power in the universe capable of deposing the dominant celestial divinity widely worshipped as the supreme being. It was only a few decades later that Attilio Hortis, Henri Hauvette, Oskar Hecker, and others began to apply the methodologies of modern scholarship that prepared the way for modern editions and translations of Boccaccio's *Genealogy*.

Sources

The sources range chronologically from Homer to Boccaccio's mid-fourteenth-century Greek contemporary Leontius Pilatus, who, not coincidentally, was helping Boccaccio learn to read Homer in Greek.[19] Indeed, incorporating the Homeric poems as mythological evidence and then citing, quoting, and translating into Latin dozens of ancient Greek passages which Western Europeans had not been able to access in centuries is the most revolutionary aspect of Boccaccio's scholarship in the *Genealogy*.

There are forty-five Greek passages quoted from Homer, ranging in length from one to six hexameters. Most of them contain minor diacritical and/or orthographic errors.[20] All but one of the twenty-four books of the *Iliad* are cited;[21] the entries involving Ulysses flesh out the many *Odyssey* passages cited in Book 13 of the *Genealogy*, although there are no citations from the last five books of the *Odyssey*. Boccaccio cites Homer directly or indirectly over 250 times, more than he cites any other author.

Boccaccio no doubt collaborated with Leontius, to whom he refers nearly one hundred times for most if not all the Homeric passages, but he gained access to additional ancient Greek sources through Paul of Perugia, who provided him source material from Barlaam of Calabria[22] as well as Theodontius. We know little

about Theodontius, whose work is lost, except that that he was knowledgeable in Greek as well as Latin, offered otherwise unknown variants and interpretations of pagan myths, and antedated Boccaccio by at least two centuries.[23] But Boccaccio cites him almost two hundred times and through him gained limited access to Pronapides and still other Greek sources.

Another important Greek source, the *Chronicle* of Eusebius, which Boccaccio cites nearly one hundred times, had been translated into Latin and adapted long before by Jerome. Boccaccio employs the *Chronicle* to add chronological precision to his historical analyses, and in most instances he regards it as an unimpeachable source. Following in the Scholastic tradition, Boccaccio cites as well eight different works by Aristotle (some already translated into Latin) and also makes reference to such ancient Greek poets as Theognis, Euripides, and Apollonius of Rhodes, such natural scientists as Thales, Anaxagoras, and Anaximander, and the historian Thucydides, cited or epitomized by such Latin intermediaries as Cicero, Valerius Maximus, Servius, Macrobius, Fulgentius, and Isidore. For European scholarship in the fourteenth century, the collection and use of such an extensive array of original Greek sources and intermediary ancient and medieval Latin sources was unparalleled.

The ancient Latin poets Boccaccio most frequently cites or quotes are Ovid, Vergil, and Statius, who supplied him with hundreds of well-known narratives and memorable descriptions of divinities and mythical mortals. The most frequently cited Roman prose author is Cicero, whose *On the Nature of the Gods* confirmed for Boccaccio that the chief Olympian gods featured by these poets were actually euhemerized homonymous pluralities, e.g., the three men who shared the name Jupiter. As with the multiple Greek authors, Boccaccio cites and quotes a variety of additional ancient Roman poets and prose authors, e.g., Seneca (tragedian and philosopher, cited as two different authors), Pliny,

Pomponius Mela, Horace, Livy, and Lucan, not to mention such late ancient writers as Solinus and Claudian. To balance and contradict the ancient pagans, Boccaccio cites scripture over one hundred times.

Although he had access to a number of comprehensive mythological compilations, Boccaccio only sporadically cites the ancient collection of myths attributed to Hyginus, Papias' medieval *Lexicon*, or the late twelfth-century *Great Book of Etymologies* by Uguccione da Pisa. Writing in the fourteenth century, Boccaccio preferred to use the late antique and early medieval compilations and commentaries by Servius, Lactantius Placidus, Macrobius, Augustine, Fulgentius, Isidore, Albericus, and Rabanus, because such secondary works offered him not only variants and summaries of divine descriptions and mythological narratives but also allegorical and rationalizing interpretations which he found either convincing or worthy of discussion and refutation in his own treatise.[24] Similarly, through his elder contemporaries Paul of Perugia and Barlaam he had direct and indirect access to additional interpretations developed in the rich twelfth- to fourteenth-century tradition of mythographic commentaries, all of which now are of relatively obscure or anonymous authorship and many of which survive in only fragmentary states.[25] For analyses which required astronomical perspective, he made use of the ninth-century Arab astronomer Albumasar, whose *Introduction to Astronomy* John of Seville had translated into Latin in the twelfth century, and the poet Andalò di Negro of Genoa, whom Boccaccio identifies (15.5) as the man who taught him astronomy.

Throughout the first thirteen books of the *Genealogy* Boccaccio often submits these authorities to source criticism, juxtaposes contrasting assertions, and applies a broad palette of investigative and exegetical methodologies. At 2.60 he prides himself on offering a very different, i.e., non-Vergilian, account of Dido, and in repeated demonstrations of his scholarly integrity, he admits when he can-

not find a source or remember reading anything more about a character. Boccaccio makes clear his goal—to remove the "veil" (*velum*) from a story (*fabula*) to reveal its true meaning (*sensum*)— and he specifies in the final two books of the *Genealogy* that underneath the ancient veil one can discover sound philosophy and valuable ancient wisdom.

But in addition to collecting, reporting, and analyzing his multiple sources, Boccaccio accommodated the humanistic spirit by adding an additional and essential element: he clearly identified his sources so his readers could benefit more fully from his research. At a time when few books were carefully prepared with scholarly guides, Boccaccio had already experimented by appending informative glosses to his pseudo-ancient tale of Theseus (*Teseida delle nozze d'Emilia*). To provide additional guidance for his *Genealogy*, he not only included a table of contents at the outset of the treatise but also recorded the name of each of the authors cited within the paragraph in the outer margins of the autograph.

Boccaccio demonstrates a different approach to his sources in the final two books designed to explain, theorize, and justify the methodology he has applied to the mythological materials he has examined in Books 1–13. Here the author becomes an advocate of the proposition that the pagan poetry he has been discussing throughout the work has great value in revealing divinely inspired truths to the reader who has been properly guided through allegorical hermeneutics.[26] When Boccaccio writes of ancient poets in Book 14, it is not to recount and interpret their fables but to cite the lives of the authors as moral and ethical exempla superior to the contemporary icons revered by his detractors (14.4.15–17) or to compare the value of their fables with those told by and about Christ (14.9.12). Throughout he calls upon the ancient tradition of literary criticism found in Latin authors from Cicero to Macrobius. By contrast, near the center of the final book (15.6) he concentrates exclusively on demonstrating the value of such modern

sources as Andalò, Dante, Barlaam, Paul of Perugia, Leontius, and the revered Petrarch.

Aware of the different spiritualities underlying his chronologically broad spectrum of sources, Boccaccio accommodates his methodical organization of ancient source material and his allegorical, historical, and scientific exegeses of what he considers to be pagan irrationality within a traditional Christian context. His synthesis depends upon still another source tradition that had been nurtured by Scholastic theologians and continued in Trecento Italy by Albertino Mussato and Petrarch, a tradition which would regularize the acceptance of art and poetry as expressions of the sensible world and thus as veiled expressions of divine truth.[27] Perhaps no passage in the *Genealogy* is more indicative of Boccaccio's ability to reconcile his pagan and Christian sources than the chapter in Book 15 (15.9) in which he affirms eloquently and at length his commitment to Christ by citing stories about a fictitious pagan character in Terence and the historical pagan King Mithridates of Pontus. This synthesis allowed Boccaccio, who at first seems to have circulated Books 14 and 15 separately from the mythological genealogy, to incorporate the two parts into a comprehensive but integrated treatise.

Precedents and Achievement

More than a millennium after ancient Greek arguments about the value and uses of poetry originated with Archaic critiques of Hesiod and Homer, Christian apologists and moralists would argue over whether to embrace or condemn pagan literature itself. When a secondary set of arguments about the use and relative value of Latin and vernacular language resonated early in the fourteenth century, Boccaccio's humanist predecessors, particularly Mussato and Petrarch, summoned up the well-known arguments Plato presented in the second and third books of his *Republic* (known via

intermediate sources). Boccaccio addresses these arguments at 14.16–19, applying them to a wide-ranging justification for reading ancient poetry and fiction, adding exegetical analysis, and continuing the contemporary scholarly momentum. The commitment, learning, and passion Boccaccio poured into his defense of poetry and the study of pagan literature in Books 14 and 15 contributed to making the *Genealogy* a standard text for literary critics, scholars, and poets of the Renaissance, and it remained an intellectual highwater mark for Sidney, Wordsworth, and Goethe, who was reportedly reading the *Genealogy* during the final days before his death.[28]

In antiquity, the corpus of Greco-Roman myths had continued to develop over the course of a millennium, as such exceptional poets as Homer, Pindar, Sophocles, Vergil, and Ovid produced mythological poetry and Hellenistic and Roman scholars identified their literary sources and origins in archaic ritual. But pagan antiquity failed to produce a comprehensive scholarly collection of Greco-Roman myths that also analyzed the mythological corpus as a whole. Many ancient prose authors, from Thucydides and Plato to the paradoxographer Heraclitus and Flavius Philostratus, analyzed, allegorized, and reformulated mythological material, but none produced a comprehensive collection, and Cicero's well-known *On the Nature of the Gods* was a philosophical study of pagan theology, not a scholarly collection of myths. The two most important extant compilations of the mythological corpus were those attributed to Hyginus and Apollodorus, but even though those authors both collected and arranged mythical narratives and summaries and the latter was even chronologically comprehensive, they lacked exegesis.

At the end of the fourth century the official Christianization of the Roman Empire not only hastened the elimination of the worship of the pagan gods but in doing so disengaged the mythical corpus: now these once sacred gods and their enormous progeny would be merely collected and studied. The euhemeristic demo-

tion of the gods to human status and an increased tendency to allegorize enabled this process to thrive in the medieval period, which produced several widely promulgated works. The sixth-century *Mythologies* of Fulgentius nonetheless is not comprehensive and rarely cites sources. The learned *Etymologies* of Isidore of Seville is relatively comprehensive and contains whole sections devoted to grammar, rhetoric, mathematics, medicine, law, and other well-established ancient rubrics, but it does not offer a systematic analysis of pagan mythology. Toward the end of the ninth century, the Carolingian Renaissance inspired the learned commentaries of Remigius of Auxerre, a forerunner of an additional number of commentaries and glosses on various works by Vergil, Ovid, Macrobius, Martianus Capella, and others written by William of Conches, Arnulf of Orleans, and the Third Vatican Mythographer, whom Boccaccio equated with Albericus. The early fourteenth-century mythological creatures and humans consigned to Dante's *Inferno* derive from a number of these earlier Latin sources, and Boccaccio's earlier contemporary Pierre Bersuire (Petrus Berchorius) completed his influential mythographical *Moralized Ovid* when Boccaccio was still studying with Paul of Perugia.

Boccaccio then incorporated many facets of this rich, variegated mythographic tradition into his *Genealogy*. Demonstrating extraordinary research skills for his era, he compiled a wealth of information and ideas from the notes he made during his Neapolitan studies with Paul of Perugia, which would have included most of the references to Barlaam and Theodontius; sorted through Albericus, Isidore, Fulgentius, Macrobius, and other strains of the medieval tradition; incorporated ideas from Cicero's *On the Nature of the Gods*; collected a fairly extensive series of quotations from ancient Latin poetry; worked for three years with Leontius to learn a sufficient amount of Homeric Greek; and received additional input from Pietro Piccolo da Monteforte. By modern stan-

dards he lacks precision as a copyist, his research is not exhaustive, and the value of his analyses varies. But it was by collecting and organizing this amount of material, comparing interpretations and then enthusiastically arguing for his own interpretations, identifying and incorporating ancient Greek quotations, and zealously defending the importance and benefit of doing so that Boccaccio helped to establish a new standard of classical scholarship. In addition, he promulgated the results of his studies not only by writing the *Genealogy* and lending a copy to fellow humanists in Naples, but by adding a number of features to make the work accessible to readers, including the table of contents, carefully painted genealogical trees, the prose descriptions which explain the arrangement of the root and leaves of the trees that preface each of the first thirteen books, the marginal Latin translations of the Homeric passages, and the marginal lists of ancient and medieval sources cited.

Boccaccio's comprehensive collection and study of Greco-Roman myths soon became a principal source for one of the ancient world's most intellectually and artistically alluring cultural products. The Greco-Roman myths would for the next two centuries inspire countless works of poetry, prose, painting, sculpture, and drama. For humanists and literati of the period, Boccaccio's *Genealogy* helped to establish the scholarly parameters for the study of Greco-Roman myths; it also provided an authoritative essay promoting the beneficial artistic and philosophical qualities of ancient poetry.

Nonetheless, the *Genealogy* is still a product of the mid-fourteenth century and retains a number of quintessentially medieval features: allegorizing and euhemerizing exegeses, portmanteaus and false etymologies, incomplete and inaccurate source citations, limited and imprecise Greek quotations, and an underlying Christian presumption laced with a firm reliance on astrological determinism. Boccaccio accepted the erroneous traditions that

there were two different younger Senecas and only one Lactantius. The mythologically rich Greek tragedies are almost entirely ignored, as are Hesiod and Pseudo-Apollodorus. Finally, the genealogical framework of the work is another traditional element.[29] But Boccaccio's scholarly achievement was to combine these variegated elements into an expansive treatment of an important and alluring subject that was to yield a substantial legacy during one of the most innovative and productive artistic periods in the Western arts.

Prefaces

Boccaccio begins with a general Preface (*Prohemium*) dedicated to King Hugo IV of Jerusalem and Cyprus.[30] That Hugo claimed title to two kingdoms over two thousand kilometers southeast of Florence is not without significance for the geographical and spiritual compass of the *Genealogy*. Hugo was the ninth monarch of the dynasty founded by the French crusader Guy de Lusignan in the aftermath of the failed Third Crusade. One century later the fall of Acre may have reduced the hereditary Lusignan title "king of Jerusalem" to an idle claim, but the Kingdom of Cyprus, now the easternmost extension of Christendom, flourished as the trade and manufacturing center of the eastern Mediterranean. Hugo was a beneficiary of this continuing prosperity. A patron of the arts educated in both Latin and Greek, he commissioned this illuminating compilation of mythical divinities, which includes the Greco-Roman goddess of love said to have emerged from the sea on the shores of the very island he ruled. But as an antidote to the underlying pagan content of the *Genealogy*, Boccaccio repeatedly affirms the primacy of Christ, who was said to have been crucified at the Church of the Holy Sepulchre, where Guy de Lusignan had first crowned himself king of Jerusalem in 1186.[31] Conscious of this dual tradition, Boccaccio differentiates his patron the Cypriot

monarch from the pre-Christian Greeks (and Cypriots) who be-lieved in the pagan "evil":

> Paul of Perugia . . . sometimes stated in my presence that he had learned from Barlaam, the Calabrian exceedingly learned in Greek letters, the name of no preeminent man, whether identified by his important position or other distinction, liv-ing anywhere in Greece, its islands, or along the aforemen-tioned shores during that era in which this foolishness flour-ished, who did not claim that he originated from one god or another. So what can I say, or what can you say, as we look at such an ancient evil that spread so far and wide? (1.P1.12–13)

Toward the end of this first preface Boccaccio introduces the travel motif he will develop in the subsequent prefaces introducing each of the fifteen books:

> . . . as a new sailor on a rather frail skiff I will descend into the vertiginous sea encircled by ubiquitous cliffs, uncertain as to whether the labor will be worth the effort of reading all the books. The shores and mountain woodlands, the chan-nels and caves I will traverse by foot if need be. I will de-scend to the nether regions, and I will become another Daedalus and fly into the ether.[32] To carry out your project, not otherwise than if I were collecting fragments along the vast shores of a huge shipwreck, I will collect the remnants of the pagan gods strewn everywhere in a nearly infinite number of volumes. (1.P1.40)

As he crosses Hellenic waters in his imaginary little skiff, he weathers monstrous storms, descends into the abyss, and rides the crest of a gigantic wave in vivid prose:

I was still navigating the waters surrounding your town of Paphos, splendid Prince, . . . when, behold, as if Aeolus' prison had broken open, all the winds flew forth onto the sea and began to grow angry, and impelled by the greatest force the waves surged toward the sky, but, repelled from there, dove into the depths to Erebus . . . I was carried down to where from the deep I spied approaching me, not otherwise than if the iron walls of Dis had been destroyed and their chains had been thrown off, the immense progeny of ancient Titan. (4.P.1–2)

Boccaccio braves the elements of a pre-Christian nature and crosses the horizontal barriers of space to decrease the barriers of time. Most of the prose in the *Genealogy* is purposely restrained and emotionless, as befits its encyclopedic and scholarly intent. But as he visits ancient realms in the prefaces at the outset of each book, Boccaccio regales us with dramatic Dantesque passages that lend literary authority to his mythological project.

Structure of the Genealogy

Like many of its predecessors dating back to Hesiod's *Theogony* and the Book of Matthew, Boccaccio's genealogy unfolds in a descending direction from progenitor to progeny. He frequently expands his lineages internally, inserting secondary and tertiary lineages as they unfold, not hesitating to proceed into one or more later generations of one descendant before completing the descendant's contemporaries. But he does not always do so, particularly if one of the progeny is a major progenitor with a complicated legacy or is worthy of an expanded narrative. He traces the lineage of Ulysses, for instance, in Book 2, from Ether to the first Jupiter to Liber to the second Mercury to Autolycus to the first Sinon to

Aesimus to Anticleia, who was Ulysses' mother, but Boccaccio saves his account of the Odyssean voyage for Book 13 in connection with his father, Laertes.

The mythological material begins in Book 1, Preface 2, in which Boccaccio asks the essential question, "Who was regarded as first among the pagan gods?" Identifying a father or mother for all the obvious candidates who had considerable and well-known progeny — Jupiter, Sky, Ocean, Earth, Sun, and Ether — Boccaccio declared the parentless Demogorgon as the ultimate progenitor.

Demogorgon, whom Boccaccio discusses briefly in Preface 3, differed significantly from the traditional Olympian and pre-Olympian divinities of the Greco-Roman religious system.[33] He represented a type of divinity found mostly at the theological fringes of Greco-Roman spirituality. In his *Timaeus* (40c) Plato writes of a *demiourgos*, an "artificer," who more so than any genuine Greek divinity performs the mythographical role of the creator god of Genesis. This *demiourgos* was developed into a mysterious spiritual force in later Platonic and Gnostic thought. Like the "uncertain Judaean god" described by Lucan (*Pharsalia* 2.592–93) and the aniconic Cypriot stone described by Tacitus (*Histories* 2.2–3), the Demiurge was not anthropomorphic and lacked the usual mythological elements and votive epithets. He resurfaces in late antiquity and takes on a revised identity as Demogorgon through Lactantius Placidus' commentary on Statius' *Thebaid* (4.516–17). Ironically, his original nonmythological essence provided the parentless status that Boccaccio found to be unique. It is primarily through Theodontius and obscure, lost Greek sources that Boccaccio is able to attribute to him the progeny that will connect him to the remaining genealogical history of the pagan divinities.

From Demogorgon Boccaccio will ultimately derive Erebus, who produces the first Jupiter and Sky, who in turn produce the second and third Jupiters, Titan, Ocean, and Saturn. These pro-

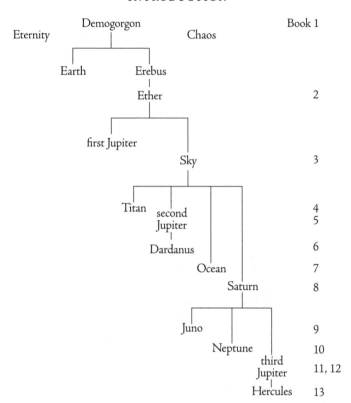

The Major Branches of the *Genealogy*

duce all the remaining lesser "gods" other than the primordial Eternity and Chaos and the eight offspring of Demogorgon. The large branches consume more than one book, and individual books generally contain information about more than one sub-branch of the genealogical tree. Boccaccio describes each pagan figure in a single entry, and he distributes the 723 entries among the first 13 books, ranging in number from the 19 entries in Book 8 to the 86 in Book

2. Each entry is prefaced by one of the rubrics Boccaccio extracted and listed in the autograph's table of contents and then usually commences by specifying the parents and the source of the information, often supported by a quotation from an ancient source. Thereafter Boccaccio usually expands the entry, either by quoting source materials or by listing any relevant fables, attributes, and epithets, and then analyzes the material he has laid out.[34]

Summary by Book

Book 1 accounts for the two additional primordial contemporaries, Eternity and Chaos (1.1–2), and then initiates Boccaccio's rigorous genealogical concatenation with the interesting collection of nine offspring of Demogorgon, e.g., Strife (1.3), Pan (1.4), and the Fates (1.5), the eighth being Earth (1.8), who in turn produces five children, and the ninth being Erebus (1.14), who produces twenty-one, twenty of whom are described here (1.15–34).

Book 2 begins with Ether, the twenty-first child of Erebus, who in turn fathered the first Jupiter and Sky (2.1). The first Jupiter's thirteen progeny (2.2–86) include Liber (2.11), who fathers the second Mercury (2.12). The twelfth child of this Jupiter is Epaphus (2.19), whose son Belus fathered Danaus, Aegyptus, and Agenor (2.21). Boccaccio offers chapters on three of Danaus' fifty daughters (2.22–26) and one of the fifty sons of Aegyptus, who fathers Lynceus, father of Abas, Iasius, and Acrisius, the latter being the father of Danae, the mother of Perseus, the others producing Atalanta, Amphion, Parthenopeus, and several others (2.27–43). Agenor fathers seven predominantly Levantine children, including Cilix, who fathers Pygmalion, king of the Cypriots, and the rest of the Cypriot tradition through Adonis (2.44–53) — no doubt to the intended delight of King Hugo. Boccaccio proceeds to the eastern branch that produced Dido (2.55–61)

and the Theban tradition that produced the line of Oedipus (2.62–86).

Book 3 begins the focus on Sky, who fathered twelve children, only eight of whom are treated in this book because several — e.g., Ceres (3.3), Mercury (3.20–21), the Cypriot Venus and the second Venus (3.22–24) — were important divinities who either produced many descendants or require lengthy exegeses to account for all their fables, attributes, and epithets. Ceres (3.4) was the mother of the infernal river Acheron, who also had a large progeny (3.5–17).

Book 4, the longest other than the nonmythological Book 14, continues with the children of Sky but is limited to the progeny of Titan. Titan alone fathered an additional thirteen as well as a brood of giants. First of the thirteen is Hyperion, who fathered Sun (4.2–15), and this generates a discussion about the element of time and Sun's better-known offspring, especially Pasiphae (4.10), Medea (4.12), Circe (4.13), and Moon (4.16–17). Coeus, the third child of Titan, fathered Latona, who in turn produced Apollo and Diana (4.19–20). The eighth child of Titan is Iapetus, who engendered Atlas (4.31), the father of whole groups of star figures (Hyades, 4.32; Pleiades, 4.34–40), Epimetheus (4.42–43), and Prometheus (4.44). The discussion on Prometheus and humankind is one of the longest in the entire *Genealogy*. The Winds (4.54–61) and the Giants (4.68) warrant comprehensive entries toward the end of the book.

Boccaccio devotes Book 5 to fifteen of the progeny of the second Jupiter, the ninth son of Sky. These fifteen children include additional well-known Olympian deities: Diana (5.2); Apollo and his progeny (5.3–23), notably Orpheus (5.12), Aesculapius (5.19), and Psyche (5.22), Apuleius' account of whom is discussed at some length; Bacchus and his Theban progeny (5.25–33); and Minerva (5.48).

Book 6 focuses on the progeny of Dardanus, the sixteenth child of the second Jupiter by Electra, daughter of Atlas. This subbranch was of particular interest to Boccaccio because as the ancestor of the Trojan royal line, Dardanus and his progeny include many of the characters included in Homer's *Iliad*. Boccaccio inserts Greek texts into a dozen of the entries in Book 6. The first part of the book includes the two large groupings in this lineage, the progeny of Laomedon (6.6–13) and the prolific Priam (6.14–48). Thereafter Boccaccio changes his focus to the segment of the Trojan lineage that produced the mythological ancestors of Rome, beginning with the eponymous Tros, his son Assaracus (6.49), his great-grandson Aeneas, who warrants an extended discussion derived from Homer, Livy, Vergil, and others (6.53), and continuing all the way to Ilia, daughter of Numitor and the mother of Romulus and Remus (6.73).

Having completed the offspring of the second Jupiter, Boccaccio in Book 7 now picks up the succession from Book 5 by delineating the progeny of Sky's tenth child, Ocean (7.1), who in several earlier genealogies was identified as the ultimate progenitor of gods and men. According to Boccaccio's research, Ocean produced thirty-four offspring, and he seems to assign them to four general categories: well-known Oceanids, e.g., Phaethon's mother Clymene (7.6); anthropomorphized sea creatures like Triton (7.7) and Proteus (7.9–11); Nereus (7.13) and the many nymphs he fathered, including Thetis (7.16), Galatea (7.17), and Arethusa (7.18); and rivers. Boccaccio focuses on two important Greek rivers: Achelous, who fathered the Sirens (7.19–20), and Inachus, whose daughter Io is compared to Isis (7.21–22). Continuing this Egyptian line, Boccaccio then discusses the Nile, who fathered a number of Egyptian children who have been syncretized with Greco-Roman equivalents, including the fourth Mercury, Hermes Trismegistus (7.34). This Egyptian excursus also inspires Boccaccio's scientific analysis of Phaethon's solar catastrophe (7.41). The remaining riv-

ers range geographically from the western Tiber (7.50) to the Asian Axius (7.52) and Meander (7.60).

Book 8 introduces a branch of the Sky tradition that descended from his eleventh child, Saturn. Saturn's ten children include Juno, Neptune, and the third Jupiter, who are reserved for the ensuing five books. As a primordial figure who castrated his father and experienced a well-documented afterlife, Saturn himself undergoes a lengthy analysis (8.1), as does his daughter, an alternate Ceres, along with her daughter Proserpina (8.4), and Pluto (8.6). The second half of the book features the progeny of Picus (8.10), whose lineage through his son Faunus (8.11) leads to King Latinus (8.17) and Lavinia (8.18) and elicits a discussion about such Arcadian creatures as fauns, satyrs, Pans, and Silvani (8.13). This is the shortest book of the *Genealogy*.

Book 9 is limited to the complete lineage descended from the Saturnian Juno. After an extended discussion of Juno herself (9.1), Boccaccio continues with her parthenogenetic issuance of Hebe (9.2) and a discussion of Mars as a god of war (9.3). Mars in turn fathered fifteen children. First is Cupid, and Boccaccio neatly juxtaposes this extended discussion of desire with the previous discussion of war (9.4). Other offspring descended from Mars include Oenomaus and his daughter Hippodamia, wife of Pelops (9.6–7); Tereus, father of Itys (9.9–10); and the Calydonian King Oeneus, who fathered Deianira, Meleager, and Tydeus, father of Diomedes (9.16–23), among others. Somewhat like the entries involving woodland figures in the latter segments of Book 8, the final third of Book 9 introduces the offspring of Ixion (9.27), many of whom were centaurs (9.28–32). The final entries in this book involve the most famous and chronologically latest Roman offspring of Mars, Romulus and Remus (9.40–41).

Book 10 delineates the thirty-five children of Neptune (10.1). Many of these are lesser figures to whom Boccaccio devotes short paragraphs, but he expands the entries on Scylla (10.9) and

Polyphemus (10.14), well known from the accounts by Homer and Vergil; Medusa (10.11); the Cyclopic trio of Brontes, Steropes, and Pyragmon (10.16); and Pegasus (10.27). Neleus, the twenty-second child listed (10.35), produced four children, including the Homeric Nestor, who in turn produced eight (10.36–41). Neptune also produced the giants Otus and Ephialtes (10.47), as well as Aegeus (10.48), father of Theseus (10.49), father of Hippolytus (10.50). Boccaccio leads to the conclusion of this portion of the genealogy with the lineage of Nauplius and Palamedes (10.59–60) and the Harpies (10.61).

Books 11, 12, and 13 are required to accommodate the thirty-nine children of the more familiar third Jupiter, that is, the son of Saturn and brother of Juno. In Book 11, after a full discussion of Jupiter himself (11.1), Boccaccio discusses twenty-nine offspring and their progeny, featuring extended entries on the nine Muses (11.2); Castor and Pollux (11.7); the Homeric Helen (11.8); Orion (11.19); Minos and his well-known progeny (11.26–32); and the Homeric Ulysses (11.40). The unextended passage on Clytemnestra (11.9) reflects the general lack of interest in the tradition of ancient Greek tragedy, even through Seneca *tragicus* served as an intermediary.

The first of the eight Jovian children covered in Book 12 include the six generations of Tantalids: Tantalus, Niobe/Pelops, Atreus/Thyestes, Agamemnon/Menelaus, Electra/Orestes, and their offspring (12.1–23). Thereafter Boccaccio features Perseus, the thirty-second child of Jupiter, and his genealogical legacy leading down through Amphitryon and Alcmena to but not including Hercules (12.25–40), who is reserved for the following book; the Aeacids, including Achilles (12.45–56); the lineage of Mercury, the thirty-sixth child, including the Lares (12.62–69); and the lineage of Vulcan, the thirty-seventh child, which leads to the quasi-historical Tullius Servilius (Servius Tullius) and his two daughters, for whom Livy is the major source (12.70–79).

Book 13 then completes the Jovian section of the *Genealogy* by delineating the progeny of Hercules, who fathered seventeen sons (13.1–19), and Aeolus, who fathered ten children (13.20–70). The initial entry on Hercules is one of the longest in the entire *Genealogy*, presenting thirty Herculean labors (13.1). None of the sons warrants an extended treatment, but Jason was great-grandson of Aeolus, and his quest for the golden fleece is described in some detail (13.26). Boccaccio then features two more of his descendants, Sisyphus (13.56) and Bellerophon (13.58). The last entry offers Boccaccio's explanation for why he does not include either Alexander the Great or Scipio Africanus as a son of Jupiter (13.71). Boccaccio ends the genealogy itself here.

Book 14 offers the author's general response to "the enemies of the name of poetry." After an address to the king (who may well have predeceased its writing) (14.1), Boccaccio denigrates many of his critics for their ignorance and lack of taste (14.2–3). He also attacks the wealthy in an extensive defense of poverty (14.4). The second half of the book offers a more positive approach, defining poetry and discussing its origin, function, and usefulness (14.6–10). He then justifies the obscurity of poetry, asserting that one's inability to understand poetry does not validate critical condemnation (14.11–15). Boccaccio then compares poetry and philosophy, concentrating on Plato's apparent condemnation of poetry in his *Republic* (14.16–19). Boccaccio finishes with an address to the enemies of poetry in the hope of reforming them (14.22).

In Book 15 Boccaccio anticipates the criticism that his *Genealogy* will engender and attempts to defend its worth. Fables, he argues, are natural forms of adornment, and because his book lifts the veil from these fables, it should have enduring value (15.1–2). Boccaccio allows that others might prefer a different genealogical arrangement or the insertion of fables he has omitted, but perfection is impossible (15.3–4), and he has selected only ancient stories, some of them long forgotten (15.5), and cited such knowledgeable mod-

ern authorities as Andalò, Dante, Barlaam, Paul of Perugia, Leontius, Paul the geometer, and Petrarch (15.6). He explains that he has quoted ancient Greek poetry not to be ostentatious with his learning but in imitation of ancient writers like Cicero and Macrobius, and because he and his contemporaries have much to learn from the ancient Greeks (15.7). Then he affirms the value of studying ancient theology (15.8), and in the next passage he eloquently expresses his firm belief in the Christian god to challenge any threat his contemporaries feared from the examination of paganism (15.9). He also addresses his own natural inclination to pursue this project and reviews the process by which the king commissioned the work (15.10–13); he then concludes humbly and apologizes for any defects (15.14).

NOTES

1. Two years later, in a letter to Petrarch dated July 18, 1353, Boccaccio fondly remembered the latter meeting, for which see Giovanni Boccaccio, *Epistole,* ed. Ginetta Auzzas, vol. 5 of Vittore Branca, ed., *Tutte le opere di Giovanni Boccaccio* (Milan: Mondadori, 1992), 574 [10.4].

2. For the influence of Petrarch and the transformation of Boccaccio's output in this period, see M. L. McLaughlin, "Humanism and Italian Literature," in Jill Kraye, ed., *The Cambridge Companion to Renaissance Humanism* (Cambridge: Cambridge University Press, 1996), 228–29.

3. Many of Boccaccio's influential works — *Decameron, Genealogia deorum gentilium, De casibus virorum illustrum, De mulieribus claris,* and *De montibus* — date from the late 1340s to the early 1360s. Boccaccio was also sent on a number of diplomatic missions during this extremely busy and productive period. He worked with Leontius from 1360 to 1362; Leontius departed from Florence in October 1363.

4. For the letter, see Giuseppe Billanovich, "Pietro Piccolo da Monteforte tra il Petrarca e il Boccaccio," in *Medioevo e Rinascimento: Studi in onore di Bruno Nardi* (Florence: G. C. Sansoni, 1955), 59–65, esp. 61 n. 101.

5. Zaccaria, *Genealogie*, 1592–1594, offers a chronology. (This and other titles cited only in abbreviated form in these notes may be found in the Bibliography.)

6. For a recent account of the confusion surrounding Boccaccio's alleged discovery of the Monte Cassino Tacitus and Apuleius manuscripts, see Julia Haig Gaisser, *The Fortunes of Apuleius and the* Golden Ass: *A Study in Transmission and Reception* (Princeton: Princeton University Press, 2008), 93–99.

7. Cf. David Anderson, "Which Are Boccaccio's Own Glosses?" in Michelangelo Picone and Claude Cazalé Bérard, eds., *Gli Zibaldoni di Boccaccio: Memoria, scrittura, riscrittura* (Florence: F. Cesati, 1998), 327–31.

8. For a recent discussion of Boccaccio's colorful and instructive genealogical trees, see Maria Grazia Ciardi Dupré dal Poggetto, "L'iconografia nei codici miniati boccacciani dell'Italia centrale e meridionale," in Vittore Branca, ed., *Boccaccio visualizzato: Narrare per parole e per immagini fra Medioevo e Rinascimento*, vol. 2 (Torino: Einaudi, 1999), 3–52, 57–62 (fig. 5), and 78–88 (figs. 12–18).

9. For the trees as well as marginal sketches, see Giovanni Morello, "Disegni marginali nei manoscritti di Giovanni Boccaccio," in Picone and Bérard, *Gli Zibaldoni di Boccaccio*, 169–71.

10. See A. T. Hankey, "Domenico di Bandino of Arezzo (?1335–1418)," *Italian Studies* 12 (1957): 110–28.

11. In most instances the alphabetical ordering was carried out only to the second or third letter. Boccaccio's autograph does not contain chapter numbers; he simply lists the chapter headings in order, divided by a space and the *incipit* and *explicit* for each book.

12. To Zaccaria's list of partial manuscripts, add St. Florian, Bibliothek des Chorherrenstifts, Hs.XI.79 and SB. Hs.XI.108, for which see Michael Dallapiazza, *Die Boccaccio-Handschriften in den deutschsprachigen Ländern* (Bamberg: Stefan Wendel Verlag, 1988), 59–60 (Nos. 110, 111). For a relatively recent discovery, see Livio Petrucci, "Lasciti della prima circolazione della 'Genealogia deorum gentilium' in un manoscritto campano del quattrocento," *Studi medio-latini e volgari* 27 (1980): 162–81.

13. For probable influence in contemporary visual art as well, see Catherine King, "Mnemosyne and Calliope in the 'Chapel of the Muses,' San Francesco, Rimini," *Journal of the Warburg and Courtauld Institutes* 51 (1988): 186–87.

14. The ISTC (ib00750000) lists two printers, Louvain's Johann Veldener and Cologne's Printer of the 'Flores Sancti Augustini,' i.e., Johann Schilling. In 1970 Allan Stevenson, "The First Book Printed at Louvain," in D. E. Rhodes, ed., *Essays in Honour of Victor Scholderer* (Mainz: Pressler, 1970), 402–6, demonstrated, by examining paper composition and watermarks, that the printer was Veldener in Louvain.

15. Cf. Anne Dawson Hedeman, *Laurent de Premierfait and Boccaccio's De casibus* (Los Angeles: J. Paul Getty Museum, 2008); and Patricia May Gathercole, ed., *Laurent de Premierfait's Des cas des nobles hommes et femmes, Book 1, Translated from Boccaccio* (Chapel Hill: University of North Carolina Press, 1968).

16. For a biographical summary, see Irma B. Jaffe, *Zelotti's Epic Frescoes at Cataio: The Obizzi Saga* (New York: Fordham University Press, 2008), 24–35.

17. For Martín de Avila's Catalan translation and a survey of the history of Boccaccio's *Genealogy* in humanist Spain, see Álvarez and Iglesias, *Los Quince Libros*, lxvii–lxx, and Michael McGaha, "Boccaccio and Cervantes: The Influence of the *Genealogia Deorum* on *Don Quixote*," *Hispano-Italic Studies* 2 (1979), 6–16.

18. See also George F. Butler, "Boccaccio and Milton's 'Manlike' Eve: The *Genealogia Deorum Gentilium Libri* and *Paradise Lost*," *Milton Quarterly* 37 (2003): 166–71. For additional borrowings, see Herbert G. Wright, *Boccaccio in England from Chaucer to Tennyson* (London: Athlone, 1957): 36–45, and Edmund Reiss, "Boccaccio in English Culture of the 14th and 15th Centuries," in Giuseppe Galigani, *Il Boccaccio nella cultura inglese e angloamericana* (Florence: L. S. Olschki, 1974), 24.

19. See Agostino Pertusi, *Leonzio Pilato fra Petrarcha e Boccaccio: Le sue versioni omeriche negli autografi di Venezia e la cultura greca del primo umanesimo* (Venice: Instituto per la collaborazione culturale, 1964), and Cornelia

C. Coulter, "Boccaccio's Acquaintance with Homer," *Philological Quarterly* 5 (1926): 44–53.

20. Some letters are written only in majuscule; aspirates and accents are often interchanged. At 5.43, phrases are reversed and an important word is omitted. Hecker, *Boccaccio-funde*, 137–53, analyzes the Greek passages and their Latin translations in detail.

21. Book 17 is the lone exception.

22. Barlaam was the Calabrian Greek who taught Greek language, literature, and mythology to Paul of Perugia and Leontius Pilatus as well as Petrarch, albeit briefly. Boccaccio refers to him over two dozen times.

23. For a thorough investigation, see Pade, "The Fragments of Theodontius," 149–82.

24. For context, see Tobias Foster Gittes, *Boccaccio's Naked Muse: Eros, Culture, and the Mythopoeic Imagination* (Toronto: University of Toronto Press, 2008), 16–21.

25. E.g., Frank, T. Coulson, ed., *The 'Vulgate' Commentary on Ovid's Metamorphoses: The Creation Myth and the Story of Orpheus* (Toronto: Pontifical Institute of Mediaeval Studies, 1991), and Virginia Brown, "An Edition of an Anonymous Twelfth-Century *Liber de natura deorum*," *Mediaeval Studies* 34 (1972): 1–70. For a general survey, see both volumes of Jane Chance, *Medieval Mythography* (Gainesville: University Press of Florida, 1994 and 2000).

26. Giovanni Gullace, "Medieval and Humanistic Perspectives in Boccaccio's Concept and Defense of Poetry," *Mediaevalia* 12 (1989, for 1986): 225–48, differentiates Boccaccio's humanistic methodology fromf his medieval theology.

27. For Mussato, see Michael Papio, trans., *Boccaccio's Expositions on Dante's Comedy* (Toronto: University of Toronto Press, 2009), 19–20. Ronald G. Witt, *In the Footsteps of the Ancients: The Origins of Humanism from Lovato to Bruni* (Boston: Brill, 2003), 252–60, differentiates the more traditional assumption made by Boccaccio that pagan poets were inspired by divine truths from the humanistic assumption made by Petrarch that the human element was also of considerable importance.

28. For its influence in specific instances, see R. W. Maslen, ed., *Sir Philip Sidney: Apology for Poetry, or, The Defence of Poesy*, 3rd ed. (Manchester: Manchester University Press, 2002), 18–19; Alan G. Hill, "Wordsworth, Boccaccio, and the Pagan Gods of Antiquity," *Review of English Studies* 45 (1994): 26–41; and Willi Hirdt, "Boccaccio in Germania," in Francesco Mazzoni, *Il Boccaccio nelle culture e letterature nazionali* (Florence: L. S. Olschki, 1978) 31; cf. Lionello Sozzi, "Boccaccio in Francia nel cinquecento," in Carlo Pellegrini, *Il Boccaccio nella cultura francese* (Florence: L. S. Olschki, 1971), 211–349, esp. 236–52.

29. For genealogical trees, see Christiane Klapisch-Zuber, "The Genesis of the Family Tree," *I Tatti Studies: Essays in the Renaissance* 4 (1991): 105–29, and Ernest Hatch Wilkins, "The Trees of the *Genealogia Deorum*," *Modern Philology* 23 (1925): 61–65.

30. Boccaccio uncharacteristically places three prefaces after the *incipit* of Book 1. Only the third preface introduces Book 1 itself.

31. After being ousted from the Levant, subsequent Lusignan kings of Cyprus and Jerusalem had to be satisfied with being crowned in the Church of Saint George in Famagusta. The Angevin line in Naples also claimed the title of king of Jerusalem.

32. *GDG* 11.26.1.

33. For historical surveys, see Wolfgang Fauth, *Demogorgon: Wanderungen und Wandlungen eines Deus Maximus Magorum in der abenländischen Literatur* (Göttingen: Vandenhoeck & Ruprecht, 1987); Maria Pia Mussini Sacchi, "Per la fortuna del Demogorgone in età umanistica," *Italia medioevale e umanistica* 34 (1991): 300–310; and Carlo Landi, *Demogorgone* (Palermo: R. Sandron, 1930).

34. In some entries Boccaccio analyzes details of stories he has not fully explained, e.g., the story of Theseus and the Minotaur in the chapter on Pasiphae (4.10).

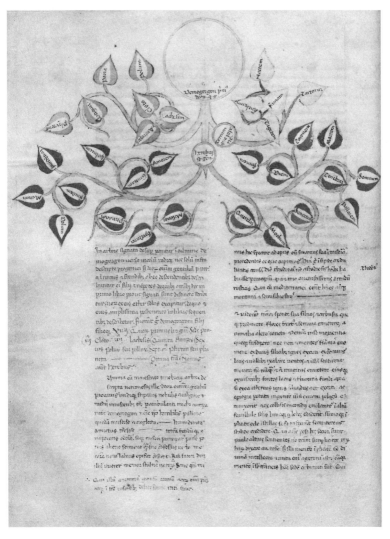

Boccaccio's illustration of the genealogical tree of Book 1 in the autograph manuscript of the Genealogy of the Pagan Gods, Florence, Biblioteca Medicea Laurenziana, Ms. Plut. 59.2, f. 11v. Image courtesy of the Biblioteca Medicea Laurenziana.

GENEALOGIA DEORUM GENTILIUM
AD UGONEM INCLITUM
IERUSALEM ET CYPRI REGEM
SECUNDUM IOHANNEM
BOCCACCIUM DE CERTALDO

GENEALOGY OF THE
PAGAN GODS
FOR THE ILLUSTRIOUS HUGO
KING OF JERUSALEM
AND CYPRUS BY
GIOVANNI BOCCACCIO
OF CERTALDO

LIBER PRIMUS

Prohemium[1] 1

1 Si satis ex relatis Domnini Parmensis egregii militis tui vera per-
cepi, Rex inclite, summopere cupis genealogiam[2] deorum gentilium et heroum ex eis iuxta fictiones veterum descendentium, atque cum hac quid sub fabularum tegmine illustres quondam
senserint viri, et me a celsitudine tua, quasi expertissimum atque
eruditissimum hominem in talibus, selectum tanto operi autorem.

2   Sane ut omiserim desiderii tui admirationem, non enim parvum hominem decet, quid regem moveat perscrutari, et adversus
electionem mei quid sentiam dicere pretermictam, nedum insuffi-
cientiam meam monstravero per subterfugia arbitreris imposititi laboris onus evitem, antequam ad sententiam meam circa impositum
opus deveniam, libet, serenissime regum, apponere, etsi non omnia, quedam saltem que inter Domninum insignem militem tuum,
dum iussa tue celsitudinis explicaret, et me intervenere verba, ut
eis perlectis satis de me iudicium tuum videas et temeritatem
meam, dum in obedientiam tue maiestatis devenio.

3   Cum igitur ille facundo ore sacra tue sublimitatis studia et
opera regalis officii admiranda nec non et insignes atque gloriosos
quosdam tui nominis titulos longa dicacitate explicuisset, eo devenit ut conatu plurimo me in tuam sententiam deducere niteretur,[3]
nec unica tantum ratione sed multis ex quibus, fateor, valide videbantur quedam.

BOOK I

Preface 1

If I have understood correctly from the reports of your eminent 1
officer, Donnino of Parma, you, glorious King, greatly desire a
genealogy of the pagan gods and the heroes the fictions of the ancients tell us were descended from them, and you want to learn
what meaning once illustrious men found hidden at the core of
these fables. And for this considerable task Your Highness has
chosen me to be the author, as if I were the most knowledgeable
and erudite in such matters.

It will be best if I disregard my surprise at your request, for it is 2
not fitting for a little man to examine a king's motives. And I will
overlook what I might have to say against your choosing me: as I
demonstrate my insufficiency I do not want you to think that I am
using subterfuge to avoid the task you have assigned me. But before I come to my decision about undertaking the project you have
assigned me, allow me, most serene King, to relate at least some,
but not all, of the exchange that took place between your distinguished officer Donnino and myself as he was delivering Your
Highness's orders, so that after reading this you may have a better
perspective on your decision to choose me as well as my foolhardi-
ness in complying with Your Majesty.

After he at length had catalogued in eloquent speech Your Maj- 3
esty's studies of sacred subjects and admirable royal achievements
as well as your distinguished and glorious titles, he then made every attempt to entice me to comply with your proposal — not by
one method only but by many, some of which, I confess, seemed
compelling.

4   Verum postquam tacuit et michi respondendi copia facta est, sic dixi:

'Arbitraris[4] forsan, facunde miles, seu rex tuus de proximo noster futurus, prestante Deo, hanc insaniam veterum, scilicet cupientium se haberi divino procreatos sanguine, angulum terre modicum occupasse et tanquam ridiculum quoddam, ut erat, parvo perseverasse temporis tractu et veluti etiam recentissimum opus facile colligi posse?

5   'Attamen bona semper tua pace dicam: longe aliter est. Nam, ut omictam Cicladas et reliquas Egei maris insulas, Achaiam et Ylliricum atque Traciam, quas penes fomenta huius stultitie emicuere plurimum, et potissime dum Grecorum respublica floruit, Eleuxini maris, Hellespontiaci, Meonii, Ycarei, Pamphylii, Cilicii, Phenicis et Syri atque Egyptiaci litora sua contagione infecit. Nec Cyprus nostri regis insigne decus ab hac labe fuit immunis.

6   'Sic et omnem Libye atque Syrtium et Numidie oram labefactavit et Athlantiacos occiduique maris[5] sinus et remotissimos Hesperidum ortos. Nec Mediterranei tantum maris fuit contenta litoribus; quin imo et ad incognitas mari[6] nationes etiam penetravit.

7   Decidere enim in perniciem hanc cum litoralibus accole omnes Nyli, fonte carentis, et harene libyce una cum suis pestibus, et antiquissimarum Thebarum solitudines, nec non et superiores Egyptii, atque Garamantes fervidi et calentes nimium hirsutique Ethyopes, et odori Arabes Perseque dites atque Gangarides populi et nigredine insignes Yndi, Babilones et celsa Caucasi cacumina, eiusque tam in fervidum solem quam in gelidas arthos scabrosa declivia, Caspium mare Hyrcanique truces et omnis Tanais ac nivosus

8   semper Rhodopes et Scytharum etiam inculta barbaries. Et cum orientalis occeani fluctus et Rubri maris infecisset insulas, pos-

After he fell silent and gave me an opportunity to respond, I 4
replied as follows:

"Do you, eloquent soldier, or your king, who soon will be ours
by the grace of God, believe perhaps that this foolishness of the
ancients by which they fancied themselves as the offspring of divine blood, occupied only a small corner of the earth? That because it was so ludicrous it endured for only a small amount of
time? And that one could gather information about it as easily as
something quite recent?

"I will respond politely: it is far otherwise. Even if I were to 5
omit the Cyclades and other islands of the Aegean Sea, Achaea,
Illyria, and Thrace, where to a large extent the kindling for this
folly blazed forth, especially while the Greek state was flourishing,
this contagion infected the shores of the Black Sea, the Hellespont, Maeonia, Icaria, Pamphylia, Cilicia, Phoenicia, and Syria as
well as Egypt. Nor was Cyprus, worthy splendor of our king, immune from this malignancy.

"In the same way it infected all of Libya, Syrtis, and the shore 6
of Numidia as well as the Atlantic bays of the western sea and the
most distant gardens of the Hesperides. Nor was it contained only
by the shores of the Mediterranean Sea; it penetrated even to
peoples unfamiliar with the sea. Falling victim to this ruin along 7
with the costal inhabitants were those who dwelled along the Nile
of unknown source, and the plague-ridden Libyan sands, and the
far reaches of most ancient Thebes, and also upper Egypt, and the
scorching Garamantes and hot-blooded, shaggy Ethiopians as well
as the scented Arabs, rich Persians, people of the Ganges, and Indians distinguished by their dark skin, and Babylonians, and the
high peaks of the Caucasus, with its rugged cliffs facing both the
hot sun and icy valleys, the Caspian Sea, the savage Hyrcanians,
the entire Tanais, the ever-snowy Rhodope, and also the uncivilized Scythian barbarians. And after it had infected even the waves 8
of the Eastern ocean and the islands of the Red Sea, finally it

tremo ad nos usque Ytalos declinavit, adeo ut Roma, rerum domina, huius caliginis offuscata nube sit.

9   'Et ne passim per regiones omnes, in quibus plurimum hec inscitia potuit, evager, ut satis potes advertere, portiuncula sola fuit orbis inter triones et cadentem solem, que deitatis huius modi non fuit nobilitata progenie, esto nephande credulitatis sicuti et reliqua fuerit infecta.

10   'Nec ista evo fuere nostro. Erat forsan adhuc adolescens Abraham dum apud Sicyonios cepit ista proserpere et insipientium hominum subintrare animos; heroum tamen tempestate ferbuit et in maximum devenit decus et nomen, et in dies usque superbi Ylionis ruine perseveravit. Nam in Troiano bello quosdam deorum filios cecidisse et Hecubam in canem et Polydorum in virgulta conversos legisse meminimus.

11   'Quod quidem et vetustissimum est et plurium seculorum tempus. Nec dubitandum insuper quin, quocunque hec viguerit stultitia, ibidem ingentia sint descripta volumina, ut maiorum divina

12   nobilitas monimento licterarum veniret ad posteros. Et esto nunquam existimaverim talium parvum fuisse numerum, quod permaximus fuerit, Paulus Perusinus, vir gravis et talium solertissimus atque curiosissimus exquisitor, non nunquam asseruit, me presente, se a Barlaam, quodam calabro homine Grecarum licterarum apprime erudito, habuisse neminem insignem virum, principatu aut preminentia alia, tota in Grecia insulis et litoribus premonstratis, eo fuisse seculo, quo hec fatuitas viguit, qui ab aliquo deorum huius modi duxisse originem non monstraret.

13   'Quid igitur dicam, quid tu, spectantes tam longe lateque diffusum malum tam vetus, tot perseveratum seculis, tot explicatum voluminibus et in tam grandi virorum numero ampliatum? Cre-

reached us in Italy, until even Rome, mistress of the world, was clouded in its murky fog.

"I will not wander through all the regions everywhere influenced by this ignorance, but as you can easily see, there was only a small portion of the world between the northern Plough Oxen and the setting sun which was not part of the progeny of this kind of divinity, although that remainder was infected by ineffable credulity as well.   9

"But these things do not apply to our era. Perhaps Abraham was still a young man when it began to creep among the Sicyonians and steal into the minds of foolish humans.[2] It raged during the era of the heroes and reached its full glory and fame, lasting even until the ruin of proud Ilium, for we remember reading that during the Trojan War certain sons of divinities fell, Hecuba was transformed into a bitch,[3] and Polydorus into a shrubbery.[4]   10

"This was a most ancient period of many generations ago. And there can be no doubt that wherever this folly flourished, lengthy books were written, literary monuments to commemorate among subsequent generations the divine nobility of their ancestors. Although I would certainly never underestimate the number of these books, which happens to be quite large, Paul of Perugia,[5] a dedicated man most expert in such matters and a most inquisitive investigator, sometimes stated in my presence that he had learned from Barlaam, the Calabrian exceedingly learned in Greek letters, the name of no preeminent man, whether identified by his important position or other distinction, living anywhere in Greece, its islands, or along the aforementioned shores during that era in which this foolishness flourished, who did not claim that he originated from one god or another.   11   12

"So what can I say, or what can you say, as we look at such an ancient evil that spread so far and wide, one that was so persistent through the ages, prevalent in so many books, and promulgated among such a great number of men? Do you believe I could ac-   13

14   disne me regis optata posse perficere? Equidem[7] si prestent montes faciles transitus et solitudines invie apertum notumque iter, si flumina vada et maria tranquillas undas, ac transfretanti emictat ab antro Eolus ventos tam validos quam secundos, et, quod maius est, sint Argiphontis talaria aurea volucri cuicunque homini alligata pedibus, et pro votis, quocunque libuerit evolet, vix tam longos terrarum marisque tractus, etiam si illi prestetur permaxima seculorum annositas, nedum aliud agat, solum poterit peragrasse.

15   'Concedam amplius; detur[8] cui velis hec omnia posse contingere in momento loca et, divina insuper favente gratia, caractherum ac ydiomatum variarum nationum notitia, et coram accedenti integra preparentur volumina; quis, ut me pretermiserim, mortalium erit cui sint vires tam solide, tam perspicax ingenium tanque tenax memoria, ut omnia videre queat apposita, et intelligere visa et intellecta servare, et demum calamo etiam exarare et in opus collecta deducere?

16   'Addebas preterea ut explicarem quid[9] sub ridiculo cortice fabularum abscondissent prudentes viri, quasi rex inclitus arbitretur stolidum credere homines, fere omni dogmate eruditos, simpliciter circa describendas fabulas nulli veritati consonas nec preter licteralem sensum habentes, trivisse tempus et inpendisse sudores.

17   'Non inficiar, delectavit me regalis ista discretio et argumentum certissimum prebuit quoniam, ut tu ante dicebas, sit illi divinum ingenium, meque in votum inpulit suum, dum modo vires sufficerent.

18   'Sane circa huiusmodi explicationes longe plus quam putes difficultatis et theologi hominis labor est; nam, dato, iuxta Varronis sententiam, ubi *De divinis et humanis rebus* multa descripsit, genus

complish what the king wishes? Indeed, if mountains prepared   14
easy passage and impenetrable deserts offered a well-marked, well-
disclosed journey, rivers shoals, and the seas tranquil waves, and if
for the maritime traveler Aeolus from his cave issued forth winds
as strong as they were favorable, and, even more, if the golden
ankle-wings of Argeiphontes[6] were bound to the feet of some swift
human and he was granted his wish to fly wherever he wanted,
scarcely could even he cover such vast regions of lands and sea
even if he spent the greatest possible fullness of years extended to
him and he did nothing else.

"I will concede further: if someone were to be given the ability   15
to have all these places accessible in a moment and, with divine
favor, knew of the characters and traits of the various peoples, and
was supplied with whole books when required, what mortal — do
not include me — would have such considerable abilities, natural
insight, and tenacious memory to envision all that was required,
and then to understand what he had seen and to remember what
he understood, and, finally, to set it all down in writing and organize the work?

"You added in addition that I should explain the meaning wise   16
men had hidden under the outer layers of these inane fables, suggesting that the illustrious king thought it nonsensical for men
who were learned in nearly every doctrine to spend time and effort
simply telling fables unrelated to the truth and lacking a deeper
meaning.

"I do not deny it: such royal discretion of his delights me, and   17
he provided me with the most convincing proof that he, as you
were saying earlier, possesses divine ability, and this compels me to
grant his wish, but only if I have the ability to do so.

"Explications of this sort are certainly more difficult than you   18
would think and are the task of a theologian. In this regard, although, according to the opinion of Varro, who wrote much about
this in his *On Divine and Human Matters*,[7] this is a kind of theology

hoc theologie sit, quod mithicon, seu, ut aliis placet et forte melius, physicon dicitur, etsi plurimum ridende falsitatis habeat, multum tamen ad illam eliciendam artis exquirit. Et ob id, miles elegantissime, pensande sunt hominum vires et examinanda ingenia, et sic illis convenientia onera imponenda. Potuit Athlas sustinere capite celum, eique fesso sub onere Alcides potuit prestare vicem, divini homines ambo, et invictum fere robur fuit ambobus. Ast ego quid? Brevis sum homuncio, nulle michi vires, ingenium tardum et fluxa memoria; et tu meis humeris, non dicam celum, quod illi tulere, quin imo et terram super addere cupis et maria, ac etiam celicolas ipsos, et cum eis sustentatores egregios. Nil aliud hoc est nisi velle ut pondere premar et peream.

'Verum si tantum regi hoc erat animo, erat onus aptum, si inter mortales ullus est tanto labori sufficiens, viribus preclarissimi viri Francisci Petrarce, cuius ego iam diu auditor sum. Homo quippe est celesti ingenio preditus et perenni memoria, ac etiam facundia admirabili, cui familiarissime quarumcunque gentium hystorie sunt, sensus fabularum notissimi, et breviter quicquid phylosophie sacro iacet in gremio, manifestum est.'

Tacueram iam, cum sic ille vultu placido et comto sermone secutus est:

'Credo, longe melius quam noverim, ea vera esse, que narras, et difficultates video; sed queso, mi Iohannes, an putes regem nostrum circumspectione carere? Oculatus quippe dominus est et mitis ingenii, et regia facilitate laudabilis. Et absit ut quenquam, nedum te, premere velit, quin imo vetus est illi mos leviare quoscunque, et idcirco sane intelligenda atque assumenda iussa ipsius.

which is called mythical or, as others prefer to call it, perhaps more accurately, natural, and if it contains a significant amount of ludicrous falsehood, it nevertheless demands much skill to elicit. And 19 for this reason, my fine soldier, the abilities of men must be weighed and their talents evaluated if they are to be burdened with suitable tasks. Atlas was able to sustain the heavens with his head, and then when he was weary from this burden Alcides was able to take his turn.[8] Both of them were divine men, and both of them had nearly indomitable strength. But what about me? I am a little 20 man, absent of strength, with a slow wit and a fluid memory. And upon my shoulders you want to add, not the heavens they bore, but both the earth and the seas, and even the heavenly dwellers themselves along with their distinguished companions. This is to 21 wish nothing upon me other than that I be crushed by their weight and perish.

"If this was what was in the king's mind, the burden was fitting—if there is any mortal prepared for such a task—for the abilities of the famous Francesco Petrarch, whose disciple I have been for a long time now. This man is indeed endowed with divine genius and unfailing memory, as well as admirable eloquence; and he knows intimately the histories of these peoples, the best-known interpretations of the fables, and, in short, whatever lies in the sacred lap of philosophy."

I had now fallen silent when with a calm demeanor and well- 22 ordered speech he responded:

"I believe, much better than I could have known, that you are speaking the truth, and I see the difficulties. But I ask you, my Giovanni, do you think our king lacks circumspection? Indeed, our lord is sharp-sighted and gentle in nature, and his kingly ability is laudable. Far be it from him to wish to pressure you or anyone; it has long been his way to be patient, and that is how his orders are to be understood and accepted.

23 'Edepol facile credi potest inaccessibiles esse eas, quas predixeras, nationes et eorum codices, si qui sunt, omnino Latinis incognitos; verum, si qua ex Grecis, que ad Latinos usque devenerint, seu apud Latinos ipsos, quorum licteris non parum honoris et glorie maiorum attulere studia, comperiantur, etsi non omnia, que sal-

24 tem tua cura haberi possint, ista desiderat. Eia ergo, liberali animo, bene de Deo sperans, laborem subi, et quod potes facito, cum ad impossibile requiratur nemo. Non enim michi virum illum subli-mem et, nedum apud Cyprios, sed fama super ethera notum, Franciscum Petrarcam dedit fortuna obvium, credo sic volente Deo, ut et illi maximis occupato parcerem, et iuventuti tue hones-tum laborem inferrem, ex quo nomen tuum, nuper in auras exire incipiens, inclita gloria[10] elucescat clarius apud nostros.'

25 Tunc ego inquam:

'Iam satis video, strenue miles, quod, pretermissis barbarorum remotissimis libris, existimes ex Grecis Latinisque opus hoc inte-grum perfici posse. O bone Deus! Nonne ipse, Domnine, vides

26 quia hac ipsa concessione maximam partem operi demas? Sed fa-ciamus uti iam dudum nostri fecere principes, Romanum impe-rium dividentes in orientale et occiduum; sint monstro huic cor-pora duo, barbaricum unum et Grecum atque Latinum reliquum,

27 ad Grecum Latinumque, quos ipsemet nominas, libri. Nec istud etiam poterit ut quod postulas consequatur; antiquam enim hanc pestem monstravimus. Tu nunc tecum volve quot labentibus secu-lis hostes habuere volumina. Confiteberis equidem quoniam et[11] incendia et aquarum diluvia, ut de particularibus taceam, bib-liothecas assumpserint plurimas; etsi non alia deperisset quam Alexandrina, quam iam dudum Phyladelphus summa cum diligen-tia fecerat, esset librorum diminutio maxima, cum in ea testimonio antiquorum poteras reperire quod velles.

"By Pollux, it is easy to believe that these peoples are inaccessi-   23
ble, as you have outlined, and that whatever texts they have are
altogether unknown to the Latins. Indeed, he requests that you
investigate any Greek material which has reached the Latins or
belongs to the Latins themselves, whose pursuits have brought not
a little honor and glory to literature; if you cannot find all, then he
wants you to investigate at least those under your care. So, be gra-   24
cious, and with the will of God, undertake the task; accomplish
what you can, since no one is asking you to do the impossible. I
have never had the good fortune to meet that sublime man whose
fame has spread not only throughout Cyprus but among the heavens, that is, Francesco Petrarch, and I think God wills that I do
not add to his busy schedule but bring the honorable task to you.
As a young man your reputation, already beginning to rise aloft,
would shine among us with greater renown and glory."

Then I said: 25

"Now I see clearly, spirited soldier, that you think this task can
be accomplished entirely from Greek and Latin books without
consulting the most obscure books of barbarians. Good God! Do
you not see, Donnino, that by conceding this you are eliminating
the greatest part of the work? But let us do as our rulers did now   26
long ago, dividing the Roman Empire into East and West. There
are two heads to this monster, one barbaric and the other Greek
and Latin, and the books you mention are on the Greek and Latin
side. But even this will not make your demand possible, for we   27
have demonstrated this to be an ancient malady. But now you
should consider how many enemies books have had throughout
the centuries. You have to admit also that both fires and floods — I
need not discuss the particulars — have destroyed many books.
And if it were that only the library of Alexandria,[9] which long ago
Philadelphus had created with such diligence, had perished, books
would be extremely scarce, since our ancient witnesses tell us that
there you could find whatever you wanted.

28 'Preterea, invalescente gloriosissimo Christi nomine, eiusque doctrina sincere veritatis perlucida letiferi erroris et potissime gentilicii tenebras amovente, ac etiam iam diu Grecorum declinante[12] fulgore, clamantibus in infaustam religionem Christi nuntiis ac eam in exterminium pellentibus, nulli dubitandum est quin secum multos deleverint libros huius materiei refertissimos, dum non multos esse deos, nec deorum filios, sed unicum Deum patrem et filium Dei unicum tam vera quam pia predicatione monstrarent.

29 'Insuper avaritiam, cui non parve sunt vires, concedes habuisse hostem; facultas enim poetica scientibus nil afferre lucri certissimum est, et apud eam nil preciosum est preter quod afferat aurum. Ex quo consecutum ut aurum non afferentia, non solum neglecta, sed despecta atque deiecta sint; et cum omnes fere in divitias totis tendant pedibus, volumina talia in desuetudinem abiere, et

30 sic etiam periere facile. Eque in eorum detrimentum quorundam principum detestabile accessit odium, nec aliter quam in hostes ab eis adversus ea conspiratum est. Et quot hoc deleverit odium non solum fabularum, sed quarumcunque facultatum volumina, non

31 leviter exprimeretur numerus. Ceterum si cetera pepercissent, non eis, restauratore carentibus, perpercisset labile tempus, cui et taciti et admamantini sunt dentes, nedum libros, sed saxa corrodentes[13]

32 durissima et ferrum ipsum, domans cetera. Hoc hercle tam Greca quam Latina multa redegit in pulverem!

'Etsi hec et alia plura passa sint, et ea potissime, que nostro labori oportuna essent, negari tamen non potest quin multa supersint, sed nullum tamen, quod ego noverim, in hoc, quod optas, conscriptum. Vagantur igitur tam deorum quam progenitorum

33 nationes et nomina, huc illuc dispersa per orbem. Habet enim liber hic ex his aliquid, et aliquid liber alter. Que quis, queso, pro minime, seu saltem parum fructuoso labore velit exquirere et tot

"In addition, when the most glorious name of Christ began to   28
prevail, with its pure, lucid doctrine of truth removing the dark-
nesses of mortal, and especially pagan, error, and when the splendor of the Greeks was already in decline for a long time, as the
messengers of Christ railed against the unpropitious religion and
drove it to extinction, doubtlessly they destroyed many books
filled with this pagan material as they demonstrated with their
true and pious preaching that there were not many gods nor sons
of gods but only one God, the father, and one son of God.

"In addition, you will admit that avarice, a powerful entity, was   29
another hostile force, for poetic skill assuredly brings no profit to
those who possess it, and avarice finds nothing worthwhile unless
it brings gold. Since literature did not provide gold, it was not only
neglected but despised and discarded. And with nearly all in lock-
step and eager for riches, these books fell into disuse and thus also
perished easily. Equally detrimental was the detestable animosity   30
of certain rulers, conspiring against books no differently than
against their enemies. And no number could easily express how
many—not only books of fables but of various subjects—this animosity destroyed. But even if they had been spared, the passing of   31
time, with its silent but adamantine teeth, and which is the master
of not just books but other things—eating away at the hardest
stone and even iron—would not have spared the other books,
which lacked anyone to repair them. By Hercules this reduced   32
many Greek and Latin volumes to dust!

"And if these and many others have suffered, and especially
those which would have been useful for our task, it is nonetheless
not possible to deny that many survive, even if none I know of is
written on the subject you have chosen. Therefore the origins and
names of both gods and progenitors range here and there, dispersed throughout the world. One book contains one bit of infor-   33
mation, another contains another. So who, I ask you, would want,
for a labor apt to bear very little, if any, fruit, to seek out and leaf

volumina volvere, legere et hinc inde excerpere perpauca? Credo satius desistendum.'

34   Ast ille, in me defixis luminibus inquit: 'Non me latebat quin adversum moderatam petitionem meam haberes quid diceres; sed non adeo me repelles quin loculus remaneat aliquis, in quem fugiam. Non equidem negabo quod asseris. Verum iam secundo

35 dixisse velim: quod potes, facito! Hanc portiunculam, quam hinc inde excerpsisse poteris, rex noster exoptat. Poterisne istud etiam denegasse? Sed heu! Timeo non has tibi torpor ignavus rationes preparet, ut laborem effugias. Nil nempe turpius ocioso iuvene. Etsi laborandum est, cum ad laborem nascamur omnes, cui melius

36 quam regi optimo potes laborem inpendere? Surge igitur, et inertiam hanc pelle, et ad opus ingenti accingere animo, ut regi pariter pareas et tuo nomini ad inclitam famam viam facias! Venies profecto, si prudens es, ultro eo quo ego te conor inpellere. Nosti enim quoniam labor improbus vincat omnia, audentesque iuvet fortuna,[14] et multo magis Deus ipse nunquam deserens sperantes

37 in se. Vade igitur, et bonis avibus volve et revolve[15] et exentera libros, calamum arripe, et, dum regi obsequeris, tuum nomen in longissimum deduc evum!'

38   Tum ego:

    'Vincor, inquam, magis fere lepiditate verborum quam viribus rationum; urges etenim, me inpellis, trahis, et ut paream, si nolim velim, necesse est.'

39   Et sic, clementissime Rex, ut ad te aliquando calamum flectam, aliquandiu altercati sumus, Domninus tuus et ego; et, seu valeam seu non valeam, ad ultimum victus in tuam sententiam inpulsus

40 venio; quibus tamen viribus, tu vides. Iussu igitur tuo, montanis Certaldi cocleis et sterili solo derelictis, tenui licet cymba in vertiginosum mare crebrisque implicitum scopulis novus descendam nauta, incertus nunquid opere precium facturus sim, si omnia

16

through so many volumes, and read them and then extract so little? I believe that it would be better if I did not."

But fixing his eyes on me, he said: "I suspected that you would   34
have something to say against my modest request, but you will not
deny me a small place of refuge. I will not deny your assertion. But
now for the second time I would say to you: do what you can!
Our king desires the small portion you can excerpt from here and   35
there. Can you refuse even that? But alas! I fear that idleness and
inactivity do not provide you with reasons for avoiding the task.
Surely nothing is lazier than an inactive youth.[10] But if you have
to set to work, and we are all born for work, to whom would you
be able to better direct your work than to a noble king? Rise,   36
therefore, and rid yourself of this inertia, gird your great spirit for
the task so you might equally serve the king and pave the way for
the great renown of your name! If you are prudent you will surely
achieve our goal. You know that 'remorseless labor conquers all,'[11]
that 'fortune helps the daring,'[12] and, even more, that 'God himself
never deserts those who have hope in him.'[13] So come on, begin   37
with good portents, turn your books over and over, and disembowel them, take up the reed pen, and as you obey the king, lead
your name into time everlasting."

My response: 38

"I am defeated," I said, "nearly more by the facility of your
words than by the strength of your reasoning, for you are urging,
forcing, and dragging me, and so I have to obey, willingly or not."

And in this way, most merciful King, Donnino and I debated   39
for quite some time as to whether I would finally set my pen to
writing on your behalf. But whether I debated well or not, I was
ultimately vanquished and have been won over to your idea, although you see how much effort it took. Therefore, by your order   40
I will leave behind the mountain snails of Certaldo and its sterile
soil, and as a new sailor on a rather frail skiff I will descend into
the vertiginous sea encircled by ubiquitous cliffs, uncertain as to

legero; litora et montuosa etiam nemora, scrobes et antra, si opus sit, peragravero pedibus, ad inferos usque descendero, et, Dedalus alter factus, ad ethera transvolavero; undique in tuum desiderium, non aliter quam si per vastum litus ingentis naufragii fragmenta colligerem sparsas, per infinita fere volumina deorum gentilium reliquias colligam, quas comperiam, et collectas evo diminutas atque semesas et fere attritas in unum genealogie corpus, quo potero ordine, ut tuo fruaris voto, redigam.

41   Horresco tamen tam grande opus assumere, et vix credam, si resurgat et veniat Prometheus alter seu is idem, qui poetarum assertione prisco tempore consueverat homines ex luto componere, nedum ego, huius operis sit artista sufficiens. Sane ne, Rex inclite, mireris in posterum, dixisse velim:

'Non expectes, post multum temporis dispendium et longis vigiliis elucubratum opus, corpus huiusmodi habere perfectum; mutilum quippe, et utinam non membrorum plurium et fortasse distortum seu contractum gibbosumque, habendum est iam rationibus premonstratis.'

42   Porro, Princeps eximie, uti componendo membra deveniam, sic sensus absconditos sub duro cortice enucleando procedam, non tamen ad unguem iuxta intentionem fingentium fecisse promictam. Quis enim tempestate nostra antiquorum queat terebrare pectora et mentes excutere, in vitam aliam iam diu a mortali segregatas, et, quos habuere, sensus elicere? Esset edepol divinum potius quam humanum! Veteres quippe, relictis licteris suis nominibus insignitis, in viam universe carnis abiere, sensusque ex eis iuxta iudicium post se liquere nascentium, quorum quot sunt cap-

whether the labor will be worth the effort of reading all the books.[14] The shores and mountain woodlands, the channels and caves I will traverse by foot if needs be. I will descend to the nether regions, and I will become another Daedalus and fly into the ether.[15] To carry out your project, not otherwise than if I were collecting fragments along the vast shores of a huge shipwreck, I will collect the remnants of the pagan gods strewn everywhere in a nearly infinite number of volumes, and once found and collected, even if they are ravaged and half eaten by time and nearly worn to nothing, I will reduce them into a single corpus of genealogy, arranged to the best of my ability, to satisfy your wish.

Nonetheless, I dread undertaking such a large task, and if another Prometheus or even Prometheus himself, who in a bygone era the poets said could form men from mud,[16] were to rise up and present himself, I scarcely believe that he, much more than I, would have the skills for this work. In truth, illustrious King, so that in the future you will not be astonished, I will want to go on record, stating: 41

"Do not expect a work of this kind, even if it has consumed much time and toil late at the night, to have a perfect shape; indeed, for the reasons already discussed, you should think of it as maimed, but hopefully without extra limbs or misshapen, withered, or bulging."

Further, distinguished Prince, to produce the exegetical component, I will proceed by peeling back the hard outer layer and finding the hidden meanings underneath, but I still do not promise to do this in precise accord with the author's intentions. For who in our day can penetrate the hearts and examine the minds of the ancients, who long since have been moved from mortal life into another, and elicit their interpretations? By Pollux that would be a task more divine than human! Indeed, the men of the past, having left behind names made famous by their literature, have gone the way of all flesh, and they left their interpretations to the judgment 42

43

ita, fere tot inveniuntur iudicia. Nec mirabile. Videmus enim divini voluminis verba ab ipsa lucida, certa ac immobili veritate prolata, etiam si aliquando tecta sint tenui figurationis velo, in tot interpretationes distrahi, quot ad illa devenere lectores.

44 Et ob id in hoc minus pavescens accedam; nam, etsi minus bene dixero, saltem ad melius dicendum prudentiorem alterum excitabo; et hoc faciens, primo, que ab antiques hausisse potero scribam; inde, ubi defecerint seu minus iudicio meo plene dixerint, meam apponam sententiam; et hoc libentissimo faciam animo, ut quibusdam ignaris atque fastidiose detestantibus poetas a se minime intellectos appareat eos, etsi non catholicos, tanta fuisse prudentia preditos, ut nil artificiosius humani ingenii fictione velatum sit, nec verborum cultu pulchrius exornatum. Ex quibus patet liquido eos plurima mundana sapientia imbutos fuisse, qua sepis-

45 sime carent stomachosi reprehensores eorum. Ex quibus enucleationibus, preter artificium fingentium poetarum et futilium deorum consanguinitates et affinitates explicitas, naturalia quedam videbis tanto occultata misterio, ut mireris; sic et procerum gesta moresque non per omne trivium evagantia.

46 Post hec, quoniam in longe maius volumen quam existimes progredietur opus, oportunum arbitror, ut facilius invenias quod exquires et melius possis retinere que velis, illud in partes distin-

47 guere plures, easque nuncupare libros. Quorum unius cuiusque principio arborem apponendam censeo, cuius in radice pater assit propaginis, in ramis vero iuxta degradationis seriem apponere omnem dilitatam propaginem, ut per hanc videas de quibus et quo ordine in sequenti libro perquiras. Quos libros etiam debitis com-

of those born after them, who have nearly as many opinions as there are interpreters. Nor is this remarkable. We see the words of the divine book, clear by themselves, revealed with certain and unshakable truth, even if they are covered somewhat by a thin veil of literary figures, divided by as many interpretations as there are readers.

For this reason I will fear less as I approach this project, for although I may not say it as well, at least I will stimulate a better response from another person more skilled than I. My plan is, first, to write what I have extracted from the ancients, and then I will offer my interpretation where they have offered none or have done so less, in my opinion, than the text deserves. I do this most readily so that those who in ignorance fastidiously detest poets hardly known to them will see clearly that these ancient poets, despite not being Christians, were gifted with such prudence that no creation of human genius was ever veiled in fiction more cleverly, nor adorned more beautifully in the splendor of words. This makes it clear that they were imbued with the great worldly wisdom their peevish detractors very frequently lack. Once the outer layer is peeled back for you, beyond the artifice of the poets who fashion them and the relationships and affinities of the meaningless gods you will see aspects of nature, once shrouded in mystery, that will amaze you, as will the deeds of great men and customs now relatively obscure.

In addition, because the work will extend into a volume larger than you might suppose, I think it a good idea, so that you will find more easily what you seek and will be more able to remember what you like, to divide the work into a number of parts which I have designated as books. At the beginning of each of these books I thought it best to append a tree: the father is located at the roots; in the branches in descending order I have spread out all the progeny so you can see from whom they are born and in what order you will find them later in the book. You will also find these

44

45

46

47

21

peries distinctos rubricis ampliori sermone pandentibus, quod
48   unico tantum nomine per frondes arboris primo perlegeris. Demum[16] duos super addam libellos, et in primo quibusdam obiec-
tionibus in poesim et poetas factis respondebo; in secundo, qui
totius operis erit ultimus, quedam que in me forsan obicientur,
amovere conabor.

Sane, ne omiserim, nolo mireris aut errore meo contigisse putes
(veterum crimen est), quod sepissime leges, multa scilicet adeo
veritati dissona et in se ipsa non numquam discrepantia, ut nedum
a phylosophis oppinata, sed nec a rusticis cogitata putes, sic et
49   pessime temporibus congruentia. Que quidem et alia, si qua sunt
a debito variantia, non est mee intentionis redarguere vel aliquo
modo corrigere, nisi ad aliquem ordinem sponte sua se sinant redigi;[17] satis enim michi erit comperta rescribere et disputationes
phylosophantibus linquere.

50   Postremo, si sane mentis homines, tam ex debito quam ex Platonis consulto in quibuscunque etiam minimarum rerum principiis divinam opem imprecari consuevere, ac eius in nomine agendis
initium dare, eo quod, illo pretermisso, Torquati sententia nullum
rite fundetur exordium, satis advertere possum quid michi facien-
dum sit, qui inter confragosa vetustatis aspreta et aculeos odiorum,
membratim discerptum, attritum et in cineres fere redactum ingens olim corpus deorum procerumque gentilium nunc huc nunc
illuc collecturus et, quasi Esculapius alter, ad instar Ypoliti conso-
51   lidaturus sum. Et ideo, cum solum cogitans iam sub pondere titu-
bem nimio, eum piissimum patrem, verum Deum rerumque omnium opificem et cuncta potentem, cui mortales vivimus omnes,

books divided into appropriate chapter headings that will be more memorable because you will have already read that single name on one of the leaves in the tree. At the end I will also add two small 48 books. In the first I will respond to certain objections that have been made against poetry and poets; in the second, which concludes the entire work, I will attempt to dismiss any potential criticism against me.

Lest I forget, I certainly do not wish for you to be surprised or to think it is my error — it is the fault of the ancients! — when you read a number of things throughout the work that are so discordant with the truth and persistently self-contradictory that you will think that they were not thought up by philosophers or even pondered by simple folk, and that they were hardly fitting even for the ancients. It is not my intention to refute these and other in- 49 congruities if they differ from what is expected, nor will I correct them in any way unless they allow themselves to be returned to some sense on their own accord. It will be enough for me to recount what I have found and leave the disputes to the philosophers.

Finally, if wise men, whether because it was expected or because 50 Plato so advises, were accustomed to invoking divine assistance at the outset of even the smallest enterprises and to dedicate the beginning of a project in his name, since, in the opinion of Boethius,[17] if he is omitted no beginning can be properly undertaken, then I too can understand what I must do, as I venture over the rough terrain of antiquity and among the stingers of hatred, in order to collect from here and there the huge corpus of gods and noble princes, torn limb from limb, beaten, and reduced nearly to ashes, and to consolidate this corpus as if it were Hippolytus and I another Aesculapius.[18] And so, since the mere thought of the 51 undertaking makes me stagger under its excessive weight, I humbly pray that the most sacred Father, true God and omnipotent creator of all things, for whom all mortals live, favor my grand and

supplex precor ut grandi superboque ceptui meo favens assit. Sit michi splendens et immobile sydus et navicule dissuetum mare sulcantis gubernaculum regat, et, ut oportunitas exiget, ventis vela concedat ut eo devehar quo suo nomini sit decus, laus et honor et gloria sempiterna, detrectantibus autem delusio, ignominia, dedecus et eterna damnatio!

Prohemium 2

Quis primus apud gentiles deus habitus sit?

1 Mare magnum et dissuetum navigiis intraturus novumque sumpturus iter, ratus sum prospectandum fore solerter quo ex litore cymbe proresia solvenda sint, ut rectius, secundo spirante vento, eo devehar quo cupit animus. Quod quidem tunc comperisse reor dum eum comperero quem sibi primum deum finxere priores, ut, ab eo inito propaginis sumpto, debito possim ordine in posteritatem procedere.

2 Conveneram igitur mecum omnes animi vires et e sublimi mentis speculo omnem fere orbis intuebar ambitum, surgentesque extemplo plurimos vidi nec unius tantum religionis homines cuiuscunque tamen veritatis fidedignissimos testes, gravitate asserentes sua deum unicum esse, quem nemo vidit unquam, et hunc verum esse principio fineque carentem, potentem omnia, rerum patrem

3 atque creatorem tam patentium quam non patentium nobis. Quod cum optime crederem et ab ipsis puerilibus annis crediderim semper, cepi mente revolvere veterum quam plurium circa hunc varias atque diversas opiniones; visumque michi est hoc idem fere ipsos credere gentiles, sed eos decipi dum creature creatoris attri-

lofty enterprise. May he be a splendid and unmovable star for me and guide the rudder of my small ship as it ploughs through the unfamiliar sea, and, as the opportunity requires, bring winds to my sails so that I can be conveyed where there is grace, praise, and honor and everlasting glory for his name, and to my detractors deception, ignominy, disgrace, and eternal damnation!

Preface 2

Who was regarded as first among the pagan gods?

About to begin a new journey and embark upon a great sea unaccustomed to navigation, I thought I should use my skill and survey from which shore I should loosen the prow of my skiff in the hope that a favorable wind might better convey me where my spirit desires. I think I will have found it when I find who it was the ancients thought was their first god; if I could commence with the beginning of the lineage, I could then proceed to its posterity in the proper order. 1

I therefore had summoned up all the powers of my spirit and began to look at the expanse of nearly the whole world in the sublime mirror of my mind, and suddenly I saw several men rising up. Even if they were of different beliefs, they offered the most worthy evidence of every truth, authoritatively asserting that there is one god whom no one ever sees, the true God, without beginning or end, omnipotent, the father and the creator of everything visible and invisible to us. Because I believe this thoroughly and have always believed it since the years of my youth, I chose various and diverse opinions of many ancient men to reflect upon in my mind. It appeared to me that the pagans themselves believed nearly this same thing, but they were deceived in that they attributed the dignity of the creation to a something that was created, and di- 2 3

buunt dignitatem nec omnes uni sed diversi diversis conantur inpendere.

4   Cui errori causam intulisse phylosophantes et diversimode sentientes existimo, dum ostenderent prisce ruditati et post eos poete, quos primos theologizantes Aristotiles dicit, secundum suas credulitates eos esse deos primos quos ipsi arbitrabantur rerum primas fuisse causas. Et hinc, si plures et diversimode opinantes fuere, de necessitate secutum est ut plures et diversos deos diverse haberent nationes vel secte, quarum unaqueque suum exstimavit verum et primum et unicum esse deum aliorum patrem et domi-

5 num. Et sic non solum ad instar Cerberi tricipitem fecere[18] beluam, quin imo in monstrum longe plurium capitum describere conati sunt.

    Quorum dum antiquissimum investigarem, Thaletem Milesium obvium habui, suo evo sapientissimum hominem et celo astrisque familarissimum et quem ego audieram multa de vero deo ingenio magis quam fide iam dudum exquisivisse. Hunc ego rogavi ut diceret quem ratus sit deorum fuisse primum.

6   Qui evestigio inquit:

    'Rerum omnium causam primam aquam fuisse reor, eamque in se divinam habere mentem, omnia producentem nec aliter quam apud nos plantas humectet, sic ex abisso scaturiginibus emissis in celum usque sydera et ornatum reliquum manu madida fabricasse.'

7   Hinc Anaximenem, alium doctissimum virum, conveni et, dum hoc idem quod a Thalete percontor, respondit: 'Aerem rerum omnium productorem eo quod animantia aere perdito moriantur illico et absque eo nequeant procreari.'

8   Post hos Crisippus affuit, inter priscos famosus homo, qui rogatus ait ignem se rerum omnium conditorem credere, eo quod

verse men attempted to attribute it to diverse gods and not all to one.

I think the philosophers, who also had diverse opinions, gave 4 impetus to this error and revealed their ancient lack of sophistication, and after them the poets, whom Aristotle says were the first theologians,[19] in their mistaken belief that the first gods were those whom they considered to be the primary causes of things. And from this it necessarily followed, since there were even more who had different opinions, that different peoples and schools of thought had different gods, each of them thinking their god was the true, primary, and unique god who was father and master of the others. The result was that they created a beast not only like 5 triple-headed Cerberus[20] but in fact tried to describe a monster of many more heads.

It was when I was investigating the most ancient of them that I encountered Thales of Miletus,[21] the wisest man of his era, most knowledgeable about the sky and the stars. I had heard that long ago he had made many inquiries about the true god, albeit more by natural ability than by faith. I asked him to speak about who he thought was the first of the gods.

He immediately said: 6

"I think water was the first cause of all things, and that it has in itself a divine mind which produces everything much as it does in moistening our plants. Spring waters from the abyss were sent into the sky and formed the stars and the rest of the cosmos with its moist hand."

After this I addressed Anaximenes,[22] another very learned man, 7 and when I asked him the same question I asked of Thales, he responded, "Air produces all things; when deprived of air, living things die immediately, and without it they are unable to be created."

Following them came Chrysippus,[23] well known among the an- 8 cients, and after being asked he said he believed that fire was the

absque calore nil appareat posse gigni mortale, vel genitum posse consistere.

9   Alcinoum autem Crotoniensem cum convenissem, ceteris celsioris animi hominem comperi. Nam elementis transvolatis repente intellectu se miscuit astris, inter que, que noverit nescio, sed retulit se arbitrari solem, lunam et stellas et omne celum rerum omnium fuisse fabros. O liberalis homo! Quam uni tantum elemento ceteri dederant, hic omnibus supercelestium corporibus deitatem largitus est.

10   Post hos ego Macrobium iuniorem omnium adorior. Ille autem solo soli attribuit quod dederat Alcinous toti celo. Theodontius vero, ut arbitror, novus homo sed talium investigator precipuus, neminem nominando respondit vetustissimorum Arcadum fuisse opinionem terram rerum omnium esse causam, eique, ut de aqua dicit Thales, mentem inesse divinam existimantes, crediderunt eius opere omnia fuisse producta atque creata.

11   Porro ut de reliquis taceamus, poete qui Thaletis opinionem secuti sunt, aque elementum Occeanum vocavere et rerum omnium hominum atque deorum dixere patrem, et ab eodem genealogie deorum dedere principium. Quod et nos fecisse poteramus nisi invenissemus secundum quosdam Occeanum filium fuisse Celi.

12   Et qui Anaximenem et Crisippum vera dixisse credidere, eo quod Iovem pro elemento ignis et non nunquam ignis et aeris sepissime ponant poete, ei principatum deorum omnium tradidere et suis genealogiis deorum primum omnium ascripsere;[19] quos ideo in hoc secuti non sumus, quia Iovem nunc Etheris nunc Celi nunc Saturni fuisse filium legisse meminimus.

foundation of all things, for without heat it is apparent that nothing mortal could be born or that anything born could survive.

When I addressed Alcmeon of Croton,[24] however, I found a 9
man of loftier thought than the others, for among the flying elements he suddenly mingled his mind with the stars, becoming familiar with I know not what, but he reported that he thought that the sun, moon, and stars and entirety of the heavens were the makers of all things. Oh noble-minded man! The divinity the others attributed to only a single element, he bestowed upon all the supercelestial bodies.

After these I approached Macrobius,[25] the youngest of all. He, 10
however, attributed to only the sun what Alcmeon had given to the whole sky. Then Theodontius,[26] who I believe is a more contemporary man but a distinguished investigator in such matters, responded by naming no single person's opinion: "It was the opinion of the most ancient Arcadians that earth was the origin of all things; as Thales said regarding water, they proposed that it contained a divine intelligence which they believed produced and created everything."

We may skip over the others, but the poets who followed the 11
opinion of Thales called the element of water Ocean and said he was the father of all things, gods and men; from him they began the genealogy of the gods.[27] We might have done that too, except that we had found that according to some, Ocean was the son of Sky.[28]

Those who believed Anaximenes and Chrysippus to have spo- 12
ken the truth, whereby the poets very often make Jupiter stand for the element of fire and sometimes of fire and air, award the leadership of all the gods to him and begin their genealogies with him. We have not followed them in doing so because we recall reading that Jupiter was the son of Ether, and elsewhere of Sky, and elsewhere of Saturn.[29]

13   Qui vero Alcinoo prestitere fidem, Celium seu Celum genealogie sue principem voluerunt. Quod cum Ethere genitum legissemus, ultro omisimus. Sic et qui Macrobium primoresque suos, Soli genealogie concessere primatum. Quem multos habuisse parentes ipsi testantur poete, nunc illi Iovem patrem, nunc Yperionem, nunc Vulcanum attribuentes.

14   Qui autem terram rerum omnium productricem voluere, ut Theodontius dicit, inmixtam illi divinam mentem Demogorgonem nuncupavere. Quem profecto ego deorum gentilium omnium patrem principiumque existimo, cum neminem illi secundum poeticas fictiones patrem fuisse compererim, et cum Etheris non tantum patrem, sed avum extitisse legerim, et deorum aliorum plurium, ex quibus hi orti sunt, de quibus supra mentio facta est.

15   Sic igitur omnibus circumspectis, aliis abscisis tanquam superfluis, capitibus et in membra redactis, adinvenisse itineris principium rati, facientes Demogorgonem non rerum patrem sed deorum gentilium, duce deo scabrosum intrabimus iter per Trenaron aut Ethnam in terre viscera descendentes et ante alia Stygie paludis vada sulcantes.

Arbor

In arbore signata desuper ponitur in culmine Demogorgon versa in celum radice, nec solum infra descripte progeniei sed deorum omnium gentilium pater, et in ramis et frondibus ab eo descendentibus describuntur eius filii et nepotes de quibus omnibus hoc in primo libro prout signati sunt distincte scribitur.[20] Verum ex eis Ether solus excipitur, de quo et eius amplissima posteritate in li-

Those who entrust their belief to Alcmeon prefer to have Sky 13 at the beginning of their genealogy, but because we have read that he was the son of Ether, we have omitted him too. The same is true for those who follow Macrobius and his sources in making Sun the beginning of their genealogy. The poets attest that he has many parents, whether they attribute fatherhood to Jupiter, or Hyperion, or Vulcan.

Those who make the earth the mother of all things, as Theo- 14 dontius holds, prefer to name the divine mind intermingled with it Demogorgon.[30] But I think that he was certainly the father and beginning of all the pagan gods. I have found no one, according to the poetic fictions, to be his father, and in my readings I have found him to appear as not only the father of Ether but as his grandfather as well, and of many other of the gods, from whom were born the others mentioned above.

And so, having considered all these things, eliminating what 15 was superfluous, and returning the heads to the limbs, thinking that we have found the beginning of our journey and making De- mogorgon the father not of things but of the pagan gods, with God as our leader we will embark upon the rough journey through Tenarum[31] and Etna, descending into the viscera of the earth and plowing first through the shallows of the Stygian swamp.

Tree

In the tree illustrated above, the roots are turned upward toward the sky and Demogorgon is placed at the top. He is father of not only the progeny described below but of all the pagan gods. His sons and grandsons are shown in both the branches and the leaves extending from this; accordingly in this first book there is a sepa- rate chapter for each of them. Ether alone is not included; he and

bris sequentibus describetur. Fuerunt ergo Demogorgoni filii filie-
que VIIII. Quorum primus Litigium, secundus Pan, tertia Cloto,
quarta Lachesis, quinta Atropos, sextus Polus seu Pollux, septi-
mus Phyton seu Phaneta, octava Terra, nonus autem Herebus.

Prohemium 3

1 Summa cum maiestate tenebrarum, arbore descripta, veternosus
ille deorum omnium gentilium proavus, undique stipatus nebulis
et caligine, mediis in visceribus terre perambulanti michi comparuit Demogorgon, nomine ipso horribilis, pallore quodam mus-
coso et neglecta humiditate amictus, terrestrem tetrum fetidumque
evaporans odorem, seque miseri principatus patrem potius alieno
sermone quam suo confessus verbo, me coram novi laboris opifice
2 constitit. Risi, fateor, dum illum intuerer, memor stultitie veterum
qui illum a nemine genitum eternum et rerum omnium patrem
atque in terre visceribus delitescentem rati sunt. Sane quoniam
minus hoc spectat ad opus, eum sinamus sua in miseria, proceden-
tes eo quo cupimus.
3 Huius igitur insipide credulitatis causam dicit Theodontius non
a studiosis hominibus habuisse principium, quin imo a vetustissi-
mis Arcadum rusticis. Qui cum mediterranei essent homines atque montani et semisilvestres et viderent terram sponte sua, sil-
vasque et arbusta queque[21] producere, flores, fructus et semina
emictere, animalia alere cuncta et demum in se morientia queque
suscipere, nec non et montes flammas evomere, ex duris silicibus
ignes excuti, ex concavis locis et vallibus exalare ventos, et illam

his abundant posterity will be described in the following books. Demogorgon had nine sons and daughters: the first of them was Strife, second Pan, third Clotho, fourth Lachesis, fifth Atropos, sixth Polus or Pollux, seventh Phyton or Phanetes, eighth Earth, and ninth Erebus.

Preface 3

Once I described the tree, that languid forefather of all the pagan gods, surrounded everywhere by clouds and gloom and accompanied by the greatest majesty of darkness, appeared to me as I passed through the center of the earth's viscera, Demogorgon—the name alone is horrible—enveloped in a certain slimy pallor and relentless humidity, exhaling an earthy, foul, and fetid odor, acknowledging more in another's voice than in his own that he was the father of this wretched realm; he stood before me, master builder of this new undertaking. I laughed, I confess, as I gazed upon him, mindful of the stupidity of the ancients who thought him to be born from no one, eternal, and father of all things, lurking in the bowels of the earth. But because this pertains less to the task, let us leave him in his misery and proceed toward where we wish to go.

Theodontius says that the cause of this dim-witted credulity originates not with scholars but with very ancient Arcadian peasants. Because they were landlocked dwellers of the mountains and woodlands, and because they saw the land spontaneously produce forests and all kinds of bushes, blossom with flowers, fruits, and seeds, nourish all the animals, and then receive all of them back when they die, and because they saw the mountains vomit forth flames as well, fires chipped out from hard flints, and winds issuing forth from hollows and valleys, and because they felt it move

33

sentirent moveri nonnunquam et etiam mugitus emictere eiusque
ex visceribus fontes, lacus et flumina fundi, quasi ex ea ethereus
ignis et lucidus aer exorti ac egregie potata ingentem illum occeani
pelagum eminxerit, et ex collisis incendiis evolantes in altum favil-
lule solis luneque globos ediderint, summoque implicite celo in
stellas sese infixerint sempiternas stolide credidere.

4   Qui autem post hos secuti sunt paulo altius sentientes, non
terram simpliciter rerum harum dixere autorem, sed illi mentem
implicitam esse divinam intellectu et nutu cuius agerentur ista,
eamque mentem in subterraneis habere sedem arbitrati sunt. Cui
errori auxit fidem apud rusticos antra ac profundissimos terrarum
abditus intrasse non nunquam in quibus[22] cum in processu lan-
guescente luce silentium augeri videatur, subintrare mentes cum
nativo locorum horrore religio consuevit et ignaris presentie alicuius divinitatis suspicio quam a talibus suspicatam divinitatem,
non alterius quam Demogorgonis existimabant, eo quod eius man-
sio in terre visceribus crederetur ut dictum est.

5   Hic igitur cum esset apud vetustissimos Arcades in honore
precipuo, rati taciturnitate sui nominis divinitatis eius augeri
maiestatem, seu existimantes indecens esse tam sublime nomen in
buccas venire mortalium, vel forte timentes ne nominatus irritare-
tur in eos, consensu publico vetitum est ne impune nominaretur a
quoquam.

6   Quod quidem testari videtur Lucanus ubi Erictum manes invo-
cantem describit dicens:

                    Paretis, an ille
compellandus erit, quo nunquam terra vocato

sometimes and even emit roars as it pours out from its viscera springs, lakes, and rivers, as if ethereal fire and bright air rose out from it and, having drunk so much it urinated that huge sea of the ocean, and because they saw that from clashing fires tiny sparks flying upward brought forth the spheres of the sun and moon, and, interwoven at the top of the sky, fastened themselves into stars, they stupidly believed them to be eternal.

Those who came after them had somewhat loftier thoughts. 4 They said it was not simply the earth that was the author of these things but that inextricably connected to it was a divine mind, and that those actions were performed upon its command by its intellect, and they thought that this mind was situated in subterranean regions. Entering into caves and the deepest recesses of the earth often increased the rustics' faith in this misconception. There, when during a ceremony in the diminishing light the silence seemed to be increased, religion used to steal into their minds along with their innate awe of such places and, in their ignorant fear, they imagined the presence of some divinity. Such peoples used to think that this supposed divinity was none other than Demogorgon, since he was believed to dwell in the bowels of the earth, as has been said.

Because he was of such chief importance among the most an- 5 cient Arcadians, they believed that by not uttering his divine name they were augmenting his majesty. Whether they thought it would be unseemly for such a sublime name to come into mortal mouths, or perhaps feared that by naming him they would incur his wrath, it was forbidden by the community for anyone to utter his name with impunity.

Lucan seems to provide evidence for this when he describes 6 Erichtho calling upon the shades, saying:[32]

> Will you appear? Or must he
> be summoned at the utterance of whose name the earth

non concussa tremit qui Gorgona cernit apertam
verberibusque suis trepidam castigat Erinem?

etc.

7   Sic et Statius ubi cecum senem Tiresiam iussu Ethyoclis belli
Thebanorum exitum perscrutatur, dicit:

Scimus enim et quicquid dici noscique timetis
et turbare Hecatem, ni te, Tymbree, timerem
et triplicis mundi summum quem scire nephastum;
illum sed taceo,

etc.

8   Hunc, de quo duo poete loquuntur nomine non expresso, Lactantius insignis homo doctusque super Statium scribens liquido
dicit esse Demogorgonem summum primumque deorum gentilium. Et nos etiam satis sumere possumus, si verba carminum
ponderare velimus. Dicit enim apud Lucanum femina malefica et
gentiles, ad preminentiam atque subterraneam huius mansionem
demonstrandam, terram tremere eo vocato, quod nunquam alias
facit nisi concussa. Subsequenter hoc idem, quia videt Gorgonem,
id est terram apertam, id est ad plenum eo quod in visceribus ha-
bitet terre, nos autem respective ad eum superi superficiem tantum
9   videmus. Vel videt apertam Gorgonem, monstrum illud vertens
aspicientes in saxa, nec propterea in saxum vertitur, ut appareat
preeminentie eius signum aliud.

Tercio potentiam eius ostendit etiam circa inferna, dum eum
dicit castigare verberibus Erinem pro Erinas, id est Furias, eas
scilicet potentia sua et reprimendo et irritando. Hunc autem cognosci a superis ideo dicit Statius, ut illum et subterraneum et

unstruck always trembles, who looks openly at the Gorgon,
and terrifies the Erinyes when he whips them?

So does Statius, where he has old, blind Teiresias, by order of   7
Eteocles, forecast the outcome of the Theban war, saying:[33]

For we know what you fear will be said and known:
how to confound Hecate (if I feared not you, Thymbraean)
and the great one of the triple world, an abomination to
   know —
but I shall say nothing about him.

Lactantius,[34] a distinguished and learned man writing about   8
Statius, says that this god, about whom two poets speak without
expressing his name, is certainly the great Demogorgon and the
first of the pagan gods. And we, too, can rightly assume this if we
choose to value what it says in the texts of the poems. In Lucan,
for example, the nefarious, pagan woman demonstrates that he has
a preeminent, subterranean dwelling by saying that the earth trembles when his name is called, something which never happens unless it is shaken by an earthquake. The next passage says the same
thing: he looks at the Gorgon, that is, "open" land, and that means
"vast" because he lives in the bowels of the earth while we are
looking for him up here only on the surface. Or, he sees the "Gor-   9
gon openly," that monster who turns those looking at her into
stone, meaning that he is not turned into stone and that this is
another symbol of his preeminence.

Third, it again shows how powerful he is in the infernal region
when he is said to punish the Erinyes, or Erinas, that is, Furies,
with whips, both restraining and enraging them with his power.
And Statius says that he is so well known among the celestial gods

cunctorum demonstret principem, et invocatum posse cogere ma-
10 nes in desideria mortalium, quod ipsi nollent. Eum autem cognosci ideo nephas dicit, quia scire secreta dei non spectat ad omnes; nam si cognita sint, in vilipensionem fere veniet potentia
deitatis. Huic preterea ne tedio solitudinis angeretur, liberalis et
circumspecta vetustas, ut ait Theodontius, socios[23] dedit Eternitatem atque Chaos, et inde filiorum agmen egregium; novem enim
illi inter mares et feminas fuisse voluere, ut infra apparebit distinctius.

11   Erat hic locus detegendi, si quid fuisset poetica fictione recondi-
tum. Sed cum nudus sit huius deitatis erronee sensus, explicare
quid nomen eius horridum sonare videatur tantummodo superest.
Sonat igitur, ut reor, *Demogorgon* Grece, 'terre deus' Latine. Nam
demon 'deus,' ut ait Leontius, *gorgon* autem 'terra' interpretatur, seu
potius 'sapientia terre,' cum sepe *demon* 'sciens' vel 'sapientia' expo-
natur, seu, ut magis placet aliis, 'deus terribilis,' quod de vero Deo
12 qui in celis habitat legitur: 'Sanctum et terribile nomen eius.' Verum iste aliam ob causam terribilis est, nam ille ob integritatem
iustitie male agentibus in iudicio est terribilis, iste vero stolide
existimantibus.

    Postremo, antequam de filiis aliquid, de sociis pauca videnda
sunt.

that he represents him as the subterranean leader of all the gods, and that when called upon he can compel the shades to do the bidding of mortals even if they are unwilling. He also says that he 10 is known as such an abomination, because it is not for all to know the secrets of the gods; if they were known, the power of divinity would be considerably depreciated. In addition, lest he be angered by the tedium of solitude, a befittingly circumspect and long-lasting old age, as Theodontius says, provided him with Eternity and Chaos as companions, and after that an illustrious line of children; they believed they had determined that he had nine, counting males and females, who will appear separately below.

Thus far we have uncovered what was hidden beneath the po- 11 etic fiction. But now that the meaning of this obscure divinity has been exposed, it remains only to explain why the sound of his name seems to means something horrid. I think his Greek name, Demogorgon, means "god of the earth": *daemon* means "god," as Leontius[35] says, and *gorgon* means "land," or perhaps "wisdom of the land," since *daemon* is often explained as "knowing" or "knowledge," or, as others would have it, "terrible god," since it is said about the true God who lives in heaven, "Holy and terrible is his name."[36] But he is terrible for another reason, for he is terrible in 12 judgment by virtue of the integrity of his justice against those who are evil; Demogorgon is terrible for those believing in him out of ignorance.

Finally, before discussing his children, a few things need to be said about his companions.

: I :

De Eternitate[24]

1 Sequitur de Eternitate, quam ideo veteres Demogorgoni sociam dedere, ut is qui nullus erat videretur eternus. Que quid sit suo se ipsa pandit nomine, nulla enim temporis quantitate mensurari potest, nullo temporis spatio designari, cum omne contineat evum et contineatur a nullo.

2 Quid enim de illa[25] scripserit Claudius Claudianus, ubi heroico carmine Stilliconis laudes extulit, libet inserere. Dicit enim sic:

> Est ignota procul nostreque impervia menti,
> vix adeunda diis annorum squalida mater,
> immensi spelunca evi, que tempora vasto
> suppeditat revocatque sinu; complectitur antrum,
> omnia qui[26] placido consumit numine serpens
> perpetuumque[27] viret squamis, caudamque reducto
> ore vorat tacito, relegens exordia lapsu.
> Vestibuli custos vultu longeva decoro,
> ante fores Natura sedet cunctisque volantes
> dependent membris anime; mansura verendus
> scribit iura senex, numeros qui dividit astris
> et cursus stabilesque moras quibus omnia vivunt
> ac pereunt fixis cum legibus, ille recenset,

etc.

:   I   :

On Eternity

Here follows a discussion on Eternity, whom the ancients gave as   1
companion to Demogorgon in order to make him—who did not
exist—seem eternal. Her name explains who she is, for no quantity of time can measure her, nor is she designated by any expanse
of time; she embraces every era, and is contained by none.

It is worth quoting Claudius Claudianus where he sings her   2
praises in his heroic *On the Consulship of Stilicho.*[37] He says this:

> Far off, unknown, and impassible for the human mind,
> scarcely accessible for the gods, is the squalid mother of the
>   years;
> in a cave of immense age she bestows and recalls time
> from her vast lap. Encircling the cave—
> a serpent with a placid spirit who devours everything,
> perpetually green in his scales, and his tail,
> his mouth turned back, he devours silently, recovering his
>   slithery beginning.
> The aged custodian of the vestibule, with a beautiful
>   countenance,
> Nature, sits before the doors, flying spirits hanging on every
>   limb.
> A venerable old man writes enduring laws, enumerates
>   divisions for the stars,
> and reckons their steadfast courses and pauses, by which all
>   things live
> and die, with set regulations. . .

3   Antro demum sic descripto subsequitur idem:

> Hic habitant vario facies distincta metallo
> secula certa locis, illic glomerantur aena,
> hic ferrata rigent, illic argentea candent;
> eximia regione domus,
>
>   etc.

Hec ille; ex quibus reor, serenissime regum, possis advertere quam suavi stilo quamque accurata atque explicita oratione quid Eternitas et que intra Eternitatem contineantur poeta describat.

4   Qui, ut eius ostendat omnium temporum excessum, dicit speluncam ispius, id est gremii profunditatem, incognitam atque procul stantem, et nedum mortalibus, sed vix adeundam diis, id est beatis creaturis que in conspectu dei sunt; eamque demum dicit tempora suppeditantem atque revocantem, ut appareat intra eam omne tempus initium sumpsisse ac sumere et sumpturum esse, et ultimo in finem devenire suum; et ut appareat quo ordine describit serpentem perpetuo viridem, id est quantum ad eam nunquam in senium tendentem, eumque dicit revoluto in caudam ore eam devorantem, ut ex hoc actu percipiamus temporis circularem lapsum.

5   Nam semper anni unius finis principium est sequentis, et sic erit durante tempore. Quo exemplo usus est, eo quod per illud fuerit olim Egyptiis, antequam licteras suscepissent, consuetudo describendi annum. Subsequenter autem hoc fieri tacite dicit eoquod non advertentibus nobis paulatim labatur tempus. Naturam autem animarum circumvolantium plenam eo quod assidue multis animantibus animas infundat, ideo ante fores Eternitatis describit ut intelligamus quod quicquid intrat Eternitatis gremium, seu parum mansurum seu multum, natura rerum agente intrat, et sic

After describing the cave in this way, he continues: 3

> Here also, their faces distinguished by various metals, live
> the Ages, each assigned a place. There bronze is formed; here
>   iron stands unbending;
> there silver sparkles; and in the most extraordinary part of the
>   house. . .

So Claudian writes. I think that from this quotation, most serene of kings, you can see how the poet used such a graceful language and accurate and specific details to describe Eternity and her attendants.

To depict the full range of the elements of time, he says that   4 her cave, that is, the depth of her lap, is "unknown" and standing "far off," and "scarcely accessible for the gods," let alone mortals, which is to say for blessed creatures in the sight of god. Then he says that she "bestows and recalls time" to describe how within her confines every kind of time has commenced, commences, and will commence, and ultimately comes upon it own end. The arrangement of time he describes as a perpetually green serpent, which is to say that she never advances into old age. And he says that the tail in its mouth is devoured to represent the cyclical passing of time.

The end of one year is always the beginning of the next, and it   5 will remain so as long as time endures. He used this example because the Egyptians, before learning to write, were accustomed to describing a year like this. Subsequently, however, he said it was done silently because time passes little by little without our noticing. He describes bountiful Nature with spirits fluttering around her because she tirelessly enlivens living things with sprits. He describes her as sitting before the doors of Eternity so that we understand that what enters into the lap of Eternity, whether for a short or long duration, enters under the agency of the nature of

quasi ianitrix hic est, et est intelligendum de natura naturata, nam quod natura naturans immictit nunquam egreditur.

6   Senem autem, qui in antro numeros stellis dividit, Deum verum credo, non quia senex sit, non enim in eternum cadit etatis ulla descriptio, sed mortalium loquitur more, qui longevos etiam immortales senes dicimus. Hic numeros stellis dividit ut intelligamus quia eo agente et ordinante per certum et constitutum ab eo syderum motum nobis tempora distinguantur, ut puta per solis totius celi circuitum habemus annum, sic per eandem lune circumvolutionem mensem, et per integram octave spere revolutionem diem. De seculis autem, que ibidem esse dicit, infra ubi de Eonis satis late scribetur.

: 2 :

De Chaos

1   Chaos, ut Ovidius in principio maioris sui voluminis asserit, fuit quedam omnium rerum creandarum inmixta et confusa materia. Dicit enim sic:

> Unus erat toto nature vultus in orbe,
> quem dixere Chaos, rudis indigestaque moles
> necquicquam nisi pondus iners congestaque eodem
> non bene iunctarum discordia semina rerum,
>
> etc.

2   Hunc seu hanc tam speciosam forma certa carentem effigiem voluere non nulli, alias insignes phylosophi, sociam atque coeternam fuisse Demogorgoni, ut si quando in mentem illi venisset

44

things, and so she is like a custodian. We should know this about created nature, for what nurturing nature admits never leaves.[38]

The old man in the cave who "enumerates divisions for the 6 stars" I believe to be the true God—not because he is an old man, for in regard to the eternal age descriptions mean nothing—but because he speaks like one of us mortals, who say that the long-living are also immortal. He "enumerates divisions for the stars" to help us understand that by his agency and ordering we can determine time by the precisely established motion of the stars. As an example we have the year, which is the solar circuit of the entire sky, and similarly the month, which is the circumvolution of the moon, and the day, which is the revolution of the whole octave sphere. Generations, which he says are also there, will be described more fully below in the chapter treating the Aeons.[39]

∴ 2 ∴

On Chaos

Chaos, as Ovid asserts in the beginning of his greater work, was a 1 kind of commingled and disordered substance from which all things were to be created. He said it this way:[40]

> There was one face of nature in the whole orb,
> which they called Chaos, an unformed and undigested mass,
> nothing other than an inert weight and an amassing in one
>   place
> of discordant seeds of disparate things.

Some otherwise eminent philosophers have wanted him or 2 such a splendid image lacking any specific form, to have been the companion and contemporary of Demogorgon, so that when it

creaturas producere, non deesset materia, quasi non posset qui poterat rebus variis formam dare, materiam ex qua daret producere. Ridiculum est, sed iam neminem redarguere professus sum.

∴ 3 ∴

De Litigio primo Demogorgonis filio

1 His premissis ad inclitam prolem primi dei gentilium veniendum est. Cuius primum filium voluere Litigium, eo quod primum eum ex Chaos pregnantis utero, ex incerto tamen patre eductum velint.

2 De cuius eductione talis a Theodontio recitatur fabula. Dicit enim a Pronapide poeta in *Prothocosmo* scribi quod semel residente Demogorgone, ut quiesceret in Eternitatis antro, sensit in utero Chaos tumultuari, quam ob rem commotus extensa manu Chaos ventrem aperuit, et evulso Litigio tumultum faciente, eo quod turpem et inhonestam haberet faciem, abiecit in auras. Qui confestim evolavit in altum; non enim poterat ad inferiora descendere, cum omnium rerum inferior is esse videretur, qui illum ex utero

3 matris exemerat. Ast inde Chaos acri fessa labore, cum non haberet quam invocaret Lucinam, madens tota in sudorem videbatur resolvi debere, ignita exalans infinita suspiria, insistente forti manu Demogorgone, ex quo factum est ut iam divulso Litigio, tres Parcas et Panem educeret una cum eis. Inde autem cum illi Pan rebus gerendis videretur ceteris aptior, eum domui prefecit sue et sorores

came into his mind to produce living beings the material would not be lacking—as if it would not have been possible for him who was able to give form to various things to produce the material from which he could do so. This is ridiculous, but I have already professed that I would not disprove anyone.

: 3 :

On Strife, first child of Demogorgon

Having finished with the preliminaries, we must now turn to the 1 famous offspring of the first god of the pagans. They want to make his first child Strife since they think he was the first born from the womb of pregnant Chaos; his father, however, is uncertain. Theodontius tells this fable about his birth. He says, citing 2 the *Protocosmus* of the poet Pronapides,[41] that once while Demogorgon was resting in the cave of Eternity, he sensed a disturbance in Chaos' womb. As a result he opened the belly of Chaos with his outstretched hand and plucked out Strife, who was causing the disturbance; he had such a repulsive and dishonest face, that Demogorgon threw him into the air above. Strife immediately flew up; after all, he could not descend any lower, since the one who took him from his mother's womb was thought to be the lowest of all things. Meanwhile Chaos, without any Lucina to call upon but 3 fatigued by labor pains and covered in sweat, seemed ready to release. She exhaled endless breaths of fire, and, assisted by the strong hand of Demogorgon after Strife's departure, she gave birth to the three Parcae and Pan along with them. However, since he thought Pan was more suited than the others for managing things, he put him in charge of his home and gave his sisters to him as

illi dedit pedissequas. Chaos autem liberata pondere, iussu Panis, Demogorgonis cessit in sedem.

4   Litigium vero, quod nos vulgatiori vocabulo Discordiam dicimus, ab Homero in *Yliade* Lis vocatur, et Iovis dicitur filia, quam ipse ait, eo quod a Iunone per eam Iesus fuerit circa nativitatem Euristei et Herculis de celo in terras eiectam. Theodontius autem de Litigio plura insuper recitat, que ubi decentius in processu ponenda videbuntur, apponam, que hic de eo adpresens omictantur.

5   Habes, Rex inclite, ridiculam fabulam, verum eo ventum est, ubi oportunum sit a veritate amovere fictionis corticem. Sed prius respondendum est persepe dicentibus, 'Quid poete Dei opera vel nature vel hominum hoc sub fabularum velamine tradidere? Non erat eis modus alter?' Erat equidem, sed uti non equa facies omnibus, sic nec animorum iudicia. Achilles arma preposuit ocio, Egystus desidiam armis, Plato phylosophiam omissis ceteris secutus est, statuas celte sculpere Phydias, Apelles pinnaculo ymagines pingere. Sic ut reliqua hominum studia sinam, poeta delectatus est tegere fabulis veritatem, cuius delectionis Macrobius super *Somnio Scipionis* scribens satis apte causam videtur ostendere dum dicit:

> De diis autem, dixi ceteris, et de anima; non frustra se, nec ut oblectent ad fabulosa convertunt, sed quia sciunt inimicam esse nature apertam undique expositionem sui, que sicut vulgaribus hominum sensibus intellectum sui vario rerum tegmine operimento subtraxit, ita a prudentibus arcana sua voluit per fabulosa tractari. Sic ipsa misteria fabularum cuniculis operiuntur, ne vel hoc adeptis nudam rerum talium

servants. Relieved of her burden, Chaos went by order of Pan to the seat of Demogorgon.

Incidentally, Strife, which in our common speech we call "Discord," Homer in the *Iliad* calls Lis;[42] she is said to be a daughter of Jupiter who was thrown, Homer says, from the heavens down to earth because at the time of the birth of Eurystheus and Hercules she had offended Jupiter by carrying out Juno's deceit. The several additional things Theodontius said about Strife, omitted here for the present, I will discuss where they seem more appropriate later on.[43] 4

You have here, distinguished King, a ridiculous fable, but it provides an opportunity for removing the layer of fiction covering the truth. But first I must respond to those who frequently ask, "Why did poets treat the works of God, nature, or men under this veil of fables? Did they not have an alternative?" Yes, there was, but as all things are unequal among men, so are their judgments. Achilles preferred arms to tranquility; Aegisthus, idleness to arms; Plato followed philosophy to the exclusion of everything else; Phidias, the sculpting of statues with a chisel; and Apelles, the painting of images with a brush. Just so — and I will leave aside other human pursuits — a poet delights in covering the truth in fables. Writing about this delight in his *Dream of Scipio*, Macrobius seemed to explain the reason quite sufficiently when he said:[44] 5 6

> I have spoken about the other gods and about the soul; they turn to the fabulous not without purpose or for personal amusement but because they know that in all matters a clearly literal exposition is antagonistic to nature; just as she removes any understanding of herself from the comprehension of common people by hiding beneath various covers and an outer layer, so she wishes prudent people to treat her mysteries in fables. In this way the very mysteries of the fables are hidden deeply away so that nature does not lay her-

49

natura se prebeat, sed summatibus tantum viris sapientia interprete, veri arcani consciis, contenti sunt reliqui.

Hec Macrobius.

7   Quibus etsi multa plura dici possent, satis responsum arbitror exquirentibus. Insuper, Rex precipue, sciendum est his fictionibus non esse tantum unicum intellectum, quin imo dici potest potius polisenum, hoc est multiplicium sensum. Nam sensus primus habetur per corticem, et hic licteralis vocatus est; alii per significata per corticem, et hi allegorici nuncupantur.

Et ut quid velim facilius assummatur, ponemus exemplum.

8   Perseus Iovis filius figmento poetico occidit Gorgonem, et victor evolavit in ethera. Hoc dum legitur per licteram hystorialis sensus prestatur. Si moralis ex hac lictera queritur intellectus, victoria ostenditur prudentis in vicium, et ad virtutem accessio. Allegorice autem si velimus assumere, pie mentis spretis mundanis deliciis ad celestia elevatio designatur. Preterea posset et anagogice dici per fabulam Christi ascensum ad patrem mundi principe superato figurari.

9   Qui tamen sensus etsi variis nuncupentur nominibus, possunt tamen omnes allegorici appellari, quod ut plurimum fit. Nam allegoria dicitur ab *allon*, quod alienum Latine significat, sive diversum, et ideo quot diversi ab hystoriali seu licterali sint sensu, allegorici possunt, ut dictum est, merito vocitari. Verum tamen non est animus michi secundum omnes sensus enucleare fabulas que sequuntur, cum satis arbitrer unum ex pluribus explicasse, esto aliquando apponentur fortasse plures.

10   Nunc autem quid Pronapidem sensisse putem, explicabo paucis. Videtur etenim michi Pronapidem mundi creationem designare voluisse, secundum erroneam eorum opinionem, qui rati

self bare for even those who understand such things, but only for superior men, using their wisdom as their guide, who are privy to her arcane truths. The rest are content. . .

So writes Macrobius.

Much more could be said about this, but I think it responds 7 sufficiently to the question. Besides, eminent King, you must know that there is no unique interpretation for these fictions; rather one can say that they are *polisenus*, or, "of multiple interpretations."[45] The outer cover contains a first layer of understanding, which is called "literal." It also reveals other interpretations under its covering, and these are called "allegorical."

And let us offer an example so you can more easily understand the point. Perseus, the son of Jupiter, killed the Gorgon in the 8 poetic fiction, and, victorious, he flies up into the air.[46] When one reads this in the literal sense, it offers historical meaning. If one seeks a moral understanding from a reading, it reveals how the prudent conquer vice and accede to virtue. If we wish to treat it allegorically, it means that by spurning earthly delights the pious mind ascends to the heavens. In addition, an anagogical interpretation would say that the fable reconfigures the ascension of Christ to the Father after overcoming the ruler of the world.

These interpretations, although labeled differently, could all be 9 called allegorical, as they very often are, for "allegory" comes from *allon*, which means "different" or "diverse." Therefore as diverse as they are in the historical and literal sense, they can be called allegorical, as I have said. But even so, I do not intend to open up the following fables to every kind of interpretation; I think it will be sufficient to offer one of many explanations, although on occasion I might offer several.

Now I will use a few words to explain what I think Pronapides 10 meant. He seems to me to have wished to signify the creation of the world, according to the erroneous opinion of those who be-

sunt deum ex materia preparata produxisse que creata sunt. Nam sensisse Demogorgonem tumultum fieri in utero Chaos, nil aliud reor quam divinam sapientiam, aliqua eam movente causa, ut puta maturitatem ventris, id est temporis propositi horam, advenisse, et sic cepisse velle creationem et que immixta erant certo ordine segregare, et hinc extendisse manum, id est operam voluntati dedisse, ut ex informi colluvie formosum atque ordinatum produceret opus, et ante alia evulsit ex utero laborantis, id est laborem confusionis patientis, Litigium, quod totiens aufertur a rebus quotiens, amotis discordantie causis, illis debitus imponitur ordo.

11   Patet igitur hoc ante alia fecisse, disgregasse scilicet que inter se erant elementa confusa, calida enim frigidis, sicca humidis, et levia gravibus repugnabant. Et cum primus dei videretur actus a discordantibus ordinando subtraxisse Litigium, Demogorgonis primus filius dictus est. Eum abiectum ob turpem faciem, quia turpe sit ut plurimum litigare, evolasse ad sublimia potius videtur fabuloso

12   ordini prestare decorem, quam aliud velle significare. Preterea eiectum quo se efferret ni in altum tenderet non habebat, cum in inferioribus iam producti orbis partibus in lucem constet eum fuisse productum. Quod a superis in terras demum deiectum sit, scribit Homerus ob id factum, quod opere suo ante Herculem Euristeus natus sit, ut suo narrabitur loco.

13   Verum quantum ad intrinsecum sensum, hoc ego sentio, quod a motu superiorum corporum apud mortales persepe[28] oriantur litigia. Insuper dici potest illud in terras eiectum a superis, cum apud superos omnia certo et perpetuo agantur ordine, ubi apud mortales vix inveniatur aliquid esse concorde.

14   Deinde cum dicit sudore madefactam Chaos et ignita emictentem suspiria, nil aliud intelligat reor quam elementorum segrega-

lieved that a god produced the creation from preexisting substance. That Demogorgon sensed a tumult in the womb of Chaos I think is nothing other than divine wisdom. Some cause stimulated it, for example, the belly reaching maturity; that is, the appointed hour arrived, so divine wisdom wished to take control of the creation and separate and arrange the elements within. To do this it extended its hand, that is, to give action to its will so as to produce from a formless cesspool a beautiful and ordered work. And before everything else it tore it out from the womb of the laboring mother, that is, the labor of enduring disorder, Strife, and once strife is taken out of things, the causes of discord are removed and the proper order can be imposed on them.

Clearly this was accomplished before anything else, namely, 11 thoroughly separating the commingled elements that were battling between opposites: hot and cold, dry and moist, and light and heavy. Since the first act of the god seems to have been to remove Strife and create order from discord, he is said to be the first son of Demogorgon. He was thrown out on account of his repulsive face because to engage in strife is extremely repulsive. That he flew higher seems to add a nicety to the telling of the fable rather than signify anything else. Besides, when he was thrown out he had no 12 direction to go other than up because we know he had recently been produced into the light in the lower parts of the world. That the gods later threw him down to earth Homer wrote because it was by his efforts that Eurystheus was born before Hercules, as will be described later.[47]

I understand this intrinsically since even human strife arises 13 very often from the movement of heavenly bodies. And it can be said that he was thrown down to earth by them as well, for among the heavenly bodies all things are securely and perpetually ruled by order while among mortals scarcely anything peaceful exists.

Then, when he says that Chaos was covered in sweat and exhal- 14 ing fiery breath, I think he means nothing other than the first

tionem primam, ut per sudorem sentiamus aquam, per ignita vero suspiria aerem atque ignem, et que desursum sunt corpora, et per grossitiem molis huius terram, que Panis consilio confestim creatoris sui domus et sedes facta est. Eductum autem Pana post Litigium credo ratos veteres ea in separatione elementorum naturam naturatam habuisse initium et evestigio domui, id est orbi, Demogorgonis prepositam, quasi eius opere sic volente deo omnia producantur mortalia.

15 Parcas autem eodem partu productas et pedissequas fratri datas ideo fictum existimo, ut intelligatur naturam his cum legibus productam ut procreet seu gignat, nutriat et in finem nata deducat. Que tria sunt Parcarum officia, in quibus continuum nature prestant obsequium, ut latius in sequentibus apparebit.

: 4 :

De Pane secundo Demogorgonis filio

1 Pana Demogorgonis fuisse filium iam satis supra monstratum est. De quo talem Theodontius recitat fabulam. Dicit enim eum verbis irritasse Cupidinem et inito cum eo certamine superatum, et victoris iussu Syringam nynpham Arcadem adamasse, que cum satyros ante lusisset, eius etiam sprevit coniugium. Pan autem cum illam urgente Amore fugientem sequeretur, contigit ut ipsa a Ladone fluvio impedita consisteret, et nynpharum auxilium precibus imploraret, quarum opere factum est ut in palustres calamos vertere-
2 tur. Quos cum Pan motu ventorum sensisset, dum invicem colli-

separation of elements: we understand the sweat to mean water, the fiery breath to mean air and fire, and the bodies from above amassed together to mean earth, which at the advice of Pan was immediately made the seat and home of its creator. In that Pan was born after Strife I believe the ancients were thinking that created nature had its beginnings in this separation of the elements and that it was immediately put in charge of the home of Demogorgon, that is, the earth — as if all mortal things are produced by his work, and thus by divine will.

Moreover, that the Parcae were produced from this same birth   15 and given to their brother as servants I think was invented to mean that nature was produced with these laws governing everything that is procreated, born, nurtured, and brought to its end. The three functions of the Parcae, who are continually in the service of nature, will be presented more fully below.[48]

: 4 :

On Pan, second child of Demogorgon

We have already fully accounted for Pan as the son of Demogor-   1 gon. Theodontius tells the following fable about him. He says that Pan spoke words that angered Cupid, engaged him in a contest, and lost, and that the victorious Cupid commanded him to fall deeply in love with the Arcadian nymph Syrinx, who, although in the habit of teasing satyrs, spurned his advances. With Love urging him on, however, Pan pursued the fleeing nymph, who had to halt when she reached the river Ladon, implored with prayers the nymphs for their assistance, and was turned with their help into swamp reeds. When Pan noticed that the motion of the wind   2

derentur, esse canoros, tam affectione puelle a se dilecte quam delectatione soni permotus, calamos libens assumpsit, et ex eis septem disparibus factis fistulam, ut aiunt, composuit, eaque primus cecinit, ut etiam testari videtur Virgilius:

Pan primus calamos cera coniungere plures
instituit,

etc.

3   Huius preterea poete et alii insignes viri mirabilem descripsere figuram. Nam ut Rabanus in libro *De origine rerum* ait:

Is ante alia fronti habet infixa cornua in celum tendentia, barbam prolixam et in pectus pendulam, et loco pallii pellem distinctam maculis, quam nebridem vocavere prisci, sic et manu virgam atque septem calamorum fistulam.

Preterea inferioribus membris hirsutum atque hispidum dicit, et pedes habere capreos et, ut addit Virgilius, purpuream faciem.

4   Hunc unum et idem cum Silvano arbitrabatur Rabanus, sed diversos esse describit Virgilius dicens:

Venit et agresti capitis Silvanus honore,
florentes ferulas et grandia lilia quassans.

Et illico sequitur:

Pan deus Arcadie venit.

Et alibi:

Panaque Silvanumque senem nynphasque sorores.

5   His igitur premissis, ad intrinseca veniendum est. Et quoniam supra Pana naturam naturatam esse dictum est, quid sibi voluerint fingentes eum a Cupidine superatum, facile reor videri potest. Nam quam cito ab ipso Creatore natura producta est, evestigio

caused these to collide with one another and make melodious sounds, moved as much by his affection for the girl as by his delight in the sound, he merrily collected the reeds and from them, as they say, made a pipe of seven unequal lengths. He was the first to make music with this, as Vergil also bears witness:[49]

Pan was the first to show how to join several reeds
with wax.

In addition, poets and other famous men described his remark- 3 able shape. For, as Rabanus said in his *On the Nature of Things*,[50]

Most remarkable were the upwardly curving horns implanted into his forehead, his long beard reaching all the way down to his chest, and in place of a cloak a pelt marked with spots which the ancients called a *nebris*, as well as the wand in his hand and his pipe of seven reeds.

In addition he said that his lower legs were hairy and shaggy and that he had goat like feet, and, as Vergil added, a purple face.[51]

Rabanus thought he was one and the same as Silvanus, but 4 Vergil describes them differently, saying:[52]

And Silvanus came with a rustic honor on his head,
shaking flowering fennel plants and tall lilies.

And he continues with this:[53]

Pan, the god of Arcadia, came.

Also elsewhere:[54]

Both Pan and aged Silvanus and their sister nymphs.

These are the preliminaries, so we should move deeper. Because 5 we said earlier that Pan was created nature, I think it we can easily understand what they intended to mean by the fiction that he was conquered by Cupid, for as soon as nature was produced by the

cepit operari, et suo delectata opere, illud cepit amare, et sic a delectatione irritata amori succubuit. Syringa autem, quam aiunt a Pane dilectam, ut dicebat Leontius, dicitur a *syren* Grece, quod Latine sonat 'deo cantans,' et sic poterimus dicere Syringam esse celorum seu sperarum melodiam, que ut Pictagore placuit, ex variis inter se motibus circulorum sperarum conficiebatur, seu conficitur, et per consequens tanquam deo et nature gratissimum, a

6 natura conficiente diligitur, seu volumus potius Syringam esse circa nos agentibus supercelestibus corporibus nature opus tanto organizatum ordine, ut dum in certum et determinatum finem continuo deducitur tractu, non aliter quam faciant rite canentes armoniam facere, quod deo gratissimum fore credendum est.

7 Cur autem hanc nynpham Arcadem fuisse dixerint et in calamos versam, ideo dictum puto quia, ut placet Theodontio, Arcades primi fuere, qui, excogitato cantu, emictentes, per calamos longos et breves, spiritum, quatuor vocum invenere discrimina, et demum addidere tria, et ad postremum quod permultos faciebant calamos, in unam contraxere fistulam, foraminibus ori flantis

8 proximis et remotioribus excogitatis. Macrobius vero hoc repertum dicit Pictagore, ad ictus malleorum gravium atque levium. Iosephus vero in libro *Antiquitatis Iudaice* dicit longe vetustius Iubal inventum fuisse ad tinnitum malleorum Tubalcayn fratris sui, qui ferrarius faber fuit. Verum quoniam fingentibus verius visum est Arcades invenisse, eo quod illo forsan evo ceteros excederent fistula, arcadem nynpham fuisse voluere.

Syringam autem lusisse satiros et Pana fugientem, atque a Ladone moratam et ninpharum suffragio in calamum versam, circa nostros cantus iudicio meo aliquid bone considerationis abscondit. Hec enim spretis satyris, id est ingeniis rudibus, fugit Pana, id est

Creator himself, it immediately began its work and, delighting in that work, fell in love with it, and so, stirred by its delight, succumbed to love. Leontius used to say that Syrinx, whom they say was loved by Pan, is so called from *syren* in Greek, which means "singing to god," and so we can say that Syrinx is the melody of the heavens and spheres, that which, according to Pythagoras, was effected, or is effected, by the various interconnected motions of the orbits of spheres. Because this is so pleasing to God and nature, it is loved by the nature that creates it. Or, we might suggest 6 rather that Syrinx is a work of nature, with supercelestial bodies moving all around us, organized in such order that when it is forced continually into a certain and predetermined end, it makes harmony, just as if it were singing properly. And one would have to believe that this was most pleasing to God.

As to why they said this nymph was Arcadian and turned into 7 reeds, I think they said this because, according to Theodontius, after the invention of song, the Arcadians were the first people to blow through long and short reeds and discover four distinct tones, and then add three more, finally fitting many reeds onto one pipe by adding holes closer and further from the mouth of the player. Macrobius says that Pythagoras discovered this while strik- 8 ing heavy and light hammers.[55] Josephus, however, in his book, *Jewish Antiquities*, says that Jubal discovered it much earlier in the pings of the hammers belonging to his brother Tubalcain, who was a blacksmith.[56] But because the more accurate story tellers say it was the Arcadians who invented it—perhaps because in their day they excelled at playing the pipe—they want the nymph to be Arcadian.

As for Syrinx sporting with satyrs and fleeing Pan, as well as being delayed by the Ladon and turned into a reed with the approval of the nymphs, I think these seem to hide something of great interest about our songs. For, spurning the satyrs, that is, unrefined instincts, she flees Pan, that is, man who is by nature fit

hominem natura aptum natum ad musicalia; nec equidem actu fugit sed existimatione cupientis cui in dilatione videtur cessari
9   quod optat. Hec tunc a Ladone sistitur donec instrumentum ad emictendam meditationem perficitur.

Est enim Ladon fluvius in ripa nutriens calamos, in quos versam Syringam aiunt, ex quibus postmodum confectam fistulam novimus; ex quo sumere debemus, uti calamorum radix terre infixa est, sic et meditatio musice artis et compertus exinde cantus tam diu latet in pectore inventoris, donec emictendi prestetur organum, quod ex calamis suffragio humiditatis a radice emissis conficitur; quo confecto, sonus premeditatus emictitur suffragio humiditatis spiritus emictentis. Nam si siccus esset, nulla sonoritatis dulcedo, sed mugitus potius sequeretur, ut videmus ex igne per fistulas emisso contingere; et sic in calamos versa videtur Syringa, eo quod per calamos resonet. Possibile preterea fuit a compertore fistule calamos ad hoc primo fuisse compertos Ladonem[29] secus, et sic a Ladone detenta.

10   Restat videre quid sensisse potuerint circa Panis ymaginem, in qua ego arbitror veteres universale nature corpus tam scilicet agentium quam patientium rerum voluisse describere, ut puta sentientes per cornua in celum tendentia supercelestium corporum demonstrationem, quam duplici modo percipimus, arte scilicet, qua discursus syderum investigantes cognoscimus et sensu quo eorum in nos infusiones sentimus.

11   Per ignitam autem eius faciem ignis elementum, cui annexum aerem voluere, sumendum reor, quos sic iunctos Iovem dixere non nulli. Per barbam autem, per quam virilitas demonstratur, virtutem activam horum duorum elementorum sic iunctorum intelligi

for making music, and she does not flee in reality but in the belief of the one who is desirous, to whom a delay means that the object of one's desires seems to be slipping away. Then she is stopped by the Ladon until the instrument producing the contemplated music was finished. 9

The Ladon is a river that nurtures along its banks the reeds into which they say Syrinx was transformed and which later were made into the pipe we know. From this we should posit that the root of the reeds was fixed in the earth just as the contemplation of the musical art and then the song found later resided for a while in the heart of the inventor until the instrument of release presented itself; this came from reeds released upward from their root with the help of moisture, and once that happened, the premeditated sound was released with the help of moisture from the breath of the person who released it. If it were dry, not a sweetness of sonority but a noise would have followed, like the sound released from reeds in a fire. And so, Syrinx seems to have been turned into reeds because she makes her sound through reeds. I might add that it was also possible that the discoverer of the pipe found reeds for the first time near the Ladon, and that in this sense she was detained by the Ladon.

It remains to see what meaning they might be able to derive from the image of Pan. Here I think the ancients wished to describe the universal body of nature of things that act rather than are acted upon, thinking, for example, of his horns directed toward the sky as an identification of the supercelestial bodies. We perceive of this demonstration in two ways: by the skill with which we investigate and learn of the paths of the stars, and by the sense with which we feel their influence upon us. 10

As for his inflamed face I think we should assume the element of fire, with which they wished to join air—a union some called Jupiter. In his beard, which demonstrated virility, I think they wanted to recognize the positive actions of these two joined ele- 11

voluisse existimo, et eorum opus in terram et aquam, dum demissam illam in pectus et ad partes inferiores traxere. Eum autem maculosa pelle tectum descripsere, ut per illam ostenderetur octave spere mirabilis pulchritudo, crebro stellarum fulgore depicta, a qua quidem spera, sicuti pallio tegitur homo, sic omnia ad naturam rerum spectantia conteguntur.

12   Per virgam autem nature regimen intelligendum reor, quo omnia et potissime ratione carentia reguntur et in determinatum finem in suis operibus etiam deducuntur. Fistulam vero ad armoniam celestem designandam illi apposuere. Quod illi circa inferiora sit hispidum corpus et hyrsutum, terre superficiem montium et scopulorum gibbosam et silvarum virgultorum et graminum tectam intelligo.

13   Alii vero sensere aliter. Solem scilicet per hanc ymaginem designari, quem rerum patrem dominumque credidere, quos inter fuit Macrobius. Et sic eius cornua volunt lune renascentis indicium, per purpuream faciem aeris mane seroque rubescentis aspectum, per prolixam barbam ipsius solis in terram usque radios descendentes, per maculosam pellem celi ornatum a solis duce derivantem, per baculum, seu virgam, rerum potentiam atque moderamen, per fistulam celi armoniam a motu solis cognitam, etc., prout supra.

14   Credo, Rex magnifice, videas quam summotenus exponendo transeam, quod duplici de causa facio. Primo quidem quia confido, quoniam tibi nobile sit ingenium, quo possis, quantumcunque parvis datis indiciis, in quoscunque profundissimos sensus penetrare. Secundo quia sequentibus cedendum est. Nam si omnia que ad expositionem huius fabule possent induci describere vellem, invidia[30] forte posteritatis fecisse viderer, et ipsa sola fere totum excogitatum volumen occuparet.

ments and, since it hung down to his chest and lower parts, their effect on earth and water as well. They described him as covered in a spotted skin so they could show the wondrous beauty of the octave sphere resplendent in the ubiquitous gleam of its stars, and how this sphere, just as a cloak covers a man, covers everything pertaining to the nature of things.

I think his wand must signify the rule of nature by which ev- 12 erything, especially that which is utterly lacking in rationality, is regulated in their individual tasks and led to their predetermined end. In this way the pipe was added to designate celestial harmony. That his lower body is hairy and shaggy I think is the earth's surface contoured with mountains and cliffs and covered with forests, thickets, and grasses.

Others think differently, for instance, that this image designates 13 the sun, which they believed to be the father and master of things. Among these is Macrobius.[57] Therefore they want his horns to represent the waxing moon, his purple face the aspect of the reddish morning and evening sky, his long beard the rays of the sun reaching down to earth, his spotted pelt the sky decorated by the light of the sun, his staff or wand, power and control of things, and his pipe the harmony of the sky which we recognize from the motion of the sun, and so on, as above.

I believe, magnificent King, that you can see how I am proceed- 14 ing with full explanations. I do this for two reasons, first because I am assured that your noble nature allows you to penetrate into the deepest meanings even if provided with only a small amount of information, and second because you must agree with the following—that if I wanted to describe everything that could be used to explain this fable, I might seem to have done so out of malice toward posterity, and it alone would occupy nearly the entire projected volume.

15   Et ut redeam ad omissa, hunc Pana, seu quod in processu eundem cum Demogorgone arbitrarentur Arcades, ut Theodontio visum est, seu quod illo neglecto in istum totos verterent animos, sacris etiam horrendis, ut puta humano, imo natorum illi litantes sanguine, precipue coluere, eumque dixere Pana a *pan*, quod 'totum' Latine sonat, volentes ob hoc quod omnia quecunque sint in nature gremio concludantur, et sic ipsa totum sit.

Iuniores inde, eo quod innovata placeant, Pana Lyceum vocave-
16   runt. Alii, dempto Panis nomine, Lyceum tantum dixere. Et non nulli Iovem Lyceum, existimantes nature seu Iovis opere lupos a gregibus amoveri quibus ipsi fere vacabant omnes, et sic a lupis fugatis cognomen meruisse videtur; Grece enim lupus dicitur *lycos*. Augustinus vero, ubi *De civitate Dei* scribit, dicit non ob hoc contigisse Pana Lyceum vocari, quin imo propter crebram mutationem hominum in lupos, que in Arcadia contingebat, quod nisi divina operante virtute fieri non posse arbitrabantur.

17   Hinc preterea videtur Macrobium sumpsisse Pana non Iovem sed Solem esse, eo quod sol omnis mortalis vite sit pater, eoque surgente consueverint lupi dimissis insidiis adversus greges in silvas abire, et sic ob istud beneficium eum dixere Lyceum.

And so I return to address what I omitted. Whether because 15 the Arcadians thought him worthy of the same awe as Demogorgon, as it seemed to Theodontius, or because by not worshipping Demogorgon they could devote their entire attention to Pan, they worshipped this Pan primarily with horrible sacrifices of human blood and even their sons' blood in his honor. They called him Pan from *pan*, which is the Greek word for "all," wishing in this to understand as a totality all the things that are included in the lap of nature.

More recent writers, because they are influenced by newer things, call him Pan Lyceum. Others, taking away the name Pan, 16 call him simply Lyceum. And some call him Jupiter Lyceum after observing that wolves, whether nature or Jupiter was at work, shied away from the flocks nearly all of them tended. And so he merited this name from the elimination of wolves: in Greek the word "wolf" is *lycos*. Augustine in his *City of God* says that Pan was called Pan Lyceum not for this reason but because of the frequent transformation of Arcadian men into wolves that used to occur in Arcadia, and which they thought could not have occurred without divine power.[58]

In addition, it seems that Macrobius assumed that Pan was not 17 Jupiter but the sun, for the sun was the father of every mortal life and wolves usually finish attacking flocks and return to the forest when the sun rises, and so for this benefit they call him Lyceum.[59]

: 5 :

De Cloto, Lachesi et Atropu
filiabus Demogorgonis

1   Cloto, Lachesis et Atropos, ut supra, ubi de Litigio, filie fuere
Demogorgonis. Cicero autem has Parcas vocat, ubi *De naturis deo-*
rum scribit, et filias Herebi Noctisque fuisse dicit. Verum ego ideo
Theodontio potius adhereo, qui illas cum rerum natura creatas
dicit, quod longe magis veritati videtur conforme, eas scilicet nature rerum esse coevas.

2   Has easdem ubi supra vocat Tullius in singulari Fatum illudque
Herebi Noctisque filium dicit, quod ego longe magis quam Parcas,
habito respectu ad id quod de Fato scribitur, ut post sequetur,
Demogorgonis filium dicam. Seneca vero, has in *Epistulis ad Luci-*
lium Fata vocat, dato Cleantis dictum dicat, dicens:

Ducunt volentem Fata, nolentem trahunt.

Circa quod non solum earum[31] describit officium, eas scilicet sorores omnia ducere, sed etiam trahere, non aliter quam si de necessitate contingant omnia.

3   Quod longe apertius sentire videtur in tragediis Seneca poeta
tragicus, et in ea potissime cui titulus est *Edipus*, ubi dicit:

Fatis agimur, credite fatis.
Non sollicite possunt cure
mutare rati stamina fusi.
Quicquid patimur mortale genus
quidquid facimus venit ex alto,
servatque sua decreta colus
Lachesis dura revoluta manu,
omnia septo tramite vadunt

: 5 :

On Clotho, Lachesis, and Atropos, daughters of Demogorgon

Clotho, Lachesis, and Atropos, as I said above in the chapter on 1
Strife, were daughters of Demogorgon. In his *On the Nature of the Gods* Cicero calls them Parcae and says they were daughters of Erebus and Night.[60] I favor the account of Theodontius, however, who says they were created with the natural universe, for it seems to conform much better with the truth that they were coeval with the natural universe.

In the aforementioned passage Cicero calls them Fate in the 2
singular, and says "he" was the son of Erebus and Night. I prefer this much to "Parcae," and when I write about Fate subsequently, I will say that he is the son of Demogorgon. Seneca in his *Epistles to Lucilius* calls them Fates, although he cites Cleanthes, saying:[61]

The Fates lead the willing; they compel the unwilling.

Here he not only describes their duties, namely, that these sisters command all things, but also that they compel, as if they touch everything of necessity.

The tragic poet Seneca seems to suggest this more openly, most 3
effectively in the tragedy of the title *Oedipus*, where he says:[62]

By the Fates we are driven; believe in the Fates.
Our anxious cares cannot
change the thread of the fixed spindle.
Whatever we, the mortal species, endure,
whatever we do comes from on high.
Lachesis serves the hard decrees
of her distaff with her hand turned;

primusque dies dedit extremum.
Non illa deo vertisse licet
que nexa suis currunt causis.
It cuique ratus prece non nulla
mobilis ordo, multis ipsum
timuisse nocet, multi ad fatum
venere suum dum Fata timent,

etc.

Hec ille.

4 Quod etiam Ovidius sensisse videtur dum in maiori suo volumine dicit in persona Iovis Veneri:

Tu sola insuperabile fatum,
nata, movere putas? Intres licet ipsa sororum
tecta trium, cernes illic molimine vasto,
ex ere et solido rerum tabularia ferro,
que neque concursum celi neque fulminis iram,
nec metuunt ullas tuta atque eterna ruinas.
Invenies illic incisa adamante perenni
Fata tui generis,

etc.

5 In quibus preter iam damnatam opinionem summi potest has tres sorores esse Fatum et Fata quantumcunque Tullius in Parcas et Fatum distinxerit, volens potius, ut reor, diversitate nominum diversitatem officiorum quam personarum ostendere.

6 Nos autem de his tribus redigendis postremo in unum, quid non nulli senserint videamus. Has supra diximus servitio Panis dedicatas a patre, et causam demonstravimus. Fulgentius vero ubi *De mithologiis*, dicit eas attributas obsequio Plutonis inferorum dei, credo ut sentiamus actiones istarum circa terrena tantum versari, et Pluto terra interpretatur. Et ait idem Fulgentius, Cloto interpretari 'evocationem,' eo quod suum sit, iacto cuiuscunque rei semine,

All things walk a fenced path;
And the first day gives the last.
It is not allowed for the goddess to change
events bound by its causes.
Order, unmoved by prayer, proceeds
fixed for all. Pained, many fear it;
many come to their end while fearing fate.

This is what Seneca wrote.

Ovid in his larger book seems to have understood this when in   4
the persona of Jupiter he says to Venus:[63]

> Do you alone, daughter, think you can move
> the insuperable Fates? You may enter the house of the three
> sisters; you will see there a massive collection
> of bronze and solid iron, accountings,
> which neither the sky's thunder nor the anger of the lightning
>   bolt
> fear, nor any other destruction, secure and eternal.
> You will find there the Fates of your stock inscribed
> in indestructible adamant.

We can assume from these verses, excluding the opinion we have   5
already dismissed, that these three sisters are Fate or the Fates,
just as Cicero distinguished between Fate and the Parcae, and that
this diversity of names distinguishes, as I think, more the difference between their functions than their names.

So let us see how some have interpreted these three sisters who   6
have been reduced to one. We already said that their father put
them into the service of Pan and explained why. Fulgentius in his
Mythologies, however, says that they were assigned to serve Pluto,
god of the underworld.[64] I believe this shows that their actions
only involve terrestrial affairs, in that Pluto signifies the earth.
Fulgentius also said that Clotho means "evocation," for it is her

illud adeo in incrementum trahere, ut aptum sit in lucem emergere. Lachesis autem, ut idem dicit, interpretatur 'protractio,'[32] eo quod id quod a Cloto compositum est in lucem evocatum a Lachesi suscipiatur et protrahatur in vitam. Atropos autem, ab *a,* quod est 'sine,' et *tropos,* quod est 'conversio,' 'absque conversione' interpretatur, eo quod omne natum evestigio, quod in terminum sibi presignatum venisse cognoverit, demergat in mortem, a qua nulla retro naturali opere conversio est.

7   Apuleius vero Medaurensis non mediocris autoritatis phylosophus, de his in libro quem *Cosmographiam* cognominat, scribit sic:

> Sed tria Fata sunt numero cum ratione temporis facientia, si potestatem earum ad eiusdem similitudinem temporis referas. Nam quod in fuso perfectum est, preteriti temporis habet speciem, et quod torquetur in digitis, momenti presentis indicat spatia, et quod nondum ex colo tractum est subactumque cure digitorum, id futuri et consequentis seculi posteriora videtur ostendere. Hec illis conditio et nominum eiusdem proprietatem contingit, ut sit Atropos preteriti temporis fatum, quod non deus quidem faciet infectum; et futuri temporis Lachesis autem a fine cognominata, quod etiam illis que futura sunt finem suum deus dederit; Cloto presentis temporis habet curam, ut ipsis actionibus suadeat ne causa solers rebus omnibus desit.

Hec Apuleius. Sunt insuper qui volunt Lachesim eam esse, quam fortunam nuncupamus et ab ea omnia mortalibus contingentia
8   agitari. Nunc autem quid de fato sentiant veteres, dato non multum a precedentibus differant, videndum est.

office, once each seed is cast, to compel it to grow so it is ready to emerge into the light. Lachesis, he says similarly, refers to "protraction" or "lot," for that which is composed by Clotho and brought into the light is received by Lachesis and protracted into life. And Atropos (from *a*, meaning "without," and *tropos*, meaning "turning") refers to "turning away," for everything that is born, when it recognizes that it has come to its predetermined end, sinks immediately plunges toward death, from which there is no natural way to return.

Apuleius of Madaura, a philosopher of considerable authority, 7 wrote about these things in this way in the book he named *Cosmography*:[65]

> But there are three Fates in number representing the reckoning of time, if you relate the power of each of them to the comparable period of time. For what happens with the spindle seems like the passing of time; the turning in the fingers indicates the space of the present moment; and what has not yet been taken from the distaff and subjected to the care of their fingers seems to represent what will arrive in the future generation and subsequently. This is their circumstance. As for the propriety of each of their names, it happens that Atropos is the fate of time spent, which not even a god will undo; Lachesis is named as the end of time about to be, for god has given them even the end of what will be; Clotho has care of the present time so as to make sure by her actions that the intelligent cause is not lacking in all things.

Thus writes Apuleius. There are in addition those who wish Lachesis to be what we call Fortune and the instigator of all the things that happen to mortals. But we must understand that what 8 the ancients thought about fate does not differ much from what we just examined.

Dicit ergo de fato sic Tullius in libro quem *De divinatione* scripsit:

> Fatum id appello quod Greci *imarmenidem*, id est ordinem seriemque causarum, cum causa causam ex se gignat, ea est exomi eternitate fluens veritas sempiterna. Quod cum ita sit, nichil est futurum, cuius non causas id ipsum efficientes natura contineat. Ex quo intelligitur ut Fatum sit non id quod superstitiose, sed id quod phylosophice dicitur causa eterna rerum cur et ea que preterierint facta sunt, et que instant fiant et que sequuntur futura sint.

Hec Cicero.

Boetius autem Torquatus, vir disertissimus atque catholicus, ubi *De phylosophica consolatione* scripsit, cum diffuse de hac materia cum Phylosophia magistra rerum altercetur, dicit inter alia de Fato sic:

> Omnium generatio rerum cunctusque mutabilium naturarum progressus et, quicquid aliquo movetur modo, causas, ordinem, formas ex divine mentis stabilitate sortitur; hec in sue simplicitatis arce composita, multiplicem rebus gerendis modum statuit. Qui modus cum in ipsa divine intelligentie puritate conspicitur, providentia nominatur. Cum vero ad ea que movet atque disponit refertur, Fatum a veteribus appellatum est.

Hec ille. Poteram et apponere quid Apuleius de fato in *Cosmographia* determinet, et aliorum sententias, sed quoniam satis dictum reor.

Cur Demogorgonis aut Herebi Noctisque Parce seu Fatum vel Fata dicantur filie, breviter describam. Cum sepe eventurum sit in

Cicero says this about fate in the book he wrote *On Divination*:[66]

I call fate that which the Greeks call *heimarmene*, that is the order and succession of causes when a cause gives birth to another cause from itself; it is an eternal truth flowing from all eternity. Therefore nothing will exist if its nature fails to   9 contain the causes that make that very thing itself. From this it is understood that Fate is not that which is superstitiously but philosophically said to be the eternal cause of things, why things that have happened have been, why things that are are, and why things that will follow will be.

This Cicero writes.

Boethius Torquatus, a man most learned and Christian, when   10 he was arguing variously with Philosophy, master of things, about this material in his *Consolation of Philosophy*, said, among other things, this about Fate:[67]

The generation of all things and the entire progression of mutable nature, and whatever is moved in some way were allotted their causes, order, and forms from the stability of a divine mind; this, while composed in the refuge of its simplicity, establishes a complex method for all that happens. This method, when it is perceived in the very purity of divine intelligence, is called providence. In fact, when it refers to those things which it moves and determines, it was called Fate by the ancients.

So wrote Boethius. I could add as well what Apuleius in his *Cos-*   11 *mography* prescribed about fate and the opinions of others, but I think I have said enough.

I will describe briefly why the Parcae or Fate or Fates are said to be the children of Demogorgon or Erebus and Night. Since it will often happen in what follows and has already happened in what

sequentibus et iam in precedentibus contigerit, quod causatus causantis dicatur filius, possumus ad presens dicere has tres sorores variis nuncupatas nominibus dei filias tanquam ab eo causatas, qui prima causarum est, ut satis per verba supra proxime Ciceronis atque Torquati videri potest. Hunc deum, ut dictum est, veteres Demogorgonem dixere.

12 Quod autem ex Herebo et Nocte, ut dicit Tullius, nate sint, talis ratio reddi potest. Est Herebus, ut apperebit latius in sequentibus, terre profundissimus et absconditus locus, quem allegorice possumus accipere pro profunditate divine mentis, in quam mortalis oculus penetrare non potest, et cum divina mens videns tanquam se ipsam, intelligens quid actura esset, et inde has actu cum natura rerum produceret, satis ex Herebo, id est ex arcano et profundissimo divine mentis penetrali, natas dicere possumus.

13 Noctis autem filie dici possunt quantum ad nos, quia omnia in que acies oculorum nostrorum penetrare non potest, obscura dicimus et noctis luce carentis similia, et sic cum ad intrinseca divine mentis intellectu transire nequeamus, mortali offuscati caligine, cum in se ipsa splendidissima sit, et vive atque indeficientis lucis corusca, vicium illi nostre hebetudinis nominando attribuimus noctem perennem diem nuncupantes; et sic Noctis erunt filie; seu volumus dicere, quia nobis incognite sunt dispositiones earum, eas obscuras et Noctis filias vocitamus.

14 De nominibus propriis predictum est, de appellativis dicendum. Vocat igitur has Tullius Parcas, ut reor per antiphrasin, quia nemini 'parcant'; nulla enim apud eas est acceptio personarum; solus deus potest pervertere earum vires et ordinem. Fatum autem aut Fata a 'for faris' tractum nomen est, quasi velint, qui id imposuere nomen, quod ab eis agitur a Deo quasi irrevocabile dictum sit seu

has preceded this — namely, that which is caused is said to be the son of that which causes — we can say for the present that these three sisters called by various names are daughters of the god in that they are caused by him who is the first cause, as we can see just above in the words of Cicero and Boethius. This god, as has been said, the ancients called Demogorgon.

That they were born from Erebus and Night, as Cicero says, 12 can be explained in this way. Erebus, as will be explained more fully later, is the deepest and most hidden place on earth. Allegorically we can understand this as the profundity of the divine mind into which the human eye cannot penetrate. And because the divine mind can really see itself, knowing what it will do, and therefore produced them in an act with nature, we can surely say that they were born from Erebus, that is, the from the arcane and most profound inner sanctum of the divine mind.

They can call them daughters of the night also in the same way 13 as we label obscure and nightlike things which lack light and which the sharpness of our eyes is not able to penetrate; and so, we are also unable by means of our intellect to delve into the inner workings of the divine mind, obfuscated by our mortal cloud, although to itself it is actually very bright and shines with a vivid and unfailing light; we attribute imperfection to it because of our own dimness and call its daytime perennial "night." And so, they are daughters of Night, or we wish to call them that because their dispositions are unknown to us and therefore we call them obscure and daughters of Night.

We have talked about their individual names; now we must talk 14 about their group appellations. I think Cicero[68] calls them Parcae by antiphrasis because "they spare [*parcant*] no one," for they consider no one to be an exception; only god can overturn their power and control. Those who use the name Fate or Fates, which are derived from the word "to speak" [*fatus*] do so because what is spoken by God is irrevocable and preordained, as we saw in the words

previsum, ut per verba Boetii satis assumitur, et etiam sentire videtur Augustinus, ubi *De civitate Dei.* Sed abhorret ipse vocabulum,
admonens ut, si quisquam voluntatem Dei seu potestatem nomine
Fati appellet, sententiam teneat, linguam coerceat.

: 6 :

De Polo sexto Demogorgonis filio

1   Dicunt[33] insuper Polum Demogorgonis fuisse filium, et hoc in
Prothocosmo asserere Pronapidem, talem ex hoc fabulam recitan-
tem: quod dum secus undas in sede sua consisteret Demogorgon,
et ex exili limo sperulam composuisset, eam nuncupavit Polum.
Qui, spretis patris cavernis et inertia, evolavit in altum, et eo quod
adhuc mollis esset, in tam grande corpus evolans conflatus est, ut
2   omnia que a patre fuerant ante composita circumdaret. Verum
nondum sibi aliquis erat ornatus, cum fabricanti patri lucis globum assistens, videretque ignitas plurimum ad ictum mallei fabrilis hinc inde favillulas evolare, omnes sinu facto collegit, et in domum suam detulit, eamque ex illis ornavit omnem.

3   Haberem, Rex inclite, quid riderem, videns compositi orbis tam
ineptum ordinem, sed ante testatus sum nil velle mordere. Sequitur enim ut in ceteris Pronapides opinionem volentium ex terra a
mente divina terris inclusa cuncta fuisse producta, dum Polum,
quem ego celum intelligo, ex terra extensibile factum ait, et in
maximum ac circumplectens omnia corpus eductum. Quod autem
ex favillulis ex luce prodeuntibus domum ornaverit suam, hoc ideo
dictum reor, quia solis micantibus radiis stelle in celo composite

of Boethius and as Augustine seems to suggest as well in his *City of God*.[69] But he hesitates to use this terminology, warning that if anyone were to call the will or power of God by the name of Fate, he should control that thought and hold his tongue.

: 6 :

On Polus, the sixth child of Demogorgon

They say that Polus also was the son of Demogorgon. Pronapides 1 asserts this in his *Protocosmus* while telling the following fable.[70] While in his seat alongside the waters, Demogorgon composed a sphere from plain mud, and he called it Polus. Rejecting his father's caverns and inertia, Polus flew on high, and because he was still so soft the flying Polus blew up into such a large body that he surrounded everything his father had created. He did not yet have 2 any embellishments, but when he assisted his father in making the globe of light, he saw ignited sparks fly up everywhere from the blows of the maker's hammer, collected them all in his fold, and brought them home to decorate everything with them.

Illustrious King, I would have reason to laugh at seeing such a 3 silly ordering for the creation of the world, but I have already said that I did not wish to criticize, and yet the veil of this fiction is particularly thin. For, as in the rest of his work, Pronapides follows the opinion of those who want all things on earth to have been made by a terrestrial divine mind, while he says that Polus, whom I equate with the sky, was made from extendable earth, his body stretched to the maximum and embracing everything. That he decorated his home with the sparks emitted from light I think was said because the stars, composed in the sky and lacking light by their own nature, were made bright with the shimmering rays

natura sua luce carentes lucide facte sint. Polus autem dicitur, ut
4 arbitror, a quibusdam potioribus suis partibus. Constat enim, ut
venerabilis Andalo preceptor meus et veteres astrologie autores
asserunt, celum omne super duos polos circumflecti, quorum alterum nobis propinquiorem Articum vocant, oppositum autem Antarticum; hunc tamen aliqui Pollucem vocant, causam ego non
video.

∶ 7 ∶

De Phytone septimo Demogorgonis filio

1 Phyton Pronapidis testimonio Demogorgonis filius fuit et terre, ex
nativitate cuius talem ipse recitat fabulam. Dicit enim Demogorgonem, continue caliginis affectum tedio, Acroceraunos conscendisse montes, et ex eis ingentem nimium et ignitam evulsisse
molem, eamque primo rotundasse forcipibus, deinde in Caucaso
monte malleo solidasse; post hec ultra Taprobanem detulisse, et
globum illum lucidum sexies undis mersisse, totidemque circum
rotasse per auras, et hoc ideo ne ulla unquam posset circuitione
diminui, aut evi labefactari rubigine, et ut agilis ferretur undique.
2 Qui confestim se tollens in altum, domum intravit Poli, patrisque
sedem omnem complevit fulgore. Ex immersionibus autem eius,
aque ante dulces amaritudinem sumpsere salsedinis, et aer ad per-
cipiendos lucis radios ex rotationibus aptus effectus est.

of the sun. Polus, I think, is appointed from the best parts of each, for it is agreed, as my venerable teacher Andalò and ancient astrological authors assert,[71] that the entire sky turns upon two poles, of which the one nearer us they call the arctic, the opposite one the antarctic. Some call him Pollux, but I do not understand why. 4

: 7 :

On Phyton, seventh child of Demogorgon

According to the evidence of Pronapides, Phyton was the son of 1 Demogorgon and Earth. He tells the following fable about his birth. He says that Demogorgon, disturbed by the tedium of a continuous gloom, climbed the Acroceraunian mountains, from which he ripped off a very large, fiery mass and, after smoothing it with forceps, formed it with a hammer into Mount Caucasus. After this he then brought down Taprobane, and six times he submerged that shining globe under the waves, and six times he rotated it through the air, so that it would never be able to be diminished by rotation or damaged by the rust of age, and so that it would be nimble and carried everywhere. Immediately raising 2 himself on high, he entered the house of Polus, and he filled the entire seat of his father with glimmering light. When it was submerged, the previously sweet waters absorbed bitterness from the saltiness, and from the rotations the air was made ready for receiving rays of light.

3 Orpheus vero, qui fere poetarum omnium vetustissimus fuit, ut Lactantius in libro *Divinarum institutionum* scribit, opinatus est Phytonem hunc primum maximum et verum deum esse, et ab ipso cuncta fuisse producta atque creata. Quod forsan hoc in opere locum illi primum quesisset, tanto asserente teste, ni ipsemet Orpheus, minus advertens reor, seu quia nequiret animo concipere quenquam fuisse ingenitum, scripsisset:

Prothogonos Phyton perimetheos neros iyos.

Quod in Latinum versum sonat:

Principio genitus Phyton longo aere natus.

4 Et sic non primus ut dixerat, si aere genitus est. Hunc preterea Lactantius ubi supra Phaneta vocat.

Sed iam sumptus expetit ordo ut videamus quid contegat fictio, quod explicato sensu nominum fere apparebit liquido. Ugutio in *Libro vocabulorum* dicit, Phytonem solem esse, et hoc illi quesitum

5 nomen a Phytone serpente ab eodem superato. Sic et Paulus, in libro quem *Collectionum* intitulat, dicit, 'Phanos seu Phanet idem esse quod "apparitio."' Sic enim Phytonem hunc Lactantius vocat. Quod quidem nomen Soli optime competit, ipse enim est qui surgens apparet, eo autem cessante, nulla erit ceterarum creaturarum apparitio mortalium,[34] seu etiam syderum. Ergo solis creationem vult ostendere Pronapides.

Circa quam ut eorum sequatur opinionem qui ex terra omnia volunt condita, inducit deum, seu terre divinam mentem, ex Acroceraunis montibus sumpsisse materiam, ratus ignitam terram ad

6 componendum lucidum corpus aptiorem. Quod autem hanc mo-

Lactantius in his book *Divine Institutions*, said about Orpheus, 3
nearly the very first poet of all, that he believed that Phyton was
the first great and true god and that from him all things were produced and created.[72] Perhaps Lactantius would have ceded the first
place to Phyton in his work, with support from such a witness, if
Orpheus himself — whether, as I think, because he failed to notice
or because he was unable to grasp in his mind that someone had
been engendered — had not written,

Prothogonos Phyton perimetheos neros iyos

which means,

In the beginning was born Phyton, son of the vast air.

So he was not first, as he had said, if he was born from the air.
Also, Lactantius, in the passage already cited, called him Phaneta. 4
We must see what is covered by this new fiction about creation;
it will become clear once the meaning of the names is explained.
Uguccione in his *Great Book of Etymologies*[73] says that Phyton was
the sun and that his name was taken from that of the serpent
Phyton, which he vanquished.[74] Also Paul in his book titled *Collec-* 5
tions, says, "Phanos or Phanet are the same as 'appearance,'" so this
is what Lactantius calls Phyton. And this name is indeed appropriate for the sun, for it is he who rises and appears; when he sets,
there will be no apparition of other mortal creatures or even of the
stars. Therefore it was the creation of the sun that Pronapides
wished to describe.

In doing so and in following the opinion of those who want everything to be formed from the earth, he introduced the god, or
the divine mind of the earth, who took material from the Acroceraunian mountains, thinking fiery land more suitable for the creation of a body of light. That he smoothed this mass with forceps 6

lem forcipibus rotundasset, intelligo divinam artem, qua a Deo
solis globus adeo sphericus factus est, ut nulla superfluitate eius
superficies gibbosa sit. Equo modo et malleus dici potest summi
Artificis intentum, quo in Caucaso monte, id est in celi summitate,
adeo corpus illud solidum formavit ut nulla ex parte dissolvi aut
minui videatur.

7   Inde dicit eum delatum ultra Taprobanem, ut ostendat ubi creatum opinetur; est enim Taprobanes orientalis insula hostio Gangis
fluminis opposita, qua ex parte nobis in equinoctiis sol oritur; et
sic in Oriente compositum videtur velle. Mersum tamen[35] ibi
sexies undis dicit, imitatus fabrilis actus qui ad durandum ferrum
illud fervidum aquis immergunt. Et in hoc arbitror Pronapidem
8   voluisse perfectionem et eternitatem corporis huius designasse. Est
quidem sex perfectus numerus se ex suis partibus omnibus confi-
ciens, ex quo vult intelligamus et artificis et artificiati perfectionem. Quod autem sexies rotatum sit, puto per numerum perfectum rotationis voluerit eius circularem et indeficientem motum
describere, a quo nunquam exorbitasse aut destitisse compertum
est.

9   Quod ob ingentis et igniti corporis demersionem, aque primo
dulces amare facte sint, non ob aliud dictum puto, nisi ut ostendatur quod ob continuam radiorum solis ferventium percussionem
aquarum maris aque superficietenus salse facte sint, ut approbant
physici.

I interpret as the divine art by which the spherical globe of the sun was made by God in such a way that its surface would not be disfigured by any excess material. In a similar way the hammer can be said to be the intent of the greatest Artificer, in the Caucasus mountain, that is, in the highest part of the sky, and that it formed that body so solidly that it does not appear to be destroyed or diminished in any part.

Then he says that it was taken beyond Taprobane to show where he thought it was created, for Taprobane is an eastern island opposite the mouth of the Ganges River, where our sun rises in the equinox; and he seems to wish to have it constructed in the East. He says it was submerged six times in the waves in imitation of blacksmiths who immerse hot iron in water to make it hard. And I think in this that Pronapides wished to designate the perfection and eternity of this body, for six is a perfect number comprised of the sum of all its parts, and in this he wished that we recognize the perfection of the artificer and the artifice. In that it was rotated six times, I think that by using the perfect number of the rotation he wished to describe its circular and unfailing movement from which it is never found to deviate or desist. 7

8

That waters once sweet were made bitter by the immersion of the huge, fiery body I think was said for no other reason than to show that the surface waters of the sea are made salty by the perpetual striking of hot, solar rays, as natural scientists confirm. 9

: 8 :

*De Terra ex filiis Demogorgonis VIII^a, que ex incognitis
parentibus V genuit filios; quorum prima Nox, secundus
Tartarus, III^a Fama, IV^{us} Tagetes, V^{us} Antheus*

1 Terra, ut supra patet, Demogorgonis fuit sedes et filia, de qua Statius in *Thebaide* scribit sic:

> O hominum divumque eterna creatrix,
> que fluvios silvasque animarum semina mundi
> cuncta Prometheasque manus Pyrreaque saxa
> gignis, et impastis que prima elementa dedisti
> mutastique viros, que pontum ambisque vehisque:
> te penes et pecudum gens mitis et ira ferarum
> et volucrum requies; firmum atque immobile mundi
> robur inoccidui, te velox machina celi
> aere pendente⟨m⟩ vacuo, te currus uterque
> circumit, o rerum media indivisaque magnis
> fratribus! Ergo simul tot gentibus alma, tot altis
> urbibus ac populis subterque et desuper una
> sufficis, astriferumque domos Athlanta supernos
> ferre laborantem nullo vehis ipsa labore. . .

2   In quibus profecto carminibus satis Terre opus et laudes ostenduntur, de cuius generatione, quoniam supra ubi de Litigio dictum est reiterandum non censeo. Eam tamen veteres Titanis dixere coniugem, eamque ex patris concubitu, ut premonstratum est, quosdam suscepisse filios, et ex Occeano nepote atque ex

: 8 :

On Earth, eighth child of Demogorgon, who from
unknown parents gave birth to five children: first Night,
second Tartarus, third Rumor, fourth Tages, fifth Antaeus

As is now evident, Earth was the seat and daughter of Demogor-   1
gon. In his *Thebaid* Statius wrote about her thus:[75]

> O eternal creatrix of men and gods,
> who to the world's rivers and forests and all the seeds of
>   animals
> and the hands of Prometheus and Pyrrha's stones,
> gave birth and gave the first elements to the hungry
> and transformed men, you who carry the sea on both sides:
> in your power are the gentle herds and the anger of wild
>   animals
> and the repose of birds; firm and never-setting
> strength of the unfailing world, the swift machine of the sky
> suspended in the empty air, as do the two chariots,
> encircles you, O middle of things unapportioned to the great
>   brothers!
> Therefore you supply so many nations, so many great
> cities and peoples, sufficient by yourself below and above.
> Without toil you bear star-bearing Atlas toiling
> to support the heavenly homes. . .

In these verses the functions of Earth and her praises are amply   2
delineated, and I do not think we have to revisit her birth which
was described in the chapter on Strife. Otherwise, the ancients
say that she was the wife of Titan, and that after having sex with
her father Demogorgon, as we have described earlier, she begat
sons, as she did with her grandson Ocean, the infernal river

Acheronte infernali fluvio, nec non ex aliis incognitis, ut decenti demonstrabitur loco.

3   Vocavere eam preterea multis nominibus, ut puta Terram, Tellurem, Tellumonem, Humum, Aridam, Bonam deam, Matrem magnam, Faunam et Fatuam. Habet et preter hec cum quibusdam deabus communia nomina. Dicitur enim Cybeles, Berecinthia, Rhea, Opis, Iuno, Ceres, Proserpina, Vesta, Ysis, Maia et Medea.

4   Sed quid circa predicta theologi voluerint veteres, videndum est. Dicunt eam Titanis, qui sol est, coniugem, eo quod in eam sol agat tanquam in dispositam materiam ad producendum animantia quecunque atque metalla et preciosos lapides et huiusmodi. Non nulli volunt Titanum hominem ingentis potentie fuisse et terre virum dictum eo quod multum terre possideret, et filios suscepisset tanta prestantes fortitudine et corporis mole ut non ex muliere sed ex ingentiori corpore, ut puta terra, suscepti viderentur.

5   Et ut ad nomina veniamus, dicit Rabanus in libro *De originibus rerum*, eam terram nuncupari eo quod teratur, quod ad superficiem solam spectat. Tellus autem, ut idem testatur Rabanus, dicta est quia fructus ex ea tollamus. Servius autem dicit eam terram esse que teritur, tellurem vero deam. Et alibi dicit:

> Tellurem deam esse, terram autem elementum; sed quandoque tellurem pro terra poni, sicut pro igni Vulcanum et Cererem pro frumento.

Tellumonem vero, ut ego coniectura possum percipere, eam terre partem dixere que nec teritur nec radicibus graminum aut arbo-
6   rum usui est, eo quod longe sit tellure inferior. Humus vero, ut asserit Rabanus ea pars terre dicitur que plurimum habet humiditatis, ut puta palustris et propinqua fluminibus. Aridam autem terram vocavere, non quia sic illam a creatione creator nuncupaverit, ut eius veram complexionem ostenderet, sed eo quod aretur.

Acheron, and others unknown, as will be explained in the relevant chapters.[76]

In addition, they call her by many names, e.g., Terra, Tellus, 3 Tellumo, Soil, Arid, Good Goddess, Great Mother, Fauna, and Fatua.[77] In addition to these she shares common names with other goddesses, for she is called Cybele, Berecynthia, Rhea, Opis, Juno, Ceres, Proserpina, Vesta, Isis, Maia, and Medea.

But we must look into what ancient theologians chose to say 4 about what we have said. They call her the wife of Titan, who is the sun, because the sun treats her like a substance disposed for producing all living things as well as metals, precious stones, and the like. Some want Titan to have been a man of tremendous power and the husband of Earth because he possesses much of the earth, and he produced sons of such fine strength and size that they seem not to have been born of woman but from a huge body like the earth.

Now we come to her names. Rabanus in his *On the Nature of* 5 *Things* says she is called "earth" [*terra*] because she is "tread upon" [*teratur*] as one looks at her surface alone.[78] Tellus, however, as again Rabanus bears witness, is used because "we take [*tollamus*] fruit from her." Servius[79] says "earth" is that which is "tread upon" [*teritur*], but Tellus is the goddess. Elsewhere he says:

> Tellus is a goddess, terra an element. But when Tellus is meant as the earth, it is like using Vulcan as a substitute for fire and Ceres for grain.

They call Tellumo, as best I can conjecture, that part of the earth which is not tread upon nor of use for the roots of grasses or trees because it is far lower than Tellus. That part of the earth called 6 "soil" [*humus*], as Rabanus informs us, has the greatest "humidity," for example swamps and river wetlands. They call the earth Arid [*Arida*] not because the creator called it that upon creating it to show its true consistency, but because "it is plowed" [*aretur*]. Mac-

Bona autem dea, teste Macrobio *Saturnaliorum* ideo dicta est quod nobis omnium bonorum ad victum causa sit, cum ipsa germinantia nutriat, fructus alat, escas avibus et pabula brutis exhibeat, ex

7 quibus et ipsi nutrimur. Matrem autem magnam, ut ait Paulus, vocari voluere qui arbitrati sunt eam rerum omnium creatricem. Ego equidem arbitror, quia tanquam pia mater et maxima sua ubertate nutriat cuncta mortalia et suo gremio morientia cuncta

8 suscipiat. Cur autem Faunam dixerint Macrobius *Saturnaliorum* libro describit, dicens 'quod omni usui faveat animantium,' quod adeo manifestum est ut licteris explicari non egeat. Fatuam vero a 'fando' dictam dicit idem Macrobius veteres voluisse, eo quod infantes partu editi non prius vocem habeant vel emictant quam ipsam contigerint.

9 Que vero ex nominibus cum aliis communia sunt, ubi de illis mentio in sequentibus fiet intelligenda dicentur, et ad explicandum de filiis, quos ex incerto patre genuisse dixerunt veteres veniemus.

: 9 :

De Nocte prima Terre filia

1 Ex incerto patre dicit Paulus Noctem Terre fuisse filiam, de qua talem Pronapides in *Prothocosmo* fabulam scribit. Eam scilicet a Phanete pastore dilectam cui petenti, cum mater vellet copulare connubio, dixit se ignotum habere hominem, nec unquam vidisse, audisse tamen illum suis adversum moribus et ideo mori malle

robius[80] in his *Saturnalia* bears witness that she is called the Good Goddess because she is the cause of all "good" things for our sustenance, for she nurtures what germinates, cultivates the fruits, offers food to birds and fodder to beasts, from which we, too, receive nourishment. Those who prefer to call her Great Mother are 7 those who think, as says Paul, that she is the creator of all things. However, I think that it is because as the benevolent mother with the greatest abundance she nurtures all living things and takes them all back into her lap when they die. Why they call her Fauna 8 Macrobius describes in his *Saturnalia*, saying, "because she 'is favorable' [*faveat*] for every function 'of living creatures,'"[81] which is so obvious that it does not require explanation. Macrobius also says that the ancients wish to derive Fatua from "speech" [*fando*] because newborn infants do not have or emit any speech until they touch her.

I will supply the important information about the names she 9 has in common with others when I make mention of them in subsequent chapters; and this brings us to the explanation of her children, whom they say came from an uncertain father.

: 9 :

On Night, first child of Earth

Paul says that Night was the daughter of Earth from an uncertain 1 father. Pronapides in his *Protocosmus* writes about her in the following fable. Night was loved by the shepherd Phanetes, but when he asked to marry her, even though her mother was in favor, Night said that she did not know the man, nor had ever seen him but had heard nonetheless that he behaved differently from them and that therefore she would prefer to die rather than marry him.

quam illi nubere. Quam ob rem indignans Phanetes, ex amatore hostis factus, dum illam occisurus sequeretur, illa se copulavit He-

2 rebo, non ausa ubi Phanetes esset apparere. Dicit insuper Theodontius huic a Iove concessam quadrigam eo quod illi fautrix fuisset, dum ante lucem accederet ad Alcmenam. Hanc insuper, quantumcunque fusca sit, picta ornaverunt clamide. Et in eius laudem, et ut eius pro parte demonstraret effectus, Statius hos in *Thebaide* cecinit versus:

> Nox que terrarum celique amplexa labores
> ignea multivago transmittis sydera lapsu,
> indulgens reparare animum, dum proximus egris
> infundat Titan agiles animantibus ortus,
>
> etc.

3 Sed nunc quid sibi fabule veri tegant videamus. Dicunt igitur ante alia eam absque cognito patre terre filiam; quod ob id arbitror dictum, quia terra densitate sui corporis operatur ut radii solares nequeant in partem oppositam penetrare. Et sic causam dante terra umbra tam grandis efficitur quantum spatii a dimidio corporis terre occupatur. Que quidem umbra nox dicitur et sic tanquam a terra et non ab alia re causata absque cognito patre noctis tantum filia arbitratur.

4 Quod autem a Phanete pastore dilecta sit, hoc modo intelligendum reor. Phanetem ego solem puto ideo pastorem dictum, quia suo opere viventia cuncta pascuntur. Eum autem adamasse Noctem fictum existimo quia, tanquam dilectam sibi videre cupiens, rapido cursu sequitur, et illi videtur appetere copulari. Illa vero renuit, nec minus volucri passu fugit quam sequatur, eo quod sibi mores adversos habeat cum illuminet ille, ipsa autem obscurum faciat, nec frustra se, si illi iungatur, morituram dicit, cum sol luce

5 sua omnem dissolvat obscuritatem, et sic eius hostis efficitur. Demum Nox Herebo iungitur, id est inferno in quem cum nunquam

Consequently, the indignant Phanetes, now an enemy instead of a lover, sought Night out to kill her, while she, not daring to confront him, instead coupled with Erebus. In addition, Theodontius 2 says that Jupiter gave her a chariot because she had given him support when he approached Alcmene before daybreak. Also, they decorate her in a cloak painted as dark as she is. Singing her praises and showing in part her effects, Statius in his *Thebaid* sings these verses:[82]

> Night, embracing the labors of earth and sky,
> you send forth the fiery stars on their wandering courses,
> granting renewal to the spirit until the next Titan
> pours its enlivening sunrise onto feeble spirits.

Now let us see what truths these fables conceal. They say first 3 of all that she was the daughter of Earth from an unknown father. I think they say this because the body of the earth is so dense that the solar rays are unable to penetrate onto the opposite side. The result is shade so large that it occupies half of the earth's area. This shade is called night, and therefore it is due to the earth and no other cause that she is called the daughter of Earth from an unknown father.

That she was beloved of the shepherd Phanetes I think must be 4 understood in the following way. I think Phanetes is the sun and is called a shepherd because his function is to feed all living things. I think they devised the fiction that he dearly loved Night because, wanting to see his beloved, he chased her at considerable speed, and he seemed eager to couple with her. She rejected him and fled with no less fleetness of foot than that with which he chased her; because his behavior differed from hers, he shined while she made things dark; and not in vain did he say that she would die if she joined him, for the light of the sun makes all obscurity dissipate, and so he became her enemy. Night then united with Erebus, that 5 is, the nether region, and because the solar rays never penetrate

solares penetrent radii, nox viget atque secura consistit. Quod autem Iovi faverit fabula manifestat, ut patet per Plautum in *Amphytrione*, nam cum accessisset in diluculo Iuppiter ad Alcmenam, Nox ut illi prestaret obsequium tanquam a crepusculo nocturno inchoasset, perseveravit in longum, ex quo quadrigam meruit, per quam circuitionem terre continuam quam facit intelligo.

6 Per quattuor autem rotas ex quibus quadriga constat, quattuor arbitror significari noctis tempora solum nocturne quieti servientia. Dividitur autem nox a Macrobio in libro Saturnaliorum in septem tempora, quorum primum sole intrante incipit, et dicitur crepusculum a crepero, quod est dubium, eo quod dubitari videatur diei preterite an venienti nocti attribuendum sit, et hoc non

7 deservit quieti. Secundum autem, cum iam obscurum sit, fax prima dicitur, eo quod tunc faces accendantur, nec hoc quieti accommodum. Tercium vero, cum iam nox densior sit, nocte concubia nuncupatur, eo quod quieturi vadamus concubitum. Quartum nox dicitur intempesta, eo quod nulli operi tempus aptum sit. Quintum autem gallicinium vocitatur, eo quod a medio sui nocte in diem tendente, galli cantent. Sextum vero dicitur conticinium iam aurore proximum, et ideo sic dictum, eo quod tunc videatur ut plurimum grata quies et ob id omnia conticescunt et hec quattuor quieti prestantur. Septimum appellatur diluculum a die iam lucescente, in quo solertes assurgunt operi, quod minime somno

8 aptum est. Et sic totidemrote sunt currui Noctis quot in ea sunt tempora quieti tantummodo servientia. Seu volumus more nautarum et castrensium vigilum noctem in partes quattuor dividere, in primam scilicet et secundam et terciam atque quartam vigiliam, et sic quadrige rotas quattuor ex totidem vigiliis componemus.

Quod autem picta palla amicta sit, facile videri potest illam celi
9 ornatum significare quo tegitur. 'Nox autem,' ut ait Papias, 'ideo dicitur quia noceat oculis'; aufert enim illis videndi officium, cum

into there, night thrives and remains untroubled there. The fable specifies also that she had helped Jupiter, as we know from Plautus' *Amphitryo*,[83] for when Jupiter approached Alcmene at dawn, Night offered to help him by continuing her nocturnal twilight long enough to merit a chariot for making, I suppose, a continuous circuit of the earth.

I think the four wheels of the chariot signify the four periods of night which alone comprise the nocturnal peace. In Macrobius' *Saturnalia*, however, night is divided into seven periods, the first of which begins when the sun enters; it is called "dusk" from "dusky," that is, "doubt," since there seems to be doubtful whether this period should be attributed to the departing of the day or the coming night.[84] This is not a time for sleep. The second, because it is already dark, is called "first torch" because at that time the torches are lit, but neither is this period suitable for sleep. The third, when the night is more dense, is labeled "sleeping night" because we go to bed to sleep. Fourth is called "unfit night" because it is a time not fit for work. Fifth is called "cock-crowing" because the cocks sing from the middle of the night until day. Sixth is called the "stillness" just before dawn; it has this name because it is then that sleep seems to be the most pleasing and all things are still. These four are better for sleeping. Seventh is named "daybreak" — from "day" and "light breaking" — at which time, least suitable for sleep, accomplished people rise for work. And so there are as many wheels on the chariot of Night as there are periods used for the purpose of rest. Or, if we might wish to divide the night, as do sailors and camp watchmen, into four parts, namely, into the first, second, third, and fourth watch, then we arrive at the four wheels of the chariot from the four watches.

That she is dressed in a painted cloak appears to signify simply that she decorates the sky as she covers it. "Night [*Nox*], however," says Papias,[85] "is named because it 'harms' [*noceat*] the eyes," and night, when we see nothing, does take away the function of seeing.

nil nocte cernamus. Nocet insuper quia male agentibus apta est,
cum legamus: 'Qui male agit odit lucem'; ex quo sequitur ut tenebras amet tanquam malo operi aptiores. Et dicit etiam Iuvenalis:

Ut iugulent homines surgunt de nocte latrones.

Omerus preterea in *Yliade* eam 'domitricem deorum' vocitat, ut
sentiamus quoniam nocte magnanimes ingentia pectoribus ver-
sant, tamen nox minime talibus apta ebullientes opprimit spiritus,
eosque tanquam domitos in lucem usque coercet. Fuerunt insuper
huic tam ex viro quam ex aliis filii plures ut in sequentibus describetur.

: 10 :

De Fama secunda ex filiis Terre

1 Virgilio celestis ingenii poete, placet Famam Terre fuisse filiam,
dum dicit in *Eneide*:

Illam Terra parens, ira irritata deorum,
extremam, ut perhibent, Ceo Encheladoque sororem
progenuit,

etc.

De hac, ut appareat originis sue causa, talis a Paulo recitatur fabula. Quod cum ob regni cupidinem bellum inter Titanas gigantes, Terre filios, et Iovem esset exortum, eo itum est ut omnes
Terre filii qui Iovi adversabantur occiderentur a Iove et diis aliis.

2 Quo dolore Terra irritata et vindicte avida, cum sibi adversus tam
potentes hostes arma deessent, ut illis quibus poterat viribus ali-

Night is harmful also in that it suits those who do evil, for we read,[86] "He who does evil hates the light," from which it follows that he loves the darkness which is more accommodating for doing ill. Also, Juvenal says:[87]

To murder men thieves rise at night.

In addition, Homer[88] in the *Iliad* calls her the "subduer of the gods," for we know that at night those of mighty spirit turn over great ideas in their breasts, but since she is not at all suitable for such things, night represses ebullient spirits until she forces the "subdued" ideas into the light. Night also has children from her husband and from others, which will be described subsequently.

: 10 :

On Fame, the second of the children of Earth

For Vergil, a poet of divine genius, Fame is a daughter of Earth; in   1
the *Aeneid* he says:[89]

Her, mother Earth, provoked to anger by the gods,
produced, as they say, a sister to Coeus and Enceladus,
last.

Paul recounts a fable which details the causes of her origin in this way. When a war for control of the kingdom arose between the giant Titans, sons of Earth, and Jupiter, it reached the point at which all the sons of Earth who opposed Jupiter were killed by Jupiter or the other gods. Earth grieved at this and became angry   2
and eager for vengeance, but she opposed very powerful gods while lacking arms for herself. So she could do ill to them with whatever

quid mali ageret, coacto utero, Famam emisit scelerum superum relatricem.

Huius autem incrementum et formam describens, Virgilius ait sic:

Fama malum quo non aliud velocius ullum
mobilitate viget viresque acquirit eundo.
Parva metu primo, mox sese attollit in auras
ingrediturque solo et caput inter nubila condit.

Et paulo post hec ait:

. . . pedibus celerem et pernicibus alis.
Monstrum horrendum ingens cui quot sunt corpore plume,
tot vigiles oculi subter mirabile dictu,
tot lingue totidem ora sonant tot surrigit aures.
Nocte volat medio celi terreque per umbram
stridens nec dulci declinant lumina somno.
Luce sedet custos aut summi culmine tecti,
turribus aut altis et magnas territat urbes,
tam ficti pravique tenax quam nuntia veri.

3 Sentis, optime Rex, quanto verborum ornatu, quanto lepore, quam succi pleno, quanque industriosa fictione Virgilius quid sit Fama, quid eius augmentum, quid eius opus conetur ostendere et ostendat? Sentis equidem, sed ut qui te preter lecturi sunt ampliuscule videant, libet explicare paululum, premisso tamen quid velit fabula Pauli.

4 Dicit ergo primo irritatam Terram ira deorum. Circa quod pro iratis diis, syderum opus circa quedam intelligo. Sydera enim seu supercelestia corpora procul dubio in nos agunt potentia eis a creatore concessa secundum dispositiones suscipientium eorum influ-

powers she had, she contracted her womb and gave forth Fame, or Rumor, the narrator of the gods' crimes.

Describing her growth and her form, Vergil says this:[90]

Rumor, than whom there is no evil more swift,
thrives in her movement and gains strength from going.
Small and timid at first, she soon grows up into the air,
and she walks on the ground but hides her head among the
clouds.

A little afterward he says this:[91]

Swift of foot and on her agile wings,
a huge, fearful monster who has as many hidden but watchful
eyes
as she has feathers on her body — remarkable to describe! —
and as many tongues sound from as many mouths, so many
ears she raises.
At night as she flies between the sky and the earth,
she shrieks, nor does she lower the eyes in sweet sleep.
By day she sits as guardian either on the roof of the house
or on the tall towers and terrifies great cities,
clinging to lies and gossip as much as spreading the truth.

Do you understand, greatest King, with how much adornment 3
of words, with how much charm and spirit, and with what an industrious narrative Vergil attempted to show and did show the
essence of Fame, her growth, and her activity? You do understand,
surely, but I ought to explain a little so that those who will read
this after you will see something more expansive. I begin with
what Paul's fable wished to say.

He said first that Earth was irritated by the anger of the gods. 4
I equate the angered gods with the function of the stars, for without doubt the stars, or supercelestial bodies, by a power the creator bestowed upon them, influence us according to the disposi-

97

entias; et hinc fit quod[36] puer vel adolescens augetur eorum opere, cum diminuatur senescens, et cum nunquam a ratione gubernatoris optimi separentur, non nunquam aliqua faciunt que mortalium repentino falsoque iudicio tanquam irata fecisse videntur, ut puta dum iustum regem, dum felicem imperatorem, dum strenuum militem in finem suum deducunt. Et ideo iratos dixit deos Paulus, quia occiderint illustres viros, quos perpetuandos rebantur homines.

5   Sed quid ex hoc sequitur? Irritatur ab hoc opere, quod deorum iram vocant, Terra, id est animosus homo, nam terrei sumus omnes; et ad quid irritatur? Ut pariat Famam ultricem future mortis, id est ut id agat propter quod fama sui nominis oriatur, ut dum deorum ira ceciderit, illius nomen, agente meritorum fama, superstes sit, etiam nolentibus his, qui homines occidendo eam[37] omnino auferre conati sunt.

6   Ad quod nos idem hortatur Virgilius dum dicit:

> Stat sua cuique[38] dies breve et irreparabile tempus
> omnibus est vite, sed Famam extendere factis,
> hoc virtutis opus,
>
>   etc.

Hanc autem Famam ideo malum dixit Virgilius, quia non equo passu ad eam perquirendam tendimus omnes. Nam per fraudes ut plurimum summa occupari sacerdotia cernimus, dolo victorias obtineri, principatus possideri violentia, et ea quecunque per fas et nefas que nomina solent in lumen extollere. Nam si per virtutem agatur, tunc non malum iure dicitur Fama. Verum in hoc inproprie locutus est autor usus pro infamia vocabulo Fame, cum si fictionem inspiciamus, seu potius fictionis causam, satis advertemus ex ea infamiam non famam secutam.

tions of those who are susceptible to them. So a boy or adolescent will increase in size under their influence, while an old man will decrease. And, although they are never separate from the rationality of the greatest administrator, they sometimes do things which seem, on account of the quick and incorrect judgment of mortals, to have been done in anger, as when they lead a just king, a fortunate emperor, or a hearty soldier to their demise. And so Paul said that the gods were angry because they kill illustrious men whom other men thought should continue living.

But what does this imply? Earth, that is, spirited humankind, 5 for we are all of the earth, was angered by what they call the anger of the gods. And why is she angry? So she could give birth to Fame, the avenger of future death, that is, so she could do that for which the fame of her name arose, so that when the gods' anger fell upon us, her name, worthy of its reputation, would prevail, even among the unwilling who by murdering men have tried to eliminate her entirely.

Again Vergil emphasizes this point for us when he says:[92] 6

There stands a day for each; brief and irreparable
is the time of life is for all of us, but to continue one's fame by
    deeds,
this is the function of virtue.

Vergil calls this kind of Fame evil because we all tend toward reaching it, although with unequal strides. For we commonly see the highest priesthoods occupied through fraud, victories won by deceit, empires possessed with violence, and whatever brings one's name into the light, whether lawfully or unlawfully. And if it is done virtuously, then Fame is not rightly said to be an evil. Truly the author has spoken improperly here using the word "fame" for "infamy," for if we look into the fiction, or rather the cause of the fiction, we will discover that not fame but infamy is operative here.

7   Hanc insuper dicit metu primo parvam, et sic est; nam quantumcunque grandia sint facinora ex quibus oritur, a quodam tamen audientium metu videntur incipere. Movemur quidem auditu primo rei alicuius, et si placet eam falsam esse timemus, si vero displicet equo modo ne vera sit extimescimus. Mox sese tollit in auras, id est in ampliationem locutionis gentium evolat, seu mediocribus miscetur viris, et inde se solo infert, hoc est in vulgus et plebeios, et tunc caput inter nubila condit cum se ad reges atque

8   maiores effert. Pernix etiam est, id est velox, nil enim, ut ipsemet dicit, velocius est. Monstrum autem ingens asserit et horrendum ratione corporis quod illi describit, volens in hoc quod omnes eius plume, cum avem dicat propter eius celerem motum, habeant hominis effigiem; ad hoc ut per hoc intelligatur unumquenque de aliqua re loquentem pennam unam addere Fame, et sic ex multis, cum multe sint avium penne, non ex paucis Fama conficitur, seu potius monstrum horrendum hanc vocat quia fere nunquam superari potest. Nam quanto magis quis illam conatur opprimere tanto

9   magis exinde sit maior, quod monstruosum est. Dicit insuper omnes eius oculos vigiles esse, eo quod non nisi a vigilantibus personet fama; nam si in somnum tendet locutio, evestigio fama vertetur in nichilum. Nocte eam medio celi volitantem, ob id dicit quod sepissime contigisse compertum est sero scilicet factum aliquid, et mane etiam in remotissimis partibus cognitum, non aliter quam si nocte volaverit. Seu id dicit ut ostendat vigilantiam geru-

10 lonum. In die autem eam sedere dicit custodem, ut ostendat quod ob eius relata custodes portis territarum urbium apponantur, et in turribus ad excitandum vigiles vel ad speculandum a longe. Et cum inter veritatem et mendacium non distinguat, contenta est pro veris quecunque audita referre.

Moreover, he says she is small and timid at first, and so she is, 7
for however great the deeds are from which Fame arises, they seem
to begin with some fear of those who are listening. We are moved
when we first hear of some thing, and if it is pleasing to us, we fear
that it is false, and if it is not pleasing to us, we fear in the same
way that it might be true. "She soon grows up into the air," that is,
it rushes forth and grows among the speech of the people, or if it
is mixed in with mediocre men, from there it carries itself to the
ground, that is, into the common and lowly people, and then "she
hides her head among the clouds," when she reaches kings and
great men. She is fleet, that is, swift, for nothing is swifter, as he 8
said himself. He maintains that she is a huge monster, one to be
feared, judging by his description of her body, wanting in this that
all her feathers—he calls her a bird because of her swift movement—have a human appearance. In this respect this means that
each person who speaks about a certain thing adds another feather
to Fame, and so Fame is made of many feathers, not a few, because
birds have many feathers. Or, rather, he calls her a fearful monster
because she cannot be overcome, for the more someone tries to
overcome her, the greater she becomes, which is monstrous. In ad- 9
dition, he says that all her eyes are watchful because rumor does
not make a sound except through vigilant people, for if speech
continued during sleep, rumor would immediately be reduced to
nothing. He says, "At night she flies between the sky and the
earth," because very often something that happens in the evening
is known very far away in the morning, just as if it had flown at
night. Or he says it to demonstrate the vigilance of the famous. 10
He says that she sits as guardian during the day to show that
guardians are placed at the gates of terrified cities on account of
the information she brings, and are watchful on the towers for
rousing up or spying from afar. And since she does not distinguish
between truth and falsehood, she is content to report anything she
hears as the truth.

11   Huius preterea domum in maiori suo volumine sic describit
Ovidius:

> Orbe locus medio est inter terrasque fretumque
> celestesque plagas, triplicis confinia mundi,
> unde quod est usquam, quamvis regionibus absit,
> inspicitur penetratque cavas vox omnis ad aures.
> Fama tenet summaque locum sibi legit in arce
> innumerosque aditus ac mille foramina tectis
> addidit, et nullis iuclusit limina portis:
> nocte dieque patet, tota est ex ere sonanti,
> tota fremit vocesque refert iteratque quod audit.
> Nulla quies intus nullaque silentia parte;
> non tantum est clamor sed parve murmura vocis,
> qualia de pelagi, si quis procul audiat, undis
> esse solent, qualemve sonum, cum Iuppiter atras
> increpuit nubes, extrema tonitrua reddunt.
> Atria turba tenet: veniunt, leve vulgus, euntque
> mixtaque cum veris pariter coniuncta vagantur.
> Milia rumorum confusaque verba volutant.
> Ex quibus hi vacuas replent sermonibus aures.
> Hi narrata ferunt aliis mensuraque ficti
> crescit, et auditis aliquid novus adicit autor.
> Illic Credulitas, illic temerarius Error,
> vanaque Letitia est, consternatique Timores,
> Seditioque recens, dubioque autore Sussurri.
> Ipsa quid in celo rerum pelagoque geratur
> et tellure videt, totumque inquirit in orbem,

etc.

Ovid describes her home in his greater book in this way:[93] 11

There is a place in the middle of the earth between the earth,
    sea,
and celestial regions, the border of the three worlds.
From here whatever there is, even if it is far away,
is visible, and every voice reaches its hollow ears.
Fame lives there, having chosen the top of a peak,
and she added innumerable entrances and a thousand
    doorways,
although she did not include doors for any of the portals.
Day and night it lies open. Everything is of resonant brass,
and the whole house murmurs, echoing voices and repeating
    what it hears.
Within there is no quiet, silence nowhere.
Even so, there is no clamor but the murmur of a soft voice,
like the sea when you hear its waves from afar,
or the sort of sound the last bit of thunder makes
after Jupiter rumbles the dark clouds.
A throng fills its halls; they come, a fickle crowd, and they go,
and mixed equally with truths, lies wander about.
Thousands of rumors and confused words fly around.
With these utterings they fill empty ears;
they carry off to others what they have been told, and the
    untruths
multiply, and each new listener adds something to what he
    heard.
There lie Credulity, there imprudent Error,
vain Delight, alarmed Fears, new Sedition, and Whispers of
    dubious origin.
She herself sees all that happens in the sky, in the sea,
and on land, and scrutinizes the entire world.

12   Satis hec etiam minus erudito patentia sunt et ideo quid sibi velit Paulus dum addidit fabule famam genitam ut turpia deorum facta narraret vidisse superest; quod nil aliud autumo propter quod, cum minores in maiores nil viribus possint, illata verbis maioribus infamia conantur ulcisci. Terre autem ideo filiam vo-

13   luere, quia non aliunde quam ex gestis in terris fama sit. Quod autem patre careat, non absurde dictum est, cum ut sepissime rerum a fama gestarum, que ut plurimum falsissime sunt, ignoretur autor, qui compertus patris loco describi posset.

: II :

De Tartaro III° Terre filio

1   Tartarum asserit Theodontius absque patre Terre fuisse filium. Hunc Barlaam dicit inertem atque torpentem matris adhuc in utero iacere, eo quod invocata Lucina favere partui noluisset ob id quod Famam in deorum ignominiam peperisset. Figmentum hoc ab effectu causam sumpsit; non erat enim Lucina non nascituro seu partui non futuro prestatura favorem. Arbitrati sunt quidem veteres circa terre centrum locum esse concavum et in eodem sontium anime penis affligi, ut satis in descensu Enee ad inferos ostendit Virgilius.

2   Hunc Tartarum dici volunt, et hoc secundum Ysidorum ubi *De ethymologiis* a tremore frigoris dictum, nam ibi nec solis umquam potuit penetrare radius nec aeris motus est aliquis, confricatione cuius calefieri possit. Quod autem in utero matris torpeat, satis apparet: non enim ad superiora potest ascendere, et si ascendat

This is sufficiently clear even for someone less erudite, and so it 12 remains to find out what Paul meant by adding to the story that Fame was born to tell of the dirty deeds of the gods. I say it was for no other reason than that when the weak are powerless against the strong they try to avenge their disgrace with strong words. And they want her to be the daughter of Earth because rumor of what happens occurs nowhere else except on earth. That she lacks 13 a father is not an absurd statement, for of the things, usually quite false, which happen in the realm of fame, the author, who if found could be described as a kind of father, is very often unknown.

: II :

On Tartarus, third child of Earth

Theodontius asserts that Tartarus was a son of Earth without a 1 father. Barlaam says he was inert and torpid while still lying in his mother's womb; this was because when they invoked Lucina, she did not wish to help with the birth because she had produced Fame to the ignominy of the gods. The cause of this imaginary tale derives from the effect, for Lucina would not have favored one who was not to be born nor a birth not about to happen. The ancients thought that there was a hollow place around the center of the earth where the spirits of the condemned were afflicted with punishments, as Vergil describes well enough in Aeneas' descent to the underworld.[94]

They like to call this place Tartarus, and, according to Isidore's 2 *Etymologies*,[95] the name derives from "the tremor of cold" [*tremore frigoris*], for no ray of the sun or movement of air, which can create heat through friction, is able to penetrate there. Why he lay torpid in his mother's womb is sufficiently clear, for he was not able to

non erit amplius Tartarus. Terre autem filius improprie dicitur, nam quantumcunque conceperit mulier, nisi in lucem conceptus 3 venerit, iure filius dici non poterit. Dicitur autem absque patre conceptus, eo quod credamus terre corpus concavitates habere, non tamen satis certi sumus an a creatione an a secuto post creationem eventu habuerit.

In testimonium autem predictorum dicit Virgilius:

> Tartarus ipse
> bis patet in preceps tantum tenditque sub umbras,
> quantus ad ethereum celi suspectus Olympum,

> etc.

Nec multo post ait:

> Hic genus antiquum Terre Titania pubes,
> fulmine deiecti fundo volvuntur in imo,

> etc.

: 12 :

De Tagete IIII° Terre filio

1 Tages, ut asseruere gentiles et potissime Tusci, absque cognito genitore, Terre filius habitus est. De quo refert Paulus Perusinus quod, cum apud Etruscos in agro Tarquiniensi aliquantulum tellus intumuisset, is villicus cuius erat agellus novitate rei permotus avidusque videre quid esset ostenti monstratura turgiditas aliquandiu expectavit, tandem impatiens more, ligone sumpto, locum ce-

ascend higher, or if he had, he would cease to be Tartarus. He is not properly called a son of Earth, for whenever a woman conceives, it cannot be properly called a son unless, once conceived, it comes out into the light. He is said to have been conceived without a father because, while we believe that the body of the earth has a hollow, we are not sufficiently certain whether it dates from the time of creation or from some event that followed afterward. 3

As evidence for what we have described, Vergil says:[96]

> Tartarus itself
> lies open and stretches headlong down into the shades
> twice as far as the gaze to ethereal Olympus in the sky.

A little later he says:[97]

> Here lies the ancient brood of Earth, Titanian youth,
> downed by a thunderbolt and rolled into the profound depths.

: 12 :

On Tages, fourth child of Earth

Tages, as the pagans and, in particular, the Etruscans assert, was a son of Earth from an unknown father. Paul of Perugia reports about him that when among the Etruscans in the Tarquin territory the earth became a little swollen, the overseer of that plot, moved by the novelty of the thing and eager to see what prodigy this turgidity might reveal, waited for a while, but impatient of the delay, he picked up his mattock and began to dig the spot little 1

pit sensim effodere, nec multum effodit, et ecce ex glebis prosilivit

2 infantulus. Quo monstro perterritus rudis homo vocavit affines, nec diu et is, qui modo infans erat, etate provectus visus est, et inde senex, et cum incolas aruspicinam docuisset, repente nusquam comparuit. Auditores autem arbitrati numen et terre credidere filium et nominavere Tagetem, quod idem olim lingua sonabat Etrusca, quod Latina 'deus'; eumque postea loco summi

3 numinis coluere. Ysidorus vero ab aratore gleba vomere summota infantem compertum dicit, nec amplius una die ab Etruscis visum, et in illa eos aruspicinam docuisse et ex ea libros etiam reliquisse, quos postea Romani in linguam propriam transtulere.

4 Huius figmenti talem fuisse sensum existimo. Quendam scilicet esse potuisse qui diu studens circa aruspicinam, et ob contemplationis commodum, consortio hominum aspernato, doctus repente unde minime credebatur comparuit, et quia forsan ex antro aliquo exire visus est, Terre puerperium fictum est, vel in oculos agrum colentis inopinatus affuit, quasi prodisset ex glebis a rudi vulgo Terre filius dictus est, et ideo absque patre quia incognita eius fuerit origo.[39] Consuevere preterea veteres exteros ignotos terrestri itinere ad se venientes Terre filios vocitare, uti Neptuni qui adveherentur navigio. Infans autem dictus quia novus et confestim provectus et senex, eo quod eruditus et prudens, quod senum est, compertus sit.

5 Quod in agro Tarquiniensi contigerit, seu quia aut sic fuit ibidem, scilicet Tagetem, primo cognitum, seu quia Etrusci aruspicina clarissimi fuere. In brevi autem termino more designatur affectio grandis incolarum ad eum. Nam dilecte rei mora etiam si

by little. He had not dug much, when — behold — a tiny infant jumped out from the glebes. Utterly terrified by this prodigy, the 2 rustic fellow called his neighbors. But not long after, what had just now been an infant advanced in age and became an old man, and after he taught the locals the art of divination, he suddenly disappeared. Those who heard the story thought he was a divine spirit, believed him to be a son of the earth, and named him Tages, an Etruscan word which means "god." Afterward they worshipped him as a great divinity. Isidore says that the infant was found after 3 a farmer had moved the glebes with his ploughshare, that the Etruscans did not see him for more than one day, and that on that day he taught them divination and even left them books on the subject, which later the Romans translated into their own language.[98]

I think this inventive story has the following meaning. It could 4 be that there was someone who was studying divination for a long time, and, as the product of his contemplation, living apart from other humans, he suddenly appeared a learned man from an unknown place. And perhaps because he seemed to come out of a cave, it was said that he was the offspring of Earth. Alternatively, he appeared unexpectedly before the eyes of a man cultivating his fields, as if he came out from the glebes, and was called the son of Earth by the rustic people, and so he was born without a father because his origin was unknown. Also, the ancients were accustomed to calling unknown foreigners who arrived by land sons of the earth just as they called unknown foreigners arriving by ship sons of Neptune. He was said to be an infant because he was new and immediately got older, and an old man because he was found to be learned and prudent like an old man.

That this happened in Tarquin territory was because either 5 Tages was recognized there first, or because the Etruscans were very well known for their divination. In the hurried end to his waiting signifies the great affection the inhabitants had for him,

longissima sit, diligenti videtur brevissima. Eum autem deum habitum ob id contigisse puto, ut doctrinam quam summe colebant deo autore nobilitarent.

: 13 :

De Antheo V° Terre filio

1 Antheum omnes terre dicunt filium, et quia nemo illi patrem designat, inter genitos incerto patre eum apponere necesse fuit. De quo sic scribit Lucanus:

> Nondum post genitos tellus effeta gigantes
> terribilem libycis partum concepit in antris.
> Nec tam iusta fuit terrarum gloria Thyphon,
> aut Tityos Briareusque ferox celoque pepercit,
> quod non Flegreis Antheum sustulit arvis.
> Hoc quoque tam vastas cumulavit munere vires
> Terra sui fetus quod cum tetigere parentem,
> iam defeta vigent renovato robore membra.
> Hec illi spelunca domus; latuisse sub alta
> rupe ferunt, epulas raptos habuisse leones.
> Ad somnos non terga fere prebere cubile
> asserunt non silva torum viresque resumpsit,
> in nuda tellure iacens, periere coloni,
> arvorum Libye pereunt quos appulit equor,
> auxilioque diu virtus non ausa cadendi
> Terre spernit opes: invictus robore cunctis
> quamvis staret erat,
>
> etc.

for waiting for a beloved thing, even if it is for very long, seems very short for the lover. And I think they became to regard him as a god so that they could ennoble the doctrine they honored most by attributing it to a god.

: 13 :

On Antaeus, fifth child of Earth

All say that Antaeus was a son of Earth, and because no one speci- 1
fies a father for him, we have to place him among those born from
an uncertain father. Lucan writes this about him:[99]

> Not yet exhausted from the birth of giants,
> Earth spawned a terrible progeny in the caves of Libya.
> She did not glory so justifiably in Typhon,
> or Tityus, or fierce Briareus, and she spared the heavens
> by nurturing Antaeus afar from the Phlegrean Fields.
> Earth added to his massive powers a motherly gift:
> when he touches her his weakened limbs regain their strength.
> His home is a cave there; they say he lurks under a steep
> cliff, devouring the lions he captures.
> For sleeping he is said to make his bed not on beast skins
> or a cushion of leaves, but he renews his strength
> lying naked on the earth. Farmers of the fields
> of Libya perished, as did those brought by the sea perish,
> and his powers, for a long time not using the help of falling,
> spurned Earth's help: unvanquished against all by his strength
> even standing he was.

2   Apparet ergo per Lucani carmen quam grandis quamque fortis et ferus fuerit Antheus, ad quem, ut idem testatur Lucanus, ut cum eo luctam iniret accessit Hercules laborum victor, et cum in agone essent eumque sepius prostratum robustiorem resurgentem cerneret, advertens quod a terra vires recuperaret, iam fessum ulnis in altum extulit, tanque diu tenuit donec spiraret.

3   Fabule huius sensus duplex est, hystoricus et moralis. Videtur enim Pomponio Mele in libro *Cosmographie* placere, hunc regem in extremis Mauritanie fuisse, asserens apud Ampelusiam promontorium in occeanum Athlanticum tendens esse specum Herculi sacram et ultra eam Tingem oppidum pervetustum ab Antheo, ut ferunt, conditum; et in testimonium ostenditur ab incolis parma ingens ex elephante et ob magnitudinem nulli nunc habilis quam ab eo gestatam asserunt et summe colunt. Nec non monstratur ab eisdem collis modicus resupini hominis iacentis habens ymaginem, quem eius tumulum fuisse confirmant.

4   Adversus hunc dicit Theodontius Dyonisium Thebeum, qui ob insignem eius virtutem Hercules appellatus fuit, bellum habuisse, et qui cum advertisset eum sepius in Mauritania prostratum et evestigio exercitus restaurantem, ficta fuga eum ad se persequendum in Libyam usque traxit. Ibi vero eum superavit et occidit.

5   Leontius vero dicebat hunc Herculem fuisse Nyli filium, quem ego unum et idem cum superiori puto. Eusebius autem in libro *Temporum* dicit hunc Antheum palestrice artis fuisse doctissimum et quorumcunque certaminum que exercentur in terris, et ob id ostendit se arbitrari fictum quod Terre fuerit filius et quod viribus restauraretur ab ea.

6   Fulgentius quidem moralem sensum fictioni subesse demonstrat, dicens Antheum de terra natum libidinem esse que sola ex

We can see from Lucan's poem how huge and how strong and   2
fierce Antaeus was. Hercules, victorious in his labors, approached
Antaeus to wrestle him, as Lucan again bears witness; when they
were fighting and Hercules saw how often he knocked down his
opponent only to see him rise up again with greater strength, he
realized that Antaeus was recouping his powers from the earth; so
he raised his now weary opponent into the air with his arms and
held him there until he expired.

There are two meanings to this fable, historical and moral.   3
Pomponius Mela[100] in his *Description of the World* seems to believe
he was king in the far away regions of Mauretania, asserting that
in Ampelusia, a promontory stretching into the Atlantic Ocean,
there was a sacred cave of Hercules and, further, Tinge [Tangiers],
a very ancient town founded, as they say, by Antaeus. As proof the
inhabitants show a huge ivory shield, which on account of its size
they claim that no one wielded but him, and they greatly venerate
it. They also show a medium-sized hill having the image of a man
lying down; this they insist is his tomb.

Theodontius says that Dionysus of Thebes, who was called   4
Hercules for his great valor, fought a war against him, and when
several times in Mauretania he noticed that the defeated Antaeus
immediately restored his army, he pretended flight and drew his
pursuer all the way to Libya. There he overtook and killed him.

Leontius used to say that this Hercules was the son of the Nile;   5
I think he was one and the same as the aforementioned Hercules.
But Eusebius[101] in his *Chronicle* says that this Antaeus was very
skilled in wrestling and in whatever contests were fought on land,
and he shows that he thought that it was for this reason that this
Antaeus was a son of Earth and had his strength restored to him
by her.

Fulgentius[102] offers a moral meaning to the story, saying that   6
Antaeus, born from earth, was lust, which is born only in the

carne nascitur, qua tacta, etsi fessa sit, in vires resurgit, verum ab homine virtuoso carnis denegato tactu superatur.

7   Hunc fuisse dicit Augustinus regnante Argis Danao; Eusebius autem regnante Athenis Egeo; Leontius regnante apud Argivos Argo.

: 14 :

De Herebo VIIII° Demogorgonis filio, cui fuerunt
filii XXI. Quorum primus Amor, II ͣ Gratia,
III ͧͦ Labor, IV ͣ Invidentia, V ͧͦ Metus, VI ͧͦ Dolus, VII ͣ
Fraus, VIII ͣ Pertinacia, VIIII ͣ Egestas, X ͣ Miseria,
XI ͣ Fames, XII ͣ Querela, XIII ͧͦ Morbus,
XIIII ͣ Senectus, XV ͧͦ Pallor, XVI ͣ Tenebra,
XVII ͧͦ Somnus, XVIII ͣ Mors, XVIIII ͧͦ Caron,
XX ͣ Dies, XXI ͧͦ Ether

1   Expeditis Terre filiis, ad Herebum stilus revocandus est, qui, ut Paulus ait a Crisippo traditum, filius fuit Demogorgonis et Terre. Hunc ego arbitror unum et idem cum Tartaro, cum eum veteres omnes existimare videantur in remotissimis terre visceribus esse, et in eodem, uti de Tartaro diximus, suppliciis sontes puniri.

2   De hoc tamen multa scribuntur ab antiquis et potissime a Virgilio in sexto *Eneide* libro, que sub compendio pertransibo, eo quod fere de omnibus fiet in sequentibus prolixior mentio. Dicit ergo Virgilius quod in faucibus huius sunt terribiles visu he forme, scilicet Luctus et ultrices Cure, Morbi pallentes, et tristis Senectus atque Metus et Fames Egestasque terribilis et horribiles visu Le-

flesh: when touched, even in weakness, its strength revives, but when contact is denied by a virtuous man, the flesh is overcome.

Augustine[103] says he lived when Danaus was ruling Argos; Eusebius,[104] however, says he lived when Aegeus was ruling Athens; and Leontius says it was when Argo was ruling among the Argives.

: 14 :

On Erebus, ninth child of Demogorgon, who had twenty-one children. First of these was Love, second Grace, third Labor, fourth Jealousy, fifth Fear, sixth Deceit, seventh Fraud, eighth Stubbornness, ninth Poverty, tenth Misery, eleventh Hunger, twelfth Grievance, thirteenth Disease, fourteenth Old Age, fifteenth Pallor, sixteenth Darkness, seventeenth Sleep, eighteenth Death, nineteenth Charon, twentieth Day, twenty-first Ether

Now that the children of Earth have been accounted for, my pen must return to Erebus, who, as Paul, citing Chrysippus, says was the son of Demogorgon and Earth. I think he is one and the same with Tartarus since all the ancients seem to think he is in the most remote bowels of the earth where, as we said about Tartarus,[105] the guilty are punished with torments.

The ancients wrote much about these things, especially Vergil[106] in the sixth book of his *Aeneid*, which I will summarize because I will follow this with a longer discussion about nearly all the rest. Vergil says that in its jaws are — terrible to behold — these figures, namely, Griefs and avenging Cares, pallid Diseases, and mournful Old Age and Fear and Hunger and terrible Poverty and Death

tum Laborque, Sopor et mala mentis Gaudia, Bellumque letiferum ac Eumenides et Discordia et ulmus Somniorum sedes, Cen-
tauri, Scylle, Briareus, Lerneusque serpens et flammis armata
Chimera una cum Gorgonibus, Arpiis et tricorporeo Gerione et
trifauce Cerbero limina servante Ditis.

3   Preterea hunc Herebum quattuor rigari fluminibus, Acheronte
scilicet Flegetonte Stygeque atque Cocito; et Acherontis nautam
dicit esse Caronem, morientium animas ad profundiora Herebi
transferentem. Insuper Minoem, Radamantum Eacumque versan-
tes urnis merita intrantium inesse describit, et prostratos fulminibus Titanas, Gigantes et Salmeonem ac Tityon discerptum a vulture; Ysiona perpetua circumvolutum rota, nec non et Sysiphum in
altum ingentia pectore impingentem saxa, ac Tantalum inter undas
et poma siti fameque pereuntem, et Theseum perpetuo damnatum
ocio, aliosque; et hos omnes intra Ditis ferrea menia sub ultrice
Thesiphone cruciari.

4   Similiter et hunc idem preter Herebum multis vocavere nominibus ut puta Tartarum, Orcum, Ditem, Avernum, Baratrum et
Infernum. Sic et eundem multorum filiorum patrem faciunt.

5   Ceterum his premissis ad detectionem ascondite veritatis veniendum est. Volunt igitur eum Demogorgonis et Terre filium, eo
quod Demogorgonem rerum Omnium creatorem arbitrati sunt;
Terre autem quia ut patet eius in utero conditus est. Verum eum
locum esse penarum non solum gentiles sed non nulli illustres
Christiani existimavere hac forte ducti ratione. Nam cum summa
bonitas Deus sit, et qui peccatum commictit, quod malum est, et
sic malus effectus sit, ut a Deo tanquam a suo contrario remotissi-
mus sit, necesse est. Nos autem Deum in celis habitare credimus,
et a celo nulla remotior pars est centro terre, et ob id tanquam in

terrible and horrible to behold, and Hardship, Sleep and the mind's evil Delights, and death-bringing War and Eumenides and Discord and the elm seat of Dreams, Centaurs, Scyllas, Briareus, the Lernean serpent and the Chimera armed with flames along with the Gorgons, Harpies, and triple-bodied Geryon and three-jawed Cerberus guarding the gates of Dis.

In addition, he says this Erebus was watered by four rivers, 3 namely, Acheron, Phlegethon and Styx as well as Cocytus, and he says that the sailor of the Acheron is Charon, who transfers the spirits of the dead deeper into Erebus. He also describes Minos, Rhadamanthys, and Aeacus, examining from urns the records of those who arrive, and the Titans, Giants, and Salmoneus prostrate from thunderbolts as well as Tityus dismembered by a vulture, Ixion spun perpetually on a wheel, and Sisyphus pushing huge boulders upward with his chest, Tantalus perishing of thirst and hunger amidst waters and fruits, and Theseus condemned to perpetual inactivity, as well as others, and he says that all these are tormented within the iron walls of Dis by Tisiphone the avenger.

Similarly, they call him by many names other than Erebus, for 4 example Tartarus, Orcus, Dis, Avernus, Barathrum, and the Infernus; also, they make him the father of many sons.

Now we must move from this to the discovery of its hidden 5 truths. They want him to be the son of Demogorgon and Earth because they believed that Demogorgon was the creator of all things, and of Earth, clearly, because he was hidden away in her womb. However, not only pagans but also some illustrious Christians have thought that Erebus was the place for punishment, following this sound reasoning: since God is the greatest good, it is necessary that those who commit a sin, which is evil and produces evil, must be as far as possible from god, its opposite. We believe God dwells in heaven, and from the sky there is no more remote place than the center of the earth, and therefore it is perhaps not

loco a Deo remotissimo, ibidem penas luant impii, forsan non inepte creditum est.

6   De hoc tamen Tullius ubi *De questionibus Tusculanis* aperte truffatur ex quo satis existimari potest aliud eruditos veteres sensisse; et ideo cum voluerint duplicem esse mundum, maiorem scilicet et minorem, maiorem eum quem generaliter mundum[40] dicimus, minorem autem hominem, asserentes omnia in minore esse que in maiori describuntur ab eis, credo eos hunc Herebum et hos cruciatus intra minorem mundum, id est hominem esse existimasse, ac voluisse illas horribiles formas, quas in vestibulo Herebi describit Virgilius, esse causas exteriores, per quas introrsum illa suplicia causantur; seu ea que ab intrinsecis causata apparent extrorsum, quem longe meliorem sensum existimo.

7   Deinceps quidem ut predictorum seriem exponendo prevertam necesse est. Fictum igitur puto in profundum huius Herebi Ditem esse ferream civitatem, ut per eam intelligamus profundam obstinati cordis partem, in qua vere pertinaces non nunquam sumus et ferrei. Titanes, id est homines terrenis dediti, et Gygantes, id est superbi prostrati, ideo vexari dicuntur, ut cognoscamus circa hoc anxiari terreos et superbos homines animo, qui dum semper extolli cupiunt, ceco suo iudicio deprimi et vilipendi arbitrantur et ex excelso deiciuntur aliquando, quod illis est acre tormentum.

8   Per Tityon autem descerptum a vulture mens cuiuscunque laborantis ut ea que ad eum non spectant agnoscat, accipienda est, seu illius qui in cumulandis thesauris continua cogitatione agitatur. Ysion autem, perpetua circumvolutus rota circum, agitationes optantis regnum ostendit. Sic et Sysiphus saxa revolvens in efficacibus ac laboriosis conatibus vitam ducentis declarat. Per Tantalum autem inter undas et poma fame pereuntem, avarorum hominum curas et angores circa infamem parsimoniam intelligere

incorrectly believed that it is in a place as far as possible from God that the wicked pay their penalties.

In this matter Cicero[107] in his *Tusculan Disputations* openly ridi- 6 cules how educated ancients might have thought that they understood something else. Since they want the world to be twofold, that is, with a greater and lesser world, the greater being that which we generally call the world, the lesser mankind, asserting that all the things in the lesser world will be described by them in the greater, I believe they thought that this Erebus and these torments were located within the lesser world, that is, mankind, and that they also wanted those horrible forms in the vestibule of Erebus, as described by Vergil, to be exterior causes through which those punishments are caused within; or, those which appear to be caused internally are external, which I think makes more sense.

Next it is necessary to proceed by explaining the aforemen- 7 tioned series. I think that in the fiction that Dis is an ironlike city in the depths of this Erebus we understand the deep part of an obstinate heart, where we are sometimes stubborn and ironlike. They say that the Titans, that is, men dedicated to earthly pursuits, and the Giants, that is the proud brought low, are vexed to make us understand how earthly and proud men have anxious minds: although they always desire to be extolled, we think they are weighed down by their blind judgment and despised, tossed down from their exaltedness at some point, which is the severest torment for them.

In Tityus' dismemberment by the vulture we should understand 8 either the mind of one who takes pains to recognize what does not regard him, or that of a person who continually thinks about amassing wealth. Ixion, spun perpetually on a wheel, demonstrates the anxieties of those who desire power. So, also Sisyphus, rolling boulders, indicates the life of someone engaged in effective and laborious struggles. We should understand Tantalus, perishing of hunger amidst waters and fruits, as the cares of avaricious men

debemus. Theseus autem ociosus temerariorum frivolos conatus ostendit, quibus misere cruciantur.

9   Dicunt autem hos sub infestatione vexari Thesiphonis, quod sic reor accipiendum. Interpretatur enim Thesiphon 'irarum vox,' et sic patet qui a talibus cruciantur in se ipsos irasci, et irarum voces non numquam emictere. Per illos autem tres iudices, hoc intelligo, tres enim personas male agendo ledere possumus, Deum, proximum et nos ipsos, et sic a triplici coscientie iudicio redarguimur et damnamur.

10   Per ianitorem autem Tricerberum canem, cuius officium est volentes intromictere, et exitum intrantibus prohibere, tres intelligendas causas puto rodentes acri morsu deceptorum mentes, letales scilicet assentatorum blandicie, falsa felicitatis opinio et inanis glorie fulgor, que quidem continue novis decipulis detrahentes ignaros, miseras curas augent, et minuere auctas non permictunt.

11   Circuitur seu inundatur Herebus a quattuor fluminibus, ut per hoc sentiamus quia hi qui se ratione deiecta ab inceptis concupiscientiis trahi permictunt, primo recti iudicii perturbata letitia Acherontem transeunt, qui 'carens gaudio' interpretatur, et sic pulsa letitia ut eius occupet mestitia locum necesse est, ex qua ob bonum letitie perditum persepe vehemens nascitur ira, aqua in furorem impellimur, qui Flegeton est, id est ardens, ex furore etiam in tristitiam labimur, que Styx est, et ex tristitia in luctum et lacrimas, per quas Cocitus accipiendus est quartus Inferni fluvius. Et sic miseri mortales angimur ceca concupiscibilis appetitus opinione seducti, intraque gerimus quod in visceribus terre a poetis stolidi arbitrantur inclusum.

anguishing about disreputable parsimony. Theseus in his inactivity demonstrates the frivolous pursuits of thoughtless men who are wretchedly tormented.

In addition, they say that these are troubled and plagued also 9 by Tisiphone, which I think we should be accepted, for Tisiphone means the "voice of anger," and so it is clear that those punished in this way are angry at themselves, and that their voices forever cry out in anger. In the three judges I understand that by doing evil we can injure three persons, God, fellow man, and ourselves, and so we are convicted and condemned by the triple judgment of conscience.

I think that in the guardian dog Tricerberus, whose function it 10 was to admit those who wished to enter and to prohibit an exit for those who already had entered, can be discovered the three causes which gnaw at the minds of deceivers with their fierce bite, namely, the lethal blandishments of obsequious followers, the false opinion of felicity, and the empty glitter of glory, which continually attract the ignorant in new snares, increase their wretched woes, and prevent them, once enlarged, from diminishing.

Erebus is encircled and inundated by four rivers. I understand 11 in this those who discard reason, allow themselves to be persuaded by the beginnings of eager desire, and for whom the happiness of good judgment has become troubled, first cross the Acheron, which means "lacking in joy"; and so with happiness driven out it is necessary that sadness takes its place. Because the goodness of happiness is destroyed, very often a vehement anger is created and this drives us into rage, which is Phlegethon, that is, "burning." From rage we often descend into sadness, which is Styx, and from sadness we descend into "lamentation and tears," which we understand as Cocytus, the fourth river of the underworld. And so we wretched mortals are in anguish, seduced by the blind opinion of desirous appetite, and within we bear what stupid people think the poets included in the bowels of the earth.

12   Nunc autem quid sibi velint nomina videamus. Herebus enim dicitur, ut ait Ugutio, quia nimis 'hereat' illi quem capit. Dis autem dicitur a 'Dite' rege suo, qui apud poetas divitiarum dicitur deus, et hoc ideo quia dives sit, id est abundans locus iste, eo quod in eum descendant ut plurimum hodie morientes, olim omnes. Tartarus autem dicitur a 'tortura,' quia torqueat quos absorbet.

13   Verum Tartarus est profundissimus infernorum locus ex quo, ut opinari videtur Ugutio, Christus neminem eduxit, Orcus enim dicitur quia 'obscurus.' Baratrum vero a forma dictus creditur; est autem Baratrum vas ex viminibus confectum a parte superiori propatulum, ab inferiori autem acutum, quo utuntur agrestes Campani, dum ex vitibus arboribus annexis vindemiantes uvas colligunt, et hoc ideo dictum ut intelligamus infernum amplissimas fauces ad suscipiendum damnatos habere, ad eos vero servandos artissimum locum atque profundum. Infernus autem dicitur quia omnium terre partium 'inferior' sit. Avernus autem ab *a*, quod est 'sine,' et *vernos* quod est 'gaudium,' dicitur, eo quod gaudeo careat et tristitia lugeat sempiterna.

: 15 :

De Amore primo Herebi filio

1   Ex filiis Herebi primus occurrit Amor, quem ab eo ex Nocte susceptum ubi *De naturis deorum* Tullius asserit. Quod forsan, regum serenissime, videretur tibi monstruosum, ni verum monstraretur ratione possibili. Antiquorum sententia fuit amorem esse animi

2   passionem, et ideo quicquid optamus id amor est. Verum quoniam

Now let us see what each of these names mean. Erebus [*Here-* 12 *bus*] warrants its name, as Uguccione[108] says, because it "adheres" [*haereat*] excessively to its captive. Dis is named after its king, Dis, whom the poets call a god of riches, and they say this because he is rich, that is, it is a place of abundance because those who die go there, some today, eventually all. Tartarus comes from "torture," because it tortures those whom it engulfs.

Indeed, Tartarus is the deepest part of the infernal regions from 13 which, as Uguccione seems to have thought, Christ restored no one. We say Orcus because it is "obscure." Barathrum is believed to come from a shape: a barathrum is a vase made of twigs, open at the top, tapered toward the bottom, which the Campanian peasants use for collecting grapes when they harvest them from vines connected to trees; and it is called this so that we understand that the inferno has very wide jaws with which to accept the condemned and a very narrow and deep place for keeping them. Infernus is named from the "lowest" [*inferior*] of all the parts of the earth. Avernus comes from *a*, which means "without," and *vernos*, which means "joy," because it lacks joy and grieves in everlasting sorrow.

: 15 :

On Love, first child of Erebus

Of the children of Erebus we first encounter Love, whom Ci- 1 cero[109] in his *On the Nature of the Gods* claims was born to Erebus from Night. Perhaps this might seem to be monstrous to you, most serene King, unless I can demonstrate the truth with a plausible explanation. The opinion of the ancients was that love was a passion of the mind, so whatever we desire is love. But because 2

in diversum nostre affectiones feruntur finem, ut amor non idem circa omnia sit, necesse est, et ob id in parvum numerum redactis mortalium desideriis, triplicem illum maiores dixere.

Et ante alios Apuleio teste, eo in libro quem *De dogmate Platonis* scripsit, asserit Plato tres, non amplius amores fore. Quorum primum dixit esse divinum, cum incorrupta mente et virtutis ratione convenientem. Alterum degeneris animi corrupteque voluntatis passionem. Tertium ex utroque permixtum.

3   Post quem auditor eius Aristotiles, mutatis potius fere verbis quam sententia, eque triplicem voluit, primum dicens propter honestum, secundum propter dilectabile, tertium propter utile moventem captos a se. Sane quoniam, nec is, de quo sermo, divinus aut propter honestum est, nec ex duobus aliis permixtus, aut propter delectabile, verum degeneris animi, et propter utile, merito eum iuxta sententiam Ciceronis, filium Herebi Noctisque dicemus, id est cece mentis et obstinati pectoris.

4   Ab hoc enim in execrabilem auri famem impellimur. Ab hoc in cupidinem imperii inexplebilem. Ab hoc in stolidum periture glorie desiderium. Ab hoc in funestam amicorum cedem. Ab hoc in periclitationes urbium, furta, fraudes, violentias et dolosa consilia miseri trahimur. Hac peste afficiuntur gnatonici, histriones, assentatores et huiusmodi perniciosa manus hominum ridentem insipientium sequentes fortunam, et eo utuntur ad enudandos blanditiis et falsis laudibus milites gloriosos. Eum igitur rite pensatis omnibus non amorem, quin imo odium rectius vocaremus.

our affections are carried to different ends, love must not be the same in everything, and because of that, reducing mortal desires to a small number, the ancients said he was triple.

Based on the evidence from Apuleius'[110] *On the Doctrine of Plato*, Plato said before others that there were no more than three loves. Of these three he said the first was divine, converging with an incorruptible mind and the reason of virtue. Second was the passion of the degenerate mind and a corrupted will. Third was a mixture of each.

After him his pupil Aristotle,[111] changing the words but not the thought, also wanted love to be triple, saying that it compels its captives first because of that which is honest, second because of that which is delightful, and third because of that which is useful. But since surely love is not, as they say, divine or the result of honesty, nor mixed from the two others, or because of that which is delightful, that of a degenerate mind, and because of that which is useful, we say rightly, according to the opinion of Cicero, that he was the son of Erebus and Night, that is, of a sightless mind and a stubborn heart. 3

We are compelled by him into the accursed craving for gold. We are compelled by him into the insatiable longing for power. We are compelled by him into the foolish desire for unfading glory. We are compelled by him into the deadly murder of friends. By him we are brought miserably into the dangers of cities, deceptions, frauds, violence, and deceitful plotting. This pest affects clowns, actors, flatterers, and the pernicious band of insipid men of this sort who follow comic fortune, and they use it for denuding proud soldiers with blandishments and false praises. Therefore if we consider all this correctly, we should call him not love but, more rightly, hatred. 4

: 16 :

De Gratia Herebi et Noctis secunda filia

1 Herebi et Noctis Gratiam esse filiam scribit Tullius, ubi *De naturis deorum*. Ego tamen alibi legisse memini Gratias seu Iovis et Auctonoi, seu Liberi patris ac Veneris fuisse filias. Verum ut habeamus quid in hoc senserint qui finxerunt, est sciendum, gratiam esse quandam liberalem mentis affectionem maiorum potissime in minores, qua nullo precedente merito indulgentie beneficia et obsequia aliquando etiam non poscentibus impenduntur.

2 Harum tamen multiplices esse species reor. Alie quidem dei sunt immortales, quibus amotis nulli sumus. Alie vero hominum inter se, et he in bonum possunt tendere et in malum, quamquam

3 semper in bonum sonare videatur gratia. Has omnes Herebi et Noctis filias, variatis tamen parentum sensibus, possemus ostendere, sed ut ad hanc, omissis in suum tempus reliquis, veniamus, reor ego hanc eam Gratiam esse que ob aliquod infandum facinus, vel turpes alicuius hominis mores in perverso aliquo ac detestabili viro causatur, et sic Herebi, id est obstinati pectoris, et Noctis, id est cece mentis, erit filia Gratia talis.

: 16 :

On Grace, second child of Erebus and Night

In his *On the Nature of the Gods* Cicero[112] writes that Grace was a 1
daughter of Erebus and Night. However, I recall reading elsewhere
that the Graces were either the daughters of Jupiter and Autonoe,
or father Liber and Venus. So that we can comprehend what those
who invented this intended, we should define grace as a kind of
liberal affection of the mind, especially of greater ones toward
lesser ones, by which favors and services of kindness are performed
in return for no previous benefit and often for those who did not
ask.

I think there are many types of these. Some immortal graces 2
belong to god, without which we are nothing. Others belong to
the interactions of men, and these are able to tend toward good
and evil, although grace always seems to signify tending toward
the good.

We could show that all of these graces were daughters of Ere- 3
bus and Night, although the senses in which we understand the
parents vary. But if we omit the others until later and focus specifically on this Grace, I think she is the one caused by some unspeakable crime or the disgraceful morals of some perverse and detestable man; and so, such a Grace will be the daughter of Erebus,
that is, of a stubborn heart, and Night, that is, a sightless mind.

: 17 :

De Labore tertio Herebi filio

1 Labor a Cicerone Noctis et Herebi scribitur filius, cuius quiditas
ab eodem huiusmodi designatur. Labor est functio quedam vel
2 animi vel corporis gravioris operis vel muneris. Qua inspecta, merito Noctis et Herebi filius dici potest, is scilicet qui damnosus est
et merito reprobandus. Nam uti in Herebo et Nocte perpetua
sontium est inquietudo, sic et in secretis cordium penetrabilibus
eorum qui ceca tracti cupidine circa superflua et minime oportuna
cogitatione agitantur continua; et quoniam cogitationes tales in
obscuro causantur pectore, merito Labor talis filius dicitur Noctis
et Herebi.

: 18 :

De Invidentia seu Invidia IIII ᵃ Herebi filia

1 Invidentiam dicit Tullius Herebi et Noctis fuisse filiam. Qui ubi
De questionibus Tusculanis hanc ab Invidia differentem facit, dicens
'Invidentiam ad invidum tantummodo pertinere, cum Invidia ad
eum etiam cui fertur pertinere videatur'; et de ea concludens dicit
'Invidentiam esse egritudinem susceptam propter alterius res se-
cundas que nil noceant invidenti.'

: 17 :

On Labor, third child of Erebus

Cicero[113] wrote that Labor was the son of Night and Erebus, and 1
he equally indicated his essence: Labor is a certain function of either mind or body burdened by work or duty. Upon reflection we 2
can say that he is rightly called the son of Night and Erebus specifically in that he is ruinous and rightly condemned; for as the
guilty suffer perpetual disquiet in Erebus and in the night, so suffer as well in the inner remoteness of their hearts those who are
driven by blind desire and engage in continuous plotting about
excess and what is of little advantage. And since such plotting
originates in a dark heart, Labor is rightly called the son of Night
and Erebus.

: 18 :

On Jealousy, fourth child of Erebus

Cicero[114] says that Jealousy was a daughter of Erebus and Night. 1
In his *Tusculan Disputations* he differentiates Jealousy from Envy,
saying:[115] "Jealousy seems to pertain specifically to hatred, while
Envy seems to pertain to its object." He concludes this discussion
by saying: "Jealousy is an affliction acquired on account of another's
favorable affairs which are not harmful to the jealous person."

2   Huius enim habitationes et mores sic describit Ovidius:

Protinus Invidie nigro squalentia tabo
tecta petit: domus est imis in vallibus huius
abdita, sole carens,[41] non ulli pervia vento,
tristis et ignavi plenissima frigoris, et que
igne vacet semper, caligine semper habundet.

Et paulo post:

Concusse patuere fores, videt intus edentem
vipereas carnes, viciorum alimenta suorum,
invidiam, visaque[42] oculis avertit. At illa
surgit humo pigre, semesarumque relinquit
corpora serpentum, passuque incedit inerti;
utque deam vidit formaque armisque decoram,
ingemuit, vultumque dee ad suspiria duxit
pallor in ore sedens, macies in corpore toto,
nusquam recta acies, livent rubigine dentes,
pectora felle virent, lingua est suffusa veneno;
risus abest, nisi quem visi fecere dolores,
nec fruitur somno, vigilantibus excita curis,
sed videt ingratos, intabescitque videndo,
successus hominum, carpitque et carpitur una,
suppliciumque suum est,

etc.

3   Hos versus si quis plene considerabit, et eam esse Invidentiam
quam nos ampliori licentia Invidiam dicimus, et Herebi Noctisque
filiam absque difficultate cognoscet.

Ovid describes her dwellings and characteristics in this way:[116] 2

> Immediately she sought out, squalid with a black, putrid fluid,
> Envy's house. Her home is hidden away in the deepest
> valleys, without sun, undisturbed by wind,
> a sad place, permeated by an ignoble chill, and
> ever empty of fire, with an abundance of gloom.

Afterward he adds:[117]

> She knocked and the doors opened, seeing within
> Envy eating viper flesh, nurture for her vices.
> Seen, she averted her eyes. But Envy slowly rose
> from the ground, leaving behind the half-eaten
> corpses of serpents, and approached with an unsure step:
> as she saw the goddess, beautiful in form and handsome in her
>   armor,
> she groaned, her features dropping, and sighed.
> There was a pallor on her face, her whole body emaciated.
> She could not see straight, and her teeth were discolored with
>   decay.
> Her breast was green with bile, her tongue suffused with
>   venom.
> There is no laughter except where she sees suffering,
> nor does she enjoy sleep, disturbed by her worrisome cares.
> She views as unpleasant, and pines away when she sees them,
> the successes of men, and she consumes herself and is herself
>   consumed,
> she was her own punishment.

Anyone who considers these verses carefully and observes that 3
Jealousy is, using our broader parameters, what we call Envy, will
recognize without difficulty that she is a daughter of Erebus and
Night.

: 19 :

De Metu V° Herebi filio

1   Metus, ut sepe dictus asserit Tullius, filius Herebi fuit et Noctis.
Est enim metus, ut idem ait Tullius, 'rationi adversa cautio.' Hunc
ego horum parentum filium dictum arbitror, quia ex remotis a
cognitione nostra nostris in pectoribus oriatur.

2   Eum tamen duplicem reor, et qui in discretum virum iure cadere possit, ut metuisse tonitrua, et qui nulla rationabili causa
impellente non aliter quam mulierculas non nullos exanimat. Hic
sub vocabulo pavoris unus ex ministris Martis est, ut demonstratur a Statio dicente:

Inde unum dira comitum de plebe Pavorem
quadrupedes ante ire iubet; non alter anhelos
insinuare metus animumque avertere veris
aptior, innumere monstro vocesque manusque,
et facies quecumque libet; bonus omnia credi
autor et horrificis linphare incursibus urbes.
Si geminos soles ruituraque suadeat astra
aut nutare solum aut veteres descendere silvas.
A! miseri vidisse putant,

etc.

3   Possem, Rex optime, multa verba facere huius carminis expli-
cando partes, ut mores metus aperirem, sed adeo tenuia sunt figmenta, ut plura dicere superflua ratus sim. Huic preterea ascribit
Tullius in *Tusculanis questionibus* non inadvertenter plures subesse

: 19 :

On Fear, the fifth child of Erebus

Fear, as Cicero,[118] whom I have frequently cited, asserts, was the 1
son of Erebus and Night. For as Cicero[119] himself says, fear is
"caution contrary to reason." I think he is said to be the son of
these parents because fear originates in our breasts far from our
cognition.

I think there are two types, that which can occur justifiably in a 2
discerning man, such as the fear of thunder, and that which with
no compelling rational cause scares some people to act rather
womanly. The latter, under the name of panic, is one of the ministers of Mars, as is demonstrated by Statius when he says:[120]

There one of the companions of the dire crowd, Panic,
  he ordered to ride ahead of the horses. No one is better suited
for implanting gasping fear and distracting the mind from
    truth;
that monster has innumerable voices and hands
and whatever shape he pleases. He is an author good at
    rendering everything
believable, and with horrific assaults drives cities into frenzy.
If he were to suggest that there were two suns or that the stars
    were about to fall,
or that the ground was giving way or that ancient forests were
    sinking,
alas, the wretches think they have seen. . .

I could, great King, expend many words to explain the details 3
of this poem and account for the characteristics of fear, but the
images are so transparent, I think it would be superfluous to say
more. In addition, in the *Tusculan Disputations* Cicero[121] pointedly

ministros, ut puta: Pigritiam, Pudorem, Terrorem, Timorem, Pavorem, Exanimationem, Conturbationem et Formidinem. De quibus omnibus ibidem seriose legitur.

: 20 :

De Dolo Herebi filio VI°

1 Est et Dolus, ut Tullio placet, filius Noctis et Herebi. De quo referre consueverat Barlaam quoniam ad Troianum bellum cum Grecis ivisset, et cum minus armis iretur in votum, consultantibus quibusdam ex primatibus de agendis, ab Ulixe, cui familiarissimus

2 erat, in[43] consilium fuisse deductum. Qui cum elatos animos et iactationes atque consilia quorundam audisset atque aliquandiu secum risisset, rogatus sententiam dixit, que etsi non honesta eo quod oportuna videbatur, assumpta est; et eidem cum Epoo fabricandi equi negocium evestigio commissum est, quo postmodum eo perventum ut optato iam fessi potirentur Greci.

3 Satis tenue fictionis est velum, et ideo cur Herebi et Noctis dicatur filius videamus. Quod meo iudicio Sacris ostenditur Licteris, quibus docemur ab Herebo forma serpentis assumpta humani generis hostem in terris venisse, et parentum nostrorum mentes dolosis suggestionibus offuscasse nocte tartarea, et inde tanquam in cultum agrum semen iniecisse letiferum, cuius fructus, cum in legem egissent, extemplo venit in lucem; et sic Dolus nondum in terris cognitus ab initio manavit ex Herebo, et in utero cece mentis

attributed to him other ministers, for example, Sloth, Shame, Terror, Dread, Panic, Fright, Consternation, and Alarm. I will discuss all these later in order.

On Deceit, sixth child of Erebus

Deceit [*Dolus*], as Cicero[122] thinks, is the son of Night and Erebus. 1
Barlaam often discussed the Dolus who went along with the Greeks to the Trojan War: because he embarked on the undertaking with little interest in combat, when the leaders were discussing what they should do, Dolus was brought into the plan by Ulysses, with whom he was quite familiar. When he had heard their elated 2 spirits and boasts and all their plans and had mused with himself for a while, he was asked his opinion and gave it; even if it was not honorable, it seemed opportune, and was adopted. The task of building the horse was straight away assigned to him along with Epeus, and later the war-weary Greeks finally achieved their desired conquest.[123]

The veil of this fiction is fairly thin, so let us see why he was 3 called the son of Erebus and Night. In my judgment this is shown in the Sacred Scriptures.[124] There we are taught that Erebus assumed the form of a serpent and came to earth as an enemy of the human race, and that in the Tartarean night he clouded the minds of our progenitors with deceitful suggestions; he then injected a lethal seed into the cultivated ground, the fruit of which suddenly, proceeding by its own law, came into the light. And so Deceit, not yet known on earth, from the beginning sprung from Erebus, and conceived in the womb of a sightless mind, our death and exile

conceptus, nostra morte et exilio regni celestis palam facto, ostendit liquido se filium Noctis et Herebi.

4   Sane quia quod gentiles non noverant finxisse non poterant,
arbitror eos pro Herebo intimum cordis humani recessum intellexisse: ibi enim cogitationum omnium sedes est, et ideo si eger sit
animus, virtute neglecta ut ad optatum deveniat, si desint vires,
illico dirigit ad artes ingenium. Et quoniam facilius dolo capiuntur
amentes, eo cogitationibus pessimis fabricato, et quos cupit et se
ipsum letifero alligat laqueo. Et sic ex Nocte, id est mentis cecitate,
per quam ea via qua minime decet, in desiderium suum tendit, et
egri pectoris ignominiosa concupiscentia ferventis, dolus creatur et
nascitur, et ut plurimum non ante visus in lucem, quam is in precipitium venerit in quem struitur.

: 21 :

De Fraude VII^a Herebi filia

1   Fraus et merito Herebi et Noctis a Cicerone ubi *De naturis deorum*
dicitur filia, letalis quidem et infanda pestis, et inique mentis exe-
crabile vicium. Inter hanc et dolum vix noscitur esse discrimen,
quod si quid interest hoc esse videtur, dolum scilicet quandoque in
bonum operari posse, fraudem[44] nunquam preter in malum. Seu
potius adversus hostes dolo agimus, amicos fraude decipimus.

2   Huius autem formam noster Dantes Aligerii Florentinus eo in
poemate quod Florentino scripsit ydiomate, non parvi quidem inter alia poemata momenti, sic describit: eam scilicet iusti hominis
habere faciem, corpus reliquum serpentinum variis distinctum ma-

from the heavenly kingdom made long ago, clearly shows that he was the son of Night and Erebus.

Because the pagans were of course not able to invent what they 4 did not know, I think that they understood Erebus as the hidden recess of the human heart: there is the seat of all thinking, and so if the mind is corrupted and virtue abandoned in favor of achieving one's desires, and if strength fails, our nature finds its way to the wiles of this place; and because the foolish are more easily captured by deception, which is devised by the worst kind of thinking, it desires them and with a lethal snare binds itself to them; and so from Night, that is, a blindness of the mind, through which it reaches for what it wants in the least proper way, and by the ignominious concupiscence of an afflicted and anxious heart, Deceit is created and born, and usually not seen until it has rushed headlong toward its victim.

: 21 :

On Fraud, seventh child of Erebus

Fraud, a lethal and unspeakable pestilence and an accursed sin of 1 an unjust mind, is said rightly by Cicero[125] in the *On the Nature of the Gods* to be a daughter of Erebus and Night. It is difficult to distinguish between fraud and deceit, but if there seems to be any difference it is that deceit can sometimes be used for good, but fraud is used only for evil. Said another way, we use deceit against an enemy but deceive friends with fraud.

Our Dante Alighieri,[126] the Florentine who wrote his poem in 2 Florentine idiom, a great achievement in poetry, described her form in this way: she had the face of a just man, the rest of her body was serpentlike and distinguished by colorful markings, and

culis atque coloribus, et eius caudam terminari in scorpionis aculeum, eamque Cociti innare undis adeo ut illis excepta facie totum contegat horridum corpus, eamque Gerionem cognominat.

3   In placida igitur et simili iusti hominis huius facie sentit autor extrinsecum fraudolentium habitum; sunt enim vultu et eloquio mites, habitu modesti, incessu graves, moribus insignes et spectabiles pietate; operibus vero miserabili sub gelu iniquitatis tectis, versipelles sunt, et astutia callidi, et maculis respersi scelerum, adeo ut omnis eorum operum conclusio pernicioso sit plena veneno; et inde Gerion dicta, quia regnans apud Baleares insulas Gerion miti vultu, blandisque verbis et omni comitate consueverit hospites suscipere, et demum sub hac benignitate sopitos occidere.

4   Cur autem Herebi noctisque filia dicta sit, eadem que de Dolo ratio est.

: 22 :

De Pertinacia Herebi VIII^a filia

1 Pertinacia, insipientum exitiale crimen, secundum Tullium Herebi Noctisque filia est, nec causam videre difficile est. Nam quotiens indigestus mortalium ignavie rigor, rationibus validis, et calori divini fervoris interposita offuscati intellectus caligine, molliri non potest, obstinationem seu pertinaciam oriri necesse est, imo iam exorta est, ignorantie certissimum argumentum.

2 Ergo bene Pertinacia Herebi, quem sepe gelidum diximus, et Noctis quam sepe caliginem mentis esse monstravimus, filia est.

her tale terminates in the sting of a scorpion, and that she is submerged in the waves of Cocytus so that it covers her entire horrible body except for her face; he names her Geryon.

In the face that is gentle and similar to that of a just man the 3 author means the external demeanor of fraudulence, for she has a soothing face and manner of speaking, a modest demeanor, a confident gait, distinguished manners, and an appearance of goodness. But with her works hidden under a wretched chill of iniquity, she is a double-dealer, cunning and astute; spotted with markings of crime, so that the conclusion of all her works is full of pernicious poison. And for this reason she is called Geryon, because Geryon, ruling in the Balearic Islands with a mild face, used to entertain guests with soothing words and every courtesy, and then, when they were tranquillized by his kindness, killed them.

She is said to be a daughter of Erebus and Night for the same 4 reason as Deceit.

: 22 :

On Stubbornness, eighth child of Erebus

Stubbornness, the destructive crime of fools is, according to Cic- 1 ero,[127] a daughter of Erebus and Night, nor it is difficult to see why. When the disordered inflexibility of human laziness cannot be softened by means of valid reasoning, and when the passion of divine fervor intervenes in the fogginess of an unclear intellect, obstinacy or stubbornness necessarily arises, and once it does, it is the most certain proof of ignorance.

Therefore Stubbornness is the daughter of Erebus, whom we 2 have frequently said was cold, and Night, which we have often shown to be a darkness of the mind.

: 23 :

De Egestate Herebi filia VIIII^a

1 Egestas Herebi Noctisque filia non ea est quam plurimi arbitrantur, oportunis scilicet carere (hanc enim viri fortes tolerantia superavere ut in arenis libycis Cato) sed ea est potius cui abundantes falso tracti iudicio succumbunt, ut auri custos Mida Frigum rex, qui dum omnia que tangebat iuxta votum verterentur in aurum, fame peribat.

2 Hec est ergo vere Herebi filia, id est gelidi cordis et ignavi, ac etiam Noctis, id est ceci consilii, extimantis optimum divitias augere, ut usu careamus earum.

: 24 :

De Miseria Herebi X^a filia

1 Placet insuper Tullio Miseriam Herebi Noctisque fuisse filiam.[45] Hec enim adeo extremum infortunium est, ut possit prospectantes
2 in misericordiam commovere. Quod quidem nos ipsi nobis[46] facimus dum, neglecto veritatis lumine, perituras res abeuntes quocunque modo non aliter ingemiscimus quam si perpetuas perderemus, et sic ab offuscato mentis iudicio concussum pectus suspiriis lacrimisque miseriam emictit in publicum, ut inde filia Noctis et Herebi dici possit.

: 23 :

On Poverty, the ninth child of Erebus

Poverty, a daughter of Erebus and Night,[128] is not that which most 1
think, namely the lack of ready supplies (for strong men patiently
endure it, as did Cato[129] in the Libyan desert) but it is rather that
to which those in abundance, influenced by wrong judgment, suc-
cumb, as did Midas,[130] King of Phrygia, the guardian of gold; although he turned all that he touched into gold, as he wished, he
perished of hunger.

She is therefore truly daughter of Erebus, that is, of a cold and 2
ignoble heart, and of Night, that is, of a blind plan, calculating
how most greatly to increase riches beyond the amount we can
use.

: 24 :

On Misery, the tenth child of Erebus

Cicero[131] says also that Misery is a daughter of Erebus and Night. 1
This is such extreme misfortune that it can elicit sympathy from
those who see it. Since we ourselves do this to ourselves, neglect- 2
ing the light of truth, anguishing over perishable things dying in
the same way as if we had lost something eternal, so that our
heart, struck by clouded mental judgment, outwardly emits misery
with sighs and tears, it is possible to call her a daughter of Night
and Erebus.

: 25 :

De Fame XI^a Herebi filia

1 Famem dicit Paulus iuxta Crisippum Herebi Noctisque fuisse filiam. Hec autem aut publica est, ut olim premonstrata Pharaoni, aut privata, ut Erysithonis. Publica ex universali frugum penuria consuevit contingere. Cuius rei aut divina ira causa est, vel diuturnum bellum, seu adversa supercelestium corporum dispositio, seu vermes subterranei rodentes semina, seu locuste iam sata nascentia devorantes.

2 Ex quibus causa prime a nemine mortalium nosci potest, et sic dici poterit Herebi Noctisque filia, sed non Herebi in visceribus terre latentis, aut in egris hominum pectoribus residentis; quin imo in profundo divine mentis arcano sanctissime vigilantis, quem intellectus hominum mortalitatis caligine offuscatus intueri non potest, nec etiam noctis divine mentis, in qua nil unquam fuit obscurum, (verum suo semper[47] lumine cuncta clarificat), sed nostre imbecillitatis erroris.

3 Ceteras cause huius species asserunt mathematici suis artibus etiam previderi posse. Quod utrum verum sit, tu serenissime Princeps, cum in talibus apprime te instructum audiverim, optime nosti. Si autem sic est, talis fames nec Herebi nec Noctis filia esse posset. Si autem non sic, tunc ut de deo diximus cum in arcano nature antro repositum videri non possit, linquetur ut talis Fames filia sit Noctis et Herebi ratione iam dicta.

4 Privata autem fames, aut ex penuria ciborum continget ut plurimum, aut aliquando ex fastidio stomacantium. Si ex penuria, aut

: 25 :

On Hunger, the eleventh child of Erebus

Paul, following Chrysippus, says that Hunger was a daughter of   1
Erebus and Night. This refers to either public hunger, as once revealed to Pharaoh,[132] or private, as that of Erysichthon.[133] Publicly
it usually happens because of a widespread scarcity of crops. The
cause of this is either divine anger, or a long-lasting war, or the un-
favorable disposition of the supercelestial bodies, or underground
worms gnawing at the seeds, or locusts devouring them just as
they spring forth.

The cause of the first of these cannot be known by any mortal,   2
and so she can be said to be the daughter of Erebus and Night.
She is not, however, the daughter of the Erebus hidden in the
bowels of the earth or residing in the distressed hearts of humans,
but, rather, of the one in the hidden depths of the vigilant and
most sacred divine mind, which human intelligence, obscured by
the cloud of mortality, cannot visualize. So too she is not the
daughter of the night of the divine mind in which nothing has
ever been obscure (rather, everything becomes clear in its light),
but, instead, the daughter of the error of our imbecility.

Experts in mathematics claim that their skills allow them to   3
forecast other types. Whether this is true, most serene Prince, you
know well since I have heard you have been thoroughly instructed
in such matters. If this is so, such hunger could not be the daughter of Erebus and Night. But if this is not so, then, as we speak
about the god as being invisible and hidden away in a remote cave
of nature, for the aforementioned reason it remains that this is the
Hunger who is the daughter of Night and Erebus.

Private hunger occurs often because of a shortage of food or   4
sometimes on account of digestive fastidiousness. If because of a

inertia atque desidia patientis aut egestatis crimine contingit. Si ex inertia vel desidia, ut quandoque videmus quosdam lasciviis potius et ineptiis atque ocio vacare quam rei familiaris curam gerere, hec profecto Herebi Noctisque filia est, eo pacto quo superiores sunt ceteri. Si egestatis crimine, dum modo non ob intemperantiam sit egenus qui patitur, nec hanc Herebi Noctisque filiam puto, nisi ob
5 id dixerim quia ab intrinseco stomaci esurientis procedit. Si vero ob ciborum fastidium fames sit, ut non nunquam quibusdam discolis atque prava consuetudine nauseantibus contigisse novimus, quibus nisi exquisita edulia et pulmenta accurate composita, seu regum tucceta et preciosa vina atque forensia apponantur, adeo vulgaria spernunt et respuunt, ut prius se inedia torqueri permictant quam comedant; nulli dubium quin et hec nata sit Herebi atque Noctis.

6 Huius autem mansionem et formam sic describit Ovidius:

> Quesitamque Famem lapidoso invenit in agro
> unguibus et raris vellentem dentibus herbas.
> Hirtus erat crinis, cava lumina, pallor in ore,
> labra incana situ, scabre rubigine fauces,
> dura cutis per quam spectari viscera possent,
> ossa sub incurvis extabant arida lumbis,
> ventris erat pro ventre locus, pendere putares
> pectus et a spine tantummodo crate teneri.
> Auxerat articulos macies genuumque rigebat
> orbis, et immodico prodibant tubere tali.
> Hanc procul ut vidit,
>
>   etc.

shortage, it happens because of the laziness and idleness of the one who suffers or because of poverty. If from laziness or idleness, as when we see some people spend their days in playful pursuits, foolishness, and leisure rather than care for their household, this certainly is the daughter of Erebus and Night in that the others are superior. If because of poverty, provided that the one who suffers is not lacking on account of immoderation, I do not think she is the daughter of Erebus and Night, unless it proceeds from an intrinsically hungry stomach. But if the hunger is on account of a fastidiousness for food, as we know sometimes happens to irritable people and those who are sick because of a faulty constitution, these people refuse and spit out common foods unless fine foods and condiments are arranged meticulously, or sausages fit for a king or precious wine or exotic foods are served, allowing themselves to suffer starvation rather than eat. There is no doubt that this is the offspring of Erebus and Night.

Ovid described her dwelling and her appearance:[134]

She found Hunger in a stony field
tearing up herbs with her nails and scattered teeth.
Her hair was shaggy, her eyes hollow, with a pale mouth,
lips gray from neglect, and her throat coated with sores.
Her skin was hard; her viscera could be seen through it;
her brittle bones stuck out under her curved loins;
her stomach was a place for a stomach; and you would think
her breasts dangled, held only by the framework of her spine.
Her thinness made her joints large; stiff were her
kneecap rounds; and her ankles protruded like huge swellings.
As she saw her from afar. . .

: 26 :

De querela Herebi filia XII^a

1 Querelam dicit Tullius fuisse filiam Noctis et Herebi. Quod facile concedetur si quid sit sane mentis oculo prospectetur. Est enim morbus male secum convenientis animi, ob hoc insanum veniens pectus, quia aut subtrahi quod sibi debetur autumat inconsultus homo, aut egre fert sibi non dari quod optat, vel non posse quod cupiat. Et sic quod suum crimen est, alienum lumine mentis priva-

2 tus existimat. Hinc queritur lascivus amans, hinc auri cupidus, hinc honorum avidus, hinc sanguinis sitibundus et alii plures malum quod introduxerunt ipsi, et prudentes eiecisse poterant, flentes.

: 27 :

De Morbo XIII° Herebi filio

1 Est et Morbus Herebi Noctisque filius, ut placet Tullio et Crisippo. Hic autem mentis et corporis potest esse defectus, et uti in corpore ab humorum discordantia, sic in mente a morum inconvenientia causatur, et tunc merito huiusmodi parentum, id est cecitatis intrinsece filius nuncupatur, et quoniam in mortem salutis tendere videatur, Morbus, ut placet pluribus, appellatur.

: 26 :

On Grievance, the twelfth child of Erebus

Cicero[135] said that Grievance was a daughter of Night and Erebus. 1
One could easily agree with this when looking at it prudently with
the mind's eye. For it is a sickness of a mind not in harmony with
itself, and from there it extends to a demented heart, whether because an injudicious man insists that he is missing what is owed to
him, or because he can hardly bear not being given what he hopes
for, or because he is not able to get what he wants. And so, deprived of mental lucidity, he thinks his sin belongs to someone
else. For this reason the lascivious lover complains, as does he who 2
is desirous of gold, as does he who is avid for honors, as does he
who is thirsty for blood, and many others, weeping about an evil
they introduce themselves but which prudent people are able to
reject.

: 27 :

On Disease, the thirteenth child of Erebus

Disease is a son of Erebus and Night, as Cicero[136] and Chrysippus 1
think. This can be a defect of the mind and body. As a discor-
dance of the bodily humors, which is caused by a dissonance of
principles in the mind, he is rightly named for such parents, that
is, as the son of intrinsic blindness, and because he seems to strive
for the death [mortem] of health, he is called, as most think, Disease [Morbus].

: 28 :

De Senectute Herebi XIIII^a filia

1 Senectus etatum ultima et morti contermina solo contingit corpori, cum rationalis anima tendat viriditate perpetua in eternum. Hec, ut ait Tullius, Herebi fuit Noctisque filia. Quod quidam facile concedi potest, cum illi sit in complexione conformis, frigida scilicet et sicca, et filii similes consueverunt esse parentibus.

2 Est insuper Herebus iners et tremulus a quibus non degener est senectus, cum, ut cernimus, tremula sit et tarda. Porro quia hebetes offuscatosque sensus habet corporeos, non incongrue illi Noctem dixere matrem. Attamen hoc habet insigne, quia quantum illi subtrahitur virium, tantum menti augetur consilii, ex quo fit ut veneranda sit, et eius cani iuvenum preponantur lacertis.

: 29 :

De Pallore Herebi filio XV°

1 Pallor faciei atque totius corporis exsanguis est color, exausti sanguinis seu egri seu repentini timoris certissimus testis. Hic Noctis
2 et Herebi filius est, teste Crisippo. Et hoc ideo quia quicquid a luce solis non cernitur aut a minus bona vegetatione nutritur, pallore facile occupatur; et supra dictum est quia neque solem videat neque calorem sentiat Herebus, et ob id, ubi ista contingunt, frigescere sanguinem, et adversa digestione corrumpi et per consequens oriri pallorem necesse est, ut satis videmus in eis qui, diu

: 28 :

On Old Age, the fourteenth child of Erebus

Old age, the last age, conterminous with death, touches only the 1
body while the rational spirit strives toward eternity in perpetual
vigor. As Cicero[137] says, she is a daughter of Erebus and Night.
This can easily be conceded since she is similar to Night in complexion, that is, lifeless and dry, and children are often like their
parents.

Erebus in addition is weak and trembling, not unlike old age 2
which, as we know, is trembling and slow. Furthermore, because it
has dulled and clouded bodily senses, they say correctly that Night
was her mother. And it has this distinction, because as much as
strength is absent from old age, council is increased in the mind,
wherefore it happens that she must be respected and that her gray
hairs are placed before youthful strength.

: 29 :

On Pallor, the fifteenth child of Erebus

Pallor of the face and the whole body is bloodless color, the surest 1
evidence of drained or diseased blood or of sudden fear. He is a
son of Night and Erebus, as Chrysippus[138] testifies. This is so be- 2
cause whatever is not seen by the light of the sun or is nourished
with less than proper vegetation, is easily taken over by pallor. It is
also said that Erebus does not see the sun or feel heat, and therefore, in such circumstances, the blood grows cold and becomes
corrupted with adverse digestion, and pallor necessarily proceeds

ceco carcere clausi, in lucem veniunt, aut qui ab egritudine corporea fatigati resurgunt, vel subito correpti pavore pallescunt.

: 30 :

De Tenebra XVI^a Herebi filia

1 Herebi Noctisque filiam esse Tenebram nullo interveniente teste credetur. Sane ne idem mater et filia videantur, in hoc differunt. Nocte aliqualis luminosa res cernitur, ut luna et sydera seu ignis
2 aliquando. In tenebra autem nil unquam apparet luminis, et si appareat usquam, desistet esse tenebra.

: 31 :

De Somno Herebi filio XVII°

1 Somnus secundum quosdam est intimi ignis coertio et per membra mollita et labore relaxata diffusa quies. Secundum vero alios est quies animalium virtutum cum intensione naturalium. De hoc sic scribit Ovidius:

Somne, quies rerum placidissima, Somne, deorum,
pax animi, quem cura fugit, qui corpora duris
fessa ministeriis mulces reparasque labori,

etc.

from this. We often see this in people who, after being shut up in a dark prison for a long time, come into the light, or those who get up again after being enervated by a bodily sickness, or those who grow pale when suddenly seized by fear.

: 30 :

On Darkness, the sixteenth child of Erebus

It is believed that Darkness is a daughter of Erebus and Night, 1 although there is no source.[139] Mother and daughter seem not to be the same. They certainly differ in this way: at night some sort of luminous thing is visible, like the moon and stars or some sort of fire. In darkness, however, no light appears at all, and if it does, 2 the darkness ceases to exist.

: 31 :

On Sleep, the Seventeenth child of Erebus

Sleep, according to some, is the restraint of the innermost fire and 1 a quiet that has been diffused throughout the limbs softened and relaxed from labor. According to others it is the quiet of living powers with a tension of natural things. Ovid writes this about it as follows:[140]

> Sleep, calmest quiet of divine things, Sleep,
> peace of mind, whom our cares flee, who softens bodies
> tired from hard work and renews them for labor.

2   Sane longe plenius somni commoda describit Seneca poeta in tragedia *Herculis furentis* dum dicit:

> Tuque o domitor
> Somne malorum, requies animi,
> pars humane melior vite,
> volucer matris genus Astree,
> frater dure languide mortis
> veris miscens falsa, futuri
> certus et idem pessimus autor,
> pater o rerum, portus vite,
> lucis requies, noctisque comes,
> qui par regi famuloque venis.
> Placidus fessum lenisque fove,
> pavidum[48] leti genus humanum
> cogis longam discere mortem,
> preme devictum,

                                     etc.

3   Huic preterea Ovidius describit thalamum satis aptum dormiendi cupido, dicens:

> Est prope Cimmerios longo spelunca recessu,
> mons cavus, ignavi domus et penetralia Somni,
> quo nunquam radiis oriens mediusve cadensve,
> Phebus adire potest, nebule caligine mixte
> exalantur humo dubieque crepuscula lucis.
> Non vigil ales ibi cristati cantibus oris
> evocat auroram nec voce silentia rumpunt
> solliciteve canes canibusve sagacior anser
> garrula nec Progne stertentia pectora mulcet,
> non fera, non pecudes, non moti flamine rami,
> humaneve sonum reddunt convicia lingue.
> Muta quies habitat, saxo tamen exit ab imo,

The poet Seneca in his tragedy *Hercules Furens* describes the 2
gifts of sleep much more completely, when he says:[141]

You, O Sleep,

master of ills, rest for the spirit,
better part of human life,
fleeting offspring of mother Astraea,
languid brother of hard death,
mixing the false with the true, certain
and worst author of the future,
O father of things, harbor of life,
rest from the light and companion of night,
who comes equally to king and slave.
All of humanity fearful of passing
you compel to become acquainted with long death;
calm and mild, favor the tired
and hold the bound . . .

In addition Ovid describes his bedroom which is especially 3
suitable for one wishing to sleep, saying:[142]

Near the Cimmerians is a cave with a deep chamber,
a hollow mountain, home and inner sanctum of listless Sleep.
Whether at sunrise, noon, or sunset, never are the rays
of Phoebus able to intrude; the ground
exhales mists of darkness and the dim light of dusk.
No watchful crested bird with his tuneful cry
evokes the dawn, nor is the silence broken
by the voices of restless dogs or, wiser than dogs, geese;
nor does the garrulous Procne charm snoring breasts.
No beasts, no herds, no branches moved by the wind,
and no outcries from human tongues make any sound.
Mute quiet lives there, but from the bottom of the rock flows

rivus aque Lethes, per quem cum murmure labens
invitat somnos crepitantibus unda lapillis.
Ante fores atrii fecunda papavera florent,
innumereque herbe, quarum de lacte soporem
nox legit, et spargit per opacas humida terras.
Ianua ne verso stridorem cardine reddat,
nulla domo tota est, custos in limine nullus.
In medio thorus est ebano sublimis in antro,
plumeus, unicolor pullo velamine tectus,
quo cubat ipse deus membris languore solutis.
Hunc circa passim varias imitantia formas
somnia vana iacent totidem, quot messis aristas,
silva gerit frondes, eiectas litus harenas,

etc.

4   Hunc tam spectabili thalamo atque cubiculariis decoratum deum dicit Tullius Herebi et Noctis fuisse filium; cuius rei causa videnda est, et inde videre poterimus de ministris, cum satis sensus appareat descripti thalami.

Filius ergo Herebi Noctisque dicitur Somnus, quia a vaporibus humidis e stomaco surgentibus et opilantibus arterias, et quieta
5   obscuritate causetur. Si autem de mortali somno velimus intelligere, non difficilius parentum talium dabitur causa. Nam calore caritatis perdito et omissa rationis via, ut necessarium sit in letiferum ire somnum satis apertum est.

6   Nunc autem de assistentibus videamus, que somnia sunt multiplicium specierum, ex quibus quinque tantum super *Somnio Scipionis* ostendit Macrobius. Harum prima vocatur 'phantasma,' que

the waters of River Lethe, through which, slipping along with
   a murmur,
its waves purling above the pebbles invite sleep.
Before the doors of the cave bloom poppies in abundance and
countless herbs, from the milky juice of which dank night
gathers sleep and sprinkles it throughout the shaded lands.
There is no door, lest it make a noise creaking on its hinges
anywhere in the house, and there is no guard in the threshold.
In the middle of the cave is a raised bed of ebony,
filled with down, of solid color under a dark coverlet,
on which the god himself rests his relaxed limbs.
Everywhere around him lie many a crowd of empty dreams
taking various forms, as many as there are grains of wheat
to harvest, leaves in the forest, and sands scattered on the
   shore.

Cicero[143] says that this god adorned in his chambers with such   4
a noteworthy bedroom was a son of Erebus and Night. We must
examine the cause of this, and once the meaning of the bed chamber described above becomes sufficiently clear, then we will be able
to examine his agents.

Sleep is said to be the son of Erebus and Night because it is
caused by moist vapors, rising from the stomach and blocking the
arteries, and calm darkness. And if we want to know about mortal   5
sleep, the origin of its parents will not be more difficult to find, for
when the warmth of affection has dissipated and the way of reason
has been forgotten, it is quite clear that it is necessary to enter into
fatal sleep.

So now let us examine his assistants, that is, the dreams of   6
many types; Macrobius[144] discusses only five of them in his *Dream
of Scipio*. The first of these is called *phantasmal*. He never mixes

numquam se mortalibus miscet nisi lente, dum se incipit somnus immictere, existimantibus nobis adhuc vigilare, affertque hec horribiles visu formas, et ut plurimum a natura specie et magnitudine discrepantes, certamen noxium, aut mirabile gaudium, tempestates

7 validas, ventosque sonoros et huiusmodi. Huius in genere dicit Macrobius esse etiam *emactes* seu *ephyactes* vel *ephyaltes*, quem communis persuasio existimat quiescentes invadere et suo pondere pressos sentientesque gravare. Et huius causam opinantur multi stomachum nimio cibo vel potu gravatum, seu longo ieiunio vacuum, et nonnunquam aliquem ex humoribus ceteris predominan-

8 tem. Sunt qui superaddant hesitationes, dicantque Virgilium intellexisse Didonem vidisse phantasmata dum sorori conquesta est dicens, 'Que me suspensam insomnia terrent'; et illud 'insomnia' pro phantasmate licentia poetica improprie positum.

9   Secunda 'insomnium' nuncupatur a premeditatione causatum, ut Tullius affirmare videtur in libro *Rei publice* dicens:

> Fit enim sepe ut cogitationes sermonesque nostri pariant aliquid in somno, quale de Omero scribit Emnius, de quo videlicet sepissime vigilans solebat cogitare et loqui,

> > etc.

10 In hac igitur specie somnii amans dilectam sibi puellam in amplexus eius occurrentem aspiciet, aut fugientem miserrimus exorabit. Nauta tranquillum mare navemque pansis velis sulcantem, aut tempestate periclitantem aspiciet. Sic et agricola frustra letabitur letas arvis intuens segetes, depastasque plorabit. Ingurgitator pocula exhauriet; ieiunus cibos aut optabit, aut faucibus vacuis de-

11 vorabit appositos. De premeditatis autem a Didone saucia, visa quidam volunt, eo quod videatur a Virgilio ostensam premeditationem dum dicit:

himself with mortals except slowly—while sleep begins to set in and we think we are still awake—and it is then that he brings in figures horrible to behold, far different from any natural appearance or size: a harmful struggle, or amazing joy, powerful storms, resounding winds, and the like. Macrobius says that of this type 7 there are also *emactes*, *ephyactes*, or *ephyaltes*, which the common belief thinks invade those who are resting and burden those who are pondering, pressed down by their own weight. Many think the cause of this is a stomach disturbed by too much food or drink, or empty after a long fast, and it can happen when one of the humors predominates over the others. There are those who add as well 8 hesitation, and they say that Vergil understood that Dido saw phantasms while lamenting to her sister, saying,[145] "What apparitions [*insomnia*] frighten me in my anguish," where by poetic license *insomnia* is improperly substituted for "phantasms."

The second is called *insomnium* and is caused by premeditation, 9 as Cicero seems to assert in his *Republic*, saying:[146]

It often happens that our thoughts and conversations produce something in sleep, of the sort Ennius wrote about in regard to Homer, which we very often indeed continue to think about and discuss while lying awake.

In this type of dream, a lover will see his girl running into his 10 embrace, or he will wretchedly entreat her as she flees. A sailor will see a tranquil sea ploughed by a ship with billowing sails, or he will see it imperiled by a storm. Thus also a farmer will rejoice in vain as he sees abundant crops in his fields, and he laments their destruction. A heavy drinker will drain his cups; a starving man will either hope for food or devour with empty jaws what is served up to him. As for premeditation, some wish to see pre- 11 meditation in wounded Dido since Vergil seemed to refer to it when he said:[147]

Multa viri virtus animo multusque recursat
gentis honos, herent infixi pectore vultus
verbaque,

etc.

Et sic tamquam ex premeditatione perveniens videtur esse insomnium. Verum quoniam ex affectione procedunt, una cum somno in auras evanescunt, ut ipse idem Virgilius dicit, 'Sed falsa ad celum mittunt insomnia manes.'

12   'Somnium' species tercia appellatur, per quod placet Macrobio certa somniari, sed sub velamine, ut teste Moyse in Pentateuco, vidit Ioseph manipulos fratrum suum adorantes, et, ut ait Valerius, Astiages vitem et urinam ex genitalibus filie prodeuntem. Hoc autem fieri volunt homine existente sobrio, ut plurimum sumus propinquante die.

13   Quarta vero species 'visio' nominatur, nullas pre se ferens ambages, quin imo quod futurum est liquida patefactione demonstrat, ut vidit Arterius Rufus romanus eques dormiens Syragusis se scilicet, dum gladiatorum munus inspiceret, retiarii manu transfodi, quod die sequenti cum multis nuntiasset secutum est.

14   Quinta et ultima somniorum species 'oraculum' veteres vocavere, quod Macrobius esse vult, dum sopiti parentes maioresque nostros, gravem hominem aut pontificem, seu ipsum deum, aliqua dicentem seu premonentem nos cernimus, ut in somnis Ioseph ab Angelo premonitus est, ut acciperet puerum et matrem eius et

15   cum eis secederet in Egyptum. Sane non nulli ex priscis, ut ex verbis Porphyrii phylosophi satis percipi potest, omnia per quietem visa vera esse arbitrati sunt, sed ut plurimum minime intellecta, et ob hoc videtur Porphyrium, longe aliter quam multi alii faciant, sentire, quod per Homerum primo, deinde per Virgilium dictum est, et quoniam familiare magis Virgilii quam Homeri carmen est, illud deducamus in medium.

In her mind his great virtue and recurring often
the great honor of his line, and to her heart cling his face
and words.

And so *insomnium* seems as if it emanates from premeditation.
And because these visions derive from a mental state, they disappear along with sleep into the air, as Vergil himself says,[148] "But the Manes send false dreams to the sky."

The third type is called *somnium*, through which Macrobius[149] 12 thinks specific things are dreamt but under a veil, as, according to Moses[150] in the *Pentateuch*, Joseph sees the bundles of his brothers bowing in adoration, and, as Valerius[151] says, Astyages sees a grapevine and urine issuing forth from the genitalia of his daughter. Also, they say this happens when a man is sober, as we often are as the day approaches.

The fourth type is named "vision," which brings no ambiguity 13 with it but reveals the future in a clear manifestation, as when the Roman knight Haterius Rufus, while sleeping in Syracuse, saw himself watching a gladiatorial exhibition and being stabbed by a retiarius, which happened the next day after he had told many people of his vision.[152]

The fifth and last type of dreams the ancients call *oraculum*, 14 which Macrobius says occurs when in our sleep we see our parents or ancestors, an important man or priest, or even a god speaking or warning about something, as Joseph in his sleep was warned by an angel to take the child and his mother and depart for Egypt.[153] In fact some of the ancients, as we can understand clearly from the 15 words of the philosopher Porphyry,[154] think that everything seen in our sleep is true but usually not understood. For this reason it seems that Porphyry understood, unlike most others, what was said first by Homer and then by Vergil, and because the poetry of Vergil is more familiar than that of Homer, let us refer to that.

16   Dicit enim Virgilius:

> Sunt gemine somni porte, quarum altera fertur
> cornea, qua veris facilis datur exitus umbris,
> altera candenti perfecta nitens elephanto,
> sed falsa ad celum mittunt insomnia manes,
>
> etc.

Per hos versus vult Porphyrius somnia omnia vera esse, sentiens quod anima, sopito corpore, tanquam paululum solutior in suam divinitatem nitatur, et in latens humanitatem verum aciem omnem dirigat intellectus, et non nulla videat et discernat, et plura videat quam discernat, seu longius abdita sint, seu densiori tegmine occultata; et hinc fit ut quod discernit, esto non plene, nebula caligantis mortalitatis obsistente, dictum sit per corneam emicti ianuam, cum cornu huius nature sit, ut extenuatum pervium sit intuitu et tanquam dyaphanum corpus in se recondita videre per-
17   mictat. Quod autem obsistente carnis caligine videre non potest, id elephanto contectum dicimus, cuius quidem os a natura adeo condensatum est, ut in quantumcunque tenuitatem redigatur, videre supposita non permictat; que ideo falsa dicit Virgilius, quia minime intellecta sunt, ut ait Porphyrius.

18   Nunc autem superest de ministris videre, qui etsi forte multi sint nomina trium tantum esse cognoscimus. Quorum primum Morphea dictum volunt, quod interpretatur formatio, seu simulacrum, cuius domini iussu officium est quoscunque hominum vultus fingere, verba, mores, voces et ydiomata, ut scribit Ovidius, dicens:

> At pater e populo natorum mille suorum
> excitat artificem simulatoremque figure
> Morphea; non illo iussos solertior alter

Vergil says:[155]   16

> There are twin gates of sleep, of which the one is said to be of
>   horn, through which an easy exit is given to true shades,
> the other being perfect and shining in white ivory,
>   but from here the Manes send false dreams to the sky.

Porphyry wanted all dreams to be true in these verses, understanding that when the body was sleeping, the spirit, as if slightly
unrestrained, progressed toward its divinity, and the intellect directed its entire awareness toward the hidden truth lurking in humankind; some things it sees and understands, and it sees more
than it understands, whether because they are buried more deeply
or hidden under a thicker cover. From this it happens that what it
understands, albeit not completely because of the hindrance from
a cloud of mortal confusion, is said to be sent through the horn
gate, since the horn is of such a nature that when made thin it becomes transparent to look at and allows, as if a diaphanous body,
to see what is hidden in itself. That which is not possible to see   17
with the hindering cloud of flesh, that we say is hidden in the
ivory gate, the bone of which is naturally so dense that, no matter
how thinly it is rendered, it does not permit us to see what is underneath. Vergil therefore calls this false, because they are not
known, as Porphyry says.

Now it remains to examine Sleep's agents. Although there hap-   18
pen to be many of them, we know only the names of three. First
of these they like to call Morpheus, which means "formation," or
"likeness," whose function, by order of his master, is to recreate all
kinds of human faces, words, characteristics, voices, and idioms.
Ovid writes about this, saying:[156]

> But the father, from the crowd of his one thousand sons
> aroused the artificer and imitator of form,
> Morpheus. When ordered, no one was more expert than he

exprimit incessus vultumque sonumque loquendi,
adicit et vestes et consuetissima cuique
verba, sed hic solus homines imitatur,

etc.

19 Secundum autem Ytathona seu Phabetora quorum ego nominum signifcatum ignoro; huius tamen officium hoc in carmine dicit Ovidius:

alter

fit fera, fit volucris, fit longo corpore serpens:
hunc Ytathon superi, mortale Phabetora vulgus
nominat,

etc.

20 Tertium vero dixere Panthum, quasi totum, cuius officium est in-
sensibilia fingere, Ovidio teste, dum ait:

Est etiam diverse tertius[49] artis

Panthos: ille in humum saxumque undamque trabemque
queque vacant animo fallaciter omnia transit,

etc.

Quasi ex his velint que cernimus dormientes ab exteriori potentia
nobis allata sint. Verum utrum sic sit videant alii.

: 32 :

De Morte XVIII^a filia Herebi

1 Mors, ut voluere Tullius et Crisippus filia fuit Noctis et Herebi,
quam ultimum esse terribilium testatur Aristotiles. Ab hac enim
omnes ab ea ipsa die, qua miseri mundum intramus, sensim adeo

at portraying a gate or a face or speaking voice,
and he added both a person's clothes and characteristic
words, but imitated only humans.

The second was Icelon or Phobetor;[157] I do not know the 19
meaning of these names. Nonetheless, Ovid describes his function
in his poem this way:[158]

> The other
> becomes a beast; he becomes a bird, a serpent with a long
>   body.
> The gods call him Icelon, mortals Phobetor.

The third they call Panthus, that is, "all." It is his function to imi- 20
tate insensible objects. Ovid bears witness to this when he says:[159]

> There is also a third, of a different art.
> Phantasus.[160] Earth and stone and water and wood
> and other inanimate things he deceptively imitates.

It is as if they wish us to understand from this that when we are
sleeping external powers are brought to us. Let others determined
whether this is true.

: 32 :

On Death, the eighteenth child of Erebus

Death, as Cicero[161] and Chrysippus think, is a daughter of Night 1
and Erebus. Aristotle[162] describes her as the ultimate terror. All of
us are continuously being taken by her so gradually that we cannot

ut non advertamus, continue carpimur; et cum cotidie moriamur, tunc vulgato sermone mori dicimur, cum mori desinimus.

2 Hanc, etsi mille modis miseri rapiamur, aut violentam aut naturalem voluere priores. Violenta est que ferro vel igne, vel casu alio fugienti vel etiam postulanti infertur. Naturalis autem secundum Macrobium super *Somnium Scipionis* ea est, qua non corpus ab anima, sed a corpore anima derelicta est. Vocavere insuper veteres senum mortem maturam seu meritam, iuvenum immaturam, puerorum autem acerbam dixere.

3 Nec non et aliis multis nominibus appellata est, ut Atropos, Parca, Letum, Nex et Fatum. Huius etiam dirum opus sic breviter describit Statius:

> Stygiis emissa tenebris,
> Mors fruitur celo bellatoremque volando
> campum operit nigroque viros invitat hyatu.
> Nil vulgare legens, sed que dignissima vita,
> funera precipuos annis animisque cruento
> angue notat,
>
> etc.

4 Sed iam que pauca ficta sunt detegamus. Herebi illam dicunt filiam quia ab Herebo emissa sit, ut in prescripto carmine Statius, Stygiis emissa tenebris, seu quia calore careat, ut caret Herebus; Noctis autem ideo filia dicta est quia horribilis et obscura videatur. Mors autem dicta est, ut dicit Ugutio, quia 'mordeat' vel a 'morsu' parentis primi, per quem morimur, vel a Marte qui interfector est hominum, vel 'mors' quasi 'amaror,' quia amara sit; nil enim hominibus creditur amarius morte, eis exceptis de quibus dicit Iohannes in Apocalipsi: 'Beati qui in Domino moriuntur.'

feel it from that very day on which we wretches enter the world; and although we die daily, we die, as the common expression goes, only when we stop dying.

Although we wretches are taken in a thousand ways, the ancients speak of her as being violent or natural. She is violent when she arrives by iron or fire or accident, whether to one who flees death or one who welcomes it. Natural death, according to Macrobius[163] in his *Dream of Scipio*, is that in which the body is not left by the spirit but the spirit by the body. In addition, the ancients call the death of the elderly timely or warranted, that of the young untimely, and that of children bitter.

And she is called by many other names, such as "Atropos," "Destiny," "Ruin," "Murder," and "Fate." Statius briefly describes her dire work in this way:[164]

> Sent out by the Stygian darkness,
> Death enjoyed the sky and in her flight overspread
> the battlefield. She beckons the men with her black, gaping mouth.
> Not choosing the crowd for ruin but the most distinguished,
> those superior in years and spirit, she marked them
> with her bloody nail.

Now let us expose a few of these fictions. They say she is the daughter of Erebus because she was sent by Erebus, as in the line of Statius' poem, "sent out by the Stygian darkness," or because she lacks heat, as does Erebus. She is said to be a daughter of Night because she seems horrible and dark. They say "death" [*mors*] because, as Uguccione[165] says, she "bites" [*mordeat*]; or from the "bite" [*morsu*] of our first ancestor, through whom we die; or from "Mars" [*Marte*] who is the murderer of men; or in that death is "bitterness" [*amaror*] because it is bitter, for nothing is thought to be more bitter than death, except for those about whom John speaks in the *Apocalypse*:[166] "Blessed are they who die in God."

5   Hec ut placere videtur Servio, ab Atropu de qua supra differt, quia per hanc violentam debemus intelligere mortem, ut satis etiam colligitur proximo supra ex carmine Statii. Per Atropon autem vult intellegi naturalem rerum dissolutionem. Atropos autem dicta quia non convertitur. Parcam vero eam per antiphrasim dixere, eo quod 'nemini parcat.' Sic et Letum, cum sit mestissima rerum. Necem autem illam proprie arbitror qua aqua, vel laqueo seu modo alio spiritus intercluditur. Fatum autem dicta est, eo quod divina providentia premonstratum sit, qui nascuntur omnes mori debere.

: 33 :

De Carone Herebi filio XVIIII°

1   Charon, Acherontis nauta, Herebi et Noctis filius dicitur a Crisippo. De quo sic ait Virgilius:

Portitor has horrendus aquas et flumina servat
terribili squalore Charon cui plurima mento
canicies inculta iacet, stant lumina flamma.
Sordidus ex humeris nodo dependit amictus.
Ipse ratem conto subigit velisque ministrat
et ferruginea subvectat corpora cymba,
iam senior sed cruda deo viridisque senectus,

etc.

2   Charon, quem Servius devolvit in Cronon, tempus est. Herebus autem hic pro intrinseco divine mentis consilio intelligendus est, a quo tempus et cetera omnia creata sunt, et sic Herebus Charonis pater.

Servius seems to think that she is different from the aforemen- 5
tioned Atropos because through her we ought to know of a violent
death, as we gather from the preceding verses by Statius. By Atropos he means the natural "atrophy of life," for Atropos means "she
does not turn." They call her "Destiny" [*Parca*] by antiphrasis because she "spares" [*parcat*] no one. They call her "Ruin" [*Letum*]
because she is the "most unhappy [*letum*] of things." I think she is
more appropriately called "Murder" [*Necem*] in that the spirit is
hindered by water or a trap or some other thing. She is called
"Fate" because it is demonstrated by divine providence that all who
are born have to die.

: 33 :

Charon, the nineteenth child of Erebus

Charon, the mariner of the Acheron, is said by Chrysippus[167] to 1
be a son of Erebus and Night. Vergil says this about him:[168]

> The dreadful ferryman watches over these waters and rivers,
> Charon; frightfully filthy, a number of gray hairs lie
> unkempt on his chin; his eyes are aflame.
> A dirty garment hangs in a knot from his shoulders.
> He punts his raft with a pole and tends to the sails,
> and he conveys bodies on his rust-colored skiff;
> already old, his divine old age is fresh and green.

Charon, whom Servius[169] transforms into Chronon, is "time." 2
Erebus here must represent the intrinsic plan of the divine mind
from which time and everything else was created, and so Erebus is
the father of Charon.

3 Nox autem illi ob id mater data est, quia ante creatum tempus nulla fuit sensibilis lux, et ideo in tenebris factum est, et ex tenebris productum videtur. Apud inferos vero ideo positus est Charon, quia superi tempore non indigent, ut nos mortales, qui ab illis sumus inferi, indigemus.

4 Quod autem Charon corpora deferat ex una in alteram Acherontis ripam, ideo fictum est ut intelligamus quoniam tempus confestim ut nascimur suo nos sumit in gremio, et in ripam defert oppositam, id est in mortem, que quidem est nativitati contraria, cum illa deducat in esse, et hec corporibus auferat esse.

5 Vehimur preterea a Charone per Acherontem fluvium, qui 'absque gaudio' interpretatur, ut advertamus quoniam a tempore trahimur per vitam labilem et miseriis plenam. Eum preterea dicit Virgilius senem, sed robusta viridique fultum senecta, ut cognoscamus tempus annositate vires non perdere; hoc idem hodie potest quod potuit dum creatum est. Sordidus autem illi amictus est, ut appareat quia circa terrena, que sordida sunt, versetur.

: 34 :

De Die Herebi XX^a filia

1 Dies Herebi Noctisque fuit filia, sic, ubi *De naturis deorum*, scribente Tullio. Hanc dicit Theodontius Etheri fratri suo coniugio copulatam. Quod Herebi filia sit et Noctis, talis ratio redditur a quibusdam. Herebum enim a parte totum sumentes pro universo terre corpore sumi voluere, ex extremo cuius, quod orizonta vo-

Night is given as his mother because before time was created 3
there was no perceptible light, and so he seems to have been produced in the darkness and from the darkness. Charon is placed among the lower gods because the superior gods have no need of time as do we mortals who are lower than they.

That Charon conveys bodies from one bank of the Acheron to 4
the other was a fiction that would let us understand that as soon as we are born, time takes us into its lap and conveys us toward the opposite bank, that is, toward death, which is the opposite of birth, the one leading to existence, the other removing it from our bodies.

In addition we are carried by Charon across the Acheron river, 5
which means "without joy" [*absque gaudio*], helping us observe that we are conveyed by time through a life that is fleeting and full of miseries. Also, Vergil says that he is old but sustained by a robust and green old age, wherein we recognize that time does not lose strength by age: today he can do the same thing which was possible when he was created. His clothing is dirty, so that it appears that this involves earthy matters, which are dirty.

: 34 :

On Day, the Twentieth child of Erebus

Day was a daughter of Erebus and Night, according to Cicero[170] in 1
his *On the Nature of the Gods*. Theodontius says that she mated with her brother, Ether. That she is the daughter of Erebus and Night is the result of the following rationale: taking Erebus as the whole from the part, they want it to substitute for the entire body of earth, at the very end of which, called the horizon by the

cant Greci, non est dubium adventu solis cedente nocte diem consurgere, et eam[50] Herebum ex Nocte produxisse.

2 Eam autem Etheri coniunctam connubio ideo dicunt, quia Etherem intelligunt ignem, qui claritate carere non potest, et ob id cum dies clara sit, nil aliud volunt quam claritatem igni coniunctam ostendere. Hec autem ab antiquis, postquam a Deo dictum est, 'vespere et mane facta est dies una,' huius magnitudinis designata est, ut id tempus, quod labitur a surgente sole et mundum omnem circumeunte atque in eodem loco, unde surrexerat, redeunte, ea cum nocte que includitur, dies dicatur una, et hec naturalis, quam in xxiiii^{or} equas partes divisere, et has oras nuncupa-

3 vere. Deinde, prout eisdem visum est, artificialis est superinducta dies, que in diem et noctem divisa unicuique partium, diei scilicet et nocti xii horas, esto inequales, esse concessere, et artificialem ab artificio excogitantis eam dixere, qua in suis iudiciis ut plurimum utuntur astrologi. Inde medici Creticam invenere diem, eaque circa egritudinum observationes utuntur.

Dierum vero naturalium initium non eque a nationibus omni-

4 bus summitur. Romani autem, ut ait Marcus Varro, a nocte media incepisse et in sequentis noctis medium terminasse voluerunt, quam dimensionem adhuc servant Ytali, et potissime in iudicialibus causis. Athenienses autem olim a solis occasu incipientes diem in occasum diei sequentis finiebant. Babilonii vero ab ortu faciebant, quod ab occasu Attici. Umbri qui et Etrusci sunt, a meridie illi fecere principium, et in sequentis diei meridiem terminabant. Que consuetudo adhuc ab astrologis observatur.

5 Est preterea dies naturalis secundum varias eius qualitates variis distincta nominibus. Nam, ut Macrobius *Saturnaliorum* asserit, ab initio diei Romanorum incipiens, primum tempus diei dicitur 'medie noctis inclinatio,' eo quod nox in diem incipiat declinare. Deinde a galli cantu 'gallicinium' nuncupatum. Tertium 'contici-

Greeks, there is no doubt that day rises with the arrival of the sun and the receding night, so Erebus produced her from Night.

They say she is joined in marriage to Ether because they know 2 that Ether is fire, which is not able to lack brightness, and, since the day is bright, they wish to show nothing other than brightness joined with fire. After God said, "evening and morning were the first day,"[171] the ancients designated the magnitude of a day, that is, the time which passes from the rising of the sun, its traversing the entire world, and its return to the same place from which it had risen; including the night with it, this is called one day, and they divided this natural day into twenty-four equal parts, which they called hours. Then, as it seemed to them, the artificial day 3 was introduced, wherein it was divided into day and night, and each part, that is, day and night, was given twelve hours, albeit unequal. They said this was artificial from the artifice of those who devised it; in their judgment it was for the most part the astrologers who used it. Thereafter doctors invented the Cretan day which they use for monitoring illnesses.

The beginning of natural days is not thought of equally by all peoples. The Romans, as Marcus Varro[172] says, want it to begin 4 from the middle of the night and end in the middle of the subsequent night. The Italians still use this measurement, especially in judicial proceedings. The Athenians, beginning the day with the setting of the sun, ended it with the next day's setting. The Babylonians used to make the day begin from sunrise, the Athenians from sunset. The Umbrians, who are the Etruscans, marked the beginning of the day at noon and ended it at the noon of the following day. This custom is still observed by astrologers.

In addition, the natural day has various names to distinguish 5 between its various qualities. As Macrobius[173] in the *Saturnalia* asserts, starting from the beginning of the Roman day, the first period of the day is called "the inclination of midnight" because night begins to decline into day. Then "cockcrow" [*gallicinium*] is named

nium,' eo quod sopita omnia conticescere videantur. Quartum 'diluculum' dicitur, eo quod diei lux apparere videatur. Subsequenter quintum tempus, sole iam surgente, 'mane' vocari voluere, seu quia a manibus exordium lucis emergi visum sit, seu ab omine boni nominis, nam Lanubini mane pro bono dicunt. Sextum autem dixere 'meridium,' hoc est diei medium, quod nos 'meridiem' dicimus. Ab hac autem hora tempus in noctem tendens, quod septimum est, vocatur 'occiduum' quia cadere videatur. Octavum vero 'suprema tempestas' nuncupatum est, eo quod diei sit novissimum tempus, ut in XII tabulis est espressum: 'Solis occasus suprema tempestas esto.' Deinde nonum tempus dicitur 'vespera,' quod a Grecis tractum est. Illi enim *speran* a stella hespero, que in occasu solis apparet, dicunt. Decimum autem tempus, quod est noctis initium, dicitur 'prima fax,' eo quod tunc stelle incipiant apparere, seu, ut aliis placet, quia tunc, luce cessante diei, incipimus faces accendere, ut tenebras noctis vincamus lumine. Tempus vero undecimum 'nox concubia' dictum est, eo quod ea hora post aliqualem vigiliam cubitum consueverint ire mortales. Duodecimum quidem diei tempus, quod noctis est tertium, 'intempestum' dicitur, eo quod nullis gerendis rebus videatur accommodum. Cuius finis est circa principium eius, quod diximus 'medie noctis inclinatio.'

6

Insuper cum humana solertia respectu habito ad septenarium numerum, quem quibusdam ex causis veteres voluere perfectum, disposuerit omne tempus per septimanas dierum efflui, et dies illas septimane nominibus variis nuncupare, consuevere non nulli nominum talium exquirere causas; quas ego has puto, cum a planetis apud nos quinque denominentur, sexta *sabbatum* ab Hebreis

from the crow of the "cock" [*galli*]. Third is "still of the night" [*conticinium*] because everything seems to be "resting" [*conticescere*] in sleep. Fourth is called "daybreak" [*diluculum*] because the "light" [*lux*] of day is seen to appear. Next, the fifth period, with the sun already rising, they wish to call "morning" [*mane*] either because the beginning of the light seems to be emerging from the "shades" [*manibus*], or from the omen of a good name, for the Lanuvians say "mane" for "good. Sixth they call "meridiem," that is, the "middle" [*medium*] of the day, which we call noon. From this hour the period stretching into the night is called "sunset" [*occiduum*] because it seems to "fall" [*cadere*]. Eighth is named "the supreme period" because it is the last period of the day, as it is in the Twelve Tables:[174] "Let the falling of the sun be the last [*suprema*] period." The ninth period is then called "vespers," which is derived from the Greeks, for they call it *speran* from the star Hesperus, which appears at sunset. The tenth period, which is the beginning of the night, is called "first torch" because at that time stars begin to appear, or, as others think, because at that time, with the light of day disappearing, we begin to light torches so we can overcome the darkness of night with light. The eleventh period is called "first sleep" [*concubia*] because at that hour, after some wakefulness, mortals usually go to "bed" [*concubitum*]. The twelfth period of the day, which is the third period of night, is called "inopportune" because it seems suitable for doing nothing. The end of that period 6 leads into the beginning of the next, which we called "the inclination of midnight."

In addition, since human ingenuity distributed all of time to pass through a week of seven days — for the ancients reserved respect for the number seven, which for certain reasons they considered to be perfect — and they called those seven days by various names, some are likely to inquire about the reasons for such names, which I think are as follows. Although we name five of them after the planets, the sixth was called "Sabbath" by the He-

dicta, a Christianis postea immutata non est, eo quod 'requiem' dicant significare Latine, ut appareat cum creavisset omnia Deus in sex diebus, eum septima ab omnibus operibus suis quievisse.

7 'Dominica' autem dies, que nobis Christianis est septima, sic eo dicta est, quia ea die Christus Dei filius, non solum ab omnibus laboribus suis quievit, verum victor surrexit a mortuis et sic illam

8 a Domino nostro patres incliti vocavere dominicam. Alii volunt a sole denominatam, eo quod ipse sit planetarum princeps et inde dicatur dominus, et quia eiusdem diei hore prime principatum habeat ob id illam denominari dominicam.

Sed cum longe alius sit ordo planetarum quam in nominibus dierum habeatur, est sciendum secundum planetarum ordinem successive unicuique diei hore dari dominium, et ab eo cui contingit prime hore diei dominium habere, ab eo dies illa denominata est, ut puta si diei dominice Veneri secundam horam tribues, que Soli immediate subiacet, et Mercurio terciam, qui subiacet Veneri, et Lune quartam, que subiacet Mercurio, quintam autem Saturno, ad quem convertendus est ordo cum in Luna defecerit, sextam Iovi, et sic de singulis xxiiii^{is} horis diei dominici,[51] sub nomine vel dominio Mercurii invenietur hora xxiiii^{a}, et xxv^{a} que prima est diei sequentis sub nomine vel dominio Lune, et ideo ab ea secundus denominatus ebdomade dies, seu potius primus, ut dies domi-

9 nica septima sit ebdomade et quietis dies. A qua prima diei Lune hora, si eodem modo computaveris xxiiii^{am} eius horam invenies sub Iovis imperio constitutam, et xxiiii^{am} sub Martis dominio, a quo et ipsa secunda dies Martis denominata est, quia prime eius hore Mars imperet. Et sic successive de singulis donec ad ultimam

brews and not changed afterward by Christians; they say it means "rest," so it would appear that after God created all things in six days, he rested from all his labors on the seventh. "The Lord's Day" [*Dominica*], which is the seventh day for us Christians, is so called because on that day Christ, the son of God, not only rested from all his labors but rose in victory from the dead, and so our illustrious fathers called this day "the Lord's Day" from our "Lord." Others prefer it to be named after the sun because it is the prince of the planets and is therefore called "Lord" [*dominus*], and because it controls the beginning of the first hour, it is named the "Lord's" [*dominicam*] Day.

But since the order of the planets is far different from their order in the names of the days, we should understand that it is according to the order of the planets that dominion is given to each hour of the day in succession, and that it is from this that he happens to have dominion over the first hour of the day, and that days are named as such. For example, the second hour of the Lord's day you will attribute to Venus, which lies immediately beneath the sun, and the third to Mercury, which lies beneath Venus, and fourth to the moon, which lies beneath Mercury, and the fifth to Saturn, for which the order must be changed when it is invisible in the moon, and the sixth to Jupiter. And so of the single twenty-four hours of the Lord's day, the twenty-fourth hour is found under the name or dominion of Mercury, and the twenty-fifth is that which is the first hour of the subsequent day under the name or dominion of the moon, and so from it comes the name of the second of the seven days, or rather the first, since the Lord's day is the seventh day and the day of rest. From the first hour of the day of the moon, if you calculate in the same way, you will find its twenty-fourth hour arranged under the rule of Jupiter, and the twenty-fifth under the dominion of Mars, from which also the second day is named for Mars because Mars rules its first hour. And so it is with each succeeding day until you come to the ulti-

deveneris sabbati, que Marti subest, et subsequitur prima diei do-
10 minici ascripta Soli, a quo dies ut ante diximus dicta est. Dies
autem naturalis cum ex die constet et nocte, a die tota tanquam a
digniori parte denominata est, et dies a diis vocitata, nam *dyos*
Grece, Latine dicitur 'deus'; nam uti dii mortalibus opinione veterum adiutores sunt, sic et adiutrices sunt dies, et a diis ipsis etiam
eam ob causam denominate sunt.

11 Postquam e subterraneis latebris in diei lucem prestante Deo
devenimus, supererat nobis, ut eque de omnibus Herebi filiis dixis-
semus, etiam de Ethere, quem eiusdem filium volunt, quid sense-
12 rint veteres, descripsisse. Sane quoniam eius omne masculinum
genus, hoc excepto filio, sterile est, et huius non est parva posteritas, et in longum satis volumen protractum est, eum in secundum
servandum honestius ratus sum, et primo finem imponere.

mate hour of the Sabbath, which is under Mars and is followed by the first hour of the Lord's day attributed to the sun, which gives the day its name, as we have already said. The entire natural day, 10 although it consists of day and night, is named from the whole day, as if that were the worthier part, and the word "day" [dies] is named after "gods" [diis], which is dyos in Greek and means "god" [deus] in Latin. For as the gods, according to ancient thinking, helped mortals, so also the days were helpers, and for that reason they were named from the gods.

Now that we have arrived, by the grace of God, from subterra- 11 nean lairs into the light of day, it remains for us, since we have spoken equally about all the children of Erebus, to report what the ancients thought about Ether, whom they thought was his son. But because every masculine offspring of Erebus was sterile except 12 for him, and because Ether's posterity was not small and this book has been protracted into considerable length, I thought it would be better to save him for the second book and bring this first one to a close.

LIBER SECUNDUS

Arbor

In arbore autem signata desuper, in celum versa radice, ponitur in culmine Ether filius Herebi et Noctis; eiusque in ramis et frondibus, cum Etheri duo tantum fuerint filii Juppiter scilicet primus et Celius seu Celum, Jovis primi solum prosapia designatur omnis; Celii seu Celi prole in sequenti reservata volumine.

Prohemium

1 E cavernis Herebi fere omnem prolem eduximus, gratia Dei nostri omnipotentis et veri opitulante, et, quo concessum est ingenio, amotis figmentis, nudam in precedenti volumine coram apposuimus lectoribus, equidem non absque ingenti labore inter Stygis fumos et nebulas vacillantis hinc inde navicule. Sane postquam in patentiorem orbem ventum est, forsan minus ambigue flexus varios reciprocosque superabimus euripos, quorum superbientes in celum undas, ni fallor, aspicio. Nam inter alios arduus Ether e visceribus Herebi in sublime delatus, primus impetu occurrit suo, 2 non magna tamen prole fecundus sed spectabili quidem. Ex qua, si satis recte conspicio, primus Juppiter unus est, tam conspicui nominis gloria quam longa successione refulgens.

Quam si describere velim omnem, in Egyptum usque litus et Syrium, regnumque tuum Cyprum ut evehar impellente fluctu

BOOK II

Tree

In the tree illustrated above, the roots are turned upward toward the sky. Ether, the son of Erebus and Night, is placed at the top; in the branches and leaves, since Ether had only two sons, namely, the first Jupiter and Sky,[1] only the lineage of the first Jupiter is illustrated in its entirety, the lineage of Sky being reserved for the subsequent book.

Preface

In the preceding book, assisted by the grace of our omnipotent 1 and true God and with a bit of our own ability, we led nearly the entire progeny of Erebus out from the caverns, and, removing the fictions, laid them open for our readers — quite a task on our little boat teetering here and there amidst the Stygian vapors and clouds. Now that we have arrived in the open world, perhaps we will overcome with less uncertainty the meandering bends and reverse-flowing straits, the waters of which, unless I am mistaken, I see proudly pluming toward the sky. For lofty Ether, carried higher from amidst the others out of the bowels of Erebus, was the first to act upon impulse and produce not a large progeny but one well worthy of examination. One of them, if I am looking correctly, is 2 the first Jupiter, as resplendent in the glory of his famous name as he is in his numerous descendents.

If I wish to describe them all, a forceful wave will have to convey me to the Egyptian shore, Syria, and your kingdom of Cyprus.

necesse est. Que cum tanto sit celsitudine tue, Rex inclite, notior quanto mihi longinquior navigatio, queso per tui nominis insigne decus errores meos equo animo feras, et pii more principis emendari potius iubeas quam dentibus invidorum lacerari permictas. Ipse enim, tenso velo, ex Orci faucibus iter arripio, orans, ut ille illud dirigat qui, naufragantibus in mare Genezareth discipulis, ventis imperavit et undis.

: I :

De Ethere Herebi et Noctis XXI° filio, qui genuit Jovem primum et Celium seu Celum

1   Ether, ut placet Tullio in libro *De naturis deorum*, filius fuit Noctis et Herebi. Qui quidem etsi quandoque pro celo summatur proprie, tamen ignis elementum videtur existimari a multis. Sic enim testatur Ugucio. Sic velle videtur Ovidius ubi in principio maioris sui voluminis dicit:

> Hec super imposuit liquidum gravitate carentem
> Ethera nec quicquam terrene fecis habentem,
>
> > etc.

2   Hunc rerum omnium causam credidere quidam, ut supra dictum est, et eum similiter Demogorgonis filium fictione sua Pronapides ostendit, dum dixit Chaos ignita exalasse suspiria, sed visum est Ciceroni cedendum. Quem quantumcunque sterilem multi faciant, ipse tamen eum scribit fuisse fecundum, et Jovem genuisse primum et Celium, e quibus emanavit omnis numerosa deorum prosapia.

And since, illustrious King, the more Your Highness knows about him the longer my journey, I plead, through the eminent glory of your name, that you tolerate my errors with equanimity and that in the manner of a righteous prince you order them to be corrected instead of allowing them to be chewed by the teeth of my detractors. Now I myself, with my sails unfurled, undertake the journey from the jaws of Orcus, praying that he who gave orders to the winds and the waves when the disciples were being shipwrecked on the sea of Genezareth, guide me.[2]

: I :

On Ether, twenty-first Child of Erebus and Night, who fathered the first Jupiter and Sky

Ether, as Cicero[3] says in his *On the Nature of the Gods*, was a son of   1
Night and Erebus. While he is usually assumed with good reason to be the sky, many still seem to have regarded him as the element of fire, as Uguccione[4] bears witness. Ovid seems to mean this when in the beginning of his greater work he says:[5]

Above these he placed the clear and weightless
Ether which has nothing of earthly sediment.

Some believed him to be the cause of all things, as was said   2
before, while Pronapides similarly described him in his tale as a son of Demogorgon, where he said that Chaos exhaled fiery breath.[6] But I think Cicero ought to be trusted: however sterile many writers make him, Cicero nevertheless writes that he was fertile and that he fathered the first Jupiter and Sky, progenitors of the whole, well-populated lineage of the gods.

: 2 :

De Jove primo Etheris filio qui XIII inter filios et filias genuit.
Quorum prima Minerva, II^{us} Apis, III^{us} Sol, IIII^{a}
Dyana, V^{us} Mercurius, VI^{us} Tritopatreus, VII^{us} Ebuleus,
VIII^{us} Dyonisius, VIIII^{us} Hercules, X^{a} Proserpina, XI^{us}
Liber pater, XI^{us} Epaphus, XIII^{us} Scithas

1 Jovem primum dicit Theodontius fuisse filium Etheris et Diei. De
quo quidem Jove quantumcunque preclaro sit insignitus nomine,
legisse nichil, audisse tamen perpauca esto laudabilia, memini.
Referebat enim Leontius, Grecus homo, et talium abundantissi-
mus, hunc ante quesitum maius nomen Lysaniam nuncupatum,
hominem Arcadem, et profecto nobilem, et ex Arcadia Athenas
ivisse, et cum esset ingentis ingenii, vidissetque rudi in seculo rudi
et fere bestiali ritu viventes Atticos, ante omnia compositis legibus
illos publico instituto vivere docuit, et qui feminas fere communes
habebant, primus matrimonia celebrare monstravit, et cum iam ad
humanos redegisset mores, monuit eos deos colere, et eis aras et
templa atque sacerdotes instituit et multa insuper illis[1] ostendit
2 utilia. Que dum mirarentur silvestres Attici atque commendarent,
eum rati deum, Jovem vocavere, regemque suum fecere. Quem
etiam Cicero antiquissimum dicit Atheniensium fuisse regem. Hec
michi de isto sunt.

3   Nunc vero viso cur Etheris et Diei illum finxerint filium, et
quoniam celeberrimum fuit apud gentiles Jovis nomen, eius significatum videbimus et que potuerit esse impositionis causa et deifica-
tionis perscrutabimur. Dicunt ergo eum Etheris filium, seu ut eum

‡ 2 ‡

On the first Jupiter, son of Ether, who fathered thirteen sons
and daughters. These are first Minerva, second Apis, third
Sun, fourth Diana, fifth Mercury, sixth Tritopatreus, seventh
Eubuleus, eighth Dionysus, ninth Hercules, tenth Proserpina,
eleventh Father Liber, twelfth Epaphus, thirteenth Scythes

Theodontius says that the first Jupiter was a son of Ether and Day. 1
Despite the great fame of his name, I remember reading nothing
about this Jupiter, although what little I have heard is laudable.
Leontius, a Greek and a very rich resource in such matters, used to
say that before Jupiter acquired his greater name he was called
Lysanias, an Arcadian, no doubt a nobleman, who moved from
Arcadia to Athens. Since he had considerable ability and had seen
the people of Attica living in a primitive lifestyle with wild and
nearly bestial rituals, before anything else he composed laws and
taught them to live by using public institutions. And because they
used to regard women nearly as common property, he was the first
to tell them about the celebration of marriage. And once he had
arranged their human customs, he counseled them on worshipping the gods, and he established altars, temples, and priests for
them and showed them many other beneficial things. Because the 2
primitive people of Attica marveled at and praised such things,
they thought he was a god, and they called him Jupiter and made
him king. Cicero[7] also said that he was the most ancient king of
the Athenians. That is what I know about him.

Now that we have seen why they imagined him to be the son of 3
Ether and Day and that the name of Jupiter was famous among
the pagans, we will see its significance and examine carefully the
reason for giving him that name and his deification. They say that

nobilitent patre generoso, (putabant enim primam rerum causam ignem, et sic illi nobiliorem patrem dare non poterant), seu quod eum celestem putarent hominem seu deum, et a celo venisse ratione profunditatis ingenii, seu quia illi igneam naturam viderent, more ignis semper ad alta tendentem, ut de eo dici possit Virgilianum illud: 'Igneus est illis vigor et celestis origo.'

4   Diei vero filium ideo illum dictum puto, quia, esto nascatur quis aptus ad maxima, non tamen evestigio quod natus est, ea potest ad que natus est agere; oportet ut in dies augeantur vires, et animus in fervorem agendorum excrescat, et demum ipse operetur; cuius opera quoniam in die visa et cognita sunt, a die novo videtur editus partu, ut de talibus dici possit, quod Valerius dicit de Demostene: 'Itaque alterum Demostenem mater, alterum industria

5   enixa est.' Sic et alterum peperit Lysaniam mater, et alterum Dies operum testis. Vocatus est insuper Lysanias iste ab Atheniensibus Iuppiter, nomen eo usque nemini concessum mortalium, nec ipsi etiam deo adhuc fuerat[2] a gentilitate impositum, nec unde sumptum sit ab imponentibus satis scitur.

Arbitror ego tamen id nominis huius causam dedisse, quod et de aliis etiam planetis multis contigisse comperimus, a similitudine

6   scilicet operationum conformium huius hominis ipsi Iovi. Dicit enim Albumasar, in suo *Maiori introductorio*, Iovem planetam naturã calidum esse et humidum, aereum, temperatum, modestum atque honestum, laudabilem plurimum et patientie observatorem, ac in periculis post patientiam audacem, liberalem, misericordem, cautum, amatorem verum, magistratuum avidum, fidelem, multiloquum, bonorum amicum, malorum vero hostem, amatorem principum et maiorum, et alia plura de eo scribit, quibus annectit eum significare naturalem animam, vitam, pulchritudinem, sapientes viros, legum doctores, iustos iudices, divinum cultum, religio-

he was the son of Ether either to dignify him by giving him a noble father (for they were in the habit of thinking that fire was the primary cause of things, and therefore they could not give him a more noble father) or because they thought him to be a celestial man or god, and that on account of his profound talent he had come from the sky, perhaps because they saw a fiery nature in him. Fire always reaches for a higher place, just as Vergil says,[8] "They have a fiery strength and a celestial origin."

I think he was said to be the son of Day because, even if someone is born ready for great things, he is not immediately able to carry out that for which he was born just because he is born. His strengths must increase day after day, and his mind must develop a passion for doing things, and then he must set to work. Because his accomplishments are seen and recognized by day, he seems to have been given birth anew by day, demonstrating what Valerius said about Demosthenes:[9] "And so his mother produced one Demosthenes; diligence produced another." So in this way his mother gave birth to one Lysanias, and Day, evidence of his works, gave birth to another. In addition, the Athenians called this Lysanias Jupiter, a name which until then the pagans had not yet given to any mortal or even awarded it to a god, nor did those who used it know well whence it came. 4

5

In my opinion his name derives from what occurs also with many other planets, that is, from the similarity between the workings of the natural forces of this man and the planet Jupiter. Albumasar[10] in his *Introduction to Astronomy* says that by nature the planet Jupiter is warm and moist, airy, temperate, mild and distinguished, extremely laudable and circumspect, and amidst dangers he is first enduring, then daring, generous, compassionate, prudent, a true lover, a zealous administrator, faithful, willing to speak, friend to the good, enemy of evils, lover of princes and the powerful, and many other things he writes about intending to connect natural spirit, life, beauty, wise men, learned jurists, just 6

nem, victoriam, regnum, divitias, nobilitatem, gaudium et huiusmodi.

7   Quibus consideratis, et demum huius hominis ponderatis moribus, adeo eum cum Iove convenire discernemus, ut non incongrue
Iovem nuncupatum dicamus, et hanc convenientiam tanti nominis
illi causam fuisse credamus. Sane nomen hoc, postquam ab antiquis planete et Lysanie concessum est, non nullis aliis a recentiori-
bus etiam attributum legimus, ut puta Iovi secundo Celi filio, qui
et Arcas homo fuit et Atheniensium rex. Nec non et Iovi tercio,
homini Cretensi et Saturni filio. Sic eque et Pericli Atheniensi
principi, quem multi Jovem Olympium vocavere.

8   Preterea poete ignem elementum, et non nunquam ignem et
aerem sub Jovis nomine suis fictionibus inseruere. Adeoque in sublime conscendit, ut a prudentioribus etiam summo et vero deo
ascriberetur, nec immerito; ipsi quippe soli tam egregium competit
nomen, quod nec abhorreret Christianus considerato nominis significato nisi gentilium fuisset inventum.

9   Volunt enim aliqui et graves viri quod idem Iuppiter sonet quod
'iuvans pater,' quod soli vero Deo convenit. Ipse enim vere pater
est et ab eterno fuit et erit in sempiternum, quod de alio nemine
dici potest, similiter et iuvans est omnibus et nulli nocens, et in
tantum iuvans est, ut, si suum retrahatur iuvamen, periclitentur
confestim omnia necesse sit. Insuper hoc nomen Juppiter Grece
dicitur *zephs*, quod Latine 'vita' sonat. Et quis alter rebus et creaturis omnibus vita est nisi Deus? Ipse enim de se ipso dicens testatur: 'Ego sum via, veritas et vita'; et profecto sic est, illi enim et per
eum et in eo vivunt omnia, extra eum preter mortem et tenebras
nichil.

judges, honored divinity, reverence, victory, kingdom, riches, nobility, joy, and the like.

When we consider these qualities and then ponder the characteristics of this man, we understand that he is so like Jupiter that it is proper for us to call him Jupiter and believe that this similarity is the source of his name. Of course we read that after the ancients applied this name to the planet and Lysanias, more recent writers attributed it to several others, for example to a second Jupiter, son of Sky, who was also an Arcadian man and Athenian king, and also a third Jupiter, a Cretan man and son of Saturn, and equally as well Pericles, leader of the Athenians, whom many called Olympian Jupiter. 7

In addition, in their fictions poets grafted the element of fire and sometimes fire and air onto the name of Jupiter. In this way he was elevated until he was reckoned as the greatest and a true god by even the more prudent men, and not undeservedly: to him alone was such an excellent name fitting, and, considering its significance, a Christian might not find it so dreadful if it had not been invented by pagans. 8

Some, even important men, preferred to derive the name of Jupiter from "helpful father [iuvans pater]," because this applied only to the true God, for he is truly the father and was from the beginning and will be for eternity, because this can be said about none other, and, similarly, he helps everyone and harms no one and is so helpful that if his help were withdrawn, immediately all things would necessarily be in peril. In addition, the name Jupiter in Greek is zephs, which means "life." And who else is life for all things and creatures except God? He himself bore witness when he said about himself,[11] "I am the way, the truth, and the life." And he most certainly is, for through him all things live both by him and in him, and there is nothing outside of him except death and darkness. 9

10 Hunc, etsi non rite coluerint, veteres Romani Iovem optimum maximum vocavere, conati per hec pauca verba ostendere quoniam magnitudine et potentia ceteros excedat deos, et quod ipse solus summum sit bonum et quod ab eo vita sit et adiutorium universis. Multa preterea poteram hic apponere Iovi a poetis attributa, ut puta armigeram avem, quercum, bella, Iunonem coniugem et alia; sed quoniam ista videntur recte spectare ad ea que de Jove Cretico ficta sunt, illi censui reservanda. Porro, Rex inclite, non satis certum est utrum Athenienses Jovem hunc in deum habuerint aut

11 fecerint. Si autem fecerunt, sciendum est antiquis consuetum fuisse ad augendam originis nobilitatem conditores civitatum suarum certis suis infaustis cerimoniis numero deorum inserere, et sacris templisque colere. Sic et parentes suorum principum sic et ipsos principes ob aliquid ab eis susceptum beneficium, ut se gratos ostenderent, et alios ad bene agendum ob cupiditatem tam splendide glorie animarent. Scribunt insuper veteres multos fuisse Iovi filios, ex quibus arbitror vere non nullos Iovis fuisse filios, sed cuius Iovis, primi, secundi vel tertii de aliquibus non satis constat, sic et alios plures ob insignem virtutis preminentiam et ad gloriam generis extollendam a theologis gentilium Iovi similiter attributos, quos ego illi attribuam Iovi, cui magis videbuntur contemporanei.

Although they worshipped him inappropriately, the ancient Ro- 10
mans called him Jupiter Greatest and Best, trying with these few
words to show how he surpassed the rest of the gods in greatness
and power, and that he alone is the greatest good, because life
comes from him, and because he is the helper of all. I could append many other things attributed to Jupiter by the poets, for example, the armor-bearing eagle, the oak tree, wars, his wife Juno,
and more. But since these things seem to belong more specifically
to the fictions told about the Cretan Jupiter, I thought they should
be discussed along with him later. Further, illustrious King, it is
not sufficiently certain whether the Athenians regarded this Jupiter as their god or created him. If they created him, you should 11
know that it was customary for the ancients to increase the nobility of their origins by adding to their group of gods, albeit with
some inauspicious ceremonies, the founders of their states, and
they worshipped them in sacred temples. In this way they showed
both the parents of their leaders and even the leaders themselves
that they were grateful for some benefit they had bestowed upon
them, and they inspired others to do well if they desired equally
splendid glory. In addition, the ancients write that Jupiter had
many sons. I think some of these were genuinely sons of Jupiter
(but of which Jupiter—first, second, or third—there is no satis-
factory agreement), and that many other sons were similarly attributed to Jupiter on account of their distinguished and preeminent virtue and so that the pagan theologians could exalt the glory
of their ancestry; these sons I will attribute to that Jupiter with
whom they seem more contemporary.

: 3 :

De Minerva prima, primi Jovis prima filia

1 Minerva, vulgato fere poetarum omnium carmine, Iovis fuit filia, de ortu cuius talis fertur fabula. Quod cum videret Iuppiter Iunonem coniugem suam non ferentem filios, ne omnino absque filiis
2 esset, percusso cerebro suo armatam emisit Minervam. Quod Lucanus firmare videtur dicens, 'Hanc et Pallas amat patrio que vertice nata est.' Et in nativitate huius dicit Claudianus:

Auratos radiis imbres nascente Minerva
indulsisse Jovem perhibent,

etc.

Insuper hanc natam dicit Servius luna quinta sicuti reliqui qui steriles fuere.

Huius preterea compertum volunt lanificium ante eam incognitum, sic et texturam, et ob id placet Ovidio huic cum Aragne Colophonia de textura fuisse certamen et victoriam. Sic et cum
3 Neptuno de impositione nominis civitati Athenarum. Eam preterea non nulli armatam fingunt et arcis Athenarum presidem. Illi insuper Titus Livius attribuit numerorum inventionem et eorumdem figuras, cum ante loco numeri signis uterentur antiqui. Recitatur de hac et alia fabula, quod cum esset huic perpetue virginitatis servande propositum et Vulcanus in desiderium sui venisset, Iovi patri suo petiit loco muneris factorum a se fulminum in gigomantia Minerve matrimonium. Cui Iuppiter voti nate conscius, si obtinere possit concessit, et Minerve si illum aspernaretur versa vice concessum est ut se viribus tueretur, et sic dum totis conatibus in eam ivisset Vulcanus et ipsa in contrarium niteretur, actum est ut, emisso a Vulcano semine in terram, nasceretur puer, et ipsa

: 3 :

On the first Minerva, first child of the first Jupiter

Minerva, well known in the verses of nearly all the poets, was a 1
daughter of Jupiter. The fable about her birth is told this way:
when Jupiter realized that his wife Juno was not bearing him sons,
so that he would not be altogether childless he had his head split
open and produced Minerva. Lucan confirms this, saying,[12] "Pal- 2
las, who was born from her father's head, loved her also." And
Claudian said about her birth:[13]

> When Minerva was born, with rays of gold
> Jupiter showered, they say. . .

In addition, Servius[14] says that she was born during the fifth
moon, as are others who were sterile.

They also say she discovered wool-working, which was unknown before her, and also weaving; this is why Ovid[15] tells of her
victory in the weaving contest between her and Arachne of Colophon. She had another contest with Neptune for naming the city
of Athens. Some also depict her as armed and as guardian of the 3
Athenian citadel. In addition, Titus Livy[16] attributes to her the
invention of numbers and their figures, for previously the ancients
used signs in place of numbers. Another fable is told about her,
that although her intention was to preserve her virginity in perpetuity, Vulcan fell in love with her and asked her father Jupiter if he,
in exchange for the gift of the thunderbolts he made for the gigan-
tomachy, could marry Minerva. Jupiter, knowing the wishes of his
daughter, granted it if he could win her over, while to Minerva, if
she rejected him, he granted the opposite — that she could protect
herself by using force. And so, she countered every attempt he
made at her, with the end result that Vulcan's seed fell to the

linqueretur in pace. Triplici etiam illam indutam veste dixerunt, eique peplum pictum consecravere et eius in tutelam cornice pulsa noctuam posuere, ac pluribus eam nuncupavere nominibus, ut Minervam, Palladem, Athenam et Tritoniam.

4   His explicitis, exquirebat ordo sumptus ut detegeretur quid sensisse sub figmentis potuissent antiqui. Verum hic advertendum est, quoniam non omnia hic apposita figmenta ad hanc spectant Minervam; illa quippe nominis identitas non curantibus ex hoc poetis implicuit; nam nec arma, ut Leontius asserit, ad hanc spectant, nec Neptuni certamen, quin imo eius sunt Minerve, que Jovis secundi fuit filia, et ideo illis omissis detegemus cetera, et quedam hystorialia apponemus.

5   Voluerunt igitur Minervam, id est sapientiam, ex cerebro Iovis, id est dei natam; volunt enim physici omnem intellectivam virtutem in cerebro tanquam in arce corporis consistere. Hinc Minervam, id est sapientiam, ex cerebro natam fingunt, id est ex cerebro dei, ut intelligamus quoniam ex profundo divine sapientie arcano omnem intellectum, omnem sapientiam infusam esse, quam Iuno, id est terra, quantum ad hoc sterilis dare non poterat neque potest; nam, teste sacra pagina, omnis sapientia a domino deo est. Et ipsamet in eadem dicit: 'Ego enim ex ore altissimi prodivi.' Et sic eam profecto industriose, non ut nos gignimur sed ex Iovis cerebro natam finxere, ut ostenderent eius singularem nobilitatem ab omni terrena spurcitie feceque semotam.

6   Virginitas inde illi attribuitur perpetua et inde sterilitas ut per hoc noscatur quia sapientia nunquam labefactatur aliqua contagione mortalium, quin imo semper pura, semper lucida, semper integra et perfecta est. Et quantum ad temporalia sterilis est, cum sapientie eterni sint fructus. Quid per certamen illius senserint

ground, a boy was born, and she was left in peace. They say that she wore a triple garment; they consecrated an embroidered peplum to her; having turned away the crow, she made the owl her guardian; and they called her by several names: for instance, Minerva, Pallas, Athena, and Tritonia.

Now that I have presented these details, the process I have established demands that I reveal what the ancients could have understood as the essence of these fictions. But we should observe that not all the fictions set forth here refer to this Minerva. Identifying her by name does not mean that all the poets wrote about her, for if they refer to her arms, as Leontius asserts, or the contest with Neptune, these pertain to the Minerva who was the daughter of the second Jupiter. Omitting these, we will uncover the rest and append some historical matters.

They want Minerva, that is, wisdom, to be born from the head of Jupiter, that is, god; for physical scientists want every theoretical virtue to exist in the head as if in the citadel of the body. For this reason they say that Minerva, that is, wisdom, was born from the head, that is, from the head of god, so that we would understand that all intellect, all wisdom pours forth from the deep recess of divine wisdom, which Juno, that is, earth, insofar as she is barren in this, was not able and is not able to provide. According to Holy Scripture, all wisdom is from the Lord God. In its pages it says,[17] "For I came forth from the mouth of the highest." And they take special care to invent the fiction that she was born not as we are but from the head of Jupiter to show her unique nobility, removed from all terrestrial sediment and dregs.

They attribute perpetual virginity and then barrenness to her to make it known that wisdom is never tarnished by any contact with a mortal but in fact is always pure, always clear, always whole and complete. And she is barren in regard to temporal matters because the fruits of wisdom are eternal. What they meant by the contest

et Vulcani infra ubi de Ericthonio, ex certamine hoc nato, scribetur.

7   Triplici autem veste ideo tegitur, ut intelligatur verba sapientum et potissime fingentium multiplicem habere sensum. Illique ideo peplum pictum sacrum est, ut intelligamus sermones sapientie ornatos, floridos, lepidos et summa venustate decoros. Noctua autem ideo illi attributa est pulsa cornice, ut ostendatur sapientem premeditatione in obscuris seposita noscere, uti et noctua videt in tenebris, et loquacitate atque garrulitate repulsa ut opere agat, loca tempusque respicere.

8   Minerva enim dicitur, ut ait Albericus, a *min* quod est 'non,' et *erva* quod est 'mortalis,' ut resultet esse sapientiam immortalem. Pallas et Athene ad alias spectant Minervas, et ideo ubi de illis mentio fiet exponentur. Tritonia autem dicta est a loco seu a lacu quem penes primo comparuit, qui Triton in Affrica computatus est.

9   Fictionibus igitur sic expositis, ad hystoriam veniendum est et sciendum Minervam fuisse virginem quandam, cuius incognita fuit origo; ipsa vero, cum ingentis esset ingenii, ut Eusebius ait, regnante Argivis Phoroneo, primo apud Tritonam paludem seu lacum Affrice comparuit, ignorantibus cunctis quibus venisset ab oris. Dicit tamen Pomponius Mela in *Cosmographia,* quod incole arbitrabantur eam ibidem genitam et fabule fidem faciunt quia quam natalem illi putant diem, ludicris virginum inter se decertantium celebrant.

10   Hec autem cum lanificium et texturam et alia multa artificiosa comperisset, celebris dea habita est, et quoniam omnia eius inventa ex vi ingenii atque sapientie procedere videbantur, locus fa-

between her and Vulcan I will write about in the subsequent discussion of Erichthonius, who was born as a result of the contest.

She is covered in triple garments so it would be known that the words of the wise and especially of those inventing these tales have multiple meanings. Her sacred peplum is embroidered so that we would know that speeches filled with wisdom are ornate, florid, witty, and decorated with the greatest adornment. The owl is associated with her, once the crow was chased away, to show that by premeditation the wise man learns what has been hidden in obscurity, just as the owl sees in the darkness and, once garrulousness and loquaciousness are chased away, he considers the place and time for his work.

Minerva derives, according to Albericus,[18] from *min*, which is "not," and *erva*, which is "mortal," just as wisdom turns out to be immortal. Pallas and Athena have to do with the other Minervas, so they will be explained when we discuss them. And Tritona refers to a place or lake near to where she first appeared, and this Triton is thought to be in Africa.

Now that we have explained their fictions, we must turn to history and the information that Minerva was some maiden of unknown origin. Since her talent was considerable, as Eusebius[19] says, when Phoroneus was ruling the Argives, she first appeared near the Tritonian swamp or lake in Africa, even if no one knows whence she arrived. Pomponius Mela[20] in his *Description of the World* says that the inhabitants thought she was born there and added credence to the fable by celebrating the day they thought was her birthday with games in which maidens competed amongst themselves.

Because she invented wool-working, weaving, and many other techniques, she was honored as a goddess, and because all her inventions seemed to stem from the force of her talent and wisdom, a place was devised for the fable that she was thought to be born

II bule adinventus est ut ex cerebro Jovis genita videretur. De hac
enim dicit Augustinus in libro *De civitate Dei*, quod, Ogygio in
Actica regnante, eam in virginali etate apparuisse apud lacum Tri-
tonis, ut dictum est, et cum multorum operum esset inventrix,
tanto proclivius dea credita est, quanto minus origo eius cognita;
nec ab Eusebio differt Augustinus in tempore, nam contempora-
neos fuisse Phoroneum et Ogygium idem ostendit Eusebius, et ob
hoc ego hanc Iovi primo filiam ascripsi, eo quod illi magis quam
cum reliquis videatur convenire tempore.

: 4 :

De Api Argivorum rege, primi Jovis secundo filio

I Eusebius in libro *Temporum* dicit Apim, qui postea rex Argivorum,
filium fuisse Iovis et Niobis, filie Phoronei, cui idem Eusebius
scribit Iovem primo quam alteri mortalium immixtum, et sic primus fuit Iuppiter cum tempore longe inferiores sint alii. Leontius
autem dicit hunc Phoronei et Niobis, sororis et coniugis sue fuisse
filium, eique in regnum Sicyoniorum heredem successisse, verum
postea ab Egyptiis et deum et Iovis filium factum. De hoc Api
multa narrantur, nam, ut referunt aliqui, cum aliquandiu Argis
post Phoronei mortem imperasset, cupiditate glorie et amplioris
regni ad Egyptios transfretavit, et obtento regno, cum rudes homines multa docuisset et potissime vini usum, loco dei haberi ceptus
est, iam Yside sibi copulata coniugio.

from the head of Jupiter. Augustine[21] speaks about this in his *City* 11
of God, saying that when Ogygius was ruling in Athens she appeared of maiden age near Lake Triton, as has been said, and because she was the inventor of many works, the more readily she was believed to be a goddess, the less they knew about her origin. Augustine does not differ from Eusebius as to the time period, for Eusebius[22] shows that Phoroneus and Ogygius were contemporaneous, wherefore I have assumed she was the daughter of the first Jupiter; the time period seems to fit him more than it fits the others.

: 4 :

On Apis, king of the Argives, second son of the first Jupiter

Eusebius in his *Chronicle* says that Apis, who afterward was king 1
of the Argives, was the son of Jupiter and Niobe, daughter of Phoroneus; Eusebius[23] writes that Jupiter copulated with her before any other mortal, and so he was the first Jupiter, for the others come much later. Leontius says he was the son of Phoroneus and Niobe, his wife and sister, and that he succeeded him as heir to the kingdom of Sicyon but afterward was made into a god and the son of Jupiter by the Egyptians. Many things are told about this Apis, for, as some report, when after the death of Phoroneus he had ruled at Argos for some time, his desire for glory and increasing his territory compelled him to cross over to Egypt; and once he had gained control of the kingdom, because he had taught many things to primitive men and especially the use of wine, and since he was already paired in marriage with Isis, he began to be regarded as a god.

2   Eusebius vero eum Sicyonorum scribit fuisse regem, et ut ab eodem traditum est, de tempore eius varie sensere scriptores annalium. Nam quidam dicunt tempore Abrahe ab eo Greciam Apiam appellatam. Alii autem dicunt, nato iam Iacob, eum apud Egyptios deum habitum. Beda vero, eo in libro quem *De temporibus* scripsit, dicit, tempore Iacob ab Api in Egypto Menphim conditam. Eusebius preterea dicit secundum alios eum regem fuisse Argivorum et regnasse post centesimum annum Iacob, et ibidem dicit, Apim, cum Egyaleum fratrem regem prefecisset Achaye, in Egyptum transfretasse et Menphim condidisse civitatem.

3   Eum autem in Egyptum abisse et Ysidem habuisse coniugem satis ab omnibus creditur, verum uti de tempore eius ambigitur, sic et de morte eius varia etiam recitantur. Nam alii volunt eum apud Egyptios mortuum et sepultum; de quo in libro *De civitate Dei* sic ait Augustinus:

> Rex Argivorum Apis navibus transvectus in Egyptum, cum ibi mortuus fuisset, factus est Serapis omnium maximus Egyptiorum deus.

4   Nominis autem eius, cur non Apis etiam post mortem sed Serapis appellatus sit, facillimam rationem Varro reddit. Quia enim arca in qua mortuus ponitur, quam omnes iam sarcophagum vocant, *soron* dicitur Grece, et ibi venerari sepultum ceperant prius quam templum eius esset extructum, unde Soron et Apis Sorapis primo, deinde, una lictera commutata, ut feri assolet, Serapis dictus est.

5   Alii autem dixere eum a Typheo fratre occisum atque membratim discerptum diuque ab Yside coniuge quesitum et postremo

Eusebius[24] writes that he was king of the Sicyonians, and, according to him, the annalist writers differ as to when he lived. Some say that during the period of Abraham, Greece was called "Apia" after him. But others say that when Jacob was already alive Apis was regarded as a god among the Egyptians. Bede,[25] in fact, in his *Chronicle*, says that Apis founded Memphis in Egypt at the time of Jacob. Eusebius[26] also says that according to others he was the king of the Argives and ruled after the one hundredth year of Jacob, and at the same time he said that Apis, after he put his brother Aegialeus on the throne of Achaia, crossed over to Egypt and founded the city of Memphis.

That he went to Egypt and had Isis for a wife is sufficiently agreed upon by all, but when this happened is disputed. Various accounts are given as well about his death, for some think that he died and was buried among the Egyptians. Augustine in his *City of God* says the following about this:[27]

> When Apis, the king of the Argives who had been conveyed to Egypt, died there, he became Serapis, the greatest god of all the Egyptians.

As to why his name after he died was not said to be Apis but Serapis, Varro[28] offers the most straightforward reason: because a "box" [*arca*] in which a dead person is placed, which is now called a sarcophagus, is called *soron* in Greek, and because they began to venerate his tomb there before his temple had been constructed, therefore he was called by the names Soron and Apis Sorapis first, and then, with one letter changed, as often happens, Serapis.

Others have reported that after he was killed by his brother Typhoeus and rent limb by limb, his wife Isis searched for a long

compertum et in vanno eius membra collecta, quod postmodum in religionem versum est, in sacris scilicet februis intervenire vannum. Ysis autem ultra paludem Stygiam, que in Affrica est, in semotam insulam collecta detulit, et ibidem recondidit. Voluntque qui hoc verum arbitrantur a longa Ysidis exquisitione exortum, quam Egyptii fecere diu, non ante desistentes quam album taurum comperissent, compertoque applaudentes eum vocabant Osyrim, et quoniam singulis annis id fiebat, dixit Juvenalis, 'Et nunquam satis quesitus Osyris.'

6   Ceterum quandocunque in Egyptum iverit, seu qualitercunque occubuerit, aut quocunque sepultus sit Apis, in tanta fuit apud Egyptios veneratione, ut eo iretur ab eis ad hoc ut nulla humanitatis infectione posset illius labefactari divinitas, ut caverent instituto publico ut, si quis illum fuisse hominem diceret, capite puniretur, et ob id in quibuscunque templis erat eius simulacrum, digito labiis impresso, admonebat silentium.

7   Huius insuper tauri, quem Serapim arbitrabantur Egyptii, caput dicit Rabanus delirantes Iudeos in heremo, loco Dei coluisse. Hunc preterea Apim dicit Macrobius in libro *Saturnaliorum* apud Alexandriam Egypti civitatem[3] una cum Yside mirabili cultu venerari, seque Soli venerationem illam impendere affirmare, et sic Apim Solem esse videtur arbitrari.

time and finally found him and collected his limbs in a winnowing basket; later this was turned into a rite, specifically sacred purification feasts in which the winnowing basket played an integral part. Isis, moreover, brought the collected limbs beyond the Stygian swamp, which is in Africa, to a remote island and hid them there. Those who believe this to be true maintain that he rose up after a lengthy search by Isis; the Egyptians also searched for a long time, not stopping before they had found a white bull, and once they found this, they applauded and called him Osiris. Because that occurred on an annual basis, Juvenal said,[29] "And Osiris is never satisfactorily traced."

But yet, whenever he went to Egypt, or however he died, or 6 wherever he is buried, Apis was held in such veneration among the Egyptians that it reached the point for them where his divinity could not be undermined by any stain of humanity: they stipulated by public decree that if anyone said that he was a man, he would be executed, and therefore in whatever temples his image was placed, the image admonished silence with a finger raised to his lips.

Also, Rabanus[30] says that the Jews, when they were delirious in 7 the desert, instead of worshipping God, worshipped the head of a bull, which the Egyptians thought was Serapis. In addition, Macrobius[31] in his *Saturnalia* says that in the city of Egyptian Alexandria this bull was venerated along with Isis in an extraordinary cult, that they assert that they devote this veneration to the sun, and that therefore Apis seems to be thought of as the sun.

: 5 :

De Sole primo, primi Jovis filio III°

1 Solem primum, primi Jovis fuisse filium scribit Tullius ubi *De naturis deorum*, nec tamen dicit ex qua matre susceptum. Sunt qui velint hunc Apim fuisse, eo quod loco Solis ab Egyptiis, ut paulo supra dictum est, cultus sit.

2 Ego autem quis aliter fuerit comperisse non memini. Hominem tamen fuisse certus sum, et si alius fuit ab Api, credendum est eum insignem atque splendidum fuisse hominem et ingentis atque regii animi preditum, et eo modo quo supra de Iove dictum est tam claro nomine decoratum.

: 6 :

De Dyana prima, primi Jovis IIII^a filia

1 Dyana prima filia fuit Jovis primi et Proserpine, ut in libro quo supra Tullius idem asserit. Hanc ego reor veram huius Iovis fuisse filiam et non ascriptitiam, et cum satis sit nomen illud mulieribus
2 usitatum, possibile etiam est fuisse proprium non appositum. Verum qualiscunque fuerit, non ea est quam poete insignem virginitate perpetua voluere, cum legatur hanc ex Mercurio, Liberi et Proserpine filio, pinnatum concepisse Cupidinem.

: 5 :

On the first Sun, third Child of the first Jupiter

Cicero[32] in his *On the Nature of the Gods* says the first Sun was a son 1
of the first Jupiter, but he does not identify his mother. There are
those who want him to be Apis because the Egyptians worshipped
him in place of the sun, as I just mentioned.

I do not remember finding who he was otherwise, but I am 2
certain that he was a man, and if he was someone other than Apis,
we have to believe that he was an eminent and splendid man gifted
with a considerable, regal mind, and much like Jupiter, whom we
described before, he was distinguished with a famous name.

: 6 :

On the first Diana, fourth child of the first Jupiter

The first Diana was the daughter of the first Jupiter and Proser- 1
pina, as again Cicero[33] asserts in the book cited just above. I think
she was the true daughter of this Jupiter and not an attribution,
and because this name was used frequently by women, it is possible that it was a proper name and not an assigned name. But 2
whoever she was, she is not the Diana the poets celebrate for her
everlasting virginity, for we read that she conceived winged Cupid
by Mercury, son of Liber and Proserpina,.

: 7 :

De Mercurio primo, primi Jovis V° filio

1 Primi Jovis et Cylenis⁴ nynphe Arcadis asserit Leontius filium fuisse Mercurium. Hunc deorum nuntium seu interpretem fore poete describunt, eumque variis ornamentis insigniunt, ut per illa intelligatur eiusdem officiorum varietas. Scribit enim de eo sic Virgilius:

> Primum pedibus talaria nectit
> aurea que sublimen alis sive equora supra
> seu terram rapido pariter cum flamine portant.
> Tum virgam capit: hac animas ille evocat Orco
> pallentes alias sub tristia Tartara mittit.
> Dat somnos adimitque et lumina morte resignat.
> Illa fretus agit ventos et turbida tranat
> nubila,
>
> etc.

2 Insuper et Horatius de eo sic scribit in *Odis*:

> Mercuri facunde nepos Atlantis,
> qui feros cultus hominum recentum
> voce formasti cantus ed decore
> mere palestre,
>
> etc.

Illi insuper Statius galerum addidit dicens, 'Obnuitque comas et temperat astra galero,' etc.

3 Sane quanquam legamus plures et homines fuisse Mercurios, his inspectis que supra proximo de eo poete describunt, dato possint et ad hominem referri, de Mercurio planeta scripta potius

: 7 :

On the first Mercury, fifth child of the first Jupiter

Leontius attests that Mercury was the son of the first Jupiter and   1
the Arcadian nymph Cyllene. The poets describe him as the messenger and interpreter of the gods, and they distinguish him with various ornaments so as to make known his various duties. Vergil writes this about him:[34]

> First to his feet he binds his winged sandals,
> golden, and with their wings over both seas
> and land as swift as the wind they carry him aloft.
> Then he takes hold of his wand: with this he calls forth
> pale spirits from Orcus and sends others into gloomy Tartarus.
> He gives sleep and takes it away, and he resigns the eyes to
>   death.
> Trusting the wand he conducts the winds and crosses stormy
> clouds.

In addition, also Horace writes this about him in his *Odes*:[35]   2

> Mercury, eloquent grandson of Atlas,
> who formed the savage civilization of the first men
> with the lyrics of song and the pure
>   virtue of the palestra.

In addition, Statius gave him a cap, saying,[36] 'He covered his hair and tempered the stars with his cap.'

Although we read about several men named Mercury, consider-   3
ing how the aforementioned poets describe him, this could also apply to a human, but we presume that they were written instead about the planet Mercury, especially if we examine how the words

presumemus, et potissime si inspexerimus qualiter cum his que
4 ab astrologis scripta sunt poetarum dicta conveniant. Albumasar
autem, maxime inter antiquos autoritatis homo, asserit Mercurium
adeo flexibilis esse nature, ut evestio ad naturam eius cui adheret et ipse suam naturam convertat, et hoc propter temperamen-
5 tum eius siccitatis et frigoris. Venerabilis autem Andalo, preceptor
meus, eum complexione, dicit calidum et siccum eumque significare concubinarum delectactiones, claritatem, et oracula vatum,
eloquentiam, et hystoriarum memoriam, credulitatem, pulchritudinem, bonitatem discipline et acumen ingenii, prescientiam futurorum, arismetricam et geometriam atque astrologiam, et hinc
descriptionem tam celestium quam terrestrium rerum omnium;
preterea auguria, dulcedinem prolationis, velocitatem, et principatus desiderium, et ob illum laudem atque famam, et insuper come
tonsuram, scriptores et libros, mendacium et testimonium falsum,
speculationem semotarum rerum, paucitatem gaudii, et substantie
desolationem, negociationes et emporia, furta, contentiones, calli-
ditates et consilii profundidatem, modulationes carminum et fistu-
larum, colorationes multimodas, obedientiam, concordiam, pietatem, paupertatem, amicitie retentionem, artificia manuum, et alia
multa; et ut ipse idem asserit Andalo, cum masculis masculus et
cum feminis femineus est. Ex quibus facile comprehendere possumus, cum tam convertibilis sit nature, de eo in prescriptis carminibus intellexisse poetas, esto illud idem de hominibus mercurialibus
dici possit et dicatur, ut in sequentibus apparebit. Sane libet intentum poetarum explicare latius ut, quantum cum astrologis conveniant, manifestetur apertius.

6   Dicunt igitur, ut a capite summamus exordium, eum tectum
galero, ut per hoc sentiamus, quia, sicut qui galero tegitur ymbres
fugit et radios, sic et Mercurius solaribus tectus radiis, quibus fere
semper vinctus est, fugit aspici a mortalibus; rarissime quidem videtur, et paucis notus est, et[5] mercurialis homo calliditate suum
tegit consilium. Alata enim habere talaria, velocitatem eius non

of the poets concur with what the astrologers have written. Albu- 4
masar,[37] a man of great authority about antiquity, asserts that
Mercury was so flexible in nature that he immediately changed his
own nature to that with which he was connected, and this on account of his correct proportion of dryness and cold. The venerable 5
Andalò, my teacher, says that he was warm and dry in his constitution, and that he signified the delights of concubines, the fame
and predictions of oracles, eloquence and the memory of history,
credulity, beauty, excellence in education and a keen genius, knowledge of what will come, arithmetic and geometry and astrology,
and from this the description of all things both celestial and terrestrial, and in addition augury, sweetness of utterance, speed and
a desire for power, and on account of that, praise and fame and
also hair-cutting, writers and books, mendacity and false testimony, speculation about distant things, paucity of joy, and desola-
tion of substance, businesses and markets, thefts, disputes, shrewdness and profundity of intelligence, modulations of songs and
pipes, various colorations, obedience, harmony, piety, poverty, re-
tention of friendship, artifices of the hand, and many other things;
and, as Andalò himself asserted, he is masculine with masculine
things and feminine with feminine things. Since his nature is so
changeable, this makes it easy to understand that the poets in the
aforementioned verses knew that the same can be said about him
and is said about mercurial men; this will become clear below. But
I would like to explain the intent of the poets more fully to make
clearer how much they agree with the astrologers.

They say — let us start from the head — that he was covered by 6
a cap so that we would understand in this that, just as someone
who is covered by a cap flees the rain and solar rays, so also Mercury, protected from the solar rays, to which it is nearly always
joined, flees from human sight. In fact, the planet is very rarely
seen and noticed by few, and a mercurial man covers his intelligence with shrewdness. As for his winged sandals, its swiftness is

solum in motu, qui illi circa epiciclum velocissimus est, sed ob celerem aliorum corporum supercelestium proprietatum assumptionem atque traditionem, ex qua mercurialium etiam hominum velox versipellisque circumflexio denotatur. Virga autem illi ascripta est propter dimensiones corporum se sibi iungentium, secundum quas et ipse illico suos disponit effectus, et mercurialis homo circa quodcunque opus suum metitur obsequium.

7   Quod ab Orco animas revocet virga, id est potentia sua, est hic acutius attendendum. Fuere quidam qui arbitrati sunt omnes hominum animas a principio simul fuisse creatas et demum conceptis hominibus immissas, eas morientibus nobis ad inferos descendere ibique cruciari donec in vita commissa purgarentur, et inde transitum facere ad Elysios campos, ac inde post mille annos a Mercurio deduci ad Lethem fluvium, ut eo potato obliviscerentur presentis vite labores; et sic desiderarent iterum redire ad corpora, ad que Mercurius revocabat. Quam ridiculam opinionem optime tangit Virgilius dum dicit:

> Quisque suos patimur manes, exinde per amplum
> mittimur Elysium et pauci leta arva tenemus.
> Donec longa dies perfecto temporis orbe
> concretam exemit labem purumque relinquit
> ethereum sensum atque aure simplicis ignem.
> Has omnes, ubi mille rotam volvere per annos,
> Letheum ad fluvium deus evocat agmine magno,
> scilicet immemores supera ut convexa revisant
> rursus et incipiant in corpora velle reverti.

8   Hoc autem officium revocandi animas ad corpora ideo Mercurio attributum volunt, quia dicunt eum preesse fetui in utero ma-

not only in movement, which is the swiftest around the epicycle, but derives from the rapid assumption and transmission of the special characteristics of the other supercelestial bodies, as we see also in the swift and shape-changing flexibility of mercurial men. The wand is attributed to him on account of the dimensions of the bodies adjoining themselves to it, according to which it ordains their effects there, just as a mercurial man measures his compliance around whatever task he has.

That his wand, that is, his power, recalls spirits from Orcus, we   7 must examine more carefully here. There were those who thought that all the spirits of men were created in the beginning at the same time and then bestowed upon men as they were born, and that when upon our deaths they descended to the lower world and were tormented there until they were purged of what they committed in life, and that from there they made the crossing to the Elysian Fields, and from there after one thousand years were led by Mercury to the River Lethe so that when they drank from it they would forget the labors of their present life and thus desire to return to bodies, to which Mercury called them back. Vergil touches upon this laughable theory best when he says:[38]

Each of us endures our own shades. From there we are sent
to wide Elysium, and a few of us hold these happy meadows.
Until the long day of time's completed orb extracts
the ingrained stain and leaves purified
the ethereal perception and the fire of clear air.
All these, when they have rolled the wheel for a thousand
    years,
the god calls to the River Lethe in a long column,
now having forgotten as they revisit the upper world
again and renew a desire to be returned into bodies.

They want to attribute to Mercury this duty of calling spirits   8 back into bodies because they say that he was in charge of a fetus

tris existenti in mensi sexto, in quo opinantur multi rationalem animam infundi concepto, et hoc Mercurii predominantis opere, et sic ab Orco, id est ab inferiore loco, revocatur anima in corpus nascituri a Mercurio. Quod autem ad Tartara mictat physicum est, quia deficiente per frigidum et siccum, que est Mercurii complexio vera, calido et humido radicali, anima separatur a corpore et iuxta veterum opinionem tendit ad inferos.

9 Somnos adimere et dare idem est cum eo quod dictum est in vitam educere nascentes, quod est somnum adimere, et in mortem solvere, quod est somnum dare. Ventos agere Mercurii est, ipse enim non nunquam frigore suo suscitat illos, quibus suscitatis eis impellentibus feruntur huc illuc nubes.

10 Volunt eum preterea deum eloquentie, deum mercatorum, deum furum, et alia quedam esse, de quibus omnibus, infra protensius, ubi de mercuriis hominibus dicetur. Eum autem Iovis fuisse filium, ideo fictum est, quia Dei creatura est; Cylenis autem ad colorandam fictionem dictum est, seu eo quod apud Cylenem montem Arcadie primo cultus est.

: 8 :

De Tritopatreo VI° et Ebuleo VII°
et Dyonisio VIII°, Jovis primi filiis

1 Tritopatreum, Ebuleum et Dyonisium dicit Cicero ubi *De naturis deorum* antiquissimi Iovis, id est primi, Atheniensium regis et Proserpine fuisse filios, et Athenis Ariarches appellatos esse. Quos,

in the womb of its mother in the sixth month, at which time many think the rational spirit is infused into the conceived, and Mercury oversaw this function. And so Mercury calls a spirit back from Orcus, that is from the underworld, into a body of someone about to be born. That he sends them to Tartarus is a physical matter, for because when basic heat and cold are lacking through the cold and dry, which is Mercury's true constitution, a spirit is separated from the body and, according to the opinion of the ancients, heads toward the lower world.

Taking away sleep and giving it is the same as what was said 9 about bringing babies to life, which is to take away sleep, and releasing for death, which is to give sleep. It is for Mercury to conduct the winds, for sometimes he rouses them with his cold, and once they are aroused their force drives the clouds to and fro.

In addition, they want him to be a god of eloquence, a god of 10 merchants, god of thieves, and other things, all of which will be explained a little later along with mercurial men. That he was the son of Jupiter was invented because he is a creation of God; and he was said to be the son of Cyllene either to make the poetic fiction more elaborate or because he was first worshipped near the Arcadian Mount Cyllene.

: 8 :

On Tritopatreus, the sixth, and Eubuleus, the seventh, and Dionysus, the eighth children of the first Jupiter

Cicero[39] in his On the Nature of the Gods says that Tritopatreus, 1 Eubuleus, and Dionysus were the sons of the most ancient Jupiter, that is the first, king of the Athenians, and Proserpina, and that in Athens they were called "the Kings." Although I have found noth-

etsi nil de illis comperiam, arbitror insignes fuisse viros, cum *ariarches* sonet 'armorum principes'; nam Aris Grece, 'Mars' Latine sonat, et *archos* 'princeps,' ergo bellorum seu armorum principes
fuere: quod ea tempestate et etiam hodierna permaximum est.
Leontius vero dicit quod, cum Ebuleus ad famam tractus Anthei
Terre filii ad ineundam cum eo luctam accessisset, eo superato
Herculis meruit cognomen, quod ante eum nemo meruerat.

2   Ego autem credo longe antiquiorem Ebuleum Antheo. Similiter
et Dyonisium dicit ad Yndos, coactis in militiam mulieribus, intulisse bellum, et obtenta victoria Nysam urbem ibidem condidisse,
et cum victoriosus reverteretur primum pompam excogitasse triu-
nphi ac etiam vini usum Athenienses docuisse, eumque ab eisdem
Liberum appellatum et patrem, eo quod sese liberos eo vivente
arbitrarentur, quasi sub optimi patris tutela servatos. Que quidem
sic esse potuisse non nego, sed tamen longe post fuisse existimo.

: 9 :

De Hercule primo, VIIII° primi Jovis filio

1   Placet insuper Tullio primi Iovis ex Lysico primum et antiquissimum Herculem fuisse filium. Et huic asserit cum Apolline de tri-
pode fuisse certamen, in quo quoniam obtinuerit, dicit Paulus,
cum Dyonisius vocaretur, Hercules meruit appellari. Quod quidem et Leontius affirmat, sed causam non ostendit, et ideo quid
2   credam non habeo. Certamen autem tripodis credo de divinatione

ing about them, I think they were notable men, since *ariarches*[40] means "princes of arms." The Greek Aris means "Mars," and *archos* means "prince"; therefore they were princes of wars and arms, which at that time and even today was very important. Leontius says that when Eubuleus, drawn by the fame of Antaeus, son of Earth, approached him for the purpose of engaging in combat with him and then conquered him, he warranted the name Hercules, which no one before him had warranted.

I believe, however, that Eubuleus is much more ancient than 2 Antaeus. Similarly, he also says that Dionysus brought a war against the Indians, in which women were forced into military duty, won a victory, and founded the city of Nysa there; when he returned victorious he was the first to invent the celebration of a triumph and also taught the Athenians the use of wine; and they called him "Liber" and "father" because they thought that they were free [*liberos*] as long as he was alive, as if they were being protected under the guardianship of the best father. I do not deny that these things could have happened, but I do think they happened much later.

: 9 :

On the first Hercules, the ninth child of the first Jupiter

In addition Cicero[41] thinks that Hercules was the first and most 1 ancient son of the first Jupiter by Lysithoe. He says that he contested with Apollo over a tripod; and by taking it he warranted the appellation Hercules, says Paul, although he used to be called Dionysus. Leontius corroborates this, but he does not explain the reason, and so I am not sure what to believe. But I think the con- 2

fuerit. Nam Phebi tripodas dicit Paulus speciem esse lauri, cui tres tantum sunt radices, et has ob id in *Libris pontificum* tripodas dictas, et Apollini ob id sacras, quia cum ipse divinationis deus sit, huiusmodi lauri eandem videantur habere virtutem, cum legatur si frondes huius specie lauri dormientis capiti supponantur vel alligentur, eum procul dubio vera visurum somnia.

: 10 :

De Proserpina prima, X^a primi Jovis filia

1   Ex Proserpina Jovem non nullos suscepisse filios ostendit Tullius, et inde illius etiam fuisse filiam; quod quidem possibile est honestate servata, et Proserpinam habuisse coniugem, et ex hac eadem vel ex alia muliere Proserpinam habuisse filiam, quam Liberi fratris sui fuisse coniugem idem videtur testari Tullius, cum de ea nil aliud legisse meminerim.

: 11 :

De Libero primo, XI° primi Jovis filio,
qui genuit Mercurium secundum

1   Liberum primum primi Jovis fuisse filium Cicero ubi *De naturis deorum* testatur liquido. Hunc unum et idem cum Dyonisio superiori Leontius arbitratur, eumque preceteris fratribus insignem

test of the tripod was about divination, for Paul says that the tripods of Phoebus were a type of laurel which has only three roots; they are therefore called tripods in the *Libri pontificales*. They are sacred to Apollo because, in that he is the god of divination, laurels of this type seem to have the same power, for I have read that when the leaves of this type of laurel are placed under the head of someone who is sleeping or bound to the head, he will without doubt see true dreams.

: 10 :

On Proserpina, tenth child of the first Jupiter

Cicero[42] tells us that Jupiter had some children by Proserpina, and that he then also had a daughter of the same name. This is possible and preserves the truth in that he had a wife Proserpina and, by her or another woman, a daughter Proserpina, whom Cicero seems to testify was the wife of her brother Liber. I do not remember reading anything about her.

: 11 :

On the first Liber, eleventh child of the first Jupiter, who fathered the second Mercury

Cicero[43] in his *On the Nature of the Gods* clearly provides evidence that the first Liber was the son of the first Jupiter. Leontius thinks he is one and the same as the aforementioned Dionysus, and he attempts to show that he was a famous man before the

fuisse virum conatur ostendere, tamen Eusebius seu de hoc seu de
alio, quod ego magis arbitror, longe post hec tempora fuisse descri-
2 bit. Huius autem Proserpinam et sororem et coniugem non nulli
volunt, eumque ex ea Mercurium secundum suscepisse filium.

: 12 :

De Mercurio secundo Liberi et Proserpine filio, qui genuit Cupidinem et Auctolium

1 Mercurius alter a superiore Liberi et Proserpine fuit filius, ut
Theodontius dicit et Corvilius. De quo talis a Theodontio recitatur fabula: quod cum, vidente nemine preter Bathum quendam,
Apollinis vaccas furatus fuisset, Batho, ut hoc nemini revelaret,
unam concessit ex vaccis, demum in faciem alteram transformatus
experturus Bathi fidem ad eum rediit promisitque ei taurum si
sublatas sibi vaccas ostenderet; Bathus autem omnia que viderat
revelavit, quam ob rem turbatus Mercurius eum mutavit in saxum
quod indicem vocavere priores, nos autem paragonem vulgo dici-
2 mus. Tandem cum divinitate sua fretus hoc cognovisset Apollo,
sumpto arcu voluit Mercurium sagittis occidere, sed Mercurius
prestigio invisibilis factus ledi non potuit. Postremo, inter eos inita
concordia, citharam a se compertam Mercurius concessit Apollini.
Apollo autem virgam concessit eidem.

Dicebat insuper Paulus se alibi legisse quod Mercurius iram
precogitans Apollinis, ne ledi posset ab eo, clam illi pharetram
evacuaverat, quod cum advertisset iratus Apollo, miratus eius astu-
3 tiam risit, et in concordiam secum venit ut supra. Leontius circa

other brothers. But Eusebius[44] maintains that he—whether he was speaking about this one or, as I think more likely, another— lived long after this time. Some want Proserpina to be both his 2 sister and wife, and for him to have had a son, the second Mercury, by her.

: 12 :

On the second Mercury, son of Liber and Proserpina, who fathered Cupid and Autolycus

A different Mercury from the aforementioned Mercury[45] was the 1 son of Liber and Proserpina, as Theodontius and Corvilius[46] say. Theodontius tells the following story about him. When he had stolen the cattle of Apollo without anyone seeing except a certain Battus, he gave one of the cattle to Battus so he would not tell anyone, but then after altering his face he tested Battus' reliability by coming back to him and promising him a bull if he would reveal the stolen cattle to him. Battus revealed everything he had seen; as a result the irate Mercury turned him into the stone that the ancients called a "touchstone" but we commonly call a "paragon." Next, when Apollo, relying on his own divination, realized 2 what had happened, he picked up his bow and wanted to kill Mercury with his arrows, but Mercury, made invisible by magic, could not be harmed. Finally they came to an agreement, and Mercury gave him the cithara he invented, and Apollo gave him a wand.

In addition, Paul used to say that he had read elsewhere that Mercury, anticipating Apollo's anger, secretly emptied Apollo's quiver so that he could not harm him; when the angry Apollo noticed this, he marveled at his cleverness and laughed, therefore making peace with him, as above. Leontius used to say about this 3

hanc fabulam dicebat hunc Mercurium filium fuisse Dyonisii qui proxime supra Liber vocatur, et eum a nativitate vocatum Nysum, eo quod apud Nysam Yndie paulo ante a patre conditam natus sit, et cum adolevisset tanta pedum velocitate valuit, ut coevos suos ceteros cursu superaret, quam ob rem omisso nomine primo Stilbon appellatus est, quod 'velox' Latine sonat; demum cum illusiones magicas didicisset et latrociniis delectaretur summe, armenta rapuit Phoronidis sacerdotis Apollinis Delphici, qui ea tempestate mirande autoritatis habebatur, et ea post lapideum tumulum quon-

4 dam, cui Bathos nomen erat, seduxerat. Verum cum taurus unus, ex improviso segregatus a reliquis, socios vagus repeteret, forte conscendit tumulum illum mugiens, mugitu cuius respondentibus aliis ab exquirentibus armenta comperta sunt, et tumulus ex Batho dictus est index. Stilbon autem cum suis artibus Phoronidis irati impetum effugisset, amicus eius tandem effectus est. Verum cum in talibus perseveraret non ob avaritiam sed nature, ut aiebat, impulsu, cum alias esset et formosus homo et eloquentissimus et circa omnia manualia opera celeberrimi ingenii Mercurius nuncupatus est et furum deus.

5 Quod, ut idem asserebat Leontius, etsi a ioco habuerit initium, convaluit tantum apud Atticos et Arcades inceptum ut post eius mortem illi templa dedicarentur et sacra, quibus sibi propitium conabantur facere ii quibus furto aliquid erat subtractum, asserentes numine suo et servata multa ac etiam recuperata, eumque aiebat sicuti et ceteros insignitum. De quibus insignibus, quoniam infra ubi de tertio Mercurio late dicturus sum, hic aliquid scribere non curavi.

story that this Mercury was the son of the Dionysus who just above was called Liber, and that he was called Nysus from his birth because he was born a little before his father found him near Nysa in India. When he grew up he was so swift of foot that he excelled, surpassing all his contemporaries at running; for this reason, with his first name missing, he was called "Stilbon," which means "swift." Then, because he had learned magic tricks and delighted utterly in villainy, he seized the flock of Phoronis, the priest of Delphic Apollo, who was at that time held in high regard, and he took it behind a certain rock tomb, the name of which was Battus. But when one bull unexpectedly separated from the rest 4 and, wondering around while seeking to return to the herd, by chance climbed that tomb while lowing, he heard the lowing echoed by the rest of the lost herd and found them, and the tomb, once called Battus, was then called the touchstone. Because Stilbon had escaped the onslaught of the angry Phoronis by his arts, he finally became his friend. However, because he persevered in such things not from avarice but by the force — as he used to say — of his nature, since he was otherwise both a handsome man, quite eloquent, and very talented in all manual works, he was named Mercury and the god of thieves.

This story, as Leontius used to assert, although it began as a 5 joke, became so important in Attica and Arcadia that after his death temples and sacrifices were dedicated to him; in doing so they tried to make him propitious for those who had been robbed, claiming that his divine power preserved and even returned many stolen objects. Leontius used to say as well that he was famous like the other Mercuries, but I have not written about this here because I will discuss his fame more fully later along in my chapter on the third Mercury.

: 13 :

De Cupidine primo, secundi Mercurii filio

1 Cupido primus, ut ait cum Tullio Theodontius, secundi Mercurii
et Diane prime fuit filius, quem aiunt fuisse pinnatum. Circa quod
duo potuere sensisse fingentes; primum circa nomen, eo quod
speciosissimus fuerit puer ad instar Cupidinis filii Veneris, quem
puerum et pulcherrimum semper pinxere pictores, quasi alter Cu-
2 pido dictus est. Pinnatum autem ob id cognominatum reor, quia
velocissimus cursu fuerit adolescens.

: 14 :

De Auctolio secundi Mercurii filio,
qui genuit Synonem primum

1 Auctolius, ut Ovidio placet, Mercurii et Lychionis fuit filius. Qui
Ovidius de origine eiusdem talem recitat fabulam. Dicit enim Ly-
chionem Dedalionis speciosissimam fuisse filiam, adeo ut Apollini
et Mercurio placeret; quibus poscentibus, una et eadem die uno
tamen de altero ignorante eius, in sequenti nocte concubitum cum
promisisset, a Mercurio non expectata nocte virga tacta est et in
2 somnum soluta, et sic cum ea concubuit. Apollo autem nocte accessit ad eam. Ex quibus cum geminos concepisset, peperit Mercurio Auctolium, Apollini vero Phylemonem. Verum Auctolius inter
fures evasit clarissimus, adeo ut non videretur degenerare a patre.
Phylemon autem cytharista factus se Apollinis filium demonstravit.

: 13 :

On the first Cupid, son of the second Mercury

The first Cupid, as Theodontius says with Cicero,[47] was the son of   1
the second Mercury and the first Diana, and they say he was
winged. The creators of this story could have meant two things by
this. The first accounts for his name: inasmuch as he was a very
attractive boy in the image of Cupid, son of Venus, whom painters
always depict as a very beautiful boy, he was named as if he were
another Cupid. And then I think he was thought to be winged   2
because in his youth he was the swiftest in running.

: 14 :

On Autolycus,[48] son of the second Mercury, who fathered the first Sinon

Autolycus, as Ovid[49] believes, was the son of Mercury and Chi-   1
one.[50] Ovid tells the fable of his birth in this way. He says that
Chione was the very beautiful daughter of Daedalion who attracted both Mercury and Apollo as suitors. On one and the same
day, each unaware of the other, they promised to sleep with her
that night, but Mercury, not waiting for the night, touched her
with his wand, put her to sleep, and lay with her that way; Apollo   2
came to her at night. The result of this was that she gave birth to
twins, producing Autolycus for Mercury, and Philammon[51] for
Apollo. Autolycus grew up to become very famous among thieves,
so he did not seem to be unworthy of his father. By becoming a
citharist, Philammon proved that he was a son of Apollo.

3   Huic ego fictioni causam dedisse varium geminorum fratrum
exitum, et sic uterque eorum illi deo attributus est filius, cuius
imitatus est mores, et forsan Auctolii nascentis fuit significator
Mercurius, et sic eius dictus est filius, et Apollo eandem ob causam Phylemonem lucratus est.

: 15 :

De Synone primo Auctolii filio, qui genuit
Syssimum et Auctoliam

1   Synon Auctolii fuit filius, ut placet Paulo, et hunc idem dicit Servius insignem fuisse furem; seque ad exercenda latrocinia in diversas species adeo trasformantem, ut facile quos vellet falleret.

2   Genuit autem Syssimum et Auctoliam matrem Ulixis, et habuit
dominium penes Parnasum, ut per Homerum patet in *Odyssea*, ubi
recitat qualiter Ulixes apud Parnasum ab apro in tybia vulnera-
tus sit.

: 16 :

De Syssimo filio primi Synonis et patre⁶ secundi

1   Syssimus, ut dicit Servius, filius fuit primi Synonis, nec de eo
aliud legisse memini, nisi quia pater fuit secundi Synonis, qui
fraude sua Troianos in extremam deduxit perniciem.

I believe that the different outcomes of the twin brothers give 3
rise to this fiction, and so each of them is allotted as a son to that
god whose characteristics he imitated; and perhaps the astral signi-
fier of the birth of Autolycus was Mercury and thus he was said to
be his son, and for the same reason Apollo took on Philammon.

: 15 :

On the first Sinon, son of Autolycus, who fathered Aesimus[52] and Anticlea[53]

Sinon was the son of Autolycus, as Paul believes, and Servius[54] 1
says that this same Sinon was a famous thief, and that when com-
mitting thievery he would transform himself into different forms
so he could easily deceive whomever he wished.

He fathered Aesimus and Anticlea, the mother of Ulysses, and 2
he lorded over Parnassus, as Homer[55] makes clear in the *Odyssey*,
where he recites how Ulysses was wounded in the leg by a wild
boar on Parnassus.

: 16 :

On Aesimus, son of the first Sinon and father of the second

Aesimus, as Servius[56] says, was the son of the first Sinon, nor do I 1
remember reading anything else about him except that he was the
father of the second Sinon, whose deceit brought the Trojans to
their final disaster.

: 17 :

De Auctolia Synonis primi filia et Ulixis matre

1 Auctolia, ut Servio placet, Synonis primi fuit filia. Hec cum nup-sisset Laerti Ytachie regi, ut quibusdam placet, a Sysipho latrone ad virum vadens intercepta est atque oppressa, et ex eo concubitu sunt qui dicant eam concepisse Ulixem, et sic pregnantem ivisse in nuptias Laertis, et quem ex Sysipho conceperat Laertis filium esse dixit.

2 Quod Aiax Telamonius apud Ovidium in questione de armis Achillis illi obicit dicens:

> Quid sanguine cretus
> Sysiphio furtisque et fraude simillimus illi,
>
>   etc.

Hec autem, ut fertur, cum audisset falso nuntio apud Troiam Ulixem occisum, doloris impatiens laqueo vitam abiecit. Quam postea et apud inferos, ut in *Odyssea* scribit Homerus, Ulixes com-perit et agnovit et de multis perquisivit ab ea et predoctus est.

: 18 :

De secundo Synone filio Syssimi

1 Secundus Synon, testimonio Servii, filius fuit Syssimi et a Synone primo avo suo denominatus. Hic cum Grecis, ut per Virgilium patet, ad excidium Troianum accessit, et iam minus succedentibus

: 17 :

On Anticlea, daughter of the first Sinon and mother of Ulysses

Anticlea, according to Servius,[57] was the daughter of the first Si-   1
non. After she had been betrothed to Laertes, King of Ithaca, as
some believed, while traveling to dwell with her husband she was
captured and raped by the thief Sisyphus. There are those who say
that she conceived Ulysses during this intercourse, and so she married Laertes while already pregnant and said that the child she
conceived with Sisyphus was the son of Laertes.

Telamonian Ajax reproached Ulysses with this in Ovid during   2
the dispute over Achilles' arms, saying:[58]

> Why, born from the blood
> of Sisyphus and similar to him in theft and fraud.

Moreover, as is said, when she heard in a false report that Ulysses
had been killed in Troy, not suffering the grief, she hanged herself.
Afterward, in the land of the dead, as Homer[59] writes in the *Odyssey*, Ulysses found her, recognized her, and asked her about many
things, and she gave him instructions.

: 18 :

On the second Sinon, son of Aesimus

The second Sinon, by the testimony of Servius,[60] was the son of   1
Aesimus and named after his grandfather, the first Sinon. He
came with the Greeks to participate in the destruction of Troy, as
Vergil[61] makes clear, but when things were not progressing well,

rebus, a Grecis fingentibus reditum subornatus, volens a Troianis captus et ad Priamum regem deductus est, apud quem mira sagacitate primo se extulit, et demum fallacibus verbis in perniciosam credulitatem de recessu Grecorum regem Troianosque reliquos ad suscipiendum equum intra menia civitatis impulit.

2 Quid ex illo deinde secutum sit nescio. Scribit tamen Plinius in libro *De hystoria naturali* huius inventam fuisse significationem speculariam, ex quo satis patet eum non minimi momenti fuisse hominem.[7]

: 19 :

De Epapho primi Jovis XII° filio, qui genuit Lybiam et Belum

1 Postquam primi Liberi patris Iovis primi filii prolem omnem expedivimus, retro trahendus est sermo ad Epaphum Egyptium eiusque amplissimam progeniem.

Qui quidem Epaphus, ut testatur Ovidius, ex Yone filia Ynachi, Iovis fuit filius. Theodontius vero et Leontius eque eum Iovis fuisse filium dicunt, sed ex Yside Promethei filia, ut ubi infra, dum

2 de Yside latius patebit. Eusebius autem in libro *Temporum* dicit eum filium fuisse Thelegoni, cui post mortem Apis nupsit Ysis. Gervasius quidem Thelliberiensis in libro *Ociorum imperialium* scribit Epaphum Heleni et Ysidis fuisse filium, et Babiloniam Egyptiam condidisse, quod opus fuisse Cambisis Persarum regis certiores autores affirmant. Et sic de patre et matre huius inter se discrepant autores; ego autem vulgatiorem secutus famam Iovis et

suborned by the Greeks who pretended to return home, he willingly gave himself up for capture by the Trojans and was brought to King Priam; he first presented himself with amazing shrewdness and then used fallacious words about the Greek retreat; this induced the king and the rest of the Trojans into such destructive credulity that they dragged the horse to within the walls of the city.

I do not know what happened to him next. Pliny[62] writes in his 2 *Natural History* that the watchtower signal was his invention, so he clearly was a man of some importance.

: 19 :

On Epaphus, twelfth child of the first Jupiter, who fathered Libya and Belus

Now that we have addressed all the progeny of the first Liber, son 1 of the first Jupiter, we must turn back to Epaphus the Egyptian and his numerous progeny.

As Ovid[63] bears witness, Epaphus was the son of Jupiter by Io, daughter of Inachus. Theodontius and Leontius say equally that he was the son of Jupiter but by Isis, daughter of Prometheus, as will appear below in the chapter on Isis.[64] But Eusebius[65] in his 2 *Chronicle* says that he was the son of Telegonus, whom Isis married after the death of Apis. Gervase of Tilbury[66] in his *Recreation for an Emperor* writes that Epaphus was the son of Helenus and Isis, and that he founded the Egyptian Babylon,[67] which more reliable authorities assert was accomplished by Cambyses, King of Persia. And so, the authorities differ on his father and mother. I will follow the more common account and say that he was the son of Ju-

Yonis filium dicam, ex cuius conceptione fabula infra ubi de Yone scribitur integre referetur.

3   Huius dicit Lactantius Cassiopiam fuisse coniugem, non eam que socrus fuit Persei, sed longe antiquiorem, et ex ea quosdam suscepisse filios, ut postea apparebit. De tempore eius non minus quam de patre et matre discordes sunt veteres, nam, Eusebio ubi *De temporibus* referente, aliqui dicunt Jovem Yoni Ynachi filie mixtum, regnante Athenis Cecrope, qui regnavit circa annos mundi $\overline{\text{III}}$DCXLVII, cum constet Ynacum regnasse usque ad annum mundi $\overline{\text{III}}$CCCXCVII, et secundum hos oportuit aliam esse Yonem quam

4   Ynachi filiam. Idem autem Eusebius paulo post predictam dicit Yonem in Egyptum profectam anno xliii regni Cicropis, qui mundi fuit annus $\overline{\text{III}}$DCCX, et ibidem Ysidem nuncupatam, et Thelegono cuidam nupsisse, et ex eo Epaphum concepisse. Ego autem, discordantiis omissis, Iovis primi Epaphum filium dixi, eo quod eius tempus videatur convenire magis cum Yone Ynachi filia, et Yside Promethei, ex quibus quis potest quam malit illi matrem ascribere.

: 20 :

De Lybia filia Epaphi

1   Lybia Epaphi et Cassiopie coniugis sue, ut Lactantio placet, fuit filia. Que cum in Neptuni venisset concubitum, id est alieni hominis ab Egypto, ex eo concepit et peperit Busiridem, immanem postea tyrannum. Hec, ut dicit Ysidorus, ubi *De ethymologiis*, eius partis Affrice regina fuit que ex suo nomine Lybia dicta est.

piter and Io and tell the story of his conception in its entirety in the passage on Io.[68]

Lactantius[69] says that his wife was Cassiopeia—not the one 3 who was Perseus' mother-in-law but a much more ancient one from whom he had some children, as will be made clear later.[70] The ancients are no more in agreement about his age than they are about his father and mother, for, relying on Eusebius'[71] *Chronicle*, some say that Jupiter lay with Io, daughter of Inachus, when Cecrops was ruling Athens around the world year 3647. However, it is established that Inachus ruled until the world year 3397, and so it is necessary according to them that Io be someone other than the daughter of Inachus. Eusebius[72] again a little afterward says 4 the aforementioned Io set out for Egypt in the forty-third year of Cecrops' reign, which was world year 3710, and there she was called Isis and married a certain Telegonus, whereupon Epaphus was conceived. I, however, ignoring the disagreement, said that Epaphus was the son of the first Jupiter because his period seems to agree more with Io, daughter of Inachus, and Isis, daughter of Prometheus, and in this case one can assign for Epaphus whichever mother one prefers.

: 20 :

On Libya, daughter of Epaphus

Libya was the daughter of Epaphus and his wife Cassiopeia, ac- 1 cording to Lactantius. After she entered the bed of Neptune, that is, of a foreign man from Egypt, she then conceived and gave birth to Busiris, later a brutal tyrant. Isidore[73] in his *Etymologies* says she was queen of that part of Africa which was named Libya after her.

: 21 :

De Belo prisco Epaphi filio, qui genuit Danaum, Egysthum et Agenorem

1 Belus, quem priscum cognominant veteres, Epaphi, secundum Paulum, fuit filius, et post eum in superiori Egypto regnavit, ubi, ut aiunt, celestis discipline inventor doctorque factus, meruit ab Egyptiis, ut idem Paulus asserit, templum quod illi in Babilonia

2 fuit constructum, et Iovi Belo consecratum. Theodontius vero dicit templum hoc longe post Belum factum Cretensis Iovis astutia, qui captatis cum principibus amicitiis, quasi ad eas conservandas, templa in regnis eorum edificari et suo et amici titulo insigniri plura fecit, qua astutia summe nomen eius et deitas ampliata est.

3 Alii sunt qui dicant templum hoc non Belo prisco edificatum, nec in Babilonia Egyptia, sed Belo patri Nini regis Assyriorum in Babilonia Caldeorum, eumque ibi diu sub nomine Saturni sacris et cultu vario honoratum. Fuere preterea Belo prisco filii quidam, sed ex quibus mulieribus non constat.

: 21 :

On Belus Priscus, son of Epaphus, who fathered Danaus, Aegyptus,[74] and Agenor

Belus, to whom the ancients gave the cognomen Priscus, was, ac- 1
cording to Paul, the son of Epaphus, and ruled after him in upper
Egypt. They say that because he discovered astronomy there and
became so knowledgeable, he warranted from the Egyptians, as
Paul again asserts, a temple constructed in Babylonia and consecrated to Jupiter Belus. Theodontius says the temple was made 2
long after Belus thanks to the cleverness of Cretan Jupiter; to preserve the allegiances this Jupiter had established with the Egyptian
princes, he had numerous temples built in their kingdoms and in-
dividualized them by combining his name with that of his ally;
through such cleverness he made his name even more conspicuous
and enhanced his divinity. There are others who say that this 3
temple was built not by Belus Priscus, nor was it in Egyptian
Babylon, but by Belus, the father of Ninus, king of the Assyrians,
in Babylonia of the Chaldeans, and that under the name of Saturn
he was honored there for a long time with sacrifices and various
cults. In addition Belus Priscus had some sons, but there is no
agreement as to who their mothers were.

: 22 :

De Danao Beli prisci filio, qui quinquaginta genuit filias, ex quibus Ypermestra et Amimon atque Bona tantum nomine cognoscuntur

1   Danaus Beli prisci fuit filius, ut asserit Paulus, et illud idem confirmat Lactantius, qui etiam ante Paulum Orosium dicit Danaum Beli filium ex pluribus coniugibus quinquaginta filias habuisse. Quas cum Egysthus frater eius, cui totidem erant melioris sexus filii, postulasset in nurus, Danaus, oraculi responso comperto, se manibus generi periturum, volens evitare periculum, conscensis navibus in Argos venit.

2   Asseritque[8] Plinius in libro *Naturalis hystorie* eum primum navibus seu navi trasfretasse, cum ante ratibus inventis ab Eritra rege in mari Rubro navigaretur; esto sint, ut idem scribit Plinius, qui credant Misos et Troianos in Hellesponto priores excogitasse dum adversus Tracas transirent. Egysthus autem quod spretus esset indignans, ut illum sequerentur filiis imperavit, lege data ne unquam

3   domum repeterent, ni prius Danaum occidissent. Qui cum apud Argos oppugnarent patruum, ab eo diffidente fraude capti sunt. Spopondit enim se illis iuxta Egysthi votum filias daturum in coniuges, nec defuit promisso fides; subornate enim a patre, virorum intravere thalamos singulis cultris clam omnes armate, et cum vino letitiaque calentes iuvenes facile in soporem ivissent, obedientes patri virgines, captato tempore, iugulaverunt viros, unaqueque suum; Ypermestra excepta Lyno seu Lynceo viro suo miserta pepercit.

: 22 :

On Danaus, son of Belus Priscus, who fathered fifty daughters, of whom only Hypermnestra, Amymone, and Hesione[75] are known by name

Danaus was the son of Belus Priscus, as Paul asserts, and Lactan- 1
tius[76] confirms the same thing as well, saying even before Paul
Orosius[77] that Danaus, son of Belus, had fifty daughters from
several spouses. His brother Egyptus, who had fifty children of
the better sex, sought them as daughters-in-law. Danaus had been
warned by an oracular response that he would perish at the hands
of his son-in-law and wished to avoid that danger, so he embarked
with a few ships and sailed for Argos.

In his *Natural History* Pliny[78] claims that he was first to sail on 2
ships, or one ship, though King Erythrus navigated the Red Sea
following the earlier discovery of rafts. However, there are those,
as Pliny again writes, who believe that the Mysians and Trojans in
the Hellespont invented sailing first so they could cross over and
attack Thrace. Egyptus, indignant at the rejection, ordered his
sons to follow him, stipulating that they could never return home
until they first killed Danaus. When they tried to attack their 3
uncle in Argos, he had become suspicious and captured them by
using the following ruse. He promised to give his daughters' hands
in marriage to them in keeping with the pledge he had made to
Egyptus, nor did he renege on that promise. Suborned by their
father, each entered her husband's bed chamber armed with a
knife; inflamed with wine and rapture, the young men easily fell
asleep, whereupon the virgins, obedient to their father, seizing the
opportunity, slit their husbands' throats — each and every one except for Hypermnestra, who pitied her husband Linus or Lynceus
and spared him.

Hunc Danaum dicit Eusebius, cui et Armais nomen fuit, anno mundi ⅢDCCXVI apud Egyptios regnare cepisse. Ast inde Egypto pulsus, Argos veniens prius Stelenum Argivorum regem, cum annis regnasset XI, regno expulit, et inde Gelanorem successorem

4 eius Argivi ab imperio expulere et Danaum suscepere. Qui aquis eos abundare fecit; nam,[9] ut ait Plinius in libro *De hystoria naturali*, puteos primus ex Egypto in Greciam advectus[10] fodiendos ostendit; et eisdem fere temporibus asserit eius opere a filiabus quinquaginta Danai filios quinquaginta Egysthi fratris sui preter Lynum seu Lynceum occisos. Tandem ipse cum quinquaginta annis regnasset a Lynceo occisus est.

: 23 :

De quinquaginta filiabus Danai in generali

1 Filie Danai fratricide propriis fere nominibus incognite sunt, cum nomina trium tantum ad nos usque pervenerint; et sicuti nomina perdidimus, sic et fortunas post scelestum facinus perpetratum. Finxere tamen poete has apud inferos esse damnatas, et hoc assidue agitari supplicio ut haurientes aquas urnas absque fundis conentur implere, ut dicit Ovidius:

> Molirique suis letum patruelibus ause
> assidue repetunt, quas perdant Belides undas,
>
> etc.

2 Et[11] Seneca tragicus in *Hercule furente*, 'Urnasque frustra Danaides plenas ferunt.' Hoc ego illis iniunctum supplicium, reor, ut mulierum singularis cura describatur, que, dum suam formositatem lautitia nimia augere conantur, laborem perdunt et minuitur quod

Eusebius[79] says that this Danaus, who also had the name Armais, began to rule in Egypt in the world year 3716. But driven out from Egypt, he came to Argos and first banished Sthenelus,[80] king of the Argives, who had ruled eleven years, and then the Argives expelled his successor Gelanor from power and welcomed Danaus. He made them rich in water, for, as Pliny[81] says in his *Natural History*, when he came from Egypt he first showed the Greeks how to dig wells, and in his book he also asserts that at about the same time the fifty sons of Egyptus, except for Lynus or Lynceus, were killed by the fifty daughters of his brother Danaus. Finally, when he had ruled for fifty years he was murdered by Lynceus. 4

: 23 :

On the fifty daughters of Danaus, in general

The murderous daughters of Danaus are not really known by their 1 own names, for only the names of three of them have come down to us. And just as we have lost their names, so also we have lost track of what happened to them after they committed their wicked crime. Nonetheless, the poets invented their damnation in the netherworld, where, condemned to continual torment, they try by drawing water to fill urns without bottoms. As Ovid says:[82]

Having dared to plan death for their cousins,
the Belides continually seek the waters which they lose.

And Seneca the tragedian[83] in the *Hercules furens*, "The Danaids 2 carry urns that are full in vain." This punishment was imposed upon them, I think, because it represents the unique care women give themselves: while they try to increase their beauty by excessive splendor, they waste their labor and diminish what they intend to

3 intendunt inani solertia augere. Vel potius monstratur qualis sit
fluxorum atque effeminatorum hominum labor, qui, dum sepe repetito coitu credunt adimplere quod cupiunt, non obtento voto se
ipsos evacuasse comperiunt.

: 24 :

De Ypermestra una ex quinquaginta filiabus Danai

1 Ypermestra, ut in *Epistolis* ostendit Ovidius, filia fuit Danai, et sola
ex quinquaginta sororibus, neglecto patris imperio, Lynceo viro
suo pepercit, et ob id, ut idem dicit Ovidius, carceri tradita est.

2   Hanc, ut dicit Eusebius in libro *Temporum*, non nulli putarunt
Ysidem esse; attamen, Danao patre Argis regnante, sacerdotio
functa est.

: 25 :

De Amimone una ex quinquaginta filiabus Danai

1 Amimon, ut ait Lactantius, filia fuit Danai ex quinquaginta sororibus una. Hec, cum studiose in silvis iaculo venaretur, inadvertenter satyrum percussit, qui cum illi vim vellet inferre, Amimone
Neptuni auxilium imploravit. Neptunus autem, fugato satyro
⟨. . .⟩ quod ab illo virgo pati noluerat, a maiori deo passa concepit
et peperit ex Neptuno Nauplium.[12]

2   Quid autem de fictione sentiendum sit, infra ubi de ortu Nau-
plii apponetur.

increase with their vain skill. Or rather it demonstrates the work 3
of dissolute and effeminate men in that while they believe they are
fulfilling their desires by engaging in frequent intercourse, they fail
to obtain their wish and find themselves to be empty.

: 24 :

On Hypermnestra,[84] one of the fifty daughters of Danaus

Hypermnestra, as Ovid[85] reveals in his *Heroines*, was the daughter 1
of Danaus, and alone of the fifty sisters she disregarded her father's order and spared her husband Lynceus; on account of this,
again Ovid says, she was incarcerated.

As Eusebius[86] says in his *Chronicle*, some think she was Isis, but 2
it was because her father Danaus was the king of Argos that she
performed the duties of a priestess.

: 25 :

On Amymone, one of the fifty daughters of Danaus

Amymone, as Lactantius[87] says, was one of the fifty daughters of 1
Danaus. While happily hunting in the forest, with her spear she
inadvertently struck a satyr who desired to have his way with her.
Amymone called upon Neptune for assistance. But the maiden
Amymone, once the satyr was chased away, suffered from the
greater god what she would not suffer from the satyr, and conceived with Neptune and gave birth to Nauplius.

The meaning of this fiction appears below in the discussion on 2
the birth of Nauplius.[88]

: 26 :

De Bona una ex quinquaginta filiabus Danai

1 Bona, dicit Ditis Cretensis, ubi *De expeditione Grecorum contra Troianos* scribit, filia fuit Danai, que ut ipsemet asserit Athlanti nupsit
et ex eo Eletram peperit, que postea ex Jove Dardanum edidit.

: 27 :

De Egystho Beli Prisci filio, qui genuit
quinquaginta filios ex quibus Lynceus

1 Egysthus Beli Prisci fuit filius et Danai frater, ut supra satis monstratum est. Huic quinquaginta fuere filii, quibus cum quesisset
Danai fratris sui filias in coniuges, ab eisdem, Danai iussu, occisi
sunt omnes nuptiarum nocte preter Lynceum, ut predictum est.

: 28 :

De Lynceo ex quinquaginta filiis Egysthi uno,
qui genuit Abantem et Iasium et Acrisium

1 Lynceus, quem Lynum appellat Ovidius, filius fuit Egysthi, et solus ex quinquaginta fratribus misericordia Ypermestre coniugis
evasit a morte. Hic, ut placet aliquibus, Danao patruo pulso, pro

: 26 :

On Hesione,[89] one of the fifty daughters of Danaus

Hesione, says Dictys[90] of Crete in his *Expedition of the Greeks* ⁱ
Against the Trojans, was the daughter of Danaus, who, as he himself
asserts, married Atlas and bore him Electra; she later produced
Dardanus from Jupiter.

: 27 :

On Egyptus, son of Belus Priscus, who fathered fifty sons, including Lynceus

Egyptus was the son of Belus Priscus and brother of Danaus, as ⁱ
we have amply described above. He had fifty sons, and when he
sought to marry them to the daughters of his brother Danaus, on
their wedding night by the order of Danaus they were murdered,
all except for Lynceus, as was said above.

: 28 :

On Lynceus, one of the fifty sons of Egyptus, who fathered Abas, Iasius, and Acrisius

Lynceus, whom Ovid[91] calls Lynus, was the son of Egyptus, and ⁱ
alone of the fifty brothers he escaped death, thanks to the pity of
his wife Hypermnestra. According to others, he ousted his uncle

2 eo regnavit apud Argos; alii vero dicunt, eo occiso. Sed qualitercunque fuerit, ut Eusebius ostendit in libro *Temporum*, postquam Danaus annis quinquaginta regnasset, Lynceus eidem successit in regno, cumque regnasset annis XLI, Abante et Iasio et Acrisio filiis derelictis, diem clausit.

: 29 :

De Abante filio Lyncei, qui genuit Pritum

1 Abas, ut asserit Barlaam, filius fuit Lyncei ex Ypermestra coniuge, esto Paulus dicat eum Beli Prisci fuisse filium. Hic autem bellicosus homo et acerrimi ingenii fuit, Lynceoque patri successit in regno, annisque XXIII, ut dicit Eusebius, imperavit Argivis et mortuus est.

: 30 :

De Prito filio Abantis, qui genuit
Meran et sorores

1 Pritus seu Pretus, ut Lactantio placet et Servio, filius fuit Abantis Argivorum regis. Huic, ut fere omnes asserunt, coniux fuit Stenoboe, Homerus autem dicit Anthiope, ex qua tres sustulit filias, que iam adulte, eo quod formosissime essent, elate templum Junonis intrantes, se pretulere Iunoni; quam ob rem turbata Iuno, illis furorem immisit talem, ut se vaccas arbitrarentur, et aratra timentes

Danaus and ruled Argos in his stead; but still others say that he killed him. Whatever happened, as Eusebius[92] reveals in his *Chron-* 2 *icle*, after Danaus had ruled for fifty years, Lynceus succeeded him as king; after he had ruled for forty-one years, he died, leaving behind his sons Abas, Iasius, and Acrisius.

: 29 :

On Abas, son of Lynceus, who fathered Proetus

Abas, as Barlaam asserts, was the son of Lynceus by his wife Hy- 1 permnestra, although Paul says that he was the son of Belus Priscus. He was a bellicose man of considerable ability. He succeeded his father Lynceus as king, ruling the Argives, as Eusebius[93] says, for twenty-three years, and then died.

: 30 :

On Proetus, son of Abas, who fathered Maera[94] and her sisters

Pritus, or Proetus, according to Lactantius[95] and Servius,[96] was 1 the son of Abas, king of the Argives. His wife, as nearly all maintain, was Stheneboea, although Homer[97] says it was Antiope. She gave him three daughters. As adults, because they were very beautiful, as they entered the temple of Juno they insolently claimed superiority to her. Angered by this, Juno cast such a spell of madness upon them that they thought they were cows, and fearing the

silvas optarent, ut ait Virgilius: 'Pretides implerunt falsis mugitibus agros.'

2   Ovidius aliam refert insanie causam, dicens has in Cea insula se vaccas creditas, eo quod furto facto ex armentis Herculis prestitissent consensum. Sed quacunque causa factum sit, egre tulit infortunium Pretus, proposuitque regni partem, et quam ex eis mallet in coniugem, ei qui illas in pristinam mentem revocasset. Cuius premii cupiditate tractus Melampus Amythaonis filius curandas assumpsit, et, ut ait Vitruvius in libro *Architecture*, eas apud Clitorim Arcadie civitatem duxisse, ibidem enim spelunca est ex qua profluit aqua, ex qua si quis biberit fit abstemius et ob id apud eam in lapide epygrama Grecis carminibus scriptum est, testificans aquam non esse ydoneam ad lavandum, et vitibus inimicam. Ibi autem, peractis sacris, eas purgavit et pristine restituit menti, et sic regni partem et coniugium unius consecutus est. Pretus autem, secundum Eusebium, annis XVII regnavit, eique successit Acrisius frater.

3   Huius ego filias, si medelam Melampodis intueor, vino fuisse ultra quam deceat mulieres avidas arbitror et, potate, non nunquam se patri regi preferre ausas; quam ob rem Iunonis iram, id est regnantis patris, meruere, et castigate in partem alteram instigante vino muliebriter in furiam verse, se vaccas, id est servas et

4   iugo subditas clamitabant. Quod cum forsan sepius contigisset, vexatus infortunio Pretus eas tradidit Melampodi curandas; qui cum eas aqua predicta potasset, hostes vini fecit et furor abiit consuetus.

plow they opted instead for the forests, as Vergil says,[98] "The Pro-
etids filled the fields with counterfeit lowing."

Ovid[99] tells of another reason for their insanity, saying that they 2
believed they were cows on the island of Cea because they consented to the trick played out on the herd of Hercules. But whatever the reason was, Proetus did not bear his misfortune lightly
and offered to the man who could restore their former sanity both
part of his kingdom and whichever daughter he preferred to marry.
Attracted by a desire for such a reward, Melampus, son of Amyth-
aon, undertook their care and, as Vitruvius[100] says in his *On Architecture*, led them to Clitor, a city in Arcadia. In that place, there
was a cave from which water issued forth, and whoever drank of it
became abstemious, which is why there was an epigram in Greek
verses written on a stone nearby, warning that the water was not
suitable for washing and was an enemy of grapevines. It was there
that after performing sacrificial rites he purified them and restored
their former sanity, thus taking part of the kingdom and one of
them as a wife. Proetus, according to Eusebius,[101] ruled seventeen
years, and his brother Acrisius succeeded him.

When I think about Melampus' cure, I think Proetus' daugh- 3
ters were more ardent for wine than befits women, and when
drunk they sometimes dared to act superior to their father the
king. Therefore, they merited the anger of Juno, that is, of their
royal father, and when punished they changed, led on by the wine,
turning into feminine frenzy, screaming that they were cows, that
is, subjugated slaves. Perhaps because this happened frequently 4
Proetus was troubled by his misfortune and handed them over to
Melampus to cure; when he made them drink the aforementioned
waters, he made them averse to wine and their accustomed frenzy
disappeared.

: 31 :

De Merane Preti filia

1 Meran, dicit Leontius, filia fuit Preti et Anthie filie Anphianaste, que cum venationibus dedita Dianam per nemora sequeretur, a Iove visa atque dilecta est, et ab eo Diane sumpta ymagine, viciata. Que tandem cum ob pudorem patrati sceleris, et timens ne iterum deciperetur, vocanti eam Diane obsequi noluit, et ob id Diana commota illam sagittis occidit.

2 Hanc dicit Paulus Stenoboe fuisse filiam sicut et relique, et post susceptam sanitatem obsecuturam Diane venisse. Qua fictione dicit idem Leontius monemur, ypocritas sepe credulos dolis in eam, quam dissuadent, deduxisse perniciem, a qua, dum verax homo aliquando lapsos relevare conatur, decepti semel et omnia timentes, increduli facti, oblatam respuentes salutem, in mortem perpetuam dilabuntur.

: 32 :

De Acrisio Abantis filio, qui genuit
Danem matrem Persei

1 Acrisius Abantis fuit filius, ut dicit Lactantius et, ut Eusebius in libro *Temporum* scribit, Preto fratri successit in regno. Hic, ut idem Lactantius asserit, nec ab hoc discrepat Servius, unicam habens filiam Danem, ab oraculo in responsis habuit, se manu eius, qui ex

: 31 :

On Maera, daughter of Proetus

Maera, Leontius says, was the daughter of Proetus and Antaea,   1
daughter of Amphianaste. An avid hunter, she was following Diana through the woods, where Jupiter espied her and liked her, and, after he assumed the shape of Diana, defiled her. Shamed by the crime that was committed and fearing that she would be deceived again, Maera refused to obey Diana when she called her, and on account of this the angry Diana killed her with arrows.

Paul says she was the daughter of Stheneboea, like the others,   2
and that after recovering her sanity she became a follower of Diana. From this fiction, says Leontius, we are warned that hypocrites are often duped by trickery into that ruin which they advise against; and although the honest man tries at some point to restore those who have fallen, deceived once and fearing everything, made incredulous, disdaining help when it is offered, they slip away into perpetual death.

: 32 :

On Acrisius, son of Abas, who fathered Danae,[102] mother of Perseus

Acrisius was the son of Abas, as Lactantius[103] says, and, as Euse-   1
bius[104] writes in his *Chronicle*, succeeded his brother Proetus as king. As Lactantius asserts, nor does Servius[105] disagree, he had one daughter, Danae, and he received an oracular response that said he would die at the hands of him who was born from his

filia nasceretur, moriturum. Qui ad effugiendam prenuntiatam mortem, filiam in turri quadam[13] seposuit servarique iussit, ne quis homo ad eam posset accedere. Contigit igitur ut audita formositatis eius fama, illam concupisceret Juppiter, qui, cum ad eam accessum alium non videret, versus in auri guttam ex tegulis in

2 gremium eius se cadere permisit, et sic pregnans effecta est. Quod egre ferens Acrisius eam capi iussit, et in arcam poni atque in mari proici. Quod cum ministri fecissent, in litus usque Apulum arca delata est, et casu a piscatore capta, in qua cum comperisset Danem et parvulum filium quem enixa fuerat, eam ad Pylumnum regem detulit. Qui cum genus eius cognovisset et patriam, illam libenter sibi coniugio copulavit. Filius autem eius, cui Perseus nomen fuit, cum excrevisset et Gorgoni caput abstulisset, in Argos veniens Acrisium transmutavit in saxum.

3 Que quidem permutatio secundum Eusebium sonat, quod cum regnasset Acrisius apud Argos annis XXXI a Perseo nepote suo non sponte tamen occisus est, et in lapidem, id est in frigiditatem perpetuam, versus. Quod autem fictionis superset, infra ubi de Dane declarabitur.

: 33 :

De Dane filia Acrisii[14]

1 Danes Acrisii filia, ut supra proximo dictum est, in mare pregnans a patre demissa, cum in Apuliam impulsa venisset, Pylumno regi Apulo nupsit, et inde ad Rutulos abiere, et constructa ibidem Ardea civitate, Daunum Pylumno peperit. Sane quod supra omissum est, Iovem aurum fluxisse per tegulas intelligendum est auro pudi-

daughter. To avoid this preordained death, he isolated his daughter in a certain tower and ordered her to be guarded so that no man could come near her. But it happened that Jupiter, having heard of the fame of her beauty, desired her and, not seeing any way to reach her, turned himself into a drop of gold and allowed himself to fall from the roof into her lap, thus making her pregnant. Disturbed at this, Acrisius ordered that she be taken, put 2 into a box, and thrown into the sea. His attendants did this, and the box was carried to the shore of Apulia, where it was by chance recovered by a fisherman. Inside he found Danae and a small child to whom she had given birth, and the fisherman took her to King Pilumnus. When the king learned of her family and homeland, he gladly made her his wife. When her son, whose name was Perseus, had grown up and beheaded the Gorgon, he came to Argos and turned Acrisius into stone.

This transformation, according to Eusebius,[106] means that after 3 Acrisius had reigned in Argos for thirty-one years, he was involuntarily killed by his grandson Perseus, and turned into stone, that is, into perpetual frigidity. The rest of the story will be described below in the discussion about Danae.

∶ 33 ∶

On Danae, daughter of Acrisius

Danae, daughter of Acrisius, as was just said, pregnant, aban- 1 doned to the sea by her father, and propelled to Apulia, arrived and married Pilumnus, King of Apulia. Then they went to the Rutulians, and after the city of Ardea was constructed there, she bore Daunus to Pilumnus. What was omitted above, that Jupiter flowed as gold through the roof tiles, should be understood as a

citiam virginis viciatam, et cum non esset adultero iter permissum per ianuam, clam tectum conscendisse, et exinde se in thalamum virginis dimisisse.

2   Dicit tamen Theodontius quod cum Danes amaretur a Iove, et se ob timorem patris sciret perpetuo damnatam carceri, ut posset evadere et fugam arripere, occulte cum Iove auro concubitum mercata est, et parata navi et cum his quas potuit deferre divitiis, fugam arripuit pregnans ex Iove.

: 34 :

De Iasio Abantis filio, qui genuit Athlantam, Amphyonem et Thalaonem

1   Fuit, ut Theodontio placet, Iasius iste Abantis filius. De quo nisi quod sepissime inter Argivos reges numeratus est, et quod quosdam habuerit filios, nil legi.

: 35 :

De Athlanta filia Iasii et matre Parthenopei

1   Athlanta, ut dicit Lactantius et Theodontius, iunior fuit filiorum Iasii. Que cum speciosa virgo ex sociis esset Diane, ad aprum Calydonium perimendum una cum cetera Achaye nobilitate iuvenum a

maiden's chastity violated by gold, and since there was no way for the illicit lover to enter by the door, he furtively climbed to the roof and from there let himself down into the bedchamber of the maiden.

Theodontius, however, says that Danae had been loved by Jupiter and knew that fear of her father would condemn her to eternal imprisonment; thus, to escape and take flight, she secretly paid gold to lay with Jupiter, and, pregnant by Jupiter and having prepared a ship loaded with whatever riches she was could carry off, she took flight. 2

: 34 :

On Iasius, son of Abas, who fathered Atalanta, Amphion, and Talaus

Iasius, according to Theodontius, was the son of Abas. I have not read anything about him except that he is usually numbered among the Argive kings and had some children. 1

: 35 :

On Atalanta, daughter of Iasius and mother of Parthenopeus

Atalanta, as Lactantius[107] and Theodontius say, was the younger of Iasius' children. When she was an attractive maiden and one of Diana's companions, she came along with the rest of the noble Achaean youths summoned by Meleager to kill the Calydonian 1

Meleagro vocata venit, et in venatione prima aprum sagitta percussit, et ob suam formositatem a Meleagro dilecta; occisa belua ab ea eiusdem honorari capite meruit, ex quo eius in amicitiam venit et amplexus ipsius passa, ei Parthenopeum peperit.

: 36 :

De Amphyone Iasii filio, qui genuit Clorim

1 Amphion, alter ab illo qui Thebas clausit muro, filius fuit Iasii et regnavit, ut dicit Leontius, in Orcomeno Minyo et in Pylo, vocatus alias Argus, cui unica fuit filia nomine Cloris.

: 37 :

De Clori filia Amphyonis et Nelei coniuge

1 Cloris, ut supra dictum est, filia fuit Amphionis et, ut in *Odyssea* testatur Homerus, Neleo nupsit, eique peperit Nestorem et alios plures filios.

boar; in that hunt she shot the first arrow that struck the boar, and captured by her beauty, Meleager fell in love with her; when the beast was killed, she merited the honor of being given its head, and for this reason she befriended Meleager, endured his embraces, and produced Parthenopeus.

: 36 :

On Amphion, son of Iasius, who fathered Chloris

Amphion, a different Amphion from the one who encircled 1
Thebes with its wall,[108] was the son of Iasius and ruled, as says Leontius, in Minyan Orchomenus and in Pylos. Elsewhere he was called Argus, and he had one daughter whose name was Chloris.

: 37 :

On Chloris, daughter of Amphion and wife of Neleus

Chloris, as said above, was the daughter of Amphion, and, as 1
Homer[109] bears witness in the Odyssey, married Neleus and bore him Nestor and many other children.

: 38 :

De Thalaone Jasii filio, qui genuit Euridicem, Flegeum et Adrastum

1 Thalaon, dicit Paulus, filius fuit Iasii, et apud Argos regnavit. Quod quidem, iudicio meo, sane intelligendum est dum huiusmodi homines reges appellant veteres. Nam, cum in catalogo regum non reperiantur, existimandum est eos de stirpe regia fuisse, et aliquam regni portiunculam tenuisse, et appellatos reges magis ob decus stirpis, quam ob possessum a talibus regnum. Ex quibus Thalaonem hunc et Amphyonem et Jasium puto.

: 39 :

De Euridice Thalaonis ⟨filia⟩ et Amphyarai coniuge

1 Euridices, ut asserit Theodontius, fuit filia Thalaonis, et Amphyarao vati iuncta coniugio, cui peperit Amphylocum et Almeonem. Cumque Adrastus Polynicis generi sui causam adversus Ethyoclem et Thebanos sumpsisset bellumque pararet, vidissetque Amphyaraus oraculi responso se non rediturum si iret in bellum, latibulum 2 petiit, uxorique sue tantum suas patefecit latebras. Qui cum ab Adrasto aliisque quereretur, nec comperiretur usquam, contigit ut videret Euridices Argie coniugi Polynicis monile, quondam a Vulcano donatum Hermioni coniugi Cadmi, illudque desideraret diceretque Argie, si monile illud illi concederet, se ostensuram

: 38 :

On Talaus, son of Iasius, who fathered Eriphyle,[110] Phlegeus, and Adrastus

Talaus, says Paul, was the son of Iasius, and he ruled in Argos. In my judgment, however, we must understand that the ancients called men of this sort kings. Although they are not found in the catalogue of kings, we must assume they were of royal lineage, held some small portion of the kingdom, and were called kings rather out of respect for their lineage which entitled them to their possession of the kingdom. I think this Talaus, Amphion, and Iasius were of this sort.

: 39 :

On Eriphyle, wife of Talaus and Amphiaraus

Eriphyle, as Theodontius asserts, was the daughter of Talaus, and, by her husband, the seer Amphiaraus, she gave birth to Amphilochus and Alcmeon.[111] After Adrastus embraced the cause of his son-in-law Polynices against Eteocles and the Thebans and was preparing for war, Amphiaraus, because an oracular response revealed to him that he would not return if he went to war, sought a hiding place and revealed the location of this hiding place only to his wife. When Adrastus and others were looking for him and could not find him, it happened that Eriphyle saw the necklace of Argia, wife of Polynices, which was once given by Vulcan to Hermione, wife of Cadmus, and desired it; she said to Argia that if she would give her that necklace she would expose the where-

3 Amphyaraum, et sic factum est. Quam ob rem in bellum vadens
Amphyaraus a terra absorptus est. Euridices autem postea ab Al-
meone filio, cui vadens Amphyaraus vindictam sue mortis iniunxe-
rat, occisa est.

: 40 :

De Flegeo filio Thalaonis

1 Flegeus, ut dicit Theodontius, filius fuit Thalaonis, et iuvenis moriens, nil memoratu dignum reliquit.

: 41 :

De Adrasto rege filio Thalaonis, qui genit Deyphylem et Argiam

1 Adrastus Argivorum rex, ut ait Lactantius, fuit filius Thalaonis et
Eurimones, cui cum due essent filie Deyphyles et Argia, audissetque ab oraculo se nuptui daturum alteram apro, alteram leoni,
circa futurum infortunium filiarum affligebatur, et ecce casu factum est, ut Polynices Thebanus ex composito exul intempesta
nocte Argos appelleret, imbresque fugiens regiam subintraret por-
2 ticum. Nec mora et Tydeus, ob homicidium Calydoniam fugiens,
ibidem deveniret, et in certamen post iurgium hospitii causa
consurgerent, quam ob rem percitus senex Adrastus ad eos descendit et verbis et autoritate sua iuvenum iras composuit eosque de-

abouts of Amphiaraus, and that is what happened. Amphiaraus   3
went to war because of this and was swallowed by the earth. Afterward Eriphyle was killed by her son Alcmeon, whom Amphiaraus
had enjoined to avenge his death.

: 40 :

On Phlegeus, son of Talaus

Phlegeus, as Theodontius says, was the son of Talaus, and dying   1
young, he left nothing behind worthy of memory.

: 41 :

On Adrastus, king and son of Talaus, who fathered Deiphyle and Argia

Adrastus, king of the Argives, as Lactantius[112] says, was the son of   1
Talaus and Eurynome. Because he had two daughters, Deiphyle
and Argia, and had heard from an oracle that he would give one of
them in marriage to a boar, the other to a lion, he was devastated
by the unfortunate prospects for them both. But by chance it happened one stormy night that Polynices the Theban put ashore at
Argos for his prearranged annual exile, and to escape the rain he
entered the portico of the royal palace. Not much later Tydeus ar-   2
rived in Argos as well, fleeing Calydonia on account of a homicide.
After a quarrel about the hospitality accorded them became a
fight, old King Adrastus thought it best to come down and use
words and his authority to soothe their youthful anger, and he

duxit in regiam. Et cum vidisset alterum pelle leonis tectum, Polynicem scilicet, qui regius iuvenis insigne illud in testimonium
virtutis Thebani Herculis ferebat, et alterum cute apri, qui ob occisum a Meleagro patruo aprum[15] in decus prolis ea tectus incede-
bat, responsi ambiguitate intellecta, cognovit hos sibi generos esse
3 transmissos. Quos postquam novit, affinitate contentus, Tydeo
Deyphylem et Polynici Argiam dedit uxores. Et cum iuxta promis-
sum regnum ab Ethyocle Polynici non restitueretur, contractis viribus, adversus Thebanos bellum movit, et cum iam duces omnes
sui morte occubuissent cecidissentque mutuis vulneribus Polynices
et Ethyocles, ipse in fugam versus repetiit Argos, nec quis illi fuerit
finis inveni.

: 42 :

De Deyphyle Adrasti filia et Tydei coniuge

1 Deyphyles, ut dicit Statius, filia fuit Adrasti regis et coniunx Tydei
Calydonii, cui peperit Dyomedem.

: 43 :

De Argia Adrasti filia et coniuge Polynicis

1 Argia, secundum Statium, Adrasti regis fuit filia et Polynicis coniunx, que cum illi peperisset Thessandrum audissetque eum a

brought them back to the royal palace. When he saw that the one was wearing a lion skin, namely Polynices, who as a royal youth wore that famous skin as evidence of the valor of Theban Hercules, and that the other arrived wearing the skin of a boar, which he wore as an ancestral honor for the boar killed by his uncle Meleager, understanding the ambiguity of the oracular response, he recognized that they had been sent to him to be his sons-in-law. Once he got to know them and felt satisfied with the relation- 3 ships, he gave as wives Deiphyle to Tydeus and Argia to Polynices. When contrary to their agreement Eteocles did not restore Polynices to the throne, Adrastus assembled his forces and made war against the Thebans; and when all the leaders fell to their deaths and Polynices and Eteocles died of reciprocal wounds, he fled and returned to Argos. I have not found to what end he came.

꞉ 42 ꞉

On Deiphyle, daughter of Adrastus and wife of Tydeus

Deiphyle, as Statius[113] says, was the daughter of King Adrastus 1 and wife of the Calydonian Tydeus, to whom she bore Diomedes.

꞉ 43 ꞉

On Argia, daughter of Adrastus and wife of Polynices

Argia, according to Statius,[114] was the daughter of King Adrastus 1 and wife of Polynices. When she had given birth to his son Ther-

fratre occisum, ab Argo Thebas veniens, ut extremas lacrimas et officium funerale cadaveri viri impenderet, eo quod id faceret adversus imperium Creontis, una cum Antigona Polynicis sorore capta et, iussu Creontis, occisa est.

: 44 :

De Agenore III° Beli Prisci filio, qui genuit VII filios, quorum prima Taygeta, II^us Polydorus, III^us Cilix, IIII^us Phenix, V^a Europa, VI^us Cadmus, VII^us Labdacus

1 Post explicatas successiones Danai et Egysti filii Beli Prisci, ad ampliorem prolem Agenoris Phenicum regis, eiusdem Beli filii, ut Theodontius dicit et Paulus, stilus revocandus est. Et esto a predictis dicatur quod hic Agenor fuerit Beli filius, sunt tamen qui dicant eum Beli fuisse filium, sed non Egyptii, quin imo Phenicis, avumque huius Agenoris, Agenorem etiam nuncupatum, eumque Agenorem primum, Ninia apud Assyrios regnante, cum ingenti multitudine peste coactum patrias sedes, quasi circa extremam meridionalem Egyptum habuerat, liquisse, et duce peregrinationis Nylo in litus Syriacum devenisse navibus, et illud, pulsis veteribus incolis, occupasse, ibique regnasse sibique Belum filium successorem liquisse, quem huius Agenoris patrem volunt; alii vero nepotem ex Phenice filio.

sander and heard that Polynices had been killed by his brother, she went from Argos to Thebes so she could cry final tears over her husband and perform funeral duties for his corpse. Because she did that contrary to the orders of Creon, she was captured along with Antigone, Polynices' sister, and executed by Creon's order.

∶ 44 ∶

On Agenor, third son of Belus Priscus, who fathered seven children: first Taygeta, second Polydorus, third Cilix, fourth Phoenix, fifth Europa, sixth Cadmus, seventh Labdacus

Now that I have explicated the lineages of Danaus and Egyptus,   1
sons of Belus Priscus, I must redirect my pen for the more extensive progeny of Agenor, king of the Phoenicians, son of the same Belus, as Theodontius and Paul say. But although the aforementioned say that this Agenor was the son of Belus, there are nonetheless those who say that he was the son of Belus—not the Egyptian one but rather the Phoenician one, grandfather of this Agenor, also named Agenor. They say that at the time when Ninus was ruling among the Assyrians, this first Agenor was forced by a plague to leave his ancestral territories in the extreme south of Egypt with a great multitude; with Nilus as the leader of the migration he sailed to the shores of Syria, and, after defeating its ancestral inhabitants, occupied it and ruled there, leaving as successor his son Belus, whom they want to call the father of this Agenor. Others say he was his nephew by his son Phoenix.

2   Ex quibus comprehendi potest a similitudine nominis et forsan
temporis exortum errorem, ut qui Beli Syriaci filius fuerit, creditus
Beli Egyptiaci. Sed ex quocumque Belo natus sit, mens michi est
hic Theodontii et Pauli opinionem sequi, cum de superiori non
satis certus appareat autor. Hunc igitur dicunt ex Egypto in litus
Syrium abiisse et Phenicibus imperasse et amplissima atque gene-
rosa prole claruisse.

: 45 :

De Taygeta, prima Agenoris filia

1   Taygetam dicit Ditis Cretensis Agenoris fuisse filiam, eamque Iovi
placuisse et in eius venisse concubitum, et cum concepisset, Lacedemonem peperisse, dato sint qui eum ex Semele natum dicant.

: 46 :

De Polydoro, II° Agenoris filio

1   Polydorus ut testatur Lactantius, filius fuit Agenoris, de quo preter nudum nomen haberi nil puto, esto Theodontius de isto le-
vem faciat mentionem, sed longe antiquiorem isto Agenore illum
dicit.

From this we can understand that because of the similarity of   2
names there may also be a mistake in the time period, so that he
who was the son of the Syrian Belus was believed to be the son of
the Egyptian Belus. But whichever Belus was his father, I have a
mind here to follow the opinion of Theodontius and Paul, since
no author is sufficiently clear about the former. And so they say
that he left Egypt for the Syrian shores, ruled the Phoenicians,
and was famous for his numerous and noble offspring.

: 45 :

On Taygeta, first child of Agenor

Dictys[115] of Crete says that Taygeta was the daughter of Agenor,   1
that she was pleasing to Jupiter and had intercourse with him, and
that after she conceived she gave birth to Lacedaemon, although
there are those who say he was born from Semele.

: 46 :

On Polydorus, second child of Agenor

Polydorus, as Lactantius[116] bears witness, was the son of Agenor. I   1
think nothing is known about him other than simply his name.
Although Theodontius makes a brief mention of him, he says that
he was much more ancient than this Agenor.

: 47 :

De Cilice, III° Agenoris filio qui genuit
Lampsacium et Pygmalionem et Pyrodem[16]

1 Cilix, secundum Lactantium, filius fuit Agenoris. Hunc dicit
Theodontius hominem acris ingenii et robusti corporis fuisse, et
cum superiores sibi fratres sperneret et de successione regni etiam
desperaret, vilipenso superiorum iugo, parte copiarum sumpta,
sedes haud longe a suis sibi occupavit, et regionem a suo nomine
Ciliciam nuncupavit, ibique duos sibi filios superstites dereliquit,
2 Lampsacium scilicet et Pygmalionem. Sunt qui dicant provinciam
hanc a Cadmo occupatam antequam quesiturus Europam micteretur a patre, eamque postea a Cilice possessam, Cadmo non redeunte.

: 48 :

De Lampsacio Cilicis filio

1 Lampsacius, ut dicit Theodontius et post eum Paulus, filius fuit
Cilicis, eique successit in regno, nec ex eo aliud ulterius invenitur.

: 47 :

On Cilix, the third child of Agenor, who fathered Lampsacius, Pygmalion, and Pyrodes

Cilix, according to Lactantius,[117] was the son of Agenor. Theodon- 1
tius says he was a man with a keen mind and strong body, and
because he despised his older brothers and despaired about becoming king, holding in contempt the bond with his brothers and
taking part of their army, he occupied territories not very far away,
naming the region Cilicia after himself, leaving behind two sons
there, namely, Lampsacius and Pygmalion. There are those who 2
say that this province was occupied by Cadmus before he was sent
by his father to seek Europa, and that when Cadmus did not return, Cilix took possession.

: 48 :

On Lampsacius, son of Cilix

Lampsacius, as Theodontius says and Paul after him, was the son 1
of Cilix and succeeded him as king. Other than this I could not
find anything about him.

: 49 :

De Pygmalione, primo Cilicis filio et Cypriorum rege, qui genuit Paphum

1 Pygmalion, ut dicit Theodontius, filius fuit Cilicis, de quo refert, quod cum iuvenis esset, et gloria maiorum suorum, quos ad occiduum usque penetrasse et Affricum litus etiam occupasse audierat, infestaretur, collecta Cilicum manu, et convocatis ex Phenicibus classeque parata, in Cyprum tuam, serenissime regum, transvexit exercitum, et inde veteres Syros, qui ibidem, Agenoris vetustissimi viribus ex antiquis pulsi sedibus, confugerant, expulit et occupavit omnem atque tenuit insulam et regnavit in ea.

2 Sane, quod etiam testatur Ovidius in maiori volumine, cum ibi scelestissimas comperisset mulieres et omnino libidini obsequentes, vicio offensus vitam celibem ducere disposuerat. Attamen quia valebat ingenio et artificiosas haberet manus, finxere poete eum sibi ex candidissimo ebore femineam sculpsisse ymaginem, eamque iuxta desiderium suum lineamentis atque decore oris contraxisse

3 per omnia. In qua, cum ingeniosus homo et artem miraretur suam et venustatem ymaginis commendaret, in dilectionem eius incidit, et fervore maximo cupiebat eam esse feminam oravitque Venerem, ea tempestate celeberrimam insule deam, ut animaret eandem et suorum faceret amorum sensibilem, nec effectu caruere preces: femina vera facta est. Quod advertens Pygmalion, gaudio plenus, quoniam voti compos esset, eius usus est concubitu, et evestigio gravida facta est, eique peperit filium quem Paphum ipse postea nominavit, eumque sibi morienti reliquit heredem.

∶ 49 ∶

On Pygmalion, first son of Cilix and king of the Cypriots, who fathered Paphos

Pygmalion, as Theodontius says, was the son of Cilix. He says   1
about him that when he was young he was driven by the glory of
his ancestors, whom he had heard had advanced westward and occupied even the shores of Africa, so he assembled a Cilician army,
mustered the Phoenicians, prepared a fleet, and brought his forces
to your Cyprus, most serene King; then he expelled the ancient
Syrians, who had fled there after being driven from their ancient
territories by the forces of the most ancient Agenor, and he occupied, held, and ruled the entire island.

Of course, as also Ovid[118] testifies in his greater work, because   2
he found the women there to be very wicked and given completely
to lust, offended by their vice he decided to lead a celibate life. But
because he had great talent and skillful hands, the poets made up
the story that he sculpted for himself the likeness of a woman
from the whitest ivory, and that he concentrated exclusively on its
body contours and the beauty of its face, his own desire being his
guide. In the process of doing so, since a talented man admires his   3
own art and imparts charm to his creations, he fell in love with it
and passionately desired her to become a woman, so he prayed to
Venus, the goddess who at that time was so renowned on island,
to make her come to life and feel his love. His prayers were not
without effect: she was made into a real woman. When Pygmalion
saw this, full of joy at the fulfillment of his desire, he had intercourse with her, and she immediately became pregnant and bore
him a son whom he later named Paphos; upon his death Pygmalion left him as his heir.

4 Nunc quid sibi eburnea velit ymago ingenio potius poetico quam viri artificio fabrefacta videndum est. Arbitror enim, cum Pygmalioni suspecta provectarum etate virginum pudicitia esset, eum sibi virgunculam elegisse etate suspicione carentem, candore atque mollitie ebori similem, quam cum suis aptam fecisset moribus, excrevit ante etatem puellule concupiscentia eius, cepitque desiderare atque exposcere precibus ut cito efficeretur matura viro, qua tandem facta, in votum devenit suum.

: 50 :

De Papho Pygmalionis filio, qui genuit Cynaram

1 Paphus, ut dicit Theodontius, filius fuit Pygmalionis ex eburnea matre. Qui cum Pygmalioni successisset in regno, Cyprum insulam Paphum ex suo nomine nuncupavit. Paulus autem dicit Paphum oppidum ab eo tantum constructum et de suo nomine no-
2 minatum. Quod quidem Veneri sacrum esse voluit, constructo in eodem illi templo et ara, cui thure solo diu sacrificatum est.

: 51 :

De Cynara filio Paphi, qui genuit Myrram
et ex Myrra Adonem

1 Cynara filius fuit Paphi, prout ostendit Ovidius dum dicit:

Editus hac ille est, qui, si sine prole fuisset,
inter felices Cynaras potuisset haberi.

Now we must look at the meaning of an ivory image which was   4
made by poetic skill rather than manual artifice. I think that since
Pygmalion suspected the purity of virgins of advanced age, he
chose for himself a young virgin whose age was above suspicion
and was similar, in her whiteness and tenderness, to ivory, and he
reshaped her behavior to his liking. But his desire increased before
the age of the girl, and he began to desire her and pray so that she
would quickly become mature enough for a husband, and once
that happened, he got his wish.

: 50 :

On Paphos, son of Pygmalion, who fathered Cinyras

Paphos, as Theodontius says, was the son of Pygmalion by an   1
ivory mother. When he succeeded Pygmalion as king, he named
the island of Cyprus Paphos after himself. But Paul says that he
constructed only a city named after himself. He wanted this city   2
to be sacred to Venus, and after constructing a temple and an altar
there, he sacrificed to her for a long time with only incense.

: 51 :

On Cinyras, son of Paphos, who fathered Myrrha, and from Myrrha Adonis

Cinyras was the son of Paphos, as Ovid reveals when he says:[119]   1

He was born here, and if he had been without issue,
Cinyras could have been counted among the favored.

Est autem hic alter ab illo Cynara, qui Assyriorum rex dicitur in
2 lapidem versus, flendo infortunia filiarum. Ex hoc autem Cynara
Cyprio preter scelus unum non habemus. Nam, ut ipse recitat
Ovidius, huic ex coniuge filia fuit nomine Myrra, que cum formosa esset ac etiam matura viro, preter debitum patrem amavit et
nutricis sue opere, dum mater eius sacra Cereris celebraret, in quibus oportebat per novem dies a contactu viri abstinere, eius concubitu potita est, in quo pregnans effecta, illi Adon filius natus est.

: 52 :

De Myrra filia Cynare et matre Adonis

1 Myrram, ut supra patet, Cynare regis filiam dicit fuisse Ovidius, et
cum eum nephasto adamasset amore, opere nutricis sue, eius incognita nocte[17] habuisse concubitum. Fulgentius tamen dicit eam
cum Cynara, postquam illum ebrium effecisset, habuisse concubitum. Que ex nephario concubitu pregnans facta, cum illam vellet
noscere Cynara novissetque filiam, dolore percitus eam secutus
2 occidere voluit. Quidam dicunt eam in Sabeos fugisse, ad quos
usque secutus Cynara, cum illam gladio percussisset, ex vulnere
conceptum filium erupisse. Ovidius tamen dicit eam miseratione
deorum apud Sabeos in arborem sui nominis versam et, calore
solis aperto cortice, filium emisisse, quem nynphe liquoribus un-
xere maternis.
3   Figmento huic arbitror causam dedisse nomen arboris, que
apud Sabeos vocatur Myrra, guttas emictens, solis percussa radiis.
Ex quibus pigmentum conficitur quod *adon* vocant, quod Latine

However, he is different from the Cinyras who as king of the Assyrians was said to have been turned into stone while weeping for
his daughters' misfortune. Of this Cyprian Cinyras we know noth-   2
ing other than his one crime, for, as Ovid[120] recites, he and his
wife had a daughter named Myrrha, who was beautiful and also of
marriageable age. She loved her father beyond what was proper
and, with the help of her nurse, while her mother was celebrating
sacrifices to Ceres, during which she had to abstain from contact
with her husband for nine days, she had intercourse with him,
became pregnant by him, and gave birth to a son, Adonis.

: 52 :

On Myrrha, daughter of Cinyras and mother of Adonis

As is clear from the preceding, Ovid[121] says that Myrrha was the   1
daughter of King Cinyras, and because she lusted after an illicit
love affair with him, with the help of her nurse she had intercourse
at night without being recognized. Fulgentius[122] says that she had
intercourse with Cinyras after she made him drunk. Made pregnant from this illicit intercourse, she wanted Cinyras to know, and
when he did find out he was struck with remorse and went after
her to kill her. Some say that she fled to Sheba and that Cinyras   2
followed her there, and when he struck her with his sword her son
burst forth from the wound. Ovid,[123] however, says that the gods
pitied her and at Sheba turned her into a tree called by her name
and, when its bark opened from the heat of the sun, she exuded a
son, whom the nymphs anointed with his mother's fluids.

I think this fabrication begins with the name of the tree which   3
is called *myrrha* in Sheba; it drips sap when struck by the rays of
the sun. From this comes a pigment which they call *adon*, which

'suave' sonat, est enim suavissimi odoris, et ut videtur velle Petronius Arbiter, plurimum libidini conferens, adeo ut asserat se ad libidinis incrementum mirrinum potasse poculum.

4   Verum Fulgentius, ut in pluribus longe altius sentiens, circa hoc dicit, myrram arborem in Yndia esse et solis caloribus cremari, et quia solem patrem omnium rerum dicebant, ideo patrem Myrram amasse dictum, et cum sol ferventius illam calefaceret, eam rages ex rimis corticis emictere et sic, a patre vulnerata, Adonem, id est suavitatem odoris, emisisse.

: 53 :

De Adone filio et nepote Cynare

1   Adon Cynere regis avi sui et Myrre sororis fuit filius, ut longo carmine, in maiori volumine, testatur Ovidius. De quo talem ipse idem recitat fabulam. Dicit enim quod cum formosissimus evasisset iuvenis, a Venere casu percussa a filio summe dilectus est; que dum illum maxima delectatione sua per silvas sequeretur et nemora eiusque uteretur amplexibus, sepius eum monuit, ut sibi ab

2   armatis beluis caveret et sequeretur inermes. Verum die quadam male verborum Veneris memor, in aprum irruens ab eo occisus est. Quem Venus flevit amare, et in florem convertit purpureum.

Hoc figmentum Macrobius in libro *Saturnaliorum* conatur enodare mirabili ratione. Dicit enim Adonem solem esse, quo nil pulchrius et eam terre partem quam inhabitamus, superius scilicet hemisperium, Venerem esse, cum que in inferiori est hemisperio a

means "sweet," for it has the sweetest aroma. Petronius Arbiter[124] seemed to want it very much to assist in matters of passion, so much so that he claims that he drank a cup of myrrh to enhance his ardor.

Fulgentius, however, who in most matters has far loftier 4 thoughts, says about this that myrrh is a tree in India which burns from the heat of the sun, and because they used to say that the sun is the father of all things, so it is said that Myrrha loved her father, and that when the sun's intensity heats up the tree, it emits a liquid substance from the cracks in its bark and so, wounded by her father, she produces Adonis, that is, a sweetness of aroma.

: 53 :

On Adonis, son and grandson of Cinyras

Adonis was the son of his grandfather, King Cinyras, and his sis- 1 ter Myrrha, as Ovid[125] testifies in many verses of his greater book. He tells the following fable about him. He says that since he had grown up to be a very handsome young man, he was greatly loved by Venus, who was accidentally struck by her son's arrows. And while with the greatest delight she pursued him through the forests and woods and enjoyed his embraces, she often warned him to avoid armed beasts and to pursue defenseless ones. But one day, 2 not properly mindful of Venus' words, Adonis attacked a boar and was killed. Venus wept bitter tears and transformed him into a purple flower.

Macrobius[126] in his *Saturnalia* endeavored to unravel this fabrication with a wonderful explanation. He said that Adonis was the sun—nothing is more beautiful than the sun—and that the part of the earth we inhabit, that is, the upper hemisphere, is Venus,

3 physicis Proserpina appellata sit. Et sic apud Assyrios et Phenices, quos penes et Veneris et Adonis ingens fuit religio,[18] tunc Venus cum Adone a se dilecto delectatur, cum circa superius hemisperium sol ampliori circumflectitur ambitu et inde ornatior, quia flores frondes et fructus eo tempore terra producit. Dum vero breviores circumducit circulos de necessitate maiores apud inferius hemisperium agit, et sic autumnus et hyemps imbribus assiduis terram decore suo privatam lutosam faciunt, quo aper, qui hispidum animal est, delectatur, et sic ab apro, id est ab ea temporis qualitate qua delectatur aper, Adon, id est sol, terre, id est Veneri, sublatus videtur, et inde Venus luctuosa efficitur.

4 Quod autem sit Adon transformatus in florem, ob id fictum puto, ut nostri decoris brevitas ostendatur: mane quidem purpureus est, sero languens pallensque marcidus efficitur; sic et nostra humanitas mane, id est iuventutis tempore, florens et splendida est, sero autem, id est senectutis evo, pallemus et in tenebras mortis ruimus. Sane quicquid Assyrii sentiant vel Macrobius, hystoria tamen videtur sentire, et Tullius testatur ubi *De naturis deorum* Venerem fuisse Syria Cyproque conceptam, id est ex Syro homine et Cypria muliere, quam Astarcem vocavere Syri, eamque Adoni nupsisse, et ut dicit Lactantius in libro *Divinarum institutionum*, in *Sacra hystoria* continetur hanc meretriciam instituisse artem et stuprum mulieribus suasisse, et ut vulgato corpore questum facerent, et hoc ideo dicit imperasse, ne sola preter alias mulieres impudica et virorum appetens videretur.

5 Ex quo consecutum est et longis perseveratum temporibus, ut Phenices de prostitutione filiarum donarent antequam eas iunge-

while that which is in the lower hemisphere the natural scientists call Proserpina. And so for the Assyrians and Phoenicians, for 3 whom the reverence for Venus and Adonis was considerable, Venus and Adonis requite their love for each other just as the sun circles around the upper hemisphere in a wider orbit and is thereby more richly endowed because in that season the earth produces flowers, leaves, and fruits. When it orbits in shorter circles, it necessarily becomes more intense in the lower hemisphere, and so the autumn and winter with their relentless rains make the earth muddy and deprive it of its beauty; the boar, a bristly animal, delights in this, and so by the boar, that is, by the quality of season in which the boar delights, Adonis, that is, the sun, seems to be deprived of the earth, that is, of Venus, and therefore Venus becomes mournful.

That Adonis is transformed into a flower I think was invented 4 so that it would demonstrate the brevity of our beauty: in the early morning it is purple, but languishing and fading later it becomes withered; so also our humanity in the morning, that is, in the time of youth, is in bloom and splendid, but later, that is, in old age, we grow pale and rush into the darkness of death. In fact, what the Assyrians or even Macrobius thought, history seems to think as well, and Cicero[127] bears witness to the same in his *On the Nature of the Gods:* Venus was born in Syria and Cyprus, that is, from a Syrian man and a Cypriot woman, whom the Syrians call Astarte. She married Adonis, and as Lactantius[128] says in his *Divine Institutions,* the *Sacred History* contains the report that she instituted the practice of prostitution and persuaded women to engage in illicit sexual intercourse so they would make a profit from their prostituted bodies and also reports that she commanded this so that she would not seem to be the only woman who was shameless and eager for men.

As a long-lasting consequence of this, the Phoenicians gave 5 their daughters over to prostitution before they married them off,

rent viris, ut in libro *De civitate Dei* testatur Augustinus, et Iustinus
in *Epythoma* Pompeii Trogi, ubi Didonem LXX virgines in litore
Cyprio, que in questum venerant, rapuisse demonstrat. Fuit igitur
Adon rex Cypri et Veneris maritus, quem ego etiam seu ab apro
seu alia nece Veneri subtractum reor, eo quod ad imitationem la-
crimarum eius veteres anniversario plangore consueverint Adonis
interitum flere. Quos[19] in suis visionibus increpat Ysaias.

: 54 :

De[20] Pyrode Cilicis filio

1 Pyrodes, ut Plinius asserit, in libro *Naturalis hystorie*, filius fuit Cilicis, ex quo etsi nil aliud habeamus, eodem Plinio teste, saltem
habemus eundem primo ignem ex silice excussisse.

: 55 :

De Phenice, IIII° Agenoris filio,
qui genuit Phylistenem et Belum

1 Phenix, ut dicit Lactantius, filius fuit Agenoris. Hunc dicit Eusebius in libro *Temporum*, regnante Argivis Danao, una cum Cadmo
fratre a Thebis Egyptiis venisse in Syriam, et apud Tyrum et Sydonem imperasse, quod quidem fuisse potuit circa annum mundi
IIDCCXLVI; post paululum autem dicit eum anno primo Lyncei regis Bithiniam condidisse, que prius Mariandina vocabatur.

as Augustine[129] bears witness in his *City of God*, and Justin[130] in his *Epitome* of Pompeius Trogus, where he describes how on the Cypriot shore Dido had taken away seventy virgins who had come for profit. There was therefore an Adonis, King of Cyprus and husband of Venus, who I think was taken from Venus by a boar or some other death, because in imitation of her tears the ancients had a annual custom of lamenting the death of Adonis. Isaiah[131] scorns them in his visions.

: 54 :

On Pyrodes, son of Cilix

Pyrodes, as Pliny[132] asserts in his *Natural History*, was the son of   1
Cilix. If we knew nothing else about him, at least we would know, again with Pliny bearing witness, that he was the first to strike fire from flint.

: 55 :

On Phoenix, fourth child of Agenor,
who fathered Philistine and Belus

Phoenix, as Lactantius[133] says, was the son of Agenor. Eusebius[134]   1
in his *Chronicle* says that when Danaus was ruling the Argives he came with his brother Cadmus from Egyptian Thebes to Syria and ruled at Tyre and Sidon, which indeed could have happened around world year 3746; a little afterward he says that in the first year of the reign of Lynceus he founded Bithynia, which was ear-

2 Quod fuit anno mundi ĪĪĪDCCLXXVIIII. Huius tamen adventus in Syriam non convenit cum dictis supra, ubi de Agenore a Theodontio et etiam ab Ovidio discrepat, qui videtur velle Agenorem venisse non Phenicem, cum Cadmum missum ad perquirendam Europam ab Agenore, non a Phenice describat. Sed has ego varietates ultro concordare volentibus linquam et de Phenice quid compererim prosequar.

3 Hunc autem arteficiosum fuisse hominem ostendit Eusebius, eo quod primus quasdam licteras seu licterarum caracteres Phenicibus dederit. Deinde ad scribendum eas instituisse vermiculum, unde et color ille pheniceus dictus est, credo ab inventore qui postea, mutata lictera, est puniceus appellatus.

: 56 :

De Phylistene filio Phenicis, qui genuit Syceum

1 Phylistenem dicit Theodontius filium fuisse Phenicis. Qui cum esset Herculis sacerdos, qui persanctissime a Phenicibus colebatur, videretque, Phenice patre mortuo, Belum fratrem natu maiorem regnare, relicto Syceo filio sacerdotio et copiarum parte sumpta, naves conscendit et post multos casus cum Herculis columnas cursu superasset, ibidem in litore occeani sedes assumpsit perpetuas, condita civitate quam Gades vocavere sui et, ne sacerdotium abdicasse videretur, omnino templum ibidem constituit Herculi et sacra omnia ritu Tyrio innovavit.

lier called Mariandina. That was in the world year 3779. Nevertheless, his arrival in Syria does not fit what was said above about Agenor. Eusebius differs from Theodontius and also Ovid[135] in that whereas Ovid claims that it was Agenor, not Phoenix who sent Cadmus to search for Europa, Eusebius seems to want it to have been Agenor, not Phoenix, who arrived in Syria. But I will leave these differences to those who want to reconcile them and continue with what I have found about Phoenix. 2

Eusebius explains that he was a skillful man because he first gave the Phoenicians some letters and their shapes. Then for writing them he made vermilion, whence that color is also called "phoenician" [*pheniceus*]; it is named, I believe, after the inventor of the color which later, with the letters changed, was called "punic" [*puniceus*]. 3

: 56 :

On Philistine, son of Phoenix, who fathered Sychaeus

Theodontius says that Philistine was the son of Phoenix. Since he was a priest of Hercules, who was worshipped very devotedly by the Phoenicians, and watched his older brother Belus rule after his father Phoenix died, he left the priesthood to his son Sychaeus and, loading a part of his fortune, sailed away on a few ships and had a number of encounters when their course took them beyond the pillars of Hercules. There on the shore of the ocean he established his permanent territory, built his city, which they called Gades, and, lest he seem to have abdicated his priesthood altogether, constructed a temple to Hercules there and reinstituted all the sacrifices with Tyrian rites. 1

: 57 :

De Syceo Phylistenis filio et Didonis viro

1 Syceus secundum Theodontium fuit filius Phylistenis, cui abeunte patre sacerdotium derelictum est, ut supra dicitur, quod a rege proximus erat honor. Hunc dicit Servius Sycarbam vocatum, esto eum Syceum semper Virgilius[21] vocet. Et Iustinus insuper illum vocat Acerbam.

2 Hic autem seu relictis seu aliunde quesitis thesauris, ut Theodontio placet, et reliquis copiosus factus plurimum, Belo mortuo, Elyssam filiam eius accepit uxorem, que postea Dido vocata est, quam precipue dilexit. Verum cum Pygmalion, Beli filius, patri successisset in regno, auri avidus, eius desideratis divitiis, clam illi tetendit insidias et incautum interemit.

: 58 :

De Belo Phenicis filio, qui genuit
Pygmalionem et Didonem et Annam

1 Belus qui et Mettes secundum Servium appellatus est, ut ait Theodontius, filius fuit Phenicis, vir bello et armis insignis adeo ut Cyprios litus Phenicum pyrratica infestantes subigeret, quod Virgilius in persona Didonis perfunctorie tangit dicens:

> Genitor tum Belus opimam
> vastabat Cyprum et victor dicione tenebat,

etc.

: 57 :

On Sychaeus, son of Philistine and husband of Dido

Sychaeus, according to Theodontius, was the son of Philistine. As 1
I said above, when his father departed the priesthood, which was
next to the kingship in honor, it was left to him. Servius[136] says he
was called Sicarbas, although Vergil[137] always calls him Sychaeus;
then again, Justin[138] calls him Acerbas.

Whether he inherited his treasure or acquired it from else- 2
where, as Theodontius thinks, it was added to the balance and he
became very wealthy. After Belus died Sychaeus took as his wife
Belus' daughter Elyssa, who afterward was called Dido and whom
he loved very much. But when Pygmalion, the son of Belus, succeeded his father to the throne, eager for gold and with his eyes on
Sychaeus' riches, he secretly planned an attack on him and, catch-
ing him unprepared, killed him.

: 58 :

On Belus, son of Phoenix, who fathered
Pygmalion, Dido, and Anna

Belus, who was also called Mettes, according to Servius,[139] was the 1
son of Phoenix, as Theodontius says, a man so accomplished in
war and arms that he subjugated the piratical Cypriots who were
harassing the Phoenician shores. Vergil touches upon this superfi-
cially in the persona of Dido, saying:[140]

Then father Belus fertile
Cyprus ravaged and as victor held it under his sway.

: 59 :

De Pygmalione filio Beli

1 Pygmalion, ut Thedontio placet, filius fuit Beli regis Tyri et, patre moriente, ut ait Iustinus, una cum sororibus Tyriis derelictus est.

2 Cui, adhuc puero, populus paternum tradidit regnum. Hic vero avarissimus, cum animum ad divitias Sycei patruelis sui iniecisset, illum dolo interemit. Hoc solum scelus ex rege isto nobis reliquit antiquitas.

: 60 :

De Didone filia Beli et coniuge Sycei

1 Dido precipuum matronalis pudicitie decus, ut Virgilio placet, Beli regis fuit filia. Hanc insignis forme virginem Tyrii, Belo mortuo, Acerbe seu Sycarbe vel Syceo Herculis sacerdoti dedere in

2 coniugem, qui ob avaritiam a Pygmalione occisus est. Hec autem post longa fratris mendacia in somniis a viro premonita, sumpto virili animo, pluribus ex his quibus sciebat Pygmalionem exosum clam in suam sententiam tractis, sumptis navibus fugam cepit, thesauris secum delatis, et cum in litus devenisset Affricum, ut placet etiam Tito Livio, mercata ab incolis suadentibus, ut ibidem sedem sumeret, tantum litoris quantum posset bovino corio occupare, illudque in cartam redactum et in frusta concisum occupavit plurimum, et ostensis sociis thesauris eisque animatis, civitatem

: 59 :

On Pygmalion, son of Belus

Pygmalion, according to Theodontius, was the son of Belus, King 1
of Tyre, and, when his father died, as Justin[141] says, he was left
alone with his Tyrian sisters. The people turned his paternal king- 2
dom over to him when he was still a youth. But he was extremely
avaricious, and because he coveted the riches of his cousin Sychaeus, he used treachery to kill him. Antiquity has left us only
the crime of this king.

: 60 :

On Dido, daughter of Belus and wife of Sychaeus

Dido, distinctive icon of matronly purity, was the daughter of 1
King Belus, according to Vergil.[142] When Belus died, the Tyrians
gave this maiden of celebrated beauty in marriage to Acerbas, or
Sicarbas, or Sychaeus the priest of Hercules, who was killed on
account of Pygmalion's avarice. But a long time afterward Dido 2
was warned by her husband in a dream about her brother's mendacity, adopted a manlike spirit, and brought over to her side several men whom she knew hated Pygmalion in secret. She took
several ships and fled, bringing the treasure with her. When she
arrived at the African shore, as Livy[143] also says, she bought land
from the local inhabitants, who proposed that she take as her territory there as much of the coast as she could cover with a cow's
hide. She reduced this to thin sheets, cut these into bits, and covered a great amount of territory, and then having displayed the

composuit, quam postea vocavere Cartaginem; arcem vero eius a bovino corio, quod sic vocitant, Byrsam nuncupavit.

3   Ad hanc accessisse Eneam profugum, vi tempestatis impulsum, et hospitio thoroque susceptum ab ea, Virgilio placet, eamque, discedente a se Enea, ob amoris impatientiam occisam. Verum Justinus et hystoriographi veteres aliter sentiunt. Dicit enim Iustinus eam a Musitanorum rege sub belli denuntiatione a principibus Cartaginensibus postulatam in coniugem, quod cum ipsa rescisset et sua se ante sententia ad omnem casum pro salute patrie damnasset, egre tulit, sed terminum impetravit infra quem se ad virum

4 promisit ituram. Qui cum venisset, constructo ingenti rogo in eminentiori civitatis parte, quasi Sycei placatura manes, illum conscendit, et astantibus civibus atque expectantibus quidnam factura esset, ipsa, educto quem clam gesserat cultro, dixit, 'Optimi cives ut vultis ad virum vado,' seque hoc dicto interemit, mortem potius eligens[22] quam pudicitiam maculare. Quod etiam longe aliud est a descriptione Maronis.

: 61 :

De Anna Beli regis filia

1 Anna filia fuit Beli, ut videtur placere Virgilio, qui illam sepissime sororem Didonis[23] appellat. Hec Didonis fuge comes fuit, quam postquam mortuam vidit et Cartaginem a Iarba rege occupatam, ut Ovidius dicit, ubi *De fastis*, ad Bathum regem Corise insule aufugit, vetusti hospitii confsa iure. Tandem sentiens quia Pygma-

treasure to her companions and inspiring them, she built a city which later they called Carthage; the citadel created from the cow's hide, since they referred to it thus, she named Byrsa.

Vergil[144] suggests that Aeneas came to her as a refugee driven by the force of a storm, and that she gave him her hospitality and her bed, though when Aeneas left her she could not endure it and killed herself for love. But Justin[145] and ancient historiographers think differently, for Justin says that the Carthaginian leaders, under threat of war by the king of the Massitani, ordered her to marry; that she became distraught when she found this out, for in advance she had willingly obliged herself to do anything on behalf of her homeland, but that she requested a specific day on which she would promise to go to her husband; and when that day came, she climbed a huge pyre built on the highest part of the city, as if she were placating the shades of Sychaeus, and with the citizens standing by and anticipating what she would do, drawing a knife which she had secretly taken with her, she said, "Noble citizens, as you wish I go to my husband; and after saying those words she killed herself, choosing death rather than staining her purity. This is very different from Vergil's description.

: 61 :

On Anna, daughter of King Belus

Anna was the daughter of Belus, as Vergil[146] seems to believe: he frequently calls her the sister of Dido. She was Dido's companion in flight, and after she watched Dido's death and saw Carthage occupied by King Iarbas, as Ovid[147] says in the *Fasti*, she fled to King Battus on the island of Cosyra,[148] trusting in the justice of ancient hospitality. Learning then that Pygmalion had sent an

lion arma adversus eam moveret, hanc ob causam a Batho licenti-
ata intravit mare, et tempestatem passa, ubi Cameren petere inten-
debat, in Laurentum litus delata est, per quod dum Eneas iam
superato Turno cum Achate spatiando deambularet, eo viso, fugam cepit, tandem prestita ab Enea fide, substitit et ab eo in re-
2 giam deducta est. Cuius ob adventum suspicata Lavinia ei tetendit
insidias, verum Anna, a Didone per quietem monita, nocte regiam
exivit, et si satis potest ex Ovidii verbis concipi, in Numicum flumen sese precipitem dedit. Sane fictor Ovidius ad ulteriora pro-
cedens dicit quod cum postea exquireretur et a perquirentibus
perveniretur ad Numicum, visum est illis e fluvio vocem audisse
dicentem:

>   placidi sum nynpha Numici.
> Amne perenne labens Anna Peremna vocor.

3   Post ipsum autem Ovidium dicit Macrobius in *Saturnaliorum*
libro, aprili mense publice et privatim sacrificatum iri ut annare et
perennare comodi liceat.

: 62 :

De Europa Agenoris V^a filia

1 Europa filia fuit Agenoris, ut per Ovidium patet. Ex qua talis narratur fabula. Quod cum ob formositatem suam summe diligeretur
a Iove, ab eodem Mercurius missus est, eique imperatum ut, que
cerneret armenta in montanis Phenicum, in litus pelleret, quo cum
2 puellis ludere consueverat Europa. Quod cum Mercurius fecisset,
Iuppiter, in candidum taurum transformatus, se armentis immis-

army against her, with Battus' permission she therefore took to the sea, and, although she planned to head for Camere, she ran into a storm and was carried to the coast of Laurentum. But Aeneas—this was after the defeat of Turnus—had gone for a walk with Achates, and when she saw him she began to run away. But when Aeneas displayed his good faith, she stopped and allowed him to escort her to the palace. Lavinia became suspicious at her arrival 2 and planned to attack her, but while she was sleeping Anna was warned by Dido, left the palace that night, and, if this is how we are to understand the words of Ovid, jumped into the Numicus River. However, Ovid, the fabricator, proceeding to the end of the story says that later, when those who were searching for her reached the Numicus, they seemed to hear a voice from the river, saying:[149]

> I am a nymph of the placid Numicus.
> An ever-flowing river, I am called Anna Perenna.

Following this passage in Ovid, Macrobius[150] says in his *Satur-* 3 *nalia* that in the month of April there were public and private sacrifices to ensure annual and perennial prosperity.

: 62 :

On Europa, the fifth child of Agenor

Europa was the daughter of Agenor, as Ovid[151] makes clear. The 1 following fable is told about her. When Jupiter had singled her out for her beauty, he sent Mercury with instructions to drive any herd he might find on the mountains of the Phoenicians to the seashore where Europa was accustomed to playing with girlfriends. After Mercury had done this, Jupiter transformed himself into a 2

cuit. Hunc cum cerneret virgo, pulchritudinis et mansuetudinis eius delectata, illum primo tractare manibus cepit, at in eius conscendit dorsum, qui paulatim se in undas deducens, dum illam territam et cornibus atque dorso innitentem sensit, natans in Cretam transtulit, ubi in veram redactus formam eam oppressit et oppressu pregnantem fecit. Que illi postea peperit, ut non nullis placet, Minoem, Radamantum et Sarpedonem. Ipse vero in eius sempiternam memoriam terciam orbis partem Europam ex eius nomine nuncupavit.

3   Huius fabule figmentum adeo tenui tegitur cortice, ut facile possit apparere quid velit. Nam Mercurium armenta depellentem in litus ego eloquentiam et sagacitatem alicuius lenonis, virginem e civitate in litus deducentem, intelligo, seu mercatorem fictum se iocalia ostensurum, si navem conscenderet, pollicentem. Iovem in taurum transformatum virginis delatorem, iam apud deliras aniculas vulgatum est, navem fuisse, cui erat insigne albus taurus, qua, quacunque fraude conscensa a virgine, illico remigantium opere factum est ut deferretur in Cretam, ubi Iovi coniugio iuncta est, seu, secundum Eusebium in libro *Temporum*, Asterio regi, ex quo ipse supra dictos filios asserit procreatos. Augustino tamen placet hunc non Asterium sed Xantum appellatum fuisse.

4   Discrepant insuper de tempore huius rapine plurimum autores[24], cum sint, ut Eusebius refert, qui dicant Iovem, anno Danai regis Argivorum XL°, Europe mixtum; eamque postea Asterium Cretensium regem in coniugem assumpsisse, qui annus est mundi
5   ĪĪDCCLXVIIII. Alii vero dicunt eam a Cretensibus raptam, regnante Argis Acrisio, circa annum mundi ĪĪDCCCLXXVIIII. Quidam autem volunt eam raptam, Pandione Athenis regnante, anno

white bull and mixed himself in with the herd. When the maiden saw him, delighted by his beauty and his tameness, she began to touch him with her hands first, and then she climbed onto his back. Little by little he made his way into the waves until he sensed that she was frightened and holding onto his horns and back; then he swam across to Crete where he returned to his natural form, forced himself upon her, and thereby made her pregnant. Afterward, according to some, she gave birth to Minus, Rhadamanthys, and Sarpedon. He then named a third of the world Europe in eternal remembrance of her name.

The fiction in this fable has such a thin cover that its meaning 3 can easily be laid bare, for I think Mercury driving the flock to the shore is the persuasiveness and shrewdness of some procurer leading a maiden from the city to the shore, or a beguiling merchant promising to show her jewels if she will climb aboard his ship. Jupiter transformed into the bull that carried the maiden was already commonly known among senile old women to be a ship on which the emblem was a white bull, and it was the rowing of such a ship that brought the maiden—enticed to climb aboard by whatever trick—from there to Crete, where she coupled with Jupiter, or, according to the *Chronicle* of Eusebius,[152] to King Asterius, from whom he says the aforementioned children were procreated. According to Augustine,[153] however, he was not called Asterius but Xanthus.

In addition, authors disagree considerably about the time of 4 this abduction, for there are those, as Eusebius[154] points out, who say that Jupiter mated with Europa in the fortieth year of Danaus' rule among the Argives, and that later Asterius, king of the Cretans, married her in the world year 3769. Others[155] say that she 5 was abducted by Cretans when Acrisius was ruling the Argives around the world year 3879. Some[156] think she was abducted when

scilicet mundi $\overline{\text{III}}$DCCCCXVI. Quod quidem tempus magis convenit eis que de Minoe eiusdem Europe filio leguntur.

6 Huius ymaginem egregiam ex ere a Pictagora Tarenti positam dicit Varro, ubi *De origine lingue Latine*.

: 63 :

De Cadmo, Agenoris VI° filio qui genuit Semelem, Agavem, Auctonoem et Ynoem

1 Cadmus, antiquorum omnium vulgata fama, fuit filius Agenoris, quem una cum Phenice fratre a Thebis Egyptiorum venisse anno Danai Argivorum regis XVII°, et apud Tyrum et Sydonem regnasse scribit Eusebius in libro *Temporum*, cum, ut supra patet, longe ante ibidem venerit Agenor peste pulsus, a quo Agenorem patrem ho-
2 rum non nulli volunt duxisse originem. Qui Eusebius post hec scribit: anno regni Lyncei XVI° Cadmum Armeniam occupasse; quod a Cilyce factum supra memoravimus.

Hic tamen, ut scribit Ovidius, cum rapuisset Juppiter Europam, ad ipsius perquisitionem ab Agenore patre missus est, hac ei indicta lege, ne absque ea reverteretur in patriam. Qui, sumptis sociis, cum quorsum quereret ignoraret, novas sibi exquirere sedes statuit. Et cum haud longe a Parnaso applicuisset, oraculum consuluit et habito responso ut bovem sequeretur indomitam et ibidem, ubi consisteret, sedes sumeret, qui in destinatum sibi locum ductus acquievit, et regione a bove vocata Boetia, civitatis fundamenta iecit, eamque ab antiquis Thebis Egyptiis, ex quibus predecessores

Pandion was ruling Athens, namely in the world year 3916. This period conforms better with what we read about Minos, the son of this Europa.

Varro[157] in his *On the Latin Language* says that a fine bronze image of her by Pythagoras was located in Tarentum. 6

: 63 :

On Cadmus, the sixth child of Agenor, who fathered Semele, Agave, Autonoe, and Ino

Cadmus, whose fame was spread among all the ancients, was the 1
son of Agenor. As Eusebius[158] writes in his *Chronicle*, Cadmus came along with his brother Phoenix from Egyptian Thebes in the seventeenth year of Danaus' rule of the Argives, and he ruled in Tyre and Sidon. As explained above,[159] Agenor, forced there by a plague, had arrived long before, and some think is the origin of the Agenor who is their father. Eusebius[160] writes about this that Cad- 2
mus occupied Armenia in the sixteenth year of the rule of Lynceus, while above we recalled that it was Cilix who had done this.

Nonetheless, as Ovid[161] writes, after Jupiter had abducted Europa, Cadmus was sent by his father Agenor to search for her with the stipulation that he was not to return home without her. He took some companions, but since he did not know where to search, he decided to seek out a new home for himself. And since he put to shore not far from Parnassus, he consulted the oracle and received the response that he should follow an untamed cow and establish his home in the very place where it stopped. Led to the place destined for him, he rested, and in an area named Boeotia from the cow [*bove*] he laid the foundations of a city and named it Thebes after the ancient Egyptian Thebes, whence his

3 eius advenerant, Thebas appellavit. Sane, ut dicit Ovidius, dum
vellet sacrum conficere et ex sociis quosdam misisset ut aquam
afferrent, nec reverterentur, eos secutus, comperit a serpente ingenti devoratos. Quem cum spectaret, audivit quia et ipse serpens
inspiceretur. Eo tandem occiso, monito sumpto dentes illi evulsit
ac seruit, et repente homines in armis exorti sunt, et prelium invicem habuere spectante Cadmo nec ante cessavit prelium, quam
4 quinque tantum superstites remanerent. Qui, inita pace, sese iunxere Cadmo et cepto operi adiutorium prestitere.

Palefatus insuper scribit eum Spingam habuisse coniugem, ean-
demque propter zelum Hermione ab eo discessisse et adversus
Cadmeos bellum inisse. Sunt preterea qui velint eum secum Yppo-
crenem fontem sedentem atque meditantem, xvi literarum caracteres adinvenisse, quibus postea omnis Grecia usa est; sic[25] et Plinius in libro *Naturalis hystorie* dicit eum apud Thebas lapicidinas
invenisse et auri metallorumque conflaturam, dato Theophrastus
eum dicat hec apud Phenices egisse, verum longe post designatum
tempus. Nam quod supra de eo scribitur fuit circa annum mundi
$\overline{\text{III}}$DCCXCV, hec autem circa annos $\overline{\text{III}}$DCCCCXXXVIII. Inde dicit
Ovidius fuisse sibi coniugem Hermionem Martis et Veneris filiam,
ex qua constat quattuor genuisse filias, eidemque Hermioni a Vul-
5 cano victrico exitiale monile concessum. Post hec autem, cum
plurima ex nepotibus et filiabus evenissent infortunia, ipse iam
senex ab Amphyone et Zetho pulsus in Yllirios abiit, et ibi miseratione deorum in serpentes ipse et Hermiona versi sunt.

6 Huius hystoria fabulosa aliqua habet immixta, quorum videre
sensum superest. Serpentem igitur Marti sacrum ego senem homi-

predecessors had emigrated. Of course, as Ovid[162] says, he wished   3
to make a sacrifice and sent some of his companions to bring water, but they did not return, so he followed them and found that
they had been eaten by a huge serpent. When he looked at it, he
heard that he himself would be viewed as a serpent. Then he
killed the serpent and, as he had been forewarned, took out its
teeth and planted them. Immediately armed men sprang up, and
as Cadmus watched, they battled against each other and did not
stop the battle until only five survivors remained. These made   4
peace, joined with Cadmus, and helped him continue the task he
had begun.

In addition, Palaephatus[163] writes that he had a wife named
Sphinx and that on account of the jealousy of Hermione she left
him and initiated a war against the Cadmeans. There are also
those who think that while he was sitting by the Hippocrene
fountain and thinking, he invented the shape of sixteen letters
which were later used all over Greece. Similarly, Pliny[164] in his
Natural History says also that he discovered the Theban quarries
and how to alloy gold with metals, although Theophrastus says he
did this while he was among the Phoenicians, but long after the
specified time: what was written above about him took place
around world year 3795, but these happened around world year
3938. And then Ovid[165] says that his wife Hermione was the
daughter of Mars and Venus, by whom it is agreed that he fathered four daughters, and that this same Hermione was given a
deadly necklace by her stepfather Vulcan. After these things, how-   5
ever, when misfortune had visited heavily upon his grandchildren
and daughters, he himself, now an old man, was driven out by
Amphion and Zethus and made his way to the Illyrians, and
there, with the gods taking pity on him, he and Hermione were
turned into serpents.

It remains to examine the meaning of some of the fabulous ele-   6
ments mixed in with his story. I think the serpent sacred to Mars

nem atque prudentem olim armigerum et bellicosum intelligo, verbis suis et percontationibus Cadmi socios detinentem, cuius consilio, quod ego per dentes assummo, inter incolas seminata discordia est, qui adversus eum Spinge impulsu surrexerant. Ex qua repente sumptis adversum se armis in pugnam devenere, quorum principes, attritis cede popularibus, cum Cadmo in concordiam devenere et ex incolis atque forensibus unum fecere popu-

7 lum. Quod autem ipse exul cum coniuge serpens effectus sit, eos designat factos esse longevos; prudentes enim serpentum more sunt senes et rerum experientia cauti, et etate annosi, et si etiam evum impulerit et subsidia desint, ritu serpentum curvo incedunt pectore.

De tempore tamen regni huius etiam discordes fuere veteres. Dicit enim Eusebius in libro *Temporum*, anno regni Abantis, regis Argivorum, octavo, qui fuit mundi annus $\overline{\text{III}}$DCCCXXVII, Cadmum ab Amphyone et Zetho regno pulsum. Nec multum post dicit, regnante Argis Acrisio, Cadmum regnasse Thebis, cum Acrisius Abanti successerit, quod tamen esse potuit circa annum mundi $\overline{\text{III}}$DCCCLXXV. Cui tempori congruit quod post modum idem scribit Eusebius, scilicet Acrisio Argis regnante ea fuisse que de Spar-

8 tis memorantur. Quos dicit Palefatus quod, cum proximarum essent regionum, adversus Cadmum subito constitisse, et propter repentinos contractus quasi de terra natos, et quia ex omni confluxissent parte, Spartos vocatos. Sed tamen male convenit tempori quo supra raptam diximus Europam. Hi veritatem comperiant quibus magis est cure; ego autem nil amplius reperire potui.

is a prudent old man, once a bearer of arms and warlike, who detains the comrades of Cadmus with his words and questions. His plan, which I equate with the teeth, was to sow discord among the inhabitants, who rose up against him after being incited by the Sphinx. Then they suddenly took up arms and fought against themselves; after the slaughter had diminished the number of inhabitants, the faction leaders made peace with Cadmus and formed the inhabitants and the foreigners into a unified population. That as an exile he himself, along with his wife, was turned into a serpent, signifies their long lives, for old men are prudent like serpents, wary because of life's experiences and aged in years, and if age pursues them and they lack the means of support, like serpents they move on their curved chest.

Even the ancients disagree as to the period of his reign. Eusebius[166] in his *Chronicle* says that in the eighth year of the rule of Abas, king of the Argives, which was in the world year 3827, Cadmus was banished from the kingdom by Amphion and Zethus. Not much after that he says that when Acrisius was ruling the Argives, Cadmus ruled Thebes, when Acrisius succeeded Abas, which could have been around the world year 3875. This time period conforms with what Eusebius again writes a little later, namely, that the events involving the Sparti occurred when Acrisius was ruling the Argives. Palaephatus[167] says about these Sparti that they lived in nearby regions and suddenly formed an alliance against Cadmus; they were called Sparti because of the suddenness of this alliance, as if it had been born from the earth, and because they joined together from every part of the land. But this does not fit well with the period of Europa's aforementioned abduction. Those who engage themselves with this further might discover the truth, but I was not able to find anything else.

: 64 :

De Semele filia Cadmi

1 Semeles Cadmi filia fuit et Hermionis, ut satis per Ovidium patet
in maiori volumine. Hanc ex Iove pregnantem cum egre ferret
Iuno, ei in vetulam Beroem Epydauream transformata suasit ut
experiretur nunquid amaretur a Iove, ut ab eo postularet ut secum
prout cum Iunone concumberet.

2 Que cum Iovem per Stygias undas iurare compulisset ut sibi
postulata concederet, petiit ut secum prout cum Iunone iaceret.
Iuppiter autem dolens quia iurasset, sumpto minore fulmine, eam
percussit et mortua est, eique ex utero nondum perfectus infans
eductus est, qui Bachus postea fuit.

3 Figmenti huius ego veritatem puto hanc feminam pregnantem,
ut ipsa sonat fabula, fulmine percussam; non enim ignis, id est
Iuppiter, aeri, id est Iunoni, miscetur, nisi per fulmen ad inferiora
descendens.

: 65 :

De Agave filia Cadmi

1 Agaves, ut satis notum est, Cadmi et Hermionis fuit filia, quam
Cadmus Echioni uni scilicet ex sociis, qui illum iuvere Thebas
ponere, matrimonio iunxit, ex quo ipsa concepit et peperit filium

2 quem vocavere Pentheum, elati animi iuvenem. Qui cum sacra
Bachi spreverat, celebrantibus matre et sororibus et aliis, ab omni-

: 64 :

On Semele, daughter of Cadmus

Semele was the daughter of Cadmus and Hermione, as Ovid[168] 1
makes sufficiently clear in his greater work. Because Juno was upset that she was pregnant by Jupiter, she transformed herself into
the elderly Beroe of Epidaurus and persuaded Semele to test Jupiter's love for her by asking him to have intercourse with her just as
he does with Juno.

When she forced Jupiter to swear by the Stygian waters that he 2
would submit to what was demanded of him, she asked him to
have intercourse with her just as he does with Juno. But Jupiter,
pained because he had sworn to her, lifted a small thunderbolt and
struck her, and she died, but from her womb he took an immature
infant, who later would be Bacchus.

I think the truth in this fiction, as the story itself says, is the 3
pregnant woman struck by a thunderbolt, for fire, that is, Jupiter,
is not mixed with air, that is, Juno, unless it descends to earth in a
thunderbolt.

: 65 :

On Agave, daughter of Cadmus

Agave, as is well known, was the daughter of Cadmus and Hermi- 1
one. Cadmus gave her in marriage to Echion, that is, one of the
companions who helped build Thebes; by him she conceived and
gave birth to a son named Pentheus,[169] a youth with a proud
spirit. Because he scorned the sacrifices of Bacchus, when his 2

bus in furiam versis occisus est. Dicebat Leontius Pentheum hunc
abstemium fuisse, et ob id a temulenta matre et aliis occisum, quia
sepius ebrietatem et temulentiam damnasset earum.

: 66 :

De Auctonoe filia Cadmi

1   Auctonoe Cadmi et Hermionis fuit filia, ut ait Ovidius. Hec Aristei fuit coniunx et ex eo peperit Atheonem.

: 67 :

De Ynone Cadmi filia

1   Yno eque Cadmi et Hermionis, ut ait Ovidius, filia fuit. Que cum
nupsisset Athamanti Eoli filio, eique Learcum et Melicertem peperisset, cum ab insano patre Learcum vidisset occisum, sibi timens
et reliquo, ex prerupto saxo se precipitem dedit in mare.

2   Ex quo aiunt eam marinam deam Leucotoem factam, et Melicertem Palemonem miseratione Neptunni. Credo ego loca illa
fuisse ad que necata cadavera mare detulerit, et delatis ad solatium
superviventium imposita deitatis nomina, seu[26] potius ut infra legitur de Learco et Melicerte.

mother, her sisters, and others were celebrating them and swept into a frenzy, he was killed by all of them. Leontius used to say that Pentheus was abstemious and for that reason was killed by his drunken mother and the others because he often criticized their drunken intoxication.

: 66 :

On Autonoe, daughter of Cadmus

Autonoe was the daughter of Cadmus and Hermione, as Ovid[170] says. She was the wife of Aristaeus and produced Acteon by him. 1

: 67 :

On Ino, daughter of Cadmus

Ino was equally the daughter of Cadmus and Hermione, as Ovid[171] says. When she had married Athamas, son of Eolus, and had borne him Learchus and Melicertes, she saw Learchus killed by his demented father, and fearing for herself and the other child, she jumped headlong into the sea from a steep cliff. 1

From this they say that she became the sea goddess Leuconoe[172] and that Melicertes became Palaemon thanks to the compassion of Neptune. I believe that those were the places to which the sea carried dead bodies, and that they gave them the names of gods to console the survivors; more will be said about this below in the chapter on Learchus and Melicertes. 2

: 68 :

De Labdacio, VII° Agenoris filio
qui genuit Layum

1 Labdacius, ut dicit Theodontius, iunior fuit filiorum omnium
Agenoris. Qui cum audisset fugatum fratrem et Amphyonem propria manu peremptum, et Lycum occisum ab Hercule, ab amicis
sollicitatus precibus ut, Syria relicta, veniret in Greciam, cum esset
ob senium nimis inhabilis ad laborem, Laium ex filiis iuniorem
2 transmisit. Qui confestim, occupato regno, rex dictus est.

Paulus autem dicit Labdacium Phenicis fuisse filium, senemque
Thebas venisse vocatum, et ibidem regnasse aliquandiu et Laium
filium genuisse.

: 69 :

De Layo rege Thebarum Labdacii filio,
qui genuit Edippum

1 Laius Thebarum rex fuit et, ut satis premonstratum est, Labdacii
filius. Qui seu ex Phenice missus venerit Thebas, seu ibidem natus
sit, regnans Yocastam Creontis Thebani filiam sumpsit uxorem.
Quam cum audisset concepisse, consuluit de futura prole oraculum et in responsis habuit se nascituri manu periturum. Qui volens consilio obstare periculo, iussit Yocaste ut quicquid nasceretur

: 68 :

On Labdacus, the seventh child of Agenor, who fathered Laius

Labdacus, as Theodontius says, was the youngest of all of Ag- 1
enor's sons. When he had heard that his brother had been put to
flight, and that Amphion had been killed by his own hand, and
that Lycus had been killed by Hercules, his friends solicited him
through prayer to leave Syria and come to Greece, but since his
old age left him unable to make the journey, he sent his youngest
son Laius. He immediately took over the kingdom and was called
king.

Paul, however, says that Labdacus was the son of Phoenix, and 2
that as an old man he was invited to come to Thebes and ruled
there for a long time, and that he fathered a son, Laius.

: 69 :

On Laius, king of the Thebans, son of Labdacus, who fathered Oedipus

Laius was king of the Thebans and, as has been shown already, 1
son of Labdacus. He was either sent by Phoenix and came to
Thebes or he was born there, and once he became king he took as
his wife Jocasta, the sister of Theban Creon. When he had heard
that she conceived, he consulted an oracle about his future progeny and received the response that he would perish by the hand of
the one who was to be born. Wishing to escape this peril, he gave
it some thought and ordered Jocasta to expose whatever child was

2 exponeret. Que cum mesta infantem fecisset exponi, alitus puer ab extero, dum adolescens patrem exquireret et ab oraculo se audisset illum apud Phocim inventurum, cum venisset ibidem, patrem incognitum seditionem civium et exterorum separantem, occidit, et sic Laius occubuit.

: 70 :

De Edippo filio Laii, qui genuit Antigonam et Ysmenam et Ethyoclem et Polynicem

1 Edyppus rex Thebarum fuit et Laii filius et Yocaste, ut in *Thebaide* testatur Statius. Hunc iussu patris, ut supra dictum est, a matris utero in silvas abiciendum feris delatum, dicunt. Quem cum deferrent servi, eius etati innocue compatientes, non abiecerunt iuxta mandatum, quin imo, perforatis ei pedibus, arbori vimine alliga-
2 runt. Ad vagitum cuius tractus pastor quidam Polybi Corinthiorum regis, eum ab arbore abstulit et ad Polybum detulit. Qui, cum filiis careret, patria affectione suscepit et filii loco educavit. Is tamen cum adolevisset audissetque se non Polybi filium, perquirere patrem disposuit, et cum Apollinem consuluisset, accepit se Phocis patrem reperturum et matrem sumpturum in coniugem.

3 Qui Phocim veniens, orta inter cives forensesque seditione, dum faveret forensibus, Layum conantem sedare tumultum incognitum interemit. Tandem, tanquam ab oraculo lusus, Thebas pe-

born. She was saddened to subject the infant to exposure, but the 2
boy was nurtured by a foreigner, and upon reaching manhood, he
inquired about his father and heard from an oracle that he would
find him in Phocis; after he arrived there, while trying to separate
a riot of citizens and foreigners, he killed his father, whom he did
not recognize, and thus Laius died.

: 70 :

On Oedipus, son of Laius, who fathered Antigone,
Ismene, Eteocles, and Polynices

Oedipus was the king of the Thebans and the son of Laius and 1
Jocasta, as Statius[173] bears witness in his *Thebaid*. They say that by
order of his father, as was said above, he was taken from the womb
of his mother to be cast out to wild beasts. When the servants
were taking him away, feeling compassion for one of such an innocent age, they did not expose him as ordered but, indeed, pierc-
ing his feet, bound him to a tree with shoots. His crying drew a 2
certain shepherd of Polybus, king of the Corinthians, who freed
him from the tree and brought him to Polybus. Since he had no
children, Polybus received him with fatherly affection and brought
him up as his own son. Nonetheless, when he was an adolescent
and had heard that he was not the son of Polybus, he determined
to search for his father, and when he consulted Apollo, he heard
that he would come upon his father in Phocis and that he would
marry his mother.

When he came to Phocis during a riot between the citizens and 3
foreigners, he took the side of the foreigners and killed Laius as he
was trying to calm the tumult, not recognizing him. Then, as if he
were being tricked by the oracle, he headed for Thebes, came upon

tens, Spingem invenit, quam, solutis problematibus, cum occidisset, Thebas intravit, ubi filius Polybi creditus; illi Yocasta mater
coniugio iuncta est, quam libens sumpsit, Meroes olim Polybi coniugis, quam matrem suspicabatur, timens coniugium, et rex Thebarum factus et quattuor filiorum ex Yocasta pater. Orta letali
peste Thebis, habitum est ab oraculo non defuturam civitati pestem, ni regnantis exilio incestuosum Yocaste coniugium purgaretur.

4   Sane dum hesitaret iam infelix, venit Corinthius unus, eum
Polybo mortuo in regnum vocans. Qui, dum se matris nuptias ti-
mere diceret, quonam modo Corinthum devenisset audivit a sene.
Quod cum audisset Yocasta, memor que a servis audisset qui illum
detulerant, inspectis eius pedibus, eum extemplo recognovit in

5   filium. Quod ille audiens et a se Layum patrem occisum cognoscens, dolore percitus sibi manus iniecit in oculos, eisque eiectis se
perpetuis damnavit tenebris.

Filii vero dissidentes, eius spreta humilitate venientes in bellum
et inde in mutuam mortem, Yocasta iam gladio perempta, mestus
dolensque, altera filiarum ducente, exul Creontis imperio, in Cy-

6   theronem montem abiit. Quo autem inde abierit, michi incognitum est. Sibi tamen ab Atheniensibus, nescio quo merito, templum et sacra tanquam deo, Valerio referente, constituta sunt.

the Sphinx whom, after solving her riddles, he killed, and entered Thebes where he was believed to be the son of Polybus. He entered into a marriage with his mother Jocasta, whom he gladly accepted since he feared marriage to Meroe, the wife of Polybus, whom he supposed was his mother. He became king of the Thebans and father of four children by Jocasta, and when a deadly plague broke out in Thebes, they learned from an oracle that the plague would not leave the city unless the incestuous marriage of Jocasta were purged by the exile of the king.

While the already unfortunate Oedipus remained undecided, a 4 Corinthian arrived to invite him to assume the throne now that Polybus was dead. When he said he feared marrying his mother, the old man explained how he had come to Corinth. When Jocasta heard this, remembering what she had heard from the servants who carried him away and inspecting his feet, she immediately recognized him as her son. After hearing this and knowing 5 that he had killed his father Laius, stirred by grief he plunged his hands into his eyes, pulled them out, and condemned himself to eternal darkness.

His sons scorned his disgrace, quarreled, and fought a war leading to their mutual deaths, and with Jocasta killed already by a sword, Oedipus, saddened and grieving and with one of the daughters leading the way, went to Mount Cithaeron as an exile by order of Creon. Where he went after that is unknown to me. 6 Nonetheless, according to Valerius, the Athenians set up a temple and sacrifices to him; I do not know for what reason.

: 71 :

De Antigona Edyppi filia

1 Antigona, Statio teste, Edipi et Yocaste fuit filia. Hec patri ceco et
in exilium a Creonte pulso ducatum miseranda prestitit. Inde cum
ad exhibendas ultimas lacrimas fratribus et officium funebre noctu
adversus Creontis imperium venisset, ibique Argiam Polynicis coniugem comperisset cremarentque ambe cadavera fratrum, cum
Argia capta est, et iussu Creontis occisa.

: 72 :

De Ysmene filia Edippi

1 Ysmenes Edipi fuit filia, ut asserit Statius. De qua nil habetur nisi
quod cuidam Athys iuveni Cyrreo desponsata fuerit. Qui ante
nuptias a Tydeo occisus est.

: 73 :

De Ethyocle Edippi filio et Yocaste

1 Ethyocles Edypi filius, spreta patris humilitate, habita cum Polynice fratre de regimine regni sub hac lege concordia, ut vicissim

: 71 :

On Antigone, daughter of Oedipus

Antigone, with Statius[174] as evidence, was the daughter of Oedi- 1
pus and Jocasta. Feeling compassion, she guided her blind father
who had been driven into exile by Creon. When contrary to Creon's order she then came by night to offer the final lament and
funerary rites for her brothers, she found there Argia, the wife of
Polynices; they both cremated the bodies of their brothers, and
they were captured and killed by order of Creon.

: 72 :

On Ismene, daughter of Oedipus

Ismene was the daughter of Oedipus, as Statius[175] asserts. Noth- 1
ing is known about her except that she was betrothed to a certain
Atys, a youth from Cirrha. He was killed by Tydeus before the
wedding.

: 73 :

On Eteocles, son of Oedipus and Jocasta

Eteocles was the son of Oedipus. Scorning his father's disgrace, he 1
peacefully controlled the kingdom along with his brother Polynices
according to this stipulation: they would rule alternately, each for

singulis annis altero interim exule regnarent, repetito a Polynice
exule per Tydeum amicum regno, non solum servare legem noluit,
2 sed insidias Tydeo legato posuit. Quam ob rem septem regum
obsidionem passus est, et demum in duellum cum fratre veniens,
ab eo iam victus, illum cultro transegit, et sic mutuis cecidere vulneribus, nec eorundem ignes cremantes cadavera fuere concordes.

: 74 :

De Polynice filio Edippi, qui genuit Thessandrum

1 Polynicem Edipi fuisse filium et Yocaste notissimum est. Hic cum
fratre, ut proximo supra, inita de regimine pactione, primus in
exilium tendens, agentibus imbribus et vento, nocte Argos intravit;
et cum sub regia porticu quiesceret adveniente Tydeo, qui exul
patriam fugiebat, intrante eo sub porticum, adversus eum surrexit
in rixam, et ut supra dictum est ab Adrasto rege pacati et in regiam deducti sunt, et eius etiam generi facti.

2 Tractu autem temporis, cum Tydeus sub legationis nomine pro
Polynice Ethyocli regnum postulasset frustra, eique contra ius
gentium in mortem insidias ab Ethyocle sibi positas comperisset,
eo itum est, nato iam ex Argia Polynici parvulo filio, ut Adrastus,
congregatis Argivis principibus, adversus Ethyoclem et Thebanos

one year, during which time the other would go into exile. But when Polynices in exile sent his friend Tydeus to petition for his year of rule, not only did Eteocles not wish to observe the law but he attacked the legate Tydeus. As a result he was besieged by seven 2 kings, and finally it came down to a duel with his brother. Overcome by Polynices, Eteocles stabbed him with his knife, and so they fell from mutual wounds, nor were the fires that cremated their bodies harmonious.[176]

: 74 :

On Polynices, son of Oedipus, who fathered Thersander

It is well known that Polynices was the son of Oedipus and Jo- 1 casta. With his brother he made an agreement about ruling the state, as explained just above, and he went into exile first, driven by the winds and the rain and entering Argos by night. And when he was sleeping under the palace portico, Tydeus, an exile fleeing his native land, arrived and entered the portico; he started a quarrel with him and, as was said above, King Adrastus calmed them down and brought them into the palace, and they became his sons-in-law.

With the passing of time, Tydeus in his capacity as legate de- 2 manded in vain the kingdom of Eteocles on Polynices' behalf, and he learned that contrary to the law of nations Eteocles was planning deadly attacks against him. After a little boy was born to Polynices by Argia, Adrastus collected the Argive princes and went

iret in bellum, ubi hyatu terre absorpto Anphyarao, et Tydeo sagitta letali vulnere icto reliquisque peremptis variis mortibus pu-
gnando regibus, actum est ut in singulare certamen devenirent
fratres, in quo, cum iam victor videretur Polynices, clam a fratre
3 iacente transfixus est, et sic ambo mutuis vulneribus periere. Quorum tam efficax atque inflexibile odium fuit, ut etiam eis mortuis
inter cadavera perseveraret. Nam, eis in eodem rogo ab Argia Polynicis coniuge et Antigona sorore positis, non primo ignis accen-
sus est quam divise sint flamme, adeo ut liquido appareret cadavera recusare uno eodem igne comburi.

: 75 :

De Tessandro Polynices filio

1 Tessander Polynices fuit filius ex Argia, Statio teste. Qui, cum ro-
bustus evasisset iuvenis, inter proceres ceteros ad Troianum excidium ivit cum Grecis, et, ut ait Virgilius, unus fuit ex illis qui cum
2 Ulixe ligneum equum intravere. Quid tandem ex eo fuerit non
comperi.

to war against Eteocles and the Thebans. As for the war, after Amphiaraus was swallowed by a cleft in the earth, Tydeus was mortally wounded by an arrow, and the remaining princes were killed while fighting in a variety of ways, it came down to the brothers in single combat in which Polynices, although he seemed for the moment to be the victor, was unexpectedly stabbed by his prostrate brother, and so they both perished by their mutual wounds. Their hatred was so intense and unswerving that it even 3 continued in death to their corpses, for although they were placed on the same pyre by Argia, wife of Polynices, and their sister Antigone, no sooner was the fire lit than the flames separated, so clear was it that the corpses refused to be burned by one and the same fire.

: 75 :

On Thersander, son of Polynices

Thersander was the son of Polynices by Argia, with Statius as evidence.[177] Since he had grown into a strong young man, among the other princes he went with the Greeks to take part in the destruction of Troy, and, as Vergil[178] says, he was one of those who entered the wooden horse with Ulysses. What then happened after that I have not been able to discover.

: 76 :

De²⁷ Scitha XIII° filio primi Jovis

1 Scitha, ut Plinio placere videtur in libro *De hystoria naturali*, Iovis fuit filius. De quo nil aliud legimus, preter quod ipse asserit Plinius, eum scilicet arci sagittarumque repertorem primum fuisse; quem longe antiquiorem *Sacre* testantur *lictere*, ex quibus summitur Lamech sagittarium extitisse.

2 Supererat de stirpe Etheris Celius quem, ut in sequenti libro daret initium, reservare satius visum est.

: 76 :

On Scythes, the thirteenth child of the first Jupiter

Scythes, as Pliny[179] seems to think in his *Natural History*, was the 1
son of Jupiter. I have read nothing about him other than what
Pliny himself asserts, namely, that he first discovered the bow and
arrow; a much more ancient inventor is claimed in Holy Scripture,[180] where Lamech is on record as an archer.

Of the lineage of Ether only Sky remains, but it seems better to 2
reserve that discussion for the beginning the next book.

LIBER TERTIUS

Arbor

In arbore autem signata desuper, ponitur in radice Celius Etheris
et Diei filius et in eius ramis et frondibus pars sue posteritatis
ostenditur. Fuerunt enim Celio filii XI. Quorum prima fuit Opis,
II^a Thetis magna, III^a Ceres prima, IIII^us Vulcanus primus, V^us
Mercurius tertius, VI^a Venus magna, VII^a Venus secunda, VIII^us
Toxius,[1] VIIII^us Titanus, X^us Juppiter secundus, XI^us Occeanus, XII^us
Saturnus. Ex istis XII reservantur quattuor, de quibus nulla in
presenti libro III° mentio fiet, scilicet Titanus, de quo scribetur in
quarto, et Juppiter secundus de quo et eius prole scribetur in
quinto et sexto, et Occeanus de quo scribetur in septimo, et Saturnus de quo et eius posteritate fiet mentio in octavo et reliquis
huius operis libris.

Prohemium

1 Sulcanti michi exiguo cortice errorum vetustatis salum et ecce inter aspreta scopulorum et frequentia freta grandevus senex, Numenius phylosophus, vir quidem suo seculo autoritatis inclite, se
obtulit obvium, et placida satis voce sermoneque composito inquit: 'Quid labore tuo numina ledis, ubi quiete illis poteras pla-

BOOK III

Tree

In the tree illustrated above, Sky, the son of Ether and Day, is placed in the root and part of his progeny is shown in the branches and leaves. Sky had twelve children, of whom the first was Opis, great Thetis second, first Ceres third, first Vulcan fourth, third Mercury fifth, great Venus sixth, the second Venus seventh, Toxius eighth, Titan ninth, the second Jupiter tenth, Ocean eleventh, Saturn twelfth. No mention is made in this third book of four of these twelve, their chapters are reserved for subsequent books: Titan in the fourth, the second Jupiter along with his progeny in the fifth and sixth, Ocean in the seventh, and Saturn and his progeny in the eighth and later books of this work.

Preface

While plowing the sea of the errors of antiquity in my small bark, 1 behold, between the rough parts of cliffs and numerous straits an elderly man of great age, the philosopher Numenius,[1] a man considered in his era to be an illustrious authority, presented himself to me, and in a rather calm voice and well ordered speech said, "Why do you offend the divine spirits with your work when you

cuisse? Fuit olim michi, que tibi nunc cura est, theologizantium scilicet poetarum claustra vulgo etiam reserare, et dum Eleusiorum sacrorum arcanum totis viribus in propatulum trahere conarer, ecce sopito michi in quiete profunda vise sunt Eleusine dee, meretriciali ornatu vesteque deturpate, ipsis fornicum in faucibus se quibuscunque adeuntibus prostrantes ultro.

2 'Quod cum videretur divinitati indecens nimium, mirarerque tam pudicas deas in tam prophanum meretricium corruisse repente, quesivi tam inepte ignominie causam. Ast ille, torvis oculis et rugosa fronte in me verse, irato vultu, verbisque cepere: "Quid, leno sceleste, poscis? Tu tam obsceni facinoris causa es. Ex secessu equidem nostre integritatis atque pudicitie renitentes, vi crinibus captas, abstrahis et in publicum lupanar tu ipse castissimas olim passim subicis."

3 'Ego autem, etsi somno plurimo marcerem, non aliter quam vigilans intellexi indignantes illico, et cognovi dormiens, quod vigilando non videram, sacra scilicet misteria paucorum esse debere; et extemplo a ceptis destiti, ne indignationem acriorem incurrerem. Tu autem, longe plus cupiens quam tibi cavens, vertiginosum intrasti gurgitem, et quod omisi, presummis ipse. Sino nunquid credam tantum tibi luminis prestetur ingenii quantum operi tam 4 sublimi oportunum sit; et hoc tacuisse nolim. Cave, quid feceris, iam premonitus! Erysithones ob lesam Cererem fame periclitatus est; Pentheus Bachi sacra despiciens capite mulctatus a matre, penas dedit; Niobes ob vilipensam Latonam, perditis filiis et viro, in

could have appeased them by not doing it? It was once my concern — and now it is yours — to reveal to the uninitiated the cloisters of the theological poets. And while with all my faculties I was attempting to bring the mystery of the Eleusinian rites into the open, behold, appearing to me while in the peaceful depths of sleep were the Eleusinian goddesses, dressed and adorned like disfigured harlots offering themselves at brothel entrances to anyone approaching.

"Because this seemed so inappropriate for their divinity, and I   2
marveled that such chaste goddesses declined rapidly into such profane prostitution, I asked about the reason for such unfitting disgrace. But they, with pitiless eyes and wrinkled brows, turned toward me and with an angry expression began to say, 'Why do you ask, accursed panderer? You are the reason for such a perverted outrage. Grasping us by the hair, you dragged us out from the secluded spot where we maintained our integrity and modesty and subjected us, once completely chaste, to the public brothel.'

"Although enfeebled by my deep sleep, I was still alert and knew   3
right away that they were indignant, and I recognized while sleeping what I had not seen while awake, namely that sacred mysteries must belong to the few. So I immediately stopped what I had begun lest I incur more severe indignation. You, however, desiring much more than you have taken precautions against, have entered a vertiginous abyss, and you are taking up what I left behind. I will allow myself to believe that you have exhibited as much light of ability as it is fit for such a sublime work, and I do not wish to be silent about this. Beware of what you do; you are now forewarned!   4
Erysichthon[2] was tested by hunger because he offended Ceres; Pentheus[3] scorned the rites of Bacchus and, punished by his mother, paid the penalty with his head; and because she slighted Latona, Niobe[4] lost her children and husband and hardened into

silicem riguit. Et ne plures enumerem, tu forsan credis deorum aulas impune reserare vulgo? Deciperis, et, ni desistas, eorum iram non ante quam experiaris, agnosces.'

5   Tum ego, etsi estuantis maris obsisteret impetus, paululum tamen substiti dixique: 'Quibus te ab oris, queso, Numeni, hos inter scopulos evehis? Ab inferis arbitror, odore enim sulphureo cuncta reples, et es inferna caligine fuscus. Et hec veteris et infausti Plutonis mandata sint credo, quasi Christiano homini, uti iamdudum gentilibus consueverat talibus timorem putet incutere. Ille quidem veteres cecidere cathene, et arma hostis antiqui contrita sunt; vicimus precioso redempti sanguine, et in eo renati lotique, suas decipolas non curamus.

6   'Attamen ego dearum tuarum non resero thalamos, nec deorum tuorum secessus aperio, quasi velim illecebras eorum magis ex propinquo conspicere, sed ut appareat poetas, si bene de Deo sensissent, homines fuisse preclaros et ob mirabile artificium venerandos; et ut videas quanti pendam hos tuos fabulosos deos, similem Stratonico, sibi iram Alabandi imprecanti et Herculis in molestum exoranti, precem faciam: ipsi ergo omnes, quorum tu me hortaris iram fugere, michi irati sint, queso, tibi autem illisque et tam inepta credentibus Christus Ihesus.'

7   His dictis, evestigio evanuit ille; ast ego attentus navigio in Egeum evehar mare, Celi prolem perquisiturus amplissimam. Ille autem iter prestet placidum, qui ex Sabeis magos ad se orandum atque muneribus honorandum, stella duce, deduxit in Syriam.

stone. No need to enumerate more: do you by some chance believe that you can open up the halls of the gods with impunity? You are deceiving yourself, and, unless you desist you will not recognize their anger before you experience it."

Then, although the force of the raging sea opposed me, I halted   5
a bit and said, "Let me ask, Numenius, what shores bring you to navigating between these cliffs? I think the nether shores, for you reek of sulfuric odor and are obscured in an infernal cloud. And I think these things have been mandated by the ancient and inauspicious Pluto, as if he intends to instill the same fear in a Christian man as was common long ago among pagans. But those ancient chains have fallen, and the weapons of the ancient enemy are blunted; redeemed by precious blood, we have conquered, and reborn and cleansed by it, we have no anxiety about their deceits.

"Nonetheless, I am not opening the bedrooms of your god-   6
desses, nor am I uncovering the hiding places of your gods, as if my desire were to look at their enticements more closely. But to make it clear that your poets would have been, if they had known God well, famous men and venerable for their wondrous artifice, and so that you might see how much I depend on your legendary gods, I will make a prayer — as did Stratonicus, who invoked the anger of Alabandus upon himself and invoked the anger of Hercules upon his opponent.[5] Therefore I ask that all these gods whose anger you urge me to flee be angry at me but that Jesus Christ be angry with you and those believing in such foolish things."

Once I said these things, he immediately vanished, but I will be   7
conveyed on my ship with care to the Aegean Sea in search of the very widespread progeny of Sky. May he who guided the magi, led by the stars, from Sheba into Syria to pray for him and honor him with gifts, provide a calm journey.[6]

: I :

De Celo Etheris et Diei filio, qui genuit XII² filios,
dato quod in presenti III° libello de VIII tantum tractetur,
ut puta de Opi, de Thetide magna, de Cerere prima,
de Vulcano primo, de Mercurio tertio, de Venere magna
et de Venere secunda et de Toxio

1   Celum, non illud quidem pregrande corpus ornatum syderibus, quod dicebat Orpheus a Phanete compositum in domicilium suum atque aliorum deorum, et quod nos semper nos ambire circuitu cernimus, verum homo quidam sic vocitatus, ut ait Tullius, ubi *De naturis deorum*, filius fuit Etheris et Diei, id est ignite virtutis et claritatis eximie, a quibus eius nomen processit in lucem. Et quod homo fuerit satis in libro *Divinarum institutionum* per Lactantium patet. Dicit enim sic in *Sacra hystoria* reperiri:

Uranium potentem virum Vestam habuisse coniugem, et ex
2   ea Saturnum atque Opem et alios suscepisse. Qui Saturnus, cum regno potens efficeretur, patrem Uranium Celum appellavit et matrem Terram, ut hac mutatione nominum fulgorem sue originis ampliaret,

etc.

Huic preterea, ut in *Sacra hystoria* dicit Emnius, Juppiter nepos eius primo in Paneo monte aram statuit, atque sacrificium adolevit, et ab eo celum ipsum verum denominavit. Evemerus vero dicit hunc Celium seu Celum in Occeania mortuum, et in oppido Aulatia sepultum.

: I :

On Sky, son of Ether and Day, who fathered twelve children, although in this third book only eight will be treated, that is, Ops, great Thetis, first Ceres, first Vulcan, third Mercury, great Venus, the second Venus, and Toxius

Sky — not that huge body decorated with the stars which Orpheus[7] said was created by Phanes as the dwelling for him and the other gods, and which we always see around us in a circle — but a certain man called that, is said by Cicero[8] in his *On the Nature of the Gods* to have been the son of Ether and Day, that is, of fiery virtue and extraordinary clarity, from which his name came into the light. And that he was a man is clear enough from the *Divine Institutions* by Lactantius, for he says that it is found in the *Sacred History* that:[9]

> Uranius, a powerful man, had Vesta as his wife, and from her he received Saturn, Ops, and other children. This Saturn, when he took charge of the kingdom, called his father Uranius Sky and his mother Earth, and with this change of names he glorified the splendor of his origins.

In addition to this, as Ennius[10] says in the *Sacred History*, his grandson Jupiter first established an altar on Mount Panchaeus,[11] increased his sacrificial rite, and named the sky itself after him. Euhemerus[12] says that this Sky died in Oceania, and is buried in the town of Aulatia.

: 2 :

De Opi prima Celi filia et Saturni coniuge

1 Ops seu Opis, ut placet Lactantio libro *Divinarum institutionum*, filia fuit Celi et Veste, et Saturni fratris coniunx, et Iovis aliorumque plurium deorum mater; quam ob rem apud orbos orbis plurimum venerationis obtinuit. Sane seu antiqui theologizantes ad suos palliandos errores fecerint, seu ad occultandam vulgo fictionibus magnarum rerum veritatem, ut pretactum est, seu potius ut Jovi adularentur maximo regi, hystoria omissa, hanc miris fictionibus ornavere, atque illam eis extulere adeo ut loco maximi numinis coleretur a multis, eique templa et sacra sacerdotesque variis 2 constituerentur in locis. De quibus, ut distinctius videamus, apponenda sunt aliqua. Primo eam deorum dixere matrem, eique constituere quadrigam a leonibus tractam, eiusque capiti turritam descripsere coronam, et sceptrum manibus addidere; veste preterea ramorum circuitionibus et herbarum conspicua ornavere. Illamque incedentem sacerdotes quos, eo quod eunuchi ex instituto essent, 'gallos' vocavere, timpana tangentes et era precedere demonstrarunt, eiusque in circuitu sedes vacuas posuere, et Coribantes armatos illam ambire voluerunt.

3 Quid ex his tot senserint videamus. Deorum enim mater ideo habita est, quia terrei sint homines qui ab hominibus dii facti sunt. Turrita vero corona, qua insignita est, satis eam pro terra sumendam ostendit, cum sit terre circuitus civitatum et oppidorum ad instar corone insignitus. Vestis autem ramis herbisque distincta monstrabit silvas et fruteta et herbarum species infinitas, quibus terre superficies tecta est. Sceptrum autem, quod manibus defert,

: 2 :

On Ops, first daughter of Sky and wife of Saturn

Ops or Opis, according to Lactantius[13] in his *Divine Institutions*, 1
was the daughter of Sky and Vesta, wife of her brother Saturn,
and the mother of Jupiter and many other gods, which is the reason she received considerable veneration from the deprived. Of
course, whether the ancient theologians did this to cloak their errors, or to conceal the truth about great things with a wide range
of fictions (as we have touched upon), or rather to adulate Jupiter,
a great king, they abandoned the true story and adorned her with
strange fictions and so extolled her that many worshipped her as a
great divinity and established temples, sacrifices, and priests for
her in various places. Some things had to be appended to these, as 2
we will see clearly. First they said she was the mother of the gods,
and they established for her a chariot drawn by lions, depicted a
turreted crown on her head, and added a scepter to her hands. In
addition, they decorated her in a garment distinguished by its circuit of branches and herbs. And leading her processions they show
priests whom, because they were traditionally eunuchs, they called
galli ["roosters"], who held drums and bronze instruments; and
they placed empty thrones in a circle and liked to have armed
Corybantes encircle her.

Let us see what they meant in all this. She was thought to be 3
the mother of the gods because those who are made gods by men
are earthborn men. The turreted crown which distinguishes her
shows clearly that she must be understood as the earth, for the
circle of the earth, like the crown, is distinguished by cities and
towns. Her garment marked with the branches and herbs signifies
the forests, thickets, and limitless types of herbs which cover the
surface of the earth. The scepter she carries in her hands signifies

regna, divitias et potentiam imperantium super terram monstrabit.

4 Quod quadriga vehatur, cum sit immobilis, intellexere ordinem in operibus terre per quattuor anni tempora, circulari quodam incessu servari continue.

Cur autem a leonibus trahatur, ratio hec reddi potest, voluere quidem agricolarum in tradendis terre seminibus consuetudinem demonstrare; consuevere quidem leones, ut Solinus in libro *Mirabilium* dicit, si per pulvereum solum iter faciant, cauda pedum suorum verrentes turbare vestigia, ne venatoribus sui itineris prestent indicium. Quod et agricole, seminibus iniectis sulcis, evestigio

5 faciunt, retegentes, ne semen surripiatur ab avibus. Preterea cum sint ossa leonibus ossibus ceterorum animalium duriora, intelligi voluerunt vertentium terram membra esse oportere solidiora quam ceteris, vel potius ut ostendatur per leones, quos quadrupedum reges dicimus, iugo Opis subditos, orbis principes terre legibus esse suppositos.

Sedes autem vacue illi circumposite existimo nil aliud velint quam ostendere, quia non solum domus, sed civitates, que incolentium sunt sedes, vacuentur persepe, peste agente vel bello; seu quia in superficie terre vacue sint sedes plurime, id est loca inhabitata; seu quia ipsa terra semper sedes servet vacuas nascituris; seu ad demonstrandum quod hi ad quos pertinet terre cultum, non dico de agricultoribus tantum, sed etiam de principibus, qui civitatibus et regnis presunt, non debent se ocio et inepte quieti concedere, quin imo stare continue et vigilare, cum de novo semper emergant, que exercitio talium indigeant.

6 Coribantes autem has armatos ambire designare volunt unumquenque mortalium pro patria se debere bellis exponere, et arma

the kingdoms, wealth, and the power of those ruling the earth. Insofar as she is carried on a chariot, since the earth is immobile, they understood that the order of the works of the earth is continually preserved in a kind of circular procession throughout the four seasons of the year.   4

The reason that the chariot is drawn by lions can be furnished in this way: they wanted to demonstrate the practice of farmers in spreading seeds on the earth; in reality it is the habit of lions, as Solinus[14] says in his *On the Wonders of the World*, as they make their way through dusty soil, to spoil the tracks made by their feet by sweeping their tails so they do not reveal their trails to hunters. This is also what farmers do, who after planting their seeds in furrows immediately cover them so the seeds are not stolen away by birds. In addition, since the bones of lions are harder than the bones of other animals, they wanted it to be understood that the limbs of those who turn the earth need to be more solid than those of others. Or, rather, they wanted to show by yoking the lions — whom we call kings of the quadrupeds — to the team of Ops that they are the princes of the earth yoked to laws.   5

I think that the empty seats which surround her are intended to demonstrate nothing other than that not only homes but cities, which are the seats of inhabitants, are often empty because of plague or war; or because there are on the surface of the earth many empty seats, that is, uninhabited territories; or because the earth itself preserves empty territories for those still to be born; or for demonstrating that those to whom the worship of the earth pertains, and I mean not only farmers but also princes who are in charge of cities and kingdoms, must not yield to leisure and inordinate rest but to remain continuously vigilant since matters which require their ability ever arise anew.

They want the armed Corybantes who surround her to indicate that every mortal man ought to march out to war on behalf of his country. That they had priests called *galli* they say happened be-   6

pro salute patrie sumere. Gallos autem sacerdotes habere ob id contigisse dicunt, quod cum deum mater Athym decorum adamasset puerum, eumque cum pellice comperisset, zelo percita, illi abscidisse virilia, et ob id similes sacerdotes appetere, quos 'gallos' a contrario sensu dixere. Sane per dilectum Athim vult Macrobius *Saturnaliorum* libro solem intelligi, qui anno quolibet iuvenescere videtur, et adeo a terra diligitur, ut in se eius suscepta influentia, quas cernimus herbas flores et fructus pariat.

7   Quod eum castraverit, hoc ideo fictum credo, quia certo anni tempore solis radii videantur steriles esse, et potissime circa autumnum et hyemem in quibus temporibus nil gigni videtur ab eis. Vel ut dicit Porphyrius, Athys flos est a terra dilectus tanquam ornamentum suum, qui tunc a terra castratur cum veniente fructu flos decidit; vel si cadat ante fructum, non sit ulterius ad fructum aptus. Quod hi sacerdotes timpana ferant et era, volunt per timpanis, que vasa sunt semisperica et semper bina feruntur, duo intellegi hemisperia terre, in quibus ambobus, ut non nulli opinati, sunt, terre opus ostenditur. Per era vero intelligi voluerunt strumenta ad agriculturam accommoda, que quondam, antequam ferri usus inveniretur, ex ere confici consueverant.

8   Hanc preterea multis nuncupavere nominibus, de quibus non nulla significata exposita supra sunt ubi de Terra, et certa huic sunt cum aliquibus deabus communia, de quibus in sequentibus dicetur et ob id que sua sunt propria censui apponenda. Vocant igitur eam Opim, Berecinthiam, Rheam, Cybelem, Almam et magnam Palem. Opim autem ideo vocitatam volunt, quod ut ait Rabanus 'opem' ferat frugibus, et opere melior fiat. Berecinthiam autem dicit Fulgentius vocatam quasi montium dominam, eo quod deorum sit mater, qui pro montibus intelliguntur, id est elatis hominibus, vel, ut placet aliis et michi, a Berecinthio monte, seu op-

cause when the mother of the gods lusted after the handsome boy Attis but found him with a rival, driven by jealousy she cut off his manhood, and the priests, whom they called "roosters" in a contrary sense, sought to be similar. Macrobius[15] in his *Saturnalia* wanted the beloved Attis to be understood thoroughly as the sun which seems to be rejuvenated every year and is so beloved by the earth that the influence it receives unto itself gives birth to the herbs, flowers, and fruits that we see.

That she castrated him I think was invented because at a certain time of the year the rays of the sun seem to be sterile, especially around the autumn and winter, seasons during which nothing seems to be produced by them. Or, as Porphyry[16] says, Attis is the flower loved by the earth as its decoration, who is then castrated by the earth when, with the fruit coming, the flower falls off, or, if it falls before the fruit comes, it is no longer ready for fruit. As for the priests carrying drums and bronze instruments, they mean by the drums, which are hemispherical vessels and always carried in twos, the two hemispheres of the earth, in both of which, as some think, the work of the earth is revealed. By the bronze instruments they want us to understand agricultural tools which once, before the use of iron was discovered, used to be made from bronze. 7

In addition, they called her by multiple names, some of which we have discussed earlier in the chapter on Earth, and certain names are in common with certain goddesses who will be discussed subsequently, and so I thought I should address the ones that are appropriate here. They call her Opis, Berecynthia, Rhea, Cybele, Alma, and great Pales. They choose to call her Opis because, as Rabanus[17] says, she bears her "influence" [*opem*] upon fruits, and by her work it becomes better. Fulgentius[18] says she was called Berecynthia as if she was the mistress of the mountains because she was the mother of the gods who are understood as mountains, that is, high-level humans, or, as others think and so 8

pido Frigie, in quo persancte colebatur ab incolis. Rhea autem eo quod idem Grece sonet, quod Ops Latine. Cybelem vero voluere non nulli eam a *cibalo* quodam denominatam quem primum illi sacerdotio functum aiunt. Alii autem a Cybalo oppido, in quo dicunt sacra eius fuisse comperta. Quidam autem dictam volunt a *cibel*, quod capitis motus sonat, qui plurimus in sacris eius fiebat. Almam autem ab 'alendo' non nulli credidere dictam, eo quod suis fructibus omnes alat. Palem autem eam vocavere pastores et pabulorum dixere deam, eo quod gregibus et armentis pabula prestet.

9

: 3 :

De Theti magna, Celi II^a filia et Occeani coniuge

1   Thetim magnam dicit Paulus, a Crisippo traditum, filiam fuisse Celi atque Veste et Occeani coniugem. Quod quidem Lactantius asserit, eamque matrem dicit fuisse nynpharum. Verum Servius eam vocat Dorim, quod arbitror a Virgilio sumpserit, ubi dicit:

> Sic tibi cum fluctus subterlabere Sycanos,
> Doris amara suam non intermisceat undam,
>
> > etc.

2   In his igitur cum nil hystoriographum habeatur, allegoricus sensus videndus est. Thetis procul dubio aqua est, quam dicit Crisippus vi fervoris celestis e visceribus eductam terre, et sic ex Celo non homine Vestaque, id est terra, natam. Doris autem 'amaritudo' interpretatur, que quidem, solis agente fervore, aque marine ut physici testantur addita est; quod experientia notum videtur, nam,

do I, from Mount Berecynthia, or a town in Phrygia, in which she was worshipped devoutly by the inhabitants. Rhea in Greek means what Ops means. Some want her to be called Cybele after a certain "cymbal" which they say was made first for her priesthood. Others think it is from the town of Cybelo in which they say her rites were found. Some think it is from *cibel,* which means the movement of the head which occurred frequently in her rites. Some think she was called Alma from "nourishing" [*alendo*] because she nourishes all with her fruits. Shepherds called her Pales and said she was the goddess of fodder because she provided fodder [*pabula*] to flocks and herds.

: 3 :

On great Thetis, second daughter of Sky and wife of Ocean

Paul, following Chrysippus, says that great Thetis was the daughter of Sky and Vesta, and the wife of Ocean. Lactantius[19] confirms this, and he says that she was the mother of nymphs. Servius[20] in fact calls her Doris, which I think he took from Vergil, who says:[21]

So when you slip along under the Sicanian waters, may bitter Doris not mix her waves with you.

Because there is nothing historiographical in this, the meaning must be understood as allegorical. Undoubtedly, Thetis is water; Chrysippus says she was brought out by force of celestial warmth from the bowels of the earth, and so she was born from Sky, not from man, and Vesta, that is, earth. Doris is interpreted as bitterness, for she, in the heat of the sun, is added to sea water, as natural scientists bear witness. We know this from experience, for, as

ut aiunt naute, salsedo illa superficiei aque maris tantum immixta est, cum infra decem passus dulcis inveniatur.

3 Sed quid quod eam Occeano coniugem iungunt, cum Occeanus aqua sit, et sic idem videatur vir et uxor? Credo hoc fingentes sensisse: occeanum accipi debere pro elemento aque simplici, quod quidem agens creditur ubi aque actio requiratur. Thetim vero pro aqua elementata, seu mixturam aliorum elementorum habente, cuius mixtionis opera potest concipere et nutrire, seu cum utrumque sexum diis esse describant, ut Valerii Serrani carmine patet dicentis:

> Iuppiter omnipotens rex regum atque repertor,
> progenitor genitrixque deum deus unus et idem,
>
> etc.

4 Volunt, cum agat aliquid aqua, eam vocari Occeanum, cum vero patiatur Thetim. Seneca autem, ubi *De questionibus naturalibus* scribit, aliter videtur sentire; dicit enim, aquam virilem vocant mare, muliebrem omnem aliam.

Vocavere autem eam Thetim maiorem, ad differentiam Thetis matris Achillis, quam nynpham voluere veteres, non marinam deam, nisi et nynphas, ut quandoque fit, dixerimus deas. Hec autem magna Thetis multos ex Occeano peperit filios, de quibus postea.

: 4 :

De Cerere prima, Celi III^{a_3} *filia, que peperit Acherontem*

1 Ceres, ut placet Lactantio in libro *Divinarum istitutionum,* filia fuit Celi et Veste. Hanc dicit Theodontius Sycani, vetustissimi Sycilie regis, fuisse coniugem, Syculosque primam frumenti usum do-

sailors say, saltiness is mixed into only the surface of sea water, while ten paces below the water is found to be sweet.

But why is it that they join her to Ocean as his wife when Ocean is water, making husband and wife seem the same? I think 3 the fabricators meant this: that ocean ought to be accepted as the simple element of water which is believed to act when the action of water is sought. Thetis then ought to be accepted as elemental water either because it contains a mixture of other elements, the purpose of this mixture being to conceive and nourish, or because they describe the gods as having both sexes, as Valerius Soranus makes clear in his verses, saying:[22]

> Jupiter, omnipotent king of kings and author;
> progenitor and ancestor of the gods, one and the same god.

When water does something they want her to be called Ocean, 4 and when it is acted upon, Thetis. But Seneca,[23] as he writes in his *Natural Questions*, seems to interpret it differently, for he says that they call sea water masculine, all other waters feminine.

They call her a greater Thetis to differentiate Thetis, the mother of Achilles, whom the ancients thought to be a nymph, not a sea goddess, except that we sometimes call nymphs goddesses. This great Thetis produced many children from Ocean, who will be discussed later.

: 4 :

On first Ceres, third daughter of Sky, who produced Acheron

Ceres, according to Lactantius[24] in his *Divine Institutions*, was the 1 daughter of Sky and Vesta. Theodontius says that she was the wife of Sicanus, the most ancient king of Sicily, and first taught the

cuisse et Sycano plures peperisse filios, nullum tamen nominat.
Hanc preterea, testimonio Pronapidis, dicit Acherontem fluvium
peperisse, et ob hoc talem ex ea recitat fabulam: eam scilicet
concepisse et rubore excrescentis uteri in abditam Crete specum
secessisse, et ibidem Acherontem peperisse; qui non ausus lucem
aspicere, defluxit ad inferos, et ibidem infernalis effectus est fluvius.

    Cuius fictionis ipsemet Theodontius talem explicat rationem.
2 Dicit enim pro constanti habitum Cererem suasisse Saturno fratri
ne Titano regnum aliquo pacto restituiret, et adversus condicio-
nem inter Titanum et Saturnum initam, quos Saturnus filios masculos procreavit, clam nascentes surripuisse una cum Vesta matre,
atque educasse; quod cum detectum esset et audisset Saturnum
Opemque a Titano detineri captivos, sibi timens in Cretam abiens
latebras petiit, nec ausa est comparere donec certior facta est Io-
3 vem victoria liberasse parentes. Ex quo Cererem concepisse voluit
Pronapides Dolorem ex captivitate fratrum, eumque in specu, id
est in latebris, peperisse, id est emisisse seu reliquisse dum, victoria Iovis letata, venit in publicum.

    Eum autem Acherontem dictum ab *a*, quod est 'sine,' et *cheron*,
'gaudium,' nam absque gaudio est qui dolet; et ideo lucem videre
noluisse dicit, quia dolentes, ut plurimum, deiectis in terram oculis, recessus appetunt, et obscura loca. Ibi enim infernalis fluvius
factus est, quia apud inferos nulla unquam sit letitia. Nec illi ideo
pater ascribitur, quia nostra tantum existimatione procreetur.

Sicilians the use of grain and produced several children for Sicanus, though he names none. In addition, from the evidence Pronapides offers, he says that she produced the Acheron River, and for this reason he tells the following fable about her: namely, that she conceived, and, ashamed of her growing belly, she went into hiding in a cave in Crete and there gave birth to Acheron; not daring to see the light, he flowed down to the underworld and there became the infernal river.

Theodontius himself offers this rational explanation for this fiction. He says that it was well known that Ceres had persuaded her brother Saturn not to restore the kingdom to Titan in accordance with a certain agreement, and that contrary to the agreement between Titan and Saturn, what masculine children Saturn fathered he secretly stole away after their birth along with their mother Vesta and reared them; when this was discovered and she heard that Saturn and Opis were being held captive by Titan, fearing for herself she went to Crete to find a hiding place, nor did she dare to return to sight until she became certain that Jupiter had liberated her parents in his victory. After this Pronapides wanted Ceres to have conceived Grief from the captivity of her brothers, and in a cave, that is, in hiding, gave birth to him, that is, sent him out or left him to come out in public because she was delighted by Jupiter's victory.

He was called Acheron from *a*, meaning "without," and *cheron*, "joy," for he who grieves is without joy; and so he says he did not wish to see the light because grieving people, their eyes cast down to the ground, often seek recesses and obscure places; it is there that the infernal river originates, for there is never any happiness among the dead. And so no father is ascribed to him because he is procreated only in our thoughts.

: 5 :

De Acheronte infernali fluvio Cereris filio, qui genuit VI
filios, scilicet Alecto, Thesiphonem, Megeram,
Victoriam, Aschalaphum et Stygem

1   Acheron infernalis fluvius, absque patre, Cereris fuit filius, ut premonstratum est. Hunc Paulus Titanis et Terre filium dicebat et ob
id a Jove deiectum ad inferos, quia sitientibus Titanis limpidas
prestitisset aquas. Sane noster Dantes in prima sui poematis parte
que Infernus dicitur, aliter de origine huius sentire videtur. Dicit
enim in summitate Yde montis Cretensis statuam esse ingentem
cuiusdam senis, cuius aureum caput est, pectus vero et brachia
argentea, corpus et renes ex ere confectos, tybias atque crura et si-
nistrum pedem ex electissimo ferro factum; dextrum autem pedem
ex terra cocta consistere et in eum fere corporea moles omnis in
Romam versa inniti, et has omnes partes preter aureum caput ri-
mulas habere, ex quibus efluunt gucte aque, seu lacrime, que col-
lecte et per cavernas ad inferos descendentes, flumen faciunt Acherontis.

2   Sed quid sibi tam varie velint fictiones videndum est. Cur Cereris dictus sit filius premonstratum est. Quod Titanis et Terre fuerit etiam concedi potest, ubi Titanum solem velimus intelligere, ut
etiam veteres voluere, et sic non nulli opinati sunt agente calore
solis, aquas maris trahi in viscera terre, et ex eis a frigore terre
dulcoratas efluere, et sic cum sol causam dederit, eius filius dici
potest, ac illius cuius videtur uterum exire.

∶ 5 ∶

On the infernal river Acheron, son of Ceres, who fathered six children, namely Alecto, Tisiphone, Megaera, Victory, Ascalaphus, and Styx

The infernal river Acheron was the son of Ceres without a father, 1
as already described. Paul used to say that he was the son of Titan
and Earth, and Jupiter therefore tossed him down to the nether
world for providing clear water to the thirsty sons of Titan. Then
again our Dante[25] in the first part of his poem called *Inferno* seems
to think differently about his origin, for he says that on the summit of the Cretan Mt. Ida there is a large statue of a certain old
man of which the head is made of gold, the chest and arms of silver, and the body and kidneys of bronze; the shins, legs, and the
left foot are made of the finest iron; the right foot consists of ter-
racotta, and nearly the entire weight of the body, which is turned
toward Rome, rests on that; and all these parts except for the gold
head have small cracks from which trickle out drops of water, or
tears, which accumulate and descend through caverns to the nether
regions to make the river of Acheron.

But we must examine the meaning of such various fabrications. 2
Why he was said to be a son of Ceres has been explained. That he
was the son of Titan and Earth can be also be allowed if we are
willing to understand Titan as the sun (as even the ancients did),
and some were of the opinion that from the action of the sun's
heat, the waters of the sea are taken into the bowels of the earth
and, sweetened by the coolness of the earth, they flow out from
there; therefore with the sun providing the cause, the Acheron can
be said to be its son and of the earth from whose womb he seems
to come.

3   Quod inferorum sit fluvius hoc modo potest accipi. Sunt enim fluvii duo quibus Acheron nomen est, unus quidem apud Molossos defluit, ut dicit Titus Livius, et in stagna que 'inferna' vocantur efluit, et ex eis in Thespontium sinum mergitur. Alter vero apud Lucanos fluens, morte Alexandri Epyrote insignis, in inferum mare cadit. Et sic horum ad inferos unusquisque descendit. Nam qui apud Molossos est in regno quondam Plutonis, qui deus inferni dictus est, eo quod ob oriente sole factum esset, inferior vagatur;

4   et sic, si in regno Plutonis est, in inferno est. Attamen de secundo sic sensere quidam.

    Asserunt quippe priscis temporibus Grecis fuisse consuetudinem, damnatos exilio in Ytaliam mictere, seu ipsi exules sua sponte venire; quam eo quod apud inferum mare dicebant, seu quia inferior Grecia ab ortu sit solis, ideo et flumen et damnatos esse 'apud inferos' testabantur. Ex quo volunt locum fabule adinventum; cum etiam ethymologia nominis fluvii faveat fictioni, cum sonet 'sine gaudio' vel 'salute,' quasi exules, patria perdita, absque gaudio vel salute essent.

5   Qui vero aliter sentiunt, ut Servius et post eum Albericus, dicunt Acherontem fluvium non esse, sed locum Ytalie; verum de hoc alias. Dantes autem noster de vero Acheronte infernali intelligit, et dicens quia in Creta insula senis sit statua ex variis metallis a Damiata Syrie civitate in Romam versa, intendit loci congruentiam origini designare et tempora causasque.

6   Sed primo de loco videamus. Dicit ergo[4] statuam senis seu senem stare erectum, ut per hunc intelligamus humanum genus quod adhuc stat, esto antiquum sit, et stat in monte Yde. Yda enim idem sonat quod 'formositas,' per quam sentire vult formositatem

That the Acheron was the river of the nether regions can be 3
accepted in this way. There are two rivers which have the name of
Acheron:[26] one flows among the Molossi, as Livy[27] says, into pools
which are called "infernal," and then flows into the Thesprotian
Bay. The other flows among the Lucanians, famous for the death
of Alexander of Epirus, and falls into the Tuscan Sea.[28] And each
of these descends into the nether regions, for the one near the
Molossians in the former kingdom of Pluto, who was called the
god of the nether region, glides lower because it rises from the
east; thus, if it is in the kingdom of Pluto, it is in the nether region. But some think this about the second river.   4

They state that in ancient times among the Greeks there was a
custom of sending those condemned to exile to Italy, or the exiles
came there on their own accord; and because Italy is near what
they used to call the lower sea, or because Greece is lower on the
east, so also they bear witness that both the river and the condemned are "in the lower regions." It is from this that they want to
derive the invention of the fable, for the etymology of the name of
the river supports the fabrication: it means "without joy" or "without prosperity," just as exiles, having lost their homeland, are without joy and prosperity.

There are those who think otherwise, like Servius[29] and after 5
him Albericus,[30] who say that the Acheron was not a river but a
place in Italy, but more about that elsewhere. Our Dante knows of
the truly infernal Acheron, and in saying that on the island of
Crete there is a statue of an old man made of various metals from
Damietta, a city in Syria, turned toward Rome, he means to indicate the similarity of the place in its origin as well as its era and
causes.

But first let us look at the place. He says that a statue of an old 6
man, or an old man, stands upright so that we might understand
that the human genus still exists, although it is ancient, and it
stands on Mt. Ida. Ida means "beauty," by which he wants us to

temporalium rerum, quam ut perituram designet, dicit olim montem illum letum, hodie vero tristem atque desertum. In monte
autem Cretensi, eo quod Creta insula tripartiti orbis media videatur; nam illi, ab arthoo Egeum est mare, et ab occiduo Yonium seu
Myrtoum, que Europe sunt maria; a solis ortu est illi Ycareum
mare atque Carpatium seu Egyptium, que Asyactica maria sunt. A
meridie vero et occiduo Affro alluitur ponto, et sic tribus orbis
partibus terminus est, ut intelligamus non solam unam harum
partium, sed omnes operam dare ut Acheron concreetur. Ipse
autem ex guctis cadentibus, id est ex criminibus et operibus pravis
fluxisque antiquarum etatum et presentis confectus est olim et
conficitur hodie, ut sentiamus ex criminibus mortalium amicti
gaudium sempiternum.

7   Verum ut appareat quia non omnis etas in hoc conveniat,
aureum caput solidum esse dicit, ut per illud intelligatur innocen-
tie primi parentis tempus, et nostrum, dum renati baptismate in
infantia, simplices perseveramus. Demum venit argentea que etsi
corporeis viribus videatur validior, viciis tamen efficitur vilior, et
sic argentea, scissa rimis, id est criminibus. Tandem tercia sequitur
priorum sonorior et operum longe deterior et hec equo modo
scissa est, et in augmentum agit miserie. Inde sequitur ferrea for-
8   tior, reliquarum etiam peior et obstinatior. Ultimo sequitur testea,
in quam omnis moles corporea inclinatur, et per quam mortalium
fragilitas et senium designatur, et hec scissa est. Ex quibus quidem
scissuris fit ut lacrime effluant facientes Acherontem, id est gaudii
perditionem, ex qua acquisitio tristitie sequatur necesse est, ut
Stygis habeatur origo, et ex tristia doloris incendium, qui Flegeton
est, et ex hoc luctus et miserie, frigiditas sempiterna, quam Cocitus significat. Quod[5] autem a Damiata in Romam versus sit, des-

understand the beauty of temporal things, and to show us that it will perish he says that the mountain was once joyous but today is gloomy and deserted. He says it is a Cretan mountain because the island of Crete seems to be the middle of the tripartite earth, for it has the Aegean Sea to the north, the Ionian and Myrtoan, which are the seas of Europe, to the west; to the east is the Icarian Sea and the Carpatian or Egyptian, which are the Asiatic seas. To the south and west it is washed by the African sea, and therefore it is a boundary for the world divided into three parts. Therefore we know that not only one of these parts but all are involved in creating the Acheron. The river itself was made from falling drops, that is, from the sins and corrupt and dissolute deeds of ancient times and the present, and it happened then and it continues today because we understand that our mortal crimes have caused us to lose eternal joy.

But to show that this does not apply to every era, he says that 7 the head is of solid gold, by which we understand the time of innocence of our first father Adam as well as our era, in which we, reborn in infancy by baptism, continue in righteousness. Then comes the silver part which, if it seems stronger in corporeal strength, is made weaker nonetheless by vices, and so the silver part is marred by cracks, that is, sins. The third part follows, noisier than the former and lesser by far in deeds, and this, too, is fissured and increases our misery. Then follows the iron, stronger, worse than the rest and more resolute. Finally comes the earthen- 8 ware on which the weight of the whole body rests, through which is indicated the fragility of mortals and old age, and that is fissured. From the fissures tears flow forth to make the Acheron, that is, the ruin of joy, after which necessarily follows the acquisition of sadness, which is held to be the origin of Styx, and after sadness comes the burning of grief, which is Phlegethon, and after this sorrow and miseries, eternal frigidity, which the Cocytus signifies. That it is turned from Damietta toward Rome describes the hu-

cribit humanum genus, quod in campo Damasceno principium habuit, Romam regnorum mundi ultimum, id est finem suum, prospiciat.

: 6 :

De Furiis filiabus Acherontis in generali

1   Furias tres esse omnes videntur velle poete, de quibus in generali libet pauca prefari ut de particularibus summatur facilius intellectus. Primo igitur eas dicunt Acherontis fuisse filias atque Noctis; quod Acheron illis pater fuerit testatur Theodontius; quod autem ex Nocte matre nate sint carmine patet Virgilii dicentis:

> Dicuntur gemine pestes cognomine Dire
> quas et tartaream Nox intempesta Megeram,
> uno eodemque tulit partu,
>
> etc.

2   His insuper plura esse nomina voluere. Nam apud inferos eas vocari dixere canes, ut videtur velle Lucanus dum dicit:

> Iam vos ego nomine vero
> eliciam, Stygiasque canes in luce superna
> destituam,
>
> etc.

Apud mortales Furias ut ab effectu patet per Virgilii carmen:

> Ceruleis unum de crinibus anguem
> conicit, inque sinum precordia ad intima subdit,
> quo furibunda domum monstro permisceat omnem.

man genus, which had its beginnings in the Damascene plain,[31] and looks toward Rome, the greatest of earthly kingdoms, that is, toward its own end.

: 6 :

On the Furies, daughters of Acheron, in general

All the poets seem to want there to be three Furies. I am pleased 1
to offer briefly a general introduction to facilitate understanding
the meaning of the individual Furies. First they say that they were
the daughters of Acheron and Night. Theodontius testifies to the
fact that Acheron was their father, while Vergil in his verses makes
clear that they were born from Night, saying:[32]

> Twin plagues are known as the Dire Ones,
> born from the darkness of Night along with Tartarean Megara,
> in one and the same labor.

They give them several additional names. Among the dead they 2
say they were called the dogs, as Lucan seems to wish when he
says:[33]

> Now by your true name
> I will call you forth, Stygian dogs, and in the upper light
> I will leave you.

Among mortals they are called Furies because of what they do, as
is clear in this passage of Vergil:[34]

> A snake, one of her bluish hairs,
> she threw and set it deep into her bosom,
> confusing in her fury the whole palace with this monster.

Eumenides etiam apud nos appellari dicuntur, ut per Ovidium patet dicentem:

Eumenides tenuere faces de funere raptas,

etc.

3 Et hoc apud nos factum in infortunato coniugio satis constat. Dire etiam appellantur, et hoc apud superos, ut ait Virgilius:

At procul ut Dire stridorem agnovit et alas,
infelix crines scindit Iuturna solutos,

etc.

Nam Iuturna dea in aere stridorem Dire non in terris agnovit. Vocantur et volucres, ut idem dicit Virgilius:

Iam iam linquo acies, ne me terrete timentem,
obscene volucres: alarum verbera nosco.

Dicit preterea Theodontius, apud litorales Arpyas appellari. Post hec illas aiunt Jovis atque Plutonis obsequio[6] deputatas, ut Virgilius testatur scribens de eis:

He Jovis ad solium sevique in limine regis
apparent, acuuntque metum mortalibus egris,
si quando letum horrificum morbosque deum rex
molitur, meritis aut bello territat urbes,

etc.

4 Sed iam quid ista velint videndum. Dicunt igitur eas Acherontis et Noctis filias, et ratio videtur talis. Non succedentibus pro votis rebus et ratione cedente, ut perturbatio mentis oriatur de necessitate videtur, que non absque cecitate iudicii perseverat, et ex perseveratione fit maior, donec erumpat in actum, qui absque ra-

Humans are also said to have called them Eumenides, as is clear when Ovid says:[35]

Eumenides held torches stolen from funerals.

And certainly this happens among us in an ill-fortuned marriage. Among the gods they were called the Dire Ones, as Vergil says:[36]   3

But as she recognized from afar the sound of the Dire One's
    wings,
Juturna in her misery tore at her loosened hair.

Here the goddess Juturna recognized the sound of the Dire One in the air, not on the ground. They are also called birds, as again Vergil says:[37]

Now, now I leave the battlefield. Do not terrify me in my
    fright;
obscene birds, I know the beatings of wings.

In addition, Theodontius says that along the shores they were called Harpies. And then they say that they were obedient to Jupiter and Pluto, as Vergil bears witness when writing about them:[38]

In the threshold by the throne of cruel Jupiter
they appear, and they incite fear for wretched mortals
whenever the king of the gods incites horrible death and
    disease,
or terrifies deserving cities with war.

But now we must examine what these things mean. They call   4
them the daughters of Acheron and Night with reason: when things do not go according to our wishes, reason recedes as the mind seems necessarily to suffer a disturbance, and this persists as near blindness of judgment, and then from this persistence it becomes worse, until it erupts into action which is done without

tione factus 'furiosus' appareat necesse est; et sic ex Acheronte Furie nascuntur et Nocte. Dicuntur preterea apud inferos canes, scilicet apud homines conditionis infime, qui dum in perturbationem veniunt, non existentibus furori viribus, clamoribusque omnia complent, canum more latrantes.

5   Apud medios autem Furie vel Eumenides dicte sunt, eo quod maiori ledant incendio 'furiosum'; mediocris enim homo perturbatus, ut in se agat seque intus rodat atque consumat, quedam faciunt; nam ne in minores agat lex publica prohibet, in maiores potentia, et more vulgi inferioris clamores emictere indignatio vetat; secum igitur furit etsi eruperit vix desistet quin in maximum tendat incendium, multis opitulantibus furori. Eumenides dicuntur ab *heu*, quod est interiectio dolentis, et *men*, quod est 'defectus,' eo quod ipse qui patitur sibi ipsi pena sit, seu per antiphrasim dicuntur ab *eu* et *mane* quod utrumque sonat 'bonum.' Et ipse omni
6   bono carent. Apud superos vero appellantur Dire a sevitia maiorum in minores ad quam confestim evolat maiorum furor. Volucres autem appellantur a velocitate furoris, cum repente a mansuetudine in furorem erumpant homines. Arpye autem apud litorales a rapacitate dicuntur, tanto enim fervore litorales efferuntur in predam, ut in nullo discrepet a furore.

Plutoni autem idio obsequiosas vocant, quia divitiarum dicitur deus, ut advertamus crebro perturbationes irasque et rixas ob immoderatam auri cupidinem suscitari. Quod autem Jovi assistant
7   non est mirandum, esto illum pium mitemque dixerimus; pio enim iudici opportunum est ultores scelerum habere ministros,

reason and necessarily seems "furious." And so the Furies are born of Acheron and Night. And then they are called dogs among the dead, namely among humans of the vilest condition, who when they suffer a disturbance have no strength with which to oppose their furor and so satisfy themselves with shouting, barking like dogs.

Among living mortals they are often called Furies and Eu-   5
menides because they inflict greater passion upon the "furious" person, for they make it so that even an average man who becomes disturbed works against himself and gnaws at and consumes himself within; public law prohibits him from doing this to inferiors, power prohibits him from doing it to superiors, and his sense of dignity prevents him from screaming like common people; and so he is furious with himself, and if he erupts, he will hardly stop before he reaches the greatest passion, for many things facilitate fury. They are called Eumenides from *heu*, which is an interjection of grief, and *men*, which is a "defect" because he who suffers is his own punishment; or by antiphrasis it can be derived from *eu* and *mane*, both of which mean "good," for they lack every good. Among   6
the gods they are called Dire Ones from the violence of the more powerful to the less powerful, which is what immediately becomes of the fury of the powerful. They are called birds [*volucres*] from the swiftness [*velocitate*] of furor, since humans erupt quickly from calm into furor. In coastal regions they are called Harpies for their rapacity, for so much plundering takes place in coastal regions that furor is present in everyone.

They describe them also as subservient to Pluto because he is said to be the god of riches, and we repeatedly observe disturbances, anger, and quarrels stirred up because of an immoderate desire for gold. It is not surprising that they assist Jupiter, although   7
we have said that he was respectful and mild: it is suitable for a dutiful judge to have ministers as avengers of sins; if he does not

quibus si careat aut non utatur, legum autoritas facile dissolvetur. Est insuper aliquando ob populorum crimina divina permissio, ut in elementis misceatur furor et eis discordantibus inficiatur aer, et pestes letifere oriantur, quibus miseri absorbemur. Sic et eorundem superbia bella nascantur, ex quibus incendia, populationes et excidia consequuntur.

: 7 :

De Alectho Acherontis prima filia

1 Alectho Furiarum prima est Acherontis et Noctis filia, quam sic describit Virgilius:

> Luctificam Alectho dirarum a sede sororum
> infernisque ciet tenebris cui tristia bella,
> ireque insidieque et crimina noxia cordi.
> Odit et ipse pater Pluton, odere sorores
> Tartaree monstrum, tot sese vertit in ora
> tam seve facies, tot pullulat atra colubris.

Et paulo infra:

> Tu potes unanimes armare in prelia fratres
> atque odiis versare domos, tu verbera tectis,
> funereasque inferre faces, tibi numina mille,
> mille nocendi artes,

>   etc.

2 Satis hoc carmine huius Furie apparent officia, satis potentia, satis et truculentia, cum etiam Plutoni et sororibus odiosa sit. Sonat enim Alectho iuxta Fulgentium 'inpausabilis,' ut intelligatur omnem furiam ab animi inquietudine initiari. Que quidem inquie-

have them or does not use them, the authority of law will easily come undone. And then finally, because of human sins there is divine permission for furor to commingle with the elements and for the air to be corrupted by their discord: lethal plagues break out which devour us in our misery. So also human pride generates wars produce conflagration, devastation, and destruction.

: 7 :

On Alecto, first child of Acheron

Alecto is the first of the Furies, daughter of Acheron and Night. 1
Vergil describes her in this way:[39]

> She roused baleful Alecto from the seat of the dire sisters
> and infernal darkness, to whom sorrowful wars,
> angers, assaults, and noxious sins are dear.
> Even father Pluto himself hates and her sisters hate
> this Tartarean monster, for she turns herself into so many
>   faces,
> so many cruel looks, and, deadly, she sprouts snakes.

And a little further on:[40]

> You can arm harmonious brothers to battle each other,
> and turn homes to hatred, lash at houses,
> and bring in funeral torches; your divinity has a thousand
> forms, and you harm in a thousand ways.

This poem makes sufficiently clear the functions of this Fury, 2
her power, and her savageness, since she was hated by even Pluto
and her sisters. According to Fulgentius,[41] Alecto means "relentless," for it is understood that all fury begins with disquiet of the

tudo totiens intrat mentes, quotiens desistimus nos ipsos et Deum cognoscere.

: 8 :

De Thesiphone furia Acherontis secunda filia

1 Thesiphones Furiarum secunda est Acherontis et Noctis filia, quam sic designat Ovidius:

> Nec mora, Thesiphone madefactam sanguine summit
> importuna facem, fluvidoque cruore rubentem
> induitur pallam, tortoque incingitur angue,
> egrediturque domo. Luctus comitatur euntem
> et Pavor et Terror trepidoque Insania vultu,
>
> etc.

Quibus Claudianus addit:

> Centum illi stantes vibrabant ora ceraste,
> turba minor diri capitis; sedet intus abactis
> ferrea lux oculis, qualis per nubila Phebes
> Atracia rubet arce color; suffusa veneno.

2 Et his insuper addit Statius, dicens:

> Suffusa veneno
> tenditur ac sanie gliscit cutis; igneus atro
> ore vapor, quo longa sitis morbique famesque
> et populis mors una venit,
>
> etc.

Sic igitur uti per Virgilium Alecto qualitas, sic per hos tres vates Thesiphonis demonstrata est. Fulgentius preterea dicit, Thesi-

spirit; this disquiet enters our minds whenever we stop knowing ourselves and God.

: 8 :

On the Fury Tisiphone, second child of Acheron

Tisiphone, the second of the Furies, is the daughter of Acheron 1
and Night. Ovid describes her in this way:[42]

Without delay cruel Tisiphone seized her torch soaked
in blood, and put on her cloak red
with moist gore, girded herself with a twisted snake,
and left her house. Grief accompanied her on her way,
as did Panic and Terror and Madness with a look of horror.

Claudian adds to this:[43]

A hundred horned snakes stood there with vibrating tongues;
a smaller group upon her dire head, within her sunken eyes sat
an iron light, like Phoebus through the clouds glows red with
Atracian magic, suffused with poison.

And Statius adds to this, saying:[44] 2

Suffused with poison
her skin stretches and swells with blood; from her black
mouth
comes a fiery vapor along with thirst, disease, hunger,
and death for the multitudes.

Just as Vergil described the nature of Alecto, these three poets
described that of Tisiphone. Fulgentius[45] says otherwise, that Tisi-

phones idem quod Tritonphones, id est 'irarum vox.' In quam postquam pectus turgidum fecit inquietudo, facile devenitur, et ideo progressum talem facem sanguine madentem dicit Ovidius, eo quod ignea ira nunquam egreditur nisi in sanguinem, et ideo fluvido cruore rubentem dicit, ob colorem faciei hominis irati, et

3 ad dispositionem animi demonstrandam. Nec ante consurgit iratus quam illum amicorum comitantur lacrime, illi minus sano timentes, qui ideo a terrore comitatur, quia iratus omnis terribilis videatur. Serpentes autem eidem appositi habent ire sevitiam denotare. Hinc deveniens iratus in vocem emictit vapores, id est verba, per que sepe desolationes oriuntur, locorum et populorum mortes atque egestates.

: 9 :

De Megera furia III^a Acherontis filia

1 Megera furiarum tercia Acherontis et Noctis filia, sic a Claudiano ubi *De laudibus Stiliconis* effigiatur:

Improba mox surgit tristi de sede Megera,
quam penes insani fremitus animique prophanus
error et undantes spumis furialibus ire.
Non nisi quesitum cognata cede cruorem
illicitumque bibit patrium, quem fuderat ensis,
quem dederint fratres, hec terruit Herculis ora,
hec defensores terrarum polluit artus,
hec Atamantee direxit spicula dextre,
hec Agamennonios inter bachata penates

phone is the same as Tritonphones, that is, "the voice of angers." It easily reaches this point after disquiet swells the heart, and so Ovid says that this progresses like a torch soaked in blood because fiery anger never breaks out except into the blood; and he says that it is red with flowing gore because of the color of the face of an angry man, which must depict the disposition of the mind. Nor 3 does an angered person fly into a rage before the tears of his friends accompany him. They fear that he is not sane, and that he is accompanied by terror since every angry person seems terrifying. The serpents, fittingly, denote the savageness of the anger. And then it comes down to the angry man emitting vapors in his voice, that is, words, through which frequently come the devastation of regions and the deaths and impoverishment of people.

: 9 :

On the Fury Megaera, the third child of Acheron

Megaera, the third of the Furies, a daughter of Acheron and 1 Night, is portrayed by Claudian in his *On the Consulship of Stilicho* this way:[46]

> Wicked Megaera soon rose from her seat of sorrow,
> along with the raging of madness and the impious error
> of the mind and the angers welling up with frenzied froth.
> She drinks only blood in the murder of kin, premeditated
> and forbidden, shed by a paternal sword,
> or by brothers. She terrifies the face of Hercules,
> and defiles the arms of defenders of the land.
> She directed the javelin in the right hand of Athamas;
> she attacked two throats in the crazed house of Agamemnon;

alternis lusit iugulis, hac auspice tede
Edipodem matri nate et iunxere Thiestem,

etc.

2   Et quoniam Megera 'magna' sonat 'contentio' seu 'lis,' satis cognoscere possumus per superiores versus facta nomini convenire,
et sic fit ut ex inquietudine animi deveniamus in clamorem, et ex
clamore in odium et rixam, ex quibus furiosi in exitium sepissime
ruimus.

: 10 :

De Victoria IIII^a Acherontis filia

1   Victoriam dicit Paulus Acherontis fuisse filiam, ex Styge filia sua
susceptam. Cui adeo Iovem fuisse gratum aiunt ut, cum ei favisset
in pugna Gigantum, sibi loco muneris exhibuisse ut dii per Stygem
matrem eius iurarent, et si qui adversus iuramentum agerent, per
certum tempus a nectare abstinerent. Hanc Claudianus ubi *De
laudibus Styliconis* sic describit:

Ipsa duci sacras Victoria panderet alas
et palma viridi gaudens et amicta tropheis
custos imperii virgo, que sola mederis,
vulneribus nullumque doces sentire laborem,

etc.

Theodontius vero, fere concors Claudiano, in descriptione, eam
insuper ornat triumphalibus ornamentis. Verum Paulus discrepat,
eamque dicit letam, sed rubigine atque pulverulento squalore obsi-
tam, armis indutam, et cruentis manibus, nunc captivos, nunc

on her watch Oedipus married his mother,
and Thyestes married his daughters.

And because Megaera means "great contention" or "lawsuit," we   2
can recognize clearly from the above verses that her deeds fit her
name, and so it is that from the disquiet of the mind we descend
into shouting, and from shouting to hatred and quarreling, and
then in our fury we too often rush into ruin.

: 10 :

On Victory, fourth child of Acheron

Paul says that Victory was the daughter of Acheron by his daugh-   1
ter Styx. They say that she was so favored by Jupiter, because she
supported him in the battle against the Giants, that he granted to
her as a reward that the gods would swear by her mother Styx,
and if they broke that oath they would abstain from nectar for a
certain period of time. Claudian in his *In Praise of Stilicho* describes
her this way:[47]

> Victory herself spreads her sacred wings for the leader,
> both rejoicing in the green palm and cloaked in trophies,
> virgin guardian of the empire, you who alone heal
> wounds and teach us to not feel our hardship.

Then Theodontius, generally agreeing with Claudian's description,
adorns her in addition with triumphal decorations. Paul, however,
disagrees and says that she is joyous but covered in rust and dusty
squalor, clothed in arms, and with bloody hands counts first pris-

spolia recensentem, et ornamenta que Theodontius huic appone-
bat, filio eius, quem Honorem dicunt, exhibent omnia.

2   Sed quid senserint exquiramus. Victoriam Acherontis filiam
ideo voluisse veteres credo, quia non ex incuria et ocio acquiratur,
sed ex cogitationibus continuis, que dum ex ingenio exprimunt
utiliora consilia, angunt profecto cogitantem et ab eo gaudium
omnem amovent; et sic iam adest Acheron. Preterea nec in
comesationibus atque ioculationibus invenitur, quin imo ex vigiliis
circuitionibus et laboribus assiduis, constanti animo, et forti pectore, dolore vulnerum et tolerantia incursionum excerpitur, que
3 absque tristitia patientis evenire aut tolerari non possunt. Verum
ut differat hec tristitia a tristitia Furiarum, illa ab egritudine mentis, hec a corporea ut plurimum oritur. Et sic cui pater Acheron
venerat, Styx accedit evestigio mater. Econtra autem festantes nec
aliqua premeditantes facile deveniunt in ruinam; Troia anxia capi
non potuit, leta confestim capta est. Alatam Victoriam dicit
Claudianus, quia facile etiam una oportuna omissa vigilia non nunquam in partem evolat alteram.

4   Palma ornatur, quia nunquam lignum palme corrumpitur fron-
desque viriditatem conservant, ut victoris auctum robur et nomen
in longum virere intelligamus. Tropheis autem amicta est, ut secunda honoris species impensi victori monstretur, minor enim erat
triunphus, et quia in eo sacrificaret 'ovem' victor, 'ovatio' vocabatur,
seu vocabant veteres 'tropheum' truncum ad instar superati hostis
factum, et armis eiusdem indutum. Habitus Victorie a Paulo desi-
gnatus, aptior videtur quam is qui a Theodontio scribitur; non
enim extemplo victor ornamentis ornatur, non victorie sed ob victoriam ei postea exhibentur.

oners and then spoils; and they present all the ornaments Theodontius assigned her, to her son, whom they call Honor.

But let us look to what this means. I believe the ancients 2 wanted Victory to be the daughter of Acheron because victory is achieved not from neglect and laziness but by constant deliberation which by nature produces useful advice but also restricts one's deliberative process and removes him from any thought of joy, and so then Acheron is present. Moreover, she is found in neither merrymaking or jocularity but rather is gathered by watchmen making their rounds and unremitting efforts, true spirit and brave heart, grieving over wounds and suffering from attacks, for these are not capable of happening or being endured without the sadness of suffering. (To differentiate between this and the sadness of the Fu- 3 ries, the latter arises from an affliction of the mind, but this is mostly corporeal.) And so to whom Acheron comes as father, Styx is immediately present as mother. To the contrary, those who celebrate and plan nothing ahead come easily into ruin. Anxious Troy was not able to be captured, but cheerful Troy was captured immediately. Claudian says that Victory is winged because, simply, once the appropriate watchfulness is neglected, she always flies to the other side.

She is decorated with a palm because palm wood is never cor- 4 rupted and palm fronds remain green, telling us that the increased strength and name of a victor last a long time. She is cloaked in trophies to show the second type of honor given to a victor, for there was a minor triumph called an "ovation" in which the victor sacrificed a "sheep" [ovem], and the ancients used to call a "trophy" a tree trunk made to look like the conquered enemy dressed in their arms. Victory's dress as described by Paul seems more apt than what Theodontius depicted, for the victor is not decorated with ornaments right away, and they are exhibited afterward not for the victory but to the victor on account of his victory.

: II :

De Honore Victorie filio

1   Honorem Theodontius et Paulus filium dicunt fuisse Victorie, ex quo patre non dicunt. Hunc tamen arbitror ideo Victorie dictum filium, quia ex victoria quesita consequatur honor, qui quidem in presentia suscipientis exhibebatur, cum laudes in absentia prestarentur. Huic a Romanis templum olim constitutum fuit, templo Virtutis iunctum, ad quod nisi per templum Virtutis non erat introitus, ut appareret neminem nisi per virtutem honorem consequi posse. Etsi ob aliam causam cuiquam fiat, non honor sed ridicule atque letales blanditie sunt.

2   Huic coniugem fuisse Reverentiam volunt, et ex ea illi maiestatem exortam. Sunt tamen qui idem dicant Reverentiam et Honorem, cum differant. Est honor publicus et privatus: publicus cum alicui laurea vel triunphus decernitur; privatus is est qui a privatis impenditur, ut dum alicui privato assurgimus, eum premictimus primum in templo vel in mensa locum prestamus. Reverentia vero est quam maioribus, non ex decreto, sed sponte vel consuetudine exhibemus, cum flexis genibus et adaperto capite venerabiles viros alloquimur. Que solius Dei sunt, esto sibi ambitiosi principes occuparint.

: II :

On Honor, child of Victory

Theodontius and Paul say that Honor was the son of Victory; 1
they do not name the father. I think that Honor was said to be the
son of Victory because after the victory is won, honor follows,
which used to be exhibited in the presence of the recipient, while
praises were presented in absentia. The Romans once erected a
temple to Honor, next to the temple of Virtue; it had no entrance
other than through the temple of Virtue, so it appeared that no
one could achieve honor except through virtue. And if someone
was honored for another reason, it was not honor but ridicule and
lethal flattery.

They want Reverence to have been his wife, and he fathered 2
Majesty by her. Nonetheless, there are those who say that Reverence and Honor are the same, but they are different. Honor can
be public or private: public honor occurs when someone is awarded
laurels or a triumph; private is that which is awarded in private, as
when we extol someone in private, send him first into the temple,
or award him pride of place at the table. Reverence is what we
exhibit to our superiors, not by decree but spontaneously or by
custom, when we speak to venerable men on bended knees and
with our heads uncovered. This is the reverence we owe to God
alone, although ambitious princes claim it for themselves.

: 12 :

De Maiestate Honoris filia

1 Maiestatem Honoris atque Reverentie filiam dicit Ovidius. De qua ubi *De fastis* sic ait:

> Donec honor placidoque decens Reverentia vultu
>   corpora legitimis imposuere thoris.
> Hinc sacra Maiestas que mundum temperat omnem,
>   quaque die parta est edita magna fuit.
> Nec mora, consedit medio sublimis Olympo,
>   aurea purpureo conspicienda sinu,
>
>   etc.

2 Hanc Honoris et Reverentie filiam voluisse reor, quia ex honore impenso et exhibita reverentia sit quidam maioritatis status in suscipiente, ex quo maiestas est dicta, Deo soli competens.

: 13 :

De Ascalapho V° Acherontis filio

1 Ascalaphus Acherontis et Orne nynphe fuit filius, ut ait Ovidius:

> Ascalaphus audit[7] quem quondam dicitur Orne
> inter Avernales non ignotissima nynphas
> ex Acheronte suo fulvis peperisse sub undis,
>
>   etc.

: 12 :

On Majesty, daughter of Honor

Ovid says that Majesty is the daughter of Honor and Reverence. 1
He says this about her in his *Fasti*:[48]

> Until Honor and seemly Reverence with her calm face
>   place their bodies on their rightful couches.
> From here comes sacred Majesty who controls the entire
>   world.
>   She was great, beginning with the day she was born.
> No delay: she sat like gold up high in the center of Olympus
>   conspicuous in her purple robe.

I think they wanted her to be the daughter of Honor and Rev- 2
erence because there is a certain elevated status that accompanies
the person given honors and shown reverence, whereupon it is
called majesty, competing only with God.

: 13 :

On Ascalaphus, fifth child of Acheron

Ascalaphus was the son of Acheron and the nymph Orphne,[49] as 1
Ovid says:[50]

> [It was] heard by Ascalaphus, whom it is said that Orphne,
> by no means the least known of nymphs of the Avernus,
> once produced under the tawny waves for Acheron.

357

Hunc aiunt, rapta Proserpina a Plutone, cum quereretur nunquid aliquid apud inferos gustasset, eam accusasse atque dixisse tria grana mali punici ex viridario Ditis gustasse; ex quo factum est ut non restitueretur ex toto Proserpina, et ipse verteretur a Cerere in bubonem.

2   Circa quod figmentum nil credo aliud voluisse poetas, quam ostendere odiosissimum esse accusatoris officium; et idcirco aiunt in bubonem versum Ascalaphum, eo quod, sicut bubo funesta est avis et sinistri semper augurii reputata, sic et accusator semper laboris et anxietatis prenuntius est accusato. Preterea bubo stridula avis est, ut ostendatur clamosos esse accusatores; sic et uti bubo sub multitudine variarum pennarum modicum habet corporis et eque accusatoris sub longa verbositate ut plurimum reperitur modicum veritatis.

3   Igitur non incongrue filius dicitur Acherontis, a similitudine saltem officii, quia sicut Acheron gaudio privat quos transvehit, sic et accusator hos replet tristitia in quos invehit. Quod autem Orne mater eius dicatur, a consuetudine bubonis sumptum est, qui sepissime ut aiunt, qui de proprietatibus rerum scripsere, die mortuorum sepulcris inhabitat, que ut ait Papias *orne* vocantur. Et Lucanus ait:

Celo tegitur qui non habet urnam.

Spectantia ad Cererem et Proserpinam, ubi de eis in sequentibus apponentur.

They say that after Proserpina was abducted by Pluto, when there was a question as to whether she had tasted anything while among the dead, he accused her and said that she had tasted three seeds of a pomegranate from the garden of Dis, and it was because of this that Proserpina was not restored entirely, and he was himself turned into an owl by Ceres.

I do not believe that the poets wanted anything from this fiction other than to show that the role of being an informer is very offensive. Regarding that, they say Ascalaphus was turned into an owl because just as the owl is a funereal bird and always thought to be associated with evil omens, so also an informer is the harbinger of hardship and anxiety for the accused. In addition, the owl is a strident bird, so this suggests that informers are noisy as well; so also as the owl has a modicum of body underneath a multitude of various feathers, only a modicum of truth is found equally within the great verbosity of the informer.

Therefore it is appropriate to call him the son of Acheron, at least in the similarity of their tasks, because just as Acheron deprives of joy those who cross him, so also an informer fills those with sadness whose path he crosses. That his mother is called Orphne is derived from the behavior of the owl: as those who have written about the characteristics of things say, owls often inhabit tombs on the day of the dead and are therefore called *orne* as Papias[51] says. And Lucan says:[52]

He who has no urn is covered by the sky.

Observations on Ceres and Proserpina will follow in subsequent passages about them.[53]

: 14 :

De Styge Acherontis VI^a filia

1 Styx inferna dicitur palus et Acherontis et Terre filia extimatur a
cunctis, et secundum Albericum deum nutrix et hospita, per quam
etiam, ut supra dictum est, dii iurant, neque timore pene audent
deierare, ut ait Virgilius:

> Stygiamque paludem,
> dii cuius iurare timent et fallere numen,
>
> etc.

Privabatur enim ad tempus qui deierasset nectareo poculo. Et hoc
ideo illi concessum volunt, quia Victoria eius filia diis adversus
Titanos pugnantibus favisset. Styx enim interpretatur 'tristitia,'
ideo Acherontis, qui 'sine gaudio' est, dicta filia, eo quod, ut ait
Albericus, qui gaudio caret in tristitiam labitur facile, imo ut laba-
2 tur necesse est. Terra autem illi attribuitur mater, quia cum omnis
aqua a fonte illo aquarum unico occeano procedat, trahi per viscera
terre ad illum usque locum, unde prorumpit in publicum, necesse
est; et sic Terra Stygis dicitur mater; seu, secundum alium sensum, inter humores ab elementis impressos mortalibus, a terra
imprimitur melanconia, que procul dubio tristitie mater et altrix
est. Deorum autem nutricem et hospitam non absque misterio
Stygem voluere.

3 Circa quod advertendum est duplicem esse tristitiam; aut tristamur quia detestanda nostra desideria, quacunque ex causa sit,
consequi nequeamus; aut tristamur cognoscentes, quia aliquid seu
multa minus iuste peregimus. Tristitia prima nunquam deorum
fuit nutrix aut hospita. Secunda vero fuit et est; nam ex minus

: 14 :

On Styx, the sixth child of Acheron

Styx is said to be an infernal swamp and is thought by all to be the   1
daughter of Acheron and Earth. According to Albericus[54] she was
the nurse and hostess of the gods. Also, as was said above,[55] the
gods swear by her, nor do they dare to swear falsely for fear of being punished, as Vergil says:[56]

The Stygian swamp,
by whose divine force the gods fear to swear and deceive,

for whoever swears falsely is deprived of the cup of nectar for a
period. And they want to concede this to her because her daughter
Victory had favored the gods when they were fighting against the
Titans. Styx means "sadness," and she is called the daughter of
Acheron, who is "without joy" because he who lacks joy, as Albericus says, easily slips into sadness; in fact, it is a necessary consequence. Earth is attributed to her as mother because, while all   2
water proceeds from that single source of waters, the ocean, it
needs to be taken through the bowels of the earth to that place
from which it breaks out into the open. And so Earth is said to be
the mother of Styx, or, in another interpretation, of the elemental
humors that influence mortals, it is the earth that influences mel-
ancholy, which is with little doubt the mother and sustainer of
sadness. Mysteriously they want Styx to be the nurse and hostess
of the gods.

It should be noted that there are two kinds of sadness: first, we   3
are sad because we are unable to follow, for whatever reason, our
accursed desires, or we are sad to know that we have not properly
done something or many things. The first type of sadness was
never the nurse and hostess of the gods. But the second was and

bene commissis dolere et tristari, nil aliud est quam alimenta pre-
bere virtuti, per quam in deitates suas gentiles ivere, et nos Christiani in beatitudinem imus eternam, in qua dii, non inanes aut
4 perituri sumus. Has tristitie species optime sensisse in sexto *Eney-
dos* ostendit Virgilius, ubi perfidos et obstinatos in malum homines
mictit in Tartara, ubi nulla est redemptio, alios vero post exac-
tas ob culpam penas Elysios ducit in campos; seu volumus dicere quod forsan magis sensere poete, deos, id est sol et sydera,
ad Egyptios aliquando abiisse, quod hyemali tempore contingit,
quando sol semotus a nobis tenet solstitium antarticum, quod ultra meridionales Egyptios cenith capitis habitantium ibidem facit,
et tunc a palude Stygia pascuntur sydera secundum opinionem
eorum qui existimabant superiorum corporum ignes ex humiditate
vaporum ex aqua surgentium pasci; et apud eam hospitantur donec versus articum polum gradum non flexerint.

5 Stygem autem esse sub australi plaga demonstrat Seneca eo in
libro quem scripsit *De sacris Egyptiorum*, dicens, Stygem paludem
apud superos esse, id est apud eos qui in superiori sunt hemisperio, ostendens inde quod circa Syenem extremam Egypti partem
versus austrum locum esse, quem Phyalas, hoc est 'amicas,' incole
vocitent, et apud eas paludem esse ingentem, que cum transitu
difficillima sit, limosa nimis et papiris implicita, Styx appellata est,
quasi tristitiam ob laborem nimium transeuntibus inferens.

6 Iurare autem deos per Stygem potest esse ratio talis, consuevi-
mus enim per eas res quas timemus aut optamus iurare; sane qui
summe gaudet non videtur habere quod cupiat, cum non desit
quod timeat, et ex his dii sunt quos felices faciunt, quam ob rem
restat ut iurent per tristitiam quam sibi noscunt adversam.

is, for to feel pained and saddened from not doing things well does nothing other than provide nourishment for virtue, by means of which the pagans went to their gods and we Christians go to our eternal beatitude, where we become divine, neither empty nor mortal. Vergil explains these types of sadness best in the sixth book of the *Aeneid*, where he sends the treacherous and resolute villains to Tartarus, where there is no redemption, but the rest, after being punished for their offenses, he leads to the Elysian Fields. Or, we wish to say what perhaps the poets understand better: the gods, that is, the sun and stars, retreated at some point to the Egyptians, which happens in winter time when the sun is distant from us and occupies the southern solstice, which then makes its zenith above the inhabitants who live beyond the southern Egyptians, and then the stars feed from the Stygian swamp according to the opinion of those who used to think that the fires of the higher bodies fed on the moisture of vapors rising from water, and they were hosted by her as long as they did not change their course toward the north pole.

Seneca,[57] in the book he wrote *On Egyptian Rites*, shows that Styx was under the southern region, saying that Styx was a swamp among the gods, that is, among those who are in the upper hemisphere, proving in this that near Syene, the part of Egypt furthest to the south, is what the inhabitants call Philae,[58] that is, "friends," and there exists a large swamp there which, because it is so difficult to cross, being so muddy and entangled with papyrus, is called Styx as if it produces sadness from the excessive effort it takes to cross it.

It is possible that this is the reason the gods swore by the Styx: we often swear by those things we fear or desire; he who rejoices most does not seem to have what he wants, for he does not lack a reason to fear; and in this category are the gods, whom people regard to be happy, wherefore they are left to swear by the sadness that they know to be their opposite.

7   Quod deierantes nectareo priventur poculo, eo dictum puto, quia qui ex felicitate in miseriam devenere deierasse, id est minus bene egisse, dicebant, et sic a nectareo poculo ad amaritudinem infortunii devenisse.

: 15 :

De Cocito infernali fluvio Stygis filio,
qui genuit Flegetontem

1   Cocitus infernalis est fluvius, quem ex Styge palude natum dicit Albericus, quod ob id arbitror dictum, quia 'luctus,' quem per Cocitum intelligunt, ex 'tristitia,' que Styx est, oriatur.

: 16 :

De Flegetonte fluvio infernali Cociti filio,
qui genuit Lethem

1   Flegeton, et hic inferni fluvius est, et secundum Theodontium, Cociti filius, ob id, ut existimo, dictum, quia ex diuturno luctu quis facile veniat in furorem, quod quidem ut non nullis placet 2 natura contingit. Nam exhausto lacrimis humiditate cerebro, ferventes cordis impetus frenari non possunt, et sic quis in furiam labitur. Flegeton enim 'ardor' interpretatur, ut comprehendatur ex fervore cordis nimio hominum excitari furores.

That they are deprived of their drink of nectar I think is said   7
for this reason: those who descend from happiness into misery
swear falsely, that is, do not do it well, and so they descend from
the drink of nectar to the bitterness of misfortune.

: 15 :

On Cocytus, infernal river, son of Styx, who fathers Phlegethon

Cocytus was an infernal river which Albericus[59] says was born   1
from the Stygian swamp. I think they say this because "grief,"
which they understood as Cocytus, arises from sadness, which is
Styx.

: 16 :

On Phlegethon, infernal river, son of Cocytus, who fathers Lethe

Phlegethon was also a river of the nether region, and, according to   1
Theodontius, son of Cocytus. This was said because, as I think,
someone easily comes from lasting grief into furor, which happens
naturally, according to some. For when tears have drained the   2
brain of its moisture, those who are inflamed cannot bridle the
urging of their heart, and so they slip into fury. Phlegethon means
"burning," in which we understand that human furor is aroused
from excessive inflammation of the heart.

: 17 :

De Lethe fluvio infernali Flegetontis filio

1 Lethem inferni dicunt fluvium et Flegetontis filium. Quod ideo fictum puto, eo quod ex furore nascatur oblivio. Cernimus enim furiosos sue suorumque dignitatis oblitos, et Lethes interpretatur 'oblivio.' Hunc fluvium ponit Virgilius apud Elysios campos et eo illos potari, quos Mercurius vult reverti ad corpora, de quibus supra dictum, ubi de Mercurio primo.

2 Dantes vero noster illum describit in summitate montis Purgatorii, et ex illo dicit animas mundas et celo dignas potare, ut obliviscantur preteritorum malorum, quorum memoria felicitati perpetue prestaret impedimentum.

: 18 :

De Vulcano primo, Celi filio IIII°, qui genuit Apollinem

1 Vulcanus primus, teste Tullio ubi *De naturis deorum*, Celo natus est, de quo nil aliud reperitur, nisi quia ex Minerva secundi Iovis filia, ut dicit Theodontius, Apollinem genuerit primum. Credo ego hunc igneum et inexausti vigoris hominem fuisse et Saturni fratrem.

: 17 :

On Lethe, infernal river, son of Phlegethon

They called Lethe a river of the nether region and the son of 1
Phlegethon. I think they invented this because forgetfulness is
born from fury. We see how the furious forget their own dignity
and that of others, and Lethe means "forgetfulness." Vergil[60] places
this river in the Elysian Fields, and says that those who drink of it
are those whom Mercury wishes to be returned to bodies, which
we spoke of earlier in the discussion of the first Mercury.[61]

Our Dante[62] describes it on the summit of Mt. Purgatory, and 2
he says that spirits which are purified and worthy of heaven drink
from it to forget their past sins, the memory of which would present a hindrance to perpetual happiness.

: 18 :

On the first Vulcan, fourth child of Sky, who fathered Apollo

The first Vulcan, with Cicero's[63] On the Nature of the Gods as evi- 1
dence, was born to Sky. I have not found anything else about him
other than that, according to Theodontius, he fathered the first
Apollo by Minerva, the daughter of the second Jupiter. I think
that he was a fiery man of inexhaustible vigor, and the brother of
Saturn.

: 19 :

De Apolline, primi Vulcani filio

1 Apollo, ut Ciceroni placet et Theodontio, filius fuit primi Vulcani atque Minerve et, ut ipsemet Tullius asserit, ubi *De naturis deorum*,
2 hic omnium Apollinum fuit antiquior. Hunc dicit Theodontius fuisse medicine artis repertorem, et primum virium herbarum cognitorem, quantumcunque[8] Plinius, in libro *Hystorie naturalis*, asserat Chironem, Saturni et Phyllare filium, primum fuisse herbarum virium atque medicamentorum repertorem.

: 20 :

De Mercurio V° Celi filio

1 Mercurius qui tercius est, ut ait Tullius *De naturis deorum*, Celo patre et Die matre natus est, obscenius tamen excitata natura, eo quod aspectu Proserpine motus sit. Huic ornamenta que ceteris apponuntur, dicit tamen Theodontius Egyptios virge huius circumvolvisse serpentem, quod[9] testatur Valerius Martialis *Epygrammatum* libro septimo dicens:

> Cillenes celique decus, facunde minister,
> aurea cui torto virga dracone viret.

Aiunt insuper eum ex Venere sorore sua Hermofroditum filium suscepisse.

: 19 :

On Apollo, the son of the first Vulcan

Apollo, as Cicero and Theodontius think, was the son of the first   1
Vulcan and Minerva, and, as Cicero[64] himself asserts in his *On the
Nature of the Gods*, he was the most ancient of all the Apollos.
Theodontius says that he was the inventor of the art of medicine   2
and the first to be knowledgeable about the powers of herbs, however much Pliny[65] in his *Natural History* asserts that Chiron, the
son of Saturn and Philyra, was the first to be knowledgeable about
the powers of herbs and medicines.

: 20 :

On Mercury, the fifth son of Sky

The third Mercury, as Cicero[66] says in his *On the Nature of the Gods*,   1
was born to his father Sky and his mother Day, but in a state of
obscene arousal from the effect of having caught sight of Proserpina. He had the ornaments which were assigned to the others,
but Theodontius says the Egyptians encircled his staff with a serpent, which Valerius Martial[67] witnesses in the seventh book of his
Epigrams:

> Glory of Cyllene and the sky, eloquent minister,
>   whose golden wand with twisted serpent remains green.

In addition, they say that he had a son Hermaphroditus by his
sister Venus.

2   His premissis, quid sensisse veteres fictionibus voluerint exquiramus; et primo quid eum a Celo obscene genitum dicant. Hoc
circa multa dicebat Leontius, ut prospectum celi in terram et ra-
ram Mercurii planete apparitionem, et alia huiusmodi, que quoniam frivola visa sunt, eis omissis Barlae relatum apponere libuit.
Dicebat enim huius Mercurii a nativitate nomen Hermes fuisse,
seu Hermias, eumque ex stupro Phylonis Arcadis et Proserpine
eiusdem filie, in quam se balneantem impudicos iniecerat oculos,
procreatum; et sic satis patet quia obscene excitata natura sit, inspecta Proserpina.

    Hermetem autem eum nominatum dicit, eo quod eo nato, cum
de futuris eius successibus Phylon consuluisset mathematicum,
habuit pro responso eum divinum futurum hominem et maximum
divinarum rerum interpretem. Quam ob rem Phylon, qui illum
exponi proposuerat, servari fecit, atque cum diligentia nutriri,
eumque vocavit Hermetem, eo quod *hermena* Grece, Latine sonet
3   'interpres.' Post hec cum adolevisset, ob ruborem sceleste originis
in Egyptum secessit, ubi mirabiliter profecit in multis et potissime
in arismetrica, geometria et astrologia, adeo ut Egyptiacis ceteris
preferretur, et cum ob excellentiam predictorum iam Mercurii nomen meruisset, medicinalibus operam dedit tamque in his sublimis effectus est, ut non omisso Mercurii nomine, crederetur
Apollo, et longe profusius in sacris Egyptiorum instructus, cunctis
factus est homo mirabilis; ibique seu ad eius nobilitandam originem, seu potius ad ignominiam originis contegendam, Celi dictus
est filius et Diei, quasi a celo missus et in diei luce factus conspi-
4   cuus. De hoc preterea Hermes Trimegistus, qui se testatur eius
fuisse nepotem, mentionem facit eo in libro, quem *De ydolo* scribit

Now that we have set forth the basics, let us examine what the 2
ancients wished to signify with these fictions, the first being why
they say he was born from the indecent Sky. Leontius used to say
much about this, referring to the view from the sky toward the
earth, the rare appearance of the planet Mercury, and other things
of this sort, which seem pointless. I would like to ignore this and
refer to what Barlaam added, for he used to say that the name of
this Mercury at birth was Hermes, or Hermias, and that he was
the product of illicit intercourse between the Arcadian Philo and
his daughter Proserpina, toward whom he had cast his shameless
eyes while she was bathing. So it is sufficiently clear that he
reached an obscene state of arousal once he had seen Proserpina.

Barlaam said that he was named Hermes because after he was
born, Philo consulted an astrologer about his future outcome, and
the response he heard was that he would be a divine man and the
greatest interpreter of divine matters. For this reason Philo, who
had suggested exposing him, made sure to rescue him and nurture
him with care; and he called him Hermes because the Greek word
hermena means "interpreter." After this, when he had matured, be- 3
cause of the disgrace of his accursed birth he retired to Egypt
where he became so remarkably accomplished in many areas, especially arithmetic, geometry, and astrology, that he surpassed the
other Egyptians; and when on account of the excellence of his
predictions he now warranted the name of Mercury, he turned his
attention to medicine and became so exalted that without losing
the name Mercury he was thought to be Apollo; and more thoroughly learned in the sacred rites of the Egyptians, he became a
man who was admirable to everyone; and there, whether to ennoble his birth, or rather for concealing the ignominy of his birth,
he was said to be the son of Sky and Day, as if he was sent from
the sky and made conspicuous in the light of day. In addition, 4
Hermes Trismegistus,[68] who bears witness that he was his grandson, makes mention of him in the book *On Idols*, which he wrote

ad Asclepium, dicens, quod esto mortuus, venientes ad eius sepulcrum adiuvet et conservet.

Sed quid in hec velint insignia advertendum, cum aliud in planeta, aliud in medico, aliud in rethore et aliud in mercatore, vel
5   fure Mercurio habeant demonstrare. Dicunt ergo eum, ut premonstratum est, ubi de Mercurio primo, galero tectum, ut per illum Celum intelligamus, a quo etsi tegamur omnes a medico potissime cognosci debet, circa planetarum motus varios et eorum
dispositiones et syderum speculando, ut per ea tanquam in humana corpora agentia et causantia plurima, et egritudinum causas
et successus et oportuna remedia possit agnoscere, atque ea que ad
salutem egrotantis necessaria monstrantur disponere.

6   Talaria vero ideo illi apponuntur pennata, ut per ea noscamus
oportere medicum promptam ad remedia contingentium habere
scientiam, ne ante egritudine laborans deficiat, quam accesserit
tardi medici argumentum; preterea ut et ipsi cognoscant, cum nature ministri sint, omni alia seposita cura se debere ad necessitates
vocantium evolare. Est illi insuper virga, quam supra diximus, illi
ab Apolline fuisse concessam, ut intelligatur primo quia concessa
est ab Apolline medicine autore, id est a medico experto et doc-
tore, autoritas approbantis, absque qua nemo hercle deberet tale
officium exercere.

7   Insuper dicunt eum hac virga ab Orco pallentes evocare animas,
ut appareat multos iam dudum iudicio et arte multorum meden-
tium in mortem ituros, scientis medici adiutorio in vitam retentos,
seu a morte, id est ab Orco potius revocatos. Sic versa vice, dum
minus morborum noscuntur cause, hac eadem virga, id est autoritate vel artificio minus congrue operato, anime que stetissent emic-

for Asclepius, saying that although he was dead, he would help and save those who came to his tomb.

But we must turn our attention to what they thought notable in this since they had to represent one thing in the planet Mercury, another in the medical, another in the rhetorical, and another in the mercantile, or in the thieving Mercury. For they say, as presented before in the discussion of the first Mercury,[69] that he was covered by a cap, which we understand as the sky. Although we are all covered by the sky, the cap ought to be identified chiefly with the medical Mercury: by contemplating the various motions of the planets and their dispositions and those of the stars acting on human bodies and causing many things, it is possible through them to identify the causes of sicknesses and their progression and appropriate remedies and show what is necessary to prescribe for the health of the sick person.

Winged sandals are ascribed to him to teach us that a doctor 6 must have skill prepared to remedy emergencies, lest the person laboring in sickness expire before hearing the decision of a slow-working doctor, and that also the doctors themselves, as ministers of nature, should know to put all other matters aside and fly to the needs of those calling them. He has as well a wand, which we said before had been given to him by Apollo, so that it would be known above all that Apollo, the originator of medicine, that is, an expert and learned doctor, gave him the authority of approval, without which, by Hercules, no one ought to perform such a duty.

In addition, they say that with this wand he evoked the pale 7 spirits from Orcus because it is clear that many people who by the arts of skilled healers were long ago judged to be dead, are kept alive by the help of a knowledgeable doctor, or are called back from death, that is rather, from Orcus. Conversely, when the causes of diseases are less known well, this same wand, that is, the

tuntur ad Tartara, id est in mortem. Somnos etiam hac virga, id
est arte, dat medicus persepe in somnum declinare nequentibus, et
8 aufert in suam perniciem dormientibus nimium. Ventos insuper
hac virga medicus amovet, dum stultas egrotantium opiniones
suasionibus et rationibus veris removet, auferendo timorem, seu
etiam dum ventositates viscera in gravissimum patientis dolorem
agitantes suis aut potionibus, aut remediis aliis resolvunt in nichilum. Sic et nubila tranant dum humiditates superfluas educunt,
quasi tranantes, id est ad se trahentes e corpore languido.

9 Serpens autem ideo circumvolvitur virge, ut intelligamus medi-
cinale exercitium absque naturali et debita discretione tendere non
forte minus in perniciem quam salutem. Pendent enim non minus
ex animadvertentia medentis, quam ex arte quandoque remedia.
Iubet enim ars reubarbaro e corporibus expelli superflua, quod si
debilitato nimium dabitur, facile vita cum superfluis emictetur, et
ideo circa talia et alia omnia medentis plurimum oportuna discretio, que per serpentem prudentissimum animal designatur, virge
ideo circumvolutum, ut nunquam absque discretione exerceatur
autoritas.

10 Quod Hermofroditum genuerit dicit Paulus verum non esse,
sed ideo fictum atque appositum est, quia primus Egyptiis, qui
monstruosum arbitrabantur hermofroditos nasci atque tanquam
rem preter naturam abiciebant, si quando aliquem nasci contigisset, ostendit, quia naturali gigni ratione poterant, et qua in parte
matricis susciperentur a femina.

authority and artifice used less effectively, sends down to Tartarus, that is, to death, spirits that might have survived. By means of this wand, that is, by skill, a doctor often puts to sleep those who are unable to fall asleep, and he carries off into ruin those who sleep too much. In addition, with this wand a doctor removes flatulence, 8 when through persuasion and true reasoning he removes the foolish opinions of those who are sick by eliminating their fear, or also when his potions or other remedies resolve into nothing the windiness which stirs up the severe pain in a patient's viscera. So also they penetrate clouds of anxiety when they draw out excess moisture, as if penetrating, that is, drawing them from a languid body into itself.

The serpent wraps itself around the wand because without natural and the required discretion, the practice of medicine is more predisposed toward destruction than health. Sometimes remedies depend no less on a doctor's attentiveness than on his skill: the skill assists in expelling excess from the body when using rhubarb, but if it is given to someone who is too debilitated, it will easily remove his life as well as the excess, and so in this and other conditions the discretion of the doctor is quite useful. This is designated by the serpent, a very wise animal, so wound around the wand to make sure authority is never practiced without discretion.

Paul says that it is not true that Mercury fathered Hermaphroditus but that this was fabricated, and yet it is apposite because Mercury first showed the Egyptians, who used to regard the birth of a hermaphrodites as monstrous and disdain the occasional birth of one as a preternatural event, that their births were due to natural causes, and in which part of the female a woman could carry them.

: 21 :

De Hermofrodito Mercurii et Veneris filio

1 Hermofroditum dicit Theodontius ex Venere fuisse filium Mercurii, quod etiam testatur Ovidius dicens:

Mercurio puerum et diva Cythereide natum
Nayades Ydeis enutrivere sub antris;
cuius erat species in qua materque paterque
cognosci possent: nomen quoque traxit ab illis,

etc.

Ex quo insuper Ovidius fabulam recitat talem. Quod cum Yda monte Frigie, in quo fuerat altus, derelicto, vagans in Cariam usque devenisset, fontem limpidum vidit quem Salmacis nynpha in-
2 colebat. Que cum eum formosissimum vidisset, evestigio amavit, et blandis verbis in suam sententiam trahere conata est. Tandem cum verecundaretur adolescentulus, aspernareturque nynphe verbaque pariter et amplexus, illa, simulato recessu, post vepretum latuit. Iuvenis autem putans abiisse nynpham nudus fontem intravit. Quod Salmacis videns, abiectis vestibus, confestim et ipsa in
3 fontem se nudam dedit renitentemque tenuit. Verum cum eum inflexibilem cerneret, oravit ut ex ambobus efficeretur unus, et factum est, et sic qui masculus intraverat fontem, masculus illum exivit et femina, et deprecatus est ut qui in eo balnearentur in posterum hanc eandem ignominiam reportarent, quod obtentum est favente precibus utroque parente.

Hermofroditum ex Mercurio et Venere genitum vult Albericus lascivientem preter oportunitatem esse sermonem, qui, cum virilis esse debeat, nimia verborum mollicie videtur effeminatus.

: 21 :

On Hermaphroditus, son of Mercury and Venus

Theodontius says that Hermaphroditus was the son of Mercury 1
by Venus. Ovid also testifies to this, saying:[70]

> A boy born to Mercury and the divine Cytherid
> the Idaean Naiads nourished in their caves;
> His type was that in which both his mother and father
> could be recognized; his name also he took from both.

In addition, Ovid recites this fable about him. When he left the
Phrygian Mt. Ida, where he had been nurtured, and wandered
until he reached Caria, he saw the clear spring which the nymph
Salmacis inhabited. Seeing how extremely handsome he was, she 2
immediately fell in love and with coaxing words tried to attract
him into a mutual feeling. Because the young man was embar-
rassed and rejected equally the nymph's words and embraces, she
then pretended to withdraw and hid behind a bramble thicket.
Thinking the nymph had departed, the youth, naked, slipped into
the spring. Seeing this, and with her clothes tossed aside, Salmacis
herself, also naked, immediately entered the spring and held onto
him as he struggled. When she saw that he would not acquiesce, 3
she prayed that the two of them become one, and it was done.
And so, he who had entered the spring as masculine, came out
masculine and feminine, and he prayed that those who later bathed
in the spring suffer this same ignominy, and his prayers were favored and granted by each of his parents.

Albericus[71] wants Hermaphroditus, born from Mercury and
Venus, to represent wanton and inappropriate speech, for though
he ought to be manly, because of the excessive tenderness of his
words he seems to be effeminate.

4   Ego vero hermofroditum habere utrumque sexum ad naturam Mercurii refero, quem venerabilis Andalo aiebat, eo quod cum masculinis planetis masculus esset, cum femininis autem femina, inferre inter cetera his quorum nativitatibus preerat, ni planetarum alius obsisteret vel celi locus ut utriusque sexus concupiscientia teneretur. Sed volunt non nulli altius intellexisse poetam, dicentes in matricibus mulierum septem conceptui aptas cellulas esse, quarum tres in dextera uteri sunt, et totidem in sinistra, et una media, et ex his unaqueque duos posse concipere; quantumcunque dicat Albericus in libro *De naturis animalium*, se ab ortu cuiusdam mulie-

5   ris advertisse eam centum et L filios invicem concepisse. Ex his enim que in dextra sunt, cum semen concipiunt, masculos pariunt, que autem in sinistra feminas, cum vero in ea que media est concipitur, nascantur utrumque sexum habentes, quos hermofroditas dicimus; et sic in cellula illa tanquam in fonte utriusque sexus lucta est, et dum vincere conatur uterque, ne alter succumbat, efficitur ut utriusque victorie vestigia videantur. Et sic rata manet oratio, ut si quis fontem illum intraverit semivir exeat illum.

Sane longe aliter sensisse poetantes existimo. Est enim Salmacis Carie fons celeberrimus, qui ne hac labe pollutus appareat, et

6   purgare fontem, et quid dederit fictioni causam libet apponere. Est igitur, ut Vitruvio eo in volumine quod *De architectonica* scripsit placet, fons cui Salmacis nomen est in Caria, haud longe ab Halicarnaso, claritate precipuus et sapore egregius, circum quem barbari olim, Carii scilicet et Lelege habitabant, qui a Nyda et Arevania Arcadibus, a quibus ibi Troezen communis deducta colonia, pulsi ad montana fugere et latrociniis ac discursionibus omnia infestare cepere. Sed cum de colonis Arcas unus lucri tractus avidi-

That Hermaphroditus had both sexes I trace back to the nature   4
of Mercury. The venerable Andalò used to say that because Mercury was masculine with the masculine planets and feminine with
the feminine, he brought to births over which he presided, among
other things, unless another planet or its place in the sky inter-
fered, a desire for both sexes. But others wish to understand the
poet in a more profound way, saying that in the wombs of females
there are seven chambers suitable for conception: there are three
on the right side on the right of the uterus, and an equal number
on the left, and one in the middle, and each of these can conceive
two — even if Albericus[72] in his *On the Nature of Animals* might say
a certain woman conceived one hundred and fifty aborted children. When those on the right receive the seed, they produce   5
males, those on the left females, while those conceived in the
middle are born having both sexes, and we call them Hermaphrodites. And so in that chamber, as if in the spring, there is a struggle between the two sexes, and although each tries to conquer,
neither succumbs, so it turns out that each one's vestiges of victory
remain visible. And so the pronouncement remains valid: whoever
enters that spring leaves half a man.

But I think the poets understood it very differently, for Salmacis is a very famous spring in Caria, and so that it would not appear to have been stained by this pollution, I would like to purge
the spring and attribute a reason for the fiction. And so, as Vitru-   6
vius chose to write in his *On Architecture*, there is in Caria (not at
all far from Halicarnassus) a spring named Salmacis, distinctive
for its clarity and excellent taste. Near this spring barbarous people — namely it was Carians and the Leleges who used to inhabit
that area — had been driven away by the Arcadians of Mela and
Areuania,[73] who founded the colony of Troezen there; they fled to
the mountains and began to attack and harass everyone with pi-
racy.[74] But when Arcas, one of the colonists, compelled by avarice

tate prope fontem tabernam meritoriam edidisset, quasi aque bonitas ceptis suis esset prestatura favorem, factum est ut tam aque
delectatione quam cibi oportunitate non nunquam barbari imma-
nes descenderent in tabernam et consuetudine paulatim barbariem
ponere, et Grecorum mollioribus moribus atque humanioribus
adherere inciperent, donec ex ferocissimis mites viderentur effecti.

7   Et quoniam mansuetudo respectu feritatis videatur feminea, dictum est ut qui illo uterentur fonte effeminarentur.

: 22 :

De Venere magna VI^a Celi filia

1   Venus magna, ut ubi *De naturis deorum* scribit Cicero, Celi fuit filia
et Diei, et cum preter hanc tres alias fuisse demonstret, hanc primam omnium asserit extitisse. Attamen cum figmenta plurima
circa Veneres indistincte comperiantur, his sumptis que ad hanc
spectare videbuntur, reliqua reliquis relinquemus, non quia huic
adaptari non possint omnia, sed postquam aliis attributa sunt, illis, dum de eis sermo fiet, apposuisse decentius est.

2   Huius igitur ante alia filium fuisse Amorem geminum voluere,
ut testatur Ovidius, dum dicit, 'Alma fave, dixi, geminorum mater
amorum,' etc. De patre autem dissentiunt, cum dicant alii ex Iove
genitum, alii ex Libero patre. Sic et Gratias quas huius etiam dicunt filias. Dicunt insuper huic cingulum esse quod *ceston* nomi-
nant, quo cinctam eam asserunt legitimis intervenire nuptiis. Aliis

and greed, established a tavern near the fountain, as if the goodness of the water would bestow favor on his undertaking, it happened that sometimes the savage barbarians would come down to the tavern, as much because of their liking for the water as the opportunity to obtain a meal, and little by little they put aside their barbarian qualities and began to adhere to the more civilized and refined customs of the Greeks until the most ferocious people seemed to have been made gentle. And since their mildness seemed 7 womanly in comparison to their savagery, it was said that those who used that spring had become effeminate.

: 22 :

On great Venus, sixth child of Sky

Great Venus, as Cicero[75] writes in his *On the Nature of the Gods*, 1 was the daughter of Sky and Day, and although he mentions that there are three other Venuses in addition to her, he asserts that she was the first. But although most of the fabrications about the Venuses seem to be indistinct, we will treat those which seem to refer to her and postpone the rest — not because all of the fabrications could not be accommodated to her, but once they have been distributed to the other Venuses, it will be more appropriate to present them when they become the subject under discussion.

Above all they prefer the son of this Venus to be the twin 2 Amor, as Ovid bears witness when he says,[76] "Favor me, I said, nurturing mother of twin Amors." They disagree about his father, for some say he was born to Jupiter, others that it was Liber who was his father. This is so as well for the Graces, whom they say were also her daughters. They say in addition that she had a girdle which they called *cestos*, and they assert that she wore it when occupied with legitimate marriages; they say that she participated in

vero coniunctionibus maris et femine dicunt absque cingulo inte-
resse. Eam[10] insuper dicunt summe Solis progeniem habere odio
propter adulterium eius cum Marte, ab eo Vulcano patefactum.

3   Addunt preterea in tutelam eius esse columbas. Et cum eidem
currum tribuant, illum a cignis trahi volunt, mirtumque arborem
illi sacram statuunt et ex floribus rosam. Post hec etiam dicit
Theodontius eam in domum Martis Furias hospitio suscepisse,
seque eis familiaritate iunxisse. Et ut plurimum de reliquis diis
faciunt, eam multis appellant nominibus: ut puta Venerem, Cythe-
ream, Acidaliam, Hesperum, Luciferum et Vesperuginem. Et ut, si
qua alia sunt, omiserim, ad sensum precedentium veniamus.

4   Sane quoniam vel omnia vel fere omnia predicta a fingentibus, a
proprietatibus Veneris planete sumpta forte sunt, quid de eisdem
astrologi sentiant ante alia apponendum censui, ut facilius suma-
tur ex dictis poetantium intellectus. Et quoniam alias Albumasar
secutus sum et venerabilem Andalo, iuxta eorum sententiam eius

5   fere mores et potentiam, seu circa que versetur, describam. Volunt
igitur Venerem esse feminam complexione flegmaticam atque nocturnam, apud amicos humilem et benignam,[11] acute meditationis
in compositionibus carminum, periuria ridentem, mendacem, cre-
dulam, liberalem, patientem et levitatis plurime, honesti tamen
moris et aspectus, hylarem, voluptuosam, dulciloquam maxime,
atque aspernatricem corporee fortitudinis et animi debilitatis. Est
huius insuper significare pulchritudinem faciei, et corporis venustatem, rerumque omnium decorem, sic et usum preciosorum un-
guentorum, aromatum fragrantium, alearum ludos et calculorum,
seu latronum, ebrietates preterea et commesationes, vina, mella
et quecunque ad dulcedinem et calefactionem pertinere videntur,
eque omnis generis fornicationes atque lascivias et coitus multitu-
dinem, magisteria circa statuas et picturas, sertorum compositio-

other unions of man and woman without the girdle. In addition they say that she held the progeny of Sun in intense hatred on account of her adultery with Mars, which Sun had revealed to Vulcan. They also add that doves were under her protection; and when they give her a chariot, they want it drawn by swans. They also make the myrtle tree sacred to her, and of flowers it is the rose which is sacred to her. After this Theodontius says also that she hosted the Furies in the house of Mars and that she became intimate with them. And as with many of the other gods, they called her by many names, e.g., Venus, Cytherea, Acidalia, Hesperus, Lucifer, and Vesperugo. If there are more, I omit them so I can explain the meaning of what I have said to this point. 3

Because either all or nearly all the things mentioned by the poets are probably subsumed by the qualities of the planet Venus, I think I ought to treat first what the astrologers thought about them so that it will be easier to take up the meaning of what the poets said. And because elsewhere I have followed Albumasar[77] and the venerable Andalò, I will describe its characteristics and power in general according to their opinion, or around what it revolves. They want Venus to be a woman of phlegmatic complexion and nocturnal, humble with friends and affable, keen in thought for the composition of verses, laughing at perjury, deceitful, credulous, courteous, patient and very easygoing but of honest character and mien, cheerful, delightful, and extremely charming, and a woman who despises corporeal strength and weakness of the mind. In addition Venus signifies the beauty of the face, attractiveness of the body, and an adornment for every thing, and so the use of precious unguents, fragrant aromatics, games of dice and calculation, or of bandits, and also drunkenness and feasts, wines, honeys, and whatever seems to pertain to sweetness and warmth, equally fornication of every kind and wantonness and a multitude of coition, the guardianship of statues and pictures, the composition 4

5

nes et vestium indumenta, auro argentoque contexta, delectationem plurimam circa cantum et risum, saltationes, fidicinas, et
fistulas nuptiasque et alia multa.

6   Sed eis omissis ad auferendam fictionum corticem veniamus.
Filiam eam dicunt Celi et Diei, et cum de planeta intelligant, non
incongrue, nam quia celo videtur infixa et cum eo movetur, ab eo
videtur producta; Diei vero dicitur filia a claritate sua, qua ceteris
astris fulgidior est. Eam geminum amorem peperisse non caret
misterio, ad evidentiam cuius existimandum est, ut aliquando dicere consuevit venerabilis Andalo, Deum patrem omnipotentem,
dum omnis mundi machina ab Eo fabrefacta est, nil fecisse super-
7 fluum aut commodo carens animalium futurorum. Sic et supercelestia corpora tam grandia, tam lucida, tam ordinate suo se et
alieno motu moventia, non solum adornatum, quem nos fere ob
crebram inspectionem flocci facimus, condidisse credendum est,
sed circa inferiora illis plurimum potestatis dedisse, ad hoc scilicet
ut eorum motu atque influentia anni volventis variarentur tempora, gignerentur mortalia, genita nascerentur, et alerentur nata
atque in tempore deducerentur in finem. Nec hanc mixtim atque
confuse corporibus iniunctam debemus arbitrari potentiam, quin
imo unicuique proprium constituisse officium, et circa que eius
versaretur autoritas distinxisse, voluisseque omnia se invicem secundum plus et minus coniunctionum atque reliquarum virium,
pro varietate locorum, ad opus in finem deducendum intentum
mutuis vicissitudinibus iuvare. Et inter alia concessa pluribus, ut
testantur effectus, Veneri planete asserebat idem Andalo fuisse
concessum quicquid ad amorem, amicitiam, dilectionem, coniunc-

of wreaths and wearing of garments, weavings with gold and silver, the greatest amusement in song and laughter, dancing, music by stringed instruments and pipes, weddings, and many other things.

But let us leave these things aside and come to removing the 6 cover from the fictions. It is not incongruous that they say she is the daughter of Sky and Day, for they know that because the planet seems fastened to the sky and moves along with it, it seems to have been produced by it; she is said to be the daughter of Day from her clarity, whereby she shines more brightly than the other stars. That she gave birth to the twin Amor does not lack mystery; for proof we have to consider, as sometimes the venerable Andalò used to say, that when God the omnipotent father fashioned the machine of the whole world, he made nothing superfluous or lacking benefit for future creatures. So also we must believe that he 7 composed the supercelestial bodies, so great, so clear, and moving so regularly by their own and external motion, not only for adornment, to which we generally pay little regard because we see it frequently, but to furnish around them bodies greatly inferior to them in power so that by their motion and influence the seasons of the revolving year would be varied, living things would be begotten, what was conceived would be born, and what was born would be nourished and, in time, led toward its end. We must not think this power is mixed or joined indistinctly in bodies but that each one has its own function and that each has it own discrete and specific authority, and that it wants to help with their mutual vicissitudes all things in turn to complete their work and continue toward their intended end, varying according to greater or lesser conjunctions and the power they maintain in their various locations. And among the other things granted to many planets, as their effects bear witness, the same Andalò used to assert that to the planet Venus should be conceded anything that seems to look toward love, friendship, delight, association, society, and union

tionem, societatem et unionem inter animalia spectare videretur, et potissime ad procreationem prolis spectantia, ut esset qui segnem forte naturam in sui continuationem atque ampliationem urgeret, et idcirco causari ab ista hominum voluptates concedi potest.

8 Quo concesso egregie finxere poete, qui eius Amorem seu Cupidinem filium fuisse dixere. Sed quid illum geminum dicit Ovidius advertendum. Credo ego amorem tantum unicum esse, sed hunc totiens et mutare mores et novum cognomen patremque acquirere, quotiens in diversos sese trahi permictit affectus. Et hinc Aristotilem reor triplicem designasse, propter honestum, propter delectabile, et propter utile. Et ne discordes Aristoteles et Ovidius videantur, forsan ex duobus ultimis unum tantum faciebat Ovidius, cum etiam delectare videatur utilitas. Verum quoniam tractatus talis potius spectat ubi de Amore vel Cupidine mentio fiet, ad reliqua ad Venerem pertinentia veniendum est.

Dicunt igitur eam Gratias peperisse. Nec mirabile: quis unquam amor absque gratia fuit? Que quare tres et alia ad eas spectantia, commodius infra ubi de eis ratio apponetur. Cingulum Veneri quod vocavere *ceston* insuper esse dixere, quod illi minime a natura datum fuerat, nec a poetis fuisset ni santissima atque veneranda legum autoritate illi fuisset appositum, ut aliqua li coertione vaga nimis lascivia frenaretur. Quid enim ipsum sit *ceston* in *Yliade* describit Omerus, dicens:

ἦ καὶ ἀπὸ στήθεσφιν ἐλύσατο κεστὸν ἱμάντα
ποικίλον, ἔνθα δέ οἱ θελκτήρια πάντα τέτυκτο·
ἔνθ᾽ ἔνι μὲν φιλότης, ἐν δ᾽ ἵμερος, ἐν δ᾽ ὀαριστὺς
πάρφασις, ἥ τ᾽ ἔκλεψε νόον πύκα περ φρονεόντων.

Et a pectoribus solvit *ceston* cingulum
varium, ubi sibi voluptaria[12] omnia ordinata erant,
ubi certe amicitia atque cupido atque facundia,
blandicieque furate intellectum licet studiose scientium.

among living things, and especially things having to do with the procreation of offspring, so that it is Venus which impels a somewhat inactive nature into its continuation and expansion, and therefore it can be conceded that the delights of men are caused by her.

With this granted to her, the poets created excellent fictions, 8 saying that Amor or Cupid was her son. But we should turn to why Ovid said that he was twofold. I believe that Amor was merely single, but as often as he changed his characteristics and acquired a new name and father, he therefore let himself take upon different affects. From this I think Aristotle[78] described him as triple, namely, the honest Amor, the delightful Amor, and the useful Amor. And lest Aristotle and Ovid seem to disagree, perhaps from the latter two Ovid made only one since utility seems also to delight. But because this discussion is leading more toward Amor or Cupid, we should focus on what is pertinent to Venus.

They say that she gave birth to the Graces, nor is this remarkable: what love was there ever that lacked grace? The reason why there are three Graces and other matters referring to them will be treated more properly below.[79] They said also that Venus had a 9 girdle which they called a *cestos*;[80] this had not at all been given to her by nature, nor would it have been given to her by the poets unless it had been appropriate for her according to the most sacred and venerable authority of laws, its purpose being to provide some kind of restraint to bridle her excessive wantonness. Homer describes what this *cestos* is in the *Iliad*, saying:[81]

She loosened from her breast the *cestos* belt,
embroidered, wherein all the enchantments were crafted.
Therein surely is fondness and longing and eloquence,
and flatteries, which steal the mind even of the prudent.

10   Circa quod si rite considerentur in eo descripta, satis coniugium contingentia esse videbimus. Dicit enim ibi cupidinem esse, ut intelligatur sponsi sponseque ante nuptias desiderium; inde amicitiam que quidem ex commixtione et morum convenientia oritur, atque in longum trahitur. Si vero dissonent mores, inimicitie, iurgium, despectio, et huiusmodi nasci vidimus aliquando. 'Facundia' autem quam oportuna sit patet liquido, nam per eam affectiones panduntur cordis, amantum mulcentur aures, sedantur litigia, que sepissime inter coniuges oriuntur, et ad tolerantiam emergentium etiam animantur.

    Sunt et in eo blandicie, que habent animos attrahere et ligare, iras comprimere, et alienatum amorem etiam revocare; quarum tam grandes sunt profecto vires, ut non solum ab eis capiantur ignari, sed etiam ut ipsemet dicit Omerus, he 'furate' sunt sepissime sapientibus 'intellectum.' Hoc cingulum dicit Lactantius, uti nos ante diximus, Venerem non ferre nisi ad honestas nuptias; et ob id omnem alium concubitum, eo quod ad eum *ceston* delatum non sit, 'incestum' vocari.

11   Quod Furias in domo Martis hospitata sit et eis familiaris effecta, hanc ob causam dictum reor. Sunt enim inter signa celestia, ut dicebat venerabilis Andalo, duo que Marti ab astrologis domicilii loco attributa sunt, aries scilicet et scorpio, in quam harum domorum illas Venus duxerit non habemus. Sed si in Arietem duxerit, initium veris per Arietem designari credo, cum tunc ver incipiat quando sol Arietem intrat. Circa quod tempus animalia cuncta in concupiscientiam inclinantur, et, ut dicit Virgilius: 'In furias ignesque ruunt.' Nec solum bruta, sed et mulieres, quarum complexio ut plurimum frigida et humida est, agente veris temperie, in calorem et venerem acrius excitantur. Que quidem excitatio,

12   nisi frena rubor iniceret, verti in furiam videretur. Sino fervores

If we consider this description carefully we will see that it con- 10
cerns matters related primarily to matrimony. He speaks of fondness here, and we know there is desire in the bride and groom
before their wedding; and then there is the bond which begins
with commingling and similar habits and lasts a long time. Indeed,
if their habits are not similar, we see at some point the beginning
of enmity, dispute, disdain, and the like. It is clear how apposite
"love's utterances" are, for because of them the affections of the
heart are opened up, the ears of lovers are softened, the quarrels
which frequently arise between married couples are settled, and
they are inspired as well to endure whatever emerges.

In the cestos there is also persuasion, which can allure minds
and bind them, suppress anger, and even restore a disaffected love;
its powers are surely so great that it captivates not only the unaware but also, as Homer says, frequently "steals the mind even of
the prudent." Lactantius[82] says, as we said before, that Venus did
not wear this belt except for reputable marriages, and on account
of this every other type of intercourse, in which the *cestos* is not
worn, is called "incest."

That she hosted the Furies in the house of Mars and became 11
familiar with them I think is said for this reason: there are among
the celestial signs, as the venerable Andalò used to say, two which
astrologers assign to the place for Mars' domicile, namely Aries
and Scorpio, although we do not know into which of these houses
Venus led them. But if she led them into Aries, I believe that the
beginning of spring is designated through Aries, for spring begins
when the sun enters Aries. It is around this time when all living
creatures are inclined to longing and, as Vergil[83] says, "rush into
fury and fire." Not only brute animals, but also women, whose
makeup is extremely cold and moist, when tempered by the action
of spring, are more keenly aroused for heat and love, and this
arousal, unless modesty applies restraint, seems to be turned into
fury. I submit the fervor of youths, who unless they are stilled, or 12

iuvenum, qui nisi legum autoritate sopirentur, seu potius coerce-
rentur, in pestiferos profecto furores excederent. Et sic bene in
domum Martis a Venere deducte sunt Furie, eis familiaris effecta
est, in quantum immoderata efficitur et effrenis.

Si in Scorpionem duxisse velimus, quoniam venenificum atque
fraudulentum est animal, intelligo non nunquam amantum amaritudines anxias modice mixtas dulcedini, ob quas sepissime miseri
adeo vexantur ardentes, ut in se ipsos gladio, laqueo, precipitioque
furentes vertantur. Seu ob susceptas iniurias, lusis amoribus, vel
mutatis ob iuramenta frustrata, ob fraudes compertas, ob mendacia, ex quibus autem desperatione torquentur, aut in rixas et homi-
cidia furiosi precipitantur. Et sic a Venere in Scorpione suscepte
sunt Furie.

Venerem[13] exosam Solis prolem habere ab consequentibus ex
amore illecebri sumptum puto. Nam, ut inferius legetur ubi de
Sole Yperionis filio, producit sol formosissimos homines et mulieres, quorum pulchritudo procul dubio trahit inspicientium mentes
in concupiscientiam sui; et qui tracti sunt variis artibus persepe
trahentes trahunt, quod quidem Veneris opus esse creditur. Hi
quippe innumeris subiciuntur periculis; nam dum in libidinem
suam paribus deveniunt votis, alii occiduntur, alii letali persequun-
tur odio, alii ex ditissimis in extremam efferuntur inopiam; et non
nulle splendidum pudicitie decus turpi atque perpetua denigrave-
runt infamia; et ut alia plura sinam ignominiose occubuere postremo. Et sic patet liquido Venerem Solis prolem vetusto odio infestare et mellitis venenis suis opprimere.

Columbas insuper eius in custodiam posuere, quod taliter
contigisse legitur: lascivientibus in campis Venere et Cupidine in
contentionem devenere, quisnam scilicet ex eis plures sibi collige-
ret flores, videbaturque alarum suffragio plures Cupidinem col-

rather restrained, by the authority of laws, surely will break out into destructive furors. And so the Furies are indeed brought by Venus into the home of Mars, and she becomes familiar with them insofar as she is immoderate and unrestrained.

If we want to lead them into Scorpio, a creature that is poisonous and deceptive, I think that here the anxious bitterness of lovers is always mixed a bit with sweetness. As a result, those wretched with desire become so vexed that in their fury they destroy themselves by the sword, noose, or headlong leap, or when their loves become a mockery or are altered by broken oaths, discovered deceits, or lies, the injuries they receive cause them to be tortured by desperation or rush furiously headlong into quarrels and homicide. And in this way Venus takes the Furies into Scorpio. 13

As for Venus hating the progeny of Sun, I think that comes as a consequence of illicit love. The sun, which will be discussed below in the chapter on Sun,[84] that is, the son of Hyperion, produces very beautiful men and women, and their beauty unquestionably lures the minds of those eyeing them into desiring it; and those who are attracted by various arts very often attract those who attract them, which is believed to be the work of Venus. Indeed such people are subjected to innumerable dangers, for when they achieve their longing with equal desires, some are ruined, others plagued by lethal hatred, and others who are very wealthy are brought into extreme destitution; and some blacken the splendid honor of modesty with shameful and perpetual disgrace; and, omitting many other consequences, finally they die ignominiously. And so it is very clear that because of her old hatred Venus harassed the offspring of Sun and overwhelmed him with sweetened poisons. 14

In addition, they put doves under her guardianship, which is said to have happened this way: when Venus and Cupid were frolicking in the fields, they starting competing to see which of them would collect the most flowers, and it seemed that Cupid would

lecturum; quam ob rem vidit Cupido Peristeram nynpham in
adiutorium Veneris surrexisse, qua indignatus causa eam in columbam transformavit illico. Venus autem transformatam in tutelam
confestim assumpsit, et inde subsecutum est columbas semper
15 Veneri attributas. Huic autem fabule sensus talis prestari videtur.
Dicit enim Theodontius Peristeram apud Corinthios origine insignem fuisse puellam et longe magis notissimam meretricem, et
ideo hic Venus agens dici potest in Peristeram patientem, agentis
autem impressio in patientem amor est. Cuius agitata stimulis
virgo adhesit Veneri, id est coitui, qui fere finalis est agentis intentio, si forsan ob id vinci posset infestans cupido. Verum cum talis
appetitus actu potius accendatur quam extinguatur, eo devenit ut
non esset unius amantis contenta solatio, sed more columbe, cuius
moris est sepissime novos experiri amores, in plurium devenit amplexus.

16   Quam ob causam ab ipso Cupidine, id est luxurie stimulo, in
columbam versam voluere poete. Peristera vero Grece, Latine 'co-
lumba' sonat. Que quidem columbe eo Veneri in tutelam date
sunt, quia aves sunt coitus plurimi et fere fetationis continue ut
per eas crebro coeuntes Veneri obsequentes intelligantur. Nam hi
veniunt in tutelam alicuius, qui nondum sibi oportuna facere co-
gnovere, et tutore habito, agenda eius mandato conficiunt. Sic et
libidinosi sub tutela Veneris esse dicuntur, quia semper in lascivias
merguntur, Venere imperante.

Currus autem ideo Veneri designatur, quia sicuti ceteri planete,
17 per suos circulos circumagitur motu continuo. Quod a cignis eius
trahatur currus, duplex potest esse ratio, aut quia per albedinem
significant lautitiam muliebrem, aut quia dulcissime canant, et
maxime morti propinqui, ut demonstretur amantum animos cantu

collect the most by virtue of having wings; but for this reason, when Cupid saw that the nymph Peristera had offered to assist Venus and therefore grew resentful, he transformed her into a dove right there. Venus immediately took the transformed girl under her protection, and because of this it follows that doves were always allotted to Venus. The following seems to be the 15 meaning of this fable: Theodontius says that Peristera was a girl known among the Corinthians from birth but became much more famous as a prostitute, and therefore it can be said that Venus was acting upon Peristera, and that the action of one acting upon another is love. Spurred on by this, the maiden became an adherent of Venus, that is, of intercourse, which is generally the final purpose of action, as if somehow vexing desire can be conquered by that. In truth, since this sort of appetite is kindled rather than extinguished by this act, in reality the solace of having one lover is not sufficient, so, like the dove, whose most common behavior is to try out new loves, it finds its way into more embraces.

For this reason the poets wanted to have her turned into a dove 16 by Cupid himself, that is, by the stimulus of luxury. Peristera in Greek means "dove." These doves are put under the guardianship of this Venus because they are birds which have coitus frequently and breed nearly continuously, and so they are thought by their frequent coition to be obedient to Venus, for those come under the guardianship of another who have not yet learned to do what is right for themselves, and once they have a guardian, they do what that guardian commands. And so the libidinous are said to be under the guardianship of Venus because they are always immersed in lasciviousness, which is the domain of Venus.

A chariot is ascribed to Venus because, like other planets, Venus revolves in her paths in a continuous motion. That the chariot 17 is drawn by swans can be for one of two reasons, either because through their whiteness they signify a feminine splendor, or because they sing so sweetly, especially near death, demonstrating

trahi, et quod cantu amantes fere desiderio nimio morientes passiones explicent suas.

Mirtus autem ideo Veneri dedicata est, quia, ut ait Rabanus, a mari dicta est, quia nascatur in litoribus, et Venus in mari dicitur genita; seu quia odorifera sit arbor et Venus odoribus delectatur; seu quia huius arboris odor credatur a non nullis venerea suadere; seu, ut physici dicunt, eo quod ex ea multa mulierum commoda fiant; seu quia ex bacis eius aliquod compositum fiat per quod excitatur libido ac etiam roboratur, quod videtur testari Futurius poeta comedus, dum Dygonem meretricem inducit dicentem: 'Mirtinum michi affers quod Veneri armis occursem fortiuncula,' etc. Rosa vero ob id illius flos dicitur, quia suavis sit odoris.

18 Nominum eius plurium he possunt rationes ostendi. Dicitur primo Venus, quam Stoyci vanam rem interpretantur, quasi voluptatem abominantes, et hoc intelligendum est, eam 'vanam rem' a Stoycis dici, in quantum ad illecebrem partem illam libidinum et lasciviarum declinet. Epycuri vero Venerem bonam rem exponunt, uti voluptatum professores, nam circa voluptatem summum existi-
19 mant bonum consistere. Cicero autem dicit Venerem dici quod 'ad omnia veniat'; quod quidem non incongrue dictum est, cum amicitiarum omnium a quibusdam credatur causam prestare. Cytherea autem ab insula Cytherea, seu a Cythereo monte in quibus potissime coli consueverat, denominata. Acidalia autem dicta est, seu ab Acidalio fonte qui in Orcomeno Boetie civitate est Veneri atque Gratiis sacer, et in quo arbitrabantur olim insipidi Gratias Veneris pedissequas lavari, seu quia curas iniciat, novimus enim quot curis amantes repleat, et Greci 'acidas' curas vocant. Hesperus autem proprium planete nomen est apud Grecos, et maxime dum post solem occidit, et inde etiam Vesper dictus, ut per Virgilium

that song attracts lovers' spirits and that lovers, nearly dying in their excessive desire, display their passions through song.

The myrtle bush is dedicated to Venus because, as Rabanus[85] says, it originates along the shore and is said to be maritime, and Venus, too, was said to be born in the sea; or because the odor of this tree is believed by some to induce love; or, as doctors say, because it provides many beneficial things for women; or because from its berries a certain substance can be made to excite passion and then strengthen it, as the comic poet Sutrius seems to testify when introducing the prostitute Glycon by saying,[86] "Bring me myrtle, that I might run into the arms of Venus more vigorously." Indeed, the rose is said to be her flower because it has such a sweet odor.

These could be the reasons for her several names. First she is 18 called Venus, which the Stoics, as if detesting pleasure, interpret as "empty thing" [vanam rem], and in this we ought to know that she was said to be an "empty thing" by the Stoics insofar as she descends toward the alluring part of passion and lasciviousness. But the Epicureans, since they advocate pleasures, explain Venus as a good thing, for they think she represents the greatest good in the realm of pleasure. Cicero[87] says that Venus means what "comes 19 [veniat] to all," which is appropriate since some believe that she provides the reason for all personal relations. She is named Cytherea from the island of Cytherea, or from Mt. Cythereus where she was worshipped with the greatest devotion.[88] She was called Acidalia either from the Acidalian spring in the Boeotian city of Orchomenos, which was sacred to Venus and the Graces and in which fools used to believe that the Graces, as Venus' attendants, bathed themselves, or because "she inspired cares," since we know how she fills lovers with so many cares, and the Greeks call cares "bitter" [acidas]. Hesperus among the Greeks is a name appropriate for the planet, especially when it sets after the sun, and therefore she is also called Vesper, as is clear in Vergil:[89] "Sooner would

20 patet: 'ante diem clauso componet Vesper Olympo.' Varro autem vult ubi *De origine lingue Latine,* eam ab hora in qua apparet Vesperuginem appellari. Nam et Plautus sic etiam illam vocat dicens, 'neque Iugula neque Vesperugo neque Virgilie occident,' etc.

Lucifer autem Latine dicitur, cum apud Grecos, ut asserit Tullius ubi *De naturis deorum,* Fosferos appelletur, quasi 'lucem afferens,' et hoc quando ante solem aut auroram in oriente cernitur tanto splendore corusca, ut etiam de se merito Lucifer appelletur. Hanc et naute et ydiote Dianam persepe vocant, quia diei videatur prenuntia.

∴ 23 ∴

De secunda Venere Celi VII^a filia et matre Cupidinis

1 Venerem secundam plures Celi volunt fuisse filiam, non tamen ritu genitam quo gignimur[14] omnes, ex qua recitatur: Saturnum scilicet in Celum sevisse patrem, et, falce sumpta, ei abscidisse virilia et in mare abiecisse, quorsum autem ceciderint non habetur. Falcem vero haud longe a promontorio Lilibei Syculi deiectam aiunt nomenque dedisse loco Drepanum, eo quod sic Grece 'falx' dicta sit. Testiculi vero deiecti, quacunque in parte maris deciderint, sanguinem emisere, ex quo et maris spuma hanc procreatam Venerem voluere ac etiam a 'maris spuma' denominatam, que Grece *aphrodos* dicitur, quoniam sic et hec dicta est.

2 Macrobius autem in libro *Saturnaliorum* Venerem ex sanguine testiculorum Celi natam dicit, sed maris spuma nutritam. Dicunt insuper, ut Pomponius Mela refert, accole Palepaphos Cyprici oppidi tui, serenissime Rex, penes eos Venerem sic natam in terras

Vesper set the day's close on Olympus." Varro[90] in his *On the Origin of the Latin Language* wants her to be named Vesperugo after the hour in which Venus appears, for Plautus[91] also calls her this, saying, "Neither Orion, nor Vesperugo, nor the Pleiades are setting."

The Latin name Lucifer, which among the Greeks, as Cicero[92] asserts in his *On the Nature of the Gods*, is Phosphorus, means "bringing light"; when Venus is seen in the East before sunrise or the dawn in such twinkling splendor, it is deservedly called Lucifer as well. Both sailors and uneducated people very often call her Diana because she seems to be the harbinger of the day.

: 23 :

On the second Venus, the seventh child of Sky and mother of Cupid

Many want the second Venus to be the daughter of Sky, but she was not born in the custom in which we are all born, and there is a story about this: namely, that Saturn was angry at his father Sky, and, taking a scythe, cut off his manhood and threw it into the sea, although it was not known whither they fell. They say that the scythe was thrown not far from the promontory of Sicilian Lilybaeum and gave the place the name Drepanum which means "sickle" in Greek. They say that the discarded testicles, wherever they landed in the sea, emitted blood, and this mixed with sea foam created this Venus; she is also named after the "sea foam," which in Greek is *aphrodos*.

Macrobius[93] in his *Saturnalia* says that Venus was born from the blood of Sky's testicles but nurtured by the sea foam. In addition, as Pomponius Mela reports,[94] the inhabitants of Palaepaphos, a town in your Cyprus, most serene King, say that their Venus was

primo emersisse, et quod ob id nudam et persepe natantem eam fingant, quod et nostri etiam quandoque testantur poete. Dicit enim eius in persona Ovidius:

Et diis adde tuis! Aliqua est michi gratia ponto,
si tamen in medio quondam concreta profundo
spuma fui, gratumque manet michi nomen ab illa,

etc.

Et Virgilius Neptunum ei dicere scribit:

Fas omne est, Cytherea, meis te fidere regnis
unde genus ducis,

etc.

3   Huic preterea dicunt rosas esse dicatas, et quod marinam gestet manibus concam. Sic et ex ea et Mercurio Hermofroditum natum volunt, et ex ea sola Cupidinem. Multe quidem fictiones sunt, sed ex eis talis potest exprimi sensus. Nam pro Venere hac ego voluptuosam vitam intelligo, et in omnibus ad voluptatem et libidinem pertinentibus cum superiori unam et eandem esse, et sic etiam videtur velle Fulgentius.

4   Ex sanguine autem testiculorum a Saturno desectorum ideo natam, quia, ut ex Macrobio sumi potest, cum Chaos esset, tempora non erant; nam tempus est certa dimensio que ex celi circuitione colligitur, et sic a celi circuitione natum tempus, et inde ab ipso Caronos natus, qui et Cronos est, quem nos Saturnum dicimus, cumque semina rerum omnium post celum gignendarum de celo fluerent, et elementa universa que mundo plenitudinem facerent ex illis seminibus fundarentur, ubi mundus omnibus suis partibus atque membris perfectus est, certo iam tempore finis est precidendi de celo semina; et sic genitalia a Saturno, id est tempore, decisa videntur, et in mari deiecta, ut appareret gignendi atque propagandi facultatem, que per Venerem assumenda est, in

born and first emerged onto land this way, and so they depict her nude and usually swimming, and even our poets sometimes do this. Ovid, in her persona, says:[95]

> Add them to your gods as well. I have some favor with the
>   sea,
> since I was once conceived in the middle of the deep
> of the sea foam, and my propitious name derives from that.

And Vergil writes that Neptune said to her:[96]

> It is wholly divine right, Cytherea, for you to trust our realms, whence you trace your birth.

In addition, they say roses were offered to her and that she carried 3 a seashell in her hands. Also, they want Hermaphroditus to be born to her and Mercury, but from her alone Cupid. There are many fictions, but this is the meaning that can be rendered from them: I understand in this Venus the life of pleasure, and in everything relating to pleasure and lust she is one and the same as the preceding Venus. Fulgentius[97] also seems to think this.

She was said to have been born from the blood of Saturn's sev- 4 ered testicles because, as Macrobius can teach us,[98] when there was Chaos,[99] there was no time. Time is a certain dimension which is computed according to heavenly orbit, and therefore time was born from the orbit of the sky. From this Charon was born, also known as Cronus, whom we call Saturn, and because the seeds of all things born after the sky flowed from the sky, and the universal elements which make up the abundance of the world have their foundation in these seeds, when the world was completed with all its parts and members, there was surely then at some time an end to the appearance of seeds from the sky. And so genitalia are seen to be detached from Saturn, that is, from time, and thrown down into the sea, which would appear as the resource for producing and propagating and is assumed to be Venus, that is, into moisture

humorem translatam coitu maris et femine mediante, qui per spumam intelligitur; nam uti spuma ex aquarum motu consurgit, sic et ex confricatione venitur in coitum, et uti illa facile solvitur, sic et
5 libido brevi delectatione finitur; seu, ut placet Fulgentio, quod concitatio ipsa seminis spumosa sit, et ideo marinam dicimus spumam ob salsedinem sudoris emuncti circa coitum, seu quod ipsum sperma salsum sit. Sic ex humiditate nata Venus hec et a spuma maris, id est salsedine humiditatis, nutrita, id est aucta, donec in finem cepti operis deducta sit.

6 Sane videndum que hec sit humiditas ut clarius origo huius Veneris enodetur. Fulgentius igitur vult, ubi ab aliis dicitur, Saturnum Celo, Iovem Saturno genitalia abscidisse et sic suam exponit opinionem. Dicit enim Saturnum Grece Cronos nuncupari, quod 'tempus' Latine, cui vires abscise falce, id est fructus qui in humoribus viscerum velut in mare proiciuntur, ex quibus dicit necesse sit procreari libidinem. Nec dubium ea ex humiditate procedit Venus, que ex cibo potuque procedit, cum raro ruant in libidinem ieiunantes; et tunc procedit maxime quando cibi potusque calor vires movet et suscitat naturales, et vere in mari nascitur, scilicet in gurgite salso sanguinis calefacti et eiusdem ebullientis. Spuma, id est pruritu nutritur, cum eo tepescente libido deficiat. Falcem autem nonnulli volunt apud Drepanum fuisse deiectam, ut ostendatur sicuti falx aliquid operata est circa Veneris originem, sic et habundantia frugum, ex quibus demum cibaria componuntur, plurimum etiam operetur, que quidem abundantia plurima est et alia incitatoria multa apud insulam Sycilie, in qua et Drepanum civitas
7 est. Ego autem reor huius particule et nomen oppidi et litoris formam, que falci similis est, fabule causam tribuisse.

transferred by coition of the sea and feminine means, that is, through the foam. For as foam arises from the motion of waters, it also comes from the friction in coitus, and as it is easily released, so also does passion finish in a brief moment of delight; or, according to Fulgentius, because the stimulation of semen itself is foamy, so also we say that maritime foam is due to the saltiness of sweat emitted during coition, or because sperm itself is salty. And so this Venus was born from moisture and the foam of the sea, that is, the saltiness of moisture, and was nourished, that is, grew, until she reached the end of the task she had begun.

We must examine what this moisture is to better clarify the origin of this Venus. Fulgentius wants to say, as do others, that Saturn cut off the genitals from Sky, as did Jupiter from Saturn, and in this way he explains his opinion. He says that Saturn in Greek is named Cronos, which means "time," and that a sickle cut off his bodily forces, that is, the fruits which are thrown into the moistures of the viscera, as if into the sea, whereby he says passion must be produced. Without doubt Venus derives from this moisture, and passion proceeds from food and drink since rarely do those who fast rush into passion, and then it proceeds mostly when the heat of food or drink stirs and arouses one's natural forces, and is truly born in the sea, that is, in a salty whirlpool of warmed and bubbling blood. It nurtures the foam, that is, sexual urge, since without it passion is tepid. Some, moreover, want the sickle to have been thrown down near Drepanum to show that, as the sickle is involved in the birth of Venus, so also is an abundance of crops from which foods are then composed, and this is particularly true (and there is the greatest abundance as well as many other means of stimulation) on the island of Sicily, where the city of Drepanum lies. But I think the shape of the coast, which is like a sickle, and the name of the town produced the source for this part of the fable.

Quod autem cives Paphos apud se e mari emersisse Venerem
velint bona cum pace maiestatis tue, Rex optime, dicturus sum,
quod nisi te equum etiam in maximis rebus noscerem non aude-
rem. Est autem Cyprus insula vulgata fama, seu celo agente, seu
alio incolarum vicio, adeo in Venerem prona ut hospitium, offi-
cina, fomentumque lasciviarum atque voluptatum omnium habea-
8 tur. Quam ob causam Paphiis concedendum est primo apud eos ex
undis Venerem emersisse.

Verum[15] hoc potius ad hystoriam quam ad alium sensum pertinere ex Cornelio Tacito sumi potest. Qui velle videtur Venerem
auspitio doctam armata manu conscendisse insulam bellumque
Cynare regi movisse; qui tandem, cum inissent concordiam, conve-
nere ut ipse rex Veneri templum construeret, in quo eidem Veneri sacra ministrarent, qui ex familia regia et sua succederent.
9 Confecto autem templo, sola animalia masculini generis in holo-
caustum parabantur, altaria vero sanguine maculari piaculum cum
solis precibus igneque puro illa adolerent. Simulacrum vero dee
nullam humanam habere dicit effigiem, quin imo esse ibidem
continuum orbem latiorem initio et tenuem in ambitu ad instar
methe exurgentem, et quare hoc nullam haberi rationem. Nuda
autem ideo pingitur ut ad quid semper parata sit ostendatur, seu
quia nudos qui illam imitantur persepe faciat, aut quia luxurie
crimen etsi in longum perseveret occultum, tandem, dum minus
arbitrantur obsceni, procedit in publicum, omni palliatione re-
mota, vel potius quia absque nuditate commicti non possit.

10 Natantem autem ideo Venerem pingunt, ut infelicium aman-
tium amaritudinibus inmixtam vitam procellis agitatam variisque
et eorum naufragia crebra demonstrent, unde et Porphyrius in

As for the fact that the citizens of Paphos wish Venus to have emerged from the sea near them, I would say, with the good peace of Your Majesty, great King, that I would not act so boldly if I did not know you were impartial in great affairs. The island of Cyprus, whether in the common opinion, or by act of heaven, or by some other vice of the inhabitants, is so favorable toward Venus as to be regarded as the inn, workshop, and nurture of lasciviousness and pleasures. For this reason it must be conceded to the 8 Paphians that Venus first emerged from the waves in their vicinity.

However, we can learn from Cornelius Tacitus[100] that this pertains to history rather than any other branch of knowledge. He seems to want Venus, who was skilled in reading auspices, to have led an armed invasion of the island and made war upon King Cinyras; later, when they entered upon a truce, they agreed that the king himself would construct a temple to Venus in which the royal family and their successors would perform sacrifices to Venus. Once the temple was completed, only male animals were 9 prepared for the burnt offering, and, since they worshipped her only with prayers and pure fire, it was considered a sin to stain the altar with blood. He says that the statue of the goddess contained no human image; instead, for some unknown reason, there is a full circle wider at the bottom, lessening in circumference, and rising to the likeness of a cone. She is depicted nude to show that for which she is always prepared, either because she often makes those who imitate her nude, or because the crime of luxuriance, although it continues secretly for a long time, finally, when the depraved think it acceptable, appears in public with all its clothing removed, or rather because it cannot be committed without nudity.

They depict her swimming to show life mixed with the bitter- 10 ness of unhappy lovers, driven by various tempests, and their frequent shipwrecks, whereupon Porphyry says in an epigram,[101]

epygrammate dicit, 'Nudus, egens, Veneris naufragus in pelago.'
Sed longe melius in *Cistellaria* Plautus, dicit enim:

> Credo ego amorem primum apud homines carnificinam
>   commentum.
> Hanc ego de me coniecturam domi facio, ne foras queram,
> qui omnes homines supero atque anteeo cruciabilitatibus
>   animi.
> Iactor, crucior, agitor, vexor, vi amoris totus miser exanimor,
> feror, differor, distrahor, diripior,
> ita nullam mentem animi habeo,
> ubi sum, ibi non sum, ubi non sum, ibi est animus,
> ita michi omnia ingenia sunt,
> quod lubet non lubet, iam id continuo
> iam amor lassum animi ludificat,
> fugat, agit, appetit, raptat, retinet,
> iactat, largitur, quod dat non dat, deludit.
> Modo quod suasit dissuadet;
> quod dissuasit, id ostentat.
> Maritimis modis mecum experitur,
> ita meum fatigat[16] amantem animum,
>   etc.

Equidem bene fluctuabat in sale Veneris homo iste.

11   Sed nos ad reliqua. Illi rosas in tutelam datas aiunt, eo quod
rubeant atque pungant, quod quidem libidinis proprium esse videtur. Nam turpitudine sceleris erubescimus et conscientia peccati
vexamur aculeo; et sicut per tempusculum rosa delectat, parvoque
lapsu temporis marcet, sic et libido parve brevisque delectationis et
longe penitentie causa est, cum in brevi decidat quod delectat, et
quod officit vexet in longum. Marinam concam manibus gestat, ut

"Nude, destitute, shipwrecked in the sea of Venus." But far better is Plautus in the *Cistellaria*, where he says:[102]

> I believe that love first devised torture for humans.
> I infer this about myself at home, not needing to search outside,
> I who outshine and surpass all men in the torture-readiness of the mind.
> Disturbed, tortured, agitated, vexed, utterly wretched, I am being killed by the power of love.
> I am carried this way, I am carried that way, I am dragged apart and ripped apart.
> And so I am losing my mind:
> wherever I am, I am not there; and where I am not, there is my mind: this is my mentality:
> what pleases me does not please me; it changes so fast!
> Love now toys with my weary mind—
> it chases, drives, seeks, grabs, holds,
> tosses and corrupts me; it takes away what it gives, it deludes me,
> and dissuades me after persuading me, and then returns to its persuasion.
> For me it is an experience like the sea:
> it so wearies my loving spirit.

Indeed, that man undulated thoroughly in the sea of Venus.

As for the other things associated with Venus, they say that 11 roses were put under her guardianship because they are red and have thorns; these seem to be appropriate for lust since we grow red from the disgrace of a sin and are vexed by the thorn of a sin of which we are conscious. And as a rose delights for a brief time and then after a short while it withers, so also passion is the cause of small, brief delight and long penance, since that which one enjoys quickly fails, and that which harms vexes for a long time. She

per eam Veneris ostendatur illecebra; toto enim adaperto corpore, refert Iuba, conca miscetur in coitum.

: 24 :

De Cupidine Veneris filio

1   Cupido, ut Symonidi poete placet, Servio teste, ex Venere sola natus est. De quo, cum alibi plura dicenda veniant, satis erit mentionem fecisse tantummodo.

: 25 :

De Toxio[17] VIII° Celi filio

1   Toxius, ut ait Plinius in libro *Naturalis hystorie*, Gellio affirmante, filius fuit Celi eumque dicit lutei edificii, exemplo ab hirundinibus sumpto, inventorem. Nondum enim construxerant architecti palatia, ex quo patet eum industruosum et antiquum fuisse hominem, et merito Celi, id est claritatis, filium.

2   Supererant ex filiis Celi, Titanus, Juppiter secundus, Occeanus et Saturnus. Quorum eo quod amplissima esset posteritas, visum est ut huic libro tertio fiat finis, et Titanum quarto servare volumini, Iovem quinto et sexto, Occeanum septimo, Saturnum octavo reliquisque.

held a seashell in her hands to show the allurement of Venus, for when its whole body is open, Juba[103] reports, a mollusk has coitus with itself.

: 24 :

On Cupid, son of Venus

Cupid, according to the poet Simonides,[104] as cited by Servius, was born from Venus alone. Because the many things that have to be said about him come elsewhere,[105] it will be sufficient simply to make mention of him.

: 25 :

On Toxius, the eighth child of Sky

Toxius, as Pliny[106] says in his *Natural History*, citing Gellius, was the son of Sky, and Pliny says that he, following the example of the swallow, was the inventor of the mud structure, since architects had not yet built palaces. From this it is clear that he was an industrious and ancient man who warranted being called the son of Sky, that is, of clarity.

Of the sons of Sky, Titan, the second Jupiter, Ocean, and Saturn remain. Because their posterity is so abundant, it seemed best to me finish the third book here and to preserve Titan for the fourth volume, Jupiter for the fifth and sixth, Ocean for the seventh, and Saturn for the eighth and the rest.

LIBER QUARTUS

Arbor

In arbore autem signata desuper ponitur in radice Celius, eo quod nondum filii eius descripti sunt, sed in ea tam in ramis quam in frondibus omnis Titanis progenies demonstratur.

Prohemium

1 Fluctuabar adhuc, splendide Princeps, circa Paphum oppidum tuum, Veneris infauste describens illecebras, cum ecce, quasi Eoli carcere fracto, omnes in pelagus prodeuntes sevire venti ceperunt, et in celum surgere fluctus impetu impulsi maximo, eoque repellente, in profundum usque demergi Herebum. Qui dum ascenderent et mergerentur iterum, flatusque illos valido spiritu ex transverso confringerent, stupidus ego et semivictus novitatis horrore, quidnam tam repentine tempestati causam prestitisset excogitans, fere absorptus sum.

2 Tandem eius crebro invocans suffragium, qui ex navicula piscatoria ad se venientem periclitantemque Petrum manu sustulit, nunc dextrorsum, nunc sinistrorsum deiectum lembum, quibus poteram viribus regens, eo usque fere naufragus deductus sum, ut ex alto

BOOK IV

Tree

In the tree illustrated above, Sky is placed in the root because his sons have not yet been described, but the whole progeny of Titan is represented here in the branches as well as in the leaves.

Preface

I was still navigating the waters surrounding your town of Paphos, 1
splendid Prince, and describing Venus' baleful enticements, when, behold, as if Aeolus' prison had broken open, all the winds flew forth onto the sea and began to grow angry, and impelled by the greatest force the waves surged toward the sky, but, repelled from there, dove into the depths to Erebus. When they rose and submerged a second time and a strong lateral blast shattered them, stunned and half overcome in awe of this rarity, I was nearly swallowed while contemplating what caused this unexpected tempest.

Then, calling frequently for the assistance of him whose hand 2
supported the imperiled Peter as he approached him on his fishing boat,[1] as my small boat was being tossed now to the right, now to the left, and as I steered with what powers I could muster, albeit nearly shipwrecked, I was carried down to where from the deep I spied approaching me, not otherwise than if the iron walls of Dis had been destroyed and their chains had been thrown off, the im-

cernerem non aliter quam si dirutis ferreis Ditis muris, disiectis vinculis, Titanis antiqui immanem adventare prolem, stilo cepti operis exigente, scribendam; novique, antiqui moris eiusdem memor, eam in tumultum tam grandem hostes suos suscitasse deos.

3 O quas in superbiam suam in medio periculi excitavit iras! O quotiens Iovis fulmina non solum laudavi sed etiam imploravi! O

4 quotiens cathenas atque supplicia augeri deprecatus sum! Sed quid tandem? Postquam aliquamdiu, non aliter quam si in Olympum redivivi insultassent, unde mugitu maximo sonuere, omnesque vehementes, venti suscitavere procellas, ut arbitror iubente Deo, cui soli omnia parent, aquarum resedere montes, etsi equa tranquillitas facta non sit, tamen navigabile devenit mare; quam ob rem a Cypro separatus in Egeum veniens, a longe ingentia cepi mirabundus prospectare corpora, adhuc fulminibus exusta, et inferno pallore atque caligine turpia, et longo cathenarum circuitu pressa, adeo ut non absque difficultate nomina ex semesis elicerem descripturus; ea tamen, que novisse potui, huic apponentur cum successoribus suis volumini. Attamen, ne deficiam, Is faciat, qui populo Israel Jordanem aperuit transeunti.

mense progeny of ancient Titan, which I had to describe for this task I had already untaken. And remembering their ancient behavior, I knew that they had made enemies of their gods and roused them into a huge tumult.

O how they piled dangers upon the ires stirred up against their 3 arrogance! O how often I not only praised but even implored Jupiter's thunderbolts! O how often I prayed to add to their chains and increase their punishments! But what happened next? As if 4 they had been revived and were assaulting Olympus, the waves for some time sounded with the greatest roar, and the winds in all their vehemence stirred up gales, but then, I believe, by order of God who alone is obeyed by all things, the mountains of water subsided, and, although the water was not made tranquil, it nonetheless became navigable. All this separated me from Cyprus and brought me to the Aegean where in wonderment I began to behold from afar the huge bodies still burned by the thunderbolts, repulsive in their infernal pallor and gloom, and so restrained by a great circuit of chains that it was not without difficulty that I elicited their names from their half-eaten bodies so I could describe them. Those which I was able to ascertain I have assigned, along with their descendents, to this book. And may he who opened Jordan for the people of Israel keep me from failing.[2]

∴ I ∴

De Titano Celi filio VIII° qui genuit filios multos,
ex quibus hic XIIII nominantur. Quorum primus
Yperion, II^{us} Briareus, III^{us} Ceus, IIII^{us}
Thyphon vel Typheus, V^{us} Encheladus, VI^{us} Egeon,
VII^a Aurora, VIII^{us} Iapetus, VIIII^{us} Astreus, X^{us} Alous,
XI^{us} Pallenes, XII^{us} Runcus, XIII^{us} Purpureus,
XIIII^{us} Lycaon. Genuit preterea gigantes,
quorum nomina non habemus.

1   De Celo Etheris et Diei filio satis in precedenti volumine dictum
est. Verum cum eius explicetur proles, aiunt Titanum eius et Veste
fuisse filium theologi veteres, ut in libro *Divinarum Institutionum*
testatur Lactantius. Cuius fuisse coniugem Terram, Demogorgonis
filiam, Theodontius asserit, ex qua plures suscepisse filios in sequentibus apparebit, quos omnes quinta luna natos videtur velle
Virgilius, dum dicit:

> Tum luna scilicet quinta partu Terra nephando
> Oetumque Iapetumque creat sevumque Typhea
> et coniuratos celum rescindere fratres,

etc.

2   De hoc enim Titano multa referuntur fabulosa, inter que, quod
potissimum est, aiunt eum cum filiis adversus Iovem deosque reliquos bellum habuisse eisque celum conantes eripere, montes montibus superimposuisse sibi sternentes iter ad illud, eosque demum
a diis cesos et fulminibus interemptos atque apud inferos catenis
religatos et morti damnatos perpetue, ut in sexto *Eneidos* satis
convenienter ostendit Virgilius.

: I :

On Titan, the eighth child of Sky, who fathered many
children, of whom fourteen are named here. The first of
them is Hyperion, second Briareus, third Coeus, fourth
Typhon or Typhoeus, fifth Enceladus, sixth Aegaeon,
seventh Aurora, eighth Iapetus, ninth Astraeus, tenth Alous,
eleventh Pallenes, twelfth Rhuncus, thirteenth Purpureus,
fourteenth Lycaon. In addition, he fathered the Giants,
whose names we do not know.

Sky, the son of Ether and Day, we discussed sufficiently in the   1
preceding book. But when the ancient theologians delineate his
progeny, they say that Titan was his son by Vesta, as Lactantius[3]
bears witness in his *Divine Institutions.* Theodontius asserts that his
wife was Earth, daughter of Demogorgon. The numerous children
he received from her will be discussed in subsequent chapters, and
all of them Vergil seems to want to have been born in the fifth
month, for he writes:[4]

> Then on the fifth moon in an abominable birth, Earth created
> Oetus and Iapetus and savage Typhoeus
> and the brothers sworn to pull down the sky.

Many fabulous things are said about this Titan, the most im-   2
portant of which is that they say he and his sons fought a war
against Jupiter and the other gods and that they tried to take the
sky from him: piling mountains upon mountains they laid out
their own path to the sky, but then smitten by the gods and destroyed by thunderbolts they were bound by chains in the nether
regions and condemned to perpetual death, as Vergil[5] amply explains in the sixth book of the *Aeneid.*

3   Latentia sub hac fictione, et hystoriam continent et moralem sensum naturali mixtum. Quod ad hystoriam pertinet, verba de ea que in *Sacra* leguntur *hystoria,* apponentur ad licteram. Dicit enim sic:

> Exin Saturnus uxorem duxit Opim; Titan, qui maior natu[1] erat, postulat ut ipse regnaret, ubi Vesta mater eorum et sorores Ceres atque Ops suadent Saturno uti de regno non
> 4   cedat fratri. Ibi Titan, qui facie deterior esset quam Saturnus, idcirco et quod videbat matrem atque sorores suas opera dare ut Saturnus regnaret, concessit eis ut is regnaret. Itaque pactus est cum Saturno, uti si quis liberorum virilis sexus ei natus esset ne quem educaret. Id eius rei causa fecit uti ad
> 5   suos natos regnum rediret. Tum Saturno filius qui primus natus est, eum necaverunt. Deinde posterius nati sunt gemini: Iuppiter atque Juno. Tum Junonem Saturno in conspectum dedere, atque Iovem clam abscondunt, dantque eum Veste educandum, celantes Saturno. Item Neptunum clam Saturno Opis parit, eumque clanculo abscondit. Ad eundem modum tercio partu Opis parit geminos Plutonem et Glaucam. Pluto Latine dictus est Dispiter, alii Orcum vocant. Ibi filiam Glaucam Saturno ostendunt, ac[2] Plutonem celant, atque abscondunt; deinde Glauca parva emoritur.

6 Nec multum post hec, sequitur in eadem *Hystoria:*

> Deinde Titan, postquam rescivit Saturno filios procreatos atque educatos esse clam se, seducit secum filios suos, qui Titani vocantur, fratremque suum Saturnum atque Opem comprehendunt, eosque muro circumegit et custodiam his apponit.

Hidden under this fiction are historical and moral interpreta- 3
tions mixed with a natural interpretation. The historical interpretation is contained in the words committed to writing in the *Sacred
History*, where it says:[6]

> Then Saturn married Ops; Titan, who was older, demanded
> that he should rule. His mother Vesta and his sisters Ceres
> and Ops persuaded Saturn not to cede his kingdom to their
> brother. Then Titan, because he was inferior in appearance 4
> to Saturn and because he could see that his mother and sis-
> ters were working on Saturn's behalf, conceded that Saturn
> should reign. And so he came to an agreement with Saturn
> that if any male children should be born to him, he would
> not rear them; he did this so the kingdom would revert to
> his own sons. So, the son that was first born to Saturn they 5
> killed. Then twin children were born afterward, Jupiter and
> Juno. They presented Juno for Saturn to look at, but con-
> cealing Jupiter from Saturn, they secretly hid him away and
> gave him to Vesta for nurture. Similarly, without informing
> Saturn Ops gave birth to Neptune and secretly hid him
> away. In the same way Ops gave birth to the twins Pluto and
> Glauce in a third birth. (Pluto in Latin is called Dispiter;
> others call him Orcus.) They then showed to Saturn the
> daughter Glauce but concealed the son Pluto and hid him
> away. Glauce then died while still small.

The *Sacred History* continues a little afterward with this: 6

> Then Titan, after he learned that sons had been born to
> Saturn and brought up in secret, gathered his own sons, who
> were called Titans, and they captured his brother Saturn and
> Ops, surrounded them with a wall, and placed them under
> guard.

Post hec autem, paucis interpositis, sequitur:

> Iovem ad ultimum, cum audisset patrem atque matrem cus-
> todiis circumseptos atque in vincula coniectos, venisse cum
> magna Cretensium multitudine, Titanumque atque filios
> eius expugnasse, parentes vinculis exemisse, patri regnum
> reddidisse, atque ita in Cretam remeasse.

7 Hec Lactantius ex *Hystoria sacra*; que quam vera sint, quasi eadem
referens edocet Sybilla Erithea.

8   Viso sensu hystoriali, circa reliquos pauca dicenda sunt, et
primo quid sibi velint hunc Celi dicentes filium atque Veste, quod
preter hystorie veritatem de quocunque mortali arbitror dici posse;
nam terrenum corpus et celestem habemus animam, ex quibus

9 constat hominem esse. Sed hic altiori verborum molimine extolli-
tur ab universo mortalium grege, et nuncupatur Titan, quod, ut
placet Lactantio, idem quod 'ultio' sonat. Supra enim ostensum est
Vestam Terram esse, et Terram irritatam ira deorum in ultionem
sui peperisse Titanes; et quoniam ubi de Fama demonstratum est
que sit ira deorum ob quam Terra irritata est et qualiter Terre filii
in ultionem matris consurgant, satis est hic dicere tantum, hunc
Titanum unum ex egregiis illis viris fuisse, qui operibus conatus
est estendere famam et mortem superare suam.

10   Quod autem illi Terra coniunx fuerit, per hoc intelligo huius
hominis et cuiuscunque alterius huic similis ingentem animum,
quo sibi terram subigit uti vir uxorem, eique dominatur saltem

11 animo, si possessio desit. Ex hac enim volunt eum multos genuisse
filios, quod quidem etiam ostendit hystoria, etsi etiam possibile
sit, non nullos ob convenientiam morum sibi, ut reliquis, attributos esse. Secundum absconditum sensum nulli dubium esse debet

After this and a few intervening words, it continues:

> It is said that when Jupiter finally heard that his father and mother were encircled by guards and thrown into chains, he came with a great crowd of Cretans, fought against Titan and his sons, freed his parents from their bonds, restored the kingdom to his father, and returned to Crete.

This is what Lactantius records from the *Sacred History*. How true 7 these things are the Erythraean Sybil confirms by telling them in an almost identical account.

Now that we have examined the historical interpretation, a few 8 words must be said about the others, first what they want to suggest by saying that he was the son of Sky and Vesta. I think one can say this about any mortal without regard to the truth of the story: we have an earthly body and a celestial spirit; in essence these make us human. But the rest of the mortal crowd increased 9 his praise by using words of greater weight and called him Titan, which, according to Lactantius,[7] means the same as "retribution." Earlier we demonstrated that Vesta was Earth, and that Earth, irritated by the anger of the gods, gave birth to the Titans out of vengeance; and because in the discussion on Fame[8] we showed that the anger of the gods was the cause of Earth's irritation and explained how the sons of the Earth rose to avenge their mother, it is sufficient to say here only that this Titan was one of those exceptional men who attempted by performing great deeds to increase his fame and overcome his death.

Because Earth was his wife, I recognize a remarkable spirit in 10 this man and in any other man similar to him in that he holds sway over the earth, as a man does his wife, and even if she is not his possession, at least he controls her spirit. For this reason they 11 want him to have produced many sons, which also history shows, and, if possible, to attribute to him other sons whose characters were similar to his and the others. In an obscure sense, no one

417

quin multi fuerint olim et hodie sint insignes viri, qui eius, eo
12 quod primus describitur, filii dici possunt. Insuper dicunt hos elatos fuisse homines et adversum deos habuisse bellum, ut advertamus quoniam ex magnanimitate ad superbiam facilis sit transitus,
et ob id ut plurimum, dum minus considerate magnates agunt, ex
gloriosissima virtute in detestabile vitium cadunt, et tunc steriles
efficiuntur, id est absque fructu virtutis; et, ut intelligamus Titanis
13 filios fuisse tales, quinta luna natos dicunt. Veteri enim supersti-
tione creditum est, quicquid quinta nasceretur luna, sterile atque
damnosum fore, nec dubium elatos esse damnosos, eo quod bellorum sint semen, per que evacuantur agri colonis et civitates, et
desolantur regna.

14   Dicunt preterea eos habuisse cum diis bellum quod et magnanimes habent et superbi; magnanimes enim bonis operibus[3] similes diis effici conantur; superbi autem se quod minime sunt existimantes, verbo, etsi possent opere, ipsum verum deum calcare
15 satagunt, ex quo fit ut deiciantur et redigantur in nichilum. Est hic
tamen advertendum duplex ab hominibus bellum cum superis habitum, quorum unum fuit istud, quo Iuppiter liberavit parentes,
occisis Titanis filiis. Aliud vero fuit cum Gigantes, qui et Titanis
dicuntur filii, voluerunt Iovi celum eripere, et tunc montes montibus imposuere, quod postea ubi de Gigantibus exponetur.

should doubt that there were long ago and are today many famous men who can be said to be his sons because he was described as the first of this sort. In addition, they say that these men were exalted and fought a war against the gods so we would observe the easy transition from magnanimity to pride, and that it is on account of this that when great men become less cautious in their actions, they very often fall from the most glorified virtue into detestable vice, and then they become sterile, that is, lack the fruit of virtue. And so that we would know that such men were the sons of the Titan, they said that they were born in the fifth month, for the ancients were superstitious in believing that whatever was born during the fifth moon would be sterile and accursed; nor did they doubt that the elated would be accursed: they were the seed of wars by which fields are emptied of farmers and cities and kingdoms laid waste.

In addition by making war on the gods they represent the magnanimous and proud, for the magnanimous try to be like the gods in their good deeds, while the proud overestimate themselves and, by words and, if possible, by deeds, spend their time trampling the true God himself, which is why they are cast down and returned to nothing. But here we should take notice that there were two wars waged by men against the gods. The first of these was that in which Jupiter freed his parents and killed the sons of Titan. The other occurred when the Giants, who are said to be sons of Titan, wanted to remove Jupiter from the sky and then placed mountains upon mountains, which will be explained later in the chapter on the Giants.[9]

: 2 :

De Yperione primo Titanis filio, qui genuit Solem et Lunam

1 Yperionem Titanis et Terre fuisse filium Theodontius et Paulus voluere. De quo nil aliud credo legi, nisi quia Solem genuerit et Lunam; arbitror tamen eum magne preminentie hominem fuisse, et hoc tam a significato nominis quod 'super omnia' sonat, quam a nominibus filiorum tam claris.

: 3 :

De Sole Yperionis filio qui genuit Horas, quas loco unius filie pono et sic prima genuit Eonas, quas eque loco filie unius scribo et sic secunda, III^{am} Phetusam, IIII^{am} Salempetii, V^{am} Dyrcem, VI^{um} Miletum, VII^{am} Pasiphem,⁴ VIII^{am} Oetam, VIIII^{am} Cyrcem, X^{am} Angitiam

1 Solem Yperionis fuisse filium vulgatissima fama est, ex qua tamen matre non constat. Hunc dicunt non solum patri et fratribus adversum Iovem non favisse, sed Iovis partes secutum; quam ob causam post victoriam currum, coronam et aulam et alia multa insignia a Iove obtinuisse, que omnia insequentibus plene explicabuntur.

2   Hunc ego credo suis temporibus clarissimum fuisse hominem et vere magnanimem, et ob id dictum non favisse fratribus sed

: 2 :

On Hyperion, the first child of Titan,
who fathered Sun and Moon

Theodontius and Paul want Hyperion to be the son of Titan and 1
Earth. I believe that I have read nothing about him other than
that he fathered Sun and Moon. I think therefore that he was a
man of great preeminence, which can be assumed as much from
the significance of his name, which means "above all things," as
from the names of his children who were so famous.

: 3 :

On Sun, son of Hyperion, who fathered the Hours,
whom I count as one child and therefore the first,
and fathered the Aeons, whom I describe equally
as one child and therefore the second, and third
Phaetusa, fourth Lampetia,[10] fifth Dirce, sixth Miletus,
seventh Pasiphae, eighth Aeetes, ninth Circe, tenth Angitia

There is common agreement that Sun is the son of Hyperion, but 1
there is no agreement about his mother. They say that he did not
only fail to support his father and brothers against Jupiter but
assisted Jupiter's side. For this reason, after the victory Jupiter
awarded him a chariot, crown, and palace as well as many other
honors, all of which will be fully explained subsequently.

I believe him to have been the most famous man of his time 2
and truly magnanimous, and this is why they said he supported

Iovi, quia non superbus. Quam ob rem adeo illi fuit fama propitia, ut in eum a poetis omne decus delatum sit, quod vero soli deferendum est, nec aliter de eo quam de vero sole ut plurimum locuti sunt.

3   Sane quoniam hic fere nulla ad hominem spectantia apponi videntur, de Sole planeta loquemur. Finxerunt igitur eum ante alia regem, et forte fuit, eique regiam designavere aulam. De qua sic Ovidius:[5]

> Regia Solis erat sublimibus alta columnis,
> clara[6] micante auro flammasque imitante pyropo,
> cuius ebur nitidum fastigia summa tenebat,
> argenti bifores radiabant lumine valve,
> materiam superabat opus, nam Mulcifer illic
> equora celarat medias cingentia terras
> terrarumque orbem celumque quod imminet orbi.
> Ceruleos habet unda deos, Tritona canorum
> Proteaque ambiguum balenarumque prementem
> Egeona suis inmania terga lacertis,
> Doridaque et natas, quarum pars nare videtur,
> pars in mole sedens virides siccare capillos,
> pisce vehi quedam: facies non omnibus una,
> nec diversa tamen qualem decet esse sororum.
> Terra viros urbesque gerit silvasque ferasque
> fluminaque et nynphas et cetera numina ruris.
> Hec insuper imposita est celi fulgentis imago,
> signaque sex foribus dextris totidemque sinistris,
>
>   etc.

4   Descripta igitur aula Ovidius maiestatem regiam proceresque describit, dicens:

> Purpurea velatus veste sedebat
> in[7] solio Phebus claris lucente smeragdis.

Jupiter but not his brothers: he was not prideful. His popularity was therefore so great that the poets awarded him every honor which should have been conferred upon the sun, and they very often spoke about him no differently than if he were the true sun.

Because it seems that there is practically nothing to examine 3 about the man, we will speak about the sun as a planet. They conceived of him above all else as king, and perhaps he was, and they assigned him a royal palace. Ovid writes about this in the following way:[11]

> The palace of Sun stood high on lofty columns,
> gleaming with sparkling gold and gilt bronze like fire;
> shining ivory covered the top of the roof;
> its double doors radiated with the gleam of silver.
> The work surpassed the material, for there Mulciber
> had engraved the seas surrounding the earth in their middle,
> the orb of the lands, and the sky above the orb.
> The waters sport the cerulean gods, sonorous Triton
> and changeable Proteus and pressing on the huge backs
> of whales with his arms Aegaeon
> and Doris and her daughters: some seemed to be swimming,
> some sitting on a rock drying their sea-green hair,
> some riding on fish. They did not all have the same face,
> nor were they different, as befits sisters.
> The land bore men and cities and forests and beasts
> and rivers and nymphs and other spirits of countryside.
> Above these was placed the image of the shining sky,
> and the six signs on the right door, and as many on the left.

After describing the palace Ovid describes the royal court and 4 principals, saying:[12]

> Cloaked in a purple garment
> Phoebus sat on his throne shining with sparkling emeralds.

A dextra levaque Dies et Mensis et Annus
Seculaque et posite spatiis equalibus Hore
Verque novum stabat circumflorente corona.
Stabat nuda Estas et spicea serta gerebat.
Stabat et Autumnus calcatis sordidus uvis
et glacialis Hyemps canos hyrsuta capillos,

etc.

5 Designata regia maiestate, currum eius describit:

Aureus axis erat, themo aureus, aurea summe
curvatura rote, radiorum argenteus ordo,
per iuga crisoliti positeque ex ordine gemme
clara repercusso reddebant lumina Phebo,

etc.

Nec post multum idem describit equos:

Interea volucres Pyrous, Eous, et Ethon,
solis equi, quartusque Phegon hymnitibus auras
flammigeris implent, pedibusque repagula pulsant,

etc.

6 Huic insuper regi coronam insignem ex XII lapidibus preciosis,
ut Albericus ostendit, imponunt.[8] Eique dicunt aurora veniente ab
Horis currum parari et equis adnecti. Hunc preterea multorum
filiorum patrem volunt, ex quibus aliquos veros fuisse possibile est,
dum eum hominem fuisse dicamus, et non nullos etiam ratione
convenientie morum ei attributos, si solem planetam dixerimus.

7 Preterea,[9] ut aiunt phylosophi, in rebus procreandis tante potentie
est, ut pater omnis mortalis vite habeatur; et inter alia ex quadam
singulari potentia, dum in nativitate alicuius hominis ceteris su-

On his right and left were standing Day and Months and Year
And Centuries and the Hours equally spaced,
And young Spring stood there garlanded by a floral crown;
Standing there was Summer, naked and bearing a wreath of
    ears of grain;
Standing there was Autumn stained by trampled grapes
And icy Winter, shaggy with white hair.

After describing the royal court with majesty, he then describes his   5
chariot:[13]

Its axle was golden, golden was the tongue, golden were
    the tips of the wheel rims, the array of spokes was of silver;
topazes and gems placed in order along the yoke
reflected the bright light bouncing off Phoebus.

Not much afterward he describes the horses:[14]

Meanwhile winged Pyrois and Eous and Aethon,
horses of Sun, and the fourth, Phlegon, with their flame-
    bearing
whinnying, fill the air, their hoofs pounding against their
    restraints.

    In addition this king wears a crown decorated with twelve pre-   6
cious stones, as Albericus[15] shows. They also say that when dawn
came, the Hours prepared his chariot and attached the horses.
They want him also to be the father of many sons; it is possible
that some of these sons were real, if we say that he was a man, and
also that some, if we speak of the sun as a planet, were attributed
to him because they had similar characteristics. In addition, as the   7
philosophers say, he had such powers of procreation that he was
regarded as the father of every mortal life; and in addition to other
things, when he was prevalent over the rest of the supercelestial
bodies in the birth of some man, by some singular power the man

percelestibus corporibus prevalet, eum formosissimum, amabilem, facie alacrem atque splendidum, moribus insignem et generositate producit conspicuum. Eum similiter multis vocant nominibus, per que satis apparet de sole planeta, non de homine intellexisse poetas.

Nunc quid dicta velint explicandum est. Dicunt eum primo Yperionis natum, quod concedendum est. Diximus enim supra, Yperionem idem sonare quod 'super omnia,' et sic hic pro vero Deo accipietur, qui, cum omnia ex nichilo creaverit, solus pater Solis
8 dici potest, cum Ipse solus sit super omnia. Post hec regia huic tam splendida ideo designata est, ut intelligamus per apposita in eadem opere huius ex potentia attributa cuncta consistere, eumque omnium curam gerere. Cui inter alia propinquiora circumposita sunt tempora et temporum qualitates, ut intelligatur eum motu suo descripsisse omnia, esto aliquos ante eum fuisse dies in princi-pio *Pentateuci* scribat Moyses, quos arte sua Ille fecit, qui cuncta creavit, nondum isto creato nec eidem potestate aliqua attributa.
9 Postquam vero creatus est, volente Creatore suo motu tempora descripsit et describit omnia et horas et diem et mensem et annum et secula, ut in sequentibus latius apparebit. Sic et motu suo qua-litates temporum facit esse diversas, cuidam dans frondes et flores, alteri segetes, tertie maturos prebet fructus, et frondes incipit auferre, ultime rigorem frigoris et nivis caniciem.
10 Currus autem illi tam lucidus apparatus, indefessam eius atque perpetuam cum indeficiente lumine circa orbem terrarum volubili-tatem ostendit, qui rotarum quattuor est, ut descripta iam quat-tuor tempora sua fieri circuitione designet. Sic et illi quattuor equi ut per eos qualitates diurne circuitionis ostendat. Nam Pyrous qui primus est, pingitur et interpretatur 'rubeus,' eo quod, primo mane

he produced was most beautiful and lovable, cheerful of aspect and splendid, known for his character, and conspicuous for his generosity. Similarly, they call him by many names which the poets clearly knew in regard to the planet sun, not the man.

Now we must explain what meaning they intended in this. First they say that he was the son of Hyperion, which we must concede, for we said above that Hyperion means that which is "above all things," and so he will be taken for the true God, who, because He created everything from nothing, can alone be called the father of the sun; He Himself alone is "above all things." Then, such a 8 splendid palace is ascribed to Sun so we would know from its appropriate fittings that everything exists because of his work and by the power attributed to him, and that Sun cared for all things. Among the other things positioned near Sun are the times and divisions of time so that we would understand that he established all things by his motion, although Moses[16] in the Pentateuch writes about some days which preceded him; He who created all things made these by His art when the sun was not yet created nor was any power attributed to him. But after he was created, by 9 will of the Creator he established time by his motion and established all things and the hours and day and month and year and centuries, which will develop in sequence. So also by his motion he makes the characteristics of the seasons diverse, giving leaves and flowers to one, crops to the second; he provides mature fruits to the third and begins to take away the leaves and ultimately the numbness of cold and the whiteness of snow.

That we was provided with such a shining chariot shows his 10 indefatigable and perpetual circular motion, with his unfailing light, around the orb of the earth; it has four wheels to describe the four seasons defined by his revolutions. So also there are four horses to show the characteristics of the daily revolution, for Pyrois, who is first, is colored and means "reddish" because early in the morning, by the action of the vapors rising from the land, the

agentibus vaporibus a terra surgentibus, sol oriens rubeat. Eous, qui secundus est, cum albus effigietur, dicitur 'splendidus,' eo quod exaltatus iam sol dissolutis vaporibus splendens sit. Ethon autem tertius rubens sed in croceum tendens, 'ardens' exponitur; nam, sole iam celi medium tenente, lux eius corusca est et cunctis videtur fervidior. Phegon autem quartus ex croceo colore tendit in nigrum, et interpretatur 'terram amans,' ostendens, advesperescente

11 die, solem terram petere, id est occasum. Hos tamen equos Fulgentius, esto cum eisdem significationibus, aliter nominat, videlicet Eritreum, Actheona, Lampos et Phylegeum.

12 Per coronam autem XII lapidum ostendit Albericus longa dicacitate XII celi signa intelligi debere, per que mortalium ingenia cum anno quolibet discurrere invenere.

13 His predictis superest de nominibus solvere globum. Ex quibus, eo quod non nulla cum quibusdam aliis diis habeat communia, illis reservatis ubi de diis talibus; de his que ad eum solum spectare videntur quam brevius fieri poterit exponetur. Vocatur igitur primo Sol, eo quod inquantum planeta 'solus' est, ut testari videtur Macrobius dicens, 'Nam et Latinus eum, qui tantam claritudinem solus obtinuit, "solem" vocavit.' Et in *Thimeo* dicit Plato ubi de speris:

> Ut autem per ipsos octo circuitus celeritatis et tarditatis certa mensura et sit et noscatur, deus in ambitu supra terram syderum lumen accendit, quem nunc solem vocamus.

14 Insuper hunc Tullius ubi *De republica* vocat 'principem' atque 'ducem,' dicens:

> Deinde subter mediam fere regionem sol obtinet, dux et princeps et moderatur luminum reliquorum, mens mundi et

rising sun is red. Eous, who is second, because he is depicted as white, is called "shining" because now, with the vapors dissolved, the sun is high and is shining. Aethon, the third, red but nearly yellowish, is explained as "burning," for with the sun now holding the middle of the sky, its light is brilliant and seems hotter than everything else. Phegon, the fourth, progresses from the yellowish color to black and means "loving the land," showing that with evening approaching the sun seeks the land, that is, sunset. Fulgentius,[17] however, names these horses differently, although with the same meanings, namely, Erythraeus, Acteon, Lampus, and Philogeus.

In the crown of twelve stones, Albericus[18] with great wit points out that they must signify the twelve signs of the heavens through which, as mortals in their brilliance have discovered, the sun runs differently each year.

Now it remains to unravel the throng of the aforementioned names. Because some of these are in common with certain other gods, they will be reserved for the chapters about them; those which seem to refer to him alone will be explained as briefly as it is possible to do. First, he is called Sol because insofar as he is a planet he is "alone" [solus], as Macrobius seems to confirm when he says,[19] "For also Latin calls a 'sun' him who alone obtains such clarity." And in his *Timaeus* Plato says about the spheres:[20]

So there might be a certain measure of swiftness and slowness through the eight orbits and that it might be known, a god kindled a light, now called the sun, of the stars in the [second] orbit above the earth.

In addition to this, Cicero in his *Republic* calls him "prince" and "leader," saying:[21]

Then beneath the middle region generally is found the sun, leader, prince, and governor of the remaining lights, the

temperatio. tanta magnitudine, ut cuncta sua luce lustret et compleat.

15 Super quibus verbis sic ait Macrobius super *Somnio Scipionis*:

Dux ergo quia omnes luminis maiestate procedit, princeps quia ita eminet, ut propterea quod talis solus[10] appareat, sol vocetur.

Et post pauca sequitur:

'Mens mundi' appellatur ita ut physici eum 'cor celi' vocaverunt; inde nimirum quod omnia, que statuta ratione per celum ferri videmus—diem noctemque et migrantes inter utramque prolixitatis brevitatisque vices et certis temporibus equam utriusque mensuram, deinde veris clementem temperiem, torridum Cancri et Leonis estum, mollitiem autunnalis aure, vim frigoris inter utramque temperiem—omnia hec solis cursus et ratio dispensat.

16 Iure ergo cor celi dicitur, per quem fiunt omnia que divina ratione fieri videmus. Est et hec causa, propter quam iure cor celi vocetur, quod natura ignis semper in motu perpetuoque agitata est; solem autem ignis etherei fontem esse dictum retulimus. Sol ergo in ethere quod in animali cor, cuius ista natura est, ne unquam cesset a motu, aut brevis eius, quocunque casu ab agitatione cessatio mox animal interimat.

17 Hec Macrobius. Ex quibus satis percipi potest eum existimasse solem rerum omnium causam.

mind of the world and its temperance, of such magnitude that it illumines all things and fills them with its light.

About these words Macrobius in his *Dream of Scipio* says:[22]   15

Leader because he precedes all lights in majesty; prince because he is so eminent that he is called the sun [*sol*] because he appears so alone [*solus*].

And he continues a little further on:[23]

He is called the "mind of the world" just as the natural philosophers have called him the "heart of the sky." For without doubt all the things which we see carried out according to a fixed rule — the day and night and their changing and shifting between the lengthening and shortening of each, and, at certain times, the equal measure of each, and then the mild temper of spring, the torrid heat of Cancer and Leo, the softness of the autumnal breeze, the violence of cold between each temperate season — all these things are managed by the course of the sun and reason.

It is proper that what is called the heart of the sky is that   16
through which happen all the things we see happen by divine reason. There is also this reason for properly calling it the heart of the sky: by nature fire is always in motion and perpetually moving about, and we have reported that the sun was also said to be the source of ethereal fire. The sun therefore is in the ether what the heart is in a living creature, and its nature is never to cease from motion, for a cessation of movement, whether briefly and for whatever reason, will soon kill the creature.

So says Macrobius. From this we can see clearly that he thought   17
the sun was the cause of all things.

Loxias insuper eum appellat, ut ait Macrobius, Oenopides, quod ab occasu ad orientem tendens circulum facit 'obliquum.' Phebus etiam nuncupatur et potissime a poetis, quod a specie atque nitore dictum est. Alii dicunt Phebus quia novus, eo quod mane quolibet novus videatur ab orizonte consurgere. Lycius etiam 18 nominatur,[11] et ut aliqui dicunt a Lycio templo Deli. Macrobius ostendit Cleantem aliam rationem reddere[12] dicens, 'Cleantes Lycium Apollinem nominatum[13] scribit, quod veluti lupi pecora rapiunt, ita ipse quoque humorem rapiat radiis.'

Socomas, ut idem dicit Macrobius, a Syris sol etiam appellatur, 19 a fulgore scilicet radiorum, quos vocant 'comas' aureas solis. Sic et Argitorosus, quod nascens per summum orbis ambitum veluti arcus quidam figuratur alba et argentea specie, ex quo arcu radii in modum emicant sagittarum. Imbricitor quod lumen eius exoriens amabile amicissima veneratione oculorum sol dictus est, quia sic a physicis extimatur. Dicitur et Horus quasi magnus vel gigas; maximus quidam est ut ipsi videre possumus, et hoc illi nomen est apud Egyptios. Vocatur insuper et aliis nominibus pluribus, ut per Macrobium patet in *Saturnaliorum* libro.

: 4 :

De Horis filiabus Solis et Cronis

1 Horas Solis et Cronis dicit Theodontius fuisse filias et ab eo denominatas, eo quod Horus ipse ab Egyptiis appellatur. Has Omerus

In addition, Oenopides calls him Loxias, as Macrobius[24] says, because in moving from sunset to sunrise it makes an "oblique" [*obliquum*] orbit. He is also called Phoebus, especially by the poets, because it is described by splendor and brightness. Others say he is called Phoebus because he is new, for every morning the sun is seen to rise anew from the horizon. He is also called Lycius, as some say, from the Lycian temple of Delos. Macrobius explains 18 that Cleanthes offered another reason, saying,[25] "Cleanthes wrote that Apollo was named Lycius because, just as wolves carry off flocks, so he also carries off moisture with his rays."

According to Macrobius[26] again, the Syrians also call the sun Chrysocomas,[27] that is, from the brilliance of its rays which they call the golden "hairs" [*comas*] of the sun. So also he was called 19 Argyrotoxos[28] because when he was born through the topmost circuit of the orb a kind of bow formed of white and silver appearance, and from this bow rays shone forth like arrows. He is called Imbricitor[29] ["rainmaker"] because we greet the rising of his lovely light with the friendliest veneration of the eyes, which the natural scientists also think. He is also called Horus, as if great and gigantic; indeed, he is the greatest that we can see, and this is his name among the Egyptians. He is called by many other names in addition, as is clear in the *Saturnalia* of Macrobius.[30]

: 4 :

On the Hours, children of Sun and Cronis

Theodontius says that the Hours were the daughters of Sun and 1 Cronis, and that Sun named them Hours because he himself is called Horus by the Egyptians. Homer[31] says that at the appropriate hour they prepare the horses and chariot for the Sun, and that

dicit equos et currum in tempore parare Soli, et Diei venire volenti celi portas aperire.

2 Filias ego ideo Solis dici puto et Cronis, quod est 'tempus,' eo quod solis progressu ex certa temporis dimensione fiant. Equos autem et currum Soli parari ab eis ideo fictum est, quia eis sibi vicissim succedentibus nox labitur et dies accedit, in quem sol tanquam in preparatum sibi vehiculum a successione horarum progreditur, in cuius progressionis initio, Hore diei advenienti celi portas, id est lucis ortum, aperire videntur.

: 5 :

De Eonis filiabus Solis

1 Eonas dicit Theodontius plures esse sorores, Solis et Cronis filias, corporibus ingentes, et sub Iovis collocatas pedibus. De his ego nunquam alibi legisse memini, nisi forsan has velit intelligi secula, cum *eon* Grece, Latine 'seculum' interpretetur. Si de seculis dixisse velit, hec profecto certa et longa temporis dimensione a solis motu conficiuntur.

2 Hec supra monstravimus a Claudiano in antro Eternitatis fuisse descripta. De quantitate vero seculi plurimum inter se discrepavere veteres. Dicebant enim aliqui, ut Censorius in libro quem *De natali die* scripsit ad Cerellum, ab his potissime qui rituales Etruscorum sequebantur, hoc modo descripta secula, ut aliquo superum scilicet ostento initiaretur seculum, eo quod semper usque protenderetur, donec aliud superveniret ostentum, quod finis esset preteriti et

they open the gates of the sky for Day when she is ready to break.

I think they are said to be the daughters of the Sun and Cronis, who is "time," because as the sun progresses they come into existence as specific dimensions of time. The fiction that they prepared the horses and chariot for the Sun was invented because, as the hours succeed one after another, the night slips away and the day arrives, and the sun proceeds into this, as if riding in a vehicle which the succession of hours has prepared for him; and in the beginning of this progression the Hours seem to open the gates of the sky, that is the emergence of light, for the arriving day.

: 5 :

On the Aeons, children of Sun

Theodontius says that the Aeons were a number of sisters, daughters of Sun and Cronis, who had huge bodies and were placed under the feet of Jupiter. I remember reading nothing about them except perhaps that he wants them to be understood as centuries, since *eon* in Greek means "century." By "centuries" he must mean fixed and lengthy dimensions of time composed by the motion of the sun.

Above[32] we quoted Claudian's description of this dimension in the cave of Eternity, but the ancients disagreed considerably amongst themselves as to the size of a century. For some, like Censorinus[33] in *The Birthday Book* written to Cerellus, said that centuries were marked especially by those who followed the rituals of the Etruscans in this way: the century would begin with some divine portent and then extend until another portent arrived, which was the end of the preceding and the beginning of the next, and so

sequentis initium, et sic non certo aut determinato annorum numero constare videbatur seculum, quin imo aliquando longum et
non nunquam breve contingere.

3   Post hec ostendit alios aliter arbitrari, dicentes id temporis spatium esse quod efflueret inter unam celebrationem ludorum secu-
larium et alteram subsequentem, ex quo etiam temporis inequali-
tas sequeretur permaxima. Postremo, multis recitatis opinionibus,
dicit civile Romanorum seculum centum annis solaribus terminari.
Quod ego memini sepissime a venerabili Andalo eodem finiri
spatio.

4   Erant insuper qui vellent idem esse seculum et etatem, quod
non est verum, esto aliquando improprie scribant veteres 'seculum'
pro 'etate.' Etas enim, si eo modo sumpserimus quo sanctorum
describunt lictere, ac etiam poetarum, multa in se continet secula.
Quod vero sub Iovis pedibus secula designentur, puto fieri, ut intelligamus solius veri Dei imperio tempora labi, eique soli diutur-
5   nitatem cognitam eorumdem, et que in eis futura sint. Nec ab hoc
discrepat Claudiani descriptio, qui illa dixit in antro Eternitatis
manere, cum in ipsa trinitate personarum et unica deitate tantum
consistat eternitas, et sic quicquid in eternitate consistit in Deo sit
necesse est.

: 6 :

De Phaetusa et Salempetii III^a
et IIII^a filiabus Solis

1   Phaetusa et Salempetii nynphe Sycule, filie fuere Solis et Neere, ut
in *Odissea* scribit Omerus dicens, has in Sycilia Solis servare gre-

a century seemed not to consist of a predetermined number of years but a period that happened to be rather long and never short.

After this he pointed out that others thought otherwise, saying 3 it was a space of time which flowed between one celebration of the century games and the next, followed by a great stretch of unspecified time. After discussing many opinions he finally says that the civil century of the Romans was marked by one hundred solar years. I remember that the venerable Andalò often defined a century in this way.

There were in addition those who want a century and an age to 4 be the same, which is not true, although sometimes the ancients incorrectly write "century" for "age." An age, if we understand it by what we read in the writings of both the saints and the poets, contains many centuries within it. That centuries are described under the feet of Jupiter I think was so that we would know that time slips past only by order of the one true God, and its lengths are known only to him, as are what things will happen in them. The description of Claudian, who says they remain in the cave of 5 Eternity, agrees with this, for eternity exists only in the trinity of persons and a unique divinity, so whatever exists in eternity is necessarily in God.

: 6 :

On Phaetusa and Lampetia, the third and fourth children of Sun

Phaetusa and Lampetia, Sicilian nymphs, were daughters of Sun 1 and Neaera, as Homer[34] writes in the *Odyssey*, saying that in Sicily they protected Sun's herds. These were the herds Circe had forbid-

ges, a quibus Ulixes a Cyrce prohibitus est. Circa quam prohibitionem talis ab Omero fabula recitatur. Quod cum venisset ab inferis rediturus in patriam, a Cyrce premonitus est quod, postquam cum sociis ultra Scyllam et Caribdim in Syciliam devenisset et comperisset greges Solis servari a Phaetusa et Salempetii filiabus suis, ab eis omnino cum sociis abstineret, nam si quis ex eis comederet, occideretur; ad quos cum, postergatis aliis periculis, fessus cum sociis devenisset Ulixes, factum est ut ibidem Euriloci consilio pernoctarent, sed mane mutatis ventis abire nequivere et cum ibidem longius credito detinerentur, impellente ciborum penuria, dormiente Ulixe et Euriloco suadente, a sociis Ulixis in greges itum est, et ex eis sedata fames. Verum eis discedentibus gravi agitati tempestate, ad ultimum a Iove fulminati periere omnes, Ulixe excepto, qui ex gregibus non gustarat.

2   Huic fabule talis potest sensus exhiberi. Calor et humiditas, id est Sol et Neera, que nynpha est, silvas et pascua gignunt, que due sunt nynphe Solis et Neere filie: harum altera prestat umbras, altera vero gregibus victum, et sic servantes sunt greges Solis, qui ex omni vivente conficiuntur anima, vegetativa scilicet et sensitiva, opere enim suo nascuntur, et tegmine atque victu predictarum

3   custodum servantur. Esse tamen hos greges in Sycilia dicit Homerus, non quod alibi non sint, sed ibidem ob ingentem rerum habundantiam et celi temperiem plus vigoris videantur habere delicie, que ob corruptos loci mores etiam magis quam alibi pestifere

4   sunt.[14] Ab his omnis rationalis anima prohibetur, sane tamen ne eis immoderate fruatur, ne in mortem deveniat, aut vitam, que sit morte deterior. Quod totiens contingit quotiens, habenis appetitui

den to Ulysses, about which Homer tells the following fable. When Ulysses had come from the nether region to return to his homeland, he was warned by Circe that after he and his companions ventured beyond Scylla and Charybdis to Sicily and discovered that Sun's herds were protected by his daughters Phaetusa and Lampetia, he and his companions should hold off from them completely, for whoever ate any of them would die. When the weary Ulysses and his companions had gotten past the other perils and come upon the herds, following the advice of Eurylochus they spent the night there, but in the morning the winds changed and they were unable to depart. Being detained there longer than they had expected and compelled by a lack of food, while Ulysses was sleeping, Eurylochus persuaded the companions to set upon the herd, and they allayed their hunger. But after they departed, tossed by a powerful tempest they all finally perished at the hands of Jupiter's thunderbolt, except Ulysses, who had not partaken of the herd.

The following meaning can be applied to this fable. Heat and 2 humidity, that is, Sun and Neaera, who is a nymph, produce the forests and pasturelands, who are two nymphs, daughters of Sun and Neaera. One of these provides shade, the other sustenance for herds, and so they protect the herds of Sun, who are composed of every living creature, be they vegetative or sentient, for they are born by the work of the sun, and they are protected by the shade and sustenance of the aforementioned custodians. Homer says 3 that these flocks were in Sicily, not because they are not found elsewhere, but there in Sicily, on account of the huge abundance of things and the temper of the sky, the delights seem to be more vigorous and, on account of the corrupt morals of the place, are even more destructive than elsewhere. The rational mind is pro- 4 hibited from all these delights lest it enjoy them immoderately and lead to death, or a life which is worse than death. What happens whenever the reins of the appetite are eased is that we sink into

datis, in lascivias mergimur, quod iam apud Syculos fecere plurimi,
5 qui enerves facti post gustatas delicias non sufficere laboribus. Verum Eurilocus, id est blanda sensualitatis persuasio, dormiente
Ulixe, id est rationis robore, avidos sensus in greges, id est in delicias immictit, ex quo libidinibus soluti, maris fluctuantis, id est
mundi huius, labores ferre nequivere, et sic Iovis fulmine, id est
iusto Dei iudicio, in mare deiecti periere, id est in amaritudines et
6 miserias mortalis vite anxiati et incogniti defecere. Vel, quod forsan contigisse potuit, cum in Syciliam devenisset Ulixes et ibidem
ab adverso detineretur tempore, eo non curante, adeo socii eius
cibo potuque et mulieribus soluti sunt, ut reintrantes mare oportuna negligerent, et sic naufragium facerent.

7 Quod non solo Ulixi contigisse legimus, quin imo et Hanibali
Peno strenuissimo bellorum duci,[15] qui cum in hyberna Capuam
deduxisset eos, quos nec itinerum longitudo, nec nationum variarum barbaries, non fluminum vertiginosi gurgites, non ventorum
vehementia, nec nivium rigor, nec Alpestrium viarum asperitas,
non fames, non discrimina mille, non arma Romanorum eo usque
cuncta vincentia superasse potuerant, a Campana libidine adeo
superatos invenit, ut quos duros acresque sub autumni fine in Capuam deduxisset, enerves effeminatosque veris initio vix posset in
castra compellere, et quos semper viderat ante victores, victos post
atque fugatos sepissime deploraret.

lasciviousness, which happens often now among the Sicilians, who have become feeble after experiencing delights and are not capable of performing labors. But Eurylochus, that is, the charming persuasion of sensuality, while Ulysses, that is, the force of reason, was sleeping, set his companions, that is, eager senses, upon the herds, that is, upon delights; when he released them unto pleasures, they were unable to endure the labors of the swelling sea, that is, of this world; and so, tossed into the sea by Jupiter's thunderbolt, that is, by the righteous judgment of God, they perished, that is, sank anxious and unknown into the bitternesses and miseries of mortal life. Or, perhaps it could have happened that when Ulysses arrived in Sicily and was detained there by adverse circumstance and was not paying attention, his companions were so careless from the food and drink and women that after reentering the sea they neglected proper procedure and thus wrecked their ship.

We read that this happened to not only Ulysses but the Carthaginian Hannibal, a mighty leader in warfare.[35] One winter when he had led to Capua those whom neither the length of the journey, nor the barbarism of the various peoples, not the vertiginous whirlpools of rivers, not the vehemence of the winds, nor the severity of the snow, nor the harshness of the Alpine paths, not hunger, not a thousand crises, not the Roman arms which had conquered everything, were able to overcome, he found them so overcome by Campanian wantonness that those men he had led into Capua, hardened and fierce at the end of autumn, he was scarcely able to force back, feeble and effeminate, into camp at the beginning of spring, and those he had always seen as victors before, afterward he often criticized for being conquered and defeated.

: 7 :

De Dyrce Solis V^a filia et
Lyci regis coniuge

1 Dyrces Solis fuit filia et Lyci regis Thebarum coniunx. In quam sicuti in ceteras Solis filias Venerem sevisse dicit Fulgentius. De qua talis fertur hystoria. Stuprata per vim Anthiopa, Nictei regis filia, ab Epapho, ut placet Lactantio, seu a Iove, ut plures videntur arbitrari, a Lyco Thebarum rege marito suo abdicata est, et super

2 inducta Dyrces. Que illico suspicata ne forte Lycus Anthiopam in suam revocaret gratiam et sic, ea reassumpta, dimiceretur ipsa, impetravit a viro ut posset illam in vinculis detinere. Que cum ex Iove prolem geminam suscepisset, partus adveniente tempore, ab eo vinculis liberata est, et clam in Cytheronem montem aufugit, ibique peperit Amphyonem et Zethum, quos expositos pastor quidam pro suis aluit. Qui cum adolevissent, a matre cogniti, et sui generis certiores facti, facile in Dyrcem irritati sunt, et in matris ultionem surgentes Lycum occiderunt regem, et Dyrcem tauro indomito alligarunt, qui dum eam traheret, misera deorum auxilium imploravit, quorum subsidio in fontem sui nominis haud longe a Thebis mutata est, et sic Veneris satiavit iram.

3 Quod autem in hac hystoria fabulosum est, explicabitur facile. Anthiopam a Iove tempore partus liberatam a carcere dicit Theodontius ideo fictum, quia cum videretur Dyrci ob tumidum Anthyope uterum satis sui adulterii testimonium apparere, et ob id

∶ 7 ∶

On Dirce, the fifth daughter of Sun and the wife of King Lycus

Dirce was the daughter of Sun, and the wife of Lycus, king of the 1
Thebans. Fulgentius[36] says that Venus was angry at her, just as she
was at the other daughters of Sun. The following story is told
about her. Antiope, the daughter of King Nycteus, taken by force
by Epaphus, according to Lactantius,[37] or by Zeus, as most seem
to think, was banished by her husband, Lycus, king of the Thebans, and Dirce was brought in to replace her. Dirce was immedi- 2
ately suspicious that Lycus had allowed Antiope back into his
good graces, and when she was brought back and Dirce dismissed,
she demanded that her husband allow her to put Antiope in
chains. After Antiope conceived twins by Jupiter, when the time
for delivery was approaching, he freed her from the chains, and
she secretly fled to Mt. Cithaeron and there gave birth to Amphion and Zethus and exposed them, though a certain shepherd
brought them up as his own. When they reached adolescence,
recognized by their mother and informed of their parentage, they
became exceedingly angry at Dirce, rose to avenge their mother,
killed King Lycus, and bound Dirce to a wild bull; when she was
being dragged by the bull, the wretched woman asked for help
from the gods, and they offered relief by changing her into a fountain by no means far from Thebes and named after her, thus satisfying Venus' anger.

What is fabulous in this history will be easy to explain. Theo- 3
dontius says that the fiction about Antiope being freed from
prison by Jupiter while she was in labor was invented for this reason: because Dirce thought Antiope's swollen belly seemed to be
sufficient proof of her adultery and therefore thought justifiably

eam viro arbitraretur odiosam merito, ultro eam reliquit. Dyrcem autem mutatam in fontem satis comprehendi potest, tam ob perditum regnum quam ob supplicii illati penam, eam in multas solutam lacrimas.

4   Fuisse autem Solis filiam ideo dictum, quia aut sic de facto fuit eam alicuius insignis viri sic nominati fuisse filiam, aut ob insignem eius pulchritudinem solis filiam vocitatam.

: 8 :

De Mileto Solis VI° filio, qui genuit Caunum et Biblidem

1   Miletus, ut testatur Ovidius, Solis fuit filius. Theodontius autem dicit istum Solis Rhodii filium et Pasyphis fuisse fratrem. Hunc tamen in Mynoem senem volentem insurgere bello, perterruit Iuppiter, quam ob causam in Lesbon abiit, et ibi civitatem, quam Militenem ex suo nomine dixit, construxit; verum postea, immu-
2   tatis licteris, ex Militene Mitilena dicta est. Post hec cum Cyane nynpha Meandri fluminis filia se immiscuit, et ex ea suscepit filios duos, Caunum scilicet et Biblidem.

444

that her husband hated her, she voluntarily let her go. That Dirce was transformed into a fountain can adequately be explained by the fact that she was reduced to many tears as a consequence of losing her reign and enduring the pain of punishment.

It was said that she was the daughter of Sun because either she 4 was in reality the daughter of some famous man so named, or she was called the daughter of the sun because of her distinguished beauty.

: 8 :

On Miletus, sixth child of Sun, who fathered Caunus and Biblis

Miletus, as Ovid[38] bears witness, was the son of Sun. Theodon- 1 tius, however, says that he was the sun of the Rhodian Sun and the brother of Pasiphae. When he wished to make insurrection and war on the elderly Minos, Jupiter thoroughly terrified him, so he fled to Lesbos and there built a city which he named Miletus after himself. Later, with the letters changed around, Miletus was called Mitilene. Long after this he had intercourse with Cyane, 2 daughter and nymph of the Meander River, from whom he received two children, namely, Caunus and Biblis.

: 9 :

De Cauno et Biblide filiis Mileti

1 Caunus et Biblis filii fuerunt Mileti ex Cyane nynpha suscepti, ut
testatur Ovidius dicens:

Hic tibi, dum sequitur patrie curvamina ripe,
filia Menandri totiens redeuntis eodem[16]
cognita Cyane, prestanti corpore nynpha
Biblida cum Cauno prolem est enixa gemellam,

etc.

Et quia nil preter commune ambobus de eis legi, de ambobus scribere invicem visum est.

2 Legitur ergo Caunum speciosissimum fuisse iuvenem, et a Bi-
blide sorore infausto amore dilectum, Venere in prolem Solis irata
agente. Sane cum Biblis fratri flammas execrande libidinis detexis-
set, ipse aspernatus detestabilem sororis concupiscientiam, fugam
3 sumpsit inque peregrina ponit nova menia terra. Infelix autem Biblis confestim secuta est eum, et postquam Cariam Lyciamque et
Lelegas peragravit, labore atque dolore victa consedit, et spreta
sese dedit in lacrimas. Ex quo factum est ut in fontem Nayadum
beneficio misera verteretur, ut dicit Ovidius:

Sic lacrimis consumpta suis Phebeia Biblis
vertitur in fontem, qui nunc quoque vallibus illis
nomen habet domine, nigraque sub ylice manat,

etc.

Figmentum autem satis patet, quia a fletu continuo fons lacrimis
manans visa est.

: 9 :

On Caunus and Biblis, sons of Miletus

Caunus and Biblis were children of Miletus by the nymph Cyane, 1 as Ovid testifies, saying:[39]

> Here you, while she followed her father's curved banks,
> the daughter of Meander, so often returning to the same place,
> met Cyane, a nymph of exquisite bodily form,
> who bore you twin offspring, Biblis with Caunus.

And because I have read nothing about them except what was common to both, I will accordingly write about both of them.

One can read that Caunus was a most handsome youth, and 2 that he was loved inappropriately by his sister Biblis spurred on by Venus, who was angry at the progeny of Sun. When Biblis had revealed the flames of her ill-fated passion to her brother, he spurned the execrable desire of his sister and took flight and built new walls in a foreign land. The unhappy Biblis immediately pur- 3 sued him, however, and after traveling to Caria, Lycia, and the land of the Leleges, overtaken by hardship and grief, she rested, and the spurned woman gave herself over to tears. From this it was said that the wretched woman was turned into a spring by the good will of the Naiads, as Ovid says:[40]

> So consumed by her tears, Phoebeian Biblis
> turned into a fountain which now also in those valleys
> bears the name of its mistress, and remains under a dark ilex.

This inventive story is sufficiently transparent: in her continuous weeping she seems to be a fountain shedding tears.

: 10 :

De Pasyphe VII^a Solis filia et Mynois coniuge

1 Pasiphes Solis fuit filia, ut Senece tragici percipitur carmine aientis in tragedia *Ypoliti*:

> Quid ille rebus lumen infundens suum
> matris parens,
>
> etc.

Verba quidem nutricis sunt loquentis ad insanam amore Ypoliti Phedram, Pasiphis filiam. Theodontius autem dicit eam non fuisse
2 filiam Solis Yperionis, sed Rodii. Fuit hec Minois Cretensis regis coniunx, et vacante Mynoe bello adversus Megarenses et Athenienses ob occisum Androgeum filium, ab irata Venere in sobolem Solis, infausti amoris flammas suscepit amavitque speciosissimum taurum, in cuius concubitum Dedali artificio venisse dicitur, et ex eo suscepit quem medium hominem mediumque taurum peperit.
3 Alii vero aliam amoris huius causam describunt, aientes, quod cum orasset Mynos in bellum progressurus patrem, ut dignam se sacrificaturo sibi prepararet hostiam, evestigio illi preparatus est taurus, formositate cuius captus Mynos illum armentis suis ducem prefecit, alio consecrato; ex quo iratus Iuppiter egit ut, illo absente, reservatus deligeretur a coniuge, et hinc volunt Mynoem, ob com-
4 missum facinus, non ausum in coniugem sevire. Quod autem Pasiphes filia hominis ex tauro conceperit, vult Servius Taurum hunc scribam Minois fuisse sic nominatum, eumque in domo Dedali cum Pasyphe coisse et filium ex ea suscepisse, et tandem geminos

: 10 :

On Pasiphae, seventh child of Sun and the wife of Minos

Pasiphae was the daughter of Sun, as we learn from the tragic   1
writer Seneca, who in a verse from his tragedy *Hippolytus*, says:[41]

> What of him who pours his light on things,
> the parent of your mother?

These are the words of the nurse speaking to Phaedra, the daughter of Pasiphae, who is deranged with love for Hippolytus. Theodontius, however, says that she was not the daughter of the Sun, the son of Hyperion, but of the Rhodian Sun. She was the wife of   2
Minos, King of Crete, and when Minos was away fighting a war against the Megarians and Athenians over the death of his son Androgeus, she became inflamed with a despicable love sent by Venus, who was angry at the progeny of Sun, and fell in love with a most handsome bull, with which, by means of Daedalus' artifice, she is said to have had intercourse, and from this he received an offspring that was half human and half bull.

Others describe another reason for this love match. In prepar-   3
ing for war, Minos had asked his father to prepare a worthy victim for him to sacrifice, and he immediately prepared a bull for him, but captivated by its beauty Minos made him the leader of his own herd and sacrificed another. Angry at this, Jupiter brought it about that in Minos' absence the rescued bull became the object of his wife's love. Because of this they want to say that Minos, in light of the crime he committed, could not be angry at his wife. In   4
that Pasiphae, the daughter of a man, conceived with a bull, Servius[42] suggests that Taurus was the name of Minos' scribe, that he had intercourse with Pasiphae in the home of Daedalus and that she became pregnant and ultimately produced twins. One

peperisse, quorum alterum ex Mynoe conceptum notis apparebat, alterum vero ex Tauro eque indicantibus signis, et cum de secundo non esset certa fides, nomine ad utrumque spectante parentem Mynotauro scilicet imposito, enutritus est.

5   Ego autem longe altiorem sensum hac sub fabula tegi reor. Existimo quidem voluisse veteres ostendere qualiter vitium bestialitatis causaretur in nobis hac ratione. Pasiphem spetiosissimam feminam et Solis filiam credo animam nostram veri Solis, id est Dei omnipotentis, a quo creata est, filiam omni pulchritudine in-

6 nocentie splendidam. Hec coniunx efficitur Minois regis et legum latoris, id est rationi humane iungitur, que suis legibus eam habet regere atque in rectum iter dirigere. Huic inimicatur Venus, id est appetitus concupiscibilis, qui sensualitati adherens semper rationis est hostis; cui si adheserit anima, a ratione separetur necesse est, a qua semota, facile a blanditiis et suasionibus carnis se trahi permictit et sic precipitem se fert in concupiscientiam tauri a Iove

7 dati, ut sibi ex eo Minos sacrum conficiat. Quem ego taurum sentio mundi huius delitias prima facie pulchras et delectabiles adeo rationi concessas, ut ex eius moderamine certo vite nostre oportuna ministret; nam dum his debite utimur, rite ex eis Deo sacrum conficimus; sane dum eis iudicium sensualitatis sequentes abutimur aut abuti desideramus, in bestialem concupiscientiam devenimus, et tauro tunc obscene anima iungitur in lignea vacca, dum

8 artificio ingenii nostri naturalibus preter nature leges innitimur. Et sic ex appetitu illecebri et adoptione nepharie voluptatis causatur et nascitur Minotaurus, id est bestialitatis vitium.

   Huius autem Minotauri, hominis et tauri formam esse finxere, eo quod tali vitio laborantes intuitu primo videntur homines, si opera autem prospectemus et abscondita introrsum desideria, tales

9 esse bestias cognoscemus. Clauditur hic laberinto carceri circuitio-

somewhat resembled Minos and appeared to have been conceived by him, the other, with equally distinguishing characteristics, appeared to have been conceived by Taurus. But since they were not certain about the second child, they raised him with a name that referred to each parent, namely, Minotaurus.

I think there is a much deeper meaning hidden within this fable. I believe the ancients wished to show how the vice of bestiality is caused in us for the following reason. Pasiphae, a very beautiful woman and the daughter of Sun, I presume to be our mind, daughter of the true sun, that is, all-powerful God, by whom she was created, splendid in all the beauty of innocence. She is married off to Minos, king and legislator, that is, she is joined to human reason which uses its laws to rule and guide its journey correctly. Hostile to her is Venus, that is, desirous appetite, which in adhering to sensuality is always the enemy of reason; if the mind adheres to it, it necessarily is separated from reason, and removed from reason it allows itself to be attracted easily by the blandishments and allurements of the flesh, and so she rushes headlong into the desire for the bull Jupiter gave Minos to sacrifice to him. I think this bull is the delights of this world, at first glance so beautiful and delectable, so given to reason that when moderated carefully it favorably serves our life. For when we use them properly, we therefore righty sacrifice to God, but when in following the judgment of sensuality we abuse them or desire to abuse them, we descend into bestial desire. The mind is then lewdly joined to the bull in a wooden cow when by the artifice of our genius we depend on natural things beyond the laws of nature. And so, alluring appetite and the adoption of nefarious pleasure cause the birth of the Minotaur, that is, the vice of bestiality.

They contrived the form of this Minotaur as of both man and bull because those who suffer such a vice seem at first to look like men, but if we see their acts and hidden desires, we will recognize that they are beasts. He is enclosed in the labyrinthine prison,

num plurium implicito, et hoc ideo, quia fortissimum atque fero-
cissimum et furiosum esset animal, in quo ostenditur eum hu-
10 mano pectori, infandis desideriis intricato. Et quod eo impellente
fortem atque inmanem prestemus animum, dum infaustum aliquid audemus, quod nisi pro voto perficiamus, confestim in furiam
declinamus.

11   Hic insuper a Theseo ab Adriana predocto occiditur, id est a
prudenti viro cui virilitas, quam per Adrianam accipio, eo quod
andres Grece, 'vir' sonet Latine, ostendit detestabile tam scelesto
vitio subiacere et quibus armis etiam conficiendum sit.

:   II   :

De Oeta Colcorum rege Solis figlio VIIIº, qui genuit Medeam et Absyrthium et Calciopem

1 Oeta Colcorum rex, ut Omerus in *Odissea* testatur, Solis fuit filius
et Perse filie Occeani. Tullius autem ubi *De naturis deorum*, eum ex
Asterie sorore Latone susceptum dicit, quam Asteriem videtur
idem Tullius dicere ab eo occisam; dicit enim sic: 'Quid Medee
respondebis, que duobus avis Sole et Occeano et patre matricida
procreata est?' etc.

2   Hunc clarum ea tempestate fuisse regem testatur antiquitas
cum permaximum illi regnum fuisse describat Seneca tragicus in
tragedia *Medee*. Ad hunc novercales insidias fugiens devenit Frixus,
Athamantis filius, cum aureo vellere, quod sibi fatale ab oraculo
sentiens Oeta diligentissime servabat, ne eo perdito privaretur re-

confusing in its many paths, and, because he is a most forceful, ferocious, and furious animal, this shows him to have a human breast confused with unspeakable desires. In following this impulse we exhibit a powerful and vast spirit by daring something calamitous, and unless we accomplish it as we wished, we immediately descend into fury.

Also, with the help of Ariadne's instruction he was killed by Theseus, that is, by a prudent man to whom manliness — which I understand in the name Ariadne [*Adriana*] because *andres* in Greek means "man" — teaches that it is detestable to fall victim to such a wicked vice and shows what weapons are needed to dispose of it.

: II :

On Aeetes, King of the Colchians, eighth child of Sun, who fathered Medea, Absyrtus, and Calciope

Aeetes, King of the Colchians, as Homer[43] bears witness in the *Odyssey*, was the son of Sun and Perse, daughter of Ocean. Cicero[44] in his *On the Nature of the Gods* says that he was conceived by Asteria, sister of Latona; it was this Asteria whom Cicero again seems to say was killed by him, for he says this:[45] "How will you respond to Medea, who was born from two grandparents — Sun and Ocean — and from a matricide[46] father?"

Antiquity bears witness that he was a famous king at that time, for the tragedian Seneca[47] in his tragedy *Medea* describes the very great kingdom he had. Phrixus, son of Athamas, fleeing his stepmother's assaults, came to this Aeetes with the golden fleece, and Aeetes, having learned from an oracle that this would be fatal to him, carefully preserved it so that its destruction would not cause him to lose his kingdom. Even so, he was robbed by Jason and

3   gno; qui tamen a Iasone spoliatus est et regno pulsus. Verum iam senex ab eodem in regnum reductus est.

Dicit Theodontius hunc Oetam non fuisse filium Solis Yperionis, sed eius qui apud Colcos maximus fuit, et regnavit ibidem.

∴ 12 ∴

De Medea Oete regis filia et Iasonis coniuge

1   Medea Oete regis fuit filia ex Ipsea coniuge, ut satis patet per Ovidii carmen dicentis:

Non erat Oetes ad quem despecta rediret.
non Ipsea parens,

                                etc.

Huius Medee grandis recitatur hystoria, quandoque fabulis mixta. Aiunt enim ante alia, quod ex Appollonio sumptum est, qui *De argonautis* librum scripsit, Iasonem a Pelia patruo missum Colcos venisse, et comiter ab Oeta susceptum Medee virgini placuisse, in quam Venus irata uti in ceteram Solis prolem, omnes a filio amatorias inici flammas fecit.

2   Que amans cum pericula nosceret dilecti iuvenis euntis ad vellus aureum assumendum, miserta eius, habita sui coniugii sponsione, eum docuit, quo pacto illud absque periculo posset surripere, eoque surrepto una secum fugam arripuit, traxitque fuge

3   comitem Absyrtium seu Egyaleum parvulum fratrem. Quos cum sequeretur Oeta, ut eis spatium fuge prestaretur, in insula, que in faucibus Phasis, a scelere ab ea perpetrato Thomithania, exilio Ovidii Nasonis postea nobilitata, per quam oportebat Oetam se-

454

driven from his kingdom. But now an old man, Jason restored the   3
kingdom to him.

Theodontius says that this Aeetes was not the son of Sun, son
of Hyperion, but of the one who was greatest among the Colchians and ruled there.

: 12 :

On Medea, daughter of King Aeetes and wife of Jason

Medea was the daughter of King Aeetes by his wife Idyia,[48] as is   1
sufficiently clear from the verse of Ovid in which he says:[49]

Hated she could not return to Aeetes,
nor to her parent Idyia.

This Medea's history is recounted at length, and it is mixed with
fables. This account is taken from Apollonius, who wrote the *Ar-
gonautica*. To begin with, Jason was sent by his uncle Pelias, and
after he arrived in Colchis and was received cordially by Aeetes, he
captured the heart the maiden Medea into whom Venus, angry at
Medea because she was another of Sun's progeny, injected every
one of her son's amatory flames.

Being in love, although she knew the dangers of loving the   2
young man who had come to take the golden fleece, she took pity
on him, and having his promise of marriage, she instructed him
on how he could safely steal it; and after he stole it he took flight
along with her, also bringing as companion her little brother Absyrtus or Aegialeus. Aeetes followed them, so in order to create   3
some distance between them, on the island of Thomitania in the
mouth of the Phasis, known for the crime committed there and
later from the exile of Ovid, and which Aeetes needed to pass in

quentem transitum facere puerum Absyrthium obtruncavit, arti-
culatimque divisum passim per agros disiecit, ut patrem sisteret ad
colligenda filii membra.

4   Nec premeditatio fefellit infaustam, nam sic factum est; dumque orbatus pater flens membra colligit nati, et funeralia peragit,
abiit illa cum raptore. Et post longas, secundum quosdam, circuitiones in Thessaliam devenit, ubi precibus Iasonis Ensonem pa-
5   trem annositate decrepitum in robustiorem retraxit etatem. Et
cum Iasoni duos filios peperisset, in Pelye mortem sua fraude natas armavit. Tandem quacunque ex causa factum sit a Jasone abdicata est, et Creusa Creontis regis Corinthiorum filia desponsata.

Quod cum egerrime ferret, excogitata malitia, filios suos, quasi
ad placandam sibi novercam, cum donis in scrineolo clausis misit,
quod a Creusa non ante apertum est, quam per omnem regiam
flamma evolaverit ingens, a qua cum ipsa Creusa regia omnis
exusta est, cum iam pueri premoniti evasissent. Verum cum in
eam iratus Iason irruisset, sumpturus ex tam impio facinore penas,
eo vidente trux femina filios trucidavit innocuos et maleficiis suis
sublata Athenas abiit, ubi Egeo iam senescenti coniugio iuncta,
peperit ei filium quem a se Medum vocavit.

6   Sane cum Theseo redeunti ex longinqua atque diutina expeditione ab Egeo incognito, per eiusdem manus venenatum parasset
poculum, et illud idem ab Egeo filio iam cognito sublatum vidisset, fuga Thesei evitavit iram. Et tandem nescio quo pacto Jasoni
reconciliata, una secum in Colcos rediit, patremque senem et exu-
lem Iasonis viribus in regnum restituit; esto Gaius Celius, ut ubi

his pursuit, Medea mutilated the boy Absyrtus and scattered him piece by piece throughout the fields everywhere so that her father would have to stop to collect his son's limbs.

Nor did this plan fail the accursed woman, for this is what hap- 4 pened, and while the bereaved father wept and collected the limbs of his son and then carried out a funeral, she escaped with the thief. After long voyages, according to some, she reached Thessaly, where in responding to the prayers of Jason she restored his father Aeson, decrepit from age, to a more robust youth. And after she 5 had produced two sons for Jason, she armed Pelias' daughters so they could kill Pelias by treachery. Finally, for some reason Jason renounced her and became betrothed to Creusa, the daughter of Creon, King of the Corinthians.

Medea did not take this well and devised a malicious plan. She sent her sons, as if to appease their stepmother, with gifts enclosed in a small casket, and no sooner than this was opened by Creusa, a huge flame rushed throughout the entire palace and consumed it along with Creusa, although the boys, having already been fore-warned, escaped. When the angered Jason, intending to exact punishment for such an immoral crime, then attacked her, he watched as the savage woman slaughtered her innocent sons and then, exulting in her offenses, fled to Athens where she married the now elderly Aegeus and bore him a son whom she named Medus after herself.

She next prepared a cup of poison by her own hand for The- 6 seus, who was returning from a distant and time-consuming expe-dition and was not recognized by Aegeus, but when she saw that Aegeus now recognized Theseus as his son and took the cup away, she took flight to avoid his anger. And finally, reconciled with Ja-son — I do not know how — she returned with him to Colchis and used Jason's powers to restore her elderly father from exile to the throne, although Gaius Coelius, as Solinus[50] mentions in his *On the Wonders of the World*, says that she was buried by Jason in

De mirabilibus mundi refert Solinus, dicat eam a Iasone Bitrote se-
pultam, et Medum eius filium imperasse Marsis populis Ytalis.

7   His ergo ornata facinoribus Medea locum apud Grecos primo,
qui melius eam cognovisse debuerant, deinde apud Romanos com-
perit ut pro dea susciperetur atque sacris honoraretur ab eis, ut
liquido testatur Macrobius.

8   Que autem huius in hystoria fictiones intexte sunt, ubi de En-
sone et Pelya et Iasone scribetur, quoniam ad eos spectare videntur, passim, ubi oportunum videbitur, aperientur.

:   13   :

De Absyrthio et Calciope filiis Oete

1   Absyrthius et Calciopes frater et soror filii fuerunt Oete regis Colcorum. Nam de Absyrthio testatur Tullius in libro *De naturis deo-*
rum dicens: 'Quid huius (scilicet Medee) Absyrthio fratri, qui est
apud Pacuvium Egylaus,' etc. De Calciope autem dicit Ovidius in
Epistulis:

> Non erat Oetes ad quem despecta rediret
> non Ipsea parens Calciopesque soror,
>
> > etc.

De hac Calciope nil aliud repperi, nisi quod coniunx fuerit Frisi
eique peperit Cycorum filium.

2   De Absyrthio autem seu Egyleo iam supra dictum qualiter a
sorore sit cesus; a quo sunt qui dicant flumen illud Colcorum Absyrthium de pueri nomine nuncupatum.

Buthrotum and that her son Medus ruled the Marsi people in Italy.

Marked by these crimes, Medea found a place, first among the 7
Greeks, who ought to have known more about her, and then among the Romans, who accepted her as a goddess and honored her with rites, as Macrobius[51] clearly bears witness.

The fictions that are woven into her story will be explained 8
when Aeson, Pelias, and Jason are discussed, since these chapters will be more appropriate places to do so.

: 13 :

On Absyrtus and Calciope, sons of Aeetes

Absyrtus and Calciope, brother and sister, were the children of 1
Aeetes, King of the Colchians. Cicero in his *On the Nature of the Gods* gives us some evidence about Absyrtus by saying,[52] "What of her" — that is, Medea — "to her brother Absyrtus, who is Aegialeus in Pacuvius . . ." Ovid says about Calciope in his *Epistles:*[53]

Hated she could not return to Aeetes,
nor to her parent Idyia, nor Calciope her sister.

About this Calciope I have found nothing except that she was the wife of Phrixus and produced a son Cycorus.

As for Absyrtus or Aegialeus, I have already said above how he 2
was killed by his sister; there are those who say that the name of the river of the Colchians was named Absyrtus after the boy.

: 14 :

De Cyrce Solis filia

1 Cyrces malefica mulier, ut Omerus testatur in *Odissea,* filia fuit Solis et Perse; quo autem pacto Colcos liquerit et in Ytaliam venerit nusquam legi. Constat tamen eam habitasse haud longe a Caieta Campanie civitate, in quodam monte olim insula, qui Cyrceus ab ea in hodiernum usque diem dictus est. Circa quem adhuc aiunt incole rugire leones ferasque alias, quas ex hominibus cantato carmine fecit.

2 De hac autem sic scribit Virgilius:

Dives inaccessos ubi Solis filia lucos
assiduo resonat cantu, tectisque superbis
urit odoratam nocturna in lumina cedrum,
arguto tenues percurrens pectine telas.
Hinc exaudiri gemitus ireque leonum
vincla recusantum et sera sub nocte rudentum
setigerique sues atque in presepibus ursi
sevire ac forme magnorum ululare luporum.
Quos hominum ex facie dea seva potentibus herbis
induerat Cyrce in vultus ac terga ferarum,

etc.

3 Omerus autem in *Odissea* dicit Ulixem errantem cum sociis ad hanc devenisse et cum socios eius omnes mutasset in feras, eum a Mercurio predoctum mutare non potuisse, quin imo ab eo exterrita socios eius omnes in homines reformasse, eumque per annum ibidem tenuisse ac peperisse ei Thelegonum filium, et nonnulli

: 14 :

On Circe, [ninth] child of Sun

The wicked woman Circe, as Homer[54] testifies in the *Odyssey*, 1
was the daughter of Sun and Perse. Nowhere have I read under
what circumstances she left Colchis and came to Italy, but it is
agreed that she lived not at all far from Caieta, a city in Campania,
where there is a mountain, once an island, which has been named
Circeus after her, and the name remains today. The inhabitants
around there say that the men she turned by her songs of incanta-
tion into lions and other beasts still roar.

Vergil writes this about her:[55]   2

Where the wealthy daughter of the Sun the inaccessible groves
  fills with her incessant song, and in her proud house
she burns fragrant cedar, illuminating the night,
  as she runs the melodious comb through the delicate warp.
From here the angry roaring of lions
  battling their bonds and bellowing under the late night,
and bristly swine and bears in their pens
  rage, and the bodies of great wolves howl —
once human in appearance, the cruel goddess with powerful
    herbs,
Circe, cloaked them with the faces and backs of beasts.

In the *Odyssey* Homer[56] says that after wandering with his   3
comrades Ulysses arrived at her dwelling, and although she had
changed all his comrades into beasts, she was not able to change
him, for he had been forewarned by Mercury, and that he in fact
frightened her into transforming all his comrades back into men,
and that she held him there for one year and produced a son for
him, Telegonus — others add another son, Latinus, later king of

superaddunt, Latinum Laurentum postea regem, et demum eum predoctum multis dimisisse.

4   Refert preterea de hac Ovidius, quod amaverit Glaucum marinum deum, et quoniam ipse Scyllam nynpham amaret, zelo percitam, fontem in quo nynpha lavari consueverat, infecisse venenis. Quam ob rem dum illum intrasset nynpha, repente a marinis canibus usque ad inguina absorpta in marinum monstrum versa est.

5   Insuper dicit quod a Pyco rege spreta eo quod Pomonam amaret, eum in avem sui nominis transformasset.

6   Nunc autem quid sub his fictionibus sentiendum sit, videamus. Theodontius, harum rerum solertissimus[17] indagator, dicit hanc Solis Yperionis filiam non fuisse, sed eius qui apud Colcos regnasse creditur, sed ideo huius credita, quia, ut dicit Servius, formosissima fuit mulier et meretrix famosa, quod contigisse fingunt ob Veneris odium in prolem Solis, de quo odio infra patebit, ubi

7   de Venere. Audiri feras mugientes in circuitu montis est, quia dum inter ingentia atque prerupta saxa, rupes et cavernas, quarum mons circumdatus est, maris unde ventorum impetu efferuntur, et demum retrahuntur, et supervenientibus illiduntur, et hinc inde franguntur, fit de necessitate rumor dissonus, et nunc mugitui nunc rugitui similis, et hinc se fingunt audire leones aprosque.

8   Quod autem herbis aut cantato carmine in beluas homines transformaret, hoc videtur a multis concedi possibile magicis illusionibus, dum Pharaonis magos ea suis artibus fecisse credimus, que faciebat Moyses virtute divina, dum homines in Arcadia lupos

9   fieri, dum Apuleium in asinum permutatum. Sed ego potius credo hanc formositate sua multos in dilectionem sui traxisse mortales,

the Laurentians—and then sent him away, having given him many instructions.

In addition, Ovid[57] reports about her that she loved the maritime god Glaucus, and because he loved the nymph Scylla, jealousy drove her to infect the spring in which the nymph usually bathed with poison; and so when the nymph entered the spring, suddenly swallowed up to the waist by marine dogs, she was turned into a marine monster. Ovid[58] also says that when she was spurned by King Picus ["Woodpecker"], who loved Pomona instead, she transformed him into a bird of that name. 4 5

Now let us look into what we should understand from these fictions. Theodontius, a most expert researcher in these matters, says that she was not the daughter of Sun, the son of Hyperion, but of the one who is believed to have ruled the Colchians. But she was thought to have been the daughter of the former because, as Servius[59] says, she was a most beautiful woman and a famous courtesan, and the stories they contrived were due to Venus' hatred for the progeny of Sun. (We will discuss this hatred below where we discuss Venus.) That beasts are heard bellowing in the circuit of the mountain is because, when between the huge and steep rocks, cliffs, and caverns that surround mountains, waves of the sea are carried forth by the force of winds and then brought back and crash against those coming on top of them, thereby breaking the waves, a strange sound necessarily occurs, sometimes similar to roaring, sometimes to bellowing, and from this they invented the fiction of hearing lions and swine. 6 7

That she transforms men into beasts by using herbs or singing incantations many seem to admit is possible through the illusions of magic, for we believe the Pharaoh's magicians accomplished by means of their skills what Moses could do by means of divine power, and that men in Arcadia become wolves, and that Apuleius was transformed into an ass. But I believe rather that with her beauty she attracted many mortals to love her, mortals who in or- 8 9

qui sese ut eius mererentur gratiam, que meretricum absque pecu-
nia consequi non potest, illecebris variis ut dona portarent mis-
cuisse, et sic eas induisse formas, que officiis congruebant, quas
Ulixes, id est prudens homo, non induit.

Hanc post hec amasse Glaucum ideo dictum puto, quia, secundum quod aliquibus placet et potissime Leontio, Glaucus idem
sonat quod 'terror,' et quoniam terribile sit audire mugitus aquarum circa Cyrceum, ut supra dictum est, et ipse terror ibidem
consistat, assidue videtur a Cyrce, id est a loco illo Cyrcis amari.

10 Quod autem Glaucus amaverit Scyllam, ob eadem causam dictum
est, eo quod apud Scyllam idem a mugitu maris sit terror assiduus,

11 et sic cum ibi moretur assidue, videtur Scyllam diligere. Quod
Scylla infectis aquis a marinis canibus usque ad inguina rapta sit,
ab effectu sumpsit fictio causam. Est enim Scylla scopulus secus
fretum Syculum aquis supereminens adeo ut medius aquas exire
videatur, et ab aquis medius occupari, et cum totus sit preruptus et
cavernosus et ibi continue maximo cum impetu mare fluat et
refluat, dum cavernas illas intrat et demum se retrahit, ad instar
canum latrantium sonum emictit, et sic scopulus a marinis canibus
rapi dicitur.

12 Que autem ad Pycum spectant, in sequentibus scribentur, ubi
de Pyco. Ego[18] autem Cyrcem hanc Oete fuisse sororem non
credo, cum diu ante Troianum bellum Colchida fuerit Cyrces; hec
autem contemporanea. Sed convenientia nominum et forsan artium ex duabus unam fecisse potuerunt.

der to earn her favor (which without money is not possible to acquire from a courtesan), mixed various enticements so they could present gifts, and so they dressed their bodies in forms that agreed with their services. Ulysses, that is, a prudent man, did not disguise himself.

I think they said that after this she loved Glaucus because, according to an interpretation preferred by some and Leontius in particular, Glaucus means "terror," and because it is terrible to hear the roaring of water near Circeus, as we said above, and terror itself exists there, he seems to be fervently loved by Circe, that is, the place of Circe. That Glaucus loved Scylla is said for the same 10 reason, because the same terror is constantly near Scylla from the roaring of the sea, and because it remains there so constantly it seems to love Scylla. That Scylla was seized by marine dogs up to 11 her waste in infected waters is a fiction that takes its cause from its effect, for Scylla is a cliff near the straits of Sicily standing above the waters in such a way that waters seem to issue from its middle and the middle seems to be filled with waters, and since its entirety is steep and cavernous, and since the sea flows in and out continuously there with the greatest force, when it enters those caverns and then withdraws, it emits a sound like that of dogs barking, and so the cliff is said to be seized by marine dogs.

What they thought about Picus I will write about subsequently 12 in the chapter about him.[60] But I do not believe that this Circe was the sister of Aeetes, since the Colchian Circe lived a long time before the Trojan war; this Circe was contemporary.[61] But the similarity of their names and perhaps their arts could have produced one Circe from the two.

: 15 :

De Angitia Solis filia

1 Angitiam seu Angeroniam Theodontius dicit Cyrcis fuisse sororem et Solis filiam et haud longe ab ea in agro Campano moratam, sed melioribus artibus operatam. De qua, non in omnibus cum eo concordans, Gaius Celius asserit eam Cyrcis fuisse sororem et vicinia Fucini lacus occupasse, et ibidem salubri scientia adversus morbos incolis deservisse; quam ob rem diem claudens dea ab eisdem habita est.

2 Macrobius autem in *Saturnaliorum* libro hanc Angeroniam deam vocat, dicitque illi apud Romanos XII Kal. Ianuarias ferias celebrari, eique a pontificibus in sacello Volupie sacrum fieri. Verrius autem Flaccus ideo dicit eam Angeroniam apellari, quod 'angores' ac sollicitudines animorum propitiata depellat.

3 Addit insuper Masurius simulacrum huius dee ore obligato atque signato in ara Volupie collocatum, ob id quod, qui suos dolores anxietatesque dissimulant, beneficio patientie in maximum oblectationem deveniant. Sane Iulius Modestus huic sacrum fieri dicit, eo quod populus Romanus morbi, qui anginia dicitur, voto promisso liberatus sit. Cur autem Solis sit credita aut dicta filia, medendi ars causam dedisse potuit.

: 15 :

On Angitia, [tenth] child of Sun

Theodontius says that Angitia or Angeronia was the sister of 1
Circe and a daughter of Sun, and that she lived not far from her in
Campanian land, but that she practiced better arts. Gaius Coelius,[62] who does not completely agree with him, claims that she
was the sister of Circe and dwelled in the vicinity of Lake Fucinus,
where she served the inhabitants with her salubrious skill in fighting diseases; for this reason at the end of her days they considered
her a goddess.

Macrobius[63] in his *Saturnalia* calls this goddess Angeronia, and 2
he says that among the Romans festivals were celebrated in her
honor on December 21, and that there was a rite for her celebrated
by priests in the shrine of Volupia. Verrius Flaccus therefore says
that she was called Angeronia because when propitiated she dis-
pelled the "distresses" [*angores*] and anxieties of the mind.

In addition, Masurius[64] adds that a statue of this goddess, with 3
its mouth bound and sealed, was positioned on an altar of Volupia
because those who conceal their grief and anxieties, if they are
patient, achieve the greatest delight. But Julius Modestus[65] says
that they sacrificed to her because the Roman people, in fulfillment of a vow, were freed of the disease which is called "angina."
Her healing art could have provided the reason for her being believed or said to be the daughter of Sun.

: 16 :

De Luna Yperionis filia

1 Lunam, ut ad Yperionis prolem redeam, eiusdem Yperionis fuisse filiam et Solis sororem vulgatissimum est. De hac veteres multa senserunt. Illi quippe ante alia bigam dixere concessam, eo quod adversus patruos cum Iove sensisset, eamque curru uti testatur Accius poeta in *Baccis*, dicens, 'Almaque curru Noctivago Phebe,'

2 etc. Et Virgilius:

Iamque dies celo concesserat almaque curru
noctivago Phebe medium pulsabat Olympum,

etc.

Hanc bigam dicit Ysidoros ubi de *Ethymologiis* a duobus equis trahi, quorum alter albus, alter vero niger est. Eam preterea a Pane Arcadie deo dilectam dicit Nicander poeta, et lane candide mu-

3 nere in suos deduxisse concubitus. Quod et Virgilius in Georgicis asserit, dicens:

Munere sic niveo lane, si credere dignum est,
Pan deus Arcadie captam te, Luna, fefellit
in nemora alta vocans, nec tu aspernata vocantem,

etc.

4 Insuper et eam dilectam aiunt ab Endimione pastore, quem dicunt primo ab ea repulsum, demum postquam aliquandiu albos suos pavisset greges, in suam gratiam susceptum. Dicit tamen Tullius eum in Lamio seu Latinio Yonie monte obdormuisse et in somnis

: 16 :

On Moon, Daughter of Hyperion

As we return to the progeny of Hyperion, all agree that Moon was   1
the daughter of Hyperion and the sister of Sun. The ancients associated many things with her. Above all they said she was given a
two-horsed chariot because she sided with Jupiter against her uncles; and the poet Accius in the *Bacchae* testifies that she used the
chariot, saying:[66] "And nourishing Phoebe, wandering the night on
her chariot." And Vergil:[67]   2

> And now the daylight yields the sky and on her chariot
> wandering the night, nourishing Phoebe was beating upon the
>   center of Olympus.

Isidore[68] in his *Etymologies* says that this chariot was drawn by two
horses, of which one was white, the other black. In addition, the
poet Nicander[69] says that she was loved by the Arcadian god Pan,
and that she went to bed with him after he offered her a white
fleece. Vergil also asserts this in the *Georgics*, saying:[70]   3

> With a gift of a white fleece, if it is worthy of belief,
> the Arcadian god Pan deceived you and took you, Luna,
> calling you into the depths of the wood; nor did you refuse
>   his call.

In addition they say that she was loved by the shepherd Endymion,   4
whom they say she at first rejected, but then after he had tended
his white flocks for some time, she took a liking to him. Cicero[71]
says that he fell asleep on Mt. Lamius or Latmus[72] in Ionia and

a Luna deosculatum. Sunt et qui illi filios tribuant. Nam Alcyna, lyricus poeta, dicit rorem ab ea et Aere genitum.

5   Similiter eam multis vocant nominibus, ut puta: Lunam, Hecatem, Lucinam, Dianam, Proserpinam, Triviam, Argenteam, Phebem, Cererem, Arthemim, Menam et aliis.

6   Sed quid ex his tot intellexerint advertendum. Cur Yperionis dicta sit filia, dici potest id quod de Sole dictum est. Puto ego illam claritate insignem fuisse mulierem, et ob eius singularem preminentiam, et quia Solis esset soror, Lunam denominatam fuisse;

7 ad quam sequentia non spectant,[19] quin imo ad veram lunam. Et ideo quod adversus Titanas Iovi faverit, id est adversus superbos, ob eius complexionem frigidam et humidam dictum est, qua multum fumositates hominum reprimuntur. Biga autem uti dicitur, ad designandum cursum suum diurnum et nocturnum, quem longe clarius equorum colores ostendunt; preterea et humiditate sua germinantia fovet desuper et desubter adiumentum radicibus in-

8 fert. Quod autem ab Arcade deo dilecta sit, poterit forsan hic talis prestari sensus, ut pro Arcade deo summatur quicunque pastor. Erant enim Arcades ut plurimum pastores omnes, pastores autem lunam amant, id est eius lumen, eo quod ex illo commodum suscipiant, et ob id eam in silvis votis vocare consueverant, ut suos greges per noctem ab insidiis ferarum facilius caverent, et ob id dum fulgida veniebat, ei in sacris agnam mactabant candidam, et

9 sic albo vellere captam dicebant. Quod autem ab Endimione dilecta sit, dicit Fulgentius hoc posse contegere quod Endimion pastor fuerit, qui, uti pastores faciunt, noctis humorem amavit, quem vaporia syderum atque ipsius lune in animandis herbarum succis insudant, et inde in pastorum commoda vertitur.

during his sleep was kissed by Moon. There are also those who attribute children to her, for the lyric poet Alcman[73] says that Dew was born to her and Air.

Similarly, they call her by many names, for example Luna, 5 Hecate, Lucina, Diana, Proserpina, Trivia, Argentea, Phoebe, Ceres, Artemis, Mena, and others.

But we should observe what all these mean. What we said 6 about Sun can also identify her as the daughter of Hyperion: I think that she was a woman celebrated for her renown, and on account of her singular preeminence and because she was the sister of Sun, she was called Moon. But for the following they do not refer to her but to the true moon. It was said that she favored Ju- 7 piter against the Titans, that is, against the gods, on account of her cool and humid complexion which often inhibits the vapors of men. She is said to use the chariot to signify her daily and nightly course, which the colors of the horses demonstrate much more clearly. In addition, with her humidity she warms sprouts from above and brings assistance to the roots below. Perhaps we can ac- 8 count for her being loved by the Arcadian god if we substitute a shepherd for the Arcadian god; the Arcadians were almost all shepherds, and shepherds love the moon, that is, its light, because they benefit from it, and so they are accustomed to calling upon her in the forest and praying so she will protect their flocks from the attacks of beasts throughout the night. And when she came out shining they use to sacrifice a white ewe to her, so they would say that she was taken because of the white fleece. That she was 9 loved by Endymion, Fulgentius says, could hide the fact that Endymion was a shepherd who loved, as shepherds do, the night's moisture; the vapors of the stars and moon itself sweat out this moisture to refresh the vital juices of the herbs, and therefore it turns into a benefit for the shepherds.

Vel aliter. Ait idem Fulgentius, quod is Endimion primus rationem cursus lune invenerit et obdormisse xxx annis dicitur, quia
stultorum iudicio meditationi vacantes dormiunt, id est tempus
10 perdunt. Seu qui meditationibus deditus est, profecto non aliter
quam si dormiret, immiscetur activis operibus, quod de Endimione dictum est, quia nil aliud eo vivente, nisi huic meditationi
operam dare peregit, uti Minastas, in eo libro quem de Europa
11 scripsit, testatur. Quod ego verum puto, nec sit qui longum temporis miretur spatium, cum circa lune cursum plurima veniant
consideranda, ut ostendit venerabilis Andalo in sua *Theorica planetarum.*

Sed quod albos ante greges paverit, ideo appositum credo, ut
loci sue meditationis qualitas ostendatur, qui in culmine montis
illius fuit quod sibi elegit, ut posset libere elevationes assumere
tanquam ex expedito loco, et montium culmina, et potissime celsa,
ut plurimum consueverunt esse nivosa, quas nives quia diu obser-
12 vavit, pastor nivei pecoris dictus est. Quod autem a luna deosculatus sit, ideo fictum reor, quia sicut amantes puellam amoris munus
osculum arbitrantur, sic et longe huius meditationis munus fuisse
lune comperisse cursum, et sic sui amoris videtur osculum suscepisse.

13 Superest de nominibus videre. Lunam a 'lucendo' dictam volunt, et maxime dum 'lucet' in sero, cum dum mane luceat velint
appellari Dianam. Hecates autem ideo dicta est, quia 'centum' interpretatur, in quo numero quasi finitum pro infinito positum sit,
14 volunt multiplicitatem eius potentie denotari. Triviam nonnulli,
esto Seneca poeta triformem dicat in tragedia *Ypoliti,* a triplici suo
nomine principali dictam volunt; vocatur enim Luna, Diana et
Proserpina. Dicunt eam etiam vocari Lucinam ut in *Odis* Oratius:

There is a very different interpretation. Fulgentius[74] says that this Endymion first discovered the regular path of the moon and is said to have slept for thirty years because stupid people assume that those who spend their time in deep thought are asleep, that is, they are wasting time; or, he who is given to deep thought, 10 which seems quite the same as sleeping, busies himself with activity and work, which is said about Endymion because he accomplished nothing else while he was alive other than to spend time in deep thought, as Mnaseas,[75] in that book he wrote about Europe, bears witness. I concur, nor should anyone be amazed at the long 11 period of time he spent on this since there are many things that have to be considered in regard to the course of the moon, as the venerable Andalò shows in his *Planetary Theory*.

But I believe it is fitting that he earlier pastured white flocks because this shows the kind of place where he meditated, which was on the top of the mountain he chose for himself so he could freely stand higher in a more or less unencumbered place, and mountain tops, particularly high ones, are usually snowy; because he looked at this snow for a long time, he was said to be the shepherd of a snowy white flock. That he was kissed by Moon I think 12 was invented because just as those loving a girl think of a kiss as the reward of love, so also to have discovered the course of the moon was the reward of his lengthy meditation, and so he seems to have been given a kiss by his love.

It remains to look at her names. They want Luna to derive 13 from "shining" [*lucendo*], especially when the moon "shines" brightly in the evening, since when it shines in the morning they want her to be called Diana. She is called Hecate because it means "one hundred," and in this number, which makes the infinite somewhat finite, they wish to denote the multiplicity of her power. Some 14 prefer Trivia (although the poet Seneca[76] in his tragedy *Hippolytus* calls her triform) to derive from her triple name, for she is called Luna, Diana, and Proserpina. They say that she was also called

'Te Lucinam probas vocari,' etc., quam parturientium deam vo-
15 cant, et cur sic dicta sit, paulo post dicetur. Argenteam autem ob
id dicunt, quia suum sit argentum in terris procreare, seu quia solis respectu, qui aureus est, videatur argentea. Phebeam autem
ideo vocavere, quia sepe nova sit. Arthemia seu Arnothemis Attica
lingua idem est quod luna, ideo sic dicta, ut refert Macrobius, quia
16 *arthemis* quasi *arnothemis*, id est 'aerem secans.' Luna a parturienti-
bus invocatur, quia proprium eius est destendere rimas corporis et
meatibus viam dare, quod est ad accelerandos partus salutare, ut
poeta Thymotheus eleganter expressit. Mena vero dicta est quia
non nunquam defectus patitur, ut puta in eclipsis et inde Mena,
quod Latine 'defectum' sonat, seu quia naturaliter luce careat et
quos habet radios mutuetur a sole, uti cetera faciunt sydera.
17 Reliqua autem nomina, quoniam ad alias pertinent deas, de
quibus singularis in hoc opere mentio fit, ex consulto donec de illis
tractetur omisi.

∶ 17 ∶

De Rore filio Lune

1 Rorem Alcina lyricus poeta Lune atque Aeris fuisse filium dicit,
teste Macrobio. Quod quidem figmentum a natura sumptum est,
agente quidem luna vapores terre humidos nequeuntes, absente
sole, consurgere altius, frigiditate aeris et lune alterati vertuntur in
tenuem aquam, que decidens ros estivo tempore appellatur, hyeme
vero condensati gelu bruma dicitur.

Lucina, as does Horace in his *Odes*: "You approve being called Lucina,"[77] as they call her the goddess of giving birth; why she is called this will be explained a little later. They call her Argentea 15 because it is she who creates "silver" [*argenteum*] in the earth, or because in respect to the sun, which is golden, she seems "silvery" [*argentea*]. They call her Phoebe because she is often "new." Artemia or Arnothemis[78] is what the moon is called in the in the Attic language, as Macrobius[79] reports, because *artemis*, and similarly *arnothemis*, means "cutting the air" [*aerem secans*]. She is called 16 Luna from parturition because it is for her to stretch a body's crevices and to make a path for movements, which is helpful in speeding the birthing process, as the poet Timotheus expresses elegantly.[80] She is called Mena because sometimes she endures defects, for example in eclipses, and therein Mena which means "defect," or because she naturally lacks light, and what rays she has she borrows from the sun, as do the rest of the stars.

I have omitted the remaining names, since they refer to other 17 goddesses; my plan is to make mention of them one by one throughout this work until they are all accounted for.

: 17 :

On Dew, son of Moon

The lyric poet Alcman[81] says that Dew was the son of Moon and 1 Air, as Macrobius testifies. This is a contrivance taken from nature: when the moon and not the sun acts upon them, the moist vapors of the earth are unable to rise higher; and altered by the coldness of the air and moon, they are changed into a delicate form of water which drips in summertime and is called dew; in the wintertime it is condensed by the cold and called frost.

: 18 :

De Briareo Titanis filio

1 Briareus ab omnibus creditus est Titanis et Terre filius, quem omnes fere Latini poete hostem Iovis infestissimum contemptoremque deorum asserunt, et ob id apud inferos detrusum volunt, eumque inter monstruosos in vestibulo inferni excubias agere scribit Virgilius, dicens, 'Et centumgeminus Briareus et belua Lerne,' etc.

2 Sane Omerus eum amicum fuisse Iovis ostendit in *Yliade*, dicens:

ὦχ᾽ ἑκατόγχειρον καλέσασ᾽ ἐς μακρὸν Ὄλυμπον
ὃν Βριάρεων καλέουσι θεοί ἄνδρες δέ τε πάντες
Αἰγαίων᾽, ὃ γὰρ αὖτε βίην[20] οὗ πατρὸς ἀμείνων.

Cito centimanum vocasti in magnum Olympum,
quem Briareum vocant dii hominesque
terrigenam post eius patrem meliorem.

3 In quibus carminibus Homerus perfunctorie tangit fabulam, quam Theodontius paulo latius refert dicens, quod commoti dii adversum Iovem, Iuno scilicet et Neptunus una cum Pallade et aliquibus aliis, in domo Nerei patris Thetidis deliberaverunt catenam facere, et dormienti Iovi inicere, et invicem trahentes omnes eum e celo eicere, quod Thetis Iovi retulit, et ob id ipse in favorem suum

4 in celum Briareum evocavit. Quem cum vidissent coniurati, eo quod fortissimus extimaretur, confertim a ceptis destitere et sic tutatus est Iuppiter; ex quibus patet Briareum amicum fuisse Iovis.

5 Huius autem fabule volens Leontius aperire sensum, aiebat ante resolutionem Chaos inferiora elementa cum superis discordare et

476

: 18 :

On Briareus, [second] son of Titan

Briareus is believed by everyone to be the son of Titan and Earth. 1
Nearly all the Latin poets assure us that he was a most hostile
enemy of Jupiter and paid no heed to the gods, wherefore they
wanted him thrown down to the nether world. Vergil writes that
he keeps guard amongst the monstrous in the vestibule of the
nether world, saying,[82] "And hundred-handed Briareus and the
beast of Lerna."

In the *Iliad*, however, Homer reveals him to be Jupiter's friend, 2
saying:[83]

Immediately you called the hundred-handed to great Olympus,
  whom the gods call Briareus and men,
Earth-born, mightier than his father.

In these verses Homer briefly mentions the fable which Theodon- 3
tius relates more fully, saying that gods who agitated against Jupiter, namely, Juno and Neptune along with Pallas and some others,
decided in the house of Nereus, father of Thetis, to make a chain,
fasten it upon Jupiter while he slept, and, after dragging him one
by one, throw him from the sky. Thetis reported this to Jupiter,
and it is for this reason that he called Briareus into the sky to assist him. But when the conspirators saw him and realized his great 4
strength, they immediately desisted from their plans, so Jupiter
was saved. From this it is clear that Briareus was the friend of Jupiter.

In his desire to reveal the meaning of this fable, Leontius used 5
to say that before the dissolution of Chaos the lower elements
disagreed with the upper until moisture acted upon them to ren-

humoris opera inisse concordiam, et alia quedam plura ridenda potius quam scribenda.

6 Theodontius autem dicit sub hac fabula tenui velo hystoriam tegi. Dicit enim Iovem post victoriam ex Titanis atque Gigantibus habitam adeo elatum, ut importabilis efficeretur amicis, quam ob causam Iuno coniunx eius et Neptunus frater clam apud insulam Nerithos convocatis quibusdam ex amicis inivere consilium, ut eum nil tale timentem e regno pellerent; quod cum illi revelatum esset a nauta conscio, Briareum ex Titanis superstitem unum et potentissimum adhuc hominem, seu potius Briarei Titanis filium eodem nomine nuncupatum evocavit, et cum eo inito societatis federe coniuratos exterruit adeo, ut in eum nil penitus auderent.

7 Dictus est enim Briareus Centumgeminus, quia multis preesset hominibus, et ponitur finitum pro infinito. Apud inferos autem non in civitate Ditis detrusus est, ut reliqui sunt, quia adhuc in adiutorium servaretur superum, ut intelligamus non esse aliquos quantumcunque perversos, quin ad meliorem vitam serventur a Deo, cum ab eodem eorum futura conversio cognoscatur.

: 19 :

De Ceo Titanis III° filio, qui genuit Latonam et Asterien

1 Ceum inter alios Titanis filios enumerat Paulus et eius matrem fuisse Terram ostendit Virgilius ubi dicit, 'Extremam, ut perhibent, Ceo Encheladoque sororem,' etc. Leontius dicit hunc Cee insule

der them agreeable, and some other things which should be laughed at more than written about.

Theodontius says history is hidden under a thin veil in this fable. He says that after his victory over the Titans and Giants, Jupiter was so ecstatic that he proved to be unbearable to his friends, wherefore his wife Juno and his brother Neptune, along with some of their invited friends, secretly formed a plan on the island of Nerithos[84] to drive him from his kingdom. When a sailor who had heard about this plot revealed it to the unsuspecting Jupiter, the latter called upon Briareus, a Titan survivor and still a very powerful man, or rather the son of the Titan Briareus who had the same name, and after forming an alliance with him so terrified the conspirators that they dared not punish him.

They said that Briareus was hundred-handed because he was in charge of many men, and a finite number was applied to an infinite number. He was thrust down to the nether world—but not in the city of Dis like the others—because he still served to assist the gods above. This tells us that there are no men, however corrupt, but that they are preserved by God for a better life, since he knows of their future conversion.

: 19 :

*On Coeus, third child of Titan, who fathered
Latona and Asteria*

Paul counts Coeus as one of the Titans, and Vergil points out that his mother was Earth when he says,[85] "Her last child, as they say, sister of Coeus and Enceladus." Leontius says that he was the very

fuisse potentissimum regem, et extreme ferocitatis hominem atque
superbie, ob quam cum antiquior fuerit Titano, inter eius numera-
tur filios.

2   Fuit enim Latone et Asterie spectabilium pulchritudine virginum pater, dicebatque Paulus pro eo, quod Iuppiter Latonam vi-
tiasset. Titanorum bellum adversus Iovem motum, sed falsum est,
ut supra demonstravimus, ex his que in *Sacra* leguntur *hystoria*.

: 20 :

De Latona Cei filia, que peperit
Apollinem et Dianam

1   Latonam filiam fuisse Cei ex Ovidii carmine sumitur. Dicit enim:

> Nescio quo audetis genitam Titanida Ceo
> Latonam preferre michi,
>
> > etc.

Hanc autem veteres a Iove dilectam pariter et oppressam volunt,
eamque ex eo geminam suscepisse prolem, Apollinem scilicet et
Dianam, quod aiunt adeo egre tulisse Iunonem, ut non solum
omnem terram ad onus uteri deponendum interdiceret illi, verum
et inmicteret Phytonem, ingentis magnitudinis serpentem, ad eam
2   fugandam atque impediendam. Que cum pavescens fugeret, neque
locum aliquem retinentem se inveniret, propinquans Ortygie insule ab ea suscepta est, et in eadem peperit primo Dianam, que
evestigio obstetricatus officium in nascituro fratre matri prestitit,
et Apollinem nascentem suscepit, qui mox sagittis Phytonem inte-
3   remit et dare cepit responsa petentibus. Preterea ob hunc partum dicunt nomen immutatum insule, nam cum primo diceretur

powerful king of the island of Ceos, a man of extreme savagery and arrogance; for this reason he is counted among his sons, although he was older than Titan.

He was the father of Latona and Asteria, maidens regarded for 2 their beauty. And Paul used to say that it was because Jupiter had violated Latona that the Titans made war against Jupiter, but this is incorrect, as we demonstrated above, according to what we read in the *Sacred History*.[86]

: 20 :

On Latona, daughter of Coeus, who gave birth to
Apollo and Diana

Latona, we learn from the verses of Ovid, was the daughter of 1 Coeus, for he says:[87]

Do you dare prefer the Titan born of some Coeus,
Latona, to me?

The ancient accounts are equal in saying that she was loved or raped by Jupiter; this produced twin offspring by him, namely, Apollo and Diana. They say this so irritated Juno that not only did she prohibit the entire earth from easing the burden of Latona's womb, but she also sent Python, a serpent of huge size, to put her to flight and obstruct her. When Latona was fleeing in fear 2 and could not find a place of refuge, she approached the island of Ortygia and was taken in and there gave birth first to Diana, who immediately presented her services as a midwife to her mother in the birth of her brother, and so Apollo was born. He soon killed Python with arrows and began to give responses to petitioners. In 3 addition, they say that on account of this birth the name of the

Ortygia, Delos postea dicta est. Dicunt insuper deferentem Latonam parvulos adhuc filios per Lyciam, dum ob estum siti laboraret, accessisse ad lacum quendam, ut biberet, quam cum vidissent circumstantes rustici, confestim lacum pedibus intrasse et omnem turbasse aquam, ex quo commotam Latonam orasse ut exterminarentur; quam ob rem rustici repente in ranas mutati locum semper incoluere.

4   Circa has fictiones dicebat Barlaam, cessante diluvio, quod Ogygii regis fuit tempore, ex humiditate terre nimia, cui calor erat immixtus, tam densas exalasse nebulas, ut apud plura loca Egei maris et Achaye nullo modo solares radii die, nec nocte lunares viderentur ab incolis; tandem eis rarescentibus et potissime apud insulas, apud quas ratione maris minus poterat exalatio terre, contigit ut nocte quadam circa horam diei proximam a circumstantibus in insula Ortygie primo viderentur lunares radii et subsequenter mane solares; quam ob rem maximo omnium gaudio, quasi reacquisissent quos perditos iam arbitrabantur, dictum est apud Ortygiam Dianam et Apollinem natos, et ob id insule mutatum nomen, et ex Ortygia Delos, quod idem sonat quod 'manifestatio,' appellata est, eo quod ibi primo manifestatio solis et lune facta sit.

5   Latonam autem eam ipsam insulam voluere fingentes, in qua manifestatio facta, eamque feminam precipue assumpsere ad figmentum conficiendum, quia contigerat eam geminos peperisse, quorum masculum Apollinem, feminam autem Dianam nuncupaverant.

6   Phytonem autem Latonam insequentem ne posset parere, nebulas densas surgentium vaporum voluere, que quidem obstabant ne possent solares atque lunares radii a mortalibus intueri; nec incongrue has vocavere serpentem; nam dum leves huc illuc a quocunque spiritu impellerentur, more serpentis serpere videbantur.

island was changed, for while before it was called Ortygia, afterward it became known as Delos. They also say that when her children were still small, Latona was carrying them through Lycia and was beset with burning thirst. She came to a certain lake to get a drink, but because the local peasants had seen her, they immediately entered the lake and agitated all the water with their feet. Upset, Latona asked that they be exterminated, wherefore the peasants were immediately changed into the frogs which have inhabited the place ever since.

Barlaam used to say about these fictions that after the flood, 4 which occurred when Ogygius was king, the excess moisture of the earth mixed with heat caused such dense clouds to arise that in many localities of the Aegean Sea and Achaea the inhabitants could not see the solar rays during the day or the moon beams at night; when they finally evaporated, especially in the islands, where because of the sea the emissions from the earth were less powerful, it happened that one night just before daybreak moon beams and then morning solar rays first became visible to bystanders on the island of Ortygia. As a result of the great joy they all experienced, as if they had reacquired what they thought they had now lost, it was said that Diana and Apollo were born on Ortygia, wherefore the name of the island was changed, and the former Ortygia was called Delos, which means "manifest," because the first manifestation of the sun and moon occurred there.

Those who invented this fiction wanted Latona to be the same 5 island in which the manifestation occurred, and to complete their invention they selected this woman in particular because she happened to give birth to twins, of which they named the male Apollo and the female Diana.

In Python pursuing Latona to prevent her from giving birth 6 they mean the dense clouds of rising vapors which indeed were hindering the solar and lunar rays from being able to be seen by mortals, nor did they inappropriately call these a serpent, for when

7 Et nunc a Iunone ideo missum dixere, eo quod non nunquam pro terra et mari intelligatur Iuno, a quibus evaporationes ille emictebantur. Dianam autem ideo ante natam dicunt, quia nocte, extenuatis iam vaporibus, primo lunares apparuere radii. Quod autem obstetricatus in nativitate fratris officio functa sit, ideo dictum est, quia sicut obstetrices consuevere nascentes suscipere, sic et luna dum paulo ante solem surrexisset, solem orientem suscipere pansis

8 cornibus visa est. Occisum autem Phytonem telis ab Apolline ideo fictum, quia solaribus radiis agentibus omnis illa terre evaporatio dissoluta est.

Quod autem ceperit Apollo dare responsa, sumptum est ab eo quod post modum contigit, scilicet ut ea in insula nescio cuius maleficio demon sub Apollinis titulo cepit et diu dedit de quesitis

9 responsa. Mutatos autem in ranas rusticos ideo dictum est, quia ut scribit Phylocorus, bellum fuit Rhodiis olim adversus Lycios, Rhodiis auxiliares venere Delones, qui cum aquatum ad lacum quendam Lyciorum ivissent, rustici loci incole aquas prohibuere, in quos Delones irruentes omnes interemere, et in lacum occiso-

10 rum corpora eiecere. Tractu tandem temporis cum montani Lycii venissent ad lacum, nec occisorum agrestium corpora comperissent et ranas in circuitu coassantes sensissent, rudes et ignari arbitrati sunt eas ranas animas esse cesorum, et dum sic referunt aliis, fabule causam adinvenere.

light things are blown here and there by puffs of air, they seem to snake like a serpent. And next they said he was sent by Juno because sometimes Juno is understood as the earth and sea which emit those evaporations. They say that Diana was born first because it was at night, when the vapors were already thinned, that the moon beams first appeared. That she performed the services of a midwife in the birth of her brother they said because, just as midwives normally deliver newborn babies, the moon also, when it rises a little before the sun, seems to deliver the rising sun with its spread horns. They invented the story that Python was killed by the weapons of Apollo because all of this evaporation on earth was dissolved by the action of the solar rays.

That Apollo began to give responses was taken from that which happened after a while, namely, that on that island as the result of some sorcery a demon using the title of Apollo began to give responses to questions and did so for a long time. It was said that the peasants were changed into frogs because, as Philochorus[88] writes, there once was a war between the Rhodians and the Lycians; Delians came as auxiliaries to assist the Rhodians; and when the Delians went to a certain lake of the Lycians to get water, the local peasants denied them the water, so the Delians attacked them and killed them all, and they threw the bodies of the dead into the lake. Then after an extent of time when the mountain dwelling Lycians came to the lake, they did not find the bodies of the dead farmers but heard frogs croaking around the lake, and being rude and ignorant they thought those frogs were the spirits of the dead men, and in telling of this to others they created the source of this fable.

: 21 :

De Asterie filia Cei et matre Herculis

1 Asteries filia fuit Cei Titanis, ut Theodontio placet. Hec, ut ait Fulgentius, post viciatam Latonam a Iove dilecta est, a quo verso in aquilam et oppressa fuit; eique eo ex concubitu Herculem peperit; que tandem ut quibusdem placet, adversus Iovem sentiens et eius fugiens iras, miseratione deorum in coturnicem versa est, que Grece vocatur *ortygia*, nomenque dedit insule in quam aufugerat, ubi a Iove in lapidem mutata est, undisque demersa et ab eisdem huc illuc agitata, que tandem ob susceptam Latonam firmata est.

2 Huius fabule talis potest esse ratio. Dicit Theodontius superato atque occiso a Iove Ceo, qui ob viciatam Latonam adversus eum arma moverat, eum in Ceam venisse insulam et ibidem Asteriem virginem Cei filiam oppressisse, tandem ea adversus eum sentiente primo volucri fuga in Ortygiam abiisse, inde vero in Colcos transfretasse, Solique ibi regnanti nupsisse, eique peperisse Oetam a quo postmodum occisa est; seu, ut Barlaam dicit, in partu Oete deficit.

3 Ex quibus fictum ideo est Iovem aquilam secum concubuisse, quia aquila Iovis erat signum dum esset in armis, et quia bello Ceam cepisset, fictum est eum in aquilam versum cum Asterie concubuisse.

4 Quod autem in coturnicem Asteries versa sit, aut ob eius volucrem fugam, cum coturnicum sit volare perniciter, aut propter longam eius transfretationem, quod etiam est coturnicum certo anni tempore transfretare.

: 21 :

On Asteria, daughter of Coeus and mother of Hercules

Asteria was the daughter of the Titan Coeus, according to Theo- 1
dontius. After violating Latona, as Fulgentius[89] says, Jupiter took
delight in Asteria and, transforming himself into an eagle, took
her by force. As a result of this intercourse she bore Hercules to
him; then, according to some, disfavoring Jupiter and fleeing his
anger, the gods took pity on her and turned her into a quail, which
in Greek is *ortygia*, and she gave her name to the island to which
she had fled; here she was turned into stone by Jupiter, submerged
into the waters which carried her to various places, and anchored
at last when Latona was received there.

This could be the reasoning behind such a fable. Theodontius 2
says that once Jupiter had overcome and killed Coeus, who had
taken up arms against him on behalf of the violated Latona, he
came to the island of Cea and there forced himself on Asteria, the
virgin daughter of Coeus. Then, holding Jupiter in disfavor, she
first escaped quickly to Ortygia, and then she crossed over into
Colchis and there married Sun, who was ruling there, and bore
him Aeetes, by whom she was later killed. Or, as Barlaam says, she
died while giving birth to Aeetes.

The fiction that Jupiter took the form of an eagle to sleep with 3
her was invented because the eagle was Jupiter's symbol when
he took up arms. And the fact that he had defeated Cea in war
created the fiction that he turned into an eagle and slept with
Asteria.

That Asteria was turned into a quail is either on account of her 4
swift flight, since quails fly quickly, or because she crossed the sea,
because quails also cross the sea at a certain time of year.

5   Quod autem in lapidem versa sit, non spectat ad eam, quin imo
ad insulam in quam primo aufugit, que Ortygia dicta est, Latine
vero 'coturnix,' que idio in lapidem versa dicitur, ut eius nova stabi-
6 litas designetur. Ferunt autem Ortygiam insulam[21] solitam una
cum undis fluctuare, quod fictum est, quia nimia et crebra terremotuum concussione agitari consueverit. Quam tandem firmatam
volunt, id est a concussione liberatam, eo quod ab Apolline responsum sit ne in ea mortuum corpus sepeliretur et quedam illi
insuper celebrarentur sacra, quibus rite celebratis cessavit terremotuum infestatio, et sic facta lapis, id est stabilis.

7   Puto ego repletis cavernis in quibus aer inclusus terremotus
causabat, hoc contigisse, eosque illo dyaboli responso deceptos.
Superaddunt quidam eidem Ortygie Mycones atque Gyaros insulas adhesisse atque firmasse, quod non sic simpliciter intelligendum est, quin imo ex insulis illis que illi proxime sunt, Ortygia
iam firmata, accessere incole et invicem quam reliquerant habita-
vere.

: 22 :

De Thyphone seu Typheo IIII° Titanis filio, qui genuit Aeos et Chimeram

1 Typhon seu Typheus, Theodontio asserente, Titani fuit filius ex
Terra, esto dicat Lactantius eum ex Tartaro genitum et Terra.
Hunc insuper dicit idem Lactantius Iovem in certamen provocasse
de regno, quam ob causam iratus Iuppiter fulmine eum prostravit
et ad eius opprimendam superbiam corpori eius superimposuisse
Trinacriam.

That she was turned into stone does not refer to her but to the 5
island to which she first fled; it is called Ortygia, or "quail," and is
said to have been turned into stone to designate its new stability.
They say also that Ortygia was an island which used to float along 6
with the waves, and they invented this because the island used to
be shaken by strong and frequent earthquakes. They want it stabilized, that is, freed from earthquakes, because there was a response
from Apollo that dead bodies were not to be buried there and that
they should also celebrate certain rites there, and when they were
properly observed and celebrated, the occurrence of earthquakes
ceased, and so it was made of stone, that is, made stable.

I think this happened because the earthquakes were caused by 7
caverns full of trapped air, and that they were deceived by that response of the devil. Some add that the islands of Myconos and
Gyaros stuck to Ortygia and stabilized; the simple explanation for
this is that once Ortygia was stabilized, the inhabitants from those
islands, which lie next to it, came over and then inhabited what
they had left behind.

: 22 :

On Typhon or Typhoeus, fourth child of Titan, who fathered Aeus and Chimera

Typhon or Typhoeus, as Theodontius asserts, was the son of Titan 1
by Earth, although Lactantius[90] says that he was born from Tartarus and Earth. In addition Lactantius says that he provoked this
same Jupiter into a battle for his kingdom, wherefore the angered
Jupiter laid him out with a thunderbolt, and that he placed Trinac-
ria on top of his body to suppress his arrogance.

2   Quod etiam sic testatur Ovidius:

> Vasta Giganteis iniecta est insula membris
> Trinacris, et[22] magnis subiectum montibus urget
> ethereas ausum sperare Thyphea sedes.
> Nititur ille quidem pugnat quoque surgere sepe.
> Dextra sed Auxonio manus est subiecta Peloro,
> leva, Pachine, tibi: Lylibeo crura premuntur.
> Degravat Ethna caput, sub quo resupinus harenas
> eiectat flammamque ferox vomit ore Typheus.
> Sepe remoliri luctatur pondere terre
> oppidaque et magnos devolvere corpore montes:
> inde tremit tellus,
>
> etc.

3 Virgilius autem non Ethnam sed Ynarimem illi dicit superiniectum, qui quidem mons est insule vicine Baiis, que hodie Yscla vocatur, haud longe a Prochita insula, et dicit sic:

> Tum sonitu Prochita alta tremit durumque cubile
> Ynarime Iovis imperiis imposta Typheo,
>
> etc.

4 Quod etiam videtur tenuisse Lucanus dum dicit:

> Undat apex, Campana fremens, cui saxa vaporat
> conditus Ynarimes eterna mole Typheus,
>
> etc.

5   Huic insuper insigne antrum fuisse in Cilicia, haud longe a Coryco oppido, dicit Pomponius Mela in suo *Cosmographie* libro, et post eum Solinus *De mirabilibus*. Nam aiunt in monte profundissimam specum per duo milia quingentos passus nemorum umbra et

6 rivulorum fluentium tinnitu amenam plurimum. Deinde post tam

Ovid bears witness to this:[91]   2

> The vast island of Trinacria was heaped upon his giant limbs
> and pressed upon Typhoeus laid under these great mountains,
> having dared to hope for heavenly seats.
> He struggled indeed and he often fought to rise,
> But his right hand was pinned under Ausonian Pelorus,
> His left under you, Pachine, his legs pressed by Lilybaeum;
> Weighing upon his head was Etna, under which, lying on his
>   back,
> Fierce Typhoeus belches sand and vomits flame from his
>   mouth.
> Often he wrestled to heave off the weight of the earth
> And to roll the towns and great mountains off his body:
> Then the earth trembles.

Vergil says it was not Etna but Inarime that was thrown upon   3
him, and this is indeed a mountain of the island neighboring Ba-
iae, which today is called Ischia, not at all far from the island of
Procida; and he says this:[92]

> Then with a sound lofty Procida trembles and the hard bed,
> Inarime, laid upon Typhoeus by the orders of Jupiter.

Lucan also seems to have held this opinion when he says:[93]   4

> The peak billows, Campania growls, where Typhoeus,
> hidden under the eternal mass of Inarime, breathes out stones.

Besides this, Pomponius Mela[94] in his *Description of the World*,   5
and after him Solinus[95] in his *On the Wonders of the World*, says
there was a well-known cave in Cilicia not far from the town of
Corycus, for they say that in the mountain there is a very deep
cave — two and one half miles deep — which is most attractive in
the shade of its woods and the tinkling of its flowing rivulets.
Then, after a steep decline, there is an entrance to another cave; as   6

longum descensum panditur specus altera, que in processu iam obscurior habet sacrum Iovi fanum, inde in eius extremo recessu Typhonis cubile positum incole asseruere. Hec de Typheo.

7   Nunc abscondita corticibus evisceranda sunt. Typheum igitur istum Titanis, ob elatum eius spiritum, filium dixere, et Terre ob potentiam, cum dicat Theodontius eum antiquissimum Cylicie fuisse regem et Osyrim fratrem superasse bello atque discerpsisse membratim, et bellum adversus primum Iovem movisse, sed ab eo superatum atque occisum.

8   Verum fictionibus, quibus hec hystoria dedisse causam satis apparet, erit explicatio ista. Videntur enim in his naturam et causam terremotuum satis convenienter, latenter tamen ostendere qui finxere. Dicit enim Papias Typhonem seu Typheum idem sonare quod 'flammas eicientem,' ut per hoc satis videre possimus eos primo exalantem in visceribus terre clausum ignem ostendere voluisse, in quantum illi superimpositos montes a Iove, id est a natura rerum aiunt; in quantum autem Typheum se erigere conan-

9   tem dicunt, terremotuum causam ostendunt. Est enim terra ut plurimum cavernosa, in quibus cavernis ut aer interclusus sit aliquando necesse est, et ibidem non nunquam contingit per subterraneos meatus aquam etiam penetrare, cuius qualicunque motu oportet ut aer etiam moveatur, qui motu suo et ob obicibus hinc inde percussus et in vehementiorem motum excitatus calefit. Eo autem calefacto, tante potentie efficitur motus eius, ut circumadiacentia cuncta concutiat et moveri faciat, et si bithuminosa atqui sulphurea terra loco tali propinqua sit, ut accendatur confestim necesse est, nec extinguitur unquam tali materia perdurante, et cum nequeat ignis teneri clausus et eo ardente multum augeatur

you enter it gets even darker and contains a sanctuary sacred to Jupiter, and there in its furthermost recess the inhabitants insist is placed the bed of Typhon. This is what we know about Typhoeus.

Now these hidden matters must be brought out into the open. 7 They said that this Typhoeus was the son of Titan, on account of his elated spirit, and of Earth, on account of his power, while Theodontius says that he had been the most ancient king of Cilicia and that he conquered his brother Osiris in war and tore him limb from limb, and made war against the first Jupiter but was defeated and killed by him.

This history appears to have provided sufficient material to 8 offer an explanation for these fictions. Those who invented them seem to show the nature and cause of earthquakes well enough, albeit in an arcane manner. Papias[96] says that Typhon or Typhoeus means "emitting flames," and in this we can see that they wished first to show him breathing fire while closed up in the bowels of the earth; when they say the mountains are piled on top of him by Jupiter, they mean by the nature of things; when they say Typhoeus tried to rise up, they are referring to the following cause of earthquakes. The earth is very cavernous, and at all times in these 9 caverns there must be some enclosed air, and it sometimes happens there that through subterranean movements water penetrates as well, and it must be that by some of this motion the air also is moved, and by its motion and because it beats back and forth against obstacles, stirred into even more violent movement, it grows warm. And when it grows warm, its motion becomes so powerful that it strikes everything around it and causes them to be moved, and if bituminous and sulphurous earth is near such a place, it necessarily ignites immediately, nor is it ever extinguished so long as such materials last, and because an enclosed fire cannot be contained and because while it burns much of the air is increased, and because the place does not have the capacity for this,

aeris, nec tanti capax sit locus, fit non solum grandis concussio terre adiacentis, sed aperiri cogitur, et exitum prestare accenso igni, qui evaporans Typhonem id est eicentem flammas locum fa-

10 cit. Et cum Sycilia et Ynarimes huiusmodi nature sint, ideo Typhoni superimpositas finxere prudentes.

: 23 :

De Aeo Typhonis filio

1 Aeos Ysidorus ubi de *Ethymologiis* scribit filium fuisse Typhonis eumque tuam Paphos, Rex Inclite, Cypri vetustissimam civitatem condidisse, quam supra Paphi filii Pygmalionis opus fuisse dixeram, et de suo nomine nuncupatam, quod an verum sit incertum habeo.

: 24 :

De Chimera Typhonis filia

1 Chimeram Papias dicit filiam fuisse Typhonis et Chedrie, quam ob causam hoc dictum sit non video, nisi quia et hec ignes evomat. Hanc tamen quidam monstruosissima describunt; dicit enim de ea Ovidius sic:

Quoque[23] Chimera iugo mediis in partibus ignem
pectus et ora lee, caudam serpentis habebat.

not only does a grand shaking of the adjacent earth occur, but it is compelled also to find an opening and provide an exit for the kindled fire, which turning into vapor makes Typhon, that is, a place emitting flames. And because Sicily and Inarime are of such a nature, therefore prudent men invented the story that they pressed upon Typhon. 10

: 23 :

On Aeus, son of Typhon

Isidore[97] in his *Etymologies* writes that Aeus was the son of Typhon 1 and that he founded your Paphos, illustrious King, the most ancient city of Cyprus, which earlier I said was the deed of Paphos, son of Pygmalion, and named after him. I am not certain whether this is true.

: 24 :

On Chimera, daughter of Typhon

Papias[98] says Chimera was the daughter of Typhon and Hectria.[99] 1 I do not see what the reason is for this except that she vomits fire. Nonetheless they describe her as most monstrous, for Ovid says this about her:[100]

Also on a ridge where the Chimera, fire in its middle parts,
had the chest and head of a lioness, the tail of a serpent.

Virgilius autem de ea sic ait:

Horrendum stridens flammisque armata Chimera,

etc.

2   Alii autem dicunt illam igneum habuisse caput, pectus leoni-
num, caprinum ventrem, et crura serpentis, et plurimum Lyciis
infestam, sed tandem a Bellorophonte superatam atque occisam.

Cuius dum absconditum sensum querit enucleare Fulgentius,
amplissimam et meo iudicio minime oportunam verborum effun-
dit copiam, cum potius hystoriale significatum quam aliud sub tenui satis cortice lateat. Est enim Chimera Lycie mons in summitate ardens, sicut et Ethna olim, postmodum ad inferiora declinans
leones dudum nutrire consueverat, subsequenter abundat capreis,
3 et in radicibus feracissimus erat serpentum. Qui a Bellorophonte
insigni viro purgatus noxiis habitabilis effectus est.

: 25 :

De Enchelado Titanis V° filio

1 Encheladum Titanis et Terre filium fuisse dicit Paulus, cum ex
Terra tantum natum dicat Virgilius ibi:

Illam Terra parens, ira irritata deorum,
extremam, ut perhibent, Ceo Encheladoque sororem,

etc.

Vergil says this about her:[101]

Dreadful, hissing, and armed with flames Chimera.

Others say that she has a fiery head, a leonine chest, the belly 2
of a goat, and the legs of a serpent, and that she infested especially
the Lycians but that finally she was conquered and killed by Bellerophon.

Where Fulgentius[102] seeks to find the hidden kernel of meaning
in this, he pours out the longest, and in my judgment, the least
apposite abundance of words, for there is a historical significance
and not some other that lurks clearly under a thin covering: Chimera is a mountain in Lycia that burns near the summit, just like
Etna in the past, and then coming down a little its lower portion
used to nourish lions, beyond that it abounded in goats, and the
bottom teemed with serpents. Cleared of its harmful animals by 3
Bellerophon, a distinguished man, the mountain was rendered
habitable.

: 25 :

On Enceladus, fifth child of Titan

Paul says that Enceladus was the son of Titan and Earth, although 1
Vergil says that he was born from Earth alone, saying:[103]

As for her, parent Earth, goaded by the anger of the gods,
last, as they say, sister to Coeus and Enceladus . . .

Fuit hic homo ingentis potentie et immanis, ut Theodontius asse-
2 rit. Hunc fulmine ictum Ethneque suppositum dicit Virgilius sic:

> Fama est Encheladi semiustum fulmine corpus
> urgeri mole hac, ingentemque insuper Ethnam
> impositam ruptis flammam expirare caminis;
> et fessum quotiens mutat latus, intremere omnem
> murmure Trinacriam et celum subtexere fumo,

etc.

3 Quem ego idem dicerem cum Typheo, ne illos esse diversos ostenderet in *Odis* Oratius, dum dicit:

> Sed quid Typheus et validus Mimas,
> qut quid minaci Porphyrion statu,
> quid Rethus evulsisque truncis
> Encheladus iaculator audax,

etc.

4 Quid ergo? Cum diversi sint, uti physica ratione Typheum subterraneum ignem ab igne elemento per iniectum a Iove fulmen
designato et a motu subterranei aeris causatum atque evaporatum
ad exteriora diximus, sic morali demonstratione hunc superbum
hominem designare dicemus, cuius mos est, ritu ignis, stolida ela-
tione semper ad excelsa contendere, verba ignita emictere, et cuncta
furore suo consumere, qui totiens Ethna premitur, quotiens a potentia divine iustitie impellitur et superatur et humilium calcari
pedibus summictitur. Preterea, si non alio pondere incur ventur
tales, sua tantum honusti rabie deprimuntur, dum minus, sic volente Deo, ab eis in votum itur.

He was a man of tremendous power and enormous, as Theodontius asserts. Vergil says he was struck by a thunderbolt and was 2
placed under Etna in this way:[104]

> We hear the body of Enceladus, half burned by a thunderbolt,
> is weighed down by this mass, and that the huge Etna
> placed above breathes out flame from its fractured furnaces,
> and as often as he grows weary and turns over, he shakes all
> Trinacria with a roar and veils the sky with fumes.

I would say he is the same as Typhoeus if Horace in his *Odes* 3
did not demonstrate them to be different when he says:[105]

> But what are Typhoeus and strong Mimas,
> or Porphyrion with his menacing stature,
> Rhoetus and daring Enceladus
> who heaves ripped out tree trunks?

So why? Although they are different, we can apply again the 4
physical reasoning that Typhoeus was a subterranean type of fire
—represented by the thunderbolt thrown by Jupiter—caused by
the motion of subterranean air and vaporized to the outside, to
offer the moral interpretation that this suggests that he was an arrogant man whose character, like that of fire, was always to reach
for the heights with senseless self-exaltation, to emit fiery words,
and to consume everything with his furor. Insofar as Enceladus is
pressed down by Etna, the arrogant man is constrained and overcome by the power of divine justice, and is placed under the trampling feet of the humble. In addition, if the arrogant are not bent
under an external weight, they are hard-pressed just the same,
burdened by their own madness when, with God so willing, things
do not go according to their desires.

: 26 :

De Egeone Titanis VI° filio

1 Egeon, si antiquitati credimus, Terre fuit filius et Titanis, ea ratione qua ceteri. Hunc Servius unum esse cum Briareo velle videtur, eo quod et Centumgeminus cognominetur. Sed huic opinioni Paulus adversatur, dicens Egeonem sevissimum et immanem fuisse pyrratam, et Egeona nominatum ab insula deserta que Ege, in Egeo mari, vocatur, in qua insidebat more pyrratarum, quibus fas non est ob latrocinium suum urbes incolere; superaddens Theodontius ab hoc, non ab Ege insula, Egeum denominatum mare, eo quod evo suo nemo in eo mari, nisi quantum huic placuisset, aliquid audebat.

2 Dicunt preterea fabule veteres hunc centum a Iove religatum cathenis. Ovidius insuper dicit de eo:

> balenarumque prementem
> Egeona suis immania terga lacertis,
>
> > etc.

ut possit per hoc comprehendi eum potentissimum fuisse, dum tot catenis eius astringuntur vires, et assiduam eius maris fuisse curam et navigiorum quibus insidebat.

Is enim ideo Centumgeminus dictus est, eo quod bis centum homines remigio deservientes haberet in navibus, ut in longis oportunos cernimus.

: 26 :

On Aegaeon, the sixth child of Titan

Aegaeon, if we believe antiquity, was the son of Earth and Titan in   1
the same way as the others. Servius[106] seems to want him to be the
same as Briareus because he was known also as Hundred-Handed.
But Paul disagrees with this opinion, saying that Aegaeon was a
most savage and frightful pirate, and was called Aegaeon from the
deserted island of Aege in the Aegean Sea, where he would lie in
ambush just like thieving pirates who have lost the right to dwell
in cities. Theodontius adds that he was named not from the island
of Aege but from the Aegean Sea since in his day no one would
dare to do anything in that sea unless it was at his pleasure.

In addition, the ancient fables say that Jupiter bound him with   2
a hundred chains. And then Ovid says this about him:[107]

> and pressing on whales'
> huge backs with his arms, Aegaeon . . .

From this we can learn that he was very powerful, since his
strength required so many chains to restrain him, and that his
unique focus was the sea and its sailors, whom he attacked.

He was called Hundred-Handed because a ship has two hundred men plying the oars, a number we think is appropriate for
long ships.

: 27 :

De Aurora VII^a Titanis filia

1 Auroram dicit Paulus filiam fuisse Titanis et Terre. Quam si mulierem voluimus arbitrari, eo quod eam Tytonis fratris Laumedon-
tis dicat Ovidius fuisse coniugem, possumus eam existimare aliquam ingentis potentie et admirandi decoris fuisse feminam.
Verum ego reor de ea intellexisse poetas quam omnes dicimus
Auroram, eum scilicet matutinum splendorem, quo cernimus ante
solem elevatum celum albescere. Quam ideo Titanis dicunt filiam,
non quia ex Titano natam credant, sed ex Sole, quem sepissime ex
nomine avi Titanum vocant; nam ex sole procedit, ut dictum est,
2 illa claritas celi quam auroram dicimus. Terre autem ideo dicitur
filia, quia, orizontem orientalem superans, videtur intuentibus ex
terra exire.

: 28 :

De Iapeto Titanis VIII° filio, qui genuit Hesperum et Athlantem et Epymetheum et Prometheum

1 Iapeti parentes Titanum et Terram fuisse Theodontius asserit. Qui
eum dicit suo tempore grandem potentemque fuisse apud Thessalos hominem, sed protervi ingenii, cognitus magis nobis filiorum
claritate quam sua virtute.

2   Huius dicit Varro *De origine lingue Latine* coniugem fuisse Asyam
nynpham, a qua Asya denominata est. Equidem huius non par-

: 27 :

On Aurora, seventh child of Titan

Paul says that Aurora was the daughter of Titan and Earth. If we 1
want to think of her as a woman because Ovid[108] says that she was
the wife of Tithonus, brother of Laomedon, we can believe she
was some woman of considerable power and admirable dignity.
But I think that the poets understood her to be what we all say
about Aurora, namely, that early morning brilliance we view preceding the sky growing bright before sunrise. They say that she
was the daughter of Titan not because they believe she was born
from Titan but from Sun, whom they very often call Titan from
the name of his grandfather; for proceeding from the sun, as we
call it, is that clarity of the sky which we call the dawn. She is said 2
to be the daughter of Earth because she seems to come out from
the earth in our perspective as we watch her rise above the eastern
horizon.

: 28 :

On Iapetus, eighth child of Titan, who fathered Hesperus, Atlas, Epimetheus, and Prometheus

Theodontius asserts that Titan and Earth were the parents of Ia- 1
petus. He says that in his day Iapetus was a great and powerful
man among the Thessalians, but of reckless character, known better to us by the fame of his sons rather than for his virtue.

Varro[109] in his *On the Latin Language* says that his wife was the 2
nymph Asia, after whom Asia was named. Indeed, her importance

vum magnitudine argumentum. Ex qua suscepisse nonnulli volunt Hesperum, Athlantem, Epymetheum et Prometheum.

: 29 :

De Hespero Iapeti filio, qui genuit tres Hesperidas

1 Hesperum dicit Theodontius filium fuisse Asye et Iapeti, primo Phylotem a parentibus appellatum. Verum cum iuvenis una cum Athlante fratre in extremos Mauros secessisset, atque Ethyopibus, qui ultra Ampelusiam promontorium litus occeani incolunt, ac insulis eo litori adiacentibus imperasset, a Grecis Hesperus appellatus est, eo quod ex nomine occidentis Hesperi omnem occiduam regionem vocent Hesperiam, et sic ab ea regione, ad quam trans-
2 migraverat, a suis perpetuo denominatus est. De hoc tamen nil habetur ulterius, nisi quod illi tres fuerint filie, rapina Herculis clare.

: 30 :

De Egle Heretusa et Hesperetusa filiabus Hesperi

1 Hesperides, ut ipsum sonat patronimicum, Hesperi fuerunt filie, esto sint qui Athlantis dicant. He tres numero fuere: Egle scilicet et Heretusa ac etiam Hesperetusa. De quibus fertur quod esset

is considerable: some think she produced Hesperus, Atlas, Epimetheus, and Prometheus.

: 29 :

On Hesperus, child of Iapetus, who fathered the three Hesperides

Theodontius says that Hesperus was the son of Asia and Iapetus, 1 and that he was first called Philotes by his parents. As a young man he and his brother Atlas withdrew to the hinterlands of Mauritania and ruled the Ethiopians, who inhabit the shores of the ocean beyond the promontory of Ampelusia, and the islands adjacent to the shore; therefore the Greeks called him Hesperus after the name of western Hesperus because they call the western region Hesperia; and so his subjects repeatedly referred to him by the name of this region to which he had migrated. Nothing more 2 is known about him except that he had three daughters who are famous because of Hercules' theft.[110]

: 30 :

On Aegle, Arethusa, and Hesperethusa, daughters of Hesperus

The Hesperides, as the patronymic indicates, were the daughters 1 of Hesperus, although there are those who say they were the daughters of Atlas. They were three in number: namely, Aegle, Arethusa, and Hesperethusa. It is said about them that they had a

illis viridarium in quo aurea mala nascebantur, cui custodem prefe-
cerant serpentem pervigilem; cuius viridarii fama cum ad Euris-
teum pervenisset, et ipse pomorum desiderio tractus, misit Herculem ut illa mala surriperet. Qui veniens, soporato seu occiso
serpente, viridarium intravit et mala sustulit atque Euristeo detulit.

2   Cuius fictionis arcanum aperuisse non erit difficile. Fuere
quippe, ut placet Pomponio, insule in occeano occidentali habentes ex opposito desertum litus in continenti inter Hesperos, Ethyopes et Athlantes populos, que quidem insule a puellis Hesperidi-
bus possesse fuerunt, erantque abundantissime ovium, lana
quarum preciosissima erat ad instar auri, et sic insule Hesperie,
que talium ovium erant pascua, viridarium fuere Hesperidum,
oves autem aurea mala; nam 'oves' a Grecis *male* seu *mala* dicuntur,

3   teste Varrone in libro *De agricultura*. Pervigil autem serpens euripi
erant, qui inter insulas estuante occeano die noctuque absque in-
termissione insulas mira cum tempestate circuibant et ad insulas
transitum prohibebant; quos Hercules, captato tempore, transiens
malis aureis, id est pecudibus, eductis, remeavit in Greciam.

4   Fulgentius autem, more suo, ex abysso conatur in ethera educere intellectum, quem, eo quod non putem fuisse de mente fingentium, omictendum censui. Sunt tamen qui velint hunc Herculem fuisse Perseum, et Hesperidas fuisse Gorgones; ipsi videant.

garden in which golden apples grew and that they put it under the guardianship of a watchful serpent. When the fame of this garden reached Eurystheus, who was drawn by his desire for the apples, he sent Hercules to steal them. When Hercules arrived, putting the serpent to sleep or killing him, he entered the garden, took the apples, and brought them to Eurystheus.

It will not be difficult to reveal the secret of this fiction. Clearly, 2 according to Pomponius,[111] there were islands in the western ocean situated opposite the desert shore on the continent between the Hesperian, Ethiopian, and Atlantic peoples, and these islands, with their great abundance of sheep, the wool of which was so precious that it was like gold, were in the possession of the Hesperides girls. Therefore the Hesperian islands, which were grazing lands for these sheep, were the garden of the Hesperides; and the sheep were the golden "apples" [*mala*], for sheep are called *male* or *mela* by the Greeks, according to the testimony of Varro[112] in his book *On Agriculture*. For the watchful serpent understand the is- 3 land straits which seethe with ocean waters day and night without interruption in an amazing tempest, surrounding them and prohibiting passage, and Hercules, seizing the proper moment to cross them, took the golden apples, that is, flocks, and returned to Greece.

Fulgentius,[113] however, in a unique approach, attempted to 4 equate them with the intellect brought from the abyss up to the heavens, but I think this interpretation should be ignored because I do not think the mind was part of this contrivance. There are, moreover, those who want this Hercules to be Perseus and the Hesperides to be the Gorgons; they are entitled to their opinion.

: 31 :

De Athlante II° Iapeti²⁴ filio, qui genuit Hyam
et VII Hyades, quarum hec sunt nomina: Eudora, Ambroxia,
Pyidile, Coroni, Phyto, Polyxo et Thyenes. Et genuit
insuper Plyades, quarum hec sunt nomina:
Electra, Maya, Steropes, Celeno, Taygeta, Alcyone,
Meropes. Et genuit Calipsonem nynpham.

1 Athlas dicit Lactantius, filius fuit Iapeti et Clymenes. Theodontius vero, Iapeti et Asye filium fuisse dicit. Plinius²⁵ autem, ubi *De hystoria naturali,* matrem huius dicit Libyam fuisse. Verum hi non videntur unum et idem, cum tres fuisse dicuntur, quorum primus creditur ex Arcadia, alter autem a primo Thessalus, inde Maurus fuit tertius, ille scilicet qui cum Hespero fratre ad Mauros trans-

2 fretavit. Est preterea et Athlas Ytalus, qui ut vulgo fertur antiquissimus, apud Fesulas imperavit, cuius quoniam parentes non comperi, non apposui. De quo istorum circa ea que de eis scripta comperiuntur, intellexerint autores, non satis certum est, dato quod aliquando possit per coniecturas intelligi.

3   Scribam igitur tanquam unius tantum acta sint omnia. Fuit ergo Athlas, ut dictum est, Iapeti seu ex Clymene, seu ex Asya filius, vel ex Lybia, ex quo talis narratur fabula. Quod cum Perseus Iovis filius iussu Polydectis regis, ut dicit Lactantius, ad occidendum ivisset Gorgonem, eamque superasset, et illi caput abscidis-

4 set, victorque rediret, contigit ut hospitium peteret Athlanti. Athlas autem, oraculo premonitus ut sibi caveret a Iovis filiis, quia ab

: 31 :

On Atlas, second child of Iapetus, who fathered Hyas and the seven Hyades, whose names are Eudora, Ambrosia, Phaesyla, Coronis, Phyto, Polyxo, and Thyone; and who fathered in addition the Pleiades, whose names are Electra, Maia, Steropes, Celaeno, Taygeta, Alcyone, Merope; and who fathered the nymph Calypso

Lactantius[114] says that Atlas was the son of Iapetus and Clymene, 1 but Theodontius says he was the son of Iapetus and Asia. Moreover, Pliny[115] in his *Natural History* says his mother was Libya. But these Atlases do not seem to be one and the same, for there are said to be three: the first of these is believed to be from Arcadia; apart from him there was a Thessalian; and then a third was a Moor, namely, the one who migrated to Mauritania with his brother Hesperus. There is in addition an Italian Atlas who, as is 2 commonly said, ruled most anciently among the Faesulians,[116] but because I have not discovered his parentage, I have not included him. Whether the authors understood to which of these Atlases they were referring in their writings about them is not sufficiently certain, although sometimes it is possible to understand by conjecture. Therefore I will write of all their deeds as if of only one person.

So we can say the following. There was an Atlas, whether the 3 aforementioned son of Iapetus by Clymene, Asia, or Libya, about whom the following story is told. When Perseus, son of Jupiter, by the order of King Polydectes, as Lactantius says, had gone to kill the Gorgon, defeated it, cut off its head, and returned victorious, it happened that he sought the hospitality of Atlas. But Atlas, 4 warned by an oracle to beware the children of Jupiter because he

aliquo eorum regno privaretur, audito eum Iovis esse filium suscipere noluit; quam ob rem turbatus Perseus, detecto Gorgonis capite, illum in sui nominis montem mutavit, damnavitque eum ut in perpetuum celum sustentaret humeris, quod et factum est.

5   Sub hac autem fictione voluere priores hystoriam occultari, cum dicat Fulgentius, quod cum superata Medusa ditissima regina, Perseus regnum invasisset Athlantis, fultus copiis atque substantiis Meduse, eum in montes compulit aufugere, et sic qui ex regia montanus factus est fuga, causam dedit fabule, ut in montem diceretur esse conversus opere eius, cuius divitiis in montes fuerat compulsus.

6   Quod celum humeris sustentaverit, alia causa fuit. Affirmat enim Augustinus in libro *De civitate Dei*, hunc maximum fuisse astrologum, et Rabanus dicit eum primum astrologie artem excogitasse, quod[26] a Plinio sumptum puto; ipse autem in libro *De naturali hystoria* dicit hunc astrologiam invenisse et hinc, ob sudores ex arte susceptos, celum humeris tolerasse dictum est. Verum

7   ignavum vulgus hoc credidit, eum scilicet celum humeris sustinere, quia cerneret montis verticem adeo extolli, ut in eum videatur inclinari celum. Huic preterea multas fuisse filias dixere veteres, quas ex variis Athlantibus natas arbitror, et huic soli attributas, ut in particulari earum descriptione clarius apparebit.

would be deprived of his kingdom by one of them, did not wish to welcome Perseus once he had heard that he was a son of Jupiter. Perseus was therefore perturbed, and uncovering the head of the Gorgon, changed Atlas into a mountain bearing his name, and he condemned him to bearing the sky on his shoulders in perpetuity, which is what happened.

The ancients wanted history to be hidden under this fiction, for 5 Fulgentius[117] says that when Perseus had conquering Medusa, who was a very wealthy queen, he invaded the kingdom of Atlas, and, relying on Medusa's riches and resources, he forced Atlas to flee into the mountains, and so the man who was chased by flight from the palace to the mountains gave rise to the fable that he was a man transformed into a mountain by the actions of a man who used his riches to force him into the mountains.

That he held up the sky on his shoulders was for another rea- 6 son: Augustine[118] affirms in his *City of God* that he was the greatest astrologer; and Rabanus[119] says that he was the first to devise the art of astrology, which I think he took from Pliny; in his *Natural History* Pliny[120] himself says that Atlas invented astrology and therefore he was said to have held the sky on his shoulders to represent the great labors he undertook in that endeavor. The ignoble 7 masses believe this — that he held the sky on his shoulders — because they see the summit of a mountain towering above them in such a way that the sky seems to lie on it. In addition, the ancients say he had many daughters, but I think they were born from the various Atlases and attributed to him alone, as will become clearer in the individual descriptions of them.

: 32 :

De Hyade Athlantis filio

1 Hyas, ut ab unico melioris sexus initium faciamus, filius fuit Athlantis et Ethre, ut placet Ovidio, ubi *De fastis* ait:

> Nondum stabat Athlas humeros oneratus Olympo,
>   cum satus est forma conspiciendus Hyas.
> Hunc stirps Occeani maturis nixibus Ethra
>   edidit, et nynphas, sed prior ortus Hyas,
>
> etc.

2 Hic iuvenis venator fuit, et in venationibus a leena occisus est, ut ipse ubi supra testatur Ovidius dicens:

> Dum nova lanugo, pavidos formidine cervos
>   terret,[27] et est illi preda benigna lepus.
> At postquam virtus animis adolevit, in apros
>   audet, et hyrsutas cominus ire leas,
> dumque petit latebras fete catulosque leene,
>   ipse fuit lybice preda cruenta lee.
> Mater Hyan, et Hyan meste flevere sorores,
>   cervicemque polo suppositurus Athlas.
> Victus uterque parens tamen est pietate sororum:
>   illa dedit celum: nomina fecit Hyas.

: 32 :

On Hyas, son of Atlas

Hyas, so that we begin with the only one from the better sex, was   1
the son of Atlas and Aethra, as Ovid says in the *Fasti*:[121]

> Atlas did not yet stand burdened by shouldering Olympus,
>   when Hyas, beautiful to behold, was conceived.
> Aethra of Ocean lineage in timely labor
>   gave birth to him and the nymphs, but Hyas was born first.

He was a young hunter, and while hunting he was killed by a lion-   2
ess, as Ovid again testifies in the same work, saying:[122]

> While his beard was new, stags scared and fearful
>   he terrified, and the gentle rabbit was his catch.
> But after his valor aged in years, boars
>   and shaggy lions he dared to fight at close quarters;
> and while he sought the lairs and cubs of mothering lionesses,
>   he became the bloodied catch of a fierce Libyan lioness.
> His mother wept for Hyas, the mournful sisters wept for
>   Hyas,
>   as did Atlas, soon to place his neck under the pole.
> But both parents were overcome by the piety of his sisters:
>   it gave them the sky; Hyas made their name.

: 33 :

De Hyadibus VII filiabus Athlantis

1 Hyades septem fuere sorores et filie Athlantis ex Ethra, quarum hec fuerunt nomina: Eudora, Ambroxia, Pyidile, Coroni, Phyto, Polyxo et Thyenes. De quibus invicem scribere necesse fuit, cum de eis in particulari nil legatur. De his autem sic scribit Ovidius:

> At simul inducent obscura crepuscula noctem,
>   pars Hyadum toto de grege nulla latet.
> Ora micant Tauri septem radiantia flammis,
>   navita quas Hyadas Graius ab imbre[28] vocat.
> Pars Bachum nutrisse putat, pars credidit esse
>   Thetios has neptes, Occeanique senis,

etc.

2 Per hos versus possumus cognoscere eas, ut supra dixerat idem Ovidius, ob pietatem mortui fratris in celum assumptas, et in fronti Tauri locatas. Videtur tamen Ovidius in fine carminum credere partem harum Hyadis fuisse filias, verum Theodontius totas Athlantis fuisse confirmat. Has autem 'succulas' appellari dicit Anselmus in libro *De ymagine mundi*.

3 Sed quid ista velint videamus. Et primo ego harum assumptionem in celum sic contigisse arbitror, quia eo quod numero convenirent cum stellis in fronte Tauri positis, ceptum sit ab his qui numerum norant filiarum Athlantis iocose illas stellas a nominibus puellarum vocare, et cum perseverarent, adeo stellis annexum est, ut in hodiernum usque perduret; seu quod verisimilius est, filias Athlantis ob convenientiam numeri nomine stellarum nuncupatas, et hinc fabule prestitisse materiam.

∶ 33 ∶

On the Hyades, seven daughters of Atlas

The Hyades were seven sisters, daughters of Atlas by Aethra. 1
These are their names: Eudora, Ambrosia, Phaesyla,[123] Coronis,
Phyto, Polyxo, and Thyone. It was necessary to write about them
as a group since nothing is said about any one of them in particular.
Ovid writes this about them:[124]

> But as soon as the dusky twilight brings in the night,
>   no part of the whole flock of Hyades lies hidden.
> The seven faces of Taurus twinkle, radiant with flames,
>   which the Greek sailor calls the Hyades from the rain.
> Some think they nurtured Bacchus, some believe
>   They are the granddaughters of Tethys and ancient Ocean.

From these verses we can recognize that they, as Ovid said 2
above, were taken up to the sky on account of their devotion to
their dead brother and located in the brow of Taurus. But at the
end of his verses Ovid[125] seems to believe that part of them were
daughters of Hyas, although Theodontius confirms that they were
all daughters of Atlas. In his *Image of the World* Anselm[126] says that
they were called "Little Cubs."

But let us examine what they wish to say. First, I think their 3
assumption into the sky resulted from their agreement in number
with the stars placed in the brow of Taurus. Initially those who
knew the number of Atlas' daughters jokingly labeled those stars
by the names of the girls, and when they kept doing that, they
were attached to the stars and so it remains until the present day;
or, what is more likely, the daughters of Atlantis were named after
the stars on account of their similarity in number, and this provided
the material for the fable.

4   Nam stellas illas Hyadas vocatas credo ab effectu earum longa animadversione percepto; Hyas enim Grece, 'pluvia' sonat Latine, quod eis nomen impositum est, eo quod incipientibus eis apparere, autumnales incipiunt pluvie. 'Succule' vero dicte, quasi 'succo
5   plene,' id est humiditate et pluviis. Quod autem Bachum nutriverint, ideo dictum reor, quod humiditate sua seu signi in quo sunt, sole existente in virgine, plurimum vinetis nocte conferant diurno fervore exhaustis.

: 34 :

De Eletra filia Athlantis et matre Dardani

1   Eletra filia fuit Athlantis et Pleionis, et uti ego arbitror, Athlantis Tusci, eo quod velint aliqui eam coniugem fuisse Corithi regis, quem Tuscum fuisse existimant plurimi; etsi Tusci non fuit, Arcadis tamen fuit; non enim ad eius concubitum Iuppiter ivisset in Mauros.

2   Hanc a Iove oppressam peperisse illi Dardanum Troie autorem volunt, et viro Jasium. Hec preterea cum sex sororibus a Pleyone matre Plyades appellate sunt; et quia Iovem seu Liberum patrem nutrivere, celum meruerunt et stelle in genu Tauri locate sunt, et a Latinis Virgilie appellate.

De quibus omnibus sic scribit Ovidius:

Plyades incipiunt humeros reserare paternos,
    que septem dici, sex tamen esse solent,

I believe that those stars were called the Hyades from their 4
effect, which was understood after a long period of observation,
for *hyas* in Greek means "rain," and they have been given this name
because when they begin to appear, the autumn rains begin. They
are called "Little Cubs" [*Succule*] as if they were "full of moisture"
[*succo plene*], that is, of humidity and rain. That they nurtured 5
Bacchus I think was said because with their moisture, or the moisture of the sign in which they are located when the sun stands in
Virgo, they bring ample moisture to vines exhausted by the day's
heat.

: 34 :

On Electra, daughter of Atlas and mother of Dardanus

Electra was the daughter of Atlas and Pleione, and, as I think, the 1
Etruscan Atlas, because some want her to be the wife of King
Corythus, whom many believe to have been Etruscan; and if he
was not the Etruscan Atlas, then he was the Arcadian, for Jupiter
would not have gone to Mauritania to lie with her.

They want her, after Jupiter forced himself upon her, to have 2
produced Dardanus, the founder of Troy, for him, and Iasius for
her husband. In addition, she with her six sisters by her mother
Pleione are called the Pleiades. Because they nurtured Jupiter, or
father Liber, they merited a place in the sky and were located as
stars in the knee of Taurus, and in Latin they were called the Virgiliae.

Ovid writes this about the whole group:[127]

The Pleiades begin to relieve their father's shoulders.
   Said to be seven, they are even so usually six:

seu quod in amplexum sex hinc venere deorum,
　　nam Steropem Marti concubuisse ferunt,
Neptuno Alcyonem, et te, formosa Celeno,
　　Mayam et Eletram Taygetamque Iovi;
septima mortali Meropes tibi, Sysife, nupsit;
　　penitet et facti sola pudore latet;
sive quod Eletra Troie spectare ruinas
　　non tulit; ante oculos opposuitque manum,

　　　　　　　　　　　　　　　　　　etc.

Astrologi autem dicunt harum unam esse nebulosam, nec posse videri.

3　　Sane ut figmenta paucis expediamus de his, quantum ad nomen et ad assumptionem in celum, dici potest quod de Hyadibus dictum est, esto velit Anselmus has Plyades non a matre, sed a pluralitate denominatas, cum dicat *plyon* Grece, 'pluralitatem' sonare
4　Latine. Virgilie autem dicuntur, quoniam oriuntur una cum sole, scilicet eo exeunte in Tauro, quia tunc virgulta augeantur. Iovem autem nutrisse ideo dicuntur, quia opinati sunt nonnulli ethereum ignem ex humiditate terrestri nutriri, quam humiditatem pluvie causant. De Libero autem ut supra ubi de Hyadibus.

　　　　　　　　　　：　35　：

De Maya Athlantis filia et matre Mercurii

1　Maya Athlantis fuit filia, ut dicit Virgilius:

At Mayam, auditis si quicquam credimus, Athlas,
idem Athlas generat, celi qui sydera tollit,

　　　　　　　　　　　　　　　　　　etc.

whether because six came into the embrace of gods —
  for they say that Sterope lay with Mars;
Alcyone with Neptune, and you, beautiful Celaeno;
  Maia and Electra and Taygeta with Jupiter;
the seventh, Merope, married you, Sisyphus, a mortal;
  she regrets it and hides alone for the shame of the deed —
or because Electra, to look at the ruins of Troy
  could not bear, and covers her eyes with her hand.

The astrologers say that one of them is nebulous and cannot be seen.

But so that in few words we might explain these inventive sto- 3
ries about their name and assumption into the sky, we can say
what we said about the Hyades, although Anselm[128] wishes these
Pleiades to be named not from their mother but from their plurality since *plyon* in Greek means "plurality." They are called Virgiliae 4
because they rise along with the sun, namely, when Taurus is setting, because then the "thickets" [*virgulta*] are growing. They are
said to have nurtured Jupiter because some thought that the ethereal fire is nourished by terrestrial moisture, and that rain causes
this humidity. Insofar as Liber is concerned, that is as it was above
with the Hyades.

: 35 :

On Maia, daughter of Atlas and mother of Mercury

Maia was the daughter of Atlas, as Vergil says:[129]   1

But Maia, if we believe anything we hear, Atlas
fathered, the same Atlas who holds up the stars of the sky.

2 Ego credo Athlantis Arcadis fuisse filiam, eamque dicit Cingius Vulcano nupsisse et argumento utitur, ut dicit Macrobius *Saturnaliorum*, quod flamen Vulcanalis Kalendis Maiis huic dee rem divinam facit. Sed Piso uxorem vulcani Maiestam non Mayam vocari

3 dicit. Hoc tamen asserunt omnes eam Iovi concubuisse atque ex eo peperisse Mercurium. Hanc insuper aiunt Iunonem ex pellicibus Iovis unam summe dilexisse eiusque filium Mercurium lactasse affirmat Martianus.

Et huius amoris causam reddunt, quia ea surgente ver et estas

4 veniunt, quibus aer pulchrior factus letari videtur. Sed quid non sic Celenum et Eletram et alias, que equo modo surgunt cum Maya? Ratio potest esse hec, quia per Mayam veteres terram intellexere, in qua divitie et regna sunt, quibus preest ipsa Iuno.

5 Hec autem Maya apud Romanos in maxima fuit reverentia, ei quidem, ut ait Macrobius, mense Mayo eo quod ab ea denominatum putarent, ut ubi *De fastis* scribit Ovidius, exhibebant mercatores una et Mercurio filio sacrum; et quia, ut Cornelius Labeo assentire videtur, terram eam putant, et Maye nomen a magnitudine sumpsisse, ei pregnantem suem mactabant, quam hostiam Terre

6 propriam dicebant, et hoc ob fecunditatem arbitror. Preterea dicit idem Labeo huic Maye, id est terre, edem Kalendis Maiis dedicatam sub nomine Bone dee, et eandem esse Bonam deam et Terram, sic et Bonam et Faunam et Opem et Fatuam pontificum li-

7 bris dicit ostendi. Rationes autem supra, ubi de Terra scripsimus, apposite sunt.

I believe she was the daughter of the Arcadian Atlas. Cingius says 2
that she married Vulcan and used as proof, as Macrobius[130] says in
his *Saturnalia*, the fact that the priest of Vulcan honored her divinity on the Kalends of May. But Piso[131] says that the wife of Vulcan
was Maiesta, not Maia. Nonetheless, all assert that she lay with 3
Jupiter and consequently bore Mercury. In addition, they say that
of Jupiter's mistresses Juno largely approved of her alone, and
Martianus[132] affirms that she nursed her son Mercury.

They offer as the cause of this love that spring and summer are
coming as she rises, so that the air, which is becoming more beautiful, seems to be joyful. But why not Celaeno and Electra and the 4
others, who rise in the same way along with Maia? The reason
could be this: in Maia the ancients understood the earth with its
riches and kingdoms, over which Juno is preeminent.

This Maia was held in the greatest reverence by the Romans, 5
for whom, in fact, merchants used to furnish a rite, as Macrobius[133] says, in the month of May, which they thought was named
after her, as Ovid[134] writes in the *Fasti*, along with her son Mercury, and because, as Cornelius Labeo[135] seems to agree, they
think she is the earth and assumed the name of Maia from its
magnitude, they slaughtered a pregnant sow for her, which is an
offering they used to say was appropriate for Earth, and I think
this is on behalf of fertility. In addition, Labeo says that to this 6
Maia, that is, Earth, a shrine under the name of the Good Goddess is dedicated on the Kalends of May, and that the Good Goddess and Earth are the same, and thus he says that the Good
Goddess, Fauna, Ops, and Fatua are listed in the priestly books. 7
Other applicable explanations are found above where we wrote
about Earth.[136]

: 36 :

De Sterope Athlantis filia

1 Steropes et hec filia fuit Athlantis et Pleiones, quam dicit Ovidius
a Marte dilectam, et ex eo peperisse Parthaonem, qui Parthaon rex
fuit Calydonie, Arcadie fere opposite.

: 37 :

De Cyleno Athlantis filia

1 Cyleno eque Athlantis et Pleyones fuit filia. Hec a Iove viciata
Mercurium peperit, alium a superiori, qui cognominatus est Cyle-
nius a matre, seu a monte Arcadie, in quo forte natus est.

: 38 :

De Thaygeta Athlantis filia

1 Thaygete patrem fuisse Athlantem volunt et Pleyonem matrem,
eamque dicunt placuisse Iovi, et in eius amplexus venisse, atque ex
eo concepisse Lacedemonem, quem filium Taygete Agenoris filie
dixerunt alii, et nonnulli eum ex Semele natum voluere.

: 36 :

On Sterope, daughter of Atlas

This Sterope was also the daughter of Atlas and Pleione, whom 1
Ovid[137] says was beloved of Mars and that from him she produced
Parthaon; this Parthaon was the king of Calydon, nearly opposite
Arcadia.

: 37 :

On Celaeno, daughter of Atlas

Celaeno was also the daughter of Atlas and Pleione. Violated by 1
Jupiter, she produced Mercury—different from the above—who
was named Cyllenius by his mother, or after a mountain in Arcadia on which perhaps he was born.

: 38 :

On Taygeta, daughter of Atlas

They want Atlas to have been the father and Pleione the mother 1
of Taygeta. They say that she was pleasing to Jupiter and came
into his embrace and thereby conceived Lacedaemon, whom others say was the son of Taygeta, daughter of Agenor; some want
him to be the child of Semele.

: 39 :

De Alcyone filia Athlantis

I   Alcyones ex Athlante et Pleyone nata est, placuitque Neptuno, ex quo peperisse volunt Alcyonem coniugem Cei regis Trachinne.

: 40 :

De Merope filia Athlantis

I   Meropes, ut reliqui Plyades, Athlantis et Plyonis filia fuit Sysiphoque Corinthiorum rege nupsit, Ovidio teste, et creditur eam Sysipho peperisse Laertem Ulixis patrem, et Glaucum, et Creontem.

: 41 :

De Calipsone Athlantis filia

I   Calypso nynpha, ut dicit Priscianus in maiori volumine, filia fuit Athlantis, ex qua tamen matre non dicit, quod etiam ante Priscianum testatur Omerus in *Odissea* dicens:

ἔνθα μὲν Ἄτλαντος θυγάτηρ δολόεσσα Καλυψὼ

ubi[29] certe Athlantis filia dolosa Calipso

: 39 :

On Alcyone, daughter of Atlas

Alcyone was born to Atlas and Pleione, and she was pleasing to 1
Neptune, by whom they want her to have given birth to Alcyone,
wife of Ceyx, King of the Trachinians.

: 40 :

On Merope, daughter of Atlas

Merope, like the rest of the Pleiades, was the daughter of Atlas 1
and Pleione and married Sisyphus, king of the Corinthians, according to Ovid.[138] It was also believed that by Sisyphus she gave
birth to Laertes, father of Ulysses, as well as Glaucus and Creon.

: 41 :

On Calypso, daughter of Atlas

The nymph Calypso, as Priscian[139] says in his greater work, was 1
the daughter of Atlas, though he does not say by what mother.
But even before Priscian, Homer bears witness to this, saying:[140]

There is Calypso, the cunning daughter of Atlas.

2 Cuius autem Athlantis ignoratur. Ad hanc, ut Omerus testatur, pervenit Ulixes naufragus, et septem annis apud eam detentus est. Fuit enim hec domina cuiusdam insule Ogygia nuncupate, seu a se Calipso denominate.

: 42 :

De Epymetheo Iapeti filio, qui genuit Pyrram

1 Epymetheus filius fuit Iapeti ex Asya coniuge, ut ait Leontius. Hic ingenio valens hominis statuam primus ex luto finxit, quam ob rem dicit Theodontius indignatum Iovem et eum vertisse in symiam, atque religasse apud insulas Pytacusas. Cuius figmenti reseratio talis est. Sunt symie animalia inter alia hoc a natura infixum habentia, ut quicquid viderint quenque agentem, et ipse facere velint, et aliquando faciant; sic visum est Epymetheum ad instar nature voluisse hominem facere et sic, symie imitatus naturam, Sy-
2 mia dictus est. Apud Pytagusas insulas ideo symiam religatam dixere, eo quod olim abundaverint symiis insule ille, seu forsan ingeniosis hominibus et in suis operibus naturam imitantibus.

: 43 :

De Pyrra Epymethei filia et Deucalionis coniuge

1 Pyrra Epymethei fuit filia, ut dicit Ovidius, et Deucalionis coniunx. De qua idem Ovidius sic:

Which Atlas is not known. As Homer[141] testifies, the shipwrecked 2
Ulysses reaches her and she detained him for seven years; she was
the mistress of a certain island called Ogygia, or it was named
Calypso after her.

: 42 :

On Epimetheus, son of Iapetus, who fathered Pyrrha

Epimetheus was the son of Iapetus by his wife Asia, as Leontius 1
says. A man of great ability, he was the first to make a statue of a
human from clay, wherefore, Theodontius says, an indignant Jupiter turned him into a monkey and relegated him to the islands of
Pithecusae. We can unlock this fabrication in the following way.
Monkeys are animals which along with their other natural characteristics have this one, that whatever they see someone doing they
also want to do themselves and then sometimes do so. And therefore it seems that Epimetheus wished to make a man in imitation
of nature, and so he was called Simia for imitating the nature of a
monkey [*simia*]. They said that Simia was relegated to the islands 2
of Pithecusae because those islands once abounded in monkeys or,
perhaps, in ingenious men who imitated nature in their works.

: 43 :

On Pyrrha, daughter of Epimetheus and wife of Deucalion

Pyrrha was the daughter of Epimetheus, as Ovid says, and the 1
wife of Deucalion. Ovid says this about her:[142]

Deucalion lacrimis ita Pyrram affatur abortis:
'O soror, o coniunx, o femina sola superstes,
quam commune mihi genus et patruelis origo,
deinde thorus iunxit, nunc ipsa pericula iungunt.'

2 Hec autem cum esset piissima mulierum una eum Deucalione viro
diliuvium passa est, eique quattuor peperit filios.

: 44 :

De Prometheo Iapeti filio, qui fecit Pandoram[30] et genuit Ysydem et Deucalionem

1 Prometheus Iapeti fuit filius ex Asya nynpha coniuge eius, ut
Varro testatur ubi *De origine lingue Latine,* et alii plures. Hunc ante
alios omnes formasse hominem ex terra dicit Ovidius:

Sive recens tellus seductaque nuper ab alto
ethere cognati retinebat semina celi.
Quam satus Iapeto mixtam pluvialibus undis
finxit in effigiem moderantum cuncta deorum.

Oratius autem aliquid superaddens dicit in *Odis:*

Fertur Prometheus addere principi
limo coactus particulam undique
desectam insani leonis
vim stomaco apposuit nostro,

etc.

Tearfully Deucalion says this to Pyrrha:
"O sister, O wife, O lone surviving woman.
Your clan is the same as mine, you are my cousin,
then the marriage couch joined us, now these dangers join us."

Because she was the most pious of women, she survived the flood 2
along with her husband Deucalion and produced four children for
him.

: 44 :

On Prometheus, son of Iapetus, who created Pandora and fathered Isis and Deucalion

Prometheus was the son of Iapetus by his wife, the nymph Asia, 1
as Varro[143] testifies in *On the the Latin Language*, as do several others. Ovid says that before all others he formed man from the
earth:[144]

Or the fresh earth recently brought down from the lofty
aether retained the seeds of the related sky.
The son of Iapetus mixed this with the rain waters
and formed an effigy of the gods who rule everything.

Horace adds something in his *Odes*:[145]

It is said that Prometheus, compelled to add
to the primordial mud a small particle
extracted from everywhere, placed the violence
Of a raging lion in our stomach.

2   Verum Claudianus in *Panegirico quarti consulatus Arcadii* fabricam istam longe plenius omnium longa tamen verborum serie describit dicens:

> Disce orbis, quod quisque sibi, cum conderet artus
> nostros,[31] ethereis miscens terrena Prometheus,
> sinceram patri mentem furatus Olympo,
> continuit claustris indignantemque retraxit.
> Et cum non aliter possent mortalia fingi,
> adiunxit geminas: ille cum corpore lapse
> intereunt, hec sola manet bustoque superstes
> evolat; hanc alta capitis fundavit in arce,
> mandatricem operum prospecturamque laborum.
> Illas inferius collo, preceptaque summe
> passuras domine, digna statione locavit.
> Quippe opifex veritus confundere sacra prophanis,
> distribuit partes anime, sedemque removit.
> Iram sanguinei regio sub pectore cordis
> protegit imbutam flammis, avidamque nocendi,
> precipitemque sui. Rabie succensa tumescit;
> contrahitur tepefacta metu; cumque omnia secum
> duceret, et requiem membris vesana negaret.
> Invenit pulmonis opem madideque furenti
> prebuit, ut tumide ruerent in mollia fibre.
> At sibi multa petens nil collatura Cupido,
> in iecur et tractus imos compulsa recessit.
> Que velut immanes reserans ut belua rictus,
> expleri pascique velit: nunc verbere curas
> torquet avaritie, stimulis nunc frangit amorum,
> nunc gaudet, nunc mesta dolet satiataque rursus
> exoritur, cesaque redit pullulantius ydra,
>
>   etc.

Then Claudian in his *Panegyric on the Fourth Consulship of Hono-*   2
rius, describes this fabrication more fully than anyone in a long
passage, saying:[146]

Learn of the world what each learns for himself.
When Prometheus composed our bodies
by mixing the terrestrial with the ethereal,
he stole the pure mind from father Olympus,
imprisoned it, and held back its resistance.
And since mortals could not be made otherwise,
he added twin parts: those failing with the body
perish; this one alone remains, and surviving
flies away from the pyre; this he set in the head's lofty citadel,
the mistress of our deeds, to oversee our works.
He located the other parts below the neck
to suffer the commands of the great mistress, a worthy status.
Indeed, fearing to confuse sacred with profane, our maker
divided the parts of the spirit and removed its seat.
The area under the blood-filled heart incorporates the anger
imbued in flames, and avid for harm,
mad within itself. Kindled with madness, it swells,
and contracts when tepid from fear. And taking everything
along in madness, it denies repose to the limbs.
He found help in the lung, and applied it moist
to the furious part so the swollen fibers rush into the calm.
But desire, seeking much for itself but bringing nothing,
withdraws by force into the liver and bottommost regions.
Like a huge beast opening its jaws,
it wants to be satisfied and fed: now with a lash
it tortures the cares of avarice, now with torments of loves it
      shatters them,
now it rejoices, now saddened it grieves, and satisfied it rises
again, and cut down it returns, a sprouting hydra.

3   Sane his a Servio et Fulgentio superadditur fabula. Dicunt enim cum Prometheus ex luto finxisset inanimatum hominem, miratam eius eximium opus Minervam eique spopondisse quic-
4   quid ex celestibus bonis vellet in perfectionem operis sui. Qui cum respondisset se nescire, nisi videret que apud superos sibi essent utilia, ab ea elevatus in celum est, ubi cum cerneret celestia omnia flammis animata, ut suo etiam operi flammam immicteret, clam ferulam rotis Phebi applicuit, et ea accensa ignem furatus reportavit in terras, et pectusculo ficti hominis applicavit, et sic animatum reddidit eumque Pandora vocavit.

5   Quam ob rem irati dii eum per Mercurium Caucaso alligari fecerunt et vulturi seu aquile iecur eius vel cor dilaniandum perpetuo dederunt, cuius conquestionem in rupe satis longo carmine Eschylus Pictagoreus poeta describit, asserens illi cor ab aquila rostro discerpi, et mox iterum restaurari, ac iterum ab ave laniari,
6   et sic indesinenter vexari. Hominibus autem, ut Saphos et Esyodus dicunt, dii ob hoc morbos et maciem ac mulieres immisere. Oratius autem dicit tantum maciem et febrem, ut in *Odis*:

> Audax Iapeti genus
> ignem mala fraude gentibus intulit.
>   Post ignem etherea domo
> subductum macies et nova febrium
>   incubuit cohors,

etc.

7   Harum fictionum involucrum, serenissime Rex, non erit leve corticem aperire; multa enim insunt longa exquirentia verba, que si non apponantur, erit paucis plurimum ingenii oportunum. Faciam igitur resecans quantum potero, ut prestabit deus. Et ante omnia

Servius[147] and Fulgentius[148] add a fable to this. They say that 3
when Prometheus had fabricated the inanimate man from clay,
Minerva admired his excellent work and promised him whatever
celestial benefits he wished for the completion of his work. When 4
he responded that he would not know unless he saw what the
gods could offer that would be useful for him, he was brought up
to the sky, and when he saw there all the whole celestial abode
animated with flames, he wanted to insert flame into his work as
well, so he secretly connected a fennel stalk to the wheels of Phoebus, and, igniting it, he stole fire, brought it to the earth, and applied it to the little breast of the human he created. In this way he
endowed him with life, and he called him Pandora.

As a result the angered gods ordered Mercury to fasten him to 5
the Caucasus and to have his liver or heart torn to pieces continually by a vulture or eagle. The Pythagorean poet Aeschylus[149] described his lament on the cliff amply in a long poem, asserting that
his heart was torn to pieces by an eagle's beak, and that it was
soon restored again, and again it was mutilated by the bird, and
thus he was troubled endlessly. It was for this reason, as Sappho[150] 6
and Hesiod say, that the gods sent men diseases, poverty, and
women. Horace speaks only of the poverty and fever, as he writes
in his *Odes*:[151]

> The bold offspring of Iapetus
> carried fire to men by an evil deceit;
>> after the thievery of fire from its ethereal home
> of poverty and fevers
>> a new cohort watched over . . .

It will not be easy, most serene King, to peel off the outer layer 7
of these fictions, for many words are required, and if I cannot
speak at great length, it will require much skill to do so in a few
words. Therefore I will make sure that I edit as much as I can, as
God will provide. Above all I think we must see who this Pro-

videndum puto quis fuerit Prometheus iste. Qui quidem duplex
est, sicut duplex est homo qui producitur. Primus autem deus verus et omnipotens est, qui primus hominem ex limo terre composuit, ut Prometheum fecisse fingunt, seu natura rerum, que ad
instar primi reliquos etiam ex terra producit, sed alia arte quam
8   deus. Secundus est ipse Prometheus, de quo ante quam aliam
scribamus allegoriam, secundum simplicem sensum, quis fuerit
videndum est.

Dicit ergo Theodontius de Prometheo isto legisse quod cum illi
Iapeti patris, eo quod natu maior esset, successio deberetur, iuvenis et dulcedine studiorum tractus ultro illam Epymetheo fratri
cum duobus parvis filiis, Deucalione et Yside derelictis, in Assy-
riam abiit et inde, postquam aliquandiu insignes eo evo audisset
9   Caldeos, in verticem Caucasi secessit. Ex quo longa meditatione et
experientia percepto astrorum cursu, procuratisque naturis fulminum et rerum plurium causis, ad Assyrios rediit eosque astrologiam docuit et procurationes fulminum, et quod omnino ignora-
bant civilium hominum mores, egitque adeo, ut quos rudes et
omnino silvestres et ritu ferarum viventes invenerat, quasi de novo
compositos civiles relinqueret homines.

10   Quibus sic premissis videndum est quis sit productus homo,
quem supra dixi duplicem esse. Est enim homo naturalis, et est
homo civilis, ambo tamen anima rationali viventes. Naturalis
autem homo primus a Deo ex limo terre creatus est, de quo et
Ovidius et Claudianus intelligunt, esto non adeo religiose, ut
Christiani faciunt; et cum ex luto illum Prometheus iste primus
formasset, insufflavit in eum animam viventem, quam ego rationalem intelligo, et cum hac sensitivam et vegetativam potentias, seu
secundum quosdam animas; verum he naturam habuere corpo-
ream, et nisi peccasset homo, fuissent eterne, sicuti et rationalis
11   est, cui divina natura est. Hunc perfectum fuisse hominem circa

534

metheus was. In fact, he was twofold, just as the man he produced
is twofold. The first is the true, omnipotent God, who first made
men from the clay of the earth, which they pretend Prometheus
did, or the nature of things, which produced the rest like the first
man, also from the earth but by another art than god's. The sec- 8
ond is Prometheus himself, but before writing another allegory we
should examine who he was in a simple sense.

Theodontius says that he read about this Prometheus that as
Iapetus' elder child he should have been his successor, but as a
young man he was attracted by the pleasure of study and voluntarily abandoned this legacy to his brother Epimetheus along with
his two small children, Deucalion and Isis, and departed for As-
syria; there, after listening for some time to the famous Chaldeans
of that era, he withdrew to the summit of the Caucasus. It was 9
there after long and profound thought and experience with the
orbit of the stars that he understood the natural causes of lightning and of much else, returned to the Assyrians and taught them
astrology and how to cope with lightning; and because they were
unfamiliar with the manners of civilized men, he made it so that
those whom he found boorish, uncultivated, and living like beasts
he left as civilized men made anew.

Having said this, we must examine who this aforementioned 10
twofold man was whom they produced. Man is natural, and man
is civilized, both still living with a rational mind. The natural man
was first created by God from the clay of the earth; both Ovid and
Claudian know about him, although not in the religious sense in
which Christians understand it. And when that first Prometheus
had formed him from the clay, he breathed into him a living spirit,
which I understand as a rational spirit, and with it the sensible
and animating powers, or, according to others, spirits. In fact,
these spirits had a corporeal nature, and if man had not sinned,
they would have been eternal just as is the rational spirit, the nature of which is divine. We must believe that he completed this 11

quoscunque actus terreos credendum est; nec opinari debet quisquam oportunum illi fuisse ad eruditionem temporalium rerum
Prometheum aliquem mortalem; verum qui a natura producta
sunt, rudes et ignari veniunt, imo ni instruantur, lutei agrestes et

12 belue. Circa quos secundus Prometheus insurgit, id est doctus
homo, et eos tanquam lapideos suscipiens quasi de novo creet,
docet et instruit, et demonstrationibus suis ex naturalibus hominibus civiles facit, moribus scientia et virtutibus insignes, adeo ut liquido pateat alios produxisse naturam, et alios reformasse doctrinam.

12a [Libet[32] ex multis unum saltem exemplum inducere. Legimus
inter scelestissimos quoscunque et perdite luxurie iuvenes Athenienses Polemonem fuisse principem, qui mane a convivio surgens
temulentus et unguentis fragrans, sertisque spectabilis et vestimentis suorum scelerum letus infamia, scolas Xenocratis pruden-
tum atque modestorum hominum refertas intrasse, risurus, arbitror, potius quam auditurus precepta legentis. Cuius adventus etsi
turbationem omnibus iniecisset, solus Xenocrates immoto vultu
perseverans, omissis de quibus erat sermo, de temperantia et mo-
destia cepit, tanteque fuit eius demostratio efficacie, ut Polemon
non aliter quam si veterem eiecisset animam et ab ore disseren-
tis aliam suscepisset, eiectis sertis, et intra pallium reducto bra-
chio, et omni conviviali letitia posita, et omni omnino eiecta lascivia, ex illecebri ganeone splendidus evasit phylosophus. Bene ergo
ostenditur homines quacunque ineptia deformes a sapientibus
reformare, et qui lutei erant nuditate aut viciorum ignavia, sacris
animari preceptis, et civiles homines effici. Sed ad ulteriora pro-
grediendum est, ut omnis fictionis aperiatur particula.]

13 Dicunt igitur[33] ante alia Minervam opus huius miratam eum in
celum traxisse, daturam si quid ad opus suum perficiendum cerneret oportunum. Quod ego sic intelligendum reor, pro Minerva,

man entirely with earthly actions; nor is it fitting for anyone to
think that Prometheus taught him about temporal things; indeed,
those who are produced by nature arrive coarse and ignorant, nay,
unless they are instructed, filthy, savage, and beastly. Among these   12
a second Prometheus arose, that is, a learned man, and taking
them as if they were made of stone and he were creating them
anew, he taught them and educated them and, by his demonstrations, turned them from natural men to civil, so distinguished in
their knowledge of customs and in their virtues that it is very clear
that nature produced some and teaching had reformed others.

[Let us introduce at least one example of many. We read that   12a
among the most wicked Athenian youths given to luxury was a
prince, Polemon, who one morning after a banquet woke up drunk
and smelling of perfume, a sight in his wreaths and clothes, rejoic-
ing in the infamy of his wickedness; he entered the school of Xenocrates filled with prudent and modest men, for a laugh, I think,
rather than to hear the teachings of the speaker. While his entrance caused a disturbance among everyone else, Xenocrates alone
maintained his reserve, and abandoning the subject of his lecture
he began to speak of temperance and modesty, and his demonstration was so effective that Polemon, not otherwise than if he tossed
away his old mind and took up another from the mouth of the
master, his wreaths tossed away, his arm brought back to within
his cloak, all his convivial enjoyment set aside, and all wantonness
completely forsaken, from a seductive debauchee emerged a brilliant philosopher. This shows clearly that wisdom transforms men
disgraced by whatever sort of foolery, and that those who were vile
in their needs and idle in their vices, can be molded into civil men
when enlivened by sacred teachings. But we must move on, so as
to explore every detail of the fiction.][152]

They say that early on Minerva admired his work and brought   13
him up to the sky to give him whatever he thought would be appropriate for completing it. I think that Minerva represents the

scilicet sapientem virum, qui nature opus admiratur, hominem,
scilicet ex luto productum, et cum eum videat imperfectum quantum ad doctrinam et mores, cupiens eum animare, id est perficere,
sapientia duce, per speculationem ascendit in celum, et omnia ibi
igne animata videt, ut intelligamus quod in celo, id est in loco
perfectionis, sunt omnia animata igne, id est claritate veritatis, sic
et perfectus homo nulla ignorantie nebula offuscatur, et medita-
14   tione continua versatur in celis. Deinde a rota solis furatur hic
ignem, et defert in terris, et pectori infert luteo homini, et vivus
efficitur. Equidem non incongrue dictum est. Non enim in theatris
vel plateis et in propatulo veritatis claritatem adipiscimur, quin
imo in solitudinibus semoti, et exquisita taciturnitate speculamur,
et crebra meditatione rerum naturas exquirimus; et quia ista talia
clam fiunt, quasi furari videmur, et ut appareat unde sapientia veniat in mortales, dicit quod a rota solis, id est e gremio Dei, a quo
omnis sapientia est. Ipse enim verus est sol 'qui illuminat omnem
hominem venientem in hunc mundum,' cuius eternitatem per ro-
tam non habentem principium neque finem designare voluere, et
hoc apposuere ut de ipso vero Deo et non de sole creato accipere-
15   mus dictum. Hanc demum flammam, id est doctrine claritatem,
inmictit pectori lutei hominis, id est ignari. Nam etsi omnibus
largitor ille munerum Deus animam bonam et perfectam infundat,
corporea moles caligine infecta terrestri adeo vires retundit anime,
ut plurimum, nisi doctrina iuventur et excitentur, adeo obtorpes-
cunt, ut potius bruta quam rationabilia animalia videantur.
16   Doctrina igitur sapientie a Deo suscepte prudens homo animat,
id est sopitam animam excitat lutei, id est ignari, hominis, qui

wise man who admires the work of nature, that is, man produced from the clay. And because Prometheus sees him as incomplete insofar as teaching and behavior are concerned, desiring to animate him, that is, to complete him, with wisdom as his guide, he ascended to the sky for the purpose of observation and saw everything animated by fire there, which tells us that in the sky, that is, in the place of perfection, all things are animated by fire, that is, by the clarity of truth, and so the complete man is obscured by no cloud of ignorance and is continuously involved in celestial contemplation. Then he steals fire from the wheel of the sun, carries it 14 down to the earth, places it in the chest of the man of clay, and he is brought alive. Indeed, this is not described inappropriately, for we do not obtain the clarity of truth in theaters or town squares or in open spaces but secluded in solitude, and it is in silence that we pursue our inquiries and investigate the natures of things with much deep thought. And because such things are done in secret, as if we seem to be stealing them, and to explain whence wisdom comes to mortals, the fable says that it is from the wheel of the sun, that is, from the lap of God, whence comes all wisdom, for He is the true sun "who illuminates every man coming into this earth."[153] They wanted to designate his eternity in that the wheel has no beginning nor end, and they add this so that we accept what was said about the true God himself and not about the created sun. He then inserted this flame, that is, the clarity of knowl- 15 edge, into the chest of his man of clay, that is, ignorant man, for even if God, the bestower of gifts to all, infused a good and complete mind, the bodily mass infected by a terrestrial cloud weakens the powers of the mind so much that unless they are aided and inspired by knowledge, they become so benumbed that men seem more like brutish than rational animals.

By the knowledge of wisdom supported by God, the prudent 16 man comes alive, that is, rouses the sleeping spirit of the man of clay, that is ignorance, who is said then to be alive, for he becomes

tunc vivere dicitur, dum ex bruto rationalis efficitur, seu effectus est. Explicito autem homine, iratos deos dicunt quedam fecisse, ut religasse Prometheum in rupe, immisisse febrem, maciem et femi-

17 nas hominibus. Circa quod quantum ad primum, advertendum est hic poetas more vulgi et improprie fuisse locutos. Existimat quidem vulgus iners, iratum Deum adversus quemcunque laborantem vident, quantuncumque circa laudabile opus fatigetur, quasi nil preter ocium detur a pacato deo, et ideo iratum putavere deum Prometheo, eo quod assiduo studio noscendarum rerum laboraret. Seu ideo iratos dixere, quia laboriosa hominibus immisere. De ista ira qualis sit, supra ubi de Fama dictum est.

18 Quod autem duci et alligari Caucaso Prometheum a Mercurio fecerint, pervertitur ordo, nam prius in Caucaso fuit Prometheus, quam hominem rapto igne animaret. Ductus est igitur futurus et iam desiderio ipso prudens homo a Mercurio interprete deorum, id est ab eruditione alicuius enucleantis secreta nature impulsus in Caucasum, id est in solitudinem, quantumcunque secundum hystoriam in Caucasum secesserit, et ibi religatus in rupe, id est a propria voluntate detentus. Ibi illi precordia aiunt ab aquila lacerari, id est a meditationibus sublimibus anxiari, que longo exhausta meditationis labore, tunc restaurantur, quando per ambages varias exquisita alicuius rei veritas reperitur.

19 Et hec quantum ad ficta de Prometheo, quem profecto maiores nostri asserunt eximium sapientie doctorem fuisse. Nam Augustinus in libro *De civitate Dei*, et post eum Rabanus et Luon Carnothensis equo fatentur consensu, eum scientia insignem fuisse virum. Eusebius preterea in libro *Temporum* dicit, Argo regnante Argivis fuit Prometheus, a quo homines factos esse commemorant, et re vera cum sapiens esset, feritatem eorum et nimiam im-

rational instead of brutish, or has been made so. Once man was set forth, they say that the angered gods did such things as to bind Prometheus to a cliff and send fever, poverty, and women to men. Of these, as for the first, we should observe that the poets here 17 have spoken like common people, inappropriately, for unresourceful common people think God is angry at whomever they see laboring, even if it is a laudable work that wearies him, as if an unangry God bestows nothing but leisure, and so they think god was angry with Prometheus because he labored in the assiduous zeal to learn things. Or, they say that the gods were so angry that they sent laborious things to men. What sort of anger this is was said previously in the chapter on Fame.[154]

They contrive that Mercury forced Prometheus to go to the 18 Caucasus and fettered him perverts the order: Prometheus was in the Caucasus before he enlivened man with the stolen fire. Therefore the future man, prudent already by that same desire, was led by Mercury, the interpreter of the gods, that is, by the erudition of someone explaining the secrets of nature, driven to the Caucasus, that is, into solitude, even if according to history he withdrew into the Caucasus, and there was bound onto a cliff, that is, restrained by his own will. There they say his vitals were torn by an eagle, that is, troubled by sublime and deep thoughts, and then, after being worn out by the long labor of profound thought, they are restored when after various ambiguities the once allusive truth about something is discovered.

There is much material involving the fictions about Prometheus, 19 whom our ancestors certainly assert was the extraordinary teacher of wisdom. Augustine[155] in his book, *City of God,* and after him Rabanus[156] and Luon of Chartres[157] also agree that he was a man distinguished in his knowledge. In addition, Eusebius[158] in his *Chronicle* says that when Argus ruled the Argives there was a Prometheus and that men remember that he created them; since in truth he was a wise man, he went about transforming their sav-

20   peritiam ad humanitatem et scientiam transfigurabat. Post hunc
Servius etiam de eo testatur quia prudentissimus vir fuit et a 'providentia' denominatus, et quod primus astrologiam Assyrios do-
cuerit, quam in altissimo residens Caucasi vertice maxima cum
cura didicerat. Hunc insuper dicit Lactantius in libro *Divinarum
institutionum*, primum simulacra ex luto componere invenisse, quod
forsan de compositione hominis ex luto fabule dedit initium. Sic[34]
et Plinius ubi *De naturali hystoria* dicit, eum primo docuisse ignem
e silice provocatum ferula servari.

21   Voluere insuper iratos deos immisisse hominibus maciem, febrem, et mulieres. Pro macie ego intelligo labores corporeos, quibus extenuamur et ad quos nascimur illius crimine, cui dictum est,

22   'Cum sudore vultus tui vesceris pane tuo.' Hic autem maciei viam
dedit intranti. Per febres vero, ardores concupiscientie, quibus angimur et vexamur assidue, voluisse reor. Mulier autem ad solatium
creata est, sed inobedientia sua facta est stimulus, nec equidem
parvus, si rite intueri velimus, quod ut potius alienis verbis quam
meis ostendam, quid preclarissimus preceptor meus, Franciscus
Petrarca, eo in libro quem *De vita solitaria* scripsit, de eis sentiat
libet apponere.

23   Dicit enim sic:

> Nullum virus adeo pestiferum vitam hanc sectantibus, ut
> muliebre consortium; femineus enim decor eo formidolosior
> funestiorque, quo blandior, ut sileam mores, quibus omnino
> nichil instabilius, nichil studio quietis infestius. Quisque re-
> quiem queris, feminam cave, perpetuam officinam litium ac
> laborum. Raro sub eodem tecto habitant quies et mulier.
> Satyrici verbum est:

agery and excessive ignorance to humanity and knowledge. After   20
him Servius[159] also offers testimony that he was the most prudent
man and named after his "foreknowledge," and that he first taught
the Assyrians astrology, which he had learned with the greatest
diligence when residing on the highest peak of the Caucasus. In
addition Lactantius[160] in his *Divine Institutions* says that he first invented making statues from clay, which perhaps inspired the story
about the composition of men from clay. Similarly Pliny[161] as well
in his *Natural History* says that he first taught how to preserve fire
coaxed from stone in a fennel stalk.

They say in addition that the angered gods sent poverty, fever,   21
and women to men. By poverty I understand corporeal labors,
which weaken us and for which we are born by the crime of him
to whom it was said:[162] "With the sweat of your face you eat your
bread." He gave a path for poverty to enter. By fevers I think they   22
mean the ardors of desire, which give us continual anguish and
vexation. Woman, however, was created as consolation, but by her
disobedience became cause of torment, and not at all a small one,
if we want to consider properly, as I will demonstrate with words
other than my own: let me insert the thoughts of my most illustrious preceptor, Francesco Petrarch, which he wrote in his book *The
Life of Solitude.*

He said:[163]   23

No poison is as destructive for those pursuing this life as
feminine companionship, for feminine charm is the more
dangerous and deadly the more it is flattering; I need not say
much about their behavior: nothing is less consistent, nothing more hostile to the desire for quiet. If you seek peace,
beware of a woman, a perpetual workshop of quarrels and
sufferings. Rarely do quiet and a woman live under the same
roof. The phrase of the satirist is:[164]

543

> Semper habitet lites, alternaqua iurgia lectus,
> in quo nupta iacet: minimum dormitur in illo.

> Nisi forte tranquillior est concubine accubitus, cuius et fides minor, et maior infamia et litigium par. Scitum est et illud clari oratoris dictum: 'Qui non litigat celebs est.'

24   Post hoc paulo infra sequitur idem.

> Quisquis ergo litem fugis, et feminam fuge. Vix alteram sine altera effugies. Femine, etsi, quod rarum est, mitissimi mores sint, ipsa presentia, utque ita dixerim, umbra nocens est. Cuius siquid fidei mereor, vultus atque verba cunctis qui solitariam pacem querunt, non aliter vitandi sunt, non dico quam coluber sed quam basilisci conspectus ac sibila. Nam nec aliter oculis, quam basiliscus interficit, et ante contactum inficit.

Hec ille.

25   Que etsi multa sint et vera, haberem que dicerem longe plura, sed quoniam non exigit intentum presens, hec de stimulo humani generis dixisse sufficiant.

∶ 45 ∶

De Pandore homine a Prometheo facto

1   Pandora dicit Fulgentius nominatum eum, quem Prometheus primum ex luto confecit, quod a Fulgentio ob id dictum puto, quia

> Always offering a quarrel, alternating with disputes, is
>   the bed
> in which a bride lies; there is no sleep there.

By chance it may be more tranquil to lie with a concubine, who is less faithful, more scandalous, and equally argumentative. We know also what was said of a famous orator:[165] "He who does not quarrel is a bachelor."

He continues a little farther down: 24

> If you are fleeing dispute, flee a woman. You can scarcely flee one without the other. Even if women, and this is rare, are most gentile in disposition, their very presence, as I am telling you, casts a menacing shadow. Her face and words, if I warrant any faith must be shunned by all who seek the peace of solitude, not otherwise than the sight and hissing, I do not say of a serpent, but of a basilisk. For she destroys with her eyes no differently from a basilisk, and poisons before contact.

These are his words.

Although these are many and true things, I would have more to   25
say at greater length, but because the present purpose does not require it, these words I have said about the torment of the human race will suffice.

: 45 :

On Pandora, a man made by Prometheus

Fulgentius says Pandora was the name of the first man Prometheus   1
made from clay; it was Fulgentius[166] who said the name Pandora

Pandore significatum sit in Latino 'omnium munus,' eo quod non ex notitia unius tantum rei componatur sapiens, sed ex multis et verius ex omnibus, sed talis solus est Deus. Posset preterea dici Pandora a *pan* quod est 'totum,' et *doris* quod est 'amaritudo,' quasi 'Pandorus omni amaritudine plenus.' Nil enim in presenti vita potest homo absque amaritudine possidere, quod utrum verum sit, se unusquisque excutiat et videbit. Iob autem vir sanctus et patientie insigne specimen, volens hoc humano improperare generi, dixit: 'Homo natus de muliere, brevi vivens tempore, multis repletus miseries,' etc.

2

: 46 :

De Yside Promethei filia

1 Ysis, ut ait Theodontius, filia fuit Promethei et parvula a patre Epymetheo patruo derelicta. De qua idem³⁵ Theodontius talem recitat hystoriam. Dicit enim quod cum virgo excrevisset et prestantissimi decoris esset, iam matura viro Iovi placuisse, et ab eo actum seu potentia seu suasionibus, ut in eius iret concubitum, ex quo Ysidem dicit Iovi Epaphum peperisse. Tandem seu tanto fidens amasio puella, seu quia natura ardentis esset animi, in regni cupidinem incidit, et auxiliariis a Iove habitis et aliunde contractis viribus, quasi in effetum viribus regem, animum iniciens, Argum Argivorum regem annositate decrepitum, sed alias oculatum hominem traxit in bellum, adversus quem cum descendisset in aciem, factum est ut, fractis Ysidis viribus, ipsa caperetur Ysis et ab Argo

2

means "gift of all," for, as I think, the wise man is composed not from the knowledge of only one thing but of many and, actually, of all things, but only God is such. In addition, Pandora could be said to be from *pan*, which is "all," and *doris*, which is "bitterness," as in "Pandorus is full of every bitterness": man cannot possess anything in the present life without bitterness, and each one of us searches out whether this is true and will find out. Job, a holy man and a famous example of endurance, wanting to reproach our human race, said:[167] "Man is born from woman, living a short while, full of many miseries." 2

: 46 :

On Isis,[168] daughter of Prometheus

Isis, as Theodontius says, was the daughter of Prometheus and still young when she was abandoned by her uncle Epimetheus. Theodontius again tells the following story about her. He says that when the maiden had grown up, she had the most extraordinary beauty; now mature enough for a husband, she was pleasing to Jupiter, and, whether because of his power or by persuasion, it happened that she entered his bed; Theodontius says that after this Isis produced Epaphus for Jupiter. Then, whether because the girl gained confidence by having a lover like Jupiter or because by nature she burned with ambition, she developed a desire for power, so, using the assistance of Jupiter and forces taken from elsewhere, she threw herself into a plot against a king whose powers were depleted, making war on Argus, King of the Argives, feeble from old age but otherwise an illustrious man. But when she went into battle against him, it happened that her forces were shattered and 1

2

3   servaretur captiva. Verum iussu Iovis patris sui Stilbon, qui postea
    Mercurius appellatus est, homo eloquentissimus et audacia atque
    industria plenus, decipulis suis egit ut, occiso a se Argo sene, a
    captivitate liberaretur Ysis. Cui cum non bene cederent res in pa-
    tria, sue confisa solertie, conscensa nave, cui vacca erat insigne, ad
    Egyptios transfretavit, et cum ea Stilbon ob perpetratum facinus
    pulsus ex Grecia; et cum ibi iam Apis potentissimus esset, eidem
    nupsit, et datis Egyptiis caracteribus licterarum atque ostenso
    terre cultu, in tam grandem devenit Egyptiorum existimationem,
    ut non mortalis femina, sed dea potius haberetur, divinique illi
    adhuc viventi impenderentur honores.

4   Leontius vero dicebat se a Barlaam habuisse, hanc Ysidem ante
    transfretationem Apis in Egyptum, eidem Api nupsisse, et post
    modum cum Iove concubuisse, et ob id cum rescisset indignatus
    Apys regno Argivorum relicto, in Egyptum abiisse, et eam post
    modum ad se accedentem ultro suscepisse.

5   In quibus tot sunt ab utraque parte operum et temporum in-
    convenientia, ut non solum auferatur hystorie fides, sed nec etiam
    aliqua possit verisimilitudo rerum adaptari, et potissime adve-
    niente Iovis obstaculo, cuius cum Api convenientia tempora huic
    hystorie plurimum auferunt fidei. Sane solertibus huius veritatis
    inquisitio relinquatur.

Isis herself was captured and held captive by Argus. Following the 3
instructions of his father Jupiter, Stilbon, who afterward was called
Mercury, a most eloquent man full of daring and industry, used
trickery to kill the old man Argus and free the captive Isis. But
things did not go well back in her native country, so she put her
faith in her own resourcefulness and, along with Stilbon, who had
to leave Greece for a crime he committed, climbing aboard a ship
marked by a cow emblem, she sailed across to Egypt. Apis was
already very powerful there, so she married him, and having given
the Egyptians the characters of their letters and having taught
them to cultivate their land, she earned such a great reputation
among the Egyptians that she was regarded not as a mortal woman
but rather a goddess, and divine honors were awarded her while
still living.

Leontius used to say that he had learned from Barlaam that 4
before Apis sailed across to Egypt, she married this same Apis and
later lay with Jupiter, so when Apis found out that she had rejected him, he left behind the kingdom of the Argives, sailed for
Egypt, and then later, when she followed him of her own accord,
took her back.

In this story there are so many contradictory aspects of both 5
the events and time periods that not only does it eliminate any
credibility in the story but it makes it utterly impossible to find
any semblance to the truth. The insertion of Jupiter especially is
an obstacle: making him contemporary with Apis makes us disbe-
lieve this story almost entirely. But the search for the truth here
can be left to experts.

: 47 :

De Deucalione filio Promethei, qui genuit Ellanum et Psythacum et Dyonisium et Phentratem

1   Deucalion, omnium veterum testimonio, Promethei filius fuit, cui adulto Epymetheus patruus Pyrram filiam iunxit coniugio. Mitis enim ingenii homo fuit et Pyrra piissima femina, de quibus Ovidius:

> Non illo melior quisquam nec amantior equi
> vir fuit, aut illa reverentior ulla deorum,
>
> > etc.

2   Huius enim tempore apud Thessalos ingens fuit diluvium, de quo fere omnes scriptores veteres mentionem faciunt; finguntque plurimi, excrescentibus aquis, Deucalionem solum cum Pyrra coniuge in navicula evasisse, et in Parnasum devenisse montem, et cum iam aque cessarent Themis adisse oraculum consulturi de humani generis restauratione; eiusque iussu, tecto capite solutisque vestibus postergasse saxa, tanquam magne parentis ossa, et ea in homines feminasque conversa.

3   Hoc figmentum a Barlaam sic explicatum referebat Paulus. Dicebat enim se legisse in Grecorum antiquissimis annalibus ob hoc diluvium territos homines, et ad suprema usque montium effugisse, atque intrasse cavernas, et antra una cum mulieribus suis expectaturos finem; et ad hos Deucalionem et Pyrram, cessantibus aquis, in mesto atque supplicum habitu accessisse, et Deucalionem hominibus et Pyrram mulieribus, non absque labore maximo, sua-

∶ 47 ∶

On Deucalion, son of Prometheus, who fathered Hellenus, Psittacus, Dionysus, and Pherecrates[169]

The testimony of all the ancients confirms that Deucalion was the 1
son of Prometheus. Epimetheus, Deucalion's uncle, married his
daughter Pyrrha to him once he had reached adulthood. He was a
man of gentle character and Pyrrha was a most devoted woman,
about whom Ovid says:[170]

> There was no one better than he, none a fairer
> man, nor was any woman more reverent toward the gods.

In his day there was a huge flood in Thessaly. Nearly all the an- 2
cient writers make mention of this, and most imagine that with
the waters rising only Deucalion and his wife Pyrrha escaped in a
small boat, and that they arrived on Mount Parnassus, and that
when the waters had already begun to recede, they went to the
oracle of Themis to consult her about the restoration of the human race, and that by her order, covering their heads and loosen-
ing their garments, they threw stones behind them, as if they were
the bones of their great mother, and that these were transformed
into men and women.

Paul used to refer to Barlaam's explanation for this fabrication, 3
for he used to say that he had read in the most ancient annals of
the Greeks that men were frightened on account of this flood and
had fled along with their women to the mountain peaks and entered caves and caverns, to wait for the end, and that when the
waters were receding Deucalion and Pyrrha approached them in
the mournful garb of suppliants, and that Deucalion convinced
the men and Pyrrha the women, and not without the greatest eff-

sisse aquas cessasse nec amplius fore timendum; et sic eos e verticibus montium atque ex saxeis antris, eis scilicet ambobus precedentibus, in habitationes et tecta reduxisse.

4   Porro Theodontius non sic; dicit enim delatum Deucalionem cum coniuge et aliis pluribus in navi ad Parnasum, et cum cessassent aque, ibi regni sui sedem statuisse, cum primo Thessalis imperaret, et ex communi consilio tanquam pro bono publico factum, ut revocatis hominibus et mulieribus e cavernis (quarum quantitas maxima longe hominum numerum excedebat, eo quod venientibus aquis pavidiores longe ante quam homines in montana confugerant, et sic ex eis nulla periit, cum ex hominibus multi absorpti sint) posita verecundia (quam per tectum caput intelligit, non enim verecundantur nisi videntes) indistincte homines quibuscunque mulieribus miscerentur, quod per solutas vestes dicit ostendi; nam ut ubi de Venere dictum est, Veneris cingulum est dictum *ceston* quod ipsa fert ad legiptimos coitus; cum vero in illicitos tendit, cingulum deponit, et sic illi solutis vestibus in illicitos ire coitus ostendebant, et hoc augende prolis causa, cum ex multitudine mulierum virorum paucitas possit amplissimam prolem suscipere.

5   Quod autem illos vocat ossa parentis, non ob aliud dictum puto, nisi quia sicuti saxa terre molem ne effluat continent, sic et ossa hominum corpora servant in robore; sic et labores agricultorum agunt, ut ea producuntur ex terra ex quibus nutricamur atque consistimus, quasi videantur ex agris assumpti qui incoluere postea civitates. Ego autem reor illos parentis ossa dictos, quia ex cavernis et antris montium uti lapides facimus, educti sunt, et ob duritiem suam saxei dicti.

ort, that the waters had receded and that they should no longer be afraid, and that in this way they returned from the mountain tops and from their rocky caves, the two of them in the lead, back to their dwellings and buildings.

Theodontius tells it differently, for he says that Deucalion with his wife and many others were carried on a boat to Parnassus, and that when the waters receded, he set up the seat of his kingdom there as the first king of Thessaly. By common deliberation, as if for public benefit, when the men and women were called back from the caverns (of which the greatest quantity by far was of women because, with the waters coming, they fled in greater fear toward the mountains before the men did, so none of them perished while many of the men were engulfed), it was ordered that their modesty be put aside (which he understood from their covered heads, for they were not ashamed unless they could see) and that the men should have sex indistinctly with whichever women. He says he understood this from the loosened garments; in fact, as we said in the chapter on Venus,[171] the girdle of Venus is called the *cestos*, which she herself wears for legitimate coitus, and she puts aside the girdle when she tends toward the illicit, and so with their garments loosened they reveal themselves to be entering into illicit coitus. They do this for the sake of increasing their offspring, since from a multitude of women a paucity of men is able to receive the greatest number of offspring.

That he calls them the bones of their mother I think is said for no other reason than that, just as stones keep the mass of the earth from vanishing, so also bones give support to human bodies. In the same way agricultural labors, which produce from the earth what we need for nourishment and subsistence, seem to be taken from fields which afterward will become cities. I think they are said to be the bones of their mother because they were brought out, as we bring out stones from mountain caverns and caves, and were called stonelike on account of their durability.

4

5

: 48 :

De Ellano Deucalionis filio

1 Ellanum dicit Theodontius filium fuisse Deucalionis et Pyrre, quem ait Barlaam, patre mortuo, adeo nomen suum et imperium ampliasse, ut fere omnis Grecia, que in Egeum mare versa est, a nomine suo Ellada nominata sit et Ellades Greci.

: 49 :

De Psytaco Deucalionis filio

1 Psytacus Deucalionis et Pyrre filius, ut ait Theodontius, Promethei avi sui doctrinis imbutus, ad Ethyopas abiit, ubi in maxima veneratione habitus cum in longissimum evasisset evum, oravit ut rebus subtraheretur humanis. Cuius precibus dii faciles eum in avem sui nominis mutavere.

2 Huius ego fictionis causam credo sui nominis et virtutis famam, que, eo cano mortuo, viriditate duravit perpetua, uti sunt perpetuo virides aves ille. Fuere qui crederent hunc Psytacum eum fuisse, qui unus ex vii sapientibus dictus est, sed Theodontius dicit eum longe antiquiorem.

: 48 :

On Hellenus, son of Deucalion

Theodontius says that Hellenus was the son of Deucalion and 1
Pyrrha. After his father died, Barlaam says, he increased his fame
and his power over nearly all of Greece bordering the Aegean Sea,
so Greece is named Hellas after him, and the Greeks Hellenes.

: 49 :

On Psittacus, son of Deucalion

Psittacus ["parrot"] was the son of Deucalion and Pyrrha, as 1
Theodontius says. Imbued with the teachings of his grandfather
Prometheus, he went to Ethiopia, where he was held in the greatest veneration, and when he had lived to an advanced age, he
prayed to be removed from human affairs. In response to his
prayers the gods easily transformed him into the bird named after
him.

I believe the reason for this fiction is the fame of his name and 2
virtue, which, although he died in his gray years, lasted in perpetual viridity—like those birds that are always green. There were
those who believed that this Psittacus was said to be one of the
seven sages, but Theodontius says he was much more ancient.

: 50 :

De Dyonisio Deucalionis filio

1 Dyonisius, ut testatur Eusebius in libro *Temporum*, Deucalionis
fuit filius, eiusque facta claruisse dicit circa initium ducatus Moy-
sis. Que tamen fuerint nusquam legisse memini, preterquam cum
in Atticam venisset, a Semaco quodam susceptus hospitio, filie
eius capree pellem largitus est.

: 51 :

De Fentrate Deucalionis filio

1 Fentratem Deucalionis fuisse filium Paulus et non nulli alii arbitrantur, eo quod de eo sic referat Tullius in libro *Tusculanarum
questionum*.

> Dycearcus autem in illo sermone, quem Corynthi habitum,
> tribus libris exponit, doctorum hominum disputantium in
> primo libro multos loquentes facit, duobus Fentratem quen-
> dam Phyotam senem, quem ait a Deucalione ortum, disse-
> rentem inducit,

etc.

2 Ex quibus preter originem apparet eum fuisse phylosophum.

: 50 :

On Dionysus, son of Deucalion

Dionysus, as Eusebius[172] testifies in his *Chronicle*, was the son of 1
Deucalion, and he says that his deeds were famous around the
time that Moses commenced his leadership. I remember reading
nothing about him other than that when he came to Attica he was
received hospitably by a certain Semachus and bestowed upon his
daughter the fleece of a goat.

: 51 :

On Pherecrates, son of Deucalion

Paul and some others think that Pherecrates was the son of Deu- 1
calion because Cicero[173] refers to him this way in his *Tusculan Disputations*:

> Dicearchus, in that dialogue which is set in Corinth and
> comprises three books, presents in the first book many
> speakers in the disputations of learned men; in the latter two
> books he brings in as a speaker Pherecrates, a certain elderly
> man of Phthia, who he says was born of Deucalion.

From this passage, as well as his lineage, he appears to have been a 2
philosopher.

: 52 :

De Astreo Titanis filio VIIII°, qui genuit Astream et Ventos

1 Astreus filius fuit Titanis et Terre, ut asserit Paulus. Hunc dicunt Servius et Lactantius cum Aurora concubuisse et ex ea genuisse Astream virginem nec non et ventos omnes. Quos dicit Paulus cum senex esset, dum fratres adversus Iovem bellum movissent, omnes armavit et emisit in superos, esto Lactantius dicat eos ab Athlante armatos.

2 Astreum potentem aliquem atque superbum fuisse hominem existimo, ideo ventorum patrem dictum, quia alicui ventose regioni prefuerit; quod illos armaverit in superos, a ventorum discursione sumptum est, qui si a terre concavitatibus veniant, ut in altum erumpant necesse est.

: 53 :

De Astrea filia Astrei

1 Astream Astrei Titanis fuisse filiam satis vulgatum est. Que quoniam diis favit adversum patrem et patruos, in celum assumpta est, et in Zodiaco locata, ea in parte, que ab ea Virgo denominata est.

2 Nunc autem quid sibi velit fictio videamus. Astreum Astree patrem ego hic non hominem, sed celum astrigerum intelligo, quod ex se iustitiam gignit, dum perpetuo ordine sibi divino mu-

: 52 :

On Astraeus, the ninth child of Titan,
who fathered Astraea and the Winds

Astraeus was the son of Titan and Earth, as Paul states. Servius[174]   1
and Lactantius[175] say that he slept with Aurora and with her produced the maiden Astraea as well as all the winds. Paul says
that when the brothers made war against Jupiter, Astraeus, even
though he was elderly, armed all of them and sent them out
against the gods, although Lactantius says that it was Atlas who
armed them.

I think Astraeus was some powerful and proud man called the   2
father of the winds because he was in charge of some windy region. That he armed the winds against the gods is taken from
winds' scattered movements, which, since they come from the hollows of the earth, are necessary for them to emerge higher.

: 53 :

On Astraea, daughter of Astraeus

It is common knowledge that Astraea was the daughter of Astra-   1
eus, son of Titan. Because she favored the gods against her father
and uncles, she was taken into the sky and located in that part of
the Zodiac named Virgo after her.

But now let us see what meaning this fiction offers. I under-   2
stand Astraeus, the father of Astraea, not to be a man here but the
star-bearing sky which produces justice by means of the perpetual
order given as a divine gift to itself while it ceaselessly grants to

nere dato inferioribus corporibus unicuique iuxta sui qualitatem
indesinenter oportuna concedit, et huius exemplo legum latores,
prout humano ingenio possibile est, nostram ordinavere iustitiam.

3   Ex Aurora autem ideo nata dicitur, quia sicuti aurore claritas
solem procedit, sic ex notitia certa rerum gestarum debet oriri seu
oritur iustitia seu iudicium. Diis favisse dicitur, quia bonis semper
favet iustitia et eicit reprobos. Ea enim in celi parte ideo posita est,
4 quia contigua est equinoctio, ut ostendatur ex iustitia rerum equi-
tatem consequi, et sicut sole ibidem existente equa temporis pars
nocti atque diei ab eodem sole conceditur, sic a iustitia eque ius
redditur depresse conditionis hominibus atque claris.

: 54 :

De Ventis filiis Astrei in generali

1   Venti, ut perhibent Servius et Lactantius, Astrei Titanis et Aurore
fuere filii. Hos dicit Lactantius a Iunone ob natum Epaphum inci-
tatos in Iovem, quam ob causam a Iove cavernis clausi sunt, et sub
imperio Eoli religati. Sed aliam causam dicit Theodontius a Pronapide monstrari in *Prothocosmo*, que talis est. Dicit enim Pronapides Litigium egre plurimum tulisse a Iove de celo fuisse deiectum,
et ob id ad inferos descendisse, et conventis Furiis orasse, si quid
unquam eorum votis suus labor posset in posterum voluptatis
afferre, irent et sua venena quiescentibus Ventis inicerent, ut Furiis
infestati, Iovis regnum infestarent atque quietem; que evestigio

each of the inferior bodies what is appropriate for its character, just as legislators, as far as possible within human ability, regulate our justice.

She is said to have been born of Aurora because, just as the 3 clarity of the dawn precedes the sun, so does justice or judgment arise, or ought to arise, from the certain knowledge of things that have happened. She is said to have favored the gods because justice always favors the good and casts out the condemned. She is 4 placed in that part of the sky where she borders on the equinox to show that the equality of things follows from justice. Similarly, just as when the sun appears there and an equal share of time is granted to the night and the day by that same sun, so it is by justice that right is rendered equally unto men of lowly condition and the illustrious.

: 54 :

On the Winds, sons of Astraeus, in general

The Winds, as Servius and Lactantius represent them, were sons 1 of Astraeus, son of Titan, and Aurora. Lactantius says that when Juno sent them to rage against Jupiter on account of the birth of Epaphus, Jupiter shut them up in caverns, bound them fast, and placed them under the rule of Aeolus. But Theodontius says this other reason was revealed by Pronapides in his *Protocosmos*. Pronapides says Strife became so upset when Jupiter threw him from the sky that he descended to the nether world and entreated the assembled Furies. He promised them that he would strive to satisfy any of their future desires if they would go and inject their venom into the pacified Winds so that they, infested by the Furies, would infest the kingdom of Jupiter and disturb his peace. As

tendentes, cum eos pacifice sedentes in domo patria invenissent, non solum furias[36] sed odia immisere, adeo ut in regiones suas abeuntes, confestim unus in alterum discursum facere, et omne celum terramque concutere incepere. Quibus perterritus primo Iuppiter, deinde commotus, eis non absque labore captis et cavernis Eoli inclusis, eos sub eius esse iussit imperio.

De quibus sic dicit[37] Virgilius:

Nymborum in patriam, loca feta furentibus austris,
Eolyam[38] venit. Hic vasto rex Eolus antro
luctantes ventos tempestatesque sonantes,[39]
imperio premit ac vinclis et carcere frenat.
Illi indignantes magno cum murmure montis
circum claustra fremunt, celsa sedit Eolus arce
sceptra tenens mollitque animos et temperat iras.
Ni faciat, maria ac terras celumque profundum
quippe ferant rapidi secum verrantque per auras.
Sed pater omnipotens speluncis abdidit atris;
hoc metuens molemque et montes insuper altos
imposuit, regemque dedit, qui federe certo,
et premere et lapsas sciret dare iussus habenas,

etc.

2 Si predictarum fictionum[40] volumus habere sensum, ante alia necesse est ut Astreum horum patrem celum credamus astrigerum, ita tamen ut unum sit celum quicquid inter lune concavum et octave spere convexum continetur; nam motum celi et planetarum tanquam a remotiori tantum paululum causa causari arbitror. Si autem Astreum hominem Ventorum patrem voluerimus, iam supra dictum est eum imperasse locis, ex quibus multi orirentur

soon as the Furies arrived, finding the Winds sitting quietly in their father's home, they sent in not only fury but hatred so that they scattered into their regions, immediately clashing one against the other, and began to harass the whole sky and the earth. Jupiter, at first frightened by them but then provoked, after spending great effort to capture and shut them into the caverns of Aeolus, ordered them to submit to his rule.

Vergil writes about them in the first book of his *Aeneid*:[176]

> Into the storm clouds' homeland, Aeolian regions teeming with
>   raging southerly winds,
> she came. Here King Aeolus in his vast cave
> the struggling winds and roaring storms
> rules under his sovereignty and bridles with chains and bars.
> Indignant with a great murmur of the mountain
> they bellow at the gates. Aeolus sits on the lofty heights
> holding his scepter, and he tames their spirit and tempers their
>   anger.
> If he did not, the seas and lands and the deep sky
> they would swiftly carry off and sweep along with their gusts.
> But the all-powerful father hid them in the dark caverns;
> fearing this, a mass and high mountains he set
> upon them, and gave them a king, who by firm agreement
> knows how to repress them and, when ordered, to loosen the
>   reigns.

If we wish to make sense of these aforementioned fictions, we 2 must above all accept Astraeus, the father of the Winds, as the star-bearing sky, in that it is one sky contained between the concavity of the moon and the convexity of the octave sphere, for I think the motion of the sky and planets is caused by a cause, so to speak, only a little more distant. If we were to wish Astraeus to be a man as the father of the Winds, we already said earlier that he ruled those regions from which many winds arise, and for this

venti, et hinc dictus est Ventorum pater. Aurore autem ideo dicuntur filii, quia ut plurimum appropinquante aurora consueverint venti oriri, quod nautarum approbat autoritas et consuetudo; illa enim hora eos surgere dicunt, et ob id eadem hora ut plurimum suas navigationes incipiunt, et hinc Aurore filii nuncupati sunt.

3 Eos autem a Junone in Iovem armatos fuisse, ideo fictum est, quia a terra emicti creduntur, que Juno est, et quadam terre respiratione impelli, et cum alibi nequeant preter in aerem inpingi, cum aer Iuppiter sit, in Iovem armatos fictum est, id est impetuosos.

Quod autem Litigium opere Furiarum eos et inquietare regnum Iovis et inter se hostes fecerit, hoc a motu eorum et opere sumptum est; nam si ab oriente ventus surrexerit, et itidem ab occidente, ut et per aerem et in se concurrant necesse est, ex quo videntur hostes et regnum inquietare Iovis. Eos autem sub imperio

4 Eoli religatos in cavernis ideo dictum est, quia Eolydes insule quibus olim prefuit Eolus, et ab eo denominate sunt, plene sunt cavernarum, caverne autem plene sunt aeris et aque, cuius motu causatur calor, et ob calorem surgunt ex aqua vapores, quos calor ipse resolvit in aerem; qui cum in loco non capaci consistere nequeat, egreditur, et si arctus sit agressus, de necessitate impetuosior et sonorior et diuturnior exit, et sic cum generati venti ex cavernis Eolidarum insularum exeant, fictum est eos in cavernis Eoli religatos atque suo sub imperio positos. Sed Virgilius sub hac fictione longe aliud sentit, quod quoniam non spectat ad propositum non appono.

5 Est preter fictiones horum pregrandis potentia. Sunt distincte regiones et nomina; sunt insuper secundum quosdam pauciores,

reason he was said to be the father of the winds. The Winds are said to be the sons of Aurora because for the most part winds usually arise as the dawn approaches; the authority and custom of sailors proves this, for they say that the winds arise in that hour, and because of this they very often begin sailing at that same hour; and for this reason they are called the sons of Aurora. The story 3 was invented that Juno armed them against Jupiter because they were believed to be sent out from the earth, that is, Juno, and driven by a kind of earthly respiration, and since they cannot rush out anywhere else except into the air, since Jupiter is the air, the detail was invented that that they were armed, that is, raging, against Jupiter.

That Strife by the work of the Furies made them disturb the kingdom of Jupiter and act in a hostile manner to each other is taken from their motion and their action, for if a wind arises from the East and another likewise from the West, it is necessary that they run together through the air and collide, which makes them seem to be enemies and to disturb the kingdom of Jupiter. It was 4 said that they were under the rule of Aeolus and bound in a cavern because the Aeolian islands, which Aeolus once controlled and are named after him, are full of caverns, and caverns are full of air and water, the motion of which causes heat, and on account of the heat vapors arise from the water, and the same heat renders the vapors into air, which, because it cannot remain in a place unable to contain it, goes out, and if its egress is narrow, by necessity it leaves more impetuous, noisier, and longer lasting; and so, because the generated winds come out from the caves of the Aeolian Islands, it was invented that they were bound in the caves of Aeolus and placed under his rule. Vergil thinks quite differently about this fiction, yet, because he does not formally propose it, I do not include it.

Regardless of the fictions, the power of the winds is very great. 5 There are distinct regions and names; in addition, there are few,

secundum vero alios plures, nec eisdem nominibus ab omnibus nuncupati sunt. De quibus antequam ad singulorum sermonem veniamus, pauca dixisse non erit incongruum.

Dicit[41] ergo de eorum potentia et regionibus atque nominibus sic Ovidius:

6   Et cum flaminibus facientes frigora ventos.
His quoque non passim mundi fabricator habendum
aera permisit: vix nunc obsistitur illis,
cum sua quisque regat diverso flamina tractu,
quin lanient mundum, tanta est discordia fratrum.
Eurus ad auroram Nabatheaque regna recessit
Persidaque et radiis iuga subdita matutinis,
Vesper et occiduo, que litora sole tepescunt,
proxima sunt Zephyro; Scithiam septemque triones
horrifer invasit Boreas, contraria tellus
nubibus assiduis pluvioque madescit ab Austro,

                      etc.

In quibus[42] carminibus, etsi multum dictum sit, est tamen eorum tam grandis violentia, ut non dicam pregrandes naves pondere honustas multiplici per maria tensis evehat velis, seu annosas quercus, evulsis e solo radicibus, in regionem alteram deferat, quin imo celsas turres arcesque sublimes perpetuo solidatas saxo impetu evertat suo, et montium altos vertices tanta concutiat rabie, ut mundum omnem, si rerum pateretur natura, extra veteres terminos videatur posse transferre.

7   Hos XII esse dicit Ysidorus *Ethymologiarum* libro, eosque sic disponit et nominat. Qui ab oriente verno in occiduum tendit ideo dicitur Subsolanus, quia sub ortu solis nascatur. Huic duos colla-

according to some, but many, according to others, and they are not called by the same names by everyone. Before we come to the discussion about them individually, it will be appropriate to say a few things.

Ovid says this about their power, regions, and names:[177]

... and the winds making the cold with their breezes;   6
neither did the fabricator of the world permit
the air to occupy every place: they can barely be withstood
   now,
since each one rules its breezes in a diverse tract;
nay, they would tear the world apart, such is the discord of
   brothers.
Eurus withdrew to the Dawn and the Nabatean realms
and Persia and the ridges subject to the morning rays;
the evening and the shores warmed by the setting sun
are next to Zephyr; Scythia and the North
chilling Boreas invaded; the earth on the other side
grows wet with relentless clouds and rain from Auster.

In these verses, even though it has been said often, the violence of the winds is so great that I will not say how it carries grand ships laden with multiple cargoes through the seas with their taut sails, or relocates aged oaks, their roots ripped out of the soil, into another area; nay, with its force it destroys tall towers and sublime citadels fortified with eternal stone, and it strikes the tall peaks of mountain with such madness that it would seem capable, if the nature of things allowed it, of carrying the whole world beyond its ancient boundaries.

Isidore[178] in his book, *Etymologies*, says there were twelve of   7 them and arranges and names them in the following way. That which stretches from the birth of spring to the west is therefore called Subsolanus because it is born "under the birth of the sun" [*sub ortu solis*]. To this he connected two on either side, namely,

teralis adnectit, Eurum scilicet a sinistris, quem sic ait vocari, eo quod ab 'Eoo' spiret, id est ab oriente estivo; a dextris vero dicit esse Vulturnum, sic dictus quod 'alte tonet.' Austrum inde a meridie flantem sic dicit dici, quod 'aquas hauriat,' eumque Grece appellari Nothum. A dextris eius dicitur esse Euroastrum, inde dictum quod inter Eurum sit et Austrum. Sic et qui a sinistris est Austroaffrum, quia inter Austrum sit et Affrum. Sic et idem Lybonothus vocatur, eo quod inde Lybs et hinc sit illi Nothus. Zephyrum autem subsequenter ab occiduo flantem dicit, eo sic appellatum quod flores et gramina eius vivificentur spiritu, atque eundem vocari Favonium Latine, quod his 'faveat' que nascuntur.

8   Cuius a dextra Affricum seu Lybim a regione unde spirat denominatum. A leva vero Chorum, eo quod ventorum circulum claudat et quasi 'chorum' faciat. Antea tamen dicit Caurum nominatum, et a nonnullis Argeston.

Septentrionem inde dicit dictum, eo quod a circulo septem stellarum consurgat. Cui ponit a dextra Circium, a vicinitate Chori sic denominatum. A sinistra vero Aquilone cuius nominis causam dicit, quia 'aquas' extinguat et dissipet nubes. Eumque dicit et Boream nominari, quod ab Yperboreis montibus egredi videatur.

9   Scribit preterea Ysidorus, his XII designatis, alios etiam esse ventos, quos ego eosdem puto, sed aliis nominibus appellatos, ut puta Ethesyas, quas ait statuto anni tempore a Borea in Egyptum efflare. Sic et Auram et Altanum. Auram vero ab 'aere' dictam, quod lenis sit quasi[43] agitatus leniter aer. Altanum in pelago fieri et ab 'alto' denominatum. Turbonem insuper a 'terra' dictum dicit; est enim ventorum circumvolutio quedam perniciosa persepe. Fragorem a 'fractarum rerum' sonitu denominari ventum ait. Sic et Procellam dictam, eo quod cum pluvia flans evellat.

Eurus on the left, which he says is called this because it blows "from Eos," that is, from the beginning of summer; on the right he says is Vulturnus, called this because it "thunders deeply" [*alte tonet*]. He says Auster, which blows from the South, is so named because it "drinks water" [*aquas hauriat*]; in Greece it is called Notus. On its right is said to be Euroauster, so called because it is between Eurus and Auster. So also that which is on the left is called Austroafricus because it is between Auster and Africus. So also the same is Libonotus, called this because it is from Libs and Notus. Further on he says later that Zephyr blows from the West so that it was called this because flowers and grasses are brought back to life by its breath, and the same is called Favonius because it "favors" [*faveat*] what is born. On its right Africus or Libya is 8 named after the region from which it blows. On the left is Corus because it closes the circle of winds as if it is making a "chorus." Before this he says it was called Caurus and Argestes by some.

He says Septentrio is so called because it rises from the circle of "seven stars" [*septem stellarum*]. To the right of this he puts Circius, so named from its proximity to Corus; he says the name of Aquilo on its left derives from the fact that it destroys "waters" [*aquas*] and scatters the clouds. He also says Boreas is named because it seems to leave from the Hyperborean mountains. After designating these 9 twelve, Isidore writes that there are other winds in addition. I think these are the same but called by different names, for example, Etesiae, which he says blow at a certain time of year from Boreas into Egypt. So also Aura and Altanus: he says Aura is named from "air" [*aere*] because it is gentle air gently stirred; Altanus occurs at sea and is named from the "deep" [*alto*]. In addition he says Turbo is named from "land" [*terra*], for it is a certain circumvolution of winds which is quite often destructive. He says Fragor is a wind named from the sound of "broken things" [*fractarum rerum*]. And Procella is so called because when it blows with the rain it uproots things.

10   Vitruvius autem, ubi *De architectonica* scripsit, XXIIII^or esse
ventos ostendit. Dicit enim Austri collaterales Leuconothum et
Altanum, Affrici Lybonothum et Subvesperum, Favonii Ergastes
et Ethesias, Cauri Circium et Chorum, Septentrionis Tracias et
Gallicum; Aquiloni Supernas et Cecias, Solano Curbas et Orin-
thias, Euro Circias et Vulturnum. Alibi autem dicit idem Vitruvius eos octo tantum esse, scribens Andronicum Cyrrestem ad
demonstrationem opinionis huius, Athenis turrim octogonam
construxisse, et singulis lateribus sculptam eius venti ymaginem,
cui illa facies muri esset adversa, posuisse, et tandem metha mar-
morea super turrim imposita, ereum trionem super imposuit illi
11   dextra virgam porrigentem. Qui cum circumageretur a ventis, virga
designabat, quis esset qui flaret, et sic dicit compertum inter Solanum et Austrum Eurum, inter Austrum et Favonium Affricum,
inter Favonium et Septentrionem Caurum seu Chorum, inter
Septentrionem et Solanum Aquilonem. Quam descriptionem tanquam optimam atque veram Mediterranei maris naute omnes servant, et potissime Ianuenses, qui profecto ceteros nautice artis ex-
cedunt ingenio.

∴ 55 ∴

De Subsolano vento et Vulturno et Euro
et collateralibus suis, filiis Astrei

1   Expedito de ventis in generali, de unoquoque secundum Ysidori
descriptionem in particulari pauca dicenda sunt; et primo de Subsolano orientali vento. Hic, ut Beda dicit, calidus est et siccus, sed

Vitruvius,[179] when writing in his *On Architecture*, explains that 10
there are twenty-four winds, for he says that on either side of
Auster are Leuconotus and Altanus, of Africus are Libonotus and
Subvesper, of Favonius are Argestes and Etesiae, of Caurus are
Circius and Corus, of Septentrio are Thracia and Gallicus, of Aquilo are Supernas and Cecias; on either side of Solanus are Carbas
and Orinthiae, of Eurus are Circius and Vulturnus. Elsewhere
again Vitruvius[180] says that there are only eight. He writes that
Andronicus Cyrrhestes constructed an octagonal tower as proof of
this opinion, and that he placed an image of a wind sculpted on
each side of the wall facing it, and then on the top of a marble
cone placed above the tower he added a bronze Triton extending a
wand in his right hand. When it is wheeled around by the winds, 11
the wand designates which wind is blowing, and so it says that
between Solanus and Auster is Eurus, between Auster and Favonius is Africus, between Favonius and Septentrio is Caurus or
Corus, between Septentrio and Solanus is Aquilo. All the sailors
of the Mediterranean Sea preserve this description as the best and
accurate, and especially the Genovese, who certainly surpass others
in their capacity for nautical skill.

: 55 :

On the Winds Subsolanus, Vulturnus, Eurus,
and their Collateral Winds, sons of Astraeus

Having accounted for the winds in general, we must now speak 1
briefly about each one of them in particular, according to the description in Isidore.[181] First is Subsolanus, the East Wind. Bede[182]

temperate et ideo calidus, quia diu sub sole moretur. Siccus autem, quia cum Occeanus orientalis multum distet a nobis, ex quo hu-
2 miditatem sumere creditur, eam omnem veniendo dimictit. Sed absit ut credam ridiculum istud, omnem scilicet ventum, qui ad nos ab orientis plaga venit, oriri in oriente extremo, cum certissimum habeatur multos apud Eolidas oriri, ut predictum est, ex quibus non nulli in nos efflant quos nos orientales et merito dicimus; quam ob causam, salva semper reverentia Bede, frustra dictum puto eos ob longinquitatem originis sue ad nos mutata
3 complexione venire. Huic eiusdem complexionis sunt a dextris Vulturnus omnia desiccans, a sinistris vero Eurus nubes aggregans seu generans.

: 56 :

De Notho vento et Euroastro atque Austroaffro collateralibus eius, filiis Astrei

1 Nothus australis est ventus, naturaliter frigidus et siccus, verum dum per torridam zonam ad nos veniens transit, calorem assumit, et ab aquarum multitudine in meridie existente sumit humiditatem. Et sic mutata natura ad nos venit calidus et humidus, et calore suo poros terre aperit, et humorem ut plurimum multiplicare, et nubes et pluvias inducere consuevit.

2 Huius formam sic describit Ovidius:

Madidis Nothus evolat alis,
terribilem picea tectus caligine vultum:

says it is warm and dry but temperate and that it is warm because it tarries under the sun. It is dry because, since the eastern ocean, from which it takes up its moisture, stands far from us, he has dispersed all of it along the way. But let no one think I believe this 2 ridiculous thing, namely, that every wind which comes to us from the eastern region rises in the extreme East, since it is held with great certainty that many arise in the Aeolian Islands, as I said earlier, some of which flow to us, and we correctly identify them as eastern. For this reason, and may our reverence for Bede be preserved forever, I think it is said to no purpose that they come to us with characteristics changed by the distance traveled from their origin. Having the same characteristics are Vulturnus on its right, 3 which desiccates everything, and Eurus on its left, which gathers the clouds or produces them.

: 56 :

On the Wind Notus and its Collaterals Euroauster and Austroafricus, sons of Astraeus

Notus is the south wind, naturally cold and dry, but when in 1 heading toward us it crosses through the torrid zone, it takes up heat, and from the multitude of waters existing in the south, it takes up moisture. And so with its nature changed it comes to us warm and moist, and with its heat it opens the pores of the earth, and greatly increasing the moisture, it often induces clouds and rain.

Ovid describes his appearance:[183] 2

Notus flies with dripping wings,
his terrifying face covered by a black cloud;

barba gravis nymbis, canis fluit unda capillis,
fronte sedent nebule, rorant penneque sinusque,

etc.

3 Huic eiusdem complexionis a dextris est Euroaster, qui tempestates in mari generat, eo quod, ut Beda dicit, ab imo sufflet. A sinistris autem Austroaffer, quem aliqui dicunt calidum et temperatum.

: 57 :

De Septentrione vento et Circio collaterali eius,
filiis Astrei

1 Septentrio ventus est a plaga in qua oritur nuncupatus. Nascitur
enim in locis aquosis et congelatis et excelsis montibus, ex quibus
ad nos usque purus flat, eo quod in locis, per que transitum facit,
nullus ob intensum frigus resolvitur vapor. Hic aerem serenum
2 facit, et quas exciverat Auster pestes, repellit et purgat. Complexione autem cum collateralibus frigidus est et siccus. Qui enim
a dextris est, Circius appellatur, nivium grandinumque productor.
A sinistris autem Aquilo est, seu Boreas, de quo latior sermo sequitur.

his beard was heavy with rainstorms, water flowed from his
    white hair;
on his brow sat clouds, his feathers and robes were moist.

On his right Euroaster, which generates tempests at sea, had 3
the same characteristic because, as Bede says, it blows from the
bottom. On the left is Austroafricus, which some say is warm and
temperate.

∴ 57 ∴

On the Wind Septentrio and its collateral Circius, sons of Astraeus

Septentrio is a wind named from the region in which it arises, for 1
it is born in areas that are watery and frozen high in the mountains. From there it blows unadulterated to us: no vapor escapes
on account of the intense cold of the terrain it crosses. It makes
the air serene, and it rouses and repels the pestilences evoked by
Auster, and purges them. Septentrio is cold and dry in character, 2
like his collaterals. Of those, the one on the right, called Circius, is
the producer of snow and hail. On the left is Aquilo, or Boreas,
about whom a more ample discussion follows.

: 58 :

De Aquilone seu Borea vento, Astrei filio et collaterali Septentrionis

1 Boreas seu Aquilo ventus collateralis est Septentrionis, et natura sua habet nubes dissipare et aquas ligare gelu, de[44] quo sic Ovidius in persona eiusdem dicit ad ostendendas vires eius:

> Apta michi vis est, quia tristia nubila pello
> et freta concutio nodosaque robora verto,
> induroque nives et terras grandine pulso.
> Idem ego cum fratres celo sum nactus aperto,
> nam michi campus is est, tanto molimine luctor,
> ut medius nostris concursibus insonet ether,
> exiliantque cavis elisi nubibus ignes.
> Idem ego, cum subii convexa foramina terre,
> supposuique ferox imis mea terga cavernis,
> sollicito manes totumque tremoribus orbem.
> Hac ope,[45]

etc.

2 Ex hoc plures dicuntur fabule. Nam Servius dicit eum amasse Yacintum puerum, qui etiam ab Apolline amabatur, et quoniam cerneret amorem pueri in amorem Apollinis magis quam in se flecti, iratus disco ludentem interemit. Preterea dicit Ovidius, eum amasse Orythiam Erichthonii regis Athenarum filiam, ac eam in coniugem postulasse, que cum non daretur, indignans se disposuit ad rapinam nec distulit quin[46] imo:

> Excussit[47] pennas, quarum iactatibus omnis
> afflata est tellus latumque perhorruit equor.

576

: 58 :

On the Wind Aquilo or Boreas, son of Astraeus and collateral of Septentrio

Boreas or Aquilo is the collateral of Septentrio, and by its nature 1
it causes clouds to dissipate and waters to bind together in ice.
Ovid speaks in its persona to demonstrates its powers like this:[184]

> Violence is suited to me. I use it to drive away gloomy clouds,
> and harass the seas and overturn knotty oaks,
> harden the snows and strike the lands with hail;
> and I, when I come upon my brothers in the open sky,
> which is our battlefield, struggle with such vehemence
> that the ether resonates with our collisions,
> and fires are forced to leap out from the hollow clouds;
> I, when I go down into the vaulted fissures of the earth
> and in my rage position my back against the bottom of the
>   caverns,
> disturb the shades and the whole orb of the earth with quakes.
> With this power . . .

Many fables are told about him. Servius[185] says that he loved 2
the boy Hyacinth who was also loved by Apollo, and because he
saw the boy's love turned more toward Apollo than himself, he
grew angry and killed him while playing with a discus. In addition
Ovid says that he loved Orythia, daughter of the Athenian king
Erichthonius, and asked to marry her; when she was not given to
him, he grew indignant, planned to rape her, and did not hesitate
to do so:[186]

> He shook his feathers, the movements of which
> aired the whole earth and frightened the broad sea.

Pulvereamque trahens per summa cacumina pallam
verrit humum, pavidamque metu caligine tectus
orithiam amans fulvis amplectitur alis.

Et sic illam rapuit, et ex ea Zethum et Calaym filios suscepit.
3 Insuper dicit Omerus in *Yliade*, inducens Eneam Achilli loquentem in pugna, Boream pulcherrimas Dardani adamasse equas et ex
eis equos XII velocissimos suscepisse.

4   A quibus si corticem fabularum amoverimus, advertemus primo
Boream Yacintum, qui flos est et ideo puer, quia nullus diu vivit
flos, amare; hac in forma, quia forte flabat sepissime per prata
plena yacintis, quasi visurus quos diligebat, uti et nos crebro visuri
vadimus quos amamus. Qui Yacintus et ab Apolline, id est a sole,
amabatur, nam et ipse productor talium et spectator, amator etiam
dicitur, et quia talium fotor est, et ideo a Yacinto amari dicitur,
quia una queque res id amare videtur, per quod ad esse deducitur
et perseverat in esse; nam flores et alia sole agente nascuntur et
5 vivunt, quam diu vivunt. A Borea autem ideo occisus dicitur, quia
Boreas horriditate sui flatus cuncta humore privat atque desiccat.

Amasse eum Orythiam hystoria est. Dicit enim Theodontius
Boream iuvenem fuisse Tracem nobilem et animosum, qui tractus
fama matrimonii contracti a Thereo, qui Pandyonis filiam habuerat in coniugem, cum audisset Orythiam Erichthonii Atheniensium regis formosissimam puellam esse, cupidine captus eius petiit
coniugium, quod cum illi negaretur, ob incestum commissum a
Thereo in Phylomenam, quasi similis illi Boreas futurus esset,

And drawing his dusty cloak along the summits and peaks,
he sweeps the ground, and covered in a cloud loves the fearful
Orythia and embraces her with tawny wings.

And so he raped her and by her had his sons Zethus and Calais.
In addition, Homer[187] in his *Iliad*, when introducing Aeneas and 3
having him speak to Achilles in battle, says that Boreas coveted
Dardanus' very beautiful mares and sired twelve of the swiftest
horses by them.

If we remove the fabulous covering from these, we will notice 4
first that Boreas loves Hyacinth, which is a flower and represents a
boy because no flower lives for a long time; he was of this form
because perchance he very often blew through meadows full of
hyacinths to look at those which delighted him, just as we also
frequently go to see those we love. This Hyacinth was loved as
well by Apollo, that is, by the sun, for as one who produces such
flowers and looks upon them, he is also called a lover; and because
he also warms them, he, too, is said to be loved by Hyacinth because each and every thing seems to love that which brings it into
existence and maintains it, for flowers and other things are born
and live, for as long as they live, because of the sun's action. He 5
was therefore said to have been killed by Boreas because Boreas,
by the brutality of its wind, deprives all things of moisture and
dries them.

That he loved Orythia is history: Theodontius says that Boreas
was a Thracian youth, noble and bold; lured by the report of the
marriage agreed upon with Tereus, who had married the daughter
of Pandion, when he had heard that Orythia, the daughter of the
Athenian king Erichthonius, was a very beautiful girl, he was overcome by desire and sought to marry her; and when this was denied to him on account of the incest Tereus forced upon Philo-
mena, thinking that Boreas might intend to imitate him, he
became angry, awaited his opportunity, and raped her, in the

iratus, captato tempore, illam rapuit, anno regni Erichthei nono, et filios ex ea suscepit, et sic fabule locum nomen iuvenis et regio adinvenit.

6   Equos autem Dardani a Borea genitos ideo dici arbitror, quia possibile fuit Dardanum fama bonitatis equorum eius regionis tractum, misisse ibidem, et proletarios assumpsisse, quibus iunctis equabus suis optimos atque veloces suscepit equos, quorum successores eius prolem semper post modum servavere, et hinc sumptum eos Boree filios extitisse.

: 59 :

De Zetho et Calay filiis Boree

1   Zethus et Calays filii fuerunt Boree et Orythie, ex quibus[48] quoniam que leguntur communia sunt, ut de ambobus invicem scriberem necesse fuit, de quibus sic Ovidius:

> Illic et gelidi coniunx Orythia tyranni
> et genitrix facta est, partus enixa gemellos,
> cetera qui matris, pennas genitoris haberent.
> Non tamen has una memorant cum corpore natas,
> barbaque dum rutulis aberat subnixa capillis,
> implumes Calaysque puer Zethusque fuerunt.
> Mox pariter penne ritu cepere volucrum
> cingere utrumque latus, pariter flavescere male,
>
> etc.

Hos insuper testatur Ovidius cum Iasone et aliis Argonautis ad Colcos ivisse. Verum ut dicit Servius, cum a Phyneo rege Arcadie (qui, eo quod suasione nove coniugis filios cecaverat, a diis cecatus

eighth year of Erechtheus' kingship, and had children by her. And so the name of the youth and the place it happened provided the occasion for the fable.

I think they said that the horses of Dardanus were engendered 6 by Boreas because it was possible that Dardanus, lured by the report of the quality of the horses of that region, sent for and received studs from there, and once they were joined to his mares, he received the best and swiftest horses, whose descendants have ever after preserved this strain, and from this it has been assumed that they were the offspring of Boreas.

: 59 :

On Zethus and Calais, sons of Boreas

Zethus and Calais were sons of Boreas and Orythia. Since things 1 are written about them in common, I find it necessary therefore to write about both. Ovid says this:[188]

> There Orythia became the wife of the icy tyrant,
> and a mother, giving birth to twin offspring:
> like their mother in all else, they had the feathers of their father.
> Yet they recount that they were not visible at birth,
> and when no tawny beard was hanging under their hairs,
> wingless was the boy Calais as well as Zetes;
> soon, as birdlike feathers began
> to gird their sides, so did their chins grow blond.

In addition, Ovid[189] bears witness that they went with Jason and the other Argonauts to Colchis. But as Servius[190] says, when they were received by Phineus, King of Arcadia (who, because his new wife had persuaded him to blind his sons, he had himself been

et ipse fuerat, eique ut escas fedarent atque surriperent, arpye obscene aves fuerant apposite) suscepti hospitio remunerationis gratia ad expellendas aves Zethus et Calays, quoniam alati erant, missi

2 sunt. Qui cum illas strictis gladiis persequerentur, ex Arcadia pulsas usque ad insulas, que Plote appellantur, persecuti sunt. Ibi vero monitu Yris ut desisterent Iovis canes ulterius persequi, ad socios redierunt. Que iuvenum conversio nomen immutavit insulis, et ubi Plote dicebantur, Strophades dicte sunt, nam *strophe* Grece, Latine 'conversio' dicitur.

3 Hec ego de istis legisse memini; quid autem habeant sub velamine fictiones, detegendum est. Dicit ergo Ovidius hos post pueritiam pennas habuisse, pro quibus ego intelligo barbam et velocitatem, que in adolescentia hominibus veniunt. Circa autem allegoriam pulsarum ab his arpiarum, dico quod divino munere omnes boni nascimur, et sic prima mortalium coniunx bonitas seu innocentia est. Sed tandem grandiores effecti ut plurimum obiecta innocentia depravamur, et tunc secunda superinducitur uxor, cum quis concupiscibilis appetitus iudicio se trahi permictit, quod in quam perniciosos deducat saltus, Phyneus testis est. Qui auri cupidine occupatus, dum avaritie credit, que secunda illi uxor fuit, filios privat luminibus.

4 Filii autem nostri laudabiles actus sunt, quos tunc privamus lumine, cum illos obscenis operibus deturpamus. Quid enim turpius agere possumus, quam bonam mentem abicere, ut divitias acquiramus? Quod teste Seneca phylosopho, facete Demetrius potenti cuidam libertino dixit, facilem scilicet sibi esse ad divitias viam, quo die penituisset bone mentis. Sic et nos ceci efficimur, quando ob census desiderium nimium in rapinas et turpia lucra delabimur.

5 Apponuntur enim talibus Arpye fede volucres atque rapaces, quas ego mordaces avarorum curas et sollicitudines intelligo, a quibus

blinded by the gods and beset with Harpies, polluted birds charged with befouling and snatching up his food), as repayment for his hospitality Zetes and Calais, because they were winged, were sent to expel the birds. After pursuing them with drawn swords, they 2 drove them from Arcadia, and pursued them to the islands which are called Plotae. There, warned by Iris to desist from pursuing the hounds of Jupiter any further, they returned to their comrades. That turning point of the young men changed the name of the islands, from Plotae to Strophades, for *strophe* in Greek means "turning point."

This is what I remember reading about them, but the veil cov- 3 ering these fictions must be lifted. Ovid says they developed their feathers after boyhood, by which I understand whiskers and swiftness, which arrive in adolescent men. About the allegory of the Harpies they drove away I say that we are all by divine gift born good, and so the first wife of mortals is goodness or innocence. But as we mature for the most part we reject our innocence and are corrupted, and then a second wife is brought in when some excessive appetite divorces itself from judgment by enticing us to make pernicious leaps toward satisfying it. Phineus provides the evidence: possessed by his desire for gold, while he trusted his avarice, which was his second wife, he deprived his sons of their sight.

The sons are our praiseworthy actions which we deprive of 4 their sight by disfiguring them with foul deeds. For what can we do that is more shameful than to discard a good mind to acquire riches? With Seneca[191] the philosopher as witness, this is what Demetrius says facetiously to a certain powerful freedman, namely, that the road to riches is easy the day one loses his good mind. So also we become blind when an excessive desire for wealth leads us to descend into plundering and shameful profiteering. Represent- 5 ing this are the foul Harpies, swift and rapacious, which I understand as the biting cares and anxieties of the greedy; and therefore

ideo avaris surripi dicuntur dapes, quia dum talibus detinentur cogitationibus, avari in tam grandem sui oblivionem veniunt, ut etiam aliquando cibum sumere efficiantur immemores, seu dum auri cumulum augere satagunt, sibi ipsis cibos extenuant et sua miseria fedos faciant.

6   Argonaute, qui apud hunc hospitantur, quoniam illustres omnes iuvenes fuere et virtute conspicui, loco salubrium consiliorum sumendi sunt, que etsi egre suscipiantur a talibus, suscipiuntur tamen aliquando, et suscepta, loco muneris retribuunt boni inquisitionem, que secundum Fulgentium pro Zetho et Calay intelligi-

7   tur. Hec autem boni, id est veritatis inquisitio agit ut canes Iovis, id est mordaces cure et alienis bonis continue inhyantes pellantur usque ad Strophades, id est usque ad conversionem animi perquirentis bonum. Que conversio esse non potest, nisi omissis viciis et concupiscientiis in virtutem quis egressus dirigat suos, et tunc remanet a sordibus desideriorum turpium immunis mensa Phynei.

8   Sane Leontius longe brevius huius sensum expedit. Dicit enim hystoriam hanc fuisse talem: Phyneum ditissimum fuisse regem Arcadie et avarum, et mortua Stenoboe coniuge, ex qua Palemonem et Phyneum susceperat filios, superinduxit Arpalycem Boree filiam et sororem Zethi et Calay, cuius precibus ipse filios excecavit; quod scientes pyrrate, qui Plotas insulas incolebant, quasi in destitutum auxiliis et odiosum suis ob scelus commissum in filios venere, et obsederunt eum, et machinis erectis usque in regiam putrida sordesque iaciebant; tandem venientibus Zetho et Calay, vocatis cum longis navibus, eum liberaverunt obsidione, pyrratasque usque ad Strophades repulere.

they are said to steal away with the food of a greedy man because the greedy, hindered by such thoughts, enter into such comprehensive oblivion that they sometimes mindlessly forget about eating, or, when busying themselves with increasing their pile of gold, they reduce the food they eat and foul themselves with their misery.

Because the Argonauts hosted by Phineus were all illustrious 6 youths and conspicuous in virtue, they must be understood to represent salubrious counsels which, although accepted badly by such people, nonetheless are accepted sometimes. And when they are accepted, in place of a gift they make an inquiry into the good which, according to Fulgentius,[192] Zethus and Calais represent. This inquiry into the good, that is, the search for truth, made it so 7 that the hounds of Jupiter, that is, the biting cares and incessant desires for others' goods, are driven as far as the Strophades, that is, to the turning point of the mind inquiring after good. This turning point cannot exist unless, with vices and grand desires forgotten, someone directs his steps toward virtue, and then Phineus' table remains immune from the squalor of shameful desires.

Leontius offered a more expeditious interpretation of this, for 8 he says that this was the history of those events. Phineus was the richest king of Arcadia and greedy, and after the death of his wife Stheneboea, from whom he received his sons Palaemon and Phineus, he brought in Harpalyce, daughter of Boreas and sister of Zethus and Calais. She pleaded with him to blind his sons. Pirates who used to inhabit the islands of Plotae knew this, and they besieged him, expecting to find him destitute of aid and in disfavor with his own people on account of his crime against his sons. With siege engines erected as far as the royal palace, they threw rotten and filthy objects. Finally, when Zethus and Calais, who had been invited in with their long ships, arrived, they freed him from the siege and drove the pirates back to the Strophades.

: 60 :

De Arpalyce Boree filia et Phynei coniuge

1 Arpalices, ut dicit Leontius, filia fuit Boree, ex qua matre non dicit. Hec Phyneo regi Arcadie nupta fuit, ut supra proximo patet, et infesta privignis.

: 61 :

De Zephyro vento et Affrico
et Coro collateralibus, filiis Astrei

1 Zephyrus ventus est occiduus, qui a Latinis vocatur Favonius, complexione frigidus et humidus, temperate tamen. Hyemem autem resolvit et germina floresque producit, et dicitur Zephyrus a Zephs Grece, quod Latine 'vita' sonat. Favonius autem eo quod 'foveat' germinantia vel 'faveat' germinibus; flat enim suaviter et placide a meridie usque in noctem, a principio veris usque ad estatis finem. A dextris eius Affricus ponitur, qui tempestuosus fulmina et tonitrua generat. A sinistris autem eius Chorus, qui, ut Beda dicit, in oriente nubilosum aerem facit, cum serenum faciat in occiduo. De Zephyro talis recitatur fabula. Nynpham fuisse scilicet nomine Clorim, a Zephyro dilectam, et in coniugem assumptam, eique ab eo in munus amoris atque violate pudicitie omne ius in flores concessum, eamque ex Clora Floram vocavit. Preterea refert Omerus in *Yliade* hunc Tyellam compressisse Arpyam, et ex ea Xantum et Balium Achillis equos suscepisse.

: 60 :

On Harpalyce, daughter of Boreas and wife of Phineus

Harpalyce, as Leontius says, was the daughter of Boreas; by what   1
mother he does not say. She married Phineus, King of Arcadia, as
was made clear just above, and was hostile to her stepsons.

: 61 :

On the Wind Zephyr and its Collaterals, Africus
and Corus, sons of Astraeus

Zephyr was the West wind, Favonius for the Latins. Cold and   1
moist in complexion, but temperate nonetheless, Favonius brings
an end to winter and produces seeds and flowers. In Greek Zephyr
is Zephs, which means "life," while the Latin Favonius "fosters"
[*foveat*] seeding or "favors" [*faveat*] the seeded, blowing gently and
calmly from the south into the night from the beginning of spring
to the end of summer. On his right is placed tempestuous Africus,   2
who generates lightning and thunder. On his left is Corus, who, as
Bede[193] says, makes cloudy air in the East, though he makes it serene in the West. The following fable is told about Zephyr, namely,
that there was a nymph by the name of Chloris loved by Zephyr
and taken as his wife, and to her as his tribute of love and for her
violated chastity he bestowed upon her the responsibility for flowers, and he changed her name from Chloris to Flora. In addition,
Homer[194] in the *Iliad* reports that he copulated with the Harpy
Thyella,[195] and from her he received Xanthus and Balius, the
horses of Achilles.

3   Harum fabularum intensio talis esse potest. Dicit Lactantius in libro *Institutionum divinarum* Floram feminam magnas ex meretricio quesisse opes, quarum moriens Romanum populum scripsit heredem, parte servata, que sub annuo fenore prestaretur, ex quo scilicet fenore voluit, ut suus natalis dies singulis annis editione lu-

4   dorum celebraretur. Qui ludi Florales et sacra Floralia a Flora nuncupata sunt, quod quia senatui tractu temporis flagitiosum visum est, cum timore plebis retractare non posset, ab ipso meretricis nomine argumentum sumi placuit, ut rei pudende dignitas adderetur, et inde finxerunt Floram floribus preesse, eam oportere ludis placare, ut fruges cum arboribus aut vitibus bene prospere-

5   que florerent; quem colorem secutus Ovidius, nynpham non ignobilem Zephyro nuptam et dotalitio munere, ut floribus preesset, accepisse a sponso. Qui ludi, ut dicit Lactantius, memorie meretricis conveniunt; nam omni lascivia et verborum licentia, quibus omnis obscenitas effunditur, positis flagitante populo a meretricibus vestimentis, que ludis in illis mymorum fungebantur officio, celebrantur.

6   Ex Tyella autem Arpya equos suscepisse, nescio quid velit Omerus, nisi id forte, quod apud Olisbonem extremum Hyspanie in occiduum oppidum equas facere consuevisse apud Plinium Secun-

7   dum legimus. Quas dicit Plinius in concupiscientiam prolis suscipiende venientes hyulco gutture consuevisse flantes Zephyros suscipere, et ex eis concipere et parere velocissimos equos brevi tamen evo valentes. Sic forsan ex equa cui nomen erat *Thyella*, que 'impetus' seu 'procella' interpretatur, factum est, vel ut supra de equis Dardani ex Borea conceptis diximus.

The purpose of these fables could be the following. Lactan- 3
tius[196] says in his *Divine Institutes* that Flora was a woman who had
acquired great wealth from prostitution, and when she died she
named as heir the Roman people, reserving a portion which made
annual interest, and she wanted this interest to pay for her birthday celebration annually with a performance of games. These 4
games were named the Florales and the sacred Floralia were named
after Flora. After some time the senate thought of this as scandalous. Because their fear of the common people prevented them
from canceling it, the senate decided upon a stratagem that would
bring dignity to the name of this shameful thing: they fabricated
the story that Flora was in charge of flowers and needed to be appeased with games so that fruits, along with trees and vines, would
prosper and flower productively. Lactantius says that Ovid[197] fol- 5
lowed this coloring of the fable in saying that she was a noble
nymph who married Zephyr, and as a wedding gift her husband
put her in charge of flowers. These games, as Lactantius continues,
accord with the memory of a prostitute, for they were celebrated
with every wantonness and license of words; the people poured
out every obscenity and demanded that the prostitutes, who in
those games performed the function of mimes, take off their
clothes.

In that he received horses from the Harpy Thyella, I do not 6
know what Homer wanted unless it was perhaps that which we
read in the second Pliny, that in Lisbon, the last town of Spain in
the west, they used to breed mares. Pliny[198] says that when they 7
developed a desire for having offspring, they would inhale blowing
Zephyrs into their gaping throat; this would cause conception and
they would foal horses that were extremely swift, although short-
lived. So perhaps this comes from a mare named Thyella, which
means "force" or "gale," or, as we said above, from the horses of
Dardanus sired by Boreas.

: 62 :

De Aloo Titanis X° filio

1 Alous, ut ait Theodontius, filius fuit Titanis et Terre, cui coniunx fuit, ut etiam Servius asserit, Yphymedia. Quam cum violasset Neptunus, duos ex eo peperit filios, Othum et Ephyaltem, quos Alous educavit ut suos, et cum novem digitis, ut dicit Servius, singulis mensibus crescerent, parantibus Gigantibus bellum adversus superos, nec ob senium Alous ad illud posset accedere, hos misit geminos adiutores, de quibus ubi de filiis Neptuni dicemus.

: 63 :

De Pallene XI° Titanis filio, qui genuit Minervam

1 Pallenem seu Pallantem unum fuisse ex filiis Titanis dicit Paulus, insulamque in Egeo mari tenuisse, et a se denominasse Pallenem, hominem immanem et superis adversum plurimum, cuius Luca-
2 nus meminit dicens, 'Pallenea Iovi mutavit fulmina cyclops.' Hunc dicit idem Paulus a Minerva in bello adversus Iovem facto occisum, et ob id eam Palladem cognominatam. Et alibi dicit idem
3 Paulus eum ob eius sevitiam ante bellum a Iove fulminatum. Sane Theodontius ei dicit fuisse filiam, nomine Minervam, a qua, cum illi conaretur virginitatem surripere, occisus est.

: 62 :

On Alous, tenth child of Titan

Alous, as Theodontius says, was the son of Titan and Earth, and 1
his wife, as also Servius[199] asserts, was Iphimedia. After Neptune
violated her, she produced two sons by him, Otus and Ephialtes,
whom Alous brought up as his own. Because they grew, as Servius
says, by nine fingers every month, when the Giants were preparing
their war against the gods and Alous could not join in because of
his old age, he substituted his two sons, whom we will discuss in
the chapter on the sons of Neptune.[200]

: 63 :

On Pallene, eleventh child of Titan, who fathered Minerva

Paul says that Pallene or Pallantes was one of the sons of Titan, 1
that he ruled an island in the Aegean Sea, that it was named Pallene after him, that he was a huge man, and that he was very
hostile to the gods. Lucan made mention of him, saying,[201] "Cyclops changed the Pallenean thunderbolts for Jupiter." Paul also 2
said that he was killed by Minerva in the war waged against Jupiter, and for this reason she received the epithet Pallas. Also, elsewhere Paul again says that before the war he was struck by Jupiter's thunderbolt on account of his savagery. But Theodontius says 3
that he had a daughter, Minerva by name, who killed him when he
attempted to steal away her virginity.

: 64 :

De Minerva Pallenis filia

1   Minerva, ut supra proximo patet iuxta Theodontium, filia fuit Pallantis, a se ob virginitatem tutandam occisi. Hec, ut Tullius dicit, ubi *De naturis deorum*, inter plures alias Minervas quinta fuit, eique ait ab antiquis pinnata apponi talaria, seu quia occiso patre velox fuerit ad fugam, seu ob aliam causam factum sit.

: 65 :

De Runco et Purpureo XII° et XIII° filiis Titanis

1   Runcus et Purpureus, ut asserit Priscianus in maiori volumine, filii fuere Titanis et Terre, quorum ait Nevium poetam meminisse aientem:

> Inerant signa expressa quomodo Titani,
> bicorpores Athlantes
> Runcus atque Purpureus filii terras (pro 'terre'),
>
> > etc.

2   Et Oratius in *Odis* ait, 'Aut quid[49] minaci Porphyrion statu.' De his autem aliud legisse non memini.

: 64 :

On Minerva, daughter of Pallene

Minerva, as Theodontius makes clear just above, was the daughter   1
of Pallantes, who was killed by her to protect her virginity. She, as
Cicero[202] says in his *On the Nature of the Gods*, was fifth among
several other Minervas. He also says the ancients assigned her
winged sandals either because she fled quickly after killing her father, or for another reason.

: 65 :

On Rhuncus and Purpureus, twelfth
and thirteenth children of Titan

Rhuncus and Purpureus, as Priscian[203] asserts in his larger book,   1
were sons of Titan and Earth, about whom he says that the poet
Naevius made mention, saying:

Therein were images representing how the Titans,
two-bodied Atlases,
Rhuncus and Purpureus, sons of earth . . .

And in his *Odes* Horace says,[204] "Or what Porphyrion with his   2
menacing stature . . ." But I do not remember reading anything
else about them.

: 66 :

De Lycaone XIIII° Titanis filio, qui genuit Calystonem

1 Lycaonem Arcadie regem dicit Theodontius, quod nusquam alibi legi, filium fuisse Titanis et Terre, seu ob splendorem regium, seu ob insigne aliquod facinus, seu, quod potius credo, quia nequam fuit homo et deorum spretor atque vilipensor, sicut plurimum legimus fuisse Titanes.

2 Ex eo autem talem refert Ovidius fabulam. Cum ascendisset in celum mortalium clamor quoniam omnia male agerentur in terris, voluit Iuppiter experiri presentia, et forma hominis sumpta devenit in regiam Lycaonis, egitque ut adverterent populi quia deus esset in terris; qui cum sacris operam darent, a Lycaone risi sunt omnes.

3 Qui tamen ut experiretur nunquid, ut dicebantur, hospes suus Iuppiter esset, conspirassetque in nocturnam eius necem, nec peregisse potuisset, ad aliud facinus repente intendit animum, et occiso ex obsidibus Molossorum uno, undis partim, partimque prunis excoqui iussit, et illum comedendum Iovi apposuit. Qui cum cognovisset scelus sprevissetque cibum, ignem in regiam Lycaonis iniecit et abiit. Lycaon autem territus abiit in silvas, et in lupum versus morem rapine pristinum servare cepit, in greges seviens sanguinis aviditate.

4 Sub hac fabula hystoriam esse talem dicebat Leontius. Fuit olim inter Epyros, ex quibus aliqui postea a Molosso Pyrri filio Molossi dicti sunt, et Pelasgos, qui postea Arcades, controversia, de qua cum in concordiam itum esset, petiit Lycaon, qui tunc preerat Pelasgis, ut sibi in robur inite concordie daretur saltem

: 66 :

On Lycaon, fourteenth child of Titan, who fathered Callisto

Theodontius says that Lycaon, the King of Arcadia — something I   1
have not read elsewhere — was the son of Titan and Earth, be it on
account of the royal splendor or on account of some conspicuous
crime, or, what I prefer to believe, because he was a wicked man,
who despised and scorned the gods, very much as we have read
about most of the Titans.

Ovid[205] tells the following story about him. When the clamor   2
of mortals suffering from all the evils occurring across the earth
had risen to the sky, Jupiter wanted firsthand experience. And so,
after assuming human form, he came down to the palace of Lycaon and acted in such a way that people would notice that there
was a god on earth. But when they went about making sacrifice,
Lycaon laughed at all of them. To test whether, as was being re-   3
ported, his guest was Jupiter, he had planned to kill him at night
but was not able to succeed, so he immediately planned another
crime: killing one of the Molossian hostages, he gave orders to
cook him, first boiling him in water, then grilling him over char-
coals, and then he served him as a meal to Jupiter. Jupiter recognized the crime and refused the meal, and then he set Lycaon's
palace on fire and departed. Terrified, Lycaon went into the forest,
and turned into a wolf, thereby preserving his former habit of rapacious behavior, raging against flocks in his desire for blood.

Leontius used to say that behind this fable there is the follow-   4
ing history. There was once a dispute among the Epirotes, some of
whom were later said by Molossus, son of Pyrrhus, to be Molossians, and the Pelasgians, who afterward were called Arcadians.
Lycaon was in charge of the Pelasgians when they reached an
agreement, but because the Molossians were initially responsible

obses unus ab Epyris, eo quod ab eis fuisset primitus exorta discordia. Cui a Molossis usque ad certum tempus iuvenis unus ex nobilioribus concessus est. Qui cum non remicteretur in termino a
5 Lycaone, per legatos gentis sue requisitus est. Lycaon autem, seu quia superbe requisitus videretur, seu ob aliam causam turbatus, eo quod pessimus esset homo et inflati animi, respondit legatis se in sequenti die obsidem redditurum, iussitque ut mane sequenti secum in convivio essent, et clam obside occiso atque decocto legatis aliisque convivantibus iussit apponi.

6   Erat forte inter eos epulans iuvenis adhuc Lysanias, is qui postea Iuppiter dictus est, homo ea tempestate apud Arcades existimationis permaxime, qui cum membra humana novisset, eiectis mensis turbatus atrocitate facinoris, prosilivit in publicum et in Lycaonem, sibi faventibus popularibus omnibus, evestigio conspiravit, et congregatis viribus eum traxit in pugnam, superatumque regno privavit.[50] Lycaon autem deiectus exul et inops cum paucis fugit in silvas, et cepit itineribus insidiari et raptu vivere, quod fabule locum dedit, quod in lupum versus sit.

    Nam si rite velimus inspicere, nulli dubium esse debet, quin quam cito ad avaritiam et rapinam mentem apponimus, humanitate exuti, lupum e vestigio induamus atque tam diu perseveramus in lupum, quam diu talis appetitus perseverat in nobis, humana
7 tantum reservata effigie. Dicebat insuper Leontius alios affirmare Lycaonem in verum lupum fuisse conversum, asserentibus talibus in Arcadia lacum fore, quem si quis transnatasset, illico transformabatur in lupum, et si a carnibus abstinuisset humanis, et anno nono transacto lacum eundem iterum transnatasset, ei forma pris-

for the disagreement, Lycaon sought to strengthen this initial accord by demanding at least one Epirote hostage. The Molossians did offer him one of their young nobles for a certain amount of time, but when Lycaon did not send him back at the end of the period, envoys from their people sought his return. Lycaon, 5 whether it was that the request seemed arrogant or that he was troubled for some other reason, proved to be the worst and most prideful of men by promising the legates to return the hostage the next day, ordering them to join him for a banquet the next morning, and, having secretly killed and cooked the hostage, ordered him to be served to the legates and other banqueters.

There was by chance among them a young diner, Lysanias — he 6 was afterward called Jupiter — a man who at that time was held in the highest esteem by the Arcadians, who had recognized the human limbs, and, disturbed by the atrocity of the crime, turned over the tables and rushed out into public and immediately conspired against Lycaon and gained the support of all the people; with his forces gathered, he dragged Lycaon into a fight, defeated him, and forced him from the kingdom. Forced into exile and without resources, Lycaon fled with few things into the forests and began to live by ambushing travelers and robbing them, and this gave rise to the fable that he was turned into a wolf.

If we wish to examine this properly, without question we should immediately turn our attention to avarice and rapine, which is to say that when we cast off humanity we immediately clothe ourselves as the wolf, and we continue as the wolf for a long time, as long as that sort of appetite continues in us, preserving only our human likeness. In addition, Leontius used to say that others 7 affirm that Lycaon was turned into an actual wolf, for they assert that in Arcadia there was a lake and that whoever swam across it would be transformed into a wolf, and that if he abstained from human meat and swam across the same lake a second time after a period of nine years, he would be restored to his original form.

tina reddebatur. Quod sciens Lycaon et plurimum Iovis iram timens atque suorum, et ob suam perfidiam ignorans quo satis tutam posset habere latebram, ad expectandum absque suspicione vite rei exitum, lacum transnavit et verus lupus effectus, inter alia eiusdem speciei animalia, abitavit in silvis, relicta filia unica virgine Calistone.

8   Preterea[51] scribit Plinius in libro *Naturalis hystorie*, bellorum indutias huius Lycaonis inventum fuisse, ludorumque gimnicorum in Arcadia.

: 67 :

De Calystone filia Lycaonis et matre Arcadis

1 Calisto filia fuit Lycaonis, ut satis per Ovidium patet. Hec, ut scribit Paulus, iam patre fugato inter rerum tumultum adhuc virgo, clam regiam exivit et aufugit ad nemora, ubi se virginibus Diane dicatis sociam iunxit, apud quas a Iove, in habitu transformato Diane, oppressa est. Et cum turgescente utero appareret crimen,

2 pulsa peperit Arcadem. De quibus ambobus plene infra ubi de Arcade dicetur, et ea potissime, que a Leontio de fictione relata sunt.

3   Sane hec pluribus est appellata nominibus. Nam Grece Arthos dicitur, quod Latine sonat 'ursa.' Preterea et Elyce dicitur a giri circuitione, nam Grece *elyaci* dicuntur 'giri.' Nuncupatur etiam Cynosura, quod nomen ante duo fuerunt nomina, *cynos* scilicet quod sonat Latine 'canis' (nam ymago celestis, que postea ursa dicta est, canis dicebatur, et forte adhuc apud quosdam dicitur), et

4 *uros*, quod Latine 'silvestris bos' sonat. Nam et eodem nomine dicta

Knowing this and fearing the wrath of Jupiter and his people, and not knowing where he could hide safely enough after all his treachery, hoping above all to save his life, Lycaon swam across the lake and became a true wolf, living among the other animals of his species in the forest, leaving behind a single maiden, Callisto.

In addition, Pliny[206] in his *Natural History* writes that military 8 truces were the invention of this Lycaon, as were gymnastic games in Arcadia.

: 67 :

On Callisto, daughter of Lycaon and mother of Arcas

Callisto was the daughter of Lycaon, as Ovid[207] makes clear. She, 1 as Paul writes, still a maiden when her father had already fled amidst the tumult of events, secretly left the palace and fled to the woods, where she joined the maidens consecrated to Diana; while she was their companion she was impregnated by Jupiter after he had transformed himself into the appearance of Diana. When her belly began to swell her condition became apparent, so after she was driven out, she gave birth to Arcas. There will be a full discus- 2 sion about both of these below in the chapter on Arcas,[208] especially what Leontius said about this fiction.

Callisto is called by several names, for in Greek she is called 3 Arthos which means "bear." In addition, she is also called Helice from "in the course of the circuit," for in Greek *elici* mean "circuits." She is also called Cynosura, a name which before was two names, namely, because *cynos* means "dog" — her celestial image, which afterward was called the bear, used to be called the dog, and perhaps still is by some — and *uros* which means "wild ox." She is called by 4

est, propter elevatam caudam ad semicirculi formam, quod magis ad silvestrem bovem spectat, quam ad canem faciat, aut ursam; nam sic, ut dicitur, fert silvestris bos caudam elevatam, ut semicirculum facere videatur. Appellatur et Phenix, sic volente Thalete inventore, qui Phenix et ipse fuit, seu quia Phenices, qui instructissimi fuere naute, ea in navigatione primi sint usi. Dicitur et Septentrio quod etiam Arcadi, seu maiori urse, nomen est, eo quod a septem denotetur stellis, nam *tryon* seu *teron* 'stella' interpretatur.

: 68 :

De Gigantibus ex sanguine Titanorum procreatis et Terra

1 Gigantes, ut Paulus et Theodontius testantur, nati sunt ex sanguine Titanorum et Terra, quod etiam testari videtur Ovidius, dicens:[52]

Obruta mole sua cum corpora dira iacerent,
perfusam[53] multo natorum sanguine Terram
immaduisse ferunt calidumque animasse cruorem,
et, ne nulla sue stirpis monimenta manerent,
in faciem vertisse hominum; sed et illa propago
contemptrix superum seveque avidissima cedis
et violenta fuit: scires de sanguine natos,

etc.

2 Hos Theodontius dicit pedes anguium habuisse et bellum movisse Iovi, ut patres fecerant; verum nil ausus, donec Egla speciosissima mulierum et coniunx Panis a Terra matre eorum celaretur in specu. Qua occultata, extemplo in deos fecere impetum atque eos adeo terruere, ut in Egyptum usque formis mutatis expellerent.

that same name on account of her tail raised in the form of a semicircle, which looks more toward the wild ox than it does the dog or bear, for it is said, that a wild ox carries its tale as if forming a semicircle. She is also called Phoenix; the inventor Thales,[209] who was himself Phoenician, wanted it so, or else the Phoenicians, who were the most skilled sailors, first used her in navigation. She is also called Septentrio which is also the name of Arcas, or Ursa Major, because she is marked out by "seven" [*septem*] stars, and *tryon* or *teron* means "star."

: 68 :

On the Giants born from the blood of the Titans and Earth

The Giants, as Paul and Theodontius bear witness, were born 1
from the blood of the Titans and Earth. Ovid seems to bear witness to this as well, saying:[210]

> When their fearful bodies lay crushed by their own mass,
> Earth, much suffused by the blood of her sons,
> they say was wet and revived the warm gore,
> and so that some monument of her offspring might remain,
> formed them in the appearance of men; but that breed as well
> was contemptuous of the gods and most avid for savage killing
> and was violent: you would know them to be born from blood.

Theodontius says they had feet of snakes and made war on Jupiter, 2
as had their fathers, but they dared nothing until Aegla, the most beautiful of women and the wife of Pan, was hidden in a chasm by their mother, Earth. Once she was concealed, they immediately made an attack on the gods and so terrified them that they drove them into Egypt and changed their shapes.

3   De quibus sic dicit Ovidius:

> Emissumque ima de sede Tiphea terre
> celitibus fecisse metum, cunctosque dedisse
> terga fuge, donec fessos Egyptia tellus
> ceperit et septem discretus in hostia Nylus.
> Huc quoque terrigenam venisse Typhea narrat,
> et se mentitis superos celasse figuris.
> 'Duxque gregis,' dixit, 'fit Iuppiter, inde recurvis
> nunc quoque formatus Lybie est cum cornibus Amon.
> Delyus in corvo, proles Semeleia capro,
> Phele soror Phebi, nivea Saturnia vacca,
> Pisce Venus latuit, Cyllenius ibidis ales,'

etc.

4   Verum in aliquibus Theodontius et Ovidius dissentire videntur, cum Theodontius dicat a Gigantibus hoc factum, et Ovidius dicat Typheum ex imo terre venisse atque fecisse. Preterea et in formis deorum. Nam dicit Theodontius Iovem in aquilam versum, Cybelem in merulam, Venerem in anguillam, Pana autem se in fluvium fere totum deiecisse; superiorem vero partem que remansit in ripa in hyrcum mutatam dicit, que intravit fluviam in piscem, ex qua figura postea Iovem Capricornii signum fecisse dicit. Tandem Iovem asserit oraculo habuisse, si victoriam vellet, clipeum ex Egla Panis coniuge tegeret, et caput suum Gorgone. Quo facto presente Pallade, fugati sunt atque obruti Gigantes et apud inferos a Iovi detrusi.

5   Multa his dictis superdicenda veniunt, si fictionum velimus ambages resolvere. Sed ante alia non omnino fictum est fuisse gigantes, id est homines forma seu statura ultra modum ceteros excedentes, imo constat esse verissimum et liquido his diebus apud[54] Drepanum Sycilie oppidum fortuitus demonstravit eventus. Nam

Ovid says this about it:[211]   3

> That Typhoeus, emerged from earth's bottommost seats,
> frightened the heavenly dwellers, and that they all turned
> their backs in flight until in their weariness the Egyptian land
> and the Nile with its seven distinct mouths embraced them.
> She tells how the earthborn Typhoeus came even here
> and how the gods concealed themselves in deceptive shapes;
> "Jupiter," she said, "was the leader of the flock, whence
> even now Libyan Ammon is fashioned with horns bent back;
> the Delian turned into a crow, Semele's child a goat,
> Phoebus' sister a cat, Saturn's daughter a snowy white cow,
> Venus hid as a fish, and the Cyllenian as a winged ibis."

Theodontius and Ovid seem to disagree in some matters, for   4
Theodontius says that this was done by the Giants, and Ovid says
that Typhoeus came from the bottom of the earth to do it. They
seem to disagree also in the forms of the gods, for Theodontius
says that Jupiter turned into an eagle, Cybele into a blackbird,
Venus into an eel, and that Pan almost submerged himself completely into a river. He says the upper part which remained on the
bank was changed into a he-goat, that which entered into the river
into a fish, and he says that from this figure Jupiter later made the
sign of Capricorn. Then he asserts that Jupiter heard from an oracle that if he wanted victory he should cover his shield with Aegla,
wife of Pan, and his head with the Gorgon. Doing so in the presence of Pallas, he put the Giants to flight, soundly defeated them,
and thrust them down into the nether regions.

Many things must be said in addition to this if we wish to solve   5
the mysteries of these fictions, but before anything it must be said
that it is not altogether fiction that there were giants, that is, men
surpassing others exceedingly in form or stature. In fact, it is evident that it is very much the truth, and in these days a fortuitous
event in Trapani, a Sicilian town, clearly demonstrates this: when

cum in radicibus montis, qui supereminet Drepano, haud longe ab oppido, nonnulli agrestes ad construendam pastoralem domum fundamenta foderent, apparuit caverne cuiusdam introitus, quem cum visuri, quidnam intus esset, faculis incensis fossores intrassent
6 avidi, antrum summe altitudinis atque amplitudinis invenere. Per quod incedentes in oppositum introitus ingentis magnitudinis sedentem viderunt hominem, ex quo terrefacti repente fugam arripientes exivere antrum, nec ante tenuere cursum, quam in oppidum devenissent occurrentibus quid viderant nuntiantes.

7   Mirabundi autem cives visuri quidnam mali hoc esset, incensis funalibus armisque sumptis, quasi in hostem unanimes exivere civitatem, et ultra trecentos intravere specum, videruntque non minus quam primi stupidi quem retulerant villici. Tandem proximiores facti, postquam non vivum esse hominem norunt, viderunt sedentem quendam in sede, et sinistra manu innixum baculo tante altitudinis atque grossitiei, ut excederet quemcunque pregrandis
8 navigii malum; sic et hominem invise atque inaudite amplitudinis, nulla ex parte corrosum aut diminutum. Et cum ex eis unus porrecta manu tetigisset stantem malum, evestigio malus solutus in cinerem corruit, remansit quasi veste nudatus baculus alter plumbeus ad manum usque tenentis ascendens, et ut satis adverterunt, plumbum erat ad augendam gravedinem malo infusum, quod postea ponderantes asserunt, qui viderunt, fuisse ponderis xv chintariorum Drepanensium, quorum unusquisque ponderis est librarum comunium centum.[55] Demum hominis statura tacta eque
9 corruit, et in pulverem fere omnis versa est. Quem cum non nulli tractarent manibus, tres dentes adhuc solidi comperti sunt monstruose granditie, ponderis autem erant trium rotulorum, id est centum comunium unciarum.

at the foot of a mountain which stands above Trapani not far from town some peasants building a rural house were digging its foundations, they came upon the entrance to a certain cavern. When the excavators, with their torches lit, eagerly entered this to see what was inside, they discovered a grotto of the greatest height and width. Continuing inside this grotto they saw sitting opposite 6 the entrance a man of huge magnitude. Frightened by him they quickly took flight and left the cave, nor did they stop running until they reached town, where they told those whom they encountered what they had seen.

The citizens were in wonder and wanted to see what this evil 7 was, so after lighting torches and arming themselves with weapons, they left the city together, as they would against an enemy; more than three hundred entered the grotto, and, no less astonished, they saw what the workers had reported. Then, getting a little closer, after they ascertained that the man was not living, they saw this human form sitting on a seat, resting with his left hand on a staff of such height and mass that it exceeded the mast of a great ship, and that he was a man of a size not seen or heard 8 of, and nowhere gnawed at or mutilated. When one of them stretched out his hand and touched the upright staff, the staff immediately disintegrated and turned to ash, but there remained, as if bared of its vestments, another staff of lead rising toward the hand of the one holding it. They examined this staff closely and found that lead had been poured into it to increase its weight. Later, after weighing it, those who saw it assert that it weighed fifteen Trapanese hundredweights, one of these being the weight of one hundred common pounds. Then, when the body of the 9 man was touched, it too fell apart, nearly completely turning into dust. When some of them examined it, they found still intact three teeth of monstrous size, the weight of three *rotuli*, that is, one hundred common ounces.

Quos Drepanites, in testimonium comperti gigantis et sempiternam posteritate memoriam, filo alligavere ferreo, et suspendere in quadam civitatis ecclesia in honorem Adnuntiate Virginis edita,

10 et eiusdem titulo insignita. Preterea et partem cranei anteriorem invenere firmissimam adhuc, et plurium frumenti modiorum capacem. Sic et os alterius cruris, cuius etsi ob annositatem nimia pars in putredinem devenisset, perceptum tamen in reliquo est ab his, qui totam hominis altitudinem ad mensuram cuiuscunque minimi ossis novere, eum fuisse magnitudinis ducentorum cubitorum vel amplius.

Suspicatumque est a quibusdam ex prudentioribus hunc fuisse Ericem, loci potentissimum regem, Butis et Veneris filium, ab

11 Hercule occisum et in eodem monte conditum. Quidam autem arbitrabantur Entellum, qui olim in funeribus ludis ab Enea pro Anchise patre editis pugno taurum occiderat. Alii vero unum ex Cyclopibus, et potissime Polyphemum, de quo multa Homerus. Et post quem[56] de eodem sic scripsit Virgilius:

Vix ea fatus erat, summo cum monte videmus
ipsum inter pecudes vasta se mole moventem
pastorem Polyphemum et litora nota petentem,
monstrum horrendum ingens cui lumen ademptum.
Trunca manu pinus regit et vestigia firmat.

Et post pauca sequitur:

Dentibus infrendens gemitu graditurque per equor
iam medium, nec dum fluctus latera ardua tinxit.

Et alia plura que ad magnitudinem Cyclopum designandam tendunt, et potius ad veritatem rei spectantia quam ad yperbolem, qua multi eo ibidem uti arbitrantur.

To preserve evidence of the giant they had found and to create an eternal memorial for posterity, the people of Drepanum bound the remains in an iron netting and hung them in a local church sacred to the honor of the Annunciation of the Virgin, and known by that name. In addition, they found the front part of the cra- 10 nium still very solid and large enough to hold several pecks of grain. They also found the bone of one leg, even if much of it had rotted on account of its age; nonetheless those who know how to measure the total height of a man from the tiniest bone calculated from this remnant that he was two hundred cubits or more in height.

Some of the more learned men supposed that he was Eryx, a very powerful king of that area, son of Butes and Venus, killed by Hercules and hidden in that mountain. Some thought he was 11 Entellus, who in the funeral games given by Aeneas long ago in honor of Anchises had killed a bull with his fist. Still others thought he was one of the Cyclopes, and quite possibly Polyphemus, about whom Homer[212] says much. Vergil wrote this about him:[213]

> Scarcely had he spoken when we saw on the mountain top
> among the flocks moving himself in a vast mass
> and seeking known shores the shepherd Polyphemus,
> a horrendous portent, vast, his eye taken from him.
> a pine trunk guided his hand and firmed his steps.

And after a few lines he continues:

> Gnashing his teeth with a groan, he wades through the sea,
> off shore now the waves do not yet lap his towering sides.

He says even more lines which go toward describing the size of the Cyclopes, looking rather toward the truth than toward the hyperbole many decide to use in this matter.

12   Fuere igitur ingentes stature Gigantes, quod et sacra testatur pagina, ex quibus etsi non huius tam mirande magnitudinis fuerint, duo saltem in eadem nuncupantur, Nembroth scilicet, qui turrim in Deum excogitavit, et Golias Phylisteus a Davit funda et lapidibus superatus. Hos tales Iosephus, vir alias circumspectus et eruditus, existimavit, ut ipse in libro *Antiquitatis Iudaice* scribit, ab angelis Dei mulieribus mortalibus coeuntibus procreari; quod edepol ridiculum est, cum ingentium corporum causa sint sydera celique revolutio certa, qua etiam evo nostro factum est, quod aliqui fere caput omne, vel amplius proceritate excederent etiam magnos

13   corpore viros. Sane de his ego poetas non puto locutos, si mites fuerunt homines et humane viventes. Sed de his de quibus videtur intelligere in *Saturnaliorum* libro Macrobius, ubi dicit:

> Gigantes autem quid aliud fuisse credendum est quam hominum quandam impiam gentem deos negantem, et ideo exti-
>
> 14 matam deos[57] pellere de celesti sede voluisse? Horum pedes in draconum volumina desinebant, quod significat, nil eos rectum, nil superum cogitasse, totius vite eorum gressu atque processu in inferna mergentes,

etc.

Huiusmodi ergo homines ex sanguine Titanorum et Terra productos fuisse, non debet extraneum apparere homini erudito, cum persepe similis oriatur ex simili, et ob hoc Titanorum superborum hominum rite superbos omnes, si non ex sanguine saltem ex mori-

15   bus seu vitio filios possumus nuncupare. Quorum etiam nulla rectius dici mater potest quam Terra, iam a Macrobio ratione monstrata, tales scilicet nil superum, id est celeste, nil sanctum, nil iustum cogitant, omnis vite eorum progressus ad terrena et inferiora demergitur. Attamen hos tales, seu quos tales appellamus,

And then there were the giants, huge in stature, to which Holy   12
Scripture[214] bears witness. At least two of these are named there,
although they were not of such a wondrous magnitude, namely,
Nimrod, who devised the tower to God, and the Philistine Goli-
ath, who was vanquished by David with a sling and stones. Josephus,[215] a man otherwise circumspect and learned, believed, as he
writes in his *Jewish Antiquities*, that such giants as these were
procreated by the angels of God having intercourse with mortal
women. This is of course ridiculous, for the cause of huge bodies
is the stars and a specific positioning of the sky, which is still operative today because there are those who exceed in height even
men with large bodies by nearly a whole head or more. But I do   13
not think the poets would have spoken about these if they were
meek men and living a humane life but those whom Macrobius
seems to mean in his *Saturnalia* when he says:[216]

> What else must we believe the Giants to have been other
> than a certain impious race of men who denied the gods and
> were therefore thought to desire to drive the gods from their
> celestial seat? Their feet terminate in snake coils, which   14
> means that they intended nothing upright, nothing lofty,
> sinking into the depths while advancing and proceeding
> through their whole life.

That men of this sort were the products of Titans and Earth
should not appear strange to a learned man, for very often like is
born of like, and on account of this we are rightly able to call all
the prideful men sons—if not by blood at least by morals or
vice—of the prideful Titans. No one can be said more properly to   15
be their mother than Earth for the reason already expressed by
Macrobius, namely, that such giants think of nothing lofty, that
is, celestial, nothing sacred, and nothing just, and that their whole
life progresses while sunken amidst mundane and lower matters.
Nonetheless, it is not altogether fabulous that such as these, or

bellum habuisse cum Iove homine Cretensium rege non omnino

16 fabulosum est. Constat enim ex hystoriis antiquis, Iovem duo insigna gessisse bella, primum cum Titanis, ut parentes vinculis detentos liberaret, secundum cum ipso patre suo Saturno, mortem eius, testante Lactantio, moliente et hoc Giganteum bellum dictum est, et secundum quosdam apud Flegram Thesalie agrum conflictum est, et victus atque fugatus Saturnus.

17 Quod autem oraculo Egle corio clipeum tegere illi imperatum sit, et caput suum Gorgone et Egles a terra in specu abscondita, intelligo quia subsidio gregum et armentorum, in quibus consistebant substantie veterum (que per Eglam, que idem sonat quod 'capra,' intelliguntur) et agrorum fructus, quos accipio pro Gorgone, sumptus bellorum maximi sustentati sint; et sic Iovis clipeum tectum, id est defensionem habitam, et caput coopertum, id

18 est consiliis ad oportuna fulcitum. His autem cessantibus, scilicet fructibus substantiarum, Egles dicitur abscondita, et tunc audent hostes in hostem insurgere quasi adversus inermem. Tamen his existentibus et Pallade, que pro militari disciplina intelligenda est hic, in victoriam itur. Quod autem in infernum mersi sint, humiliari atque deici superborum proterviam ostendere voluere fingentes.

19 Huic tamen bello Gigantum multa superadduntur hic non apposita, eos scilicet montes montibus imposuisse, ut in celum ascenderent, et alia quedam fecisse, que referenda sunt ad actus bellantium. Erigunt quidem arces et inponunt montibus turres, ut celum, id est regnum hostis, occupent, que omnia tandem a vic-

20 tore deiciuntur, ut a Iove factum est. De hoc Gigantum bello atque superum videbatur Varro aliter opinari. Dicebat enim hoc fuisse

those whom we call giants, made war with Jupiter, a man and king of the Cretans, for it is certain from ancient histories that Jupiter 16 waged two famous wars, the first with the Titans to liberate his parents who were being held in chains, the second with his own father Saturn, who was plotting to kill him, according to Lactantius.[217] This was called the War of the Giants, and according to some it was fought at Phlegra, a field in Thessaly, and Saturn was defeated and put to flight.

In that it was ordered by the oracle for him to cover his shield 17 with the skin of Aegla and his head with the Gorgon, and in that Aegla was hidden in a cavern, I understand that the greatest costs of war are sustained with the help of flocks and herds, that is, property for the ancients — which we understand in Aegla, meaning "she-goat" — and the fruit of the fields, which I identify as the Gorgon. Thus the shield of Jupiter is covered, that is, a defense is established, and his head covered, that is, advantageous support for the strategy. When these cease, that is, the fruits of substance, 18 Aegla is said to be hidden, and then enemies dare to rise against the enemy as if they are defenseless. Nonetheless, when they exist along with Pallas, who should be understood here as military discipline, there is victory. Their sinking into the nether regions was invented to demonstrate that impudence toward the gods is humbled and destroyed.

There is additional material about this War of the Giants 19 which is not apposite here, namely, that they piled mountains upon mountains to climb up to the sky, and they did certain other things which should be described as acts of war. They erected citadels and placed towers upon mountains to capture the sky, that is, the kingdom of the enemy; all these structures were later dismantled by the victor, which is what Jupiter did. Varro[218] seemed to 20

cum cessasset diluvium, dicens aliquos in diluvio cum utensilibus omnibus confugisse in montes, qui lacessiti postea bello ab aliis, qui de aliis descenderant montibus, tanquam superiores venientes facile repellebant; unde fictum est superiores deos esse, inferiores vero terrigenas; et quia ex vallibus ad summa scandentes premisso pectore, quasi reptare viderentur more serpentum, dictum est eos serpentum habuisse pedes.

21   Quod autem metu Typhei in Egyptum mutatis formis aufugerint dii, aliud sentit quam hystoria vel moralitas. Nam pro Thypheo, qui Terre fuit filius, terra ipsa intelligenda est, et potissime ea pars que a nobis septentrionalibus incolitur, a qua dii, id est sol, per quem, ut Macrobio placet in libro *Saturnaliorum*, reliqua deorum multitudo intelligenda est, tunc fugiunt quando ab equinoctio autumnali versus antarticum polum sol incipit declinare, quia tunc elongatur a terra sol, scilicet a regione nostra qui septemtrionales sumus, et tendit in Egyptum, id est in austrum, seu ad regiones australes.

22   Deos autem formas mutasse, forte potius ad ornatum fictionis appositum est, quam ob aliam causam. Nam, ut dicit Augustinus, ubi *De civitate Dei*:

> Non omnia que gesta narrantur, aliquid etiam significare putanda sunt, sed propter illa que aliquid significant, et ea que nichil significant attexuntur. Solo enim vomere terra proscinditur, sed ut hoc fieri possit, etiam cetera aratri membra sunt necessaria; et soli nervi in citharis atque huiusmodi vasis musicis aptantur ad cantum, sed ut aptari possint insunt et cetera in compagibus organorum que non percutiun-

think differently about this War of the Giants and the gods, for he tried to say that this happened after the flood had receded, saying that some during the flood had fled with all their household goods into the mountains. Being provoked into war afterward by others who had descended from different mountains, they attacked in superior fashion and repelled them easily. From this it was fabricated that the superior ones were gods and the inferior earth-born, and because they climbed from the valleys to the peaks with their chests pressed against the ground, as if they were seen to crawl like serpents, it was said that they had feet of serpents.

That in fear of Typhoeus the gods fled into Egypt and changed their shapes, signifies something other than history or morality, for in Typhoeus, who was the son of Earth, the earth itself should be understood, especially that part which is inhabited by us in the North, from which the gods — that is, the sun, through whom, as Macrobius[219] thinks in his *Saturnalia*, the rest of the divine group should be understood — flee when the sun begins to decline from the autumnal equinox toward the southern pole. It is then that the sun is moving away from the earth, namely, from that region of ours who live in the North, and heads toward Egypt, that is, toward the South, or the southern regions.

That the gods changed their forms is fitting perhaps to embellish the fiction for another reason, for as Augustine says in his *City of God*:[220]

> But not all things which happened are recounted, even things which should be considered somewhat significant; but on account of those things which are somewhat significant, even those things which are not significant at all are added; for the earth is opened by a single ploughshare, but so that can happen, other parts of the plough are also necessary; and single strings are fitted onto citharas and musical instruments of this sort for song, but so that they can be fitted

tur a canentibus, sed ea que percussa resonant huic connec-
tuntur.

Hec Augustinus.

23   Et ob id esto ad intentum minime spectet, ne videamur evitasse
laborem, quid in illis formis sensisse potuerint, annectamus. Dicit
ergo Ovidius Iovem mutatum in arietem, ut in hoc Iovis naturam
demonstret. Est autem aries mansuetum et benignum animal, nemini si in quiete permictatur sua infestum. Preterea utile plurimum, nam ad procreandam prolem maxime pecudum gregi solus
sufficit, et insuper non solum vir gregis est, sed dux etiam; nam si
absit pastor ipse, se pastorem pecoris previum offert, illudque iti-
24   nere recto reducit in caulas. Que Iovi convenire videntur inter alia
multa. Est autem planeta benignus et mitis, nisi coniunctione alterius depravetur; est similiter utilis, quia maturos fetus mulierum
movet ad exitum et emicit in lucem, 'omnesque iuvat' ut ipsum
nomen sonat, sic et dux gregis, id est rex et dominus deorum, ut
omnis gentilitius error affirmat.

25   Solem autem ideo in corvum versum reor, ut eque ex proprietatibus solis demonstretur una; corvum enim habere vim quandam
presagiendi credidere veteres, et ideo quia sol divinationis dictus
est deus, ut ubi de Apolline dicetur, eidem corvum consecravere,
qui, ut dicit Fulgentius, solus inter aves habet LXIIII^{or} vocis
mutationes, quam ob causam auguribus antiquis erat in auguriis
26   captandis avis gratissima. Bachum in caprum mutatum, hyemali
tempore convenit. Nam vinum, id est Bachum, a frigore hyemis
coactum, in se vires colligit suas, et cum minoris virtutis videatur
quam sit, agente frigore facilius potatur a stultis. Verum postquam

there are also other things in the framework of instruments which are not struck by the players, but those things which resonate when struck are connected to them.

This is what Augustine says.

Although this hardly addresses what they might have meant by 23 the gods changing their forms, let us connect the two lest we seem to be avoiding our task. Ovid[221] says that Jupiter changed into a ram so that he could describe the nature of Jupiter in this way. A ram is a tame and mild animal, dangerous to no one when left in peace. In addition he is very useful, for he alone sufficient for procreating a great number of offspring for the flock of sheep, and he is not only the male of the flock but also its leader, for if the shepherd is away, he acts like a shepherd in leading the rest of the group along the proper path back to the enclosure. These things 24 seem to accord with Jupiter in addition to many other things, which is a mild and meek planet unless corrupted by conjunction with another. Similarly Jupiter is useful because it moves women's mature fetuses toward birth and sends them out into the light, and Jove "assists" [*juvat*] all, as in the very meaning of his name. So also he is leader of the flock, that is king and lord of the gods, as all the pagans erroneously assert.

I think Sun was turned into a crow to reveal again one single 25 aspect of Sun's characteristics, for the ancients believed that the crow had some prophetic power, so because Sun is called the god of divination, as we will discuss in the chapter on Apollo,[222] they made the crow sacred to him. The crow, as Fulgentius[223] says, unique among the birds, has sixty-four mutations of voice, making it the most acceptable bird for ancient augurs when taking their auguries. Bacchus' mutation into a goat accords with wintertime, 26 for wine, that is, Bacchus, is congealed by the cold of winter and concentrates its power. And although it seems of less quality than it is, foolish people drink it more easily because of the action of

potatum est, calore auctum stomaci extenditur, et more hyrci ad sublimiora tendit agitque, ut calefacti homines animosiores effi-

27 ciantur, et ad celsiora contendant. Quod autem luna in felem, id est in dammam mutata sit, ut eius designetur velocitas dictum est, cum sit damma velocissimum animal, nec illi ad defensionem sui telum aliud quam fuga concessum sit a natura, et sic luna inter planetas velocissima est. Iunonem autem in candidam mutatam vaccam ideo voluere, quia vacca fertile sit animal, et sic terra, quam Iunonem aliquando volunt; et ideo candida, quia hyeme nivibus

28 tegatur. Quod Venus piscis effecta sit, eius grandis humiditas, seu quod humiditate vigeat Venus ostenditur. Mercurius autem ybis factus dicitur, eo quod ciconia sociabilis avis sit, ex quo Mercurii convenientia cum omnibus designatur, et uti serpentum hostis ciconia est, sic astutiarum dissipator Mercurius.

29 Secundum autem Theodontium Iuppiter in aquilam versus est, ut per aquilam, que altius ceteris avibus volat, eius sublimes intelligantur effectus. Cybelem vero in merulam ideo versam puto, quia cum Terra sit et merula sit avis volans continue circa terram, ut Terra per merulam designetur. Per anguillam autem in quam Venerem versam dicit, eius Veneris lubricum accipiendum est.

30 Per Pana autem in hyrcum in superiori sui parte versum, et in piscem in inferiori, intelligo orbem totum cui natura rerum, id est Pan, preest, et qui in superiori parte, id est terra, que aqua superior est, et yrcos et animalia cetera pascit; in inferiori autem parte, id est aqua, ideo piscis fingitur, quia pisces producat et nutriat.

Sed cum iam omnis Titania proles expedita sit, libello huic finem etiam faciemus.

the cold. But after it is drunk and increased by the heat of the stomach, it opens up, and, like a he-goat, reaches higher and makes it so that men become heated and more animated strive for loftier things. It was said that Moon was changed into a cat, that 27 is, a fallow deer, to designate her swiftness, for the fallow deer is the swiftest animal; it was not provided by nature with any defensive weapon other than flight, and similarly the moon is the swiftest of the planets. They wanted Juno to be changed into a white cow because a cow is an animal that is fertile, as is the earth, which they sometimes want Juno to represent, and it is white in that she is covered by the snows of winter. Venus becomes a fish to 28 indicate her great moisture or that Venus thrives with moisture. Mercury is said to have been made into an ibis because the ibis, or stork, is a sociable bird, and that designates Mercury's harmony with all, and as the stork is the enemy of serpents, so is Mercury the destroyer of the cunning.

But according to Theodontius, Jupiter was turned into an eagle, 29 for it was through the eagle, which flies higher than other birds, that they knew his lofty effects. I think Cybele was turned into a blackbird since she is the earth and a blackbird is a bird which flies continuously around the earth, so as the earth she is represented by a blackbird. He says Venus was turned into an eel, and by this we should understand the slippery deceit of this Venus.

Through Pan being turned into a he-goat in his upper part and 30 a fish in his lower I understand the whole world over which nature, that is, Pan, is preeminent; the upper part, that is, the earth, which is above the water, feeds he-goats and other animals; the lower part, that is, the water, is imagined as a fish because it produces and nourishes fish.

Since all the offspring of Titan have now been explicated, we will also bring this book to conclusion.

LIBER QUINTUS

Arbor

In arbore signata desuper ponitur in radice Celius, eo quod pater
fuerit Iovis secundi, cuius proles etsi non omnis, nam Dardanus in
librum alium hunc sequentem reservatur, in hac arbore tam in ramis quam frondibus describitur.

Prohemium

1 Nondum plene finieram superbam Titanis prolem in medium trahere, et ecce, qui adeo circa principium impetuose ab imo usque
conmoverant equora, quasi in antrum Eoli revocati imperio abiis-
sent, venti quievere omnes, et turgidum hactenus velum, langui-
dum exhaustumque adhesit malo. Quod ego prospectans, adverti
illico quia esset paululum quiescendum. Nec mirum! Quid, si ful-
minando Iuppiter fatigatus est, de me scribendo scelesti generis
elatos mores poterit arbitrari discretus?

2 Progredior ergo in litus, conscendo tumulum, visurus quonam
me vehemens liquisset spiritus; dumque in circum oculos volvo,
Atticum sub pedibus habere solum cognovi, avidusque in circuitu
cuncta passim videre, non ordine certo intuebar, quin imo, ut memoria representabat preterita, sic nunc huc nunc illuc oculos im-
pellebam. Et summos primo aliquandiu Arcadum montium consi-

BOOK V

Tree

In the tree illustrated above, Sky is placed in the root because he was the father of the second Jupiter, whose progeny is described in this tree in the branches as well as the leaves. Not all are described here: Dardanus is reserved for a subsequent book.

Preface

I had not yet completely finished bringing the haughty offspring of Titan to the forefront, and, behold, all the winds which at the beginning had so violently stirred up the seas from the bottom, departed as if called back into the cave of Aeolus at his command and quieted, and our sail, swollen until now, clung to the mast listless and exhausted. Seeing this, I immediately understood that I had to have a little repose. Nor is that amazing. What, if Jupiter is wearied from throwing lightning bolts, will a discerning man be able to think about me as I write about the arrogant behavior of a wicked race?

And so I continue to the shore and climb a hill to see where the powerful wind had left me. And while I looked around in a circle, I recognized that I had Attic soil under my feet. Eager to look everywhere around the whole circle, I was not looking in a specific order but as my memory of things past presented them, so I moved my eyes around now here and now there. At first for some time I looked at the highest peaks of the Arcadian mountains and

deravi vertices et nemorosa declivia, mecum dicens, 'Hos incoluit Mercurius puer, per illa ducebat Diana choros, discurrebat Athlas, et parvus adhuc Parthenopeus consuevit agitare cervos, in illis Calisto latuit virgo.'

3 Inde repente revolutus in litus, aspexi non dicam Athenas, sed earum dum fere consumptum parvumque vestigium intuerer, risi nostre mortalitatis insana iudicia, quibus decepta vetustas, dum illas futuras perennes arbitraretur, primo deos in litem nominis imponendi traxit, inde eas vocavit eorum sententia immortales; nunc, paucis elapsis seculis, ruinis suum finem venisse testantur.

4 In mortem profecto nos et nostra corruunt omnia celeri passu. Attamen, quantumcunque exinanita civitas, imo potius civitatis bustum esset, memorari cepi quanta phylosophorum atque poetarum luce, quanto studiorum omnium decore, quanta regum ducumque gloria, quanta insignis potentia, quanto victoriarum fulgore splendida iamdudum fuerit, et exhorrui videns omnia sub turpi ruinarum tam templorum quam edium tumulo deiecta iacere.

5 Ab hac tandem me consideratione retorsit biceps fere in conspectu positus Parnasus, plurimo celebris carmine et vatum redolens laureis, atque vetustissimum et suave Musarum hospitium. Quem dum quadam mentis veneratione conspicerem et deserto fonti Castalio compaterer, vidi antiqui hostis decipulam veterem, antrum scilicet Apollinis Delphici, ex quo prodeuntes ambages et perplexa responsa in se, tanquam in Caribdim cuncta sorbentem et in baratrum perditionis perpetue dimictentem, tam diu gentilium infelices animas contraxere—tamen mutum et elinguem, non aureis ornatum statuis, non preciosis coruscum lapidibus, sed varia fere totum serpentium radicum circumplexione

their wooded slopes, saying to myself, "The boy Mercury inhabited these mountains; Diana used to lead her dancers through them; Atlas roamed here; while still small Parthenopeus was accustomed to pursuing its deer; and here the maiden Callisto secluded herself."

Then suddenly turned toward the shore, I saw — I would say 3
Athens but I saw only its small and nearly eroded remnants. Looking at them I laughed at the demented judgments of our mortality by which deluded antiquity, believing Athens would last forever, first dragged gods into a dispute over assigning its name, and then decided to call them immortal. Now, a few centuries have gone by, and they bear witness that their end has come to ruins.

Surely we and all that is ours rush at a swift pace unto death. 4
Nonetheless, however empty that city may be, nay, even if it has become a tomb of the city, I began to recall how splendid it was long ago in the light of its philosophers and poets, in the dignity of all its scholarly pursuits, in the glory of its kings and dukes, in its illustrious power, and in the brilliance of its victories, and I shuddered to see everything lying prostrate, thrown down under the dishonorable tomb of ruins of both temples and buildings.

Capturing my attention next was twin-peaked Parnassus, just 5
now coming into sight, celebrated in much verse and fragrant with the laurels of poets, and the most ancient and charming haunt of the Muses. While I gazed upon this with a certain amount of veneration in my mind and felt compassion for the deserted Castalian fount, I saw the aged snare of the ancient enemy, that is, the cave of Delphic Apollo. The riddles it issued forth and its perplexing responses gathered unto itself the perenially unhappy souls of the pagans, as if into Charybdis swallowing up everything, condemning them to the infernal pit of perpetual perdition. But it was now mute and speechless, not decorated with golden statues nor brilliant with precious stones but almost entirely covered by a variety of entwining, creeping roots, in accord with the wishes of

contectum, sic sacro volente Lumine, quod non implicitis vocibus, sed sanctorum, qui a seculo sunt, prophetarum eius, futuris sacra misteria expectate salutis eleganti patefecit eloquio.

6   Abhinc in Thebas Boetias haud longinquas a loco se flexit intentio, quas apud, dum inter ruinarum tumulos et ingentia veterum edificia, turpi lapsu squalentia, Bachi et Herculis oculo mentis exquiro cunabula, tetrus odor tabis illisi in saxum Learci, truncati Pentei, discerpti Actheonis et germanorum vulnerum, me in partem impulit alteram, et in Lacedemonam usque protendens aciem, nedum Agamenonias arces et execrabilem decorem Helene sacrasque Lygurgi leges cernerem et imperii pregrandis insignia, sed vix locum, ubi consederit oculus alter Grecie, cognoscere potui.

    Et ob id in excedentem fere sydera Corinthiam arcem oculos
7   dedi, Lacedemonis memor et Sysiphi. Sed quid multa? Dum sic distrahor, clementissime Princeps, sensi restaurari vires, quas pridianus labor obtuderat, et me ad ceptum revocari iter ab aura tenui. Quam ob rem, omisso tumulo, quasi futuri itineris premonitus, parvam reintravi naviculam, et eius invocato nomine, qui iam dudum in suave vinum insipidas vertit aquas in Chana, secundi Iovis insignem scripturus prolem, flatibus velum dedi.

the holy Light, which not with confused voices but with the poetic pronouncements of the holy prophets, who are of the ages, has revealed for the future the sacred mysteries of our awaited salvation.

Then my concentration turned toward Boeotian Thebes, not 6 too distant from there, where, while among the tumuli of ruins and the huge edifices of the ancients, squalid in their appalling state of decline, I sought in my mind's eye the birthplace of Bacchus and Hercules, the offensive odor of putrefaction from Learchus dashed against the rock, from mutilated Pentheus, from dismembered Actaeon, and from his brothers' wounds drove me to another area. And stretching my sight to Lacedaemon, I failed to discern the citadels of Agamemnon and the accursed beauty of Helen and the sacred laws of Lycurgus or the signs of a great empire but was barely able to recognize the place where the other eye of Greece abides.[1]

And on account of this, mindful of Lacedaemon and Sisyphus, I directed my gaze toward the citadel of Corinth, nearly higher than the stars. But why so many words here? While I am so dis- 7 tracted, most merciful King, I sensed that my strengths, which the previous day's labor had beaten down, were being restored, and that a light breeze was calling me back to the journey I had begun. Therefore, leaving the tumulus behind, as if forewarned of a future journey, I once again boarded my small ship and, calling upon the name of him who long ago at Cana turned bland waters into sweet wine,[2] ready to write of the famous progeny of the second Jupiter, I gave my sail to the winds.

∴ I ∴

De Iove secundo Celi VIIII° filio, qui genuit filios XV,
quorum prima Diana, II^us Apollo, III^us Tityus,
IIII^us Bachus, V^us Amphion, VI^us Zethus,
VII^us Calathus, VIII^a Pasythea, IX^a Egyales,
X^a Euprosyne, XI^us Lacedemon, XII^us Tantalus,
XIII^us Hercules, XIIII^a Minerva, XV^us Arcas

1 Supra de Celo libro tercio dictum est, cuius fuisse filium Iovem secundum testatur Tullius in libro *De naturis deorum*, eumque dicit in Arcadia natum, ex qua tamen matre non dicit. Huius etsi credam grandia fuisse facinora, absque quibus non potuisset tam insigne meruisse cognomen, pauca tamen ad nos usque fama, seu veterum monimenta duxere, et si qua forsitan pervenere, non satis
2 certum est, an sua, an potius primi vel tercii fuerint Iovis. Verum que pauca huius fuisse Theodontius asserit, explicabo. Vult igitur Theodontius hunc insignem fuisse hominem, primo apud suos, et ibidem ob apposita a Lycaone Arcadum rege in convivio humana membra, Lycaonem vicisse prelio, regnoque privasse, et tunc primo cepisse vocari Iovem ob iustam de iniquo rege ultionem sumptam.
3 Hunc tamen Leontius Lysaniam supra, ubi de Lycaone, vocat, quem primum fuisse Iovem et Atheniensium regem diximus; et ob id quid dicam non habeo, nisi ut istas adeo inter se discrepantes opiniones prudentior me, si queat, in concordiam redigat. Post hec dicit Theodontius hunc se Athenas transtulisse et ibidem in culmine fuisse permaximo, et ob stupratam Latonam adversus Ceum ingens habuisse bellum, eoque superato maxima cum gloria,

: I :

On the second Jupiter, ninth son of Sky, who fathered fifteen
children, of whom the first was Diana, second Apollo,
third Tityus, fourth Bacchus, fifth Amphion, sixth Zethus,
seventh Calathus, eighth Pasithea, ninth Aglaea,
tenth Euphrosyne, eleventh Lacedaemon, twelfth Tantalus,
thirteenth Hercules, fourteenth Minerva, fifteenth Arcas

Above in the third book we discussed Sky,[3] whose son Cicero[4] in   1
his *On the Nature of the Gods* testifies to have been the second Jupiter. He says he was born in Arcadia, but he did not say by what
mother. Although I believe that his deeds were great, without
which he could not have merited such a famous surname, nonetheless few reports or records from the ancients have reached us,
and from those that may have, it is not sufficiently certain whether
they are his or rather those of the first or third Jupiter. But what   2
few things Theodontius asserts are his, I will explain. Theodontius
wants him to have been an important man, at first among his own
people but then, because in battle he vanquished Lycaon, King of
the Arcadians, who had served human limbs at a banquet, and
stripped him of his kingdom, he then for the first time began to be
called Jupiter on account of the righteous vengeance he exacted
from an unjust king.

Leontius, however, calls him Lysanias, as above in the chapter   3
on Lycaon,[5] whom we said was the first Jupiter and the king of the
Athenians; and on account of this I have nothing to say: let someone more skilled than I, if he can, bring such divergent opinions as
these into agreement. After this Theodontius says that he moved
to Athens and was very powerful there; he waged a massive war
against Coeus for violating Latona; having won that war and the

Athenas rediisse. Iovique primo bovem immolasse, et multa ad laudabilem civilitatem spectantia apud Athenienses instituisse; quibus agentibus causis, Iuppiter communi hominum consensu vocatus est.

4　　De tempore non constat. Sunt tamen qui credant eum Cycropem Atheniensium regem primum fuisse, sed ab hoc vulgata discordat opinio, cum Cycrops fuerit Egyptius, et Iuppiter Arcas. Alii vero antiquiorem dicunt, nec tamen ullus precisum tempus apponitur, et ideo omictamus.

: 2 :

De Diana prima Iovis secundi filia

1　Diana, omnium fere testimonio poetarum, Iovis et Latone fuit filia, et eodem partu cum Apolline edita, ut supra ubi de Latona monstratum est. Hanc veteres insignem virginitate perpetua voluere, et quoniam spreto hominum consortio silvas inhabitaret, venationibusque vacaret, eam arcu pharetraque accinctam descripsere, et nemorum montiumque dixere deam, curruque uti voluere a cervis tracto, et nynpharum societate atque officiis et obsequio uti.

2　　De[1] qua sic Claudianus ubi *De laudibus Stylliconis*:

Dixit et extemplo frondosa fertur ab Alpe
trans[2] pelagus, cervi currum subiere iugales,

greatest glory, he returned to Athens where he was the first to sacrifice a bull to Jupiter and instituted among the Athenians many things which helped establish a praiseworthy government. For doing these things he was called Jupiter by the common consent of men.

There is no agreement as to his time period. There are those 4 who believe that he was Cecrops, the first king of the Athenians, but the popular opinion differs from this, since Cecrops was Egyptian, and Jupiter Arcadian. Others say that he was more ancient, but no exact time period is assigned, so we will disregard that.

: 2 :

On the first Diana, daughter of the second Jupiter

Diana, by the testimony of nearly all the poets, was the daughter 1 of Jupiter and Latona, produced by the same birth which produced Apollo, as we showed above in the chapter on Latona.[6] The ancients wanted her to be known for her everlasting virginity and, because she spurned consorting with men, she inhabited forests and spent her idle time hunting; they portray her as being equipped with bow and quiver; they said she was the goddess of woods and mountains; and they liked to have her use a cart drawn by deer and to utilize the companionship of obedient nymphs and their services.

Claudian says this about her in his *In Praise of Stilicho:*[7] 2

She spoke, and immediately is borne from the leafy Alps,
across the sea; yoked stags pulled the chariot.

quos, decus esse dee, primi sub lumine celi
roscida fecundis concepit luna cavernis,
par nitor intactis nivibus, frons discolor auro
germinat, et spatio summas equantia fagos,
cornua ramoso surgunt procera metallo.
Opis frena tenet,

etc.

Et paulo infra sequitur:

          Sexum nec cruda fatetur
virginitas, sine lege come, duo cingula vestem
crure tenus pendere vetant; precedet amicas
flava Leonthademe, sequitur nutrita Lyceo
Neuopene telisque domat que Menala thoro,
ignea Cretea properat Bythomartis ab Yda,
et cursu Zephyris nunquam cessura Lycaste.
Iungunt se gemine metuenda feris Agapente,
et soror optatum numen venantibus Opis,
progenies Scythye, divas nemorumque potentes
fecit Yperboreis Delos delata pruinis.
He septem venere duces, exercitus alter
Nynpharum incedunt, acies formosa Diana,

etc.

Ait et hic idem:

Opis frena tenet, fert retia rara Lycaste,
auratasque plagas,

etc.

3   Hanc[3] insuper viarum voluere presidem, et una cum Luna multis vocavere nominibus.

Those, as befits a goddess, under the dewy light of the first
    sky
the moon conceived in its fertile caverns.
Their sheen resembles new-driven snow; their multicolored
    foreheads sprout,
and with gold spread like the tops of beeches,
their horns extending out with the leafy metal.
Opis holds the reins.

And a little later he continues:[8]

                        Nor does her unspoiled virginity belie
her sex. Her hair is unruly; two belts prevent her garment
from reaching the knee. Preceding her friends
is the blond Leontodeme, Nebrophone, nurtured on Lyceon,
    follows
and Thero, who tames Maenalus with her darts.
Fiery Britomartis hurries from Cretan Ida
and Lycaste, never yielding to Zephyr's course.
Joining them are the twins, Agapente[9] feared by beasts,
and her sister, desired spirit of hunters, Opis,
Scythian progeny. They were made powerful goddesses of the
    woods
by Delos, carried to Hyperborean frosts.
These seven came as leaders; another army
of Nymphs marched behind, the fair array of Diana.

He also says here:

Opis holds the reins, Lycaste carries the thin nets
and the golden snares.

In addition to this they wanted her to be the protector of roads,   3
and in addition to Luna, they call her by many names.

His igitur premissis, advertendum est que per ea sentienda sint. Fuit hec profecto femina Iovis hominis et Latone filia, et possibile est eam viraginem quandam fuisse, ut non nulle sunt, omnino hominum abhorrentem consortium, et sic virginitate perpetua claruisse et venationibus dedisse operam. Et cum hec lune convenire videantur, que suo frigore habet venereas frenare concupiscentias, et nemora montesque nocte suo lustrare lumine, ei ad lunam spectantia, tanquam si ipsa luna esset, iniunxere, seu ipsam potius insipidi credidere, eo modo quo supra sepius de quibusdam aliis dictum est.

4   Et quoniam de his, ubi de luna, nil fere dictum fuit, paululum latius prosequemur. Accingitur ergo Diana arcu et pharetra, ut per hoc intelligatur luna et ipsa radiorum iaculatrix, qui loco sagittarum intelligendi sunt, et ideo sagitte, quia non nunquam nocui atque pestiferi. Nemorum montiumque ideo dea dicta est, quia lune videatur esse plantas herbasque suis humiditatibus fecundare,

5   et in virorem servare, et etiam incrementa prestare. Currus autem ideo illi additur, non solum ut ex hoc celi circuitio assummatur, quam etiam velocius ceteris planetis peragit, quin imo ut et montium atque nemorum circuitiones venantium designentur. Qui a cervis idio trahi dicitur, eo quod a silvestribus animalibus venantium desiderium trahi videatur. Candidi autem ideo apponuntur,

6   quia albedo inter colores lune a physicis tribuatur. Quod nynphas habet socias, accipi debet pro humiditate continua, qua habundat, cum nil aliud nynpha sit quam aqua, aut complexio humida, ut infra ubi de nynphis clarius apparebit; quod nynphis sint officia attributa, ad decorem fictionis appositum est, seu velimus dicere humiditates obsequium prestare influentiis lune. Viarum vero pre-

Now that we have described these, we must pay attention to what they must mean. Surely she was the daughter of the man Jupiter and Latona, and it is possible that she was a certain virago, shunning, as some do, the consort of men altogether, whence the fame for her everlasting virginity, and devoted herself to hunting. And since these things seem to be associated with the moon, which because of its cold curtails amorous desires and with its light illumines the woods and mountains at night, they attribute lunar aspects to her as if she were the moon itself, or the foolish believe, just as they do about some of the others we have described earlier, that she herself is the moon.

And because relatively little was said about this in our discus-   4
sion of the moon, let us widen the discussion here. Diana is equipped with bow and quiver to signify that the moon, and she as well is the hurler of rays, which must represent arrows, and they are indeed arrows in that they are sometimes harmful and destructive. She is said to be the goddess of woods and mountains because the moon seems to make plants and herbs fertile with its moisture, preserve their freshness, and implement their growth. They attributed a chariot to her not only so that it would take her   5
up to her orbit in the sky, which is also completed more swiftly than the other planets, but also to represent the circuits of hunters in the mountains and woods. It is said to be drawn by stags because hunters seem to desire to be drawn by forest animals. White deer are assigned to her because among the colors whiteness is attributed by natural scientists to the moon. That she has nymphs   6
as companions ought to be understood as the perpetual moisture in which the moon abounds, for a nymph is nothing other than water, or a combination of moisture, as will become clearer below in the chapter on nymphs;[10] that duties are attributed to the nymphs helps to embellish the fiction, or we prefer to say that moistures do the bidding of the moon's influences. They wanted her to be the protector of roads because the moon renders them

sidem ideo voluere, quia lumine suo nocturnas vincens tenebras illas reddit viatoribus expeditas, seu quia vie sint Diane virgini in sterilitate similes.

7 Dianam vero vocari voluere, ut dicit Rabanus in libro *De origine rerum*, quasi Duanam, eo quod nocte et die appareat, et sic deservire videtur ambobus. Sed Theodontius aliter, ut alias dictum est: luna enim planeta iste vocatur quando de sero lucet; Diana autem, dum luce sua tendit in diem, et tunc est venationibus aptior et viatoribus, et virgo illo tunc dicitur, quia post excursum medium celi circulum, plantis nec affert nutrimentum validum, nec de novo plantatis prestat utile incrementum, uti facit dum in oppositum fertur discedens a sole.

8 Cinthia autem dicta est a Cinthio monte, in quo precipue colebatur; de reliquis alibi dictum est.

: 3 :

De Apolline II° Iovis secundi filio, qui XVI inter filias et filios genuit, quorum hec sunt nomina: prima Lapitha, II^a Eurinomes, III^us Mopsus, IV^us Lynus, V^us Phylistenes, VI^us Garamas, VII^us Brancus, VIII^us Phylemon, VIIII^us Orpheus, X^us Aristeus, XI^us Nomius, XII^us Auctous, XIII^us Argeus, XIIII^us Esculapius, XV^a Psyce, XVI^us Arabs

1 Apollo eque Iovis et Latone fuit filius et eodem enixus cum Diana partu, ut prehabitum est, ubi de Latona. De hoc multa narrantur, que forsan non minus aliena fuere quam sua, cum preter eum tres

ready for travelers by overwhelming the nocturnal darkness with its light, or because roads are similar to the virgin Diana in their sterility.

They wanted to call her Diana, as Rabanus[11] says in his *On the* 7 *Nature of Things*, as if Duana, because she appears at night and during the day, and so she seems to be of service to both. But Theodontius thinks otherwise, as has been said elsewhere, for that planet is called the moon when it shines in the evening but Diana when the light stretches toward the day, when it is more suitable for hunting and traveling; and then she is called a virgin at that point because after reaching the middle orbit of the sky, the moon offers no effective nourishment to plants, nor does it supply a useful supplement to what was planted anew, as it does when carried in opposition, departing from the sun.

She is called Cynthia from Mount Cynthus, where she is wor- 8 shipped primarily. The rest will be discussed elsewhere.

: 3 :

On the second Apollo, son of the second Jupiter, who fathered
sixteen daughters and sons; these are their names:
first Lapitha, second Eurynome, third Mopsus, fourth Linus,
fifth Philisthenes, sixth Garamas, seventh Branchus,
eighth Philemon, ninth Orpheus, tenth Aristaeus,
eleventh Nomius, twelfth Autueus[12], *thirteenth Agreus,*
fourteenth Aesculapius, fifteenth Psyche, sixteenth Arabus

Apollo was also the son of Jupiter and Latona, produced from 1 the same birth as Diana, as already discussed in the chapter on Latona.[13] Much is said about him which, however, belongs as

2   alios fuisse Apollines scribat Cicero. Verum quoniam in hunc omnes sese inclinant poete, quasi solus ipse fuerit Apollo, et ob id que aliorum fuerint, non satis apparet, in hunc omnia deferre necesse est.

    Dixere ergo post nativitatis sue fabulam, hunc divinitatis et sa-
3   pientie deum et medicine artis repertorem. Preterea dicunt eum Cyclopes interemisse, et ob id, aliquandiu privatum divinitate, armenta Admeti regis Thessalie pavisse. Voluere insuper, cum illi cytharam donasset Mercurius, eum Helyconicis preesse Musis, ut eo scilicet lyram tangente Muse canerent. Similiter et imberbem dixere, atque laurum arborem, et Yperboreas gryphes et corvum, et buccolicum carmen illi sacrum fecere; multisque illum vocavere nominibus, et plures illi filios ascripsere.

    Longa fictionum series hec est, quarum si velimus sensum excerpere, ante alia advertendum est, quoniam aliquando eum hominem, ut fuit, aliquando solem intelligamus necesse est. Fuit igitur
4   hic homo et secundi Iovis filius ex Latona, ut sepius dictum est. Verum Tullius, ubi *De naturis deorum*, dicit eum Iovis Cretensis fuisse filium, et ab Yperboreis montibus venisse Delphos. Et si sic esset, multa frustrarentur ex dictis supra. Verum, salva semper Ciceronis reverentia, ego istud non credo, cum dicat Eusebius in libro *Temporum* Apollinem et Dianam ex Latona natos, regnante Argis Steleno, regnique eius anno quarto, qui fuit annus mundi IIIDCCXI, cum longe post per eiusdem Eusebii scripta comprehendatur Iovem Cretensem fuisse.

5   Theodontius vero dicit istum Iovis secundi fuisse filium, et apud Arcades regnasse, eisque novas adinvenisse leges, et Nomium fuisse vocatum, et ob severitatem nimiam legum a subditis regno

much to the others, since Cicero[14] writes that there were three other Apollos besides this one. But since all the poets are inclined 2 toward this one, as if he were the only Apollo, and because it is not sufficiently clear what belongs to the others, it is necessary to transfer everything to this particular Apollo.

They said, after the fable about his birth, that he was the god of divinity and wisdom and the discoverer of the art of medicine. In addition, they say that he killed the Cyclopes, and on account 3 of this, deprived of his divinity for a period, he had to take care of the herds of Admetus, King of Thessaly. Also, because Mercury had given him the cithara, they wanted him to be in charge of the Heliconian Muses, so the Muses sing as he plucks his lyre. Similarly, they say he was beardless, and that the laurel tree, Hyperborean griffins, the crow, and the bucolic song were sacred to him. They call him by many names, and they ascribe many sons to him.

This is a long series of fictions, and if we wish to extract the meaning from them, we should observe before anything else that sometimes he was a man, as he was, and sometimes it is necessary that we understand him as the sun. Therefore, this Apollo was a 4 man and the son of the second Jupiter and Latona, as is often said. But Cicero[15] in his *On the Nature of the Gods* says that he was the son of Cretan Jupiter and that he came to Delphi from the Hyperborean mountains. And if this is so, many of the things said above are refuted. But, with everlasting reverence to Cicero, I do not believe this, for Eusebius[16] in his *Chronicle* says that Apollo and Diana were born from Latona in the fourth year of the reign of Sthenelus[17] in Argos, which was the world year 3711, while from the writings of this same Eusebius it is understood that Cretan Jupiter lived much later.

Theodontius says that he was the son of the second Jupiter and 5 ruled among the Arcadians, and that he devised new laws for them and was called Nomius, and that because of the excessive severity

fuisse pulsum, et ad Admethum regem Thessalie confugisse, atque ex concessione Admeti quibusdam secus Amphrisium flumen populis imperasse, ex quibus nata fabula est, quod ob occisos Cyclo-

6 pes divinitate privatus, Admeti paverit armenta. Sane dicit idem Eusebius Apollinem, ex Latona natum, non eum fuisse a quo consueverunt antiqui responsa suscipere, sed eum qui servivit Admeto; et sic ille, ut dicit Tullius, qui Delphos ex Yperboreis venit, filius potuit esse Iovis Cretensis.

De nativitate autem huius et contingentibus circa eam, multa in precedentibus, ubi de Latona, dicta sunt, et longe plura legi possent per Macrobium in libro *Saturnaliorum* scripta, que profecto utilia sunt, nec tamen multum a scriptis desuper discrepantia, et ideo non apposui.

7 Fuit insuper hic, ut Theodontius asserit, primus qui vires herbarum noverit, et ad oportunitates hominum earum virtutes adaptaverit, et ob id non solum medicine repertor habitus est, sed deus, cum egrotantes plurimi ex suis remediis sanitatem consequerentur. Et quoniam ipse pulsorum hominum concordantias repperisset, illi a Mercurio, numerorum atque mensurarum principe cytharam concessam dicunt, volentes intelligere, uti per diversas cythare voces ex diverso fidium tactu surgentes una fit melodia, si rite tangatur, sic ex diversis pulsuum motibus, si rite ordinati sint, quod ad medicum spectat, una fiat sanitatis bene dispositi corporis concordantia. Et quoniam, visis egritudinum signis, multis mortem, et multis etiam sospitatem prediceret, divinationis illi deitas attributa

8 est. Et sic illi laurus et corvus dicati sunt, cum ut alias dictum est, si lauri frondes dormientis capiti alligentur, somnia eum visurum

of the laws he was driven from the kingdom by his subordinates, fled to Admetus, King of Thessaly, and, by the grant of Admetus, ruled a group of people alongside the Amphrisus River. From this came the story that he took care of the herds of Admetus when he was deprived of his divinity for killing the Cyclopes. But Eusebius again says that Apollo, born of Latona, was not the one from whom the ancients were accustomed to receiving oracular responses but the one who served Admetus; and so, as Cicero says, the Apollo who came to Delphi from the Hyperboreans could have been the son of Cretan Jupiter.

About his birth and the events connected with it, much has been said already in the chapter on Latona, and much more can be read in what Macrobius[18] wrote in the *Saturnalia*, which is certainly profitable, but I have not included it here because it does not differ much from what was written above.

Theodontius asserts that Apollo was also the first to know the powers of herbs, and he adapted their powers for the advantage of men, and on account of this he is regarded not only as the discoverer of medicine, but as its god, for many sufferers achieved health from his remedies. And it is because he had discovered the concordances of human pulses, that they say he was given the cithara by Mercury, who was foremost in numbers and measures. What they meant to say here is that from the tones of the cithara, which differ according to how the strings are touched, a single melody can be created if the strings are touched correctly, and so from the different movements of pulses, if ordered correctly, there comes, and this is what interests a doctor, a single concordance of the health of a well disposed body. And because he predicted for many patients death as well as health by examining the symptoms of sickness, they attributed the divine power of divination to him. And for this reason they consecrated the laurel and crow to him, for, as has been said elsewhere, if laurel leaves are bound to the head of someone sleeping, they say he will see true dreams; this is

9 vera predicent, que divinitatis est species. Sic et corvum, ut etiam
dictum est, habere LXIIII vocum mutationes, ex quibus optime
augures futura se comprehendere asserebant, quod etiam ad divi-
nationem designandam apponitur.

Albericus insuper dicebat ob id fictum eum occidisse Phytonem, quia Phyton 'fidem auferens'⁴ interpretetur, que oblatio fidei
tunc de medio tollitur, cum veritatis claritas referatur, quod per
solis lumen efficitur. Sed tunc planeta est, non homo, per quem
etiam, ut mathematici asserunt, multa futura mortalibus demonstrantur. Sapientie autem ideo deus est habitus propter consilia,
que salubria circa morbos dabat poscentibus, preterea quia ubi de
sole intelligatur, lumine suo vitanda demonstrat ac etiam imitanda,
10 quod sapientis est. Imberbem autem solem planetam dicunt, quia
semper iuvenis tanquam omni die novus exoriens. Lyra canere et
Musis preesse eum ideo voluere, quia putaverint eum celestis me-
lodie moderatorem et principem et inter novem sperarum circuitiones varias, tanquam inter novem Musas, notitia et demonstratione earundem modulos exhibentem.

11   Nunc de nominibus. Dicitur Apollo, quod, ut ait Fulgentius,
'perdens' interpretatur, et ideo Ethyopum quidam sunt populi, qui
eum surgentem totis affectibus execrantur, eo quod fervore suo
nimio apud eos cuncta disperdat. Et hinc est, ut dicit Servius,
quod Porphyrius, in eo libro quem Solem appellat, dicit triplicem
esse Apollinis potestatem: eum scilicet apud superos esse Solem,
Liberum patrem in terris, et Apollinem apud inferos, et inde tria,
insigna simulacro eius ab antiquis apposita, lyram scilicet, pro qua
celestis armonie ymaginem voluere, clipeum quo eum terre numen
intelligi sensere, et sagittas quibus infernorum deus et noxius iudi-

a type of divination. In addition, as also has been said, the crow 9
has sixty-four variations of voice, which augurs used to claim was
optimal for comprehending the future; this is also said to indicate
divination.

In addition, Albericus[19] would say that it was on account of this
that the story of his killing Python was invented, because Python
means "removing faith," and the offering of faith is lifted from the
middle when the clarity of truth is restored, which is accomplished
through the light of the sun. But then it is also a planet, not a
man, through which, as mathematicians assert, many future things
are shown to mortals. And so he is regarded as the god of wisdom
because of the salubrious advice he gave to those who asked him
about their diseases, and also because when the sun is meant, it
makes clear with its light what one should avoid as well as what
one must follow, which is wisdom. They say that the sun is a 10
beardless planet because it is just like a youth, rising anew every
day. They wanted Apollo to sing with the lyre and be in charge of
the Muses because they thought him to be the moderator and
conductor of the celestial melody and that by knowledge and demonstration of their measures he produced the modes assigned to
the nine different orbits of the spheres, just as the nine Muses.

Now about the names. He is called Apollo which, as Fulgen- 11
tius[20] says, means "destroying," and so there are certain people in
Ethiopia who curse his rising with all their might because with his
excessive heat he destroys everything of theirs. And from this derives, as Servius[21] says, what Porphyry, in the book he calls *The
Sun*, identifies as the triple power of Apollo: Sun among the gods,
Father Liber on earth, and Apollo in the nether region. For this
reason the ancients placed three symbols on his statue: the lyre,
which they wanted to be the image of celestial harmony, the
shield, by which they understood that he would be known as a
spirit on earth, and arrows, by which he was declared to be a god
of the nether region and harmful. On account of this, presumably,

catus est; et ob id Omerus dixisse videtur eundem tam pestilentie
12 quam salutis autorem. Quod etiam sensisse videtur Oratius in
Carmine seculari, dum dicit:

> Condito mitis placidusque telo
> supplices audi pueros, Apollo,
>
> etc.

Vocatur et insuper Nomius, quod Latine 'pastor' sonat, inde sumptum quod pastor fingatur Admeti; et ideo tanquam pastori buccolicum illi carmen consecratum est, quia pastorale carmen est. Cynthius autem dicitur a Cynthio, in quo diligentissime colebatur.

: 4 :

De Lapitha prima Apollinis filia

1 Lapitha, ut Ysidoro placet in libro *Ethymologiarum*, filia fuit Apollinis, esto Papias virum fuisse testatur. Ab hac autem, ut Rabanus
asserit, Lapithe populi Thessalie denominati sunt. Indicium quidem est non parvi momenti, hanc scilicet insignem fuisse mulie-
2 rem, postquam ab ea egregii denominati sunt populi. Quod autem
Apollinis fuerit filia verum esse potest, tanquam hominis, si autem
tanquam solis, ob formositatem, vel sapientiam, vel augurandi peritiam fictum arbitrari potest.

Homer[22] said that he bestowed pestilence as well as health. Horace in the *Carmen saeculare* seems to think this as well, when he says:[23]

> With your spear hidden, gentle and placid,
> hear the suppliant boys, Apollo.

He is also called Nomius, which means "herdsman," wherein he is thought to have been the herdsman of Admetus; and so the bucolic song was consecrated to him, as if to a herdsman, because it is a pastoral song. He is called Cynthius from the Cynthius on which he was worshipped most devotedly.

: 4 :

On Lapitha, first child of Apollo

Lapitha, according to Isidore[24] in his *Etymologies*, was the daughter of Apollo, although Papias[25] testifies that he was a man. Rabanus[26] asserts that the Lapith people of Thessaly were named after her. That a famous group of people was named after her is a significant indication that she was an important woman. That she was the daughter of Apollo, if he was human, could be true; if of Apollo as the sun, we might suppose that the story was invented on account of her beauty or wisdom or skill in augury.

: 5 :

De Eurinome Apollinis II filia

1 Eurinomem Paulus Perusinus affirmat Apollinis fuisse filiam, eamque Thalaoni nuptam, ac eidem Adrastum Argivorum regem, et Euridicem Amphyarai postea coniugem peperisse.

: 6 :

De Mopso III° Apollinis filio

1 Mopsus, dicit Theodontius, filius fuit Apollinis et Ymantis, Iasoni summa atque fida amicitia iunctus, ut testatur Statius, 'Sepius in dubiis auditus Iasone Mopsus.' Hic, ut placet Lactantio, divinandi peritissimus fuit et Gryneo nemori, ubi Apollinis oraculum erat, prefectus, ut ait Servius. Fuit enim homo evo suo venerabilis adeo, ut illi post mortem templa dicata sint, et ex eorum abditis a petentibus accepta responsa.

2 Paulus autem dicit non Ymantis fuisse filium, sed Manthonis, filie Tiresie Thebani. Hunc preterea dicit Pomponius Mela Phaselim civitatem in finibus Pamphylie condidisse; nec multo post asserit idem Pomponius Manthonem fugientem Thebarum victores, Clarii fanum apud Lybedos Yonas statuisse, Caystro flumini proximum; nec longe ab eo Mopsum eiusdem filium Colophonem condidisse.

3 Eusebius autem dicit Mopsum apud Cilices regnasse, regnante Agamenone Mecenis, et ab eo Mopsicrene et Mopsistie dicti. Dicentibus Manthonem huius fuisse matrem, adversantur dicentes

: 5 :

On Eurynome, second child of Apollo

Paul of Perugia affirms that Eurynome was the daughter of Apollo, 1
that she was married to Talaon, and that she bore him Adrastus,
King of the Argives, and Eurydice, later wife of Amphiaraus.

: 6 :

On Mopsus, third child of Apollo

Mopsus, as Theodontius says, was the son of Apollo and Imas. 1
He joined in a great and steady friendship with Jason, as Statius
testifies:[27] "Mopsus was more often heard by Jason in time of
doubt." According to Lactantius,[28] he was very skilled at divination
and in charge of the Grynean woods, where there was an oracle of
Apollo, as Servius[29] says. He was in his day a man so venerable
that temples were dedicated to him after his death, and oracular
responses were received by petitioners from their secret chambers.

Paul however, says that he was not the son of Imas but of 2
Manto, the daughter of Theban Teiresias. In addition Pomponius
Mela[30] says that he founded the city of Phaselis in the territory
of Pamphylia; and again Pomponius not much later asserts that
Manto, fleeing the conquerors of Thebes, founded the sanctuary
of Claros at Ionian Lebedus next to the Cayster River, and that
not far from there his son Mopsus founded Colophon.

Eusebius[31] moreover says that Mopsus ruled among the Cili- 3
cians when Agamemnon ruled Mycenae, and from this they were
called Mopsicreni and Mopsisti. In opposition to those who say

Manthonem post Thebanum bellum in Ytaliam transmigrasse, et in Cisalpinam Galliam devenisse.

: 7 :

De Lyno IIII° Apollinis filio

1 Lynus, ut scribit Lactantius, ex Psamate filius fuit Apollinis, ex quo talem recitat fabulam: quod, cum interfecisset Apollo Phytonem serpentem et perquireret cedis acte piacula, a Crotopo rege Argivorum in domum susceptus est, ubi clam cum Psamate virgine et eiusdem Crotopi filia concubuit. Que cum concepisset et tempore debito secus Nemeum flumen occulte peperisset, filium illum Lynum appellavit, eumque, ut placet aliquibus, exposuit, et sic repertus a canibus devoratus est.

2 Alii vero dicunt quia illum pastori cuidam alendum tradidit, tamen dum quadam die incuria pastoris parvulus iaceret in herba,

3 a canibus devoratus est. Quod Statius testari videtur dicens:

> Irradiant; medio Lynus intertextus acanto
> letiferique canes,
>
> etc.

Apollo autem iratus filium fuisse a canibus devoratum, regioni monstrum immisit, cuncta devastans, quod postmodum Corebus occidit.

Arbitror fictioni huic causam dedisse aliquod pestiferum animal, quod forte eo tempore apparuit, quo puer iste a canibus discerptus est; quod cum impium visum sit, eo dictum monstrum

that Manto was his mother are those who say that Manto migrated to Italy after the Theban war and reached Cisalpine Gaul.

⁝ 7 ⁝

On Linus, the fourth child of Apollo

Linus, as Lactantius[32] writes, was the son of Apollo by Psamathe,   1
about whom he tells the following fable: when Apollo killed the
serpent Python and sought an expiatory offering for the murder
he committed, he was taken in by Crotopus, King of Argos, and
there he secretly slept with Psamathe, Crotopus' virgin daughter.
When she conceived and then in due time gave birth to a son in
secret alongside the Nemeus River, she called him Linus; according to many, she exposed him, and thereafter, he was devoured by
the dogs who found him.

Others say that she gave him to a certain shepherd to raise, and   2
then one day when the young child was lying on the grass and being neglected by the shepherd, he was devoured by dogs. Statius   3
seems to testify to this, saying:[33]

They shone, and woven amidst acanthus were Linus
and the deadly dogs.

Angered that his son was devoured by dogs, however, Apollo sent
a monster into the area, destroying everything; afterward Coroebus killed it.

I think the inspiration for this fiction was some destructive animal which appeared by chance at the same time a boy was torn
apart by dogs; because that seemed to be an ungodly act, it was

4 immissum. Fuit insuper et alter Lynus, qui Apollinis filius fuit, et in musica mirabilis habitus est, de quo Virgilius:

> Non me carminibus vincet nec Tracius Orpheus
> nec Lynus,
>
> etc.

: 8 :

De Phylistene V° Apollinis filio

1 Phylistenes, ut Servio placet, Apollinis ex Cantilena filius fuit, quem ait Oaxem oppidum in Creta insula condidisse, et ex suo nuncupasse nomine; unde Varro:

> Quos magno[5] Cantilena partus adducta dolore et geminis[6]
> cupiens tellurem Oaxida palmis scindere,
>
> etc.

2 Si ergo Oaxidem suo nomine appellavit, binomius de necessitate fuit. Ego existimo eum cantu valuisse, et inde tam Cantilene quam Apollinis filium a poetis fictum.

: 9 :

De Garamante VI° Apollinis filio

1 Garamas, ut Rabanus ait in libro *De originibus rerum*, filius fuit Apollinis, et ab eo, ut idem ait, Garamantes Ethyopie populi nuncupati sunt, et Garama oppidum apud Ethyopas constructum.

said that a monster had been sent against them. In addition, there   4
was also another Linus who was the son of Apollo, and he was
thought to be remarkable in music. Vergil says this about him:[34]

> Thracian Orpheus will not best me in song,
> nor will Linus.

: 8 :

On Philistenes, sixth child of Apollo

Philistenes, according to Servius,[35] was the son of Apollo by Can-   1
tilena, whom he says founded the town of Oaxes on the island of
Crete and named it after himself. On this Varro says:[36]

> Cantilena[37], suffering from such great labor pains, wanted to
> split Oaxes with her two hands.

If therefore he named Oaxes after himself, he by necessity had two   2
names. I think therefore that he was a fine singer, and therefore
poets invented the story that he was the son of Cantilena and
Apollo.

: 9 :

On Garamas, sixth child of Apollo

Garamas, as Rabanus[38] says in his book *On the Nature of Things,*   1
was the son of Apollo, and, as Rabanus then says, the Ethiopian
people were called Garamantes after him, and Garamas was a

2 Hunc ego ideo Apollinis filium fictum reor, quia ibidem imperavit, ubi profecto nimio estu sol omnia fere perimat, quas quia sedes elegit tanquam sterilitate et estu delectatus, filius Apollinis habitus est.

: 10 :

De Branco VII° Apollinis filio

1 Brancus, ut ait Lactantius, Apollinis fuit filius, ex filia Ioucis et Sucronis coniuge susceptus. Cuius talis est fabula, secundum Varronem, in libro *Rerum divinarum.* Cyus quidam decimus ab Apolline genus ducens, cum peregrinando pranderet in litore, ac deinde forte minus sobrius proficisceretur, oblitus Sucronem filium pue-
2 rum dereliquit. Qui Sucron, patre perdito, errans pervenit in saltum cuiusdam Ioucis, receptusque cepit cum pueris illius capras in pascua ducere. Contigit eos cignum capere, quem cum veste texissent, pueri pugnabant inter se, quisnam illum patrono muneris
3 loco deberet offerre. Tandem fatigati certamine, reiecta veste, loco cigni compererunt mulierem, quo eventu territi, cepere fugam, verum revocati ab ea moniti sunt, Iouci patrono suo dicerent, ut Sucronem puerum coleret. Illi vero et que contigerant et que audiverant patrono recitant; tunc Ioucis miratus, Sucronem habere loco filii cepit, eique filiam suam locavit uxorem, que, cum pregnans esset, vidit per quietem solem per fauces suas intrasse et exisse ex ventre. Post hec editus est filius, quem Brancum vocaverunt, qui cum Apollinis malas deosculatus fuisset, ab eo captus,

town constructed among the Ethiopians. That he was a son of   2
Apollo I think was invented because he ruled where the sun surely
destroys nearly everything with its excessive heat; and because he
chose this territory, as if he enjoyed the sterility and the heat, he
was regarded as the son of Apollo.

: 10 :

On Branchus, seventh child of Apollo

Branchus, as Lactantius[39] says, was the son of Apollo whom he   1
received from the daughter of Iouces, the wife of Sucro.[40] This is
his story, according to Varro[41] in his book of *Divine Matters*. While
traveling, a certain Cyus, the tenth descendant from Apollo, was
eating breakfast on the shore, and then, perhaps less sober, departed, forgetting his young son Sucro and leaving him behind.
Having lost his father, this Sucro wandered around and then came   2
to the territory of a certain Iouces, was taken in, and, along with
his own sons, began to pasture the goats. It happened that they
captured a swan, and after they covered it with a garment, the
boys began to fight among themselves over who ought to offer it as
a gift to Iouces. Then, wearied by the contest, when they threw off   3
the garment, they found instead of the swan a woman. Terrified by
this outcome they took flight; she called them back, however, and
admonished them to tell their patron Iouces to honor the boy
Sucro. They told Iouces what had happened and what they had
heard; amazed, he began to regard Sucro like a son and gave his
daughter to him as a wife, who, when she became pregnant, saw in
her sleep the sun entering into her jaws and exiting from her
womb. After this a son was born whom they called Branchus, and
when he had kissed the cheek of Apollo, he was taken by him, ac-

coronam accepit et virgam, cepitque vaticinari, et subito nusquam
4 comparuit. Post hec illi templum ingens constructum est, quod
Branchiadon nominatur, et Apollini Phylesio ob hanc rem conse-
crata sunt templa, que ab osculo Branchidis, sive certamine puerorum, Phylesia nuncupantur.

5 Alibi vero scribit Lactantius Brancum fuisse Thessalum adoles-
centem ab Apolline dilectum, quem interfectum acriter dolens sepulcro sacravit et templo et ibidem Branchiades Apollo dicitur.

In precedenti fabula pueri, id est ignari, cignum capiunt, id est
futuri vatis augurium; nam cignus avis soli dicatus est, eo quod
propinquam sibi mortem precognoscat et suavissimo cantu predi-
6 cet. Ex augurio autem sumpto in loquacitatem itur, et ideo in
mulierem, que loquax animal est, cignum versum fingitur. Ex hac
loquacitate fit ut Sucron carior efficiatur patrono, eiusque deveniat
gener, videatque in somniis coniunx pregnans solem per guttur
eius intrantem, id est celestem influentiam ad producendum procreatum aptum vaticinio, quod per solem intelligitur, qui demum
ventrem egreditur, dum nascitur, qui Apollinis tunc mala deoscu-
latur, dum delectatione absque qua nil perficitur, adheret studio
vaticinandi, et tunc coronam et virgam ab Apolline suscepit, dum
eruditus insignia doctoratus assummit. Nam per coronam, que
capitis ornamentum est, preminentia designatur, quam quis per
7 quesitam studiis scientiam consequitur. Per virgam autem potestas
intelligitur exercendi que studio quesita sunt. Eum autem nusquam comparuisse, eo factum est, quia morte de medio sublatus est.

cepted a crown and wand, and began to prophesy; and suddenly
he was not to be seen. After this a large temple was built for him   4
which is called the Branchiadon, and on account of this there are
temples consecrated to Apollo Philesius, named from the kiss of
Branchus, or the contest of the boys.

Elsewhere Lactantius[42] writes that Branchus was a Thessalian   5
youth loved by Apollo, and after he was killed, Apollo, grieving
bitterly, honored him with a tomb and a temple, and there he is
called Apollo Branchiades.

In the preceding story, the boys, that is, the ignorant, captured
a swan, that is, the prediction of the coming soothsayer, for the
swan is a bird sacred to the sun because it senses in advance the
approach of its death and foretells of it in a most lovely song. The   6
mantle of augury leads toward loquaciousness, and therefore the
swan was said to be turned into a woman, which is a loquacious
creature. It is from this loquaciousness that Sucro became dearer
to Iouces and became his son-in-law, and that his pregnant wife
saw in her dreams the sun entering through her throat, that is, the
celestial influence for producing an offspring suited for prophecy,
which is signified by the sun, and then leaving the womb in the
birth of him who then kissed the cheek of Apollo; and then because of pleasure, without which nothing is accomplished, he
dedicated himself to his zeal for prophesying. Then he took up the
crown and wand from Apollo when he was educated and assumed
the insignia of his learning. The crown, which is an ornament of
the head, designates preeminence, which someone pursues through
the knowledge sought through devotion to study. The wand signi-   7
fies the power of exercising what is sought through study. That he
never appeared comes from his being taken from the middle of
death.

: II :

De Phylemone VIII° Apollinis filio

1 Phylemon Apollinis et Lychionis, ut testatur Ovidius, fuit filius. Nam, ut ipse refert, Dedalion Luciferi filius habuit speciosissimam filiam, quam cum Apollo et Mercurius eodem tempore dilexissent, et in eius ivissent concubitum, ex ambobus concepit et Apollini peperit Phylemonem, qui carmine clarus fuit et cythara.

2 Quod autem hic fictum est, ab eventu sumptum puto; nam Lychion uno partu duos enixa est, quorum alter fuit insignis fur, quem dixerunt genuisse Mercurium, eo quod circa talia videatur astrologis operari Mercurius, alter vero cytharista fuit egregius, circa quod solem arbitrantur operam dare, et ideo Apollinis filium vocavere.

: 12 :

De Orpheo Apollinis filio VIIII°

1 Orpheus Caliopis muse et Apollinis fuit filius, ut dicit Lactantius. Huic, dicit Rabanus, Mercurius lyram, nuper a se compertam, tradidit, qua tantum valuit, ut ea movere silvas et flumina sistere et feras mites facere posset. De hoc Virgilius talem recitat fabulam: eum scilicet amasse Euridicem nynpham, quam cum suo cantu in suam traxisset gratiam, eam sibi iunxit uxorem. Hanc cepit amare Aristeus pastor, et die quadam, dum secus ripas Hebri cum Dryadibus spatiaretur, eam capere voluit, que fugiens pede serpentem inter herbas latitantem pressit, qui revolutus in eam venenato

: 11 :

On Philemon, eighth child of Apollo

Philemon, as Ovid[43] testifies, was the son of Apollo and Chione, 1
for, as he himself says, Daedalion, son of Lucifer, had a very beautiful daughter who, when Apollo and Mercury desired her at the
same time and entered her bed, conceived from both and bore to
Apollo Philemon, who was famous for his song and cithara.

I think, however, that this fiction was taken from its outcome, 2
for Chione gave birth to two sons in one birth, one of whom was
a famous thief, whom they said Mercury fathered because Mercury, as the astrologers think, influences these matters; the other
was an excellent citharist, a matter they think is under the influence of the sun, and so they call him the son of Apollo.

: 12 :

On Orpheus, ninth child of Apollo

Orpheus was the son of the Muse Calliope and Apollo, as Lactan- 1
tius[44] says. To him, Rabanus[45] says, Mercury gave the lyre he had
recently invented, which he played so well that he could move
forests with it, stop rivers, and tame wild beasts. Vergil[46] recites
the following tale about him. Orpheus loved the nymph Eurydice,
whom he had charmed with his song, and married her. The shepherd Aristaeus began to fall in love with her, and one day, while
she was walking along the banks of the Hebrus River with the
Dryads, he wanted to abduct her; while fleeing her foot landed on
a serpent lurking in the grass, whereupon the serpent twisted

2   morsu interemit. Quam ob causam gemebundus Orpheus descendit ad inferos et lyra adeo dulciter canere cepit, orans ut sibi restitueretur Euridices, quod non solum ministros inferni in sui pietatem traheret, sed et umbras in oblivionem penarum suarum deduceret. Ex quo factum est, ut illi a Proserpina Euridices restitueretur hac lege, ne illam, nisi perdere vellet, respiceret, donec devenisset ad superos, qui cum iam proximus esset, nimio videndi Euridicem suam desiderio tractus, oculos in postergantem flexit,

3   ex quo factum est, ut evestigio dilectam iterum perderet. Quam ob causam diu flevit et celibem deducere vitam disposuit. Et ob id, ut ait Ovidius, cum multas suas nuptias postulantes reiecisset, aliisque hominibus celibem vitam ducere suaderet, mulierum incidit odium, et a celebrantibus matronis orgia Bachi secus Hebrum, rastris atque ligonibus cesus atque discerptus est, et eius caput in Hebrum proiectum cum cythara in Lesbon usque delata sunt, ubi cum serpens quidam caput devorare vellet, ab Apolline in saxum versus est. Lyra autem, ut dicit Rabanus, in celum assumpta et inter alias celestes ymagines locata est.

4   Pulchre equidem et artificiose fictiones he sunt, et ut incipiamus a prima, cur Apollinis et Caliopis dicatur filius videamus.

5   Dicitur autem Orpheus quasi 'aurea' *phones*, id est 'bona eloquentie vox', que quidem Apollinis, id est sapientie, et Caliopis, que 'bonus' interpretatur 'sonus,' filia est. Lyra autem illi a Mercurio data est, quia per lyram diversa vocum habentem discrimina, debemus intelligere oratoriam facultatem, que non una voce, id est demonstratione, conficitur, sed ex multis, et confecta non omnibus convenit, sed sapienti atque eloquenti, et bona voce valenti, que cum

around and killed her with its poisonous bite. With a groan Or- 2
pheus descended to the nether region but began to sing so sweetly
with his lyre, pleading that Eurydice be restored to him, that not
only did he charm the ministers of the underworld into having
pity for him but he also lured the shades into forgetting their punishments. As a result Eurydice would be restored to him by Proserpina albeit with this condition, that until they reached the upper world he would not look back at her, unless he wished to lose
her. When he was already near, compelled by an excessive desire
for seeing Eurydice, he turned his eyes toward her as she was following him, and this immediately caused him to lose his beloved
again. For this reason he wept for a long time and committed him- 3
self to lead a life of celibacy. And on account of this, as Ovid[47]
says, after rejecting many women who sought to marry him and
persuading many other men to lead a life of celibacy, he incited the
hatred of women, and alongside the Hebrus he was killed and
dismembered with hoes and mattocks by matrons celebrating the
orgies of Bacchus; his head, along with his cithara, was thrown
into the Hebrus and carried to Lesbos; and there, when a serpent
wished to devour the head, Apollo turned it into stone. The lyre,
though, as Rabanus[48] says, was taken up to the sky and placed
among the other celestial images.

These fictions are indeed beautiful and skillful, and so that we 4
begin from the beginning, let us see why he is called the son of
Apollo and Calliope. He is called Orpheus as if "golden sounds" 5
[aurea phones], that is, "the good voice of eloquence," which indeed
is the daughter of Apollo, that is, wisdom, and Calliope, which
means "good sound." The lyre was given to him by Mercury because it is through the lyre, which has a variety of distinctions of
tone, that we ought to understand the faculty of oratory, which
reaches perfection not by one voice, that is, by one descriptive
mode, but by many; and in its most perfected form it properly
belongs only to the wise, eloquent, and those with a good, strong

omnia in Orpheum convenirent, a Mercurio mensuratore tempo-
6 rum eidem concessa dicuntur. Hac Orpheus movet silvas radices
habentes firmissimas et infixas solo, id est obstinate opinionis
homines, qui, nisi per eloquentie vires queunt a sua pertinacia re-
moveri. Sistit flumina, id est fluxos et lascivos homines, qui, nisi
validis eloquentie demonstrationibus in virile robur firmentur, in
mare usque defluunt, id est in perpetuam amaritudinem. Feras
mites facit, id est homines sanguinum rapacesque, quos sepissime
eloquentia sapientis revocat in mansuetudinem et humanitatem.

7   Hic insuper Euridicem habet in coniugem, id est naturalem
concupiscientiam, qua nemo mortalium caret. Hanc per prata va-
gantem, id est per temporalia desideria, amat Aristeus, id est virtus, que eam in laudabilia desideria trahere cupit. Verum ipsa fugit, quia naturalis concupiscientia virtuti contradicit, et dum fugit
virtutem a serpente occiditur, id est a fraude inter temporalia la-
tente. Nam apparet minus recte intuentibus temporalia virere, id
est posse beatitudinem prestare, cui apparentie si quis credat, se in
perpetuam deduci mortem comperiet.

8   Sed quid tandem? Cum naturalis concupiscientia ad inferos, id
est circa terrena, omnino lapsa est, vir prudens eloquentia, id est
demonstrationibus veris, eam conatur ad superiora, id est ad vir-
tuosa, reducere. Que tandem aliquando restituitur, et hoc dum
appetitus ad laudabiliora dirigitur, sed redditur pacto, ne retro
suscipiens respiciat, donec ad superos usque devenerit, id est ne
iterum in concupiscentiam talium relabatur, donec, cognitione veritatis et superum bonorum intelligentia roboratus ad damnandam
scelestorum operum spurcitiem, oculos possit in concupiscientiam
9 flectere. Quod autem ob id Orpheus ad inferos descenderit, debemus accipere prudentes viros non nunquam ratione contempla-

voice. And since Orpheus had all these qualities, they were said to have been given him by Mercury, the measurer of time. With this 6 Orpheus moves the forests which have roots very firmly fixed in the earth, that is, men of obstinate opinions who cannot be swayed from their stubbornness except through the power of eloquence. He stops rivers, that is, dissolute and wanton men who, unless they are emboldened by demonstrations of strong eloquence that lead them toward manly strength, that flow into the sea, that is, into perpetual bitterness. He tames wild beasts, that is, rapacious and bloodthirsty men, whom very often the eloquence of wisdom redirects into gentleness and humanity.

In addition, he marries Eurydice, that is, natural concupiscence, 7 which no mortal lacks. As she wanders through the meadow, that is, through temporal desires, she is loved by Aristaeus, that is, virtue, which wishes to lure her toward laudable desires. But she flees because natural concupiscence opposes virtue, and while she is fleeing virtue she is killed by a serpent, that is, by fraud lurking among temporal matters, for it appears to those seeing incorrectly that temporal things thrive, that is, are able to offer beatitude, and whoever believes in such a false appearance will find himself led into eternal death.

But then why? Because natural concupiscence descends alto- 8 gether to the nether region, that is, the earthly world, the prudent man attempts to restore it through eloquence, that is, true demonstration, to the upper world, that is, to virtue. It is finally restored at some point, and this happens when the appetite is directed toward the more praiseworthy, but it returns with the understanding that it not look back in suspicion until it reaches the upper world, that is, lest it slip back again into the concupiscence of such things, until, strengthened by the awareness of truth and the knowledge of heavenly good for damning the filth of wicked works, it is able to turn its eyes toward concupiscence. In that Orpheus descended 9 to the nether region we ought to understand that prudent men

tionis in perituras res et hominum ignavias oculos meditationis
deflectere, ut, dum que damnare debeant viderint, que appetenda
sunt ferventiori desiderio concupiscant.

10   Fulgentius autem longe aliter sentit; dicit enim dilecte ac perdite et demum reassumpte Euridicis esse musice designationem,
cum Orpheus dicatur quasi *orenphone*, quod interpretatur 'vox op-
tima.' Euridices autem 'profunda diiudicatio,' et ideo cum in musicis aliud sit armonia ptongorum, et aliud effectus tonorum virtus-
que verborum etc. ut ubi *De mitologiis*.

11   Sed ut ad ea veniamus, que ad Orphei videntur spectare mortem, est sciendum, ut dicit Theodontius, Orpheum primo Bachi
sacra comperisse, et ea iussit apud Traces choris Menadum, id est
mulierum patientium menstruum, ut illas illo tempore auferret a
commixtione virorum, cum non solum abominabile sit, sed etiam
12   perniciosum viris. Quod cum mulieres post tempus advertissent,
et existimassent hoc adinventum ad turpitudinem earum viris de-
tegendam, in Orpheum coniuravere, illumque nil tale suspicantem
interfecere ligonibus, et in Hebrum fluvium deiecere. Lactantius
autem, in libro *Divinarum institutionum*, dicit de eo sic:

Sacra Liberi patris primus Orpheus induxit in Greciam,
primusque celebravit in monte Boetie Thebis, ubi Liber natus est, proximo, qui cum frequenter cythare cantu persona-
13   ret, Cytheron appellatus est. Ea sacra etiam nunc Orphyca
nominantur, in quibus ipse postea dilaceratus et carptus est,

etc.

sometimes for reason of contemplation deflect the eyes of their profound thought toward perishable things and the faintheartedness of men, so that while they see what they ought to damn, they seek after the things which must be sought with a more fervent desire.

Fulgentius[49] thinks very differently, for he says that Eurydice, 10 loved, lost, and then recovered, describes music, while Orpheus is named as if from *orenphone*, which means "best voice." Eurydice, moreover, means "profound distinction;" because in music one aspect is the harmony of sounds, and the other is the effect of tones and the virtue of the words, etc., as in the *Mythologies*.

But as we come to the details of the death of Orpheus, it 11 should be known, as Theodontius says, that Orpheus first discovered the rites of Bacchus, and he ordered them performed among the Thracians by the choruses of Maenads, that is, women undergoing menstruation, so that he took them at that time from the company of men, since their state was not only abominable but also harmful to men. When the women after some time thought 12 about this and believed that he invented the practice to expose their turpitude to men, they conspired against Orpheus, and they killed him totally unsuspecting with mattocks and threw him into the Hebrus River. In his *Divine Institutions* Lactantius says this about it:[50]

> Orpheus first introduced the rites of Father Liber into Greece, and he first celebrated them on the mountain of Boeotia near Thebes, where Liber was born; this mountain is called Cithaeron, for it frequently resounds with the "song of the cithara" [*cythare cantu*]. Now these are also called the 13 Orphic rites, in which he himself was later torn to pieces and dismembered.

Quod caput eius et cythara Lesbos delata sint, dicebat Leontius fabulam non esse, quia sic fama ferebat Lesbium quendam ex auditoribus eius ea secum devotionis causa Lesbos usque portasse.

14 Quod autem serpens, qui caput Orphei devorare volebat, in lapidem versus sit, intelligo pro serpente annorum revolutiones, que caput, id est nomen Orphei, seu ea que ingenio Orphei composita sunt, cum in capite vigeant vires ingenii, consumere, ut reliqua faciunt, conate sint. Sed in saxum ideo versus dicitur serpens, ut ostendatur nil illi posse tempus obsistere, quod quidem huc usque non potuit egisse, quin adhuc famosus existat cum cythara sua, cum ex poetis fere antiquior reputetur.

15 Preterea[7] sunt qui velint, et inter hos Plinius in libro *Hystorie naturalis*, huius inventum fuisse auguria ex ceteris animalibus sumi, que primo tantum ex avibus sumebantur. Equo modo opinati sunt quidam eum primum cytharam excogitasse, quantumcunque Amphioni aut Lyno attribuant alii. Fuit enim ex gente Cycona Tracie natus, que, ut Solinus *De mirabilibus mundi* affirmat, in evum usque suum in maximum sui decus sumebat.

16 De tempore eius non videtur ambigi. Multi enim testantur quod inter Argonautas Colcos cum Iasone accesserit, ut Statius. De hoc tamen scribit Lactantius in libro *Divinarum institutionum*.

Et fuit per eodem fere tempora quibus Faunus, sed quis etate processerit potest dubitari. Si quidem per eosdem annos Latinus Priamusque regnarunt, item patres eorum Faunus et Laomedon, quo regnante Orpheus cum Argonautis ad Yliensium litus accessit.

17 Hec Lactantius. Eusebius autem in libro *Temporum* dicit eum fuisse regnante Athenis Egeo. Que quidem satis convenire viden-

That his head and cithara were carried to Lesbos Leontius used to say was not a fable, because there was a story that one of his Lesbian listeners carried them to Lesbos out of devotion. As for the serpent that wished to devour the head of Orpheus being turned to stone, I understand the serpent as the revolutions of the years which attempted to consume, as they do other things, the head, that is, the name of Orpheus, or the things composed by the talent of Orpheus, since the powers of genius thrive in the head; but the serpent is said to have been turned into stone so as to show that it was not possible for him to stop time; up to this point he indeed could not have done that because Orpheus with his cithara is still famous even though the poets thought he was quite ancient.

In addition there are those, among whom is Pliny[51] in his *Natural History*, who prefer to believe that it was his discovery to take auguries from the other animals, since previously auguries were only taken from birds. In the same way some thought that he first devised the cithara, even if others attribute that to Amphion or Linus, for he was born in the Thracian nation of Sithonia, which, as Solinus[52] affirms in his *On the Wonders of the World*, regarded this as its greatest glory, even as late as his own day.

His era does not seem to be in doubt. Many, including Statius,[53] bear witness that he sailed to Colchis among the Argonauts with Jason. Lactantius writes about this in his *Divine Institutes*:[54]

> And Faunus lived at nearly the same time as they did, but there can be some doubt as to who was prior in age. If Latinus and Priam ruled during the same years, then likewise their fathers Faunus and Laomedon, the latter ruling when Orpheus with the Argonauts reached the shores of Ilium.

Thus says Lactantius. Eusebius[55] in his *Chronicle* says that he lived when Aegeus ruled Athens, and these seem to agree sufficiently.

tur. Leontius[8] autem dicebat hunc non eum fuisse, qui orgica adinvenit, cum illum assereret longe antiquiorem.

: 13 :

De Aristeo Apollinis X° filio, qui genuit Actheonem et Yolaum

1 Aristeus filius fuit Apollinis et Cyrenis, filie Penei fluminis, ut testatur Virgilius in persona Aristei in *Georgicis* dicens:

> Mater, Cyrene mater, que gurgitis huius
> ima tenes, quid me preclara stirpe deorum,
> si modo, quem perhibes, pater est Tymbreus Apollo,
> invisum fatis genuisti?

etc.

2 Quod etiam Iustinus in *Epythomate Pompei Trogi* confirmat, talem hystoriam recitans. Quod Cyrus, scilicet rex Coramis insule, filium habuit, cui nomen Bathos propter lingue obligationem. Verum cum Cyrus ad oraculum Delphos propter dedecus adolescentis filii deprecaturus venisset, habuit in responsis Bathos Affricam petere, Cyrenem urbem condere, et ibidem lingue usum accepturum; quod ob solitudinem Coramis insule omissum est, quasi non ha-
3 berent unde colonos in Affricam deducerent. Tandem tractu temporis peste compulsi adeo paucos misere, ut vix navis compleretur una. Hi in Affricam venientes, montem Cyrum, loci amenitate et ubertate fontium capti, occupavere. Ibique Bathos, solutis lingue nodis, dux eorum loqui primum cepit. Quam ob rem oraculi pro-

Leontius, moreover, used to say that he was not the Orpheus who invented the secret mysteries, for he asserted that this Orpheus was more ancient by far.

: 13 :

On Aristaeus, tenth child of Apollo,
who fathered Acteon and Iolaus

Aristaeus was the son of Apollo and Cyrene, daughter of the Pe- 1
neus River, as Vergil testifies in the persona of Aristaeus, saying in the *Georgics*:[56]

> Mother, mother Cyrene, who at this pool's
> bottom dwells, why to me, illustrious scion of the gods,
> if only, as you suggest, my father is Thymbrean Apollo,
> did you give birth so hateful to the fates?

Justin in his *Epitome of Pompeius Trogus* confirms this in telling the 2
following history:[57] Cyrus, that is king of the island of Coramis, had a son whose name was Bathos because he was tongue-tied.[58] But when Cyrus had come to entreat the Delphic oracle on behalf of his adolescent son's disgrace, the oracle responded that Bathos should seek Africa and found the city of Cyrene, and there he would gain the use of his tongue; this was not done because the island of Coramis was so isolated that they did not know how to lead colonists to Africa. After some time passed they were forced 3
by a plague to send so few that they scarcely filled one ship. When they arrived in Africa, attracted by the pleasant location and the abundance of springs, they occupied Mount Cyra; and there their leader Bathos, the knots of his tongue loosened, first began to speak, wherefore, confident in the response of the oracle, they

4   missis certi urbem condidere Cyrenem. Porro sic a posteris fictum est, Cyrenem eximie pulchritudinis virginem a Pelio monte Thessalie ab Apolline raptam, perlatamque in eius montis iuga, cuius collem occupaverant qui filium secuti sunt, et ab eo repletam quattuor peperisse filios: Aristeum, Nomium, Auctoum et Argeum.

5   Fictio[9] autem hec ab hystoria non recedit. Nam ab Apolline ideo rapta dicitur nynpha, quia eius mandato, dum responsum dedit oratus, seu eius opera, dum pestis invasit insulam, in Cyrum montem delata est, ibidem etsi non omnes peperit, quia iam Bathos dux itineris fuerat, sed in etatem, sub fervido sole, id est Apolline, virilem forte deduxit. Verum a Speo Thessalie rege, qui apud Peneum fluvium regnum habuit patre Cyrenis, missi sunt qui perquirerent quonam abiisset filia. Qui, ea comperta a loci amenitate detenti, in iisdem terris aiunt cum Cyrene remansisse. Ex his tantum pueris tres aiunt adultos in Thessaliam rediisse et avita regna recepisse. Inter quos dicunt Aristeum in Arcadia late regnasse, eumque primum apis et mellis usum et lactis coagulum tradidisse, atque[10] trapetis oleas premere, oleum educere et eius usum ostendisse, ut refert Plinius de *Hystoria naturali*. Preterea

6   sciens factus, syderis solstitialis ortus primum invenisse. Quibus consideratis, non absurde Virgilius fabulam Aristei, de recuperatione apium, in fine *Georgicorum* descripsit.

Hunc insuper volunt Auctonoem Cadmi filiam in coniugem accepisse, et ex ea suscepisse Actheonem. Sane, ut Salustio placet, matris consilio relictis Thebis, in Cheam insulam, illo usque ab hominibus inhabitatam, abiit, eamque[11] tenuit, esto reliquerit postea, et cum Dedalo in Sardiniam abierit, in qua, ut dicit Solinus *De*

founded the city of Cyrene. Later their descendants invented the 4
story that Cyrene was a maiden of exceptional beauty ravaged by
Apollo from Mount Pelion in Thessaly and taken to the summit
of that mountain, the foothills of which the son's companions had
occupied; and impregnated by Apollo, she gave birth to four sons:
Aristaeus, Nomius, Autucus, and Agreus.[59]

This fiction[60] resembles history, which tells us again that the 5
nymph was ravaged by Apollo but that it was by his order, which
he gave as a response to a prayer, or because of his deed that she
was taken to Mount Cyra when a plague invaded the island: it is
not that she gave birth to all there — Bathos had already become
leader of the journey — but that perhaps he reached manhood under the hot sun, that is, Apollo. Meanwhile Speus, King of Thessaly, the father of Cyrene who ruled near the Peneus River, sent
them to ask where his daughter had gone. Having found her, but
detained by the pleasantness of the place, they say that they remained there with Cyrene. Of these boys they say that three returned as adults to Thessaly and received their ancestral kingdom.
Among them, they say that Aristaeus ruled a great kingdom in
Arcadia and that he was the first to teach the use of the bee and
honey, the coagulation of milk, and how to apply the press to olives and make olive oil, and he demonstrated its uses, as Pliny[61]
reports in his *Natural History*. In addition, by developing his knowledge he became the first to discover the solstitial rising of the sun.
Taking all this into consideration, I think Vergil appropriately re- 6
counted the story of Aristaeus and the recovery of the bees at the
end of the *Georgics*.[62]

They also want him to be married to Autonoe, daughter of
Cadmus, and to have produced Acteon by her. But, according to
Sallust,[63] following his mother's advice, he left Thebes for the island of Cea, uninhabited until then, and occupied it, although
later he left and went with Daedalus to Sardinia, where, as Soli-

mirabilibus, urbem Caralim condidit. Quid inde ex eo contigerit legisse non memini.

: 14 :

De Actheone filio Aristei

1 Actheon filius fuit Aristei ex Auctonoe coniuge, Statio[12] teste:

> Nec dum ille habitus aut[13] verse crimina forme
> mutat Aristeo genitus; frons aspera cornu
> tela manu reicitque canes in vulnus hyantes.

Hic etiam, ut ait Ovidius, Yanthius appellatus est. Scribit enim, 'Cum iuvenis placido compellat Yanthius ore.'

2 Et sunt qui dicant hoc illi nomen a puella sepulta eo in loco in quo natus est. Hic, ut ostendit idem Ovidius, venator fuit, et cum die quadem venatione fessus in valle Gargaphie descendisset, eo quod in ea fons esset, recens et limpidus, et ad eum forte potatu-

3 rus accederet, vidit in ea Dianam nudam se lavantem. Quod cum egre Diana tulisset, sumpta manibus aqua, in faciem eius proiecit dicens, 'Vade et dic, si potes.' Is autem repente in cervum conver- sus est, quem cum canes eius vidissent, confestim irruerunt in eum, illumque in mortem coactum atque dentibus laceratum comederunt.

nus[64] says in his *On the Wonders of the World*, he founded the city of Carales [Cagliari]. What happened to him after that I do not remember reading.

: 14 :

On Acteon, son of Aristaeus

Acteon was the son of Aristaeus by his wife Autonoe, according to   1
Statius:[65]

> He has changed neither appearance nor the reproach
> of his transformation, the son of Aristaeus; his forehead jagged
>   with horns,
> in his hand he repels by spear the dogs gaping to wound him.

He was also called, as Ovid says, Hyantius, for he writes,[66] "When the youth Hyantius compels with his gentle speech."

And there are those who say that his name comes from that of   2
a girl who was buried in the place where he was born. As Ovid again shows, he was a hunter, and one day when he was tired from hunting he had descended into the valley of Gargaphia because there was a fresh, clear spring there. And when he approached it simply to take a drink, he saw there the naked Diana taking a bath. Because Diana became upset at this, taking water into her   3
hands, she threw it into his face, saying: "Go and speak, if you can." He immediately was changed into a stag, and when his dogs saw him, right away they attacked him, killed him, tore at him with their teeth, and ate him.

4   Circa quod figmentum sic scribit Fulgentius:

> Anaximenes, qui de picturis antiquis disseruit, ait libro se-
> cundo venationem Actheonem dilexisse, qui cum ad matu-
> ram pervenisset etatem, consideratis venationum periculis, id
> est quasi nudam artis sue rationem videns, timidus factus
> est.

Et paulo post:

> Sed cum venandi periculum fugeret, affectum tamen canum
> non dimisit, quos inaniter pascendo, pene omnem substan-
> tiam perdidit. Ob hanc rem a canibus suis devoratus dicitur.

Hec Fulgentius.

: 15 :

De Yolao Aristei filio

1   Yolaum dicit Solinus *De mirabilibus* filium fuisse Aristei, et post
eum in Sardinia dominium tenuisse. Supra autem dixit in suo volumine Yolaum filium fuisse Yphiclei, filii Amphytrionis, et eque in
Sardinia imperasse, nescio an idem sit vel alius.

Fulgentius[67] writes the following about this invented story: 4

> Anaximenes, who discussed ancient pictures, says in his second book that Acteon loved hunting, and that when he reached a mature age, having thought about the dangers of hunting, that is, as if seeing the stark reality of his skill, became fearful.

And a little further:

> But although he fled the danger of hunting, he did not abandon his love for his dogs: feeding them foolishly, he spent nearly everything he had. It is on account of this that it was said that he was eaten by his dogs.

This is what Fulgentius says.

: 15 :

On Iolaus, son of Aristaeus

Solinus[68] in *On the Wonders of the World* says that Iolaus was the   1
son of Aristaeus, and that he held dominion in Sardinia after him. But earlier in his work he said that Iolaus was the son of Iphicles, son of Amphitryon, and, again, ruled in Sardinia. I do not know if he is the same Iolaus or another.

: 16 :

De Nomio Apollinis XI° filio

1 Nomius, ut scribit Iustinus in *Epythoma*, filius fuit Apollinis et Cyrenis. Hunc dicit Leontius Apollinem nominatum, quicquid supra dixerit Theodontius, eumque Arcadibus imperasse, eisque leges dedisse, que quoniam quosdam ex optimatibus viderentur offendere, orta seditione inter Arcades, Aristeo favente, pulsus est,

2 et loco eius regnavit Aristeus. Is autem ad Admetum Thessalie regem confugit, et eius armenta septem annis pavit, tandem viribus reassumptis, Aristeum fugavit et Arcadum verum obtinuit principatum, cum abiisset Aristeus in Ceam insulam, et quoniam armenta pavisset, Nomius appellatus est, quod apud Arcades 'pastor' sonat.

3 Et hinc dicit fictionem traxisse locum, Apollinem scilicet ob occisos Cyclopes divinitate spoliatum, Admeti regis armenta pavisse. Ego autem nescio quid credam potius, cum et vetustate et ignavia librariorum adeo periere codices, ut subtractum sit posse de quam plurimis veritatem cernere, et hinc amplissimus vagandi locus mendacio relictus est, cum scribat de antiquis unusquisque quod libet.

: 16 :

On Nomius, eleventh child of Apollo

Nomius, as Justin[69] writes in his *Epitome*, was the son of Apollo   1
and Cyrene. Leontius says he was called Apollo, which Theodontius had said earlier, and that he ruled the Arcadians and issued
laws for them; because these laws seemed to offend some of the
noblemen, a rebellion arose among the Arcadians, which Aristaeus
supported, and he was driven out, Aristaeus ruling in his stead.
Nomius fled to Admetus, King of Thessaly, and he tended his   2
herds for seven years. Then, regathering his forces, he put Aristaeus to flight and assumed the legitimate rule of the Arcadians;
Aristaeus went to the island of Cea. And because he fed the herds,
he was called Nomius, which among the Arcadians means "herdsman."

And it is from this he says that they derived the fiction that   3
Apollo was deprived of his divinity for killing the Cyclopes and
had to tend the herds of Admetus. But I do not know which to
believe, for because of both their great age and neglect of the copy-
ists the codices are so ruined that it prevents me from being able
to make a final decision about their accuracy: as a result there is
more than ample room for someone who writes whatever he wants
about the ancients to wander from the truth.

: 17 :

De Aucthoo XII° Apollinis filio

1 Aucthous filius fuit Apollinis et Cyrenis, ut supra monstratum est. Hunc sunt qui dicant, discedentibus fratribus ex Affrica, et in Greciam venientibus, Cyrene remansisse, et his imperasse, qui una secum ibidem remansere.

: 18 :

De Argeo XIII° Apollinis filio

1 Argeus, ut supra a Iustino monstratum est, Apollinis fuit filius et Cyrenis. Hic de se, quod ego noverim, nil preter nudum nomen posteritati reliquit.

: 19 :

De Esculapio XIIII° Apollinis filio, qui genuit Macaonem

1 Esculapius, ut fere prisci testantur omnes, Apollinis et Coronidis nynphe fuit filius. Dicit enim Ovidius hanc ex Laryssa fuisse et Flegie filiam, quam cum summe Apollo diligeret et in eius ivisset concubitum, pregnans effecta est. Porro corvus Apollinis avis ad Apollinem detulit, quia comperisset eam iuveni cuidam Hemonio commisceri. Quam ob causam turbatus Apollo eam sagittis occi-

: 17 :

On Autucus, twelfth child of Apollo

Autucus was the son of Apollo and Cyrene, as was shown above. 1
There are those who say that when his brothers departed from
Africa and came to Greece, he remained in Cyrene and ruled those
who remained there with him.

: 18 :

On Agreus, thirteenth child of Apollo

Agreus, as was shown above by Justin, was the son of Apollo and 1
Cyrene. He left nothing about himself to posterity that I know of
except his name alone.

: 19 :

On Aesculapius, fourteenth child of Apollo,
who fathered Machaon

Aesculapius, as nearly all the ancients testify, was the son of 1
Apollo and the nymph Coronis. Ovid[70] says she was from Larissa
and the daughter of Phlegyas. Apollo loved her greatly, and after
he entered into her bed she became pregnant. A little later a crow,
the bird of Apollo, informed Apollo that it had discovered that she
had sex with a certain youth named Haemonius. Apollo was dis-

dit, et facti tandem penitens, cum remediis suis illam nequiret ab inferis revocare, secto eius utero, conceptum ex se eduxit infantem, eumque Esculapium appellavit, et, ut fertur, Chironi centauro

2 tradidit educandum. Quem cum vidisset Alchyroe Chironis filia, vaticinii docta, vaticinata est quia mortuum hominem ab inferis revocaret in vitam, et ipse fulminatus deiceretur ad inferos. Quod effectu non caruit. Aiunt enim hunc arte sua cum eximius evasisset medicus, Diane precibus, Ypolitum, membris collectis undique, in vitam revocasse et pristine restituisse sanitati; quam ob causam turbatus Iuppiter, eum fulmine interemit, ut liquido testatur Virgilius dicens:

> Peoniis revocatum herbis et amore Diane.
> Tum pater omnipotens, aliquem indignatus ab umbris
> mortalem infernis ad limina surgere vite,
> ipse repertorem medicine talis et artis
> fulmine Phebigenam Stygias detrusit in undas,
>
> etc.

3 Que huc usque dicta sunt, ut satis patet, hystoria mixta poeticis est. Ast ut pura consistat hystoria, excutiende sunt fictiones. Et ideo corvum accusasse Coronidem sic accipiendum arbitror: Apollinem scilicet augurandi peritia fornicationem novisse Coronidis, et iratum interfecisse pregnantem. Quod autem Ypolitum, seu ut placet Plinio, Castorem Tyndari filium, ob raptas Lynceo et Yde sponsas a Lynceo seu Yda occisum, in vitam herbis et arte revocaverit, taliter contigisse puto. Hos, seu eorum alterum, non mortuos, quia a morte in vitam aliquem revocare solius Dei est, sed vulnerum immanitate et ob perditum sanguinem mortuos existi-

turbed by this and killed her with his arrows, and then regretting the deed, because he was not able to use his own remedies to recall her from the nether world, he cut open her womb, brought the infant to life, and called him Aesculapius, giving him over, as we read, to the centaur Chiron for his nurturing. When Ocyrrhoe,[71] the daughter of Chiron and expert in prophecy, saw him, she prophesied that he would return to life a dead man from the nether world, and that he would himself be struck by a thunderbolt and thrown down to the nether world. This actually happened, for they say that when he had become a doctor who excelled at his art, Diana prayed to him and he returned Hippolytus to life, collecting his limbs from everywhere, and restoring him to his original health. Disturbed by this, Jupiter killed him with a thunderbolt, as Vergil testifies clearly, saying:[72]

> [He was] restored by the herb peony and Diana's love.
> Then the omnipotent father, indignant that some mortal
> rose from the infernal shades to the thresholds of life,
> thrust by thunderbolt the discoverer of such medical art,
> Phoebus-born, down to the Stygian waves.

What has been said up to this point is clearly history delivered in poetic fashion. But so that the historic basis may laid bare, the fictions must be examined. Thus I think that the crow that accused Coronis must be understood in this way, namely, that Apollo, who was expert in augury, learned of the fornication of Coronis, became angry, and killed her while she was pregnant. As for the report that Aesculapius used herbs and his skill to restore to life Hippolytus, or, according to Pliny,[73] Castor, son of Tyndareus, who on account of ravaging the brides of Lynceus and Idas was killed by Lynceus or Idas, here is what I believe happened: these, or at least one of them, was not dead, because it is for God alone to restore someone to life from death, but because of the extent of their wounds and their loss of blood they were thought

matos, quos cum arte et sollicitudine sua in sanitatem revocasset
pristinam, dictum est eum illos ab inferis in vitam retraxisse.

4   Quod autem ob id a Iove fulminatus sit, non est credibile, sed
ideo fictum credo, quia possibile est ob eam curam eum laborasse
plurimum in exquisitione herbarum et aliarum oportunitatum, et
sic propter vires fatigatus in febrem incidisse, que profecto letale
fulmen et ignitum est, et ex ea febre defecerit; seu forte casu fulminatus est, et opinatum ab ignaris hoc illi contigisse ob revocatos ab
inferis mortuos, et hinc fabule datum principium.

5   Sane Theodontius negat Apollinem dilexisse Coronidem, et ex
eo Esculapium fuisse conceptum, asseritque eum ex Hemonio iuvene et Coronide natum. Sed Apollinis filius dictus est altera ex
duabus causis, seu quia matre mortua ante partum et eius secto
utero eductus est, quod non absque opere medici sit, per quem
fingitur Apollo, quia medicine repertor, et sic Apollinis filius, quia
Apollinis opere natus sit, seu quia qui sic nascuntur Apollini
sacros fore voluere veteres, eo quod, ut dictum est, Apollinis opere
lucem sortiti videntur. Et ob id aiunt Cesarum familiam sacra
Apollinis observasse, quia primus eorum, qui ex familia Iulia Ce-
sar dictus est, ob eam causam cognomen adeptus est, et factus
Apollini sacer, quia execto matris utero in lucem venerit.

6   Preterea potuit Apollinis haberi filius, quia clarissimus evaserit
medicus. Theodontii autem opinio aliqualiter dictis roboratur
Lactantii, qui de Esculapio in libro *Divinarum institutionum* dicit
sic:

to be dead, and when he restored them with his skill and his care to their former health, it was said that he brought them back to life from the nether region.

That he was struck by Jupiter's thunderbolt for this reason is 4 not believable, but I think they invented this because it is possible that he worked hard searching for herbs and other things advantageous for that cure, and, tiring himself to excess, contracted a fever — which certainly is a lethal and fiery thunderbolt — and died from that fever; or, by chance he was actually hit by a thunderbolt, and it was thought by the foolish that this happened to him on account of his restoring the dead from the nether region, and from this derived the beginning of the fable.

But Theodontius denies that Apollo loved Coronis and that 5 Aesclepius was conceived by him, claiming that he was born to the youth Haemonius and Coronis. But he was said to be the son of Apollo for one of two reasons: either because he was taken from the cut-open womb of the mother who died before his birth, which is not too different from the work of a doctor, for whom Apollo, the inventor of medicine, is fictitiously substituted, and so too he is made the son of Apollo, in that he was born through his work or because the ancients wished those who were thus born to be sacred to Apollo because, as has been said, they seemed to come into the light through his work. And they say that this is why the family of the Caesars observed the sacrifices of Apollo, because the first from the family Julia to be named Caesar adopted the cognomen for this reason, and he was made sacred to Apollo because he came into the light from the cut womb of his mother.

In addition, he could have been regarded as the son of Apollo 6 because he became a very famous doctor. The opinion of Theodontius is strengthened somewhat by the words of Lactantius, who says this about Aesculapius in his *Divine Institutes:*[74]

Hunc Tarquitius, de illustribus viris disserens, ait incertis parentibus ortum, expositum, et a venatoribus inventum, canino lacte nutritum, Chironi traditum, didicisse medicinam. Fuisse autem Messenium sed Epydauri moratum,

etc.

7 Post hec dicit Lactantius, hunc enim fuisse, qui Ypolitum curavit.

Ceterum ne ob diversitates relatorum, ubi minime oportunum est, mendaces credantur scriptores, est advertendum, ut placet Tullio *De naturis deorum*, quia tres fuere Esculapii. Quorum primum dicit ipse filium fuisse Apollinis, eumque speculum invenisse, et primum obligasse vulnus, et hunc ab Arcadibus asserit

8 summe coli. Secundum vero dicit fratrem fuisse secundi Mercurii ex Valente patre atque Coronide matre natum, eumque percussum

9 fulmine interisse, et Cynosuris humatum. Tercium vero filium fuisse dicit Asyppi et Arsynoe, eumque primum alvi purgationem et dentis evulsionem comperisse, eiusque sepulcrum esse in Arcadia, non longe a Lusio flumine, circa quod et lucus ostenditur eius.

10 Et sic erit possibile ex his aliquem ex matris utero cesum, aliquem ex incerto patre natum atque expositum, nec obstat omnium parentes a Tullio nominari. Vidi ego in patria et nonnunquam ex principibus patrie hominem, qui infans fuit expositus, et demum a nutritore tanquam a patre cognominatus.

11 Sed quid multa? Qualiscunque seu quicunque fuerit ex istis, tanta veneratione apud Epydauros habitus est, ut etiam Romani iam fere omni Ytalia occupata, pestilentia egretudinum agitati, quasi pro singulari et certo subsidio legatos ad Epydauros micterent, orantes ut illis de oportuno remedio subvenirent, permicterentque ut Esculapium tanquam salutare subsidium Romam deferrent, concessumque in forma serpentis, dyabolo operante,

Tarquitius, writing about ancient men, says that he was born of uncertain parentage, exposed, and found by hunters; nurtured with dog's milk, given over to Chiron, he acquired a knowledge of medicine. He was Messenian but spent time in Epidaurus.

After this Lactantius says that it was he who cured Hippolytus. 7

Lest the writers be thought of inappropriately as liars because the stories they relate differ, we must point out that Cicero[75] in his *On the Nature of the Gods* thinks that there were three Aesculapii. Of these the first he says was the son of Apollo and that he invented the mirror, was the first to bind a wound, and he adds that he was worshipped greatly by the Arcadians. The second he says 8 was the brother of the second Mercury, born of Valens as father and Coronis[76] as mother, and that he died when struck by a thunderbolt; he was buried at Cynosurae. The third he says was the 9 son of Arsippus and Arsinoe, and that he first discovered how to purge the stomach and extract teeth, and that his tomb is in Arcadia not far from the Lusius River, near which as well is shown his sacred grove. And so it could be possible that among these one 10 was cut from the womb of his mother, and one born of an uncertain father and exposed. And it does not matter that Cicero names the parents of all of them: in my own homeland I have seen once a man born of the local aristocracy who was exposed as an infant and then named by his foster father as if he were his father.

But why so much about him? Of whatever sort or whoever he 11 was of these, he was so venerated at Epidaurus that even the Romans, already controlling nearly all of Italy, when stricken by epidemic diseases, sent ambassadors to Epidaurus to ask them to offer help in the form of a suitable remedy, thinking they would acquire a single, specific form of relief. And they allowed them to carry Aesculapius to Rome as a relief and salvation, and in particular to carry him to Rome on a ship in the form of a serpent — the

Romam in navi deveherent, illique templum insigne in insula Tyberis construerent, et loco salutaris dei diu colerent, dato illi impune Dyonisius Syragusanus novacula auream abstulerit barbam.

12   *Esculapius* autem 'dure agens' interpretatur, quod forsan nomen labori suo circa curam Ypoliti conforme fuit.

: 20 :

De Macaone Esculapii filio, qui genuit Asclepium

1   Macaon, ut dicit Papias, filius fuit Esculapii, evo suo insignis medicus, quod ego utrum credam nescio, eum saltem fuisse medicum, cum scribat Ysidorus post fulminatum Esculapium interdictum fuisse medendi exercitium, et ut ait Plinius, ubi *De hystoria naturali*, cum claruissent opera Esculapii 'temporibus Troianis; sequentia eius in nocte densissima latuere usque ad Peloponnesiacum bellum, et tunc ea revocavit in lucem Ypocrates,' etc.

2   Quod tempus, ut dicit Ysidorus, fuit annorum fere quingentorum. Hinc ego sumptum puto quod fictum est, Solem ob fulminatum Esculapium noluisse aliquandiu lucis currum ducere, ut ostenderetur Solis inventum, scilicet medicinam, eclipsim passum per secula plura, et tandem in lucem revocatum.

3   Ego hunc Macaonem auctoritate Papie non apposuissem, cum eum in multis circa talia minus curiosum sepissime invenerim scripsisse dissona veritate, sed ut ponerem me traxit solertia Pauli, qui non solum Macaonem Esculapii filium scribit, sed et Asclepium quendam Macaonis filium fuisse confirmat.

work of the devil—and to construct a famous temple for him on the Tiber Island, and to venerate him as a god of salvation for a long time (although with impunity Dionysius of Syracuse removed his golden beard with a razor).

Aesculapius means "working hard," perhaps because this name 12 conforms with his work in curing Hippolytus.

: 20 :

On Machaon, son of Aesculapius, who fathered Asclepius

Machaon, as Papias[77] says, was the son of Aesculapius, a famous 1 doctor in his day. I do not know if I believe this, even that he was a doctor, for Isidore[78] writes that he was prevented from practicing medicine after Aesculapius was hit with a thunderbolt, and Pliny[79] says in his *Natural History* that although the works of Aesculapius were famous "during the time of the Trojans. After this his works were hidden in the densest night until the Peloponnesian War, and then Hippocrates called them back into the light."

That interim, Isidore says, was nearly five hundred years. From 2 this I think that they invented the story that because Aesculapius was struck by a thunderbolt, Sun was not willing to drive his chariot of light for some time, in order to demonstrate that the invention of Sun, that is, medicine, endured an eclipse of several centuries, and then was recalled into the light.

Based on the authority of Papias I would not have included this 3 Machaon, for I have very often found Papias in many ways to be careless about such matters and to have written statements that contradict the truth; but the skill of Paul, who not only writes that Machaon was the son of Aesculapius but also confirms that a certain Asclepius was the son of Machaon, convinced me to add it.

: 21 :

De Asclepio Macaonis filio

1 Asclepius, ut dicit Paulus, fuit filius Macaonis, credo, Augustinum secutus, qui hunc Esculapii nepotem videtur dicere, scribens, ubi *De civitate Dei*, Hermetem Trimegistum Asclepio loquentem sic:

> Avus enim tuus, o Asclepi, medicine primus inventor, cui templum consecratum est in monte Libye, circa litus croco-dilorum, in quo eius iacet mundanus homo, id est corpus; reliquus vero, vel potius totus[14] in sensu vite melior remeavit in celum, omnia etiam nunc hominibus adiumenta prestans infirmis numine nunc suo, que solet medicine arte prebere.

2 Et paulo infra idem sequitur Augustinus: 'Ecce duos deos dicit homines fuisse Esculapium et Mercurium,' etc.

Verum ego librum hunc Hermetis Trimegisti, quem *De ydolo* intitulat, vidi, nec tamen, qualiter Esculapius fuerit Asclepiadis avus, per verba Hermetis precedentia atque sequentia dictis ab Augustino percipere queo, certus tamen quoniam potius ingenium deficiat meum, quam accusari possit animadversio Augustini.

: 21 :

On Asclepius, son of Machaon

Asclepius, as Paul says, was the son of Machaon, I believe, follow- 1
ing Augustine, who seems to say that he was the grandson of
Aesculapius. Augustine writes in his *City of God* that Hermes Trismegistus said this to Asclepius:[80]

> For your grandfather, O Asclepius, was the first inventor of
> medicine; a temple is dedicated to him on a mountain in
> Libya near the shore of crocodiles, where lies his earthly
> man, that is, his body; the remainder, or rather the entirety
> in the sense of life, returned fortunately to the sky, and by
> his divinity provides even now to ill men all means of assis-
> tance which the medical art usually provides.

And a little later the same Augustine continues, "Behold, he says 2
that the two gods, Aesculapius and Mercury, were men."

I have seen this book of Hermes Trismegistus, which has the
title *On Idolatry*, but I am nonetheless not able to grasp through
the words of Hermes that precede and follow in what was said by
Augustine how Aesculapius was the grandson of Asclepius; even
so, I am certain it was my ability that was deficient rather than
that any reproach can be assigned to Augustine.

: 22 :

De Psyce XV[a] Apollinis filia

1 Psyces, ut dicit Martianus[15] Capella in libro, quem *De nuptiis Mercurii et Phylologie* scripsit, filia fuit Apollinis et Endelichie. Ex qua Lucius Apuleius, in libro *Methamorphoseon*, qui, vulgariori vocabulo, *Asinus aureus* appellatur, longisculam recitat fabulam talem: regem scilicet fuisse et reginam, quibus tres fuere filie, quarum due maiores natu, etsi forma spectabiles essent, iunior, cui Psyces nomen erat, in tantum pulchritudine ceteras excedebat mortales, ut non solum admiratione teneret spectantes, sed infigeret animis ignaris rei miraculo credulitatem, ut Venus esset que descendisset in terris. Et fama longe lateque vulgata invise formositatis egit, ut non solum cives sed exteri ad visendam Venerem et sacris honorandam accederent, templis vere Veneris neglectis.

2 Quod egre Venus ferens, in Psycen accensa, Cupidini filio suo[16] iussit, ut eam amore ferventissimo hominis extreme sortis incenderet. Interim pater de nuptiis virginis Milesium Apollinem consuluit, qui respondit, ut illam in vertice montis deduceret, ibique divina stirpe creatum, esto pessimum et vipereum, nancisceretur virgo maritum.

Quo responso parentes affecti, cum lacrimis et merore totius civitatis, virginem in predestinatum deduxere culmen, ibique so-
3 lam liquere. Que etsi solitudine et incerto timore futuri coniugis anxiaretur, non tamen diu perstitit. Et venit Zephyrus mitis, et suavi spiritu eam sumens, in floridam detulit vallem, in qua cum aliquali somno lenisset erumnam, surgens vidit gratum oculis nemus et argenteis undis manantem fontem, atque palatium non

: 22 :

On Psyche, fifteenth child of Apollo

Psyche, as Martianus Capella[81] says in his book *On the Marriage of* 1
Mercury and Philology, was the daughter of Apollo and Entelechia.
Lucius Apuleius[82] in his *Metamorphoses*, which is commonly called
The Golden Ass, tells the following lengthy fable about this. There
was a king and queen who had three daughters, of whom, although the two elder by birth were beautiful in appearance, the
younger, whose name was Psyche, exceeded the rest of mortals in
beauty so much that not only did those who looked at her hold
her in admiration, but she implanted in the minds of the foolish
the belief in the miracle that she was Venus descended to earth.
The fame of her unseen beauty spread far and wide, causing not
only citizens but foreigners to come to see this Venus and honor
her with sacrifices, neglecting the temples of the true Venus.

Venus became irritated at this, grew angry at Psyche, and or- 2
dered her son Cupid to inflame her with a most passionate love for
a man of a humble destiny. Meanwhile her father consulted the
Milesian Apollo about the maiden's wedding. The response was
that he should lead her to a mountain top, and there the maiden
would find her husband, born of divine stock, although of a very
base and viperous sort.

The parents, struck by this response, and with the tears and
sorrow of the whole city, led the maiden to the predetermined
summit and left her there alone. Although she was anxious about 3
her solitude and had an uncertain fear about her future husband,
this did not last long: a gentle Zephyr came, picked her up in his
pleasant breeze, and carried her to a valley of flowers. There she
eased her distress by taking a short nap, and upon waking up she
saw a wood pleasing to the eyes, a spring flowing with silvery wa-

solum regium sed divinum, miris ornatum divitiis. Quod cum intrasset et ingentes invenisset thesauros absque custode, et miraretur plurimum, obsequentium vocibus absque corporibus auditis,
4 intravit lavacrum, invisis sibi assistentibus obsequiosis. Inde cena
divinis conferta dapibus sumpta, cubiculum intrans, conscendit
genialem thorum, et soporate maritus affuit.

Qui cum eam sibi fecisset coniugem, veniente luce invisus abiit,
et sic sepius magna Psycis consolatione continuans. Factum est ut
sorores, eiusdem audito Psycis infortunio, e domibus maritorum
ad lugubres parentes accederent, et una cum eis sororis infelices
5 nuptias deflerent. At Cupido presentiens quid invidia sororum
pararetur Psyci, eam premonuit, ut earum omnino flocci faceret
lacrimas, nec in suam perniciem pia atque credula esset. Quod
cum spopondisset Psyces, se cepit deplorare captivam et quod sorores videre et alloqui non posset, et venientem atque redarguen-
tem Cupidinem precibus in eam sententiam traxit, ut cum eis loqui posset, Zephyroque iuberet, ut eas ad se leni deferret flatu.
Qui cum fecisset, concessit etiam ut ex thesauris, quos liberet, as-
portare permicteret, sed earum suasionibus nullo modo crederet,
6 nec suam videre formam alicuius consilio exoptaret. Tandem com-
plorata domi Psyce a sororibus, scopulum conscendere, et ululatu
femineo redintegrato a Psyce audite sunt, atque paucis consolate
verbis, et postremo illas Zephyrus Psycis imperio in vallem detulit
amenam.

Ibi a Psyce festiva[17] caritate suscepte, divinum nemus et regiam,
thesaurosque mirate, et lavacro atque cibo refecte, percontari scru-
pulose cepere, quisnam eius vir ac tantarum rerum dominus esset.
Illa autem memor precepti coniugis, iuvenem finxit venationibus

ters, and a palace not only royal but divine, decorated with ornate riches. After she had entered and found a large treasury without a guard, she gazed in wonderment and heard the incorporeal voices of obedient subordinates, and she entered a bath with the assistance of invisible servants. Then after eating a meal filled with divine foods, she entered a bedroom and mounted a nuptial couch, and her husband came to her once she was asleep.

After he had made her his wife, he left unseen upon the arrival of dawn. And he often did this, which was great consolation to Psyche. Then her sisters, having heard about the misfortune of Psyche, left the homes of their husbands and visited their mourning parents, lamenting together the unhappy nuptials of their sister. But Cupid, foreseeing what her sisters' envy might do to Psyche, warned her not to pay attention to their tears and not to be gullible or a devoted sister to her own detriment. Although Psyche promised to do this, she began to deplore her captivity and that she was not able to see and talk with her sisters; Cupid returned and when they argued she pleaded with and convinced him to allow her to talk with them and to order Zephyr to carry them to her on a gentle breeze. Cupid did this, and he also agreed to permit them to carry off as much from the treasury as they wanted, but Psyche was warned not to be persuaded by them or hope to follow anyone's scheme to see his shape. Then, after lamenting Psyche's situation at home, the sisters climbed the cliff: Psyche heard the repeated wailing of the women, and after a few words of consolation, Zephyr, following Psyche's orders, finally brought them into the pleasant vale.

There Psyche received them warmly[83] and affectionately, and they marveled at the divine woods and the palace with its the treasures. After they were refreshed by a bath and a meal, they began to make pointed enquiries as to the identity of her husband and the master of these domains. But she was mindful of her husband's instructions, so she made up a story that he was a young

intentum, et concessis eis que vellent ex thesauris, a Zephyro illas in summitate montis iussit deferri. Que, post longas infortuniorum suorum querelas, felicitati Psycis invidentes, celatis thesauris fictisque lacrimis ad parentes rediere, et inde inito de pernicie Psycis consilio abiere ad viros. Psyces autem iterum premonetur a viro ut sororum evitaret insidias, et nullius consilio eum videre conetur.

Revertuntur interim sorores invide, et obsequio Zephyri ex vertice montis deferuntur ad Psycem, et letanter suscepte felicitati et pregnationi congratulantur sue, captamque verbis mellifluis aggrediuntur venenosis colloquis, inquirentes iterum quisnam vir eius esset. Psyces autem pridiani oblita mendacii, in fictionem alteram devertit, eumque dixit mediocris etatis hominem et vacantem negociationibus, datisque muneribus iussit illas Zephyro reportaret. Que cum advertissent eam, non ea forma qua pridie dixisset, virum designasse, illum ab ea invisum, et perconsequens arbitrate deum sunt, et sic acrius exarsere.

7   Et inde die redeuntes seguenti, affectu pio verbis se maximam salutis eius curam gerere monstravere, asseverantes post multa se pro comperto habere a circumvicinis incolis, non hominem, sed serpentem tortuosum illas edes incolere, eiusque virum esse, nec illum aliud expectare quam maturitatem eius quem gerebat in utero, ut ex ea illoque se ampliori sagina saturaret. Quibus terrefacta Psyces et eis ultro aures prebens, eo quod ille adeo se videri recusaret, eis remissis ad scopulum, consilio earum novaculam paravit, et lucernam abscondit sub modio, nocte seguenti visura,

man devoted to hunting, and after giving them whatever treasure they wanted, she ordered Zephyr to carry them to the peak of the mountain. Lamenting at length their own misfortunes and jealous of Psyche's happiness, they hid their treasures and pretended tears when they returned to their parents, and after devising a plan to cause mischief for Psyche, they then went back to their husbands. But Psyche was again forewarned by her husband to ward off her sisters' intrigues and not to attempt a scheme to see him.

Meanwhile the jealous sisters return and Zephyr obediently carries them from the peak of the mountain to see Psyche, who happily welcomes them, and they rejoice in her pregnancy. The sisters now assault her with honey-sweet words and venomous talk, inquiring once again as to who her husband was. But Psyche had forgotten the previous day's lie and changed her story, saying that he was a man of middle age who was engaged in business, and then she gave them gifts and ordered Zephyr to take them back. When they realized that she had described her husband differently from the way she had on the previous day and that she had never seen him, they consequently believed that he was a god and their curiosity raged all the more.

Returning the following day, they pretended a devoted affect 7 and showed the greatest concern for her well-being, declaring after much inquiry that they had ascertained from the nearby inhabitants that the owner of these dwellings was not a man but a twisting serpent, that this was her husband, and that he wanted nothing from her other than to bring to maturation what was growing in her womb so that he could fatten himself by feeding on both of them. As she listened to them intently, Psyche grew frightened; after all, he had refused her permission to see him, so when her sisters were sent back to the rock, she followed their plan by preparing a dagger and hiding an oil lamp under a bushel, thereby intending to see the following night who it was who shared her

689

quisnam esset is cuius uteretur concubitu, et ut illum perimeret si verbis responderet forma sororum.

Intrat igitur more suo lectum Cupido, et in somnum solvitur. Psyces vero, aperto lumine, vidit illum mira formositate conspicuum iuvenem, alis pernicibus insignitum, et ad eius pedes arcum et pharetram sagittis confertam, e quibus cum unam mirabunda eduxisset, expertura aciem, adeo digito impressit suo, ut aliqualis scaturiret e vulnere sanguis. Quo facto, miro dormientis adhuc amore flagravit. Dumque illum mirabunda conspiceret, favillula ex lucerna prosilivit in dexterum dormientis humerum, quam ob rem expergefactus Cupido repente fugam arripuit. Verum Psyces cum illum cepisset crure atque fortiter teneret, tam diu ab eo per aerem delata est, donec fessa, eo dimisso, caderet. Cupido autem in viciniam cupressum evolans, longa querela eam redarguit, seipsum damnans, quod a matre missus, ut illam extremi hominis amore incenderet, et ipse se ipsum ob eius pulchritudinem vulnerasset, et inde evolavit. Psyces[18] vero postquam illum videre non potuit, se in propinquum deiecit fluvium mortem cupiens. Fluvius autem aspernatus eam deduxit in ripam, ubi a Pane deo verbis solata aliquantisper est.

A quo tandem discedens in civitatem venit, in qua altera sororum nupta, quam cum convenisset illi casum suum recitavit omnem. Verum vindicte avida in perniciem sororis consultricis astutule mentita est circa extremum verborum Cupidinis, asserens eum dixisse, '"Abi hinc et res tuas affer, postquam imperium meum servare nequisti, ego autem sororem tuam," teque nominavit, "meis nuptiis coniugabo,"' et me fecit inde confestim a Zephyro deferri in culmen ex quo sustulerat. Quod cum audisset illa, confestim evolavit in montem, et alio flante vento inquit, 'Accipe Zephyre dominam tuam meque deducito in viri cubiculum,' et cum verbis

bed and ready to kill him if he should be of the form his sisters described.

Cupid entered the bridal bed in his usual way and fell asleep. But by the light of the lantern Psyche saw him to be a youth, remarkably striking in his handsomeness, distinctive in that he had agile wings, and at his feet were a bow and quiver filled with arrows; taking out one of these arrows and entranced by it, she tested the point but pressed so hard with her finger that some blood spurted out. In doing so she burned all the more with love for her sleeping husband, and while she was gazing upon and admiring him, a little spark leapt from the lamp onto his right arm. The sleeping Cupid suddenly woke up and took flight. But because Psyche had seized hold of his leg and held on tightly, she was carried by him through the air for quite a long time until, fatigued, she let go of him and fell. Flying to a nearby cypress, Cupid repudiated her, complaining at length but blaming himself: his mother had sent him to inflame Psyche with love for the worst man, but because of her beauty he had wounded himself. And then he flew away. Because[84] she had not been able to see him, Psyche threw herself into a nearby river hoping to die. But the river rejected her and deposited her on its bank, where the god Pan consoled her with words for some time.

Finally she left him and came to the city where one of her married sisters lived. Psyche met with her and recounted her whole story, but, being eager for vengeance and the destruction of a sister who had given her such cunning advice, she lied about Cupid's last words, claiming that he said, "'Go from here and take your things, since you are not able to obey my commands, I will marry your sister'—and he named you—'and then had Zephyr immediately carry me back to the peak from which he had brought me.'" When her sister had heard this, she immediately flew to the mountain and said to a contrary wind, "Zephyr, take your mistress and bring me down to the bedroom of my husband," and with these words

sumpto saltu maximo, se in ingens precipitium dedit, quassatoque corpore toto, alitibus esca effecta est. Psyces inde equo modo et aliam sororem misit in saltum. Demum cum primo Cereris inde Iunonis precibus exquisisset subsidium, et ab utraque repulsam habuisset, audissetque, iubente Venere, Mercurium voce preconia mortalibus cunctis iussisse, ut nemo eam occultaret, et dona indicanti preponeret, se ad fores Veneris presentavit. A qua obiurgata diu et capillis tracta, sollicitudini et tristitie ancillis suis ut excruciaretur tradita est.

10a   A quibus cum esset verberibus lacessita, eidem a Venere cumulus segetum multiplicium appositus est, iussumque ut in seguenti vespere grana seminum omnium discreta representaret eidem. Quo iussu, abeunte Venere, obstupefacta Psyces riguerat, sed advenientibus formicis ab eis confestim iussa Veneris peracta sunt. Secundo autem Venus precepit eidem, ut floccum aurei velleris ostensi pecoris eidem portaret, quod Psyces, secuta monitum palustris arundinis, cum obtinuisset, imperanti reportavit. Tercio Venus urnulam tradidit iussitque, ut plenam ex undis Stygiis ei deferret confestim. Que cum locum videret inaccessibilem, aquile volantis subsidio mandatum dire socrus implevit. Quarto Venus, data ei pixide, iussit illi ad inferos descenderet Proserpineque sua 10b ex parte paululum sue formositatis exposceret. Que cum iret ad turrim se precipitatura, ab eadem monita descendit ad inferos, et legationi peracta, pixidem plenam atque coopertam assumpsit, et ad superos remeavit. Sed immemor mandatorum turris, sumptura aliquantulum divine formositatis, ut amanti suo pulchrior videretur, aperuit pixidem ex qua prosilivit somnus infernus, qui in eam

she took a great leap and threw herself off the cliff, her battered body providing food for birds. Similarly, Psyche then sent her other sister as well to take that leap. Finally, after she had sought the assistance of first Ceres and then Juno and had her prayers rejected by both, and then heard that Mercury, following Venus' orders, had made a general proclamation to all mortals forbidding anyone from hiding her and offering gifts to anyone who revealed her, Psyche presented herself at Venus' door. Venus upbraided her for a long time and dragged her by her hair, and then she was handed over to her handmaids Anxiety and Sadness to be tortured.

After they had whipped her to exhaustion, Venus put before 10a her a heap of various grains and ordered her to present her with the individual grains of every seed by the following evening. After Venus issued that order and then departed, the astonished Psyche grew numb, but ants arrived and immediately carried out Venus' commands. Second, Venus pointed out a flock of sheep and ordered her to bring a tuft of golden fleece to her; Psyche, followed the advice of a marsh reed, obtained the tuft, and brought it back to Venus. Third, Venus gave her a small urn and ordered her to fill it with the waters of the Styx and immediately bring it back to her. Although Psyche saw that the place was inaccessible, she received assistance from a flying eagle to fulfill the command of her cruel mother-in-law. Fourth, Venus gave her a box and ordered her to descend to the netherworld and to ask Persephone on her behalf for a bit of her beauty. Psyche went to the tower to throw herself 10b off, but the tower gave her advice; she descended to the netherworld, and, having accomplished her mission, she filled the box, closed it, and returned to the divine realm. However, Psyche did not heed the warnings from the tower and, wanting to take a little of the divine beauty so she would seem more beautiful to her lover, she opened the box; infernal sleep leapt out of it and jumped onto her, putting her into a sleep that made her appear as dead.

iniectus, eam non aliter quam corpus mortum soporavit. Sed Cupido iam convalescens a vulnere, casum sue Psycis advertens, per fenestram cubiculi evolavit ad dormientem, detersoque ab ea somno et in pixidem redacto, redarguit eam presuntionis adversus monitus habite, dixitque ut mictenti deferret, quod et factum est.

10c Cupido autem impatiens infelicitatum et laborum puelle a se dilecte, Iovem oravit, ut pateretur illam sibi coniugem fore. Qui precibus annuens, congregatis diis, eorum in presentia iussit ut Psyces coniunx esset perpetua Cupidinis. Quam Mercurius Iovis iussu devexit in celum et ibidem, immortalis effecta, nuptie celebrate sunt. Ipsam autem Cupidini peperit Voluptatem filiam.

11 Serenissime Rex, si huius tam grandis fabule ad unguem sensum enucleare voluerimus, in ingens profecto volumen evaderet, et ideo cur Apollinis et Endilichie filia dicatur Psyces, que eius sorores, et cur Cupidinis dicatur coniunx, cum paucis ex contingentibus dixisse satis sit.

12 Psyces ergo 'anima' interpretatur. Hec autem Apollinis, id est solis, filia dicitur, eius scilicet qui mundi vera lux est Deus, cum nullius alterius potentie sit rationalem creare animam, nisi Dei. Endelichia autem, ut dicit Calcidius super *Tymeo* Platonis, 'perfecta etas' interpretatur, cuius ideo rationalis anima dicitur filia, quia etsi in utero matris illam a patre luminum suscipiamus, non tamen eius apparent opera, nisi in etate perfecta, cum potius naturali quodam instinctu usque ad etatem perfectam feramur, quam iudicio rationis, etate vero perfecta agere incipimus ratione. Ergo bene Apollinis et Endelichie filia dicitur.

13 Sunt huius due sorores maiores natu, quarum[19] una est anima vegetativa, altera vero sensitiva. Sed Psyces pulchritudine illas excedit, et hoc ideo quia vegetativa anima communicamus cum plan-

But Cupid, by now recovering from his wound and learning of Psyche's plight, flew through the window of his bedroom to the sleeping girl, and removing the sleep from her and putting it back into the box, he repudiated her for not heeding the warnings of its owner. He said that she should carry it to Venus, and she did. Cupid, finding the unhappiness and tasks of the girl he loved to be 10c unbearable, asked Jupiter to allow them to marry. Jupiter nodded in assent to these prayers, and in an assembly of the gods he decreed that Psyche would be the everlasting wife of Cupid. By the order of Jupiter Mercury carried her into the sky and there, with immortality conferred, the wedding was celebrated. And she bore Cupid a daughter named Pleasure.

Most serene King, if we wished to write about what meaning 11 rested under the shell of such a grand fable, it would certainly turn into a great many words, so let it suffice to have said a few relevant words about why Psyche is said to be the daughter of Apollo and Entelechia, who her sisters were, and why she was said to be the wife of Cupid.

Psyche means "the rational spirit." She is said to be the daughter 12 of Apollo, that is, the sun, namely, of him who is the true light of the world, God, since no other power can create the rational spirit except God. Entelechia, as Calcidius says in discussing Plato's *Timaeus*, means "mature age."[85] The rational spirit is said to be daughter of this because, although we receive her in the womb of the mother from the father of lights, nonetheless her effect does not appear until we mature in age, for up until then we are carried more by a certain natural instinct than by the judgment of reason, whereas at a mature age we begin to use reason. Therefore she is appropriately said to be the daughter of Apollo and Entelechia.

She has two older sisters.[86] One is the vegetative spirit; the 13 other, perceptive. But Psyche exceeds them in beauty, for we share the vegetative spirit with plants, the perceptive spirit with animals,

tis, sensitiva autem cum brutis, rationali quidem cum angelis et Deo, quo nil pulchrius. Psyces vero ideo dicitur iunior, quia longe ante eam vegetativa conceditur fetui, et inde tractu temporis sensitiva, postremo a Deo rationalis infunditur. Ille ante nubunt, quod ideo dictum est quia corporeis sunt annexe virtutibus. Huius autem coniugium divine stirpi servatur, id est amori honesto, seu ipsi Deo, cuius inter delicias a Zephyro, id est a vitali spiritu, qui sanctus est, defertur et matrimonio iungitur.

14 Hic coniugi prohibet, ne eum videre cupiat, ni perdere velit, hoc est nolit de eternitate sua, de principiis rerum, de omnipotentia videre per causas, que soli sibi nota sunt; nam quotiens talia mortales perquirimus, illum, imo nosmet ipsos deviando perdi-

15 mus. Sorores autem non nunquam ad methas usque primas deliciarum Psycis deveniunt, et ex thesauris eius reportant, in quantum penes rationem viventes melius opus suum vegetatio peragit, et sensitive virtutes clariores sunt, et longius perseverant. Sane invident sorori, quod minime novum est, sensualitatem cum rationem discordem, et dum illi blandis verbis suadere non possunt, ut virum videat, id est velit naturali ratione videre quod amat et non per fidem cognoscere, eam terroribus conantur inducere, asserentes eum immanem esse serpentem, seque eam devoraturum. Quod quidem totiens sit, quotiens sensualitas conatur rationem sopire et ostendere anime contemplationes incognitarum rerum per causam, non solum delectationes sensitivas auferre, sed labores maximos et angores minime oportunos ingerere, et nil demum placide retributionis afferre.

16 Anima autem, dum minus prudens talibus demonstrationibus fidem adhibet, et quod negatur videre desiderat, occisura, si voto non conrespondeat forma, videt effigiem viri pulcherrimam, id est

but the rational spirit with angels and God, than whom nothing is more beautiful. And therefore Psyche is younger because a child is granted the vegetative spirit long before the rational, and then the perceptive spirit after the passage of time, and finally the rational spirit is conferred by God. The sisters marry first because it is said that they are joined to corporeal virtues, while Psyche's marriage is reserved for a divine offspring, that is, for an honest love, or God himself. And she is conveyed to his delights by Zephyr, that is, by the vital spirit, which is sacred, and joined in marriage.

He forbade his wife the desire to see him, under penalty of los- 14 ing him; that is, he did not wish her to inquire about his eternity, the beginnings of things, or his omnipotence, for reasons which are known to him alone. For as often as we mortals seek after such things, we lose him, nay, we lose ourselves, as we lose our way. The 15 sisters sometimes come to the first limit of Psyche's delights and carry them back from her treasuries insofar as among those living according to reason the vegetative accomplishes its work better, the perceptive virtues are clearer, and they last longer. But the sisters are envious because — and this is nothing new — sensuality is dis-cordant with reason. And when they are not able to persuade her with flattering words to see her husband, that is, to wish by natu-ral reason to see what she loves and not to know it by faith, they try to influence her by scaring her, asserting that he was a huge serpent and would devour her. This happens whenever sensuality attempts to put reason to sleep and to reveal mental contempla-tions about the cause of unknown things, not only stealing away sensitive delights but heaping on the greatest distress and the very unpleasant anxieties, and bringing no calm as recompense.

But when Psyche, the rational spirit, being less prudent and fol- 16 lowing this kind of persuasion, desiring to see what is denied and intending to kill it if its form does not correspond to her desire, sees her husband's very beautiful image, that is, the external works

697

extrinseca Dei opera; formam, id est divinitatem, videre non potest, quia Deum nemo vidit unquam. Et cum favillula ledit et vulnerat, id est superbo desiderio, per quod inobediens facta et sensualitati credula, bonum contemplationis amictit, et sic a divino separatur coniugio.

17　　Tandem penitens et amans, perniciem sororum curat astutia, easque adeo opprimit, ut adversus rationem nulle sint illis vires. Et erumnis et miseriis purgata presumptuosa superbia atque inobedientia, bonum divine dilectionis atque contemplationis iterum reassumit, eique se iniungit perpetuo, dum perituris dimissis rebus in eternam defertur gloriam. Et ibi ex amore parturit Voluptatem, id est delectationem et letitiam sempiternam.

: 23 :

De Arabe XVI° Apollinis filio

1　Arabs, ut placet Plinio in libro *Naturalis hystorie*, Apollinis et Babillonie fuit filius, quem medicine artis dicit etiam repertorem.

2　Puto ego hunc seu Babilonem fuisse hominem, et ibidem medicinam ostendisse prius, seu apud Babilonios didicisse, et ad Arabes primum detulisse, et hinc Apollinis filius dictus, quia medicus, et Babillonis, quia in Babillonia natus vel eruditus sit.

of God, she cannot see a form, that is, divinity, because no one ever sees God.[87] And when she hit him and wounded him with the little spark, that is, with haughty desire, which makes her become disobedient and trusting in sensuality, she loses the benefit of contemplation, and so she is separated from her divine husband.

Finally, repentant and loving, through cunning she concerns 17 herself with the ruin of her sisters and so overwhelms them that they have no resistance against reason, and purged of afflictions and miseries as well as presumptuous pride and disobedience, she reassumes once again the benefit of divine pleasure and contemplation. She joins herself to it forever, and while ridding herself of perishable things she is borne to eternal glory, and there she gives birth to Pleasure, that is, delight and eternal happiness.

: 23 :

On Arabus, the sixteenth child of Apollo

Arabus, according to Pliny in his *Natural History*, was the son of 1 Apollo and Babylonia, and he says also that he was the discoverer of medical arts.[88] I think that he was either a Babylonian man and 2 was the first to reveal medicine there, or he became acquainted with it among the Babylonians and first brought it to the Arabs, and from this he was said to be a son of Apollo, because he was a doctor, and from Babylonia, because he was either born or educated in Babylonia.

: 24 :

De Tityo filio Iovis III°

1   Postquam Apollinis longa posteritas expedita est, ut ad Iovis filios revertamur ordo postulat. Ex quibus sese ante alios Tityus offert. Quem dicit Leontius filium fuisse Iovis ex Hellare Orcomeni filia, quam pregnantem Iuppiter, iram Iunonis timens, occultavit in terram, ex quo factum est, ut nascens puer ex Terra natus videre-

2   tur, ut Servius asserebat. Que quidem Terra postmodum eum enutrivit, et sic non mater, sed nutrix. Is tamen cum ad integram venisset etatem, Latonam Apollinis matrem amavit, eamque de stupro interpellavit. Quam ob rem turbatus Apollo eum sagittis occidit, et apud inferos religavit, atque eius iecur vulturibus lanian- dum apposuit hac lege, ut consumptum restauraretur illico, et sic nunquam vultures a discerpendo cessarent, nec ipse a patiendo.

3   Restat nunc huic fictioni velum eripere, ut quod contegat videa- mus. Dicit enim primo Iovem pregnantem in terris abscondisse. Nil enim occultius tegitur, quam quod infoditur, et ideo debemus intelligere hanc secretissime fuisse servatam, et hoc timore Iuno- nis, id est maioris potentie, cum dea regnorum sit Iuno. Terram autem aluisse Tityum non est novum, cum omnes alamur a terra. Quod Latonam Apollinis matrem amaverit, ingentem eius de- monstrat animum, celsitudinem enim appetiit, que claritatis mater est, sed ab Apolline, id est a regio splendore, deiectus est apud in- feros, id est apud plebeios, quos penes semper curarum plenus fuit, qualiter posset in gradum, ex quo deciderat, reascendere.

: 24 :

On Tityus, third son of Jupiter

Now that we have detailed the lengthy posterity of Apollo, our   1
genealogical progression requires us to return to the sons of Jupiter. Of these Tityus presents himself before the others. Leontius
says that he was the son of Jupiter by Elara, daughter of Orchomenus. When she was pregnant, Jupiter feared Juno's anger, so
he hid her in the earth; this accounts for how the son who was
born seemed to be born from Earth, as Servius[89] asserted. After-   2
ward this Earth nurtured him, and so she was not his mother but
his nurse. When he matured he fell in love with Latona, the
mother of Apollo, and attacked her and took her by force. Angered at this, Apollo killed him with his arrows and relegated him
to the nether region, and he offered his liver up for vultures to tear
to pieces with this stipulation: that what was eaten would be restored to him, and so the vultures never ceased from ripping it
apart, nor him from suffering.

It remains now to remove the veil from this fiction and see what   3
it covers. He says first that Jupiter hid the pregnant woman in the
earth, for nothing is covered more secretly than something buried,
and so we should understand that she was secluded in the upmost
secrecy and that it was by fear of Juno, that is, of a greater power,
since she was the goddess of royal power. There is nothing new in
Earth nurturing Tityus, for we are all nurtured by the earth. That
he loved Latona, the mother of Apollo, shows a mighty spirit, for
he seeks loftiness, which is the mother of clarity, but Apollo, that
is, royal splendor, threw him down to the nether region, that is,
among the common people, and there he was always filled with
worry as to how he could reascend to the level from which he had
fallen.

4   Recitat ex isto Tityo Leontius brevem hystoriam, et dicit hunc apud Boetios magnum fuisse hominem, et viribus temptasse ex Delpho Apollinem eicere, a quo ipse eiectus est, et fere ad priva-
5   tam vitam redactus. De pena autem illi apposita dicit ubi *De somnio Scipionis* Macrobius sic:

> Vulturem iecur immortale tondentem, nichil aliud intelligi volentes quam tormenta conscientie obnoxia flagitio viscera interiora rimantis, et ipsa vitalia indefessa admissi sceleris admonitione laniantis, semperque curas, si requiescere forte tentaverint excitantis, tanquam fibris renascentibus inherendo, nec ulla sibi miseratione parcentis, lege hac, qua se iudice nemo nocens absolvitur, nec de se suam potest vitare sententiam.

Hec Macrobius.

: 25 :

De Bacho secundi Iovis IIII° filio, qui genuit Hymeneum, Thyoneum et Thoantem

1   Bachus Iovis filius et Semeles ab Ovidio et reliquis omnibus poetis dicitur. Ex cuius origine talis recitatur fabula. Cum amaret Iuppiter Semelem Cadmi filiam, et ipsa concepisset ex eo, accessit ad eam Iuno, formam gerens Beroe Epydaurie anus, et inito cum
2   ea colloquio, perquisivit numquid diligeretur a Iove. Cui dixit Semeles arbitrari se diligi; tunc Iuno: 'Non potes, filia, nisi uno modo cognoscere, scilicet si, Stygis interposito iuramento, promic-

Leontius relates the brief history of this Tityus and says that he   4
was a great man among the Boeotians, and that he attempted to
drive Apollo from Delphi by force, but he was himself driven out
by Apollo and reduced to an almost completely private existence.
Macrobius in his *Dream of Scipio* says this about the punishment   5
assigned to him:[90]

> They want the vulture gnawing on the immortal liver to be
> understood as nothing other than the torments of conscience
> probing within our viscera guilty of shame, pulling apart our
> very vitals wearied by the admonition of admitted sin, and
> always rousing up cares, if perchance they have attempted to
> subside, as if clinging to reborn entrails, nor with any pity or
> mercy, with this law — that no one is absolved when judging
> himself, nor is it possible to avoid one's own sentence.

Thus says Macrobius.

:   25   :

On Bacchus, fourth child of the second Jupiter, who fathered
Hymenaeus, Thioneus, and Thoas

Bacchus was said to be the son of Jupiter and Semele, according to   1
Ovid[91] and all the rest of the poets. The following fable is told
about his origin. After Jupiter had made love to Semele, the
daughter of Cadmus, and conceived, Juno came to her disguised as
Beroe, an old woman of Epidaurus, and during the course of the
conversation she struck up with her, Juno asked if she had been
loved by Jupiter. Semele told her that she thought she had; then   2
Juno said, "You cannot know, daughter, except in one way, namely,
if you get him to swear an oath by the Styx and then he promises

tat tecum eo pacto coniungi, quo Iunoni iungitur.' Semeles expe-
rientie avida, venienti iuramentum et inde munus poposcit. Iuppiter autem dolens, eam, ne adversus iuramentum ageret, fulminavit
et mortue filium traxit ex utero, suoque apposuit femori, donec
tempus perficeretur, quod eum esse in ventre matris oportunitas
3   exigebat. Hunc primo clam nutrivit Yno matertera eius, postmodum nynphis tradidit, que etiam ei alimenta dederant, ut ait Ovidius:

> Furtim[20] illum primis Yno matertera cunis
> educat, inde datum nynphe Nyseides antris
> occuluere suis lactisque alimenta dedere.

Et alibi:

> Nysiadas nynphas, puerum querente noverca,
>   hanc frondem cunis opposuisse ferunt,

scilicet ederam, que, ut idem dicit Ovidius, fuit postea 'gratissima
Bacho.' Huic insuper alumnum dicunt fuisse Sylenum, qui captus
a rusticis, a Myda Bacho restitutus est, ut[21] ait Ovidius. Rex venit
et Iunoni Sylenum reddit alumno.

4   Hunc preterea curru et sociis honorant; de quibus sic refert
Statius:

> Promovet, effrene dextra levaque sequuntur
> Lynces, et uda mero lambunt retinacula tygres.
> Post exultantes spolia armentalia portant,
> seminecesque lupos, scissasque Mimallones ursas.
> Nec comitatus iners, sunt illic Ira Furorque
> et Metus, et Virtus et nunquam sobrius Ardor,
> succiduique gradus et castra simillima regi,

> etc.

to join with you in the way he does with Juno." Eager to put this to the test, when Jupiter arrived Semele demanded the oath from him as well as a gift. Pained but unwilling to break his oath, he struck her with lightning and took the child from the womb of the dead woman and put it into his thigh for as much time as it would require in the womb of the mother. At first Ino, his maternal aunt, 3 nurtured him in secret, and then she handed him over to the nymphs who also gave him nourishment, as Ovid says:[92]

> In secret during his earliest years his maternal aunt Ino
> raised him, then the nymphs of Nysa hid the child
> in their caves and nursed him with their milk.

And elsewhere:[93]

> That the nymphs of Nysa, while his stepmother searched for
> the boy,
> screened his cradle with this leaf.

That is, ivy. Afterward, as again Ovid says,[94] "Bacchus liked this plant best of all." Also, they said that his ward was Silenus, who, after being captured by peasants, was restored to Bacchus by Midas.

In addition, they honor him with a chariot and companions, 4 about whom Statius reports this:[95]

> He drives; on the right and left follow unbridled
> Lynxes, and tigers lap at the reins moist with unmixed wine.
> Behind the exultant Mimallones carry rustic spoils,
> half-dead wolves and mutilated bears.
> Nor is his retinue inert: there are Anger and Furor
> and Fear and Courage and Ardor never sober,
> steps infirm, camp followers like their king.

5   Dicunt insuper eum primum vitem plantasse, ut ait Accius in *Bachis*:

O Dyonise,
pater optime, vitisator, Semela
genitus, euhia!

Et hinc vini deum asserunt. Ederam ei sacram et vannum et Marsyam in tutelam eius ascribunt eique Adryanum Mynois filiam coniugem copulant. 'Baculum' ab eo repertum atque denominatum affirmat Rabanus, ut eo homines vino graves uterentur.

6   Multis et illum nominibus vocant, de quibus Ovidius:

Tura dabant, Bachumque vocant Bromiumque Lyeum
Ignigenamque, satumque iterum, solumque bimatrem.
Additur his Nyseus intonsusque Thyoneus,
et cum Leneo genialis consitor uve,
Nictiliusque Eleusque parens et Yacus et Euan,
et que preterea per Graias plurima gentes
nomina, Liber, habes, tibi enim inconsumpta iuventa est,
tu puer eternus et formosissimus alto
conspiceris celo, tunc cum sine cornibus astas,

                    etc.

7   Addit etiam alia nomina Albericus, vocatumque dicit: Euchium, Bryseum et Bassareum. Lactantius etiam eum vocari dicit Dytirambum. Dicit insuper Servius, Orpheum dicere hunc a Gigantibus membratim discerptum. Quod Albericus affirmat, addens quod ab eis ebrius sit inventus, eumque dicit sepultum et postea
8 surrexisse integrum. Pingebant etiam eum antiqui in habitu mulie-

In addition they say that he was the first to plant the vine, as 5
Accius says in his *Bacchae*:[96]

Oh Dionysus,
greatest father, planter of the vine, of Semele
born: euhia!

And for this reason they assert that he was the god of the vine.
They ascribe the ivy and the winnowing basket as sacred to him
and put Marsyas under his protection, and they marry him to
Ariadne, daughter of Minos. Rabanus[97] affirms that he discovered
the walking stick and that he was named "walking stick" [*baculus*],
which men weighed down by wine would use.

They call him by many names, about which Ovid says:[98]   6

They offer frankincense and call upon Bacchus, Bromius, and
     Lyaeus
and 'fire-born' and 'sown-twice' and the sole 'two-mothered';
added to these are Nyseus and unshorn Thyoneus,
and with Lenaeus the planter of the festive grape,
also Nyctelius and father Eleleus and Iacchus and Euhan,
and all the many names you might have in addition,
Liber, among Greek peoples. Because your youth is
     undiminished,
you are ever a boy; you are considered the most beautiful
in the high heaven, then you appear without horns.

Albericus[99] adds still other names and says he was called Evius, 7
Briseus, and Bassareus. Lactantius[100] says he was also called Dithyrambus. In addition Servius[101] says that Orpheus says he was
torn limb from limb by giants. Albericus affirms this, adding that
they found him enebriated, and he says that he was buried and
then rose up intact. The ancients used to depict him in the cloth- 8

bri, et nudum atque puerulum, ei nocturno tempore tybiis et cymbalis et clamore sacrum, quod orgia vocabant, celebrantes.

9 Preter hec alia etiam recitantur, sed quoniam non comperta sunt omnia que queruntur, que videri possunt de appositis videamus. Primo igitur, et ante omnia, pro constanti videntur tenere hystoriographi Dyonisium hominem ex Iove et Semele natum, adeo ut de tempore inter antiquos plurima fuerit varietas. Ex quibus alii Dyonisium, alii Liberum Patrem vocant; et quoniam non constat cuius Iovis fuerit filius, ego secundo ascripsi Iovi, eo quod eius evum melius videatur convenire cum secundo, quam cum aliquo aliorum. Dicit enim Eusebius in libro *Temporum,* a quibusdam arbitrari, Danao Argis regnante, Dyonisium in Yndia Nysam condidisse, et suo nomine nuncupasse, et eodem tempore eum in Yndia militasse, et eius in exercitu fuisse mulieres, Bachas cognominatas ob furorem potius quam ob virtutem, quod quidem fuit

10 circa annos[22] mundi ⅢDCCXXVIIII. Paulo post idem Eusebius dicit, regnante Danao Argis, Cadmus regnavit Thebis, ex cuius filia Semele natus est Dyonisius, id est Liber Pater, quod secundum eius annorum descriptionem comprehenderetur fuisse circa annos[23] mundi ⅢDCCLXVI. Nec multo post dicit anno xxxv° Lycei regis Argivorum, Dyonisius, qui Latine dicitur Liber Pater, nascitur ex Semele, quod contigisse videtur anno mundi ⅢDCCCXIIII. Inde subsequitur, Acrisio regnante Argivis, Dyonisius qui et Liber Pater, adversus Yndos dimicans, Nysam urbem iuxta Yndum flumen condidit, quod factum colligitur anno mundi ⅢDCCCLXX.

11 Quanta hec sit temporis diversitas, ab Eusebio ex comentariis veterum collecta, facile comprehendi potest; nostrum autem est per coniecturas arbitrari, quod verius potuerit ex dictis tempus attribui evo Bachi. Ego autem, omissis causis me moventibus, arbitror Bachi dies fuisse circa antiquius horum tempus, seu saltem

ing of a woman as well as nude and boylike, and they celebrated his rite nocturnally with flutes and cymbals and shouting, and they used to call this an orgy.

Other things are recounted besides these, but because I could 9 not find all that I searched for, let us examine what we can from what we have already established. First and above all, therefore, while all the historiographers seem to maintain that Dionysus was a man born to Jupiter and Semele, there is much variety among the ancients about the period. Some call him Dionysus, others Father Liber; and because there is no agreement as to which Jupiter was his father, I have assigned him to the second Jupiter because his era seems to coincide better with the second than with any of the others. Eusebius[102] says in his *Chronicle* that some believe that when Danaus was ruling in Argos, Dionysus founded Nysa in India, named it after his own name, and made war in India at the same time, and that there were women in his army named Bacchae on account of their furor rather than their valor; this was around world year 3729. A little afterward Eusebius says 10 that when Danaus was ruling in Argos, Cadmus ruled Thebes, and Dionysus, that is, Father Liber, was born from Cadmus' daughter, Semele; according to his description of the years this is understood to have happened circa world year 3766. Not far beyond that he says that in the 35th year of Lynceus' reign in Argos, Dionysus, who is called Father Liber in Latin, was born from Semele, and this seems to have happened in the world year 3814. Still further he says that when Acrisius was ruling the Argives, Dionysus, who is also Father Liber, while fighting against the Indians founded the city of Nysa near the Indus river, which he computed as an event of the world year 3870.

One can easily see how much disparity between time periods 11 there is in the ancient commentaries gathered by Eusebius; it is left for us to determine by conjecture which period can be more accurately assigned to Bacchus' era. I will not elaborate on my ra-

quod de proximo sequitur, eumque ea tempestate natum egisse que ab eo gesta narrantur.

12   Sed his curiosioribus derelictis, ad figmenta tendamus. Fulminatam Semelem a casu sumptum credo, eam scilicet a fulmine, seu ab ignita febre in mortem deductam, quarum utramque a Iove, id est ab elemento ignis, emissam non mirabitur eruditus. Evulsum ab utero mortue matris fetum et Iovis femoribus applicitum, notissimum obstetricibus officium designatur; necesse enim est, ut caloribus extrinsecis, qui per Iovem debent intelligi, faveatur[24] qui ante tempus intrinsecis aufertur.

13   Sed cum sit hec expositio physica, hystoricam recitat Pomponius Mela in *Cosmographia*, dicens:

> Urbium quas incolunt Yndi, sunt autem plurime, Nysa est clarissima et maxima, montium, Meros Iovi sacer, famam hinc precipuam habent in illa genitum, in huius specu Liberum arbitrantur esse nutritum, unde Grecis autoribus, ut femori Iovis insitum dicerent, aut materia ingessit aut error.

Hec ille.

14   Albericus autem addit, dicens a Remigio affirmari apud Nysam Liberi Patris haberi crepundia in testimonium quod ibidem altus sit. Quod si sic est, extimo[25] de altero intelligendum sit, quam de eo, qui ex Semele natus est; ex quo etiam sequi posset temporum diversitates a diversis Dyonisiis exortas esse. De hoc enim, si is fuit, dicit Orosius sic:

tionale here, but I believe that the days of Bacchus were the most ancient of these times, or at least the period following this, and that he was born at that time and carried out the actions which he is said to have carried out.

But leaving these problems behind to the more curious, let us 12 proceed to the fabrications. I believe that Semele's being struck by a thunderbolt was taken from an event, namely, that she was struck by a thunderbolt or killed by a fiery fever, both coming from Jupiter, that is, from the element of fire, something which will not amaze one who is educated. That as a fetus he was plucked from the womb of his dead mother and placed into the thigh of Jupiter signifies a procedure well known to midwives, for when a fetus is taken out before its time, it needs external warming, which is known to be one of the functions of Jupiter.

While this is a physical explanation, Pomponius Mela recounts 13 a historical one in his *Description of the World*, saying:[103]

Of the cities the Indians inhabit — there are many — Nysa is the most famous and the greatest; and of the mountains, Meros, which is sacred to Jupiter. The Indians attribute the chief fame there to the fact that they believe Liber was born on its slopes and nurtured in its cave, which caused, whether by the situation or by mistake, the Greek authors to say that he was inserted into the thigh of Jupiter.

This is what he says.

Albericus[104] adds, saying it was affirmed by Remigius, that at 14 Nysa they preserve the rattle of Father Liber as evidence that he was nurtured there. If this is so, I think we must understand that it is someone other than he who was born from Semele, and therefore it might follow that the different time periods represent different people named Dionysus. As for this one, if he existed, Orosius says this:[105]

Subactam Yndiam Liber Pater sanguine madefecit, cedibus opplevit, libidinibus polluit, gentem utique nulli hominum unquam obnoxiam, vernacula tantum quiete contentam.

15 Ceterum, ut ad sensus physicos tectos sub fabula redeamus, dico quod non nulli volunt pro Bacho vinum intelligi, et sic Semeles pro vite sumetur, que ex Iove (id est ex calore in altum humorem terre immixtum per vitis poros trahente) se pregnantem, id est turgidam facit, et in palmites botrosque sucos, tanquam in conceptum fetum emictit. Tunc autem fulminatur, cum adveniente autumnali calore, non in ampliorem maturitatem sed potius in corruptionem et putredinem fructum conceptum deduceret, ut auferatur necesse est, et femori Iovis, id est calori altero, applicetur.

16 Quod quidem sit, dum pressum ex uvis vinum aut igni ipsismet pressis bulliendum concedimus iterum, donec defecatum tali bullitione reddatur potui aptum. Deinde Yno, id est vas, illud servat occultum, id est contectum, ne a Iunone inveniatur, id est ne ab aere corrumpatur. Seu pregnantem tunc Semelem dicimus ex Iove, cum vitem agente calore turgidam cernimus vere primo; verum tunc fulminatur, dum estivo calore preter consuetum exuritur; tunc autem apertis poris conceptum emitit in botros, quod femori Iovis, id est diurno calori, applicatur, ut quam ex matre non habuerat, a patre maturitatem accipiat; et tunc Yno illud servat occulte, dum a pampinis tegitur, ne ab aere nimis calido offendatur; et illud tunc nutriunt nynphe, dum nocturnis humiditatibus restauratur, quod calore diurno fuerat exhaustum.

Father Liber conquered India and soaked it with blood, filled it with slaughter, befouled it with lust, a nation which surely never harmed anyone and was utterly content in its indigenous peacefulness.

As for the rest, so that we can return to the physical meanings 15 hidden within this fable, I say that some want Bacchus to be understood as wine, and so Semele is understood as the vine; she was impregnated, that is, was made swollen, by Jupiter, that is, by the heat which brings to the surface the moisture of the earth mixed through the porous vines; and he sends the juices into the young vine branches and the grapes as if into the conceived fetus. Then he strikes like lightning when, as the autumnal heat arrives and he brings the conceived fruit not into greater maturation but rather into corruption and rot, it is necessary to remove them to the thigh of Jupiter, that is, another source of heat. This happens if we 16 allow that the wine pressed from the grapes must be bubbled up again either with fire or the pressed grapes themselves until, with the impurities removed by this bubbling, it is rendered fit to drink. Then Ino, that is, the container, protects it hidden away, that is, covered, lest it be found by Juno, that is, lest it be corrupted by air. Or, we say that Semele was impregnated by Jupiter when we perceive the vine swollen by the action of the heat at the onset of spring; then there is lightning when in the summer heat it burns excessively; then it sends what it conceives through the open pores into the grapes, which is inserted into the thigh of Jupiter, that is, diurnal heat, so that it receives from its father the maturation which it did not receive from its mother; and then Ino protects it secretly, when it is covered by vine leaves, lest it be harmed by the excessively hot air; and then the nymphs nurture it, when what had been exhausted by the diurnal heat is restored by the nocturnal moistures.

17   Sylenus senex eius alumnus dicitur, eo quod senes fere potu magis quam cibo sustententur. Qui illi a Myda avarissimo homine ideo restituitur, quia avarus potationibus non delectatur. Curru et sociis uti ideo a poetis dictum est, ut non nulli ex suis demonstrentur effectus. Nam pro curru ebriorum volubilitas assumenda est.

18   Lynces autem illi attribuuntur, ut intelligatur vinum moderate sumptum vires, audaciam et perspicaciam augere. Tygres autem ideo currum trahunt, ut ebriorum ostendatur sevitia. Nemini enim parcit onustus vino. Sunt preterea temulenti temerarii adeo, ut in quodcunque periculum inconsiderate irruant, quod per semineces lupos et scissas ursas, que in predam Bachi deportantur, intelligo. Quod irascantur facile et inde veniant in furorem, satis liquido patet, et sic non sobrio comitantur Ardore. Meticulosi etiam sunt vinolenti, quia perdito recto rationis iudicio sepissime non timenda pavescunt. Virtus autem cur currui Bachi iungatur pretactum est ubi de lyncibus diximus. Succidui gradus ideo inter Bachi numerantur comites, ut ebriorum titubantia designetur, qui adeo titu-

19   bando incedunt, ut cadere credantur continue. Superadditur Bacho castra esse simillima regum, nec immerito; nam si cernamus tabernas meritorias, ibidem tabernacula frondium, cupidinarios, lurcones et edulia, potationes hinc inde, atque tumultuantes rixantesque videbimus, que castris regum simillima sunt.

Bachum autem apud Grecos primum plantasse vitem, seu vineam, et vinum fecisse, possibile est, cum longe ante apud Hebreos

20   id fecisse Noe certissimum habeamus. Dicunt tamen aliqui Bachum vitem non plantasse, sed incognitum Thebanis vini usum introduxisse, atque illud variis liquoribus immiscuisse, ut amabi-

They say that the elderly Silenus is his ward because the elderly   17
are sustained by drink more than by eating. He is restored to him
by Midas, the most miserly of men, because a miser does not delight in drink. The poets said he employed a chariot and his train
so they could demonstrate some of the effects he has. The chariot
should be assumed to represent the whirling of drunks.

Lynxes are attributed to him so that we understand that wine   18
taken in moderation increases our strength, boldness, and perspi-
cacity. Tigers draw his chariot so that we see the savagery of
drunks, for someone heavy with wine spares no one. There are in
addition inebriants so reckless that they rush thoughtlessly into
any danger whatsoever, which I understand in the half-dead wolves
and mutilated bears carried as the spoils of Bacchus. That they
anger easily and then become furious is sufficiently clear, and so
they are not accompanied by sober Ardor, for inebriants are full of
fears: having lost the correct judgment of reason, they very often
become alarmed at what they ought not fear. We touched on why
courage is joined to Bacchus' triumph where we discussed the
lynxes. Infirm steps are counted among the companions of Bacchus to designate the staggering of inebriants who stagger as they
walk in such a way that they are continuously thought to be falling. Encampments very similar to those of kings are also attached   19
to Bacchus, and not without good reason, for if we examine the
commercial taverns and their tents of leaves, idlers, gluttons, and
foods, drinking everywhere, we will see commotions and quarreling, just as in the encampments of kings.

It is possible that among the Greeks it was Bacchus who first
planted the vine, or a vineyard, or made wine, although we know
with great certainty that Noah did this much earlier among the
Hebrews. But some say that Bacchus did not plant the vine but   20
introduced this unknown use of the vine to the Thebans by mixing it with various liquids to make it more pleasant; since that
seemed marvelous, he was believed to be a god of wine at first

lius foret, quod quoniam mirabile visum est, deus vini apud rudes primo creditus est. Ederam preterea Bacho sacram dicunt, credo quia vites edere tramites luxuriantes plurimum et botros uvarum imitentur corimbi, nec non quia vireat viriditate perpetua, per quam ostenditur vini iuventus continua; nunquam enim quantum ad vires senescit vinum. Hac etiam poete coronari consuevere, eo quod Bacho ob facundiam sacri sint, et ad perpetuitatem carminum demonstrandam.

21   Vannus autem illi sacer est mistica ratione. Ait autem Servius Liberi Patris sacra ad purgationem anime pertinere, et sic homines eius misteriis purgabantur, sicut vanno frumenta purgantur. Fuere tamen qui voluere hec purgamina viventibus hominibus fieri per extremam ebrietatem, que sacrum Bachi est, asserentes, si quis in tantam ebrietatem procederet, ut in vomitum usque veniret, post preteritum cerebri stuporem, animum, exutis curis tediosis atque eiectis, remanere tranquillum. Cui opinioni Seneca phylosophus in libro, quem *De tranquillitate animi* scripsit, adhesisse videtur.

22   Marsyam in suam tutelam positum ideo voluisse reor, quia audax imo temerarius in Apollinem fuit, per quam temeritatem vinolentorum loquacitatem in quoscunque tendentem intelligo, qua in conspectu rudium sepe prudentes ab ignaris confundi videntur, non advertentium quia nullo talium oratio incedat ordine, sed more satyri, uti Marsyas fuit, huc illuc saltitando procedat. Tandem in conspectu eruditorum nudatus Marsya, id est patefacta calefactorum presumptione, in flumen vertitur, id est in lapsum, quasi nil dixerint, talium sermo solvatur.

23   Quod ad Adrianam coniugem pertinet, in sequentibus, ubi de ea scribetur. Hunc autem a Gigantibus fuisse discerptum et inde

among uncultured people. In addition they say that ivy was sacred to Bacchus. I believe this was because their vines produce an abundance of shoots and ivy berries are similar to the berrylike grapes, and because it remains green in perpetual verdure; in this way wine reveals its continuous youth, for wine never grows old insofar as its power is concerned. Also, poets used to be crowned with it because they were sacred to Bacchus on account of their eloquence, and because this demonstrated the long life of their poetry.

The winnowing basket is sacred to him for a mystical reason. Servius[106] says that the rites of Father Liber had to do with the 21 purgation of the spirit, and men used to be purged by his mysteries just as grains are purged by a winnowing basket. There were those who preferred these purgings for living men to occur during extreme drunkenness, which is a rite of Bacchus; they asserted that if anyone should become so enebriated that he vomited, after he got past the stupor of the brain, his mind would remain tranquil, his wearisome cares cast off and expelled. Seneca[107] the philosopher in his book *On the Tranquility of the Mind* seems to adhere to this opinion.

I think they wanted Marsyas to be under his guardianship be- 22 cause he was daring, in fact, rash, toward Apollo, and in this rashness of the intoxicated I understand a loquaciousness toward everyone. Because of this, wise men often seem to be confused by the ignorant in the eyes of the uneducated, who do not notice that the speech of the wise does not proceed in any order but moves in the manner of a satyr like Marsyas, proceeding by leaping here and there. In the end, in the eyes of the learned, Marsyas is stripped bare, — that is, the presumption of hotheaded people is made plain — and is turned into a river, that is, the speech of the ignorant dissolves and collapses, as if they had said nothing.

That which pertains to his wife Ariadne will be presented sub- 23 sequently in the chapter on her.[108] That he was torn limb from limb by giants and then buried I think was said because the

sepultum, ideo dictum reor, quia ab Eusebio in libro *Temporum* scribitur, quod regnante Athenis Pandione, anno scilicet mundi ⅢDCCCXCVI, Marco Varrone poeta teste, hic Liber Pater adversus Perseum pugnans in prelio occisus sit, eiusque videri sepulcrum apud Delphos, iuxta Apollinem aureum. Et hoc quantum ad hystoriam dictum sit.

24 Sed fictioni superadditur a quibusdam, eum scilicet quantuncumque discerptum sepelierint, integrum surrexisse. Quod ego arbitror debere intelligi, quod ex pluribus ingurgitationibus ab elatis calore vini bibionibus factis, una consurgat ebrietas, per quam Bachum vivere et aliquid agere satis patet. Dicebat tamen circa hoc Albericus:

> Bachum animam mundi intelligendum, que quamvis membratim per mundi corpora dividatur, tamen se reintegrare videtur de corporibus emergens, et se reformans, et semper una eademque perseverans, nullam simplicitatis sue patiens sectionem.

Hec ille. Ast ego puto hunc Bachum Alberici, solem intelligendum Macrobii, in quem ipse Macrobius transfert deorum omnium deitates.

25 Pictus autem in habitu muliebri est, quia in expeditione adversus Yndos secum habuit mulieres, ut predictum est, vel quia continuate potationes, enervent vires debilesque reddant ad ultimum potatores. Nudus vero ideo fingitur,[26] quia ebrius omnia pandat secreta, vel quia multos iam ad inopiam et nuditatem deduxerit, vel quia calorem potationes ingerant. Puer quidem dicitur, quia non aliter sint lascivi ebrii quam pueri, quibus nondum integer est intellectus.

26 Restat nunc de nominibus videre. Dicitur igitur primo Bachus, quod idem sonat quod 'furor,' eo quod vinum, et potissime novum, tam ferventis furoris est, ut nullo queat claustro continere, et immoderate sumentes, ut predictum est, facit etiam furiosos. Dici-

Chronicle of Eusebius'[109] indicates that when Pandion was ruling in Athens, namely in the world year 3896 according to the poet Marcus Varro,[110] this Father Liber was killed in battle fighting against Perseus, and that his tomb was seen at Delphi next to golden Apollo. And this is what was said insofar as history is concerned.

Some again also add to the fiction that even though he was 24 dismembered and then buried, he rose again whole. I think that this must be understood in that after many imbibings, the heat of the wine produces small insects, and the combined result is drunkenness; from this it is quite clear that Bacchus lives and does something. About this Albericus said:[111]

> Bacchus should be understood as the spirit of the world which, although it is divided into members throughout the bodies of the world, nevertheless seems to reintegrate itself when emerging from bodies, reforming itself, and always remaining unique and the same, not suffering its single nature to be subdivided.

He says this. But I think that this Bacchus of Albericus must be understood as Macrobius' sun, to whom Macrobius[112] transfers the divinities of all the gods.

He is depicted in women's clothing because in his expedition 25 against the Indians he had women with him, as was said earlier, or, because continuous drinking saps the strength and continually debilitates drinkers. He is a nude figure because a drunk reveals all secrets, or because he has already led many into poverty and nudity, or because drinking generates heat. He is said to be a boy because lascivious inebriants are none other than boys to whom the intellect is not yet fully formed.

It remains now to see about his names. First he is called Bac- 26 chus because it means the same as "furor," for wine, and especially new wine, has such burning furor that it cannot be held in any container and fills those consuming it immoderately with furor, as

tur etiam Bromius a *bromin*, quod est 'consumere'; modesta quidem boni vini potatio consumit superfluitates ciborum, et digestionem adiuvat, ut physicis placet, sed intemperate sumptum, humiditatem bonam desiccat et nervorum hebetat vires, adeo ut plurimum ingurgitatores tremulos effetosque reddat.

27   Vocatur insuper et Lyeus a *lyen*, quod est 'tractus,' tractim enim bibitur. Vel dicitur Lyeus a 'ligo ligas'; modeste autem sumptum dispersas vires colligit augetque, immoderate sensus ligat et rationem. Vel secundum Fulgentium Lyeus dicitur, quia 'lenitatem' prestat; sumus enim post aliqualem potationem magis exorabiles.

28   Nuncupatur et Ignigena, seu quia ex 'igne genitus' sit, seu quia 'ignem,' id est calorem, 'generat'; videmus enim capita potantium fumantia eosque ob calorem vestimenta quandoque deponere.

29   Appellatur etiam 'Satus iterum,' et ob id eum vocari Dytirambum, quod idem sonet, dicit Lactantius; quia autem iterum natus sit, supra monstratum est, et inde merito Bimater.

Nyseus preterea a Nysa civitate, in qua colitur, vel a Nysa, uno ex verticibus Parnasi eidem consecrato, vocatus est. Thyoneus quod 'intonsus' sonat, ideo dicitur, quia vites ex quibus oritur longas habent palmites, vel quod melius puto, ad suam pueritiam ostendendam, quia intonsi sint pueri. Consitor uve dicitur a vite a se primo plantata. Nictilus vero vocitatur, quia 'noctem,' id est tenebras, sensibus ingerat. Eleus ab Elea civitate, in qua potissime colebatur. Yacus autem ea de causa nominatus est, quia homines 'hyare' faciat. *Euan* interiectio laudantis Bachum est, et sonat 'bonus puer.' Briseus ideo dictus, ut ait Albericus, quia primus vinum

said before. He is called Bromius from *bromin*, that is, "to consume." The modest drinking of good wine eats up a superfluity of food and aids digestion, as natural scientists think, but when consumed immoderately it dries out the good moisture and deadens the powers of the muscles so that it often makes guzzlers shaky and exhausted.

In addition he is called Lyeus from *lyen*, which is "drawn out," 27 for one drinks in a drawn-out manner. Or he is called Lyeus from "binding" [*ligo ligas*]: drinking in moderation gathers dispersed strengths and increases them, but immoderate drinking binds the senses and reason. Or, according to Fulgentius,[113] he is called Lyeus because he exhibits "lenience" [*lenitatem*], for after some drinking we are more capable of being lenient. He is also named Fire-28 born [*Ignigena*] either because he was "born [*genitus*] from fire [*igne*]" or because he generates fire [*ignem . . . generat*], that is, heat, for we see the heads of drinkers steaming and we then see them taking their clothes off on account of the heat. He is also referred 29 to as "Sown again," and on account of this Lactantius[114] says he is called Dithyrambus, which means the same; that he was born again was demonstrated above, and from that he is appropriately called "Two-mothered" [*Bimater*].

In addition, he was called Nyseus from the city of Nysa where he was worshipped, or from Nysa, one of the peaks of Parnassus consecrated to him. He is called Thyoneus, which means "unshorn," because the vines from which he is born have long shoots; or, as I prefer to think, to reveal his boyhood, because boys are unshorn. He is called the Planter of the Grape from the grapevine first planted by him. He is said to be Nictilius because the "night" [*noctem*], that is, darkness, he brings to the senses. Eleus is from the city of Elea, where he was greatly worshipped. He was named Iacchus for this reason — that he makes men "gape" [*hyare*]. *Euan* is an interjection of one praising Bacchus, and it means "good boy." He is called Briseus, as Albericus[115] says, because he first "pressed"

30   ex uva 'pressit,' vel Briseus, quasi 'hyrsutus,' id est superbus. Hinc aiunt eum apud veterem Greciam duas habuisse statuas, unam hyrsutam Briseim vocatam, alteram vero 'lenem,' Lenei vocitatam. Bassareus autem appellatus est a specie vestium, quibus ministre eius utebantur in sacris, et ab eisdem ministre Bassarides nuncupate.

31   Liber autem pater dicitur, quia hominibus 'libertatem' videatur inferre; nam potati servi, etiam ebrietate durante, arbitrantur se fregisse vincula servitutis. Liberat preterea a curis, et in agendis securiores facit, pauperes ab oportunitatibus reddit immunes, deiectos extollit etiam in sublime. Et dicit Albericus quod cum inter initia condendarum civitatum diis ceteris pro auspicibus ceptorum fierent sacra, Libero Patri fiebant, ut libertatem future patrie conservarent.

32   Preterea civitates imperantibus orbi Romanis aut stipendiarie erant, aut federate, aut libere; in liberis autem civitatibus in signum libertatis simulacrum Marsye habebatur, quem supra diximus in tutelam esse Liberi Patris. Insuper mos fuit Romanis liberam togam adolescentibus in festis Liberalibus exhibere, ad significationem liberioris vite in posterum concesse. Cuius quidem sacra dicit Servius a Julio Cesare Romam primum translata, in quibus hyrcus immolabatur, et hoc ideo, quia aliquando capelle palmites vitium crescentes vastassent. Dicit enim M. Terentius Varro, ubi *De agricultura*, eidem tanquam repertori vitis hyrcos immolari, ut penas capite pendant.

33   Ego autem huius sacra non puto a Iulio primum in Romam translata, sed eius Liberi Patris, de quo intellexisse videtur Tullius, dum ubi *De naturis deorum* dixit, 'Hunc dico Liberum Semele natum, non eum, quem nostri maiores auguste sancteque censent

wine from the grape; or Briseus, as if "shaggy," that is, proud. From 30
this they say that had two statues in ancient Greece, a shaggy one
called Briseus, the other smooth [*lenem*] called Leneus. He was
referred to as Bassareus from the type of vestments his ministers
used to wear during his rites, and from these his ministers were
named Bassarids.

He is called Father Liber because he seems to have brought 31
"liberty" [*libertatem*] to men, for drunken servants, so long as their
inebriation lasts, think they have broken the bonds of their servi-
tude. In addition, he frees from cares, and he makes doing things
more secure, the poor he renders immune to chance, and he raises
the dejected toward the sublime. Also, Albericus says that when at
the commencements for the foundations of states sacrifices were
made to the rest of the gods for auspicious undertakings, sacrifices
were made to Father Liber to preserve the liberty of the future
homeland.

In addition, when the Romans ruled the world, states were ei- 32
ther tributary, allied, or free; in free states there stood as a sign of
liberty a statue of Marsyas, whom we said above was under the
guardianship of Father Liber. In addition, it was a custom among
Roman youths to wear the toga of liberty during the festivals of
Liber to signify the freer life expected in the future. Servius[116] in
fact says that his rites were first brought to Rome by Julius Caesar,
and in these rites a he-goat was sacrificed, and they did this because sometimes kids desolate the growing shoots of grapevines.
M. Terentius Varro[117] in his *On Agriculture* says that he-goats were
sacrificed to him, as the founder of the vine, so as to pay the price
by losing their heads.

I do not think the rites of this Liber were first brought to Rome 33
by Julius Caesar but those of Father Liber whom Cicero seems to
have understood when he said in his *On the Nature of the Gods*,[118] "I
say that this Liber was born of Semele, not the one whom our

34 Liberum,' etc. Quem ego arbitror iuxta sententiam Macrobii Solem, quem arbitrati sunt rerum omnium patrem, et hinc Liberum
Patrem dictum. Et sic etiam intellexisse Virgilium puto dum
dixit:

> Vos, o clarissima mundi
> lumina, labentem celo que ducitis annum,
> Liber et alma Ceres,
>
> etc.

Non enim Bachus labentem annum celo ducit, sed sol; et hec
equidem ea duo fuerunt numina, que Etrusci potissime colue-
runt.

35 Sed quicunque hic fuerit Liber, ostendit Augustinus in libro *De
civitate Dei*, ei a priscis obscena celebrata sacra, et inter alia dicit,
quod eius in honorem pudenda virilia colebantur in patulo, adeo
ut festis diebus Liberi membrum virilem elevatum ex compitis
deferretur in urbem, verbis flagitiosissimis omni concessa licentia;
inde per forum transvectum et in locum eidem deputatum deposi-
tum, oportebat ut honestissima omnium mater familias illi coronam imponeret.

36 Insuper et Dyonisius appellatur Bachus, de quo ubi de Dyonisio.

: 26 :

De Hymeneo filio Bachi

1 Hymeneum dicit Albericus filium fuisse Bachi et Veneris, et sequitur autoritate Remigii ob id habitum, quia ex nimia petulantia

ancestors solemnly and piously thought was Liber." I think, fol- 34
lowing the opinion of Macrobius,[119] that he was the sun, whom
they thought to be the father of all things, and from this he was
called Father Liber. And I think Vergil meant this when he
said:[120]

> You, O world's most clearest
> lights, who lead the year gliding through the sky,
> Liber and nourishing Ceres.

It is not Bacchus who leads the year gliding through the sky but
the sun, and these indeed were the two divinities which the Etruscans especially worshipped.

But whichever Liber this was, Augustine[121] reveals in his *City of* 35
God that the ancients celebrated obscene rites to him, and among
other things he says that in his honor masculine genitals were
worshipped in public to the extent that on the festival days of
Liber a masculine member was lifted from the crossroads and carried into the city, and every license was given to use the most disgraceful words; after it was transported from there into the forum
and deposited in a grove reserved for it, the most reputable mother
of all was obliged to put a crown on it.

In addition, Bacchus was also called Dionysus, who will be 36
discussed in the chapter on Dionysus.[122]

: 26 :

On Hymenaeus, son of Bacchus

Albericus[123] says that Hymenaeus was the son of Bacchus and 1
Venus, and he accepts the authority of Remigius in thinking that
passion is usually aroused by the excessive wantonness of wine.

vini[27] libido soleat excitari. 'Hymen' autem Grece dicitur *membrana,* que est proprie muliebris sexus, in qua puerperia fieri dicuntur. Inde Hymeneus nuptiarum deus dictus est.

2 Sane Lactantius ab hystoria tractum dicit, scribens quia Hymeneus puer fuerit Atheniensis mediocri genere natus, qui cum annos puerilis etatis excederet, nec dum virum posset implere, ea pulchritudine fuisse preditum dicitur, ut feminam mentiretur. Istum cum una ex civibus suis virgo nobilis adamasset, is quia nuptias desperabat, puellam tamen versa vice diligebat extreme, et animo saltem aspectu satisfaciebat suo. Cumque nobiles femine cum virginibus sacra Cereris Eleusine celebrarent, subito adventu pyrratarum rapte sunt, inter quas etiam Hymeneus, qui illo a se

3 dilectam secutus fuerat. Cum igitur per longinqua maria predam pyrrate vexissent, ad quandam tandem regionem devoluti, et ibi somno oppressi, ab insequentibus interempti sunt omnes. Hymeneus autem, relictis virginibus, evolavit Athenas, pactus a consanguineis dilecte sue nuptias, si illis filias nuper raptas restitueret,

4 quas ubi pro voto restituit, exoptatam accepit uxorem. Quod coniugium quia felix fuerat, placuit Atheniensibus nomen Hymenei misceri nuptiis. Sunt tamen qui dicant eum die quadam nuptiarum ruina oppressum, et piationis causa id adinventum, ut nomen eius celebraretur in nuptiis. Quod omnino Servius damnat.

5 Ego autem eum ob id Bachi et Veneris filium dictum reor, quia propter duo fiant nuptie seu duo interveniunt in nuptiis: festum et carnalem copulam. Per festum Bachus intelligendus est, ut per Virgilium patet, dum dicit, 'Assit letitie Bachus dator,' etc. Per Venerem autem carnalem copulam, cum ad eam spectare videatur

"Hymen" in Greek is *membrana*, which is proper to the female sex and is where childbirths are said to occur. Therefore they said that Hymenaeus was the god of marriages.

But Lactantius[124] says the name is derived from history, writing that Hymenaeus was an Athenian boy born of a moderate family background and that when he had grown out of his boyhood years but had not yet reached manhood, he was said to have been gifted with such beauty that he could be mistaken for a woman. Once a noble maiden, one of his fellow citizens, had fallen in love with him, and he in turn intensely loved the girl, but because he had no hope of marriage, he used to satisfy himself by just looking at her. One day when noble women as well as maidens were celebrating the rites of Eleusinian Ceres, pirates suddenly appeared and seized them, and among the captured was Hymenaeus, who had followed his beloved there. When the pirates had carried their booty over distant seas, they arrived at some land where, overcome by sleep, they were all killed by their pursuers. The maidens were left alone, however, so Hymenaeus made his way to Athens and bargained for a marriage with the family of his beloved if he would restore their daughters who had just been abducted; when he did as promised, he took the hand of the wife he had hoped for. Because this wedding ceremony was a happy event, the Athenians decided to associate Hymenaeus' name with weddings. There are nonetheless some who say that he was overcome by some disaster on the day of his marriage, and by way of expiation they connected his name to wedding celebrations. Servius[125] completely discredits this.

I think that he was said to be the son of Bacchus and Venus on account of this: marriages occur for two reasons or two things occur at marriages — a celebration and carnal copulation. Bacchus should be recognized in the celebration, as is apparent in Vergil when he says,[126] "May Bacchus, bestower of happiness, be present." Carnal copulation occurs through Venus, for she appears to

ad procreandam prolem marem et feminam copulare, et ex his duobus conficiuntur nuptie, seu Hymeneus, qui pro nuptiis intelligendus est.

: 27 :

De Thyoneo Bachi filio

1 Thyoneum Bachi filium dicit Ovidius, et de eo brevem recitat fabulam. Dicit enim quod cum bovem fuisset furatus, et ob id opprimeretur a rusticis, invocato forte patris auxilio, factum est, ut a Bacho Thyoneus in venatorem converteretur, et bos permutaretur in cervum.

2 Arbitror ego hunc fuisse furem, et potatis optime rusticis, bovem suum repetentibus facile ostendisse eis et se venatorem et bovem cervum fuisse.

: 28 :

De Thoante Bachi filio, qui genuit Ysiphilem

1 Thoantem Bachi fuisse filium carmen demonstrat Ovidii dicentis:

Tum primum sese trepidis sub nocte Thyoneus
detexit nato portans extrema Thoanti Subsidia,

etc.

Paulus autem eum ex Adriana Minois susceptum testatur.

be connected with the copulation of masculine and feminine for procreating offspring, and these two things comprise marriage, or Hymenaeus, who must be understood to represent marriage.

: 27 :

On Thyoneus, son of Bacchus

Ovid[127] says that Thyoneus is the son of Bacchus, and he recounts 1 a brief fable about him. He says that when he had stolen a cow and was therefore being pursued by peasants, he perchance called upon his father for help, so Bacchus converted Thyoneus into a hunter and transformed the cow into a stag.

I think that he was a thief, and because the peasants were 2 drinking heavily when they went to find their cow, he demonstrated to them with ease that he was a hunter and the cow a stag.

: 28 :

On Thoas, son of Bacchus, who fathered Hypsipyle

The poem of Ovid proves that Thoas was the son of Bacchus in 1 saying:[128]

> Then first under cover of night to us in our fear Thyoneus revealed
> himself, carrying outside aid to his son Thoas.

Paul testifies that Ariadne, daughter of Minos, had given birth to him.

Sed miror qualiter hoc fieri potuerit, cum Thoas, ut infra monstrabitur, genuerit Ysiphylem, que tempore Thebani belli nutrix Opheltis Lygurgo Nemeo serviebat. Et Adriana antequam Bacho nupserit, a Theseo rapta est, post Ypolitum susceptum, qui paulo ante initium suscepti belli Thebani in Ytaliam abiit, et sic 2 longe antiquior fuit Thoas quam Adriana. Is quidem, ut testatur Statius, iam senex, cum Lemniades, apud quos rex fuit, a se minis sui communi consilio occisi sunt, a filia Ysiphyle ficto rogo salvatus est, et in Chyum insulam nocte transmissus.

: 29 :

· *De Ysiphyle Thoantis filia*

1 Ysiphyles filia fuit Thoantis, teste Statio, dum dicit:

Cui regnum genitorque Thoas et lucidus Euan
stirpis avus,

etc.

Hec autem, ut idem refert Statius, cum adhibuisset consensum in publico mulierum Lemniadum consilio de occidendis masculis suis et suis legibus vivere, ea nocte, qua scelus a ceteris feminis perpetratum est, Thoantem patrem navi imposuit, eumque Bacho patri commendavit, et in insulam Chyum transmisit, et constructo in regia rogo, se patrem interemisse monstravit, eiusque loco homicidis mulieribus imperavit.

But I wonder how this could be possible, for Thoas, as I will show below, fathered Hypsipyle, who at the time of the Theban war was serving Lycurgus of Nemea as the nurse of Opheltes. And before Ariadne married Bacchus, she had been abducted by Theseus after Hippolytus had been born, and a little before the beginning of the undertaking of the Theban War he had gone to Italy; thus Thoas was far more ancient than Ariadne. In fact, according to Statius, Thoas was already an old man when the Lemnians, whom he ruled as king, were killed by a conspiracy of their women, and he was saved by his daughter Hypsipyle, who constructed a false funeral pyre and sent him by night to the island of Chios. 2

: 29 :

On Hypsipyle,[129] *daughter of Thoas*

Hypsipyle was the daughter of Thoas, according to Statius, who says:[130] 1

> She ruled, and Thoas was her father, and shining Euhan,
> ancestor of her line.

As again Statius[131] reports, although she consented in the public debate among the Lemnian women about killing their men and lived by their laws, on the night the rest of the women perpetrated the crime, she demonstrated that she had killed her father Thoas by building a funeral pyre in the palace while putting her father aboard a ship, entrusting him to his father Bacchus, and sending him to the island of Chios; then she ruled over the homicidal women in his stead.

2   Qua regnante, ut altisono[28] carmine ostendit Statius, factum est ut tendentibus cum Iasone Argonautis in Colcos ad Lemni litus applicarent, et seu quia non reciperentur, seu quia ultores criminum accessissent, vi insulam cepere, et sic suscepti inter alios Iason ab Ysiphyle receptus est, et eius amicitia usus, sociis orantibus et exigente tempore reditu promisso, navem conscendens, eam pregnantem reliquit, que postea geminos peperit, Thoantem scilicet et Euneum. Et cum minime reverteretur Iason, et casu cognitum foret a Lemniadibus eam Thoanti pepercisse patri, regno pulsa est, et a pyrratis capta in litore, in servitium regis Nemee deducta est.

3   Qui eidem[29] Opheltem parvum filium suum alendum exhibuit. Que dum operi vacaret, venientibus Argivis in Thebanos in Nemea silva siti pereuntibus, ab his qui aque exploratores venerant,

4 seu ab ipso Adrasto rege comperta et interrogata est. Que evestigio Langiam fluvium ostendit, ubi sitim posuere reges et qui illos sequebantur populi, et cum quenam esset explorassent, et ea casus recitasset suos, contigit ut medio ex agmine Thoas et Euneus iuvenes filii eius prosilirent, matre cognita, eiusque solarentur dolores. Sed dum ipsa fortunas suas recitat, alumni oblita, quem inter herbas floresque ludentem liquerat, infelici eventum contigit ut is a serpente caude repercussione occideretur, quam ob rem turbatus exercitus est. Verum[30] Lygurgus egre filii necem ferens, dum in eam impetu agereretur, ab Adrasto reliquisque regibus, et a filiis suis servata est. Quid tandem ex ea contigerit nusquam legisse memini.

During her rule, as Statius[132] makes clear in his lofty poem, it 2
happened that the Argonauts, when making their way with Jason
to Colchis and reaching the shores of Lemnos, whether because
they were not welcomed or because they were avengers of those
crimes, took the island by force, and, received among the others in
this way, Jason had an audience with Hypsipyle and established a
bond with her. But when his companions demanded the return
promised them, with time growing short, he climbed aboard his
ship and left her pregnant. She later gave birth to twins, namely,
Thoas and Euneus, and when Jason did not return and the Lemnian women had by chance learned that she had spared her father,
she was driven from the kingdom and, captured by pirates on the
shore, was taken to serve the King of Nemea.

He made her the nurse of Opheltes, his small son. One day 3
while she was taking care of him, the Argives attacked the Thebans in the Nemean forest. Perishing of thirst, the scouts who had
come to find water, or King Adrastus himself, discovered her and
questioned her. Immediately she showed them the river Langia, 4
and the kings, as well as the people who followed them, quenched
their thirst; after they had asked who she was and she explained to
them her circumstances, it happened that Thoas and Euneus, her
young sons, leapt out from the middle of the group, and, recognizing their mother, assuaged her grief. But while she was recounting
her fortunes, she had forgotten about her ward, whom she had left
playing among the grasses and flowers, and it happened that the
unfortunate youth was killed by a blow from the tail of a serpent.
This roused the army. Lycurgus, quite upset about the death of his
son, attacked her, but she was saved by Adrastus and the rest of
the kings as well as her sons. I do not remember reading what
happened to her after this.

: 30 :

De Amphione rege Thebarum,
V° Iovis secundi filio, qui VII genuit filios
et totidem filias

1 Amphion filius fuit Iovis et Anthiope, ut in *Odissea* testatur Homerus. Ex cuius creatione, ubi de Anthiopa scribitur, fabula recitatur. Dicit tamen Ovidius quod ibidem non scribitur, a Iove in taurum verso oppressam Anthiopam et gravidam factam. Et alibi dicit:

> Addidit et satyri celatus imagine pulchram
> Iuppiter implerit gemino Nicteida fetu,
>
> > etc.

2 Omerus preterea, ubi supra, dicit Iovem tres ex Anthiopa suscepisse filios, Amphionem scilicet et Zethum, atque Calathum.

Hos preterea volunt expositos a matre, pulsa a Lynceo, rege Thebarum, ob stuprum cum Epapho, seu Iove, commissum, et grandes tandem a pastore quodam nutriti, insurrexisse in Lynceum et eum occidisse atque Dyrcem coniugem eius, et demum,

3 pulso Cadmo sene, apud Thebas regnasse. Ex istis autem, secundum Servium, Amphion musice artis adeo peritus fuit, ut iuxta Lactantium a Mercurio cytharam meruerit, cum qua Thebanos muros construxit, ut Seneca poeta in tragedia *Herculis furentis* dicit:

> Cuiusque muros natus Amphion Iove
> struxit canoro saxa modulatu trahens,
>
> > etc.

: 30 :

On Amphion, King of the Thebans,
fifth child of the second Jupiter, who fathered seven sons
and an equal amount of daughters

Amphion was the son of Jupiter and Antiope, as Homer[133] testifies   1
in the *Odyssey*. The fable concerning his birth is told in the chapter
written about Antiope.[134] Ovid says what is not written there, that
Jupiter, who had transformed himself into a bull, ravaged Antiope
and impregnated her. And elsewhere he says:[135]

> She added, and concealed by the image of a satyr
> Jupiter filled the beautiful daughter of Nycteus with twin
>   offspring.

In addition, Homer[136] in the same account says that Jupiter re-   2
ceived three sons from Antiope, namely, Amphion, Zethus, and
Calathus.

In addition they want them to have been exposed by their
mother, who was banished by Lynceus, King of the Thebans, on
account of her shameful intercourse with Epaphus or Jupiter.
Then, raised by a certain shepherd, as grown-ups they rose against
Lynceus and killed him as well as his wife Dirce, and finally, after
the elderly Cadmus had been banished, they ruled Thebes. Of   3
these, according to Servius,[137] Amphion was so skilled in the art of
music that, according to Lactantius,[138] he warranted a cithara from
Mercury, and he used this to construct the walls of Thebes, as the
poet Seneca says in his tragedy *Hercules furens*:[139]

> Its walls Amphion, born of Zeus, built
> hauling stones by tuneful modulation.

4 Eumque[31] Lydios modulos invenisse scribit Plinius. Huic insuper coniunx fuit Niobes Tantali filia, ex qua, secundum Omerum
in *Yliade*, XII suscepit filios, secundum vero Latinos poetas, et Ovidium potissime, suscepit XIIII. Quos cum ob superbiam Niobis ab
Apolline et Diana vidisset occisos, se ipsum gladio interemit.

5 Nunc autem declarande fictiones veniunt. Dicunt igitur hunc a
tauro Iove, seu satyro conceptum, quod fictum puto ad fervorem
libidinis opprimentis demonstrandum, cum scribatur alibi Anthiopam violenter oppressam. Theodontius tamen dicit Amphionem
et fratres non Iovis sed Epaphi fuisse filios ex Anthiopa, et ob hoc
a Lynceo Thebarum Egyptiorum rege Anthiopam repudiatam, in
quem Lynceum iam adulti iuvenes insurgentes, eum interfecere, et
aufugerunt in Greciam, et a Cadmo suscepti eum senem regno
privaverunt, et se Iovis dixere filios.

6 Floruit enim, ut dicit Eusebius in libro *Temporum*, in musicis,
Lynceo regnante Argis. Eum autem cythara movisse saxa in muros
Thebanos construendos dicit Albericus, nil aliud fuisse, quam
melliflua oratione suasisse ignaris atque rudibus et duris hominibus et sparsim degentibus, ut in unum convenirent et civiliter vive-
rent, et, in defensionem publicam, civitatem menibus circumda-
rent, quod et factum est. Quod autem a Mercurio cytharam
susceperit, est quod eloquentiam ab influentia Mercurii habuerit,
ut mathematici asserunt.

Pliny[140] writes that he discovered the Lydian mode. In addition,   4
his wife was Niobe, daughter of Tantalus, from whom, according
to Homer[141] in the *Iliad*, he received twelve children, but according
to the Latin poets, particularly Ovid,[142] he received fourteen. After
seeing them killed by Apollo and Artemis on account of Niobe's
pride, he killed himself with a sword.

Now we have come to the point where the fictions must be ex-   5
plained. They say that he was conceived by Jupiter as a bull or satyr, a fiction which I think demonstrates the heat of overwhelming
passions, for it is written elsewhere that Antiope was violently ravaged. Theodontius says that Amphion and his brothers were not
the sons of Jupiter by Antiope but of Epaphus, and on account of
this Antiope was repudiated by Lynceus, the King of Egyptian
Thebes; and it was against this Lynceus that the young men rose
up, killed him, and fled to Greece, where, taken in by Cadmus,
they robbed the old man of his kingdom and said they were sons
of Jupiter.

He flourished in music, as Eusebius[143] says in his *Chronicle*,   6
when Lynceus was ruling the Argives. His constructing the walls
for the Thebans by moving the stones with his cithara Albericus
says was nothing other than that by means of mellifluous oration
he persuaded the men who were ignorant, rude, and rough, as well
as those living in the country, to convene in one place and live a
civilized life by surrounding the city with walls for public defense,
which is what happened. That he received a cithara from Mercury
is, as the mathematicians assert, that he mastered eloquence by
the influence of Mercury.

: 31 :

De XIIII filiis Amphionis

1 Amphioni ex Niobe septem fuere filii, et filie totidem, quorum hec fuere nomina: Archemorus, Anthegorus et Tantalus, nec non et Phadimos, Sypilos et Semarcus atque Epynithos. Demum filie sic dicte sunt: Asticratia, Pelopia et Cheloris, et post has Cleodoxe ac Ogune et Phythia atque Neera. Horum ludentes masculi, dicit Ovidius, ob superbiam Niobis in Latonam obloquentem ab Apolline occisi sunt, femine autem a Diana, Niobe[32] matre vidente.

2 Sane Ovidius discrepat in aliquibus[33] nominibus a Lactantio; nam pro Archemoro, Anthegoro, Xemarco atque Epynitho, ponit Ovidius Ysmenum, Alphenorem et Damasyconem et Ylioneum. Ex his autem omnibus nescio quem Omerus vocabat Amaleam. Qui hos dicit sic occisos novem annis sepulcro caruisse, tandem conversis a Iove populis in lapides, eos contexisse, esto alibi dicat eos in Sypilo monte conditos extitisse.

3 Quod autem isti tam repente perierint, peste factum credo, cum sit exterminator Apollo, et hinc contigisse deficientibus hominibus defecisse qui illos sepelirent, qui mortui homines, et in lapidem, id est pulverem conversi, eos etiam resolutos texere, aut texisse credi-
4 tum, vel, quod melius dictum puto, populos lapideos factos, id est malis duratos, illos adinventis urnis, ut ait Homerus, apud Sypilum sepelisse. Non enim aliquando ob pietatem nimiam possumus quod debemus. Seu[34] aliter potuit contigisse hos, imminente peste,

: 31 :

On the fourteen children of Amphion

Amphion had seven sons by Niobe, and as many daughters, and 1
these were their names: Archemorus, Antagorus and Tantalus, as
well as Phaedimus, Sipylos, Xenarchus, and Epinicus. The daughters were called this: Astycratia, Pelopia and Chloris, and after
these Cleodoxe, Ogime, Phthia, and Neaera. Ovid[144] says that because of Niobe's prideful insult to Latona, Apollo killed the males
while they were playing; and Diana killed the females while their
mother Niobe was watching. Ovid disagrees with some of the 2
names used by Lactantius:[145] for Archemorus, Antagoras, Xenarchus, and Epinicus Ovid puts Ismenus, Alphenor, Damasycon,
and Ilioneus. I do not know which of these Homer[146] calls Amalea. Homer says that after they were killed like this they were
denied burial for nine years; finally after the Theban people were
turned into stones by Jupiter, the Niobids were buried, although
he says elsewhere that they were laid to rest on Mount Sipylus.

That they perished so quickly I believe was caused by a plague, 3
for Apollo was the destroyer, and because of this it happened that
there was a shortage of men who could bury them, and that these
dead men were turned into stone, that is, dust, and that they buried them, or were thought to have buried them, in this pulverized
state. Alternatively, and I think this is better, the people were 4
made stonelike, that is, were hardened by troubles, and thus buried them in impromptu urns, as Homer says, on Sipylus. For
sometimes on account of excessive piety we cannot do what we
ought. Or perhaps there is a different explanation: with the plague

populari ritu sepultos et novem annis neglectos, demum regio more lapideis urnis immissos.

: 32 :

De Zetho secundi Iovis filio VI°, qui genuit Ythilum et Thyim

1 Zethus filius fuit Iovis et Anthiope, ut ubi de Amphione satis dictum est. Hunc dicit Lactantius super *Achilleide*, et Servius similiter, rusticum fuisse hominem, esto cum fratrem regnaverit.

: 33 :

De Ytilo et Thyi filiis Zethi

1 Ytilus et Thyis, ut testatur Omerus in *Odissea*, filii fuerunt Zethi regis ex Aydona coniuge. Ythilum autem per errorem nocte Aydona mater interfecit, putans eum Amalea Amphionis filium; invidebat quidem uxori Amphionis, eo quod sibi sex essent filii mas-
2 culi. Que, ut ait Leontius, crimen suum cognoscens, optavit mori; miseratione tamen deorum in carduelem versa Ythilum deflet. De Thyi autem nudum superest nomen.

at hand, they were buried in the manner of common people and then neglected for nine years, after which they were finally placed in stone urns, in royal fashion.

: 32 :

On Zethus, sixth child of the second Jupiter,
who fathered Itylus and Thyis

Zethus was the son of Jupiter and Antiope, as we discussed suffi- 1
ciently in the chapter on Amphion. Lactantius[147] in his commentary on the *Achilleid*, and Servius[148] as well, says that he was a
rustic man, although he ruled with his brother.

: 33 :

On Itylus and Thyis, sons of Zethus

Itylus and Thyis, as Homer[149] testifies in the *Odyssey*, were the 1
sons of King Zethus by his wife Aedon. His mother Aedon killed
Itylus at night by mistake, thinking him to be Amalea, the son of
Amphion; she was jealous of the wife of Amphion because she
had six sons. As Leontius says, when she realized the crime she 2
had committed she hoped for death; pitied by the gods she was
turned into a finch and weeps for Itylus. Of Thyis only his name
remains.

: 34 :

De Calatho secundi Iovis filio VII°

1 Calathus filius fuit Iovis et Anthiope, ut Omerus in *Odissea* describit. De quo nil preter nomen legisse memini.

: 35 :

De Pasythea et Egyale et Euprosyne
Gratiis secundi Iovis filiabus

1 Pasythea, Egyales et Euprosyne, que Gratie seu Carites appellantur, ut placet Lactantio, Iovis et Auctonoes fuere filie. Has dicunt
Veneris esse pedissequas, affirmantque quia se lavent in Acidalio
fonte, qui in Orcomeno Boetie civitate est, et inde nudas incedere,
et invicem iunctas, ac ex eis duas facie ad nos esse conversas, cum
tergum tercia vertat.

2 Quid autem in hoc senserint veteres, excutiendum est. Cum
enim gratia semper in bonum sonet, merito Iovis dicentur filie,
cuius effectus semper in bonum tendunt. Et cum coniunctionum
omnium ex attributa potentia causatrix Venus sit, ut supra dictum
est, illi merito obsequuntur, cum semper videatur, aliquali Gratia
precedente, quis in unionem seu amicitiam ire alterius, ut puta
ratione benefici inpensi, vel complexionis et morum conformitate,
seu studiorum similitudine et huiusmodi.

∴ 34 ∴

On Calathus, seventh child of the second Jupiter

Calathus was the son of Jupiter and Antiope, as Homer[150] writes   1
in the *Odyssey*. I do not remember reading anything about him
other than his name.

∴ 35 ∴

On the Graces Pasithea, Aglaea, and Euphrosyne, daughters of the second Jupiter

Pasithea, Aglaea, and Euphrosyne, who were called Graces or   1
Charities, according to Lactantius,[151] were the daughters of Jupiter
and Autonoe. They say that these were the attendants of Venus,
and they assert that they washed in the Acidalian font in the
Boeotian city of Orchomenus, which together they entered naked,
and that two of them are turned facing us, while the third turns
her back.

We must search for what the ancients meant in this, for since   2
grace always means something good, they are rightly called daughters of Jupiter, for his effect always results in good. And because by
her allotted powers Venus is the cause of all unions, as we said
earlier, they rightly follow her, for someone always seems, with
some Grace leading the way, to enter into a union or friendship
with another because, for example, of some kindness performed,
or because their constitution and manner conform, or because
their spirit or some such is similar.

3   Et ideo, ut placet Fulgentio, Pasythea, que Gratiarum prima
est, interpretatur 'attrahens,' eo quod ante alia quacunque movea-
4   mur causa, ad aliquam rem desiderandam attrahimur. Secunda
autem Egyales interpretatur 'demulcens,' et hoc ideo, quia nisi de-
lectaret in processu, quod appetivimus ante, non iretur in perseve-
rantiam amicitie, imo dissolveretur illico, et idcirco ut demulceat et
5   delectet necesse est, quod attraxerat ante. Tercia autem Euprosy-
nes appellatur, quod 'retinens' sonat, ut per hoc intelligatur in vacuum quis in dilectionem alicuius rei attrahi, atque se attractum
delectari, nisi quis opere suo teneat quod attraxerat et delectat. Et
hinc potes advertere duas in te Gratias venientes, terciam vero a te
6   in illas euntem, et sic due in nos faciem, tercia tergum vertit. Vel
aliter. Si quid enim in hominem gratum miseris, ab eo in te du-
plum, seu maius redire videbit, et ob id dicit Ylioneus Didoni
apud Virgilium,[35] 'Nec te certasse priorem peniteat,' quasi velit intelligi, si nobis boni aliquid feceris, et vivat Eneas, duplicatum ab
eo recipies.
7   In Acidalio autem fonte ideo balneari dicuntur, quia *acida* Grece
Latine 'cura' est, et hoc ideo fictum, ut sentiamus quia, dum trahimur, dum mulcemur, dum retinere conamur, variis curis angimur.
Nudas autem eas incedere non ob aliud voluere, nisi ut videremus,
quia in captandis amicitiis, nil fictum, nil fucatum, nil palliatum
intervenire debeat; quin imo simplici et pura mente, atque aperta
in hoc debemus incedere; nam qui aliter exquirunt, amicitiarum
mercatores potius quam factores dici possunt.

And so, according to Fulgentius,[152] Pasithea, who is the first of the Graces, means "attracting" because above all we are moved by some cause: we are attracted in our desire for a certain thing. The second, Aglaea, means "charming," because if what we have sought at first does not continue to delight, pursuit of the alliance will not occur; nay, it will then dissolve, and so what had been attractive before must now charm and delight. The third is named Euphrosyne, which means "retaining," by which it is known that someone is attracted to the love of something and, if attracted, beloved, in vain unless someone expends the effort to hold on to what has been attractive and loved; and in this you can recognize two Graces coming into yourself, and the third going from you into them, and so two turn toward us and the third turns her back. Alternatively, if you commit some kindness toward a man, it will seem to come back to you double, or more. On account of this Ilioneus says to Dido in Vergil,[153] "You would not be sorry to compete first;" it is as if he wants it to be known that if you do some good to us, and Aeneas lives, you will receive double from him.

They are said to bathe in the Acidalian font because the Greek *acida* means "care," and so this fiction was invented so that we could understand that when we are attracted, when we are charmed, and when we try to retain, we are distressed by various cares. They want them to enter nude for no other reason than that we see that in seeking alliances nothing fabricated, nothing colored, and nothing cloaked ought to intervene; in fact, we ought to enter into them with a simple, pure, and also open mind, for those who pursue them otherwise could be said to be merchants, rather than makers, of alliances.

: 36 :

De Lacedemone XI° secundi Iovis filio,
qui genuit Amiclatem

1 Lacedemon, ut scribit Ditis Cretensis eo in libro, quem *De expeditione Grecorum in Troianos* composuit, filius fuit Iovis ex Taygeta, filia Agenoris Phenicum regis, esto Eusebius in libro *Temporum* dicat eum filium fuisse Semeles, patre non nominato, eumque, Crotopo Argivis regnante, Lacedemonem condidisse civitatem.

: 37 :

De Amiclate filio Lacedemonis, qui genuit Argulum

1 Amiclas, ut predictus Ditis asserit, filius fuit Lacedemonis, esto sint libri in quibus legatur Lacedemonam feminam fuisse, et ex ea
2 Amiclatem natum. Ego tamen hominem fuisse puto.

: 38 :

De Argulo filio Amiclatis, qui genuit Oebalum

1 Argulus, ut idem Ditis dicit, filius fuit Amiclatis, quem Theodontius dicit primum iunxisse apud Acheos quadrigam, sed timeo ne

: 36 :

On Lacedaemon, eleventh child of the second Jupiter,
who fathered Amiclas

Lacedaemon, as Dictys[154] of Crete wrote in the book he composed 1
on the *Expedition of the Greeks Against the Trojans*, was the son of
Jupiter by Taygeta, daughter of King Agenor of the Phoenicians,
although Eusebius[155] in his *Chronicle* says that he was the son of
Semele from an unnamed father, and that he founded the city of
Lacedaemon when Crotopus was ruling the Argives.

: 37 :

On Amiclas, son of Lacedaemon, who fathered Argulus

Amiclas, as the aforementioned Dictys stated, was the son of 1
Lacedaemon, although there are books in which Lacedaemona is
said to be a woman and that Amiclas was born from her. But I 2
think he was a man.

: 38 :

On Argulus, son of Amiclas, who fathered Oebalus

Argulus, as again Dictys says, was the son of Amiclas, whom 1
Theodontius says was the first among the Acheans to assemble a
chariot, but I fear that he is fooled by the similarity of the name:

2 similitudine fere nominis deceptus sit. Is enim, qui primus quadrigam iunxit in Grecia, Arogilus dictus est, et id adinvenit, regnante
Argis Phorbante, qui diu ante Argulum fuit.

: 39 :

De Oebalo Arguli filio, qui genuit Tyndarum et Ycarum

1 Oebalus, ut dicit Ditis et Theodontius, filius fuit Arguli, quem
regnasse dicit Paulus apud Laconas, quos a se Oebalos nominavit.
2 Huic duos fuisse filios comperimus, Tyndarum scilicet et Ycarum.

: 40 :

De Tyndaro Oebali filio

1 Tyndarus, ut Ditis scribit et Theodontius, filius fuit Oebali, illique
successit in regno, ex quo, etsi nil aliud habeamus, hoc saltem legimus, eum Ledam habuisse coniugem, que, si non ex eo, ex Iove
tamen eius in regia Castorem et Pollucem et Helenam et Clitemestram peperit, dato sint, qui Castorem et Clitemestram non
2 Iovis, sed Tyndari filios dicant. Ego omnes quattuor Tyndari fuisse
arbitror, sed absit ut auferam tam pudicissimo deo filios, quos illi
liberalis dicavit antiquitas.

he who first assembled a chariot in Greece was called Arogilus, 2
and he invented it when Phorbas was ruling the Argives, and he
lived long before Argulus.

: 39 :

On Oebalus, son of Argulus, who fathered
Tyndareus and Icarius[156]

Oebalus, as Dictys and Theodontius say, was the son of Argulus; 1
Paul says he ruled among the Laconians, whom Oebalus named
after himself. We found that he had two sons, Tyndareus and 2
Icarius.

: 40 :

On Tyndareus, son of Oebalus

Tyndareus, as Dictys and Theodontius write, was the son of Oe- 1
balus and succeeded him as king. Although we have nothing else
about him, we have at least read this about him: he married Leda,
who, if not by him, by Jupiter gave birth in the palace to Castor,
Pollux, Helen, and Clytemnestra, although there are those who
say that Castor and Clytemnestra were not children of Jupiter but
of Tyndareus. I think that all four belonged to Tyndareus, but let 2
me not subtract sons from such a virtuous god to whom antiquity
has attributed them so liberally.

: 41 :

De Ycaro Oebali filio, qui genuit Erigonem, Ypthimam et Penelopem

1 Ycarus, ut dicit Leontius, Oebali fuit filius. Hunc Lactantius dicit comitem fuisse Liberi patris, et ab eo accepisse uti vinum exhiberet mortalibus. Qui cum pastoribus seu, secundum alios, messoribus suis exhibuisset, et hi, seu quia ultra debitum, seu quia insueti potassent, ebrii facti, et inde existimantes sibi venenum exhibitum, Ycarum apud Marathonem venationi vacantem interemerunt.

2 Quem dicit Servius a cane suo diu servatum; tandem, ut dicit Theodontius, cum canis fame impulsus domum redisset, eique Erigones virgo, Ycari filia, panem dedisset, et ipse illico ad cadaver reverteretur domini, Erigones eum secuta, patrem occisum comperit.

3 Cuius tandem precibus in celum Ycarus assumptus est et in Boothem conversus, et cum eo canis, qui Assyrius nuncupatur. Possibile est, cum in octava spera ab antiquis astrologis multe sint ymagines quadam stellarum designatione figurate ex his aliquas in consolationem remanentium post Ycarum nomine Ycari et canis sui denominatas. Verum ego non credo hunc eum Ycarum fuisse, qui Oebali filius fuit aut Penelopis pater.

: 41 :

On Icarius, son of Oebalus, who fathered Erigone, Ipthima, and Penelope

Icarius, as Leontius says, was the son of Oebalus. Lactantius[157]   1
says that he was the companion of Father Liber and received from
him the wine he provided to mortals. When he had revealed it to
shepherds or, according to others, to his reapers, and they, either
because they had drunk too much or because they were unaccustomed to it, became drunk, and because of this, thinking that he
had given them poison, they killed Icarius while he was hunting at
Marathon. Servius[158] says that he was protected for a while by his   2
dog, but then, as Theodontius says, when his dog, driven by hunger, returned home, the maiden Erigone, the daughter of Icarius,
gave him bread, and he returned there to the to the corpse of his
master. Erigone followed him and found her dead father. In re-   3
sponse to her prayers Icarius was taken into the sky and converted
into Boötes and with him his dog who is called Sirius. It is possible, since there are in the eighth sphere many images configured
from the disposition of their stars by ancient astrologers, that
some of these were named after the names of Icarius and his dog
as consolation to those who remained after Icarius. But I do not
think this was the Icarius who was the son of Oebalus or the father of Penelope.

: 42 :

De Erigone filia Ycari

1 Erigones filia fuit Ycari, ut Lactantius affirmat et Servius. Que cum Bacho placuisset, ab eo in specie uve, ut dicit Ovidius, decepta atque oppressa est. Hec tamen, ut dicit Servius, cum ductu canis in Marathoniam silvam patrem a rusticis occisum comperisset, flevissetque diu; tandem doloris impatiens in arborem laqueo se suspendit. Sed seu corporis pondere nimio, seu laquei vel rami debilitate factum sit, in terram cecidit. Cuius tamen miserti dii eam inter sydera transtulerunt, feceruntque ex ea in zodiaco sig-
2 num illud, quod adhuc Virginem appellamus. Tractu tamen temporis, cum secundum Lactantium umbra eius regionem illam infestaret, ad eius iram mitigandam compertum est ex cera humanam formare speciem, et in eadem arbore appendere, et a pastoribus canibusque diem illam celebrem facere, ex quo Virgilius:

Tibique
oscilla ex alta suspendunt mollia pinu.

3   Sane Servius aliter. Dicit enim, quod cum post aliquantum temporis Atheniensibus morbus esset immissus talis, ut etiam virgines furore quodam compellerentur ad laqueum, essetque ab oraculo responsum, sedari posse pestem illam, si requirerentur Erigoni et Ycari cadavera. Qui illa quesivere diu, et cum reperiri non possent, ad ostendendam devotionem suam Athenienses, quasi in elemento etiam alieno querere viderentur, suspendebant in arboribus funes, ad quas se tenentes homines hac atque illac

: 42 :

On Erigone, daughter of Icarius

Erigone was the daughter of Icarius, as Lactantius and Servius as-   1
sert. When Bacchus took a liking to her, he deceived her, as
Ovid[159] says, in the guise of a grape, and ravaged her. But, as
Servius[160] says, when she was led by a dog into the Marathonian
woods and found that her father had been killed by provincials,
she had wept for a long time, and then no longer tolerating her
grief, she put a noose around her neck and hanged herself from a
tree. But either because of the excessive weight of her body or because of the weakness of the noose or the branch, she happened to
fall to the ground. Taking pity on her, the gods transferred her
among the stars, and they made her into that sign of the zodiac
which we still call Virgo. After some time passed, according to   2
Lactantius,[161] when her shade was haunting that region, they
found that to mitigate her anger they could make a human image
in wax and to attach it to the same tree, and they turned it into a
celebratory day for shepherds and dogs, whence Vergil's:[162]

                                              For you
they hang small images from the heights of the pine.

Servius[163] offers a different version, for he says that when shortly   3
after her death such a plague came upon the Athenians that a kind
of frenzy drove even the maidens to the noose, and that an oracular response said that the pestilence could be alleviated if they
would recover the corpses of Erigone and Icarius. They searched
for them for a long time, but because they could not find them,
the Athenians, to show their dedication, as if they seemed to be
searching for them in a different element, would hang ropes from
trees, and the men holding onto them were shaken here and there

agitabantur, ut quasi per aerem illorum cadavera petere viderentur.
Sed quia plurimi cadebant, invenere formas ad sui oris similitudi-
nem, et eas pro se suspensas movebant; unde oscilla dicta sunt ab
eo, quod in his oscillarentur, id est moverentur ora, et eo modo
4 pestis purgata est. A Bacho autem eam in specie uve deceptam,
ideo dictum credo, quia possibile fuit insuetam, dum uvas comederet, ebrietatem incidere.

: 43 :

De Yphtima filia Ycari

1 Yphtima filia fuit Ycari, ut in *Odissea* testatur Omerus dicens:

᾿Ιφθίμῃ, κούρῃ μεγαλήτορος ⟨᾿Ικαρίοιο⟩
τὴν Εὔμηλος ὄπυιε Φερῆς

Yphtime puelle magnanimi Ycari
que Eumilo nupsit Feris.

: 44 :

De Penelope filia Ycari et uxore Ulixis

1 Penelopes filia fuit Ycari, ut in *Odissea* testatur Omerus, dum
dicit:

κούρη ᾿Ικαρίοιο, περίφρων Πηνελόπεια

Filia Ycari Penelope puella

much as if they seemed to be seeking their corpses through the air. But because many used to fall, they created likenesses of themselves and hung them and moved them about instead of themselves; they called them small images [*oscilla*] because with these they were put into motion [*cillerentur*], that is, their faces were moved and in that way the plague was eliminated. That she was deceived by Bacchus in the guise of a grape I believe was said because while she was eating a grape she suffered from an unusual kind of drunkenness. 4

: 43 :

On Iphthima, daughter of Icarius

Iphthima was the daughter of Icarius, as Homer testifies in the *Odyssey*, saying:[164] 1

> Iphthime, great-hearted daughter of Icarus
> who married Eumelos at Pherae.

: 44 :

On Penelope,[165] daughter of Icarius and wife of Ulysses

Penelope was the daughter of Icarius, as Homer testifies in the *Odyssey*, saying:[166] 1

> Daughter of Icarius, wise Penelope

Hec quidem, ut satis vulgatum est, nupsit Ulixi, et ex eo Thelemacum filium peperit. Postea cum ivisset Troiam Ulixes, et inde diu
post Troiam deletam errasset, multa passa est, tam ob pudicitiam
suam tutandam, quam procatores plurimi sollicitabant assidue,
quam ob timorem insidiarum adversus Thelemacum a procatori-
bus positarum, et dolorem non redeuntis Ulixis. Tandem eis ser-
vatis, virum rehabuit. In quem tandem finem iverit, non satis certum habeo.

Dicit tamen Leontius Lycophronem Grecum poetam dicere,
Penelopem concubitum omnium procantium passam, et ex uno
eorum genuisse quendam filium, cui Pana nomen fuit. Quod cum
in reditu cognovisset Ulixes, statim abiit ad insulam Gortinam, et
2 ibidem habitavit. Quod absit, ut credam pudicitiam Penelopis, a
tot tamque egregiis celebratam autoribus, ab aliquo fuisse macula-
tam, quicquid Lycophron loquatur maliloquus.

: 45 :

De Tantalo XII° Iovis secundi filio

1 Lacedemonis expedita prosapia, ad reliquos Iovis secundi filios re-
deundum est, ex quibus XII Tantalum scilicet dicit Leontius Iovis
fuisse filium, non eum tamen qui Pelopis pater fuit, sed alium.
Fuit enim hic antiquissimus Corinthiorum rex, et pius homo, at-
2 que deorum mensis sepe accubuit. Quod ideo fictum puto, quia
celsissima sit arx Corinthiorum, adeo ut, si quis eam ascendat, in
celum videatur conscendere et esse cum superis.

As is widely known, she married Ulysses, to whom she bore a son, Telemachus. Afterward, when Ulysses had gone to Troy and then wandered for a long time after Troy was destroyed, she suffered much, not only in protecting her modesty as numerous suitors continuously harassed her, but also from her fear of the suitors attacking Telemachus, as well as because of her grief over Ulysses' prolonged absence. Finally everyone was saved and she got her husband back. I do not know for sure to what end she came.

Leontius says that the Greek poet Lycophron[167] said that Penelope endured having intercourse with all of the suitors and bore by one of them a son whose name was Pan. When Ulysses learned of this upon his return, he immediately left for the island of Gortyna and lived there. I can hardly believe that Penelope's modesty, 2 celebrated by so many and such great authors, was stained by anyone, as the slanderous Lycophron reports.

∶ 45 ∶

On Tantalus, twelfth child of the second Jupiter

With the lineage of Lacedaemon taken care of, we must return to 1 the remaining children of the second Jupiter. Leontius says that the twelfth, namely Tantalus, was the son of Jupiter, though not the Tantalus who was father of Pelops but a different one. He was a very ancient king of the Corinthians and a pious man who often reclined at the tables of the gods. I think the reason for this fabri- 2 cation is that the citadel of Corinth is very high, so much so that if someone were to climb it he would seem to climb into the sky and be with the gods.

: 46 :

De Hercule, XIII° secundi Iovis filio, qui genuit Cartaginem

1   Hercules hic a Cicerone in libro *De naturis deorum* cognominatur quartus, et ab eodem dicitur Iovis filius ex Asterie sorore Latone susceptus. Hunc preterea summe a Tyriis coli dicit, et ex eo Cartaginem filiam genitam.

: 47 :

De Cartagine, IIII^a Herculis filia

1   Cartago, ut proxime supra monstratum est, Herculis quarti filia fuit, quam ego mulierem fuisse non credo, sed eam civitatem quam nos Cartaginem nuncupamus, que ideo Herculis filia dicta est, quia a Phenicibus, qui Herculem summe colebant, posita Herculis dei sui auspicio.

: 48 :

De Minerva, secundi Iovis filia XIIII^a

1   Minerva, non ea cui cognomen Tritonia fuit, Iovis secundi fuit filia, ut scribit Tullius *De naturis deorum*; quam idem Tullius inventricem asserit fuisse bellorum atque principem, et ob id a non

: 46 :

On Hercules, thirteenth child of the second Jupiter, who fathered Carthage

This Hercules is listed fourth by Cicero[168] in his *On the Nature of* 1
the Gods, where he says that he was the son of Jupiter taken
from Asteria, sister of Latona. In addition he says that he was
worshipped by the Tyrians and that he produced a daughter,
Carthage.

: 47 :

On Carthage, daughter of the fourth Hercules

Carthage, as was pointed out just above, was the daughter of the 1
fourth Hercules. I do not believe that she was a woman but that
city which we call Carthage: it is called the daughter of Hercules
because the Phoenicians, who used to venerate Hercules greatly,
founded the city under Hercules' divine auspices.

: 48 :

On Minerva, fourteenth child of the second Jupiter

Minerva, not the one who had the cognomen Tritonia, was the 1
daughter of the second Jupiter, as Cicero[169] writes in his *On the*
Nature of the Gods. Cicero also asserts that she was the inventor of
war and a leader, and it was for this reason that many called her

nullis Bellona appellata est et soror Martis et auriga, ut testari videtur Statius dicens:

> Regit atra iugales
> sanguinea Bellona manu, longaque fatigat
> cuspide,

etc.

Nec ea fuit hec, quam veteres virginem et sterilem asseruere, quin imo, ut idem dicit Tullius, ex Vulcano, Celi filio antiquissimo,

2 Apollinem primum peperit. Preterea, ut dicit Leontius, hec est quam armis insignem finxere, oculis torvam, hastamque gerentem longissimam cum cristallino clipeo, et hoc magis ad ostentationem inventi a se belli, quam ob aliquod aliud significatum.

3 Quod ego non credo, quin imo insignia illa ad aliquod misterium ostendendum apposita omnia puto. Nam cum omnes assiduis infestemur bellis, armatam fingi puto, ut doceamur providos viros semper in armis consistere, id est consiliis, quibus ad emergentia possit obsistere. Quod oculos habeat torvos, ostendit sapientem de facili capi non posse, cum ut plurimum exterioribus actibus longe aliud se ostendat agere quam gerat animo, uti torvus

4 alibi respicit quam intuentes eius faciem arbitrentur. Hasta autem idio illi dicatur longissima, ut noscamus prudentem virum etiam longinqua cognoscere, et ex longinquo ictus infigere, atque a se insidiantes repellere. Cristallinum autem ideo illi clipeum attributum esse, ut appareat in transparenti cristallo atque solido corpore sapientem virum eque simul et hostis videre opera et se ipsum remediis oportunis protegere.

5 Huic insuper dicit idem Leontius, cum Neptuno de impositione nominis civitati Athenarum fuisse certamen, illudque presentibus diis in Ariopago agitatum, actumque eorum sententia, ut

Bellona; and the sister of Mars and his charioteer, as Statius seems to witness, saying:[170]

> She drove the yoked pair, dark Bellona, with her bloody hand and stirs them on with her long spear.

Nor was she the one whom the ancients claim was a virgin and barren; in fact, as again Cicero[171] says, she gave birth to the first Apollo by Vulcan, the very ancient son of Sky. In addition, as Leontius says, she is the one they depict distinctively in armor, with a fierce gaze, and bearing a very long spear with a crystal shield, and this is more for the portrayal of the war she invented than it is for any other significance.

I do not believe this; in fact, I think all those insignia were attributed to her to explain some mystery. For instance, because we are all vexed by continuous wars, I think she was depicted armed to make it clear to us that men of forethought are ready in arms, that is, have plans that will enable them to confront unexpected attacks. That she had a fierce gaze points out that the wise man cannot be easily captured, for he frequently feigns doing something quite different externally from what is going on in his mind, just as a fierce gaze does not look in the same direction as those watching his face believe it is looking. She is given the very long spear so that we would know that the prudent man recognizes things from a distance, strikes a blow from a distance, and repels those who attack him. They attribute a crystal shield to her so that it would appear that in the transparent crystal and the solid body the wise man equally and at the same time sees the work of his enemy and protects himself with opportune remedies.

In addition, Leontius also says that she participated in a contest with Neptune for bestowing a name on the Athenians' city that was held in the presence of the gods on the Areopagus, and that the outcome of the contest was to be that whoever produced the

quis eorum terra percussa laudabiliorem produxisset effectum, is civitati nomen imponeret. Ob quam rem Neptunus, percusso tridente solo, equum produxit. Minerva autem, hasta proiecta, produxit olivam. Que quoniam utilior visa sit equo, Minerva deorum iudicio civitatem ex suo nomine nuncupavit Athenas; nam Minerva a Grecis Athena vocitata est.

6   Quod hic figmenti est, sic Albericus exponit. Dicit enim Cecropi conditori, qui et huic Minerve contemporaneus fuit, et, iuxta Theodontium, pater, fuisse aliquandiu ambiguum, an illa a commoditate maris, qua plurimum valebat, an a commoditate terre qua etiam pluribus abundabat, denominaretur; quam maris commoditatem per equum designare voluere, quia et mare vehat ut equus, et equus ut mare velox sit, et non nunquam impetuosus et furore nimio plenus, ut mare. Terre vero olivam, seu quia locus olivarum habundans sit, seu quia pingue sit solum et fertile. Tandem dum cerneret circumspectus homo maris commoda variis ex causis posse subtrahi, et terrestria qualiacunque esse continua, a terrestribus perpetuis denominandam censuit, eamque vocavit Athenas, quod Latine 'immortales' sonat.

7

8   Ego autem puto, cum maritima civitas sit Athene, dissensionem hanc inter nautas et mechanicos fuisse homines, ostendentibus nautis rem plurimum augeri navigiis, que per equum intelligenda sunt. Mechanici autem contra artibus et agricultura civitates substentari et augmentari, que per olivam demonstrantur, cum eius sit liquor mitis et ampliativus. Quam ob rem a diis, id est a iudicibus, in hoc datis, pro mechanicis, sententia lata est, et hic pro nautis

most laudable effect by striking the earth would bestow their name onto the city. For his part Neptune struck the ground with his trident and produced a horse. Minerva, however, thrusting forth her spear, produced an olive tree. Because this seemed to be more useful than a horse, by the judgment of the gods Minerva named the city Athens after herself, for Minerva is called Athena by the Greeks.

Albericus[172] explains this fabrication in this way. He says that 6 the founder Cecrops, who was contemporary with this Minerva and, according to Theodontius, her father, was for some time in doubt as to whether he should name the city after the utility of the sea, which was much mightier, or after the utility of the land, which was very much abundant. The utility of the sea they wished to designate in the horse because the sea like a horse is a means of conveyance, and a horse is swift like the sea, and it is sometimes impetuous and full of excessive fury like the sea. The olive was used for the land either because the area was teeming with olives or because the soil was rich and fertile. Ultimately, when the judi- 7 cious man realized that they could be deprived of nautical utility by various circumstances while the terrestrial would endure no matter what, he decided that it should be named after the perpetual terrestrial utility, and he called it Athens, which means "immortal."

I, however, think that because Athens is a maritime city, this 8 reflects a disagreement between seamen and engineers, with the seamen pointing out that the city was enhanced more by shipping, and the horse must represent this. The engineers on the other hand pointed out that the citizens of the city subsisted on and were enhanced through the arts and agriculture, which are signified by the olive, because its liquid is mild and promotes growth. For this reason, the opinion given by the gods, that is, the judges, in this contest favored the engineers, and here Neptune was rightly

optime Neptunus inductus est, pro mechanicis autem Minerva, que artium omnium fere repertrix fuit.

9   Posset hic quis obicere Iovem primum regem Athenarum dictum longe antiquiorem Cecrope, et hic Cecropem conditorem dicimus Athenarum; hanc obiectionem paucis absolvit Leontius. Dicit enim non de novo edificatas Athenas a Cecrope, sed mari propinquiores factas, et hac tempestate sponte sua olivam in arcem natam.

: 49 :

De Arcade XV° filio secundi Iovis,
qui genuit Yonium

1   Arcas Iovis fuit filius et Calistonis nynphe, ut clare testatur Ovidius. Huius enim mater post Lycaonem patrem e regno pulsum a Iove, ut refert Paulus, se choris Diane sociavit, et in venationibus vitam agens, cum etate valeret et forma, a Iove dilecta est, et, ut dicit Ovidius, ab eodem sub specie Diane inter umbras nemorum decepta et oppressa est. Que cum concepisset, et iam excresceret uterus, a puellis sociis ad lavacrum evocata est, se lavante Diana.

2   Hec autem timens, ne crimen appareret suum, si vestimenta poneret, lavari renuebat; tandem a virginibus nudata, cum turgidum ventrem Diana vidisset, confestim eam a consortio suo reppulit, que postea Arcadem peperit. Quod facinus cum cognovisset Iuno, irata in eam, illam diu traxit crinibus, et tandem transformavit in ursam.

brought in for the seamen, and Minerva, who was the inventor of nearly all the arts, for the engineers.

Someone could object here that Jupiter was said to be the first 9 king of the Athenians and was more ancient than Cecrops, while we say here that Cecrops was the founder of the Athenians. Leontius obviates this objection in a few words, for he says that it was not that Cecrops built Athens anew by but that he extended it closer to the sea, and that at that time an olive sprang up on the citadel on its own accord.

∴ 49 ∴

On Arcas, fifteenth child of the second Jupiter, who fathered Ionius

Arcas was the son of Jupiter and the nymph Callisto, as Ovid[173] 1 testifies. As Paul reports, after her father Lycaon was expelled from the kingdom by Jupiter, his mother associated with the chorus of Diana, and as she spent her days hunting, Jupiter fell in love with her youth and beauty, and, as Ovid says, disguised as Diana he deceived her amidst the shadows of the woods and ravaged her. After she conceived and the size of her belly had already begun to increase, she was invited by her fellow girls to the bath where Diana was washing. But fearing that her condition would be exposed 2 if she took off her clothes, she refused to bathe, but then the maidens stripped off her clothes, and when Diana saw her swollen abdomen, she immediately expelled her from her fellowship; afterward she gave birth to Arcas. When Juno learned of her crime, she grew angry, dragged her at length by the hair, and ultimately transformed her into a bear.

Arcas autem cum iam grandis esset, eam sibi incognitam et ad
se venientem voluit occidere. Ast ipsa pavida, ut ait Theodontius,
in Iovis templum, cuius semper erant aperte ianue, nec illud propterea aut fera aut avis intrabat ulla, aufugit, in quod et Arcas secutus est. Quos cum vellent incole occidere, a Iove prohibiti sunt, et
mutato eque in ursum Arcadem, ambos in celum transtulit, et
circa polum articum locavit. Calisto autem ursa minor dicta est,
ubi maior vocatus est Arcas. Iuno autem ex hoc turbata, quod pe-
lex in celum suscepta esset una cum filio, accessit ad Thetydem
magnam nutricem suam, oravitque, ne has ursas more aliorum
syderum suis in undis lavari pateretur, quod Thetis ultro se factu-
ram promisit, et servat usque in hodiernum.

Sub hac fictione ut plurimum latet hystoria. Nam, superato a
Iove Lycaone, Calisto filia aufugit ad virgines Pani Lyceo sacras, et,
cum his emisso perpetue virginitatis voto, contigit, ut audita a Iove
eius formositate caperetur, et incideret in desiderium potiundi, et
cum se in habitum sociorum transformasset, clam noctu accessit
ad illam, et, cum variis suasionibus in suum desiderium traxisset,
eam vitiavit atque pregnantem fecit. Postremo cum partu crimen
appareret Calistonis, evestigio cum maximo dedecore suo, nil ulterius timore Iovis audentibus virginibus sacris, una cum filio claus-
tris exclusa est. Que ob ruborem clam secessit in silvas, et in eis
latuit diu incognita. Sane cum adolevisset filius, essetque ingentis
animi, nec posset perpeti matris imperium, eam voluit occidere.
Que timore percita silvas linquens confugit ad Iovem. Qui eam in
gratiam filii reconciliavit, permisitque ut in patrium possent redire

When Arcas had grown up, he wanted to kill her because he did not recognize her, and she was moving toward him. But according to Theodontius, she herself was fearful and fled into the temple of Jupiter, the doors of which were always open, but which, nonetheless, no beasts or birds ever entered, and Arcas pursued her there. Although the inhabitants wished to kill them, Jupiter prevented them, and once he had changed Arcas as well into a bear, he transferred both into the sky and positioned them around the northern pole. Callisto was called Ursa Minor, while Arcas was called Ursa Major. Distressed at the fact that his mistress along with her son had been taken up into the sky, Juno came to her nurse, great Thetis, and she asked her to forbid these bears from bathing in her waves like the other stars. Thetis willingly promised to do this, and this is true even today.

As often, under this fiction lurks history, for when Lycaon was vanquished by Jupiter, his daughter Callisto fled to the virgins consecrated to Lycean Pan. Although she took with them a vow of eternal virginity, it happened that Jupiter became enamored of her reputed beauty and planned to take possession of her and satisfy his desire. He therefore disguised himself in the clothing of one of her order and came to her secretly by night, and, when through various means of persuasion he led her over to his desire, he violated her and made her pregnant. After she gave birth, Callisto's crime was finally in the open along with her great shame, and because the sacred virgins dared do nothing else out of fear for Jupiter, she as well as her son were excluded from the cloister. Disgraced, she disappeared secretly into the woods, and there she hid unrecognized for a long time. But when her son grew into adolescence, he took on grand designs and was no longer capable of submitting to his mother's authority, so he wanted to kill her. Fearful of him, she left the woods and fled to Jupiter. He reconciled her with her son and permitted them to return to the kingdom of her father and gave them assistance. It was on account of

regnum iuvitque. Quam ob rem cum Arcas ferox iuvenis Pelasgos in dicionem redegisset suam, Arcades illos ex suo nomine appellavit.

6   Arcades autem Calistonem, quam mortuam putabant, ob diuturnam latebram 'ursam' appellavere, cum ursus, ut aiunt physiologi, certam anni partem in cavernis moretur dormiens, et a nomine matris ursum filium etiam vocavere. Quos ambos postea, in gratiam Arcadis, poete in celum translatos dixere, et ex canibus eis in locis, in quibus hos locaverunt, diu ante ab Egyptiis figuratis

7   fecere ursos. Quod autem a Thetide Iunonis alumna lavari occeano non permictantur, sumptum est ab elevatione poli, qui in regione nostra adeo elevatus est, et hec sydera adeo illi propinqua, ut circuitione celi, sicuti relique que occidendo mergi videntur occeano, occeano mergi non possint, imo earum circa polum integram circuitionem videmus. Hunc Arcadem scribit Eusebius subegisse Pelasgos anno mundi IIIDCCVIII.

: 50 :

De Yonio filio Arcadis, qui genuit Nycostratam

1   Yonius fuit, ut ait Theodontius et post eum Paulus, Arcadis filius ex Selene nynpha susceptus, homo evo suo bellica arte et potissime navali peritissimus adeo, ut litora fere omnia Peloponensia, et usque ad mare Syculum sue dicioni subigeret, et a suo nomine Yonas et Yonium cognominaret mare. Qui in tam grandem venere preminentiam, ut sibi totius Grecie quartam partem subesse diceretur, et Yonicis licteris atque grammatica uti cogerent.

this, after Arcas, a savage youth, forced the Pelasgians to submit to his rule, that he called them Arcadians after his own name.

The Arcadians called Callisto, whom they thought was dead, 6 Ursa ["she-bear"] on account of her lengthy stay in hiding, since a she-bear, as those who study nature say, spends a certain part of the year sleeping in caves; they call also the son Ursus from the name of his mother. Afterward, in order to please Arcas, poets said that they were both brought up to the sky, and instead of the dogs the Egyptians had configured in those locations long before, they positioned these bears. That Thetis, the nurse of Juno, would 7 not permit them to be bathed in the ocean represents the elevation of the pole which in our region has such an elevation, as do the stars near to it, that in its celestial circuit, while the rest of the stars seem to submerge into the ocean as they are setting, these cannot submerge into the ocean; in fact we see their whole circuit around the pole. Eusebius[174] writes that this Arcas subjugated the Pelasgians in the world year 3708.

: 50 :

On Ionius, son of Arcas, who fathered Nicostrata

Ionius, as Theodontius says as well as Paul after him, was the son 1 of Arcas by the nymph Selene. He was a man who in his day was so skilled in the art of war, particularly in naval warfare, that he subjugated nearly the entire coast of the Peloponnesus all the way to the Sicilian Sea, and he named the Ionians and the Ionian Sea after himself. The Ionians came into such great preeminence that it was said that a fourth of all of Greece was under their sway, and they compelled the others to use Ionian letters and grammar.

2   Sane Leontius negat hoc cognomen genti marique inditum ab Yonio rege, affirmans diu ante illis fuisse et ab Yone Ynaci filia, cui maximum in partibus illis fuit imperium appositum, quod etiam alibi ipsemet testatur Theodontius. Fuit ergo Yonio, ut Theodontius dicit et Leontius, filia unica nomine Nycostrata.

: 51 :

De Nycostrata filia Yonii et matre Evandri

1   Nycostrata, Theodontio et Leontio asserentibus, filia fuit Yonii Arcadum regis. Que cum, secundum predictos, Pallanti, cuidam Arcadi viro nobili, nupsisset, seu secundum alios eius nurus existeret, ex Mercurio postea Evandrum Arcadie regem concepit. Et cum Grecarum licterarum esset doctissima, adeo versatilis fuit ingenii, ut ad vaticinium usque penetraret vigilanti studio, et famosissima vates evasit. Et cum querentibus non nunquam expromeret futura carmine, Nycostrate abolito nomine, Carmenta nuncupata est.

2   Que cum Evander putativum patrem seu verum potius occidisset casu, ut quidam volunt, seu ut aliis videtur, seditione suorum e regno pulsus avito, magna filio fugienti vaticinio promictens, cum eo ad Ytaliam devenit, et hostia Tyberis intrans, in Palatino monte consedit. Et cum silvestres comperisset incolas, novos licterarum caracteres adinvenit, eosque earum coniunctiones sonosque edocuit. Que etsi ab initio XVI tantum fuerint, aliis a posteris superad-

3   ditis, eis in hodiernum usque utimur. Cuius rei admirati rudes,

But Leontius denies that it was King Ionius' name that was ap- 2
plied to the people and the sea, asserting that long before it had
come from Io, daughter of Inachus, who had assumed the greatest
power in those areas; elsewhere Theodontius himself testifies to
this as well. According to Theodontius and Leontius, Ionius had a
single daughter whose name was Nicostrata.

: 51 :

On Nicostrata,[175] *daughter of Ionius and mother of Evander*

Nicostrata, as Theodontius and Leontius assert, was the daughter 1
of Ionius, King of the Arcadians. According to them, she married
Pallas, a certain Arcadian nobleman, or, according to others, she
turned out to be his daughter-in-law; with Mercury she later conceived Evander, King of Arcadia. In addition to being very learned
in Greek letters, she had more than sufficient talent to study
prophecy diligently and became a very famous prophetess. And
because she sometimes revealed the future to respondents in verse
[*carmine*], the name Nicostrata was abandoned and she was called
Carmenta.

Later Evander killed his putative father, or rather his real father, 2
by accident, as some wish, or, as others think, was driven from his
ancestral kingdom by a rebellion of his people. Prophesying great
things for her fugitive son, she came with him to Italy, sailed into
the mouth of the Tiber, and settled on the Palatine hill. And when
she met the uncivilized inhabitants, she invented new letters of the
alphabet and taught them how to combine them and make their
sounds. And although there were only sixteen at the beginning,
others were added later, and we use them to this day. In their ad- 3

non hominem sed deam potius arbitrati sunt. Et cum eam adhuc viventem divinis celebrassent honoribus, mortue sub infima Capitolini montis parte, ubi vitam duxerat, sacellum suo nomini condidere, et ad eius perpetuandam memoriam a suo nomine loca adiacentia Carmentalia vocavere. Quod quidem nec Roma iam grandis abolesse passa est, quin imo ianuam civitatis, quam ibi exigente necessitate cives construi fecerant, Carmentalem per multa secula vocavere.

4 Supererat ut omnis Iovis secundi posteritas esset apposita, Dardanum, qui ex filiis eius unus fuit, et omnem ipsius prosapiam apponere; verum quoniam volumen hoc quintum finem poscere videbatur, et illam esse longiusculam, visum est hic terminum figere, et Dardanum prolemque suam sequenti volumini reservare.

miration for such a thing, these archaic people believed her to be not a human but a goddess. And because they already honored her with divine celebrations while still living, after she died they dedicated a shrine in her name on the lowest part of the Capitoline hill, where she had led her life, and to perpetuate her memory they call the adjacent area Carmentalia after her. Even when Rome became grand, it did not allow this name to fall into disuse: in fact, the entrance to the city which the citizens had by necessity constructed there they called Carmentalis for many centuries.

In order to present the whole posterity of the second Jupiter, I 4 must still present Dardanus, who was one of his sons, as well as his whole lineage. But since this fifth book seems to demand its end, and because it is rather long, I think it best to make an end here and reserve Dardanus and his descendants for the following book.

Note on the Text

The manuscript tradition of Boccaccio's *Genealogy* divides into two groups populated by a number of closely related manuscripts of which no single witness can be considered authoritative.[1]

The first group is dominated by Florence, Biblioteca Medicea Laurenziana, Plut. 52.9 (*A*). In October 1894, Oskar Hecker identified this manuscript as an autograph, and Giuseppe Billanovich subsequently confirmed that this was the copy which Boccaccio carried to Naples in 1371 and lent to a group of humanists, including Ugo di Sanseverino and Pietro Piccolo da Monteforte.[2] In a letter to Boccaccio on February 2, 1372, Piccolo informs him that he has read the work, made some corrections, and, contrary to Boccaccio's instructions, commissioned copies for himself and the library of the convent of San Domenico. (These Neapolitan copies are presumed lost.) After a frustrating delay, Boccaccio received his manuscript back from Piccolo, who had made a number of corrections regarding orthography and sources.

The second group, comprising the "vulgate" tradition, includes a number of copies (some quite handsome) produced in the decade following Boccaccio's death in 1375. By the 1950s, Guido Martellotti, Pier Giorgio Ricci, and Giuseppe Billanovich were suggesting that the vulgate, rather than *A*, preserved the latest version of Boccaccio's own text, and in the subsequent generation, Vittorio Zaccaria proved this conclusively.[3] Through his extensive collation of the manuscripts produced in the late 1370s and 1380s, Zaccaria was able to reject the assumptions both that the vulgate tradition derived primarily from Piccolo's 1371–72 Neapolitan apographs and that the abbreviated poetic quotations and prose passages in the vulgate necessarily predated their longer counterparts in *A*. He

hypothesized instead that at least one updated redaction of *A*, perhaps a separate working copy, presumably in Boccaccio's own hand, circulated in Florence after the spring of 1372.[4] Two offspring of this later redaction—Paris, Bibliothèque Nationale, cod. lat. 7877 (*P*) and Chicago, University of Chicago Library, cod. 100 (*Ch*)[5]—have been used, along with *A*, in the preparation of the present edition.

It was the vulgate branch of the manuscript tradition that provided the text for the proliferation of manuscript copies, redactions, printed editions, and translations of the *Genealogy* during the two centuries following Boccaccio's death. In the final paragraph of his comprehensive analysis of the manuscript variants, Zaccaria recommends that the modern editor of Boccaccio's *Genealogy* prefer the vulgate because it preserves corrected text, a practice he would later follow in his own edition.[6] The present edition generally privileges the vulgate, but I have also restored a number of readings from *A*, including many of Boccaccio's marginal supplements, and I have reported others in the Notes to the Text. *A* indisputably contains Boccaccio's own words (albeit corrected and supplemented somewhat by Piccolo), and in many instances it contains the more complete, original text which Boccaccio seems to have revised and in many instances reduced for his final redaction. If Zaccaria is correct in his hypothesis that the vulgate tradition derives from a "working copy," then it may be that Boccaccio did not necessarily want to reduce the length of his poetic quotations for an eventual final version but simply saw no need to copy them out in full in the interim. Where, however, I have employed the longer versions of the quotations (as well as the lengthier account of Cupid and Psyche at 5.22), the vulgate's shorter variants are reported in the notes.

I have consulted Zaccaria's edition throughout and have reported in the Notes to the Text most instances in which his text

(*Zac.*) and the present text differ. The editions of Romano and of Álvarez and Iglesias and the study of Pertusi (see Bibliography) are sometimes referenced in the notes, as are readings from the standard texts of several ancient and medieval sources cited by Boccaccio.

QUOTATIONS

Boccaccio's quotations of Latin sources often vary from the texts found in modern critical editions; many or most of these presumably derive from the manuscripts he consulted. As a rule, I have left these variations intact except where they make meaning or syntax impracticable.

Latin translations of Homer (perhaps by or with the help of Leontius) were added into the margins of the autograph and then incorporated into the body text of the vulgate tradition, so I have included them in my edition along with the Greek passages. However, Boccaccio so struggled with the orthography and diacritical marks of his Homeric Greek quotations that here I have found it more practical to correct his Greek, usually silently.

ORTHOGRAPHY

Transliterated Greek words presented particular problems for Boccaccio, who spelled Latin equivalents inconsistently and made a number of corrections in the various phases of the development of the text. These and other orthographical tendencies in Boccaccio's Latin text have been thoroughly analyzed by Pier Giorgio Ricci[7] and by Zaccaria, so for the most part I have followed the orthography they have established, including the use of *-ct-* instead of the classically standard *-tt-* (e.g., *licteris* for *litteris*, *emictens* for *emittens*), although the tradition is not consistent. Medievalisms include *leviare* (e.g., 1.Pr.1.22) and the one-word adverb *evestigio* (e.g., 1.3.14).

For the benefit of the nonspecialist I have regularized some other things according to the norms of classical Latin and modern editorial practice, e.g., by appending the interrogative enclitic -ne to the previous word and changing *summere* to *sumere*.

Boccaccio can be quite inconsistent in the spelling of Greek proper names, even when they are nearly juxtaposed (*Pollinices* [2.41.1] and *Pollynici* [2.41.3]; *Polinices* [2.74.2]; *Iapeti* and *Iapetho* [4.44.1]). In the vulgate, *i* (*Egiptus*) often replaces the autograph's *y* (*Egyptus*); the latter tends to employ *h* when rendering the aspirates embedded in the Greek letters *theta* and *chi* (*Thalaonem* [2.34.1]), whereas the vulgate does not (*Talaonem*); both branches of the manuscript tradition erroneously tend to render Arcas, Arcadia, and its adjectival derivatives as Archas and Archadia (which I have corrected in the text). Several noun suffixes present similar difficulties, e.g., *Pigmaleonem* (2.47.1) and *Pigmalione* (2.49.1); *Psamata* and *Psamate* (5.7.1). At 2.31 in the autograph, each of the five spellings of *Dyana* has been changed to *Diana*; the names of *Bachus* throughout the work and *Oedipus* toward the end of the second book (2.69–74) have been similarly regularized. Boccaccio wavers also on how to employ *n* and *m* in Greek names, e.g., *Anphianaste* changed from *Amphianaste* (2.31.1), *Anphione* vs. *Amphyon* (5.30.1)

Because neither *A* nor the single manuscripts of the vulgate tradition maintain internal consistency, I have often regularized the Latin orthography of proper names for the reader's benefit. The "Indice dei personaggi" and the "Indice dei luoghi geografici" compiled by Zaccaria, Marina Covini, and Federica Cusseddu provided a template which I then adjusted and supplemented as necessary.[8] In the translation I have instead followed (American) English conventions, even if more than six centuries after Boccaccio's death there are still some discrepancies as to how to transliterate ancient Greek names.

NUMBERS

Inconsistencies and differences are found as well in the numbers used for chapter rubrics. The autograph distinguishes each of the books with Roman numerals I–XV but does not number the individual chapters at all. *P* numbers each chapter with Roman numerals; *Ch* with Arabic numerals. Within the chapter rubrics, the autograph juxtaposes inflected cardinal numerals and word forms, e.g. *De Terra ex filiis Demogorgonis VIII^a, que ex incognitis parentibus V genuit filios; quorum primus Nox, secundus Tartarus, III^us Fama . . .* (1.8). The vulgate exclusively uses adjectival forms. Within the text itself, the autograph demonstrates a predilection for using Roman numerals, e.g. *LXX* instead of *septuaginta* (2.53.5). In 4.33 the autograph uses both *VII* and *septem* to describe the seven Hyades. The vulgate employs Roman numerals much less often, but always when quoting the dates from Eusebius. This edition follows Zaccaria, who in turn follows the vulgate in assigning numbers to each chapter and the autograph in its chapter rubrics, though I have made (mostly silent) corrections in the inflected endings and the numbering itself. Also, the text of this edition spells out numerals through ten that occur in the text itself.

For convenience of reference, I have followed Zaccaria's divisions of each chapter into numbered sections.

TITLE

Scholars justifiably disagree as to whether Boccaccio's treatise should be called the "Genealogy" or "Genealogies" of the pagan gods.[9] The autograph does not contain a separate title page for guidance, but in just the second clause of Book 1, Preface 1, Boccaccio specifies the singular when describing the project itself:

If I have understood correctly from the reports of your eminent officer, Donnino of Parma, you, glorious King, greatly desire to have a genealogy of the pagan gods and the heroes.

In Preface 2 Boccaccio again uses the singular to describe the genealogy inspired by Thales. Finally, in the autograph Boccaccio uses the genitive singular of the title "Genealogy" in the *incipit* and *explicit* of every book.

However, in Preface 1 Boccaccio also complicates the issue by informing the king that a genealogy of the pagan gods is by nature a "corpus of genealogy":

To carry out your project, not otherwise than if I were collecting fragments along the vast shores of a huge shipwreck, I will collect the remnants of the pagan gods strewn everywhere in a nearly infinite number of volumes, and once found and collected, even if they are ravaged and half-eaten by time and nearly worn to nothing, I will reduce them into a single corpus of genealogy, arranged to the best of my ability, to satisfy your wish.

In Book 15, written some years later, Boccaccio uses the phrase *sub titulo honorabili, scilicet Genealogie deorum,* where however *Genealogie* could be either (genitive) singular or (nominative) plural.[10] But in a reference to the work in an April 1372 letter to Piccolo, Boccaccio unambiguously uses the plural to describe "my work on the genealogies of the gods" (*opus meum de genealogiis deorum*), though the insertion of the preposition "on" (*de*) is not paralleled before "genealogies" in the treatise itself. Many later copies and editions use the plural, so whether correct or not, "Genealogies" has for centuries had a significant following.[11]

Ultimately I have chosen to assume that, at least intially, Boccaccio was following the king's commission by creating a single

genealogy of the pagan gods, which, in fact, he does by tracing every character back to Demogorgon as the ultimate progenitor. Even though the treatise includes a number of important sublineages, synthesizing the great number of Greco-Roman mythological lineages into a single genealogy was one of Boccaccio's most substantial achievements. I have chosen to translate the title, therefore, as "The Genealogy of the Pagan Gods."

NOTES

1. For a full conspectus and discussion of manuscripts, see Zaccaria, *Geneaolgie*, 1594–99.

2. Oskar Hecker, ed., *Boccaccio-funde* (Braunschweig: George Westermann, 1902), vii; Giuseppe Billanovich, "Pietro Piccolo da Monteforte tra il Petrarca e il Boccaccio," in *Medioevo e Rinascimento: Studi in onore di Bruno Nardi* (Florence: G. C. Sansoni, 1955), 15 and 33–40.

3. Zaccaria, "Per il testo," 179–240; and *Genealogie*, 1592–99.

4. Zaccaria, "Per il testo," 188, follows Ricci in suggesting that Books 14 and 15 circulated separately from the group of the first thirteen.

5. On the latter, see Ernest Hatch Wilkins, *The University of Chicago Manuscript of the* Genealogia deorum gentilum *of Boccaccio* (Chicago: University of Chicago Press, 1927).

6. Zaccaria, "Per il testo," 242.

7. Giovanni Boccaccio, *Opere in versi: Corbaccio, Trattatello in laude di Dante, Prose latine, Epistole*, ed. Pier Giorgio Ricci (Milan: R. Ricciardi, 1965).

8. Zaccaria, *Genealogie*, 1725–66 and 1767–80.

9. For a recent discussion, see Wolfgang Hübner, "Nock Einmal zum Titel von Boccaccio's *Genealogia*," *Neulateinisches Jahrbuch/Journal of Neo-Latin Language and Literature* 4 (2002): 323–27.

10. Similarly, when referring to Dante's *Comedia*, Boccaccio (15.6) writes, "The work, which has the title of the *Comedia*" (*opus, quod sub titulo Comedie*). The insertion of the word *scilicet* makes the syntax unclear.

11. Zaccaria (*Genealogie*, 1592–93, and "Ancora per il testo," 243–44) argues for and employs the plural.

Notes to the Text

❧❧❧

1. *My numbering of three separate Prohemia follows Zac.*
2. Throughout the text *PCh* generally spell this word *genealogia*, replacing the *genologia* and *genoalogia* found in *A*.
3. niteretur *A* conaretur *PCh*
4. arbitratur *PCh*
5. occeani *A*
6. mari *A* maris *PCh*
7. Et equidem *P*
8. detur *Ch* dentur *AP*
9. que *PCh*
10. inclita gloria *A* inclite *Ch* gloria *om. PCh*
11. et *om. A*
12. declinante Grecorum *PCh*
13. conterentes *A*
14. fortuna iuvet *P* fortuna iuvat *Ch*
15. evolve *PCh*
16. Demum — conabor *in marg. A*
17. redigi *Zac.* redigere *mss.*
18. tricipitem hanc fecere *A*
19. assumpsere *PCh*
20. describitur *Ch* scribuntur *P*
21. quaeque *AP* quaedam et silvas *Ch*

22. in quibus *om. PCh*
23. socios *om. PCh*
24. capitulum primum *add. Ch* capitolo primo *P*
25. ea *A*
26. qui *Zac.* quo *A* que *PCh*
27. perpetuumque *Romano* perpetuum *mss.*
28. persepe *A* sepissime *PCh*
29. et sic Ladonem *A*
30. invidia forte posteritatis fecisse viderer, et *om. A*
31. earum *Zac.* eorum *mss.*
32. seu sors *add. A*
33. Aiunt *A*
34. mortalium apparitio *PCh*
35. tamen *A* enim *PCh*
36. ut *A*
37. eam *ego* eum *mss.*
38. cuique *AP* eiusque *Ch*
39. eius fuerit origo *A* fuerit eius origo *P* eius origo fuerit *Ch*
40. generaliter eum quem mundum *Ch*
41. carens *Romano* carent *ACh* caret *P*
42. visaque *Zac.* visamque *mss.*
43. eum *add. ante* in *A*

44. fraus *PCh*
45. filiam fuisse *PCh*
46. nobis *om. Ch*
47. semper suo *Ch*

48. Pavidum—mortem *ante* Placidus *Zac.*
49. tratius *mss.*
50. eum *A*
51. dominice *PCh*

LIBER SECUNDUS

1. illis insuper *PCh*
2. fuerat adhuc *PCh*
3. civitatem una cum Yside *om. PCh*
4. Cylenis *mss.* Maie nymphe in Cyllene monte qui nomen habuit a *add. Pertusi*
5. et *Romano* etiam *mss.*
6. patre *P* pater *ACh*
7. Scribit—hominem *in marg. A*
8. Asseritque—transirent *in marg. A*
9. Nam—ostendit *in marg. A*
10. advectus *add. Zac.*
11. Et—ferunt *in marg. A*
12. *The sentence as preserved in the manuscripts does not make grammatical sense, presumably as a result of carelessness original to Boccaccio.*
13. quadam turri *PCh*

14. filia Acrisii *AP* Acrisii filia Dauni matre *Ch*
15. aprum *Romano* apro *mss.*
16. et Pyrodem *P in marg. A; om. Ch*
17. nocte *om. PCh*
18. fuit religio ingens *PCh*
19. Quos—Ysaias *om. Ch*
20. De—excussisse *in marg. A*
21. Virgilius Syceum semper *PCh*
22. eligens *AP* diligens *Ch*
23. sororem Dydonis *A* Didonis sororem *PCh*
24. plurimum autores *AP* autores plurimum *Ch*
25. sic—egisse *in marg. A*
26. seu potius ut infra legitur de Learco et Melicerte *in marg. A*
27. De—extitisse *in marg. A*

LIBER TERTIUS

1. VIII Toxius *in marg. A*
2. XII *Romano* XI *A* undecim *PCh*
3. tercia *P* II*ᵃ A* secunda *Ch*

4. ergo—desertum *in marg. A*
5. quod—prospiciat *in marg. A*
6. appellari—obsequio *om. Zac., apparently in error*

7. audit *AP* vidit *Ch*
8. quantumcunque — repertorem in marg. *A*
9. quod — viret *in marg. A*
10. Eam *A* Et *PCh* Eam — patefactum *in marg. A*
11. apud amicos humilem et benignam *after* patientem *Ch*; om. *P*

12. voluptaria *Álvarez-Iglesias* voluntaria *mss.*
13. Venerem — opprimere *in marg. A*
14. gignimur *A* gignuntur *PCh*
15. Verum — haberi rationem *in marg. A*
16. fatigat *A* frangit *PCh*
17. *De Toxio* — filium *in marg. A*

LIBER QUARTUS

1. natu maior *PCh*
2. ac *om. PCh*
3. operibus bonis *Ch*
4. VII^{am} Pasiphem, VIII^{am} Oetam, VIIII^{am} Circem, decimam Angitiam *P* VII^{am} Oetam, VIII^{am} Circem, VIIII^{am} Angitiam *A* septimum Oetam, octavam Circem, nonam Angitiam *Ch*
5. in maiori volumine libro secundo *add. PCh*
6. clara — etc. *A* et infra per XVII versus *PCh*
7. in — etc. *A* et infra per septem versus *PCh*
8. imponunt *AP* imponit *Ch*
9. Praeterea — conspicuum *in marg. A*
10. solus *Macrobius*; om. *mss.*
11. nuncupatur *A*
12. redentem *PCh*
13. nuncupatum *A*

14. sunt *om. PCh*
15. duci — deploraret *A* duci cuius milites, cum nulli, longi atque difficillimi itineris ex Hispania in Italiam trascendentes labores superasse nequissent, Capuane delicie attrivere *PCh*
16. eodem *Zac.* eadem *mss.*
17. solertissimus rerum *Ch*
18. Ego — potuerunt *in marg. A*
19. expectant *A*
20. βίην *Homer*; om. *mss.*
21. insulam *om. PCh*
22. et — etc. *A* et infra per decem versus *PCh*
23. Quique *mss.*
24. II° Iapeti *Zac.* VIIII° Tytanis *A* nono Tytanis *PCh*
25. Plinius — fuisse *in marg. A*
26. quod — invenisse *in marg. A*
27. terret — Hyas *A* et infra per octo versus *Ch*; om. *P*

28. urbe *mss.*
29. id est ubi *PCh*
30. Pandoram *Romano* Pandora *mss.*
31. nostros — etc. *A* et infra per viginti sex versus *PCh*
32. Libet — particula *om. PCh*
33. Dicunt igitur ante alia *A* Insuper dicunt *PCh*
34. Sic — servari *in marg. A*
35. ipse *A*
36. solum in furias *PCh*
37. sic dicit *A* Eneidos primo scribit *PCh*
38. Eolyam — etc. *A* et infra per duodecim versus *PCh*
39. sonantes *corrected to* sonoras *A*
40. Si predictarum fictionum *A* Harum vero fictionum si *PCh*
41. Dicit — Ovidius *A* De eorum potentia regionibus et nominibus in maiori succinte scribit Ovidius *PCh*
42. In quibus — transferre *om. PCh*

43. lenis quasi *A*
44. de — eius *A* cuius vires et opera in persona sui loquens describit Ovidius dicens *PCh*
45. Hac ope *A; om. PCh*
46. nec distulit quin *A* rapuitque *PCh*
47. Excussit — rapuit *om. PCh*
48. ex quibus — insuper *A* quos *PCh*
49. qui *mss.*
50. fugavit *A*
51. Preterea — Arcadia *in marg. A*
52. dicens *A* in maiori volumine ubi dicit *PCh*
53. Perfusam — natos *A* et infra per sex versus *PCh*
54. apud — magnitudinis fuerint *in marg. A*
55. centum *Romano; om. mss.*
56. quem — arbitrantur *A* eum Virgilius ut patet circa finem iii libri Eneidos *PCh*
57. deos *A* deum *P* sive extimatam deum *Ch*

LIBER QUINTUS

1. De — *Stylliconis A* quod Claudianus ubi de laudibus stilliconis ostendit amplissime ibi *PCh*
2. trans — plagas, etc. *A* et infra per multos versus *PCh*

3. Hanc insuper *A* Praeterea hanc *PCh*
4. auferens *mss.* afferens *Myth. Vat.*
5. magno *Servius* magnos *mss.*

6. geminis cupiens tellurem
   Servius gemitus cupiens
   dolorem *mss.*

7. Preterea — alii *in marg. A*

8. Leontius — antiquiorem *in
   marg. A*

9. Fictio — filia *A* In hac nil fere
   fictionis est, nisi, ubi Penei,
   dicit Spei regis Thessalie
   filia fuit a quo missi sunt
   qui perquirerent quonam
   abiisset *PCh* Penei, dicitur
   ⟨potius quam⟩ Spei *Zac.*

10. atque — naturali *in marg. A*

11. eamque *A* illamque *PCh*

12. Statio — enim *A* ut Statius
    testatur et Ovidius qui cum
    conscribit Yanthium
    appellatum ubi dicat *PCh*

13. aut habitus aut *Statius*

14. totus *mss.* si est homo totus
    Aug.

15. Martialis *mss.*

16. suo *om. A*

17. festiva — forma sororum *A*
    festiva congratulatione
    suscepte sunt eisque omnes
    ostense delicie, ex quibus
    invide facte sorores, ei totis
    suasere viribus ut viri
    formam conaretur videre.
    Que credula, eis cum donis
    remissis, novaculam paravit
    et lucernam abscondit sub
    modio, nocte sequenti visura

quisnam esset is cuius
uteretur concubitu, occisura
eum si esset illi forma verbis
sororum conformis. *PCh*

18. Psyces — filiam *A* Psyces vero
    anxia perditi viri, mori
    voluit. Tandem fraude
    sorores ambas, quarum
    consiliis in erumnam
    venerat, in precipitium
    deduxit. Inde a Venere
    obiurgata acriter et a
    pedissequis eius lacessita
    verberibus, in labores
    mortali inexplicabiles iussu
    implicita, opera viri adiuta
    perfecit iniuncta; cuius
    postremo ad Iovem precibus
    actum est ut in Veneris
    deveniret gratiam et in celis
    assumpta, Cupidinis
    perpetuo frueretur coniugio,
    cui peperit Voluptatem. *PCh*

19. quarum — coniugium *A* non
    quia primo nate sint, sed
    quia primo potentia utuntur
    sua, quarum una vegetative
    dicitur, altera vero sensitiva,
    que non anime sunt, ut
    quidam voluere, sed huius
    anime sunt potentie;
    quarum ideo Psyces dicitur
    iunior, quia longe ante eam
    vegetativa potentia
    conceditur fetui, et inde

tractu temporis sensitiva,
postremo autem huic Psyci
conceditur ratio; et quia
primo in actu sunt, ideo
prime dicuntur iuncte
coniugio, quod huic rationali
divine *PCh*

20. Furtim — Bacho *A* eumque,
ne a perquirente Iunone
inveniretur, hederis
occultavere [collocavere
Zac.] *PCh*

21. ut — alumno *om. PCh*

22. circa annos : circa *in marg.*,
— s *supra lineam A*

23. circa annos : circa *in marg.*,
— s *supra lineam A*

24. foveatur *PCh*

25. autumo *A*

26. fingitur *A* pingitur *PCh*

27. vini *Myth. Vat.; om. mss.*

28. altisono carmine *om. PCh*

29. eidem *A* quidem *Ch*

30. Vere *A*

31. Eumque — Plinius *in marg.*
A

32. Niobe *in marg. A*

33. in aliquibus nominibus a
Lactantio *AP* a Lactantio in
aliquibus nominibus *Ch*

34. seu — immissos *om. A*

35. apud Virgilium *om. A*

Note on the Translation

❧❧❧

In the final book Boccaccio himself described the difficulty he encountered in creating the most appropriate narrative tone for a work of Latin prose scholarship:

> If you write a simple text, one that is clear, loose, and accessible, they say your style is pedestrian and has the odor of a school text; they scornfully reject it. If you compose a text with slightly more subtlety, they weary at the first step because its meaning does not immediately become clear, find fault with the author, call the text difficult, and, even if it is smoothed over by gentle artifice, deem it unworthy and disregard it. But I do not think I have written a work that is complex or ambiguous. (15.5)

Appropriately, Boccaccio's prose style in the *Genealogy* is noticeably restrained when compared even to the popular *Famous Women* (*De mulieribus claris*), despite the fact that many of the same female characters and exploits appear here as well. (Compare, for instance, the chapters here on Venus [2.22–23] with *Famous Women* 7.)[1] He does not use vivid expressions, treats sexual activity as a simple narrative or procreative event, and avoids the kind of fictional descriptions of mythical characters that so many earlier and later poets would contrive. To a certain extent this is the result of euhemerizing the gods, reducing them to humans and treating them as individual examples of the catalog of humanity we all share. And yet there is also a personal element not expected in an encyclopedic work. Boccaccio's voice is never absent for long, whether he is conveying what he has learned, where he learned it, or what he thinks about it.

I have allowed Boccaccio's statement to guide me as to how he might have wanted the *Genealogy* translated. As much as possible I have used "gentle artifice" to shorten the complex periodic sentences, which tend to proliferate in quasi-Ciceronian humanistic Latin, and anglicize the Latin word order. On the other hand, I have not softened the sober Latinity of the *Genealogy* to the point where it might seem to be anything less than a scholarly compilation written for an educated patron, albeit one which is comprehensive, authoritative, ever inventive, and filled with scores of individual fascinations.

As for the Greek passages, Boccaccio with Leontius translated the Homeric Greek into Latin, so they appear twice in the manuscripts, once in each language. I include both Greek and Latin texts but only one English translation, which favors the Latin rendering, which, even if it differs somewhat from the Greek text, is presumably how Boccaccio understood it. Similarly, I have translated the Latin quotations according to Boccaccio's text even where they differ somewhat from the modern standard texts. Despite Boccaccio's propensity to use variant spellings for proper names, I have used the modern standard spellings in the translation. This is true even where Boccaccio consistently uses variants of names and titles rejected by modern scholarship, e.g., Hermofroditus and the title of Cicero's *De naturis deorum* (*On the Natures of the Gods*). I translate these with the more familiar American English forms: Hermaphroditus and *On the Nature of the Gods*.

The Notes serve primarily three functions: they identify Boccaccio's sources; they specify his most significant errors of attribution and orthography; and they offer translations of the variant passages found in the autograph of vulgate manuscripts. In the first five books alone Boccaccio cites approximately eight hundred sources, the impressive result of his extensive research, though the number excludes three of his most frequently used sources, namely,

the material he derived from his teachers Paul of Perugia and Leontius, who also gave him access to the narratives and interpretations of Theodontius. He does properly make attributions to them in his text, but he could not formally cite them because their work was not available in written form, except, technically speaking, Leontius' translations of Homer. Relatively infrequently, when compared with the massive amount of material Boccaccio had to collect, organize, record, and cite, Boccaccio makes inaccurate citations, e.g., erroneously citing Servius for Fulgentius (1.33.2). Where he does so, I keep the name Boccaccio cites in the English translation but make the correct citation in the Notes. This is not true for the misattribution of the story of Jason and Medea (4.12.1), which does not seem to recount, as Boccaccio claims, Apollonius' version. As for the variant passages, I have provided the reader with translations of a number of alternative passages which Boccaccio himself revised after the return of his autograph from Naples in 1372. For the most part the longer versions belong to the autograph (A) while the shorter versions derive from the later vulgate tradition (PCh).

The Notes do not provide an additional glossary of mythological or historical names or geographical locations, which would exceed the scope of the ITRL. In reality, Boccaccio's *Genealogy* already serves as a unique lexicon of mythological characters representing a specific stratum of the mythological tradition that had been established already more than two millennia earlier and would then continue to develop for many more centuries. Readers interested in identifying further the names listed in the *Genealogy* in the context of the Trecento should refer to Boccaccio's own citations and the extensive notes in the second volume of Zaccaria's edition (1611–1720). See also the reference works listed below:

Bonnefoy, Yves, ed. *Greek and Egyptian Mythologies.* Trans. Wendy Doniger. Chicago: University of Chicago Press, 1991.

———. *Roman and European Mythologies*. Chicago: University of Chicago Press, 1991.

Brumble, H. David. *Classical Myths and Legends in the Middle Ages and Renaissance: A Dictionary of Allegorical Meanings*. Westport: Greenwood, 1998.

Hornblower, Simon, and Antony Spawforth, eds. *The Oxford Classical Dictionary*. 3rd rev. ed. Oxford: Oxford University Press, 2003.

Smith, R. Scott, and Stephen M. Trzaskoma, trans. *Apollodorus' Library and Hyginus' Fabulae: Two Handbooks of Greek Mythology*. Indianapolis: Hackett, 2007.

Starnes, DeWitt T., and Ernest William Talbert. *Classical Myth and Legend in Renaissance Dictionaries: A Study of Renaissance Dictionaries in Their Relation to the Classical Learning of Contemporary English Writers*. Chapel Hill: University of North Carolina Press, 1955.

This is the first complete English translation of Boccaccio's *Genealogy of the Pagan Gods*. Charles Osgood published a translation of the Preface and Books 14 and 15 originally in 1930, and this was later made widely available in a paperback edition in the Bobbs-Merrill Library of Liberal Arts. Several books, articles, and theses translate individual passages.[2]

NOTES

1. Giovanni Boccaccio, *Famous Women*, ed. and trans. Virginia Brown (Cambridge: Harvard University Press, 2001), 38–43.

2. E.g., Marianne Pade, "The *Fortuna* of Leontius Pilatus's Homer," in F. T. Coulson and A. A. Grotans, eds., *Classica et Beneventana: Essays Presented to Virginia Brown on the Occasion of her 65th Birthday* (Turnhout: Brepolis, 2008 [15.6]).

Notes to the Translation

※⟨⟩※

1. See Introduction.

2. Cf. Augustine, *City of God* 18.2; Isidore, *Etymologies* 5.39.7; and Orosius 1.1.

3. Cf. Boccaccio, *Famous Women* 34; and Ovid, *Metamorphoses* 13.423–575.

4. GDG 6.30.2.

5. See Introduction.

6. Mercury was the "Slayer of Argus"; cf. GDG 7.22.1–3.

7. Varro in Augustine, *City of God* 6.5; cf. GDG 15.8.2.

8. Cf. GDG 13.1.28.

9. Cf. Aulus Gellius, *Attic Nights* 7.17.3.

10. If this meeting took place in or a little before 1350, Boccaccio was in his thirties, Petrarch his forties. See Introduction.

11. Vergil, *Georgics* 1.145–146.

12. Vergil, *Aeneid* 10.284.

13. Judith 13:17.

14. Osgood, *Boccaccio on Poetry*, 143, suggests Gregory the Great's proem to his *Moralia in Job* as a model for Boccaccio's *Proemium* in general and specifically for the metaphor of a nautical figure tossed by the sea.

15. GDG 11.26.1.

16. Ibid. 4.44.1.

17. Plato in Boethius, *Consolation of Philosophy* 3.9.

18. GDG 10.50.2.

19. Augustine, *City of God* 18.14; cf. Aristotle, *Metaphysics* 983b.

20. Cf. GDG 8.6.4.

21. Cicero, *On the Nature of the Gods* 1.25; Augustine, *City of God* 8.2.

22. Cicero, *On the Nature of the Gods* 1.26; Augustine, *City of God* 8.2.

23. Cicero, *On the Nature of the Gods* 1.39–40.

24. Ibid. 1.27; Boccaccio, not following Augustine or Cicero exclusively, mistakes Alcinous for Alcmeon—a relatively easy confusion in semi-Gothic script.

25. Macrobius, *Saturnalia* 1.22.2.

26. See Introduction.

27. E.g., Homer, *Iliad* 14.302.

28. E.g., Hesiod, *Theogony* 126–27; cf. Hyginus *Fables* (preface) 2, Ovid, *Metamorphoses* 1.21–23.

29. Cicero, *On the Nature of the Gods* 3.53.

30. See Introduction.

31. Cape Tenarum (Matapan), the southern tip of Mani, was identified in antiquity as one of the entrances to the Underworld.

32. Lucan, *Pharsalia* 6.744–47.

33. Statius, *Thebaid* 4.514–17.

34. Lactantius Placidus on *Thebaid* 4.516–17.

35. See Introduction.

36. Psalms 111/110:9.

37. Claudian, *On the Consulship of Stilicho* 2.424–36 and 446–49.

38. Cf. Jan Bialostocki, "The Renaissance Concept of Nature and Antiquity," in *The Renaissance and Mannerism: Studies in Western Art* (Princeton: Princeton University Press, 1963), II, 19–30.

39. GDG 4.5.

40. Ovid, *Metamorphoses* 1.6–9.

41. All of Boccaccio's nearly one dozen citations of Pronapides of Athens, traditionally said (e.g., Diodorus of Sicily 3.67.5) to be the teacher of Homer, were derived from Theodontius.

42. Folly (Ate) is the goddess integral to this story in Homer, *Iliad* 19.91–133.

43. GDG 4.54.1.

44. Macrobius, *Dream of Scipio* 1.2.17–18.

45. Cf. Dante, *Epistles* 10.7.

46. Cf. GDG 12.25.1.

47. Ibid. 12.34.1.

48. Ibid. 1.5.

49. Vergil, *Eclogues* 2.32–33.

50. Boccaccio's quotation is barely recognizable in Rabanus, *On the Nature of Things* 15.6.

51. Vergil, *Eclogues* 10.27.

52. Ibid. 10.24–25.

53. Ibid. 10.26.

54. Vergil, *Georgics* 2.494.

55. Macrobius, *Dream of Scipio* 2.1.8–12.

56. Josephus, *Jewish Antiquities* 1.2.2; Gen. 4:21–22.

57. Macrobius, *Saturnalia* 1.22.2.

58. Augustine, *City of God* 18.17.

59. Macrobius, *Saturnalia* 1.22.2.

60. Cicero, *On the Nature of the Gods* 3.44.

61. Seneca, *Epistles* 107.11.

62. Seneca, *Oedipus* 980–84.

63. Ovid, *Metamorphoses* 15.807–14.

64. Fulgentius, *Mythologies* 1.8.40.

65. Apuleius, *On the Universe* 38.

66. Cicero, *On Divination* 1.125–26.

67. Boethius, *Consolation of Philosophy* 4.6.7.

68. Boccaccio erroneously cites Cicero for Servius on *Aeneid* 1.22.

69. Augustine, *City of God* 5.9.

70. Cf. Fulgentius, *Mythologies* 1.2.

71. For Andalò, see Introduction.

72. Lactantius, *Divine Institutes* 1.5.4–5.

73. Uguccione, *Great Book of Etymologies*, F 47.4.

74. The medieval tradition interchanged Phyton and Python.

75. Statius, *Thebaid* 8.303–16.

76. Including Phyton (1.7), Night (1.9), Tartarus (1.11), Tages (1.12), Antaeus (1.13), Erebus (1.14), numerous Titans in Book 4, rivers in Book 7, and Saturn (8.1); cf. Proserpina (8.4), Amycis or Amycus (10.3), and the Harpies (10.61).

77. Tellumo is usually Tellus' masculine aspect.

78. Rabanus, *On the Nature of Things* 12.1.

79. Servius on *Aeneid* 1.171 is the source for the second statement only.

80. Macrobius, *Saturnalia* 1.12.21.

81. Ibid. 1.12.22.

82. Statius, *Thebaid* 1.498–501.

83. Plautus, *Amphitryon* 271–76.

84. Macrobius, *Saturnalia* 1.3.10–12.

85. Papias, *Lexicon*, s.v. Nox.

86. John 3:20.

87. Boccaccio erroneously cites Juvenal for Horace, *Epistles* 1.2.32.

88. Homer, *Iliad* 14.259.

89. Vergil, *Aeneid* 4.178–80.

90. Ibid. 4.173–77.

91. Ibid. 4.180–88.

92. Ibid. 10.467–69.

93. Ovid, *Metamorphoses* 12.39–63.

94. Vergil, *Aeneid* 6.

95. Isidore, *Etymologies* 14.9.8.

96. Vergil, *Aeneid* 6.577–79l.

97. Ibid. 6.580–81.

98. Isidore, *Etymologies* 8.9.35.

99. Lucan, *Pharsalia* 4.593–609.

100. Pomponius Mela, *Description of the World* 1.5.26.

101. Eusebius-Jerome, *Chronicle* 57.6–12.

102. Fulgentius, *Mythologies* 2.4.76.

103. Augustine, *City of God* 18.11–13.

104. Eusebius-Jerome, *Chronicle* 55.9–57.20.

105. GDG 1.11.1.

106. Esp. Vergil, *Aeneid* 6.273–89.

107. Cicero, *Tusculan Disputations* 1.3–5.

108. Uguccione, *Great Book of Etymologies* H 17.9.

109. Cicero, *On the Nature of the Gods* 3.44.

110. Apuleius, *On the Doctrine of Plato* 2.14.

111. Aristotle, *Nicomachean Ethics* 8.3 (1115a).

112. Cicero, *On the Nature of the Gods* 3.44.

113. Ibid.

114. Ibid.

115. Cicero, *Tusculan Disputations* 4.16–17.

116. Ovid, *Metamorphoses* 2.760–64.

117. Ibid. 2.768–82.

118. Cicero, *On the Nature of the Gods* 3.44.

119. Cicero, *Tusculan Disputations* 4.13.

120. Statius, *Thebaid* 7.108–16.

121. Cicero, *Tusculan Disputations* 4.16.

122. Cicero, *On the Nature of the Gods* 3.44.

123. Ibid.

124. Genesis 3:1.

125. Cicero, *On the Nature of the Gods* 3.44.

126. Dante, *Inferno* 16.129–17.27.

127. Cicero, *On the Nature of the Gods* 3.44.

128. Not included with the seventeen children of Erebus and Night listed in Cicero, *On the Nature of the Gods* 3.44.

129. E.g., Lucan, *Pharsalia* 9.371–410, and Dante, *Inferno* 14.12–42.

130. E.g., Ovid, *Metamorphoses* 11.100–156, and Dante, *Purgatory* 20.106–8.

131. Cicero, *On the Nature of the Gods* 3.44.

132. Genesis 41:29–30.

133. Ovid, *Metamorphoses* 8.823–78.

134. Ibid. 8.799–809.

135. Cicero, *On the Nature of the Gods* 3.44.

136. Ibid.

137. Ibid.

138. Cf. Cicero, *Tusculan Disputations* 4.19.

139. Cf. Cicero, *On the Nature of the Gods* 3.44.

140. Ovid, *Metamorphoses* 11.623–25.

141. Seneca, *Hercules Furens* 1065–78.

142. Ovid, *Metamorphoses* 11.592–615.

143. Cicero, *On the Nature of the Gods* 3.44.

144. Macrobius, *Dream of Scipio* 1.3.2–8.

145. Vergil, *Aeneid* 4.9; quoted in Macrobius, *Dream of Scipio* 1.3.6.

146. Cicero, *Republic* 6.10; cf. Petrarch, *Africa* 9.193–391.

147. Vergil, *Aeneid* 4.3–5.

148. Ibid. 6.896.

149. Macrobius, *Dream of Scipio* 1.3.9.

150. Genesis 37:7.

151. Valerius Maximus, *Memorable Deeds and Sayings* 1.7, ext 5.

152. Ibid. 1.7.8.

153. Matthew 2:13.

154. Macrobius, *Dream of Scipio* 1.3.17.

155. Vergil, *Aeneid* 6.893–96; Macrobius, *Dream of Scipio* 1.3.5 and 17.

156. Ovid, *Metamorphoses* 11.633–38.

157. Boccaccio writes *Ytathona* and *Phabetora* for *Ycelon* and *Phobetora*.

158. Ovid, *Metamorphoses* 11.640–41.

159. Ibid. 11.641–43.

160. Boccaccio writes *Panthos* for *Phantasos*.

161. Cicero, *On the Nature of the Gods* 3.44 but without Chrysippus.

162. Aristotle, *Nicomachean Ethics* 3.6 (1115a).

163. Macrobius, *Dream of Scipio* 1.13.11.

164. Statius, *Thebaid* 8.376–81.

165. Uguccione, *Great Book of Etymologies* M 136.8.

166. Apocalypse 14:13.

167. Cf. Cicero, *On the Nature of the Gods* 3.43.

168. Vergil, *Aeneid* 6.298–304.

169. Boccaccio erroneously cites Servius for Fulgentius, *Exposition of the Content of Virgil* 22.

170. Cicero, *On the Nature of the Gods* 3.44.

171. Genesis 1:5.

172. Varro in Macrobius, *Saturnalia* 1.3.6.

173. Macrobius, *Saturnalia* 1.3.12.

174. Varro [et al.] in Macrobius, *Saturnalia* 1.3.

BOOK II

1. Boccaccio writes "Celius or Celum," the former an apparent theophoric version of the latter ("sky"); subsequently he uses both forms.

2. Mark 4:37–39 narrates the story of the storm on the Sea of Galilee; the variant name Boccaccio uses, Genezereth [Genneseret], appears in 6.53.

3. Cicero, *On the Nature of the Gods* 3.44.

4. Uguccione, *Great Book of Etymologies* E 140.3.

5. Ovid, *Metamorphoses* 1.67–68.

6. GDG 1.3.1.

7. Cicero, *On the Nature of the Gods* 3.53.

8. Vergil, *Aeneid* 6.730.

9. Valerius Maximus, *Memorable Deeds and Sayings* 8.7.ext.1.

10. See Introduction.

11. John 14:6.

12. Lucan, *Pharsalia* 9.350.

13. Claudian, *On the Consulship of Stilicho* 3.226–27.

14. Servius on *Georgics* 1.277.

15. Ovid, *Metamorphoses* 6.5–145; cf Boccaccio, *Famous Women* 18.

16. Livy 7.3.7.

17. Sirach 24:5.

18. Vatican Mythographer 3.10.1.

19. Eusebius-Jerome, *Chronicle* 29.17–30.26.

20. Pomponius Mela, *Description of the World* 1.7.36.

21. Augustine, *City of God* 18.8.

22. Eusebius-Jerome, *Chronicle* 30.14–26.

23. Ibid. 30.8–11.

24. Ibid. 22.3–4.

25. Bede, *On Time* 19, but Apis is not mentioned as the founder.

26. Eusebius-Jerome, *Chronicle* 32.7–33.7.

27. Augustine, *City of God* 18.5.

28. Varro in Augustine, *City of God* 18.5.

29. Boccaccio erroneously cites Juvenal (e.g., *Satires* 8.29–30), but the quotation is from Ovid, *Metamorphoses* 9.693.

30. Rabanus, *On the Nature of Things* 15.6.

31. Macrobius, *Saturnalia* 1.20.13.

32. Cicero, *On the Nature of the Gods* 3.54.

33. Ibid. 3.58.

34. Vergil, *Aeneid* 4.239–46.

35. Horace, *Odes* 1.10.1–4.

36. Statius, *Thebaid* 1.305.

37. Albumasar, *Introduction to Astronomy* 7.9.8.

38. Vergil, *Aeneid* 6.743–51.

39. Cicero, *On the Nature of the Gods* 3.53.

40. Boccaccio writes *Ariarchi* for *Anaces* or *Anactes*.

41. Cicero, *On the Nature of the Gods* 3.42; Boccaccio writes *Lysico*.

42. Ibid. 3.53 and 58.

43. Ibid. 3.53.

44. Eusebius-Jerome, *Chronicle* 54.15–17.

45. GDG 2.7.

46. Lactantius Placidus on *Thebaid* 4.481–83.

47. Cicero, *On the Nature of the Gods* 3.60.

48. Boccaccio writes *Auctolius* for *Autolycus*.

49. Ovid, *Metamorphoses* 11.293–317.

50. Boccaccio writes *Lychion* for *Chione*.

51. Boccaccio writes *Phylemon* for *Philammon*.

52. Boccaccio writes *Syssimus* for *Aesimus*.

53. Boccaccio writes *Auctolia* for *Anticlea*.

54. Servius on *Aeneid* 2.69.

55. Homer *Odyssey* 19.386–412.

56. Servius on *Aeneid* 2.79.

57. Ibid.

58. Ovid, *Metamorphoses* 13.31–32.

59. Homer, *Odyssey* 11.152–224.

60. Servius on *Aeneid* 2.79.

61. Vergil, *Aeneid* 2.57–249.

62. Pliny, *Natural History* 7.56.202.

63. Ovid, *Metamorphoses* 1.748–49.

64. GDG 4.46.

65. Eusebius-Jerome, *Chronicle* 43.12–16.

66. Gervase of Tilbury, *Otia imperialia* 2.25.

67. Boccaccio mistakes Egyptian Babylon for Memphis.

68. GDG 7.22.

69. Lactantius Placidus on *Thebaid* 4.737.

70. GDG 12.25.3.

71. Eusebius-Jerome, *Chronicle* 42.15–16.

72. Ibid. 45.

73. Isidore, *Etymologies* 14.4.1.

74. Boccaccio writes *Aegisthus* for *Aegyptus*.

75. For *Hesione* Boccaccio writes *Bona*, which seems to derive from *Iona*, a corruption of *Hesiona*; see Romano 860, n. 3.

76. Lactantius Placidus on *Thebaid* 2.222.

77. Orosius 1.11.1.

78. Pliny, *Natural History* 7.56.206.

79. Eusebius-Jerome, *Chronicle* 44.23–25; 45.21–26.

80. Boccacio writes *Stelenus* for *Stenelus*.

81. Pliny, *Natural History* 7.56.195.

82. Ovid, *Metamorphoses* 4.462–63.

83. Seneca, *Hercules Furens* 757.

84. Cf. Boccaccio, *Famous Women* 14.

85. Ovid, *Heroines* 14.15–16.

86. Eusebius-Jerome, *Chronicle* 47.22–23.

87. Lactantius Placidus on *Thebaid* 2.433.

88. GDG 10.59.1.

89. For *Hesione*, Boccaccio writes *Bona*, which seems to derive from *Iona*, a corruption of *Hesiona*; see Romano 860, n. 3.

90. Dictys of Crete 1.9.

91. Ovid *Heroines* 14.123, but Lynceus, not Lynus.

92. Eusebius-Jerome, *Chronicle* 45.22 (Danaus), 46.11–12 (Lynceus), 50.10 (Abas), 52.10 (Acrisius).

93. Ibid. 50.10.

94. Boccaccio writes *Meran* for *Maera*.

95. Lactantius Placidus on *Thebaid* 3.453.

96. Servius on *Eclogues* 6.48.

97. Homer, *Iliad* 6.160.

98. Vergil, *Eclogues* 6.48.

99. Ovid, *Metamorphoses* 15. 320–28.

100. Vitruvius, *On Architecture* 8.3.21.

101. Eusebius-Jerome, *Chronicle* 51.13–14 and 52.9–10.

102. Boccaccio writes *Danes* for *Danae*.

103. Lactantius Placidus on *Thebaid* 4.589.

104. Eusebius-Jerome, *Chronicle* 52.9–10.

105. Servius on *Aeneid* 7.372.

106. Eusebius-Jerome, *Chronicle* 54.4–6.

107. Lactantius Placidus on *Thebaid* 4.309.

108. GDG 5.30.3.

109. Homer, *Odyssey* 11.281–84.

110. Boccaccio writes *Euridice* for *Eriphyle*.

111. Boccaccio writes *Almeon* for *Alcmeon*.

112. Lactantius Placidus on *Thebaid* 1.391.

113. Statius, *Thebaid* 3.286; cf. Dante, *Purgatory* 22.110.

114. Statius, *Thebaid* 3.678–84. Cf. Boccaccio, *Famous Women* 29.

115. Dictys of Crete 1.9.

116. Lactantius Placidus on *Thebaid* 3.286.

117. Pseudo-Lactantius Placidus, *Stories from the Fables of Ovid* 3.1.

118. Ovid, *Metamorphoses* 10.243–97.

119. Ibid. 10.298–99.

120. Ibid. 10.312–518.

121. Ibid. 10.312–468.

122. Fulgentius, *Mythologies* 3.8.122–23.

123. Ovid, *Metamorphoses* 10.476–514.

124. Petronius in Fulgentius, *Mythologies* 3.8.124.

125. Ovid, *Metamorphoses* 10. 298–559 and 708–39.

126. Macrobius, *Saturnalia* 1.20.1–4.

127. Cicero, *On the Nature of the Gods* 3.59.

128. Lactantius, *Divine Institutes* 1.17.

129. Augustine, *City of God* 4.10.

130. Justin, *Epitome* 18.5.4–5, where it is eighty virgins.

131. Boccaccio erroneously cites Isaiah for Ezekiel 8:14.

132. Pliny, *Natural History* 7.56.198.

133. Pseudo-Lactantius Placidus, *Stories from the Fables of Ovid* 3.1.

134. Eusebius-Jerome, *Chronicle* 46.22–26 and 48.9–11.

135. Ovid, *Metamorphoses* 3.3–5.

136. Servius on *Aeneid* 1.343.

137. Vergil, *Aeneid* 1.343.

138. Justin, *Epitome* 18.4.5.

139. Servius on *Aeneid* 1.343.

140. Vergil, *Aeneid* 1.621–22.

141. Justin, *Epitome* 18.4.3–4.

142. Vergil, *Aeneid* 1.619–22; Cf. Boccaccio, *Famous Women* 42.

143. Livy 34.62.12.

144. E.g., Vergil, *Aeneid* 1 and 4.

145. Justin, *Epitome* 18.6.1–7.

146. Vergil, *Aeneid* 4.9.

147. Ovid, *Fasti* 3.566–654.

148. I.e., Pantelleria.

149. Ibid. 3.653–54.

150. Macrobius, *Saturnalia* 1.12.6.

151. Ovid, *Metamorphoses* 2.836–3.2; cf. Boccaccio, *Famous Women* 9.

152. Eusebius-Jerome, *Chronicle* 47.7–11.

153. Augustine, *City of God* 18.12.

154. Eusebius-Jerome, *Chronicle* 47.25.

155. Ibid. 53.16–17.

156. Ibid. 55.4–5.

157. Varro, *On the Latin Language.* 5.31.

158. Eusebius-Jerome, *Chronicle* 46.23–26.

159. GDG 2.44.1.

160. Eusebius-Jerome, *Chronicle* 49.4–5; year 17, not 16; also, Harmonia, not Armenia.

161. Ovid, *Metamorphoses* 3.1–13.

162. Ibid. 3.14–130.

163. Palaephatus in Eusebius-Jerome, *Chronicle* 56.20–24.

164. Pliny, *Natural History* 7.56.197.

165. Ovid, *Metamorphoses* 3.132; 4.563–603.

166. Eusebius-Jerome, *Chronicle* 50.23–24; 53.12–13; Acrisius succeeded Proetus.

167. Palaephatus in Eusebius-Jerome, *Chronicle* 53.19–22.

168. Ovid, *Metamorphoses* 3.256–309.

169. Cf. Ibid. 3.511–76 and 629–733.

170. Ibid. 3.719–20.

171. Ibid. 3.313; 4.512–42.

172. Boccaccio writes *Leucotoe* for *Leuconoe*.

173. Statius, *Thebaid* 11.634–44.

174. E.g., Lactantius Placidus on *Thebaid* 3.286. Cf. Boccaccio, *Famous Women* 25.

175. Statius, *Thebaid* 8.641–42.

176. Cf. Dante, *Inferno* 22.52–54.

177. Statius, *Thebaid* 3.678–84.

178. Vergil, *Aeneid* 2.259–64.

179. Pliny, *Natural History* 7.56.201.

180. Lamech is not associated with archery in the Septuagint version of Gen. 4:23 but is so in the Talmudic tradition.

BOOK III

1. Numenius in Macrobius, *Commentary on the Dream of Scipio* 1.2.19.

2. Cf. Ovid, *Metamorphoses* 8.823–78.

3. GDG 2.65.

4. Ibid. 12.2.

5. Cicero, *On the Nature of the Gods* 3.50.

6. Matthew 2:1 and 10–11.

7. Orpheus in Lactantius, *Divine Institutes* 1.5.4.

8. Cicero, On the Nature of the Gods 3.44.

9. Lactantius, *Divine Institutes* 1.11.57.

10. Ennius in Lactantius, *Divine Institutes* 1.11.63.

11. For Panchaeus, see Jackson Bryce, *The Library of Lactantius* (New York: Garland, 1990), 333.

12. Euhemerus in Lactantius, *Divine Institutes* 1.11.65.

13. Lactantius, *Divine Institutes* 1.11.38; 1.14.2. Cf. Boccaccio, *Famous Women* 3.

14. Solinus, *On the Wonders of the World* 27.13–20, discusses lions, but the anecdote is found in Isidore, *Etymologies* 12.2.5.

15. Macrobius, *Saturnalia* 1.21.7–9.

16. Porphyry in Augustine, *City of God* 7.25.

17. Rabanus, *On the Nature of Things* 15.6.

18. Fulgentius, *Mythologies* 3.5.110.

19. Lactantius Placidus on *Achilleid* 1.222.

20. Servius on *Eclogues* 10.5.

21. Vergil, *Eclogues* 10.4–5.

22. Soranus in Augustine, *City of God* 7.9.

23. Seneca, *Natural Questions* 3.14.2.

24. Lactantius, *Divine Institutions* 1.14.2.

25. Dante, *Inferno* 14.94–120.

26. Cf. Boccaccio, *On Mountains* 5.17–18: Acheron vs. Acherontus.

27. Livy 8.24.3.

28. Cf. Boccaccio, *On Mountains* 7.57 and Isidore, *Etymologies* 13.16.7.

29. Servius on *Aeneid* 6.107.

30. Vatican Mythographer 3.6.2.

31. Cf. Justin, *Epitome* 36.2.

32. Vergil, *Aeneid* 12.845–47.

33. Lucan, *Pharsalia* 6.732–34.

34. Vergil, *Aeneid* 7.346–48.

35. Ovid, *Metamorphoses* 6.430.

36. Vergil, *Aeneid* 12. 869–70.

37. Ibid. 12.875–76.

38. Ibid. 12.849–52.

39. Ibid. 7.324–329; Boccaccio discounts Vergil's suggestion that Pluto, not Acheron, is her father.

40. Vergil, *Aeneid* 7.335–38.

41. Fulgentius, *Mythologies* 1.7.39.

42. Ovid, *Metamorphoses* 4.481–85.

43. Boccaccio erroneously cites Claudian for Statius, *Thebaid* 1.103–6.

44. Ibid. 1.106–9.

45. Fulgentius, *Mythologies* 1.7.39.

46. Boccaccio erroneously cites Claudian, *On the Consulship of Stilicho* for *Against Rufinus* 1.74–84.

47. Claudian, *On the Consulship of Stilicho* 3.204–7.

48. Ovid, *Fasti* 5.23–28.

49. Boccaccio writes *Orne* for *Orphne*.

50. Ovid, *Metamorphoses* 5.539–41.

51. Papias, *Lexicon*, s.v. Orna.

52. Lucan, *Pharsalia* 7.819.

53. GDG 8.4 and 11.6.

54. Vatican Mythographer 3.6.3.

55. GDG 3.10.

56. Vergil, *Aeneid* 6.323–24.

57. Seneca in Servius on *Aeneid* 6.154.

58. Boccaccio writes *Phyalas* for *Philae*.

59. Vatican Mythographer 3.6.2.

60. Vergil, *Aeneid* 6.705–51.

61. GDG 2.7.7.

62. Dante, *Purgatory* 28.120–33.

63. Cicero, *On the Nature of the Gods* 3.55.

64. Ibid. 3.57.

65. Pliny, *Natural History* 7.56.196.

66. Cicero, *On the Nature of the Gods* 3.56, who lists this as the first Mercury.

67. Martial, *Epigrams* 7.74.1–2.

68. Hermes Trismegistus in Augustine, *City of God* 8.26.

69. GDG 2.7.

70. Ovid, *Metamorphoses* 4.288–91.

71. Vatican Mythographer 3.9.2.

72. Boccaccio writes *Albericus* for *Albertus*, *On Animals* 9.1.5.50.

73. Boccaccio writes *Nyda* for *Mela*.

74. Vitruvius, *On Architecture* 2.8.12.

75. Cicero, *On the Nature of the Gods* 3.59.

76. Ovid, *Fasti* 4.1.

77. Albumasar, *Introduction to Astronomy* 7.9.7.

78. Aristotle, *Nicomachean Ethics* 8.3 (1156a).

79. GDG 5.35.

80. Boccaccio writes *ceston*.

81. Homer, *Iliad* 14.214–17.

82. Lactantius Placidus on *Thebaid* 2.283–84.

83. Vergil, *Georgics* 3.244.

84. GDG 4.3.

85. Rabanus, *On the Nature of Things* 19.6.

86. Fulgentius, *Mythologies* 3.8.124–25. Boccaccio writes *Futurius* for *Sutrius* and *Digon* for *Glycon*.

87. Cicero, *On the Nature of the Gods* 3.62.

88. Boccaccio writes *Cythereus* for *Cynthus*.

89. Vergil, *Aeneid* 1.374.

90. Varro, *On the Latin Language* 6.2 and 7.50.

91. Plautus, *Amphitryon* 275.

92. Cicero, *On the Nature of the Gods* 2.53.

93. Macrobius, *Saturnalia* 1.8.6.

94. Pomponius Mela, *Description of the World* 2.7.102.

95. Ovid, *Metamorphoses* 4.536–38.

96. Vergil, *Aeneid* 5.800–801.

97. Fulgentius, *Mythologies* 2.1.70.

98. Macrobius, *Saturnalia* 1.8.7–8.

99. GDG 1.2.

100. Tacitus, *Histories* 2.3.

101. Porphyrius in Fulgentius, *Mythologies* 2.1.72.

102. Plautus, *Cistellaria* 203–22.

103. Fulgentius, *Mythologies* 2.1.72.

104. Simonides in Servius on *Aeneid* 1.664.

105. E.g., GDG 9.4.

106. Pliny, *Natural History* 7.56.194.

BOOK IV

1. Matthew 14:28–29.

2. Joshua 3:13–16; cf. Exodus 14:22.

3. Lactantius, *Divine Institutes* 1.14.2.

4. Vergil, *Georgics* 1.278–80; Boccaccio writes *Oetus* for *Coeus* and reconstructs from the previous line ("flee the fifth moon") the initial four words to make it relevant to the fifth month.

5. Vergil, *Aeneid* 6.580–81.

6. Lactantius, *Divine Institutes* 1.14.2–10.

7. Boccaccio erroneously cites Lactantius for Servius on *Aeneid* 6.580.

8. GDG 1.10.2.

9. GDG 4.68.

10. Boccaccio writes *Salempetii* for *Lampetia*.

11. Ovid, *Metamorphoses* 2.1–18.

12. Ibid. 2.23–30.

13. Ibid. 2.107–10.

14. Ibid. 2.153–55.

15. Vatican Mythographer 3.8.7.

16. Genesis 1:1–14.

17. Fulgentius, *Mythologies* 1.12.44.

18. Vatican Mythographer 3.8.7.

19. Macrobius, *Saturnalia* 1.17.7.

20. Macrobius, *Dream of Scipio* 1.20.2.

21. Cicero, *Republic* 6.17.

22. Macrobius, *Dream of Scipio* 1.20.4.

23. Ibid. 1.20.6–7.

24. Macrobius, *Saturnalia* 1,17.31–33.

25. Ibid. 1.17.36.

26. Ibid. 1.17.47–49.

27. Boccaccio writes *Socomas* for *Chrysocomas*.

28. Boccaccio writes *Argitorosus* for *Argyrotoxos*.

29. Boccaccio seems to have confused or miscopied two consecutive sentences from Macrobius, *Saturnalia* 1.17.49, omitting "because he brings the rain; and the sun is called Apollo Philesius."

30. E.g., ibid. 1.17.48, 1.20.16, and 1.21.13.

31. Homer, *Iliad* 5.749–52.

32. GDG 1.1.2–3.

33. Censorinus, *The Birthday Book* 17.

34. Homer, *Odyssey* 12.132–33.

35. Vulgate version: "whose soldiers, since none were able to overcome the labors of the long and difficult crossing from Spain into Italy, wore themselves out in the delights of Capua."

36. Fulgentius, *Mythologies* 2.7.82–83.

37. Lactantius Placidus on *Thebaid* 4.570.

38. Ovid, *Metamorphoses* 9.444.

39. Ibid. 9.450–53.

40. Ibid. 9.663–65.

41. Seneca, *Hippolytus* 154–55.

42. Servius on *Aeneid* 6.14.

43. Homer, *Odyssey* 10.137–39.

44. Cicero, *On the Nature of the Gods* 3.42 and 3.46.

45. Ibid. 3.48.

46. Boccaccio writes "matricide" [*matricida*] for Cicero's "mother Idyia" [*matre Idyia*].

47. Seneca, *Medea* 211–16.

48. Boccaccio writes *Ipsea* for *Idyia*.

49. Ovid, *Heroines* 17.231–32.

50. Gaius Coelius in Solinus, *On the Wonders of the World* 2.28–30.

51. Macrobius, *Saturnalia* 1.12.26.

52. Cicero, *On the Nature of the Gods* 3.48.

53. Ovid, *Heroines* 17.231–32.

54. Homer, *Odyssey* 10.136–39.

55. Vergil, *Aeneid* 7.11–20.

56. Homer, *Odyssey* 10.230–479.

57. Ovid, *Metamorphoses* 14.8–74.

58. Ibid. 14.377–96.

59. Servius on *Aeneid* 7.19.

60. GDG 8.10.

61. Boccaccio erroneously writes *Circe* for *Medea*.

62. Gaius Coelius in Solinus, *On the Wonders of the World* 2.28–30.

63. Macrobius, *Saturnalia* 1.10.7.

64. Masurius in Macrobius, *Saturnalia* 1.10.8.

65. Julius Modestus in Macrobius, *Saturnalia* 1.10.9.

66. Accius, *Bacchae* in Macrobius, *Saturnalia* 6.5.11–12.

67. Vergil, *Aeneid* 10.215–16.

68. Isidore, *Etymologies* 18.36.2.

69. Nicander in Servius on *Georgics* 3.391.

70. Vergil, *Georgics* 3.391–93.

71. Cicero, *Tusculan Disputations* 1.38.92.

72. Boccaccio writes *Latinus* for *Latmus*.

73. Macrobius, *Saturnalia* 7.16.31; Boccaccio writes *Alcina* for *Alcman*.

74. Fulgentius, *Mythologies* 2.16.99–100.

75. Mnaseas in Fulgentius, *Mythologies* 2.16.100. Boccaccio writes *Minastas* for *Mnaseas*.

76. Seneca, *Hippolytus* 412. This parenthetical addition replaces an earlier version in the autograph.

77. Horace, *Secular Hymn* 15.

78. Aerotemis.

79. Macrobius, *Saturnalia* 7.16.27.

80. Timotheus in Macrobius, *Saturnalia* 7.16.28.

81. Boccaccio again writes *Alcina* for *Alcman*.

82. Vergil, *Aeneid* 6.287.

83. Homer, *Iliad* 1.402–4.

84. Cf. Vergil, *Aeneid* 3.271.

85. Vergil, *Aeneid* 4.179.

86. GDG 4.1.3–6.

87. Ovid, *Metamorphoses* 6.185–86.

88. Probably from Theodontius; cf. GDG 10.9.

89. Probably Cicero, *On the Nature of the Gods* 3.42.

90. Lactantius Placidus on *Thebaid* 2.595–96.

91. Ovid, *Metamorphoses* 5.346–56.

92. Vergil, *Aeneid* 9.715–16.

93. Lucan, *Pharsalia* 5.100–101.

94. Pomponius Mela, *Description of the World* 1.13.71–72.

95. Solinus, *On the Wonders of the World* 38.7.

96. Papias, *Lexicon*, s.v. Typheus.

97. Isidore, *Etymologies* 15.1.48.

98. Papias, *Lexicon*, s.v. Chimaera.

99. Boccaccio writes *Chedria* for *Hectria*.

100. Ovid, *Metamorphoses* 9.647–48.

101. Vergil, *Aeneid* 6.288.

102. Fulgentius, *Mythologies* 3.1. Cf. GDG 13.58.

103. Vergil, *Aeneid* 4.178–79.

104. Ibid. 3.578–82.

105. Horace, *Odes* 3.4.53–56.

106. Servius on *Aeneid* 6.287.

107. Ovid, *Metamorphoses* 2.9–10.

108. E.g., Ovid, *Fasti* 3.403 and *Heroines* 18.111–12.

109. Varro, *On the Latin Language* 5.31.

110. GDG 13.1.17.

111. Pomponius Mela, *Description of the World* 3.10.100.

112. Varro, *On Agriculture* 2.1.6.

113. Fulgentius, *Exposition of the Content of Virgil* 20.

114. Lactantius Placidus on *Thebaid* 1.98.

115. Pliny, *Natural History* 7.56.203.

116. I.e., Fiesole.

117. Fulgentius, *Mythologies* 1.21.60.

118. Augustine, *City of God* 18.8.

119. Rabanus, *On the Nature of Things* 13.1.

120. Pliny, *Natural History* 7.56.203.

121. Ovid, *Fasti* 5.169–72.

122. Ibid. 5.173–82.

123. Of the variant spellings Boccaccio offers for the names of the Hyades, *Pyidile* for *Phaesyla* is the only one that is relatively unrecognizable.

124. Ovid, *Fasti* 5.163–68.

125. Cf. Ovid, *Fasti* 5.179.

126. Boccaccio erroneously writes *Anselm* for *Honorius Augustodunensis*, *Image of the World* 1.104 (Migne *PL*, 172.143c).

127. Ovid, *Fasti* 4. 169–78.

128. Boccaccio erroneously writes *Anselm* for *Honorius Augustodunensis*, *Image of the World* 1.104 (Migne, *PL* 172.143c).

129. Vergil, *Aeneid* 8.140–41.

130. Cingius in Macrobius, *Saturnalia* 1.12.18.

131. Piso in Macrobius, *Saturnalia* 1.12.18.

132. Martianus Capella 1.34.

133. Macrobius, *Saturnalia* 1.12.19.

134. Ovid, *Fasti* 5.129–30.

135. Cornelius Labeo in Macrobius, *Saturnalia* 1.12.20.

136. GDG 1.8.

137. Ovid, *Fasti* 4.172.

138. Ibid. 4.175.

139. Priscian, *Grammatical Foundations* 6.18 (Keil *GL* 2.210).

140. Homer, *Odyssey* 7.245.

141. Ibid. 5.21–277.

142. Ovid, *Metamorphoses* 1.351–53.

143. Varro, *On the Latin Language* 5.31.

144. Ovid, *Metamorphoses* 1.80–83.

145. Horace, *Odes* 1.16.13–16.

146. Claudian, *Panegyric on the Fourth Consulship of the Emperor Honorius* 228–54.

147. Servius on *Eclogues* 6.42.

148. Fulgentius, *Mythologies* 2.6.78–79.

149. Aeschylus in Cicero, *Tusculan Disputations* 2.23–25.

150. Sappho and Hesiod in Servius on *Eclogues* 6.42.

151. Horace, *Odes* 1.3.27–31.

152. Section 12a appears only in the autograph and thus seems to have been eliminated by Boccaccio in later redactions.

153. John 1:9.

154. GDG 1.10.1–5.

155. Augustine, *City of God* 18.8.

156. Rabanus, *On the Nature of Things* 15.6.

157. Boccaccio must mean Ivo of Chartres, but I find no mention of Prometheus in his extant works. Other possible sources include Servius on *Eclogues* 6.72; Comestor, *Scholastic History* 86; and *Vatican Mythographer* 3.10.10.

158. Eusebius-Jerome, *Chronicle* 35.6–12.

159. Servius on *Eclogues* 6.42.

160. Lactantius, *Divine Institutes* 2.10–12.

161. Pliny, *Natural History* 7.56.198.

162. Genesis 3:19.

163. Petrarch, *On the Solitary Life* 2.3.3.

164. Juvenal, *Satires* 6.268–69.

165. Varius Geminus in Jerome, *Against Jovinianus* 1.28.

166. Fulgentius, *Mythologies* 2.6.82.

167. Job 14:1.

168. Cf. Boccaccio, *Famous Women* 8.

169. Boccaccio writes *Phentrates* for *Pherecrates*.

170. Ovid, *Metamorphoses* 1.322–23.

171. GDG 3.22.9.

172. Eusebius-Jerome, *Chronicle* 44.14.

173. Cicero, *Tusculan Disputations* 1.21.

174. Servius on *Aeneid* 1.132.

175. Lactantius Placidus on *Thebaid* 2.4.

176. Vergil, *Aeneid* 1.51–63.

177. Ovid, *Metamorphoses* 1.56–66.

178. Isidore, *Etymologies* 13.11.2–22.

179. Vitruvius, *On Architecture* 1.6.10.

180. Ibid. 1.6.4–5.

181. Isidore, *Etymologies* 13.11.2–3.

182. Bede, *On the Nature of Things* 27.

183. Ovid, *Metamorphoses* 1.264–67.

184. Ibid. 6.690–700.

185. Servius on *Eclogues* 3.63.

186. Ovid, *Metamorphoses* 6.703–7.

187. Homer, *Iliad* 20.199–225.

188. Ovid, *Metamorphoses* 6. 711–18.

189. Ibid. 6. 719–21.

190. Servius on *Aeneid* 3.209.

191. Seneca, *Natural Questions* 4.7.

192. Fulgentius, *Mythologies* 3.11.133.

193. Bede, *On the Nature of Things* 27.

194. Homer, *Iliad* 16.149–51.

195. Boccaccio confuses *Thyella* for *Podarge*.

196. Lactantius, *Divine Institutes* 1.20.6–17.

197. Cf. Ovid, *Fasti* 5.195–212.

198. Pliny, *Natural History* 8.67.166.

199. Servius on *Aeneid* 6.582.

200. GDG 10.67.

201. Lucan, *Pharsalia* 7.150.

202. Cicero, *On the Nature of the Gods* 3.59.

203. Priscian, *Grammatical Foundations* 6.6 (Keil GL 2.198–99).

204. Horace, *Odes* 3.4.54.

205. Ovid, *Metamorphoses* 1.218–43.

206. Pliny, *Natural History* 7.56.202 and 205.

207. Cf. Ovid, *Metamorphoses* 2.496 and 526.

208. GDG 5.49.

209. Thales in Hyginus, *On Astronomy* 2.1–2.

210. Ovid, *Metamorphoses* 1.156–62.

211. Ibid. 5.321–31.

212. Homer, *Odyssey* 9.233–542.

213. Vergil, *Aeneid* 3.655–59 and 664–65.

214. Genesis 10:8–9, 11.3–5; 1 Samuel 17:4–51.

215. Josephus, *Jewish Antiquities* 1.3.1.

216. Macrobius, *Saturnalia* 1.20.8–9.

217. Lactantius, *Divine Institutes* 1.14.10–11.

218. Varro in Servius on *Aeneid* 3.578, and Vatican Mythographer 3.1.10.

219. Macrobius, *Saturnalia* 1.17.2.

220. Augustine, *City of God* 16.2.

221. Ovid, *Metamorphoses* 5.327–28.

222. GDG 5.3.8–9.

223. Fulgentius, *Mythologies* 1.13.45.

BOOK V

1. The two "eyes" of Greece were Athens and Sparta; cf. Justin, *Epitome* 5.8.4.

2. John 2:1–11.

3. GDG 3.1.

4. Cicero, *On the Nature of the Gods* 3.53.

5. GDG 4.66.

6. Ibid. 4.20.

7. Claudian, *On the Consulship of Stilicho* 3.246–58.

8. Ibid. 3.285–92.

9. Boccaccio writes *Agapente* for *Hecaerge*.

10. GDG 7.14.

11. Rabanus, *On the Nature of Things* 15.6.

12. Boccaccio writes *Autous* for *Autucus* and *Argeus* for *Agreus*.

13. GDG 4.20.

14. Cicero, *On the Nature of the Gods* 3.57.

15. Ibid.

16. Eusebius-Jerome, *Chronicle* 51.24–25.

17. Boccaccio writes *Stelenus* for *Stenelus*.

18. Macrobius, *Saturnalia* 1.17.52–54.

19. Vatican Mythographer 3.8.1.

20. Fulgentius, *Mythologies* 1.12.43.

21. Porphyrius in Servius on *Eclogues* 5.66.

22. Homer in Vatican Mythographer 3.8.16.

23. Horace, *Carmen Saeculare* 33–34.

24. Isidore, *Etymologies* 9.2.70.

25. Papias, *Lexicon*, s.v. Laphyta.

26. Rabanus, *On the Nature of Things* 16.2.

27. Statius, *Thebaid* 3.521.

28. Lactantius Placidus on *Thebaid* 3.520–21.

29. Servius on *Eclogues* 6.72.

30. Pomponius Mela, *Description of the World* 1.14.79 and 1.17.88.

31. Eusebius-Jerome, *Chronicle* 60.19–20.

32. Lactantius Placidus on *Thebaid* 6.64.

33. Statius, *Thebaid* 6.64–65.

34. Vergil, *Eclogues* 4.55–56.

35. Servius on *Eclogues* 1.65.

36. Varro in Servius on *Eclogues* 1.65.

37. Boccaccio writes *Cantilena* for *Anchiale*.

38. Rabanus, *On the Nature of Things* 16.2.

39. Lactantius Placidus on *Thebaid* 8.198.

40. Boccaccio writes *Iouces* for *Patro* and *Sucro* for *Smicron*.

41. Varro in Lactantius Placidus on *Thebaid* 8.198.

42. Lactantius Placidus on *Thebaid* 3.478–79.

43. Ovid, *Metamorphoses* 11.293–317.

44. Pseudo-Lactantius Placidus, *Stories from the Fables of Ovid* 11.1, although here he is the son of Calliope and the river Oeagrus.

45. Rabanus, *On the Nature of Things* 18.4.

46. Vergil, *Georgics* 4.453–527.

47. Ovid, *Metamorphoses* 10.78–85 and 11.1–66.

48. Rabanus, *On the Nature of Things* 18.4.

49. Fulgentius, *Mythologies* 3.10.130–31.

50. Lactantius, *Divine Institutes* 1.22.15–16.

51. Piny, *Natural History* 7.56.203.

52. Solinus, *On the Wonders of the World* 10.8.

53. Statius, *Thebaid* 5.344.

54. Lactantius, *Divine Institutes* 1.22.17.

55. Eusebius-Jerome, *Chronicle* 56.3; reign of Pandion.

56. Vergil, *Georgics* 4.321–24.

57. Justin, *Epitome* 13.7.

58. Boccaccio writes *Cyrus* for *Grinus* and *Coramis* for *Thera*.

59. Boccaccio writes *Autous* for *Autucus* and *Argeus* for *Agreus*.

60. One manuscript (*Ch*) continues: "In this story there is no fiction except where it is said that she was the daughter of Peneus [rather than] Speus, king of Thessaly, who sent those who asked where she had gone."

61. Pliny, *Natural History* 7.56.199.

62. Vergil, *Georgics* 4.317–18.

63. Sallust in Servius on *Georgics* 1.14.

64. Solinus, *On the Wonders of the World* 4.2.

65. Statius, *Thebaid* 4.572–74.

66. Ovid, *Metamorphoses* 3.146–47. Boccaccio conflates two verses into one.

67. Fulgentius, *Mythologies* 3.3.107.

68. Solinus, *On the Wonders of the World* 1.61 and 4.2.

69. Justin, *Epitome* 13.7.

70. Ovid, *Metamorphoses* 2.542–648.

71. Boccaccio writes *Alchiroe* for *Ocyrrhoe*.

72. Vergil, *Aeneid* 7.769–73.

73. Pliny, *Natural History* 29.1.3.

74. Lactantius, *Divine Institutes* 1.10.2.

75. Cicero, *On the Nature of the Gods* 3.57; Boccaccio mistakes "probe" [*specillum*] as "mirror" [*speculum*].

76. Boccaccio writes *Coronis* for *Phoronis*.

77. Papias, *Lexicon*, s.v. Machaon.

78. Isidore, *Etymologies* 4.3.2.

79. Pliny, *Natural History* 29.2.3–4.

80. Augustine, *City of God* 8.26.

81. Martianus Capella 1.7.

82. Apuleius, *Metamorphoses* 4.28–6.24.

83. For 5.6–8 the vulgate (*PCh*) substitutes: "There Psyche received them with genial well-wishing, and every delight was shown to them, which made the sisters envious, and with all their might they persuaded her to attempt to see her husband's form. Trusting them, and having sent them away with gifts, she prepared a dagger and hid an oil lamp under a bushel, thereby intending to see the following night who it was who shared her bed, planning to kill him if he should be of the form his sisters described."

84. From here through 5.14, one manuscript (*Ch*) substitutes: "Psyche, upset at losing her husband, wanted to die. By deceit she then led both sisters, whose advice had caused this distress, to a precipice, and then chided sharply by Venus and attacked by attendants with whips, she was ordered to be engaged in tasks that were impossible for a mortal, but assisted by her husband she accomplished the works assigned to her. Finally by praying to Jupiter she ultimately found favor with Venus and, taken up to the heavens, enjoyed her eternal marriage to Cupid, to whom she bore Pleasure."

85. Chalcidius, *On Timaeus* 236.5–6 [Waszink].

86. The vulgate (*PCh*) reads: "There are two sisters older by birth not because they were born first but because they used their power first, the one said to be vegetative, the other perceptive, which are not the rational spirit, as some would like to think, but are under the power of the rational spirit. Psyche is said to be more junior than they because a fetus is granted the vegetative spirit long before the rational, and then the percep-

tive spirit after the passage of time. Later reason is given to Psyche; and because they are first in action they are therefore said to be joined first in marriage, which is reserved for this rational, divine offspring."

87. John 1:18.

88. Pliny, *Natural History* 7.56.196.

89. Servius on *Aeneid* 6.595.

90. Macrobius, *Dream of Scipio* 1.10.12.

91. Ovid, *Metamorphoses* 3.253–315.

92. Ibid. 3.313–15.

93. Ovid, *Fasti* 3.769–70.

94. Ibid. 3.767.

95. Statius, *Thebaid* 4.657–63.

96. Accius, *Bacchae* in Macrobius, *Saturnalia* 6.5.11–12.

97. Rabanus, *On the Nature of Things* 22.13.

98. Ovid, *Metamorphoses* 4.11–19.

99. Vatican Mythographer 3.12.2.

100. Lactantius Placidus on *Thebaid* 2.71–72.

101. Servius on *Georgics* 1.166.

102. Eusebius-Jerome, *Chronicle* 52.24–26.

103. Pomponius Mela, *Description of the World* 3.7.66.

104. Vatican Mythographer 3.12.4.

105. Orosius 1.9.4.

106. Servius on *Georgics* 1.166.

107. Seneca, *Dialogues: On Tranquility of Mind* 9.17.8–9.

108. GDG 11.29.

109. Eusebius-Jerome, *Chronicle* 54.18–19.

110. Dinarchus [not Varro] in Eusebius-Jerome, *Chronicle* 54.18–19.

111. Vatican Mythographer 3.12.5.

112. Macrobius, *Saturnalia* 1.17.2.

113. Fulgentius, *Mythologies* 2.12.92.

114. Lactantius Placidus on *Thebaid* 2.71.

115. Vatican Mythographer 3.12.1–2.

116. Servius on *Eclogues* 5.29.

117. Varro *On Agriculture* 1.2.19.

118. Cicero, *On the Nature of the Gods* 2.62.

119. Macrobius, *Saturnalia* 1.17.2 and 18.1.

120. Vergil, *Georgics* 1.5–7.

121. Augustine, *City of God* 7.21.

122. GDG 12.24.

123. Vatican Mythographer 3.11.2.

124. Lactantius Placidus on *Thebaid* 3.283.

125. Servius on *Eclogues* 8.30.

126. Vergil, *Aeneid* 1.734.

127. Cf. Ovid, *Metamorphoses* 4.13.

128. Boccaccio erroneously cites Ovid for Statius, *Thebaid* 5.265–67.

129. Cf. Boccaccio, *Famous Women* 16.

130. Statius, *Thebaid* 5.675–76.

131. Ibid. 5.36–334.

132. Ibid. 5.335–753.

133. Homer, *Odyssey* 11.260–65.

134. GDG 10.29.

135. Ovid, *Metamorphoses* 6.110–11.

136. Homer, *Odyssey* 11.262.

137. Servius on *Eclogues* 2.24.

138. Lactantius Placidus on *Achilleid* 13.

139. Seneca, *Hercules Furens* 262–63.

140. Pliny, *Natural History* 7.56.204.

141. Homer, *Iliad* 24.603.

142. Ovid, *Metamorphoses* 6.182–83.

143. Eusebius-Jerome, *Chronicle* 48.8–15.

144. Ovid, *Metamorphoses* 6.146–266.

145. Lactantius Placidus on *Thebaid* 3.191–93.

146. Homer, *Iliad* 24.609–17, does not use the name Amalea, and says that the bodies went unburied for nine days, not nine years.

147. Lactantius Placidus on *Achilleid* 13.

148. Servius on *Eclogues* 2.24.

149. Homer, *Odyssey* 19.518–23.

150. Cf. Homer, *Odyssey* 11.262.

151. Lactantius Placidus on *Thebaid* 2.286.

152. Cf. Fulgentius, *Mythologies* 2.1.72.

153. Vergil, *Aeneid* 1.548–49.

154. Dictys of Crete 1.9.

155. Eusebius-Jerome, *Chronicle* 45.3–4.

156. Boccaccio writes *Icarus* for *Icarius*.

157. Lactantius Placidus on *Thebaid* 4.655.

158. Servius on *Georgics* 2.389.

159. Ovid, *Metamorphoses* 6.125.

160. Servius on *Georgics* 2.389, lacking a reference to Marathon.

161. Lactantius Placidus on *Thebaid* 11.644.

162. Vergil, *Georgics* 2.388–89.

163. Servius on *Georgics* 2.389.

164. Homer, *Odyssey* 4.797–98.

165. Cf. Boccaccio, *Famous Women* 40.

166. Homer, *Odyssey* 1.329.

167. Cf. scholiast to Lycophron, *Alexandra* 805 (254.8–20).

168. Cicero, *On the Nature of the Gods* 3.42.

169. Ibid. 3.53.

170. Statius, *Thebaid* 7.72–74.

171. Cicero, *On the Nature of the Gods* 3.55.

172. Vatican Mythographer 3.10.6.

173. Ovid, *Metamorphoses* 2.401–532.

174. Eusebius-Jerome, *Chronicle* 45.11–14.

175. Cf. Boccaccio, *Famous Women* 27.

Bibliography

❧❧❧

EARLY EDITIONS OF THE LATIN TEXT

1472 Venice: Vindelinus de Spira. Additions and corrections by Raphael Zovenzonius and Dominicus Silvester.

1473 Louvain: Johann Veldener. An anonymous compendium of Books 1–13. Also attributed to the printer of the *Flores Sancti Augustini* (Cologne), i.e. Johann Schilling.

1481 Reggio Emilia: Bartholomeus and Laurentius de Bruschis.

1487 Vicenza: Simon Bevilaqua.

1494/95 Venice: Bonetus Locatellus, for Octavianus Scotus.

1497 Venice: Manfredus de Bonellis, de Monteferrato.

1511 Paris: Dionisius Roce, Lodovicus Hornken, et al.

1511 Venice: Augustinus de Zannis.

1532 Basel: Iohannus Hervagius. Notes by Jacob Mycillus.

EARLY TRANSLATIONS

FRENCH

1498/99 *De la génénealogie des dieux*. Paris: Antoine Vérard. Translation attributed to Laurent de Premierfait.

1531 *Bocace de la génénealogie des dieux*. Paris: Jehan Petit [and Philippe le Noir]. Translation attributed to Laurent de Premierfait.

ITALIAN

1547 *La genealogia de gli dei de' gentili*. Venice: Pozzo and Comino da Trino di Monferrato. Translation by Giuseppe Betussi. Subsequent editions: Venice: Diamante, 1554; Venice: Francesco Lorenzini da Turino, 1564; Venice: Giacomo Sansovino, 1569; Venice: Giovanni Antonio Bertano, 1574; Venice: Fabio and Agostino Zoppini, Fratelli, 1581; Venice: La Compagnia degli Uniti, 1585; Venice: Marc' Antonio Zaltieri, 1588; Venice: Lucio Spineda, 1606 (revised and corrected); Venice: Il Valentini, 1627; Venice: Turini, 1644.

MODERN EDITIONS

Hecker, Oskar, ed. *Boccaccio-funde*. Braunschweig: George Westermann, 1902. Partial edition of the Proemia, Books 14 and 15, and the Conclusion.

Romano, Vincenzo, ed. *Giovanni Boccaccio. Genealogie deorum gentilium libri*. Bari: Laterza, 1951.

Muscetta, Carlo, ed. *Vita di Dante e difesa della poesia*. Rome: Edizioni dell'Ateneo, 1963. Books 14 and 15 only.

Ricci, Pier Giorgio, ed. *Opere in versi: Corbaccio. Trattatello in laude di Dante. Prose latine. Epistole*. Milan: R. Ricciardi, 1965. Book 14 only.

Reedy, Jeremiah, ed. *Boccaccio: In Defence of Poetry, Genealogiae deorum gentilium Liber XIV*. Toronto: Pontifical Institute of Mediaeval Studies, 1978.

Álvarez, María Consuelo, and Rosa María Iglesias, eds. *Genealogia de los dioses paganos*. Madrid: Editora Nacional, 1983.

Zaccaria, Vittorio, ed. *Genealogie deorum gentilium*. Vols. 7–8 of Vittore Branca, ed., *Tutte le opere di Giovanni Boccaccio*. Milan: Mondadori, 1998.

MODERN TRANSLATIONS

ENGLISH

Charles G. Osgood, trans. *Boccaccio on Poetry*. 2nd ed. Indianapolis: Bobbs-Merrill, 1956. Books 14 and 15 only.

Hoover, Melanie, trans. "Book Eleven of the Genealogy of the Pagan Gods of Giovanni Boccaccio: A Translation with Glossary." M.A. thesis, University of Florida, 1985.

Lock, Fred, trans. *Vulcan: The Genealogy of the Pagan Gods*. Kingston, Ont: Lock's Press, 1999. Book 12, chapter 70, only.

SPANISH

Álvarez, María Consuelo, and Rosa María Iglesias, trans. *Giovanni Boccaccio: Los Quince Libros de la Genealogía de los Dioses Paganos*. Madrid: Centro de Lingüística Aplicada Atenea, 2007.

ITALIAN

Zaccaria, Vittorio, trans. *Genealogie deorum gentilium*. Vols. 7–8 of Vittore Branca, ed., *Tutte le opere di giovanni Boccaccio*. Milan: Mondadori, 1998.

FRENCH

Yves Delègue, trans. *Généalogie des dieux païens: un manifeste pour la poésie*. Strasbourg: Presses Universitaires de Strasbourg, 2001. Books 14 and 15 only.

GERMAN

Hege, Brigitte, trans. *Boccaccios Apologie der heidnischen Dichtung in den Genealogie deorum gentilium: Buch XIV, Text, Übersetzung, Kommentar und Abhandlung*. Tubingen: Stauffenburg Verlag, 1997.

SELECTED STUDIES

Arnold, Luisella Bovio. "Aspetti narrativi nella Genealogia deorum gentilium di Giovanni Boccaccio." Ph.D. diss., University of California, Los Angeles, 1994.

Branca, Vittore, ed. *Boccaccio visualizzato: Narrare per parole e immagini fra Medioevo e Rinascimento*. Turin: G. Einaudi, 1999.

———, ed. *Giovanni Boccaccio: Profilo biografico*. 2nd ed. Florence: Sansoni, 1992. First edition translated by Dennis J. McAuliffe (ed.) and Richard Monges as *Boccaccio: The Man and His Works* (New York: New York University Press, 1976).

Buck, August. "Boccaccios Verteidigung der Dichtung in den *Genealogie Deorum*," in Gilbert Tournoy, ed., *Boccaccio in Europe: Proceedings of the Boccaccio Conference, Louvain, December 1975* (Leuven: Leuven University Press, 1977), 53–65.

Gullace, Giovanni. "Medieval and Humanistic Perspectives in Boccaccio's Concept and Defense of Poetry." *Mediaevalia* 12 (1989, for 1986): 226–48.

Hill, Alan G. "Wordsworth, Boccaccio, and the Pagan Gods of Antiquity." *Review of English Studies* 45 (1994): 26–41.

Hübner, Wolfgang. "Noch einmal zum Titel von Boccaccios Genealogia." *Neulateinisches Jahrbuch* 4 (2002): 323–25.

Hyde, Thomas. "The Genealogies of Myth." *PMLA* 100 (1985): 737–45.

Jocelyn, Henry David. "The Sources of Boccaccio's *Genealogiae deorum gentilium libri* and the Myths about Early Italy." In Luisa Rotondi Secchi Tarugi, ed., *Il mito nel rinascimento* (Milan: Nuovi Orizzonti, 1993).

Marino, Lucia. "Prometheus, or the Mythographer's Self-Image in Boccaccio's Genealogie." *Studi sul Boccaccio* 12 (1980): 261–73.

Martellotti, Guido. *Le due redazioni delle "Genealogie" del Boccaccio*. Roma: Edizioni di storia e letteratura, 1951.

Meltzoff, Stanley. *Botticelli, Signorelli and Savonarola: "Theologia Poetica" and Painting from Boccaccio to Poliziano*. Florence: Olschki, 1987.

Minicucci, Angela. "I libri XIV e XV della *Genealogia deorum gentilium* e gli scritti di poetica di Tommaso Campanella," in Gilbert Tournoy, ed., *Boccaccio in Europe: Proceedings of the Boccaccio Conference, Louvain, December 1975* (Leuven: Leuven University Press, 1977), 165–90.

Mulryan, John. "The Three Images of Venus: Boccaccio's Theory of Love in the *Genealogy of the Gods* and His Aesthetic Vision of Love in the *Decameron*." *Romance Notes* 19 (1979): 388–94.

———. "Venus and the Classical Tradition in Boccaccio's *Genealogia deorum gentilium libri* and Natale Conti's *Mythologiae*." *Mediaevalia* 27 (2006): 135–56.

Mussini Sacchi, Maria Pia. "Per la fortuna del Demogorgone in età umanistica." *Italia Medioevale e Umanistica* 34 (1991): 299.

Pade, Marianne. "The Fragments of Theodontius in Boccacio's *Genealogie deorum gentilium libri*," in Marianne Pade, Hannemarie Ragn Jensen, and Lene Waage Petersen, eds., *Avignon & Naples: Italy in France, France in Italy in the Fourteenth Century* (Rome: "L'Erma" di Bretschneider, 1997), 149–82.

Papio, Michael, trans. *Boccaccio's Expositions on Dante's* Comedy. Toronto: University of Toronto Press, 2009.

Pertusi, Agostino. *Leonzio Pilato fra Petrarcha e Boccaccio: Le sue versioni omeriche negli autografi di Venezia e la cultura greca del primo umanesimo*. Venice: Instituto per la Collaborazione Culturale, 1964.

Schöningh, Daniel. *Die Göttergenealogien des Boccaccio: Ein Beitrag zur Geschichte der Wissenschaftlichen Forschung im XIV. Jahrhundert.* Posen: Merzbachische Buchdruckerei, 1900.

Stone, Gregory B. *The Ethics of Nature in the Middle Ages: On Boccaccio's Poetaphysics.* New York: St. Martin's, 1998.

Wilkins, Ernest Hatch. "The Genealogy of the Genealogical Trees of the *Genealogie deorum.*" *Modern Philology* 23 (1925): 61–65.

———. *The University of Chicago Manuscript of the* Genealogia deorum gentilium *of Boccaccio.* Chicago: University of Chicago Press, 1927.

Zaccaria, Vittorio. "Ancora per il testo delle 'Genealogie deorum gentilium.'" *Studi sul Boccaccio* 21 (1993): 243–73.

———. "Per il testo delle 'Genealogie deorum gentilium.'" *Studi sul Boccaccio* 16 (1987) 179–240.

Index of Citations

ఌఄౕ

Subject Index

ঌঌঌঌ

Publication of this volume has been made possible by

The Myron and Sheila Gilmore Publication Fund at I Tatti
The Robert Lehman Endowment Fund
The Jean-François Malle Scholarly Programs and Publications Fund
The Andrew W. Mellon Scholarly Publications Fund
The Craig and Barbara Smyth Fund
for Scholarly Programs and Publications
The Lila Wallace–Reader's Digest Endowment Fund
The Malcolm Wiener Fund for Scholarly Programs and Publications